The Portable

JOHNSON
&
BOSWELL

The Viking Portable Library

Each Portable Library volume is made up of representative works of a favorite modern or classic author, or is a comprehensive anthology on a special subject. The format is designed for compactness and for pleasurable reading. The books average about 700 pages in length. Each is intended to fill a need not hitherto met by any single book. Each is edited by an authority distinguished in his field, who adds a thoroughgoing introductory essay and other helpful material. Most "Portables" are available both in durable cloth and in stiff paper covers.

The Portable

JOHNSON
&
BOSWELL

EDITED, AND WITH AN INTRODUCTION, BY

LOUIS KRONENBERGER

NEW YORK

THE VIKING PRESS

828

The excerpts from "Dialogue with Rousseau" and *Journal of a Tour to the Hebrides* included in this volume are from the manuscript versions in the Malahide Papers, first published and copyrighted in 1928 and 1936 by Ralph H. Isham; they may not be reprinted without permission from Yale University.

Set in Caledonia and Baskerville types
and Printed in U. S. A. by The Colonial Press Inc

CONTENTS

C. 3

EDITOR'S INTRODUCTION

UNWEARIED and inseparable, Johnson and Boswell move from one generation to another—the greatest social talker whose talk has been recorded, and the greatest biographer the world has ever known. Each, in the final sense, owes his celebrity to the other. But for Johnson, Boswell would surely be forgotten. But for Boswell, Johnson would simply be a man of letters important to other men of letters and not at all a figure of universal fame. As it is, perhaps no other personality has vaulted farther out of literature into life: hundreds of Johnson's remarks have passed into common cultivated speech; his eccentricities are better known than other great men's solidest achievements; his portrait is one of the very few that everybody can recognize; and he has lent his name to both a discredited style of writing and an immensely distinguished age. Boswell, with greater genius, has had far less luck. Too many people still regard him as a kind of inspired idiot, someone who had an unrivaled opportunity to hear Dr. Johnson talk, and wrote down all he said. Nothing could explain his achievement worse. Even as concerns hearing Dr. Johnson talk, Boswell had fewer opportunities than most of Johnson's other intimate friends; as for merely writing down what his hero said, rather with the most staggering skill he wrote it up.

Yet, though the story will not down that Boswell the biographer was only accidentally great, the greatness of

1

his biography no more requires demonstration than it provokes dispute; while it is Dr. Johnson himself who, outside his disciple's pages, must plead for a hearing. The popular conception of Johnson is of someone as dull in his writing as he was lively in his talk. For he wrote, tradition has it, in stupefying polysyllables on crushingly tiresome themes: his only novel has no plot, and his only play no drama; his journalistic essays suggest the pulpit far more than the press; and his criticism is loaded down with such dicta as: that *Lycidas* is "disgusting" and that *Lear* is the better for a happy ending. Thus condemned as arid or unreadable, Johnson goes on —save by scholars and literary men—being virtually unread. And in all this he is to some degree quite fairly condemned. There *are* too many polysyllables, there *is* too much preaching; Johnson's novel is a fraud if read for its story, and his play a burden, however it be read; while some of his critical remarks are as misguided as they are well known. Only it so happens that his often ponderous style can also be extraordinarily powerful; that while Johnson, in *Rasselas,* shows no merit as a story-teller, he shows considerable as a moral philosopher; that the faults which submerge *The Rambler* hardly exist in the best of the *Lives of the Poets;* and that, in spite of many wrong-headed criticisms, he is very nearly a great critic. We shall always go first to Johnson the talker and Johnson the man; but afterwards we may find a different sort of pleasure in Johnson the biographer and Johnson the critic and Johnson the poet.

It is, indeed, because he could be a magnificent writer as well as a fabulous talker and a noble human being, that there is nearly as much in this volume by, as about, him. This is not to take sides against Boswell: it was very tempting to make room for that personality of Boswell's own which he in great measure suppressed in the *Life;* to include many things from Boswell's letters and private papers. But with the problem of space so pressing, I have withstood the temptation on what seems to me sensible grounds. Boswell in his one great literary role, Boswell the biographer, is allotted well over half the space at my disposal. Boswell as autobiographer is incredibly fascinating, but his autobiographical writings have, in the last analysis, a higher psychological than artistic interest; furthermore, to become of value they must be read in bulk. A sampling of his "confessions" would distort far more than it would reveal. We represent Boswell best by representing him at his own artistic best: and so have space besides to represent Johnson justly. This means a little more than merely giving over the remaining space to Johnson's own writings. It means supplementing Boswell's great portrait with the brilliant snapshots provided by others. Without drawing on at least Mrs. Piozzi and Fanny Burney, this book would have omitted some of the most striking anecdotes and lifelike touches of Johnson that exist.

The greatness of Boswell's *Life of Johnson* rests on a number of things—one of them, very obviously, the wonderful potentialities of its subject. Johnson had, in a surpassing degree, qualities that awaken universal interest. He had massive force, all the bursting vigor of a man seldom given to fear or to forbearance, a man who was in many ways a hero, yet in certain ways a bully. He had enormous color: with his queer habits and grotesque appearance, his odd mannerisms and peculiar superstitions, he was in fact a monumental "character." He had tremendous wit: his comments are among the most striking, and his repartees among the most pulverizing, on record. To listen to him must have been—for it still is—a really notable experience; more than any other Englishman, it has been said, he raised "a life of talk to the level of a life of action." Moreover, there was something so unchartable and eruptive about Johnson as to lend to his drawing-room appearances an atmosphere of continuous drama.

To chronicle the life of such a man is clearly to start off with immense advantages. But it does not begin to explain Boswell's achievement, for other men chronicled that life without ever approaching that achievement. Nor does the fact that Boswell slaved away far harder at the job explain it much better. Boswell, to be sure, went to the great trouble of getting down much more about Johnson, and getting it down much more accurately, than anybody else. But all experience favors the judgment that stenography is rather the enemy than the ally of skill; that without selection and arrangement and shading and stress there can be no true effect of art; and few would deny that Boswell's *Life* provides a very powerful effect of art. The more familiar with it one becomes, the surer one feels (even without the evidence of the Notebooks) that it has been creatively worked up; and that even where Boswell may have been no more than faithful in what he recorded, he had earlier been discriminating in what he recalled. Sainte-Beuve said of Mme. Récamier that she "remembered with taste"; it might be said of Boswell that he remembered with wit. If nothing about Johnson seemed too trivial to him, some things may, for all that, have seemed too dull; and such things he expunged, not deliberately from his "minutes," but by instinct from his mind. Besides, Boswell's reports of Johnson's conversations are seldom purely stenographic reports; they are for the most part commotion recollected in tranquillity; they have been reconstructed, with the aid of notes, from memory, and are in the final sense the product of Boswell's artistic "ear," of his unerring sense of what constituted the Johnsonian statement and the Johnsonian style.

Thus, in what appears as the most slavish element in the writing of the *Life*—the word-for-word setting down of Johnson's talk—industry was abetted by ingeniousness; and from that known fact we may proceed to facts less knowable in contending that Boswell was far more an artist than an ape. An ape might have caught Johnson's single statements, but only a man of great capacities could have written up, as Boswell wrote them, many-voiced and rounded scenes. Here, in the pauses, the changes of pace, the build of the argument and the sting of the rejoinders, there exists an expert dramatic sense for controlling dialogue. In the most famous of the scenes—Johnson's interview with George III, his first encounter with Wilkes, his meeting with his old schoolfellow Mr. Edwards—Boswell is very great, but we may also concede that the circumstances are very showy: it is rather where the situation is less certainly dramatic that Boswell reveals his true mettle. And of course he reveals it in yet another way on those numerous occasions when he acts as Dr. Johnson's straight man, holding the match to set off the fireworks (and often getting badly burned).

Yet, without industry, without even the worst kind of drudgery, Boswell could never have brought off such a *Life;* for second only to his efforts to get down what he heard were his efforts to get down what he did not hear; his running "half over London . . . to fix a date correctly"; his shaking every tree of knowledge for its possible fruit; his badgering one man for a letter of Johnson's and another man for an anecdote; his sitting up till all hours to rifle his memory and recast his jottings: it was only such assiduity that made possible such a

Life as Boswell's, composed on such as Boswell's methods.

Though Boswell himself may have idealized Johnson, Boswell's *Life* set out to portray him exactly as he was —to paint in every wart, and every hair on every wart, which at once indicates how realistic the portrait was to be, how intimate, and how detailed. To Boswell himself, Johnson seemed so transcendently great that his foibles and failings could do nothing worse than make him human; but to us, the miracle of Boswell's exact and unsparing portrayal is that Johnson did not issue forth a monster. It is often forgotten, and often perhaps not known, how revolutionary a biographer Boswell was: never before had any biography treated its subject at such close range, in so strong a light, so largely in his own words, so strikingly on his own terms. Despite Boswell's frequent irruptions into eulogy—which oftener than not defeat their purpose by their fatuousness— Johnson must ultimately fend for himself, for he is never accorded either the dignity or the glamour of distance. "I will not," Boswell asserted, "make my tiger a cat to please anybody." In the matter of brushwork, no biographer has ever come close to Boswell, though most subsequent biographers have been in some degree Boswellian. The pudgy Scot is one of the very few men in literature who have managed both to formulate a method and to carry it through to perfection; he is one of even fewer men who, though monstrous egoists, have remained consistently objective artists.

For all its greatness, Boswell's *Life* provides an incomplete and perhaps too simple view of Johnson— other contemporaries saw him in a pretty different light, and later biographers in much clearer perspective. Boswell's *Life* is also, in a sense, too static; and as I venture to think, too long. This second judgment is not brought forth to suit the occasion, to justify the abridged version offered here. Everybody owes himself the experience of reading Boswell through. But the uncut *Life* does suffer from outright *longueurs* as opposed to mere extensive length. Boswell did remember some things that are dull, and did (for all his wariness) include some things that interested himself much more than other people, or his own age much more than ours. We could do, I think, without a single one of the lawsuits on which Boswell sought Johnson's advice; with much less about religion, with fewer eulogies, without certain of Johnson's letters and some of other people's.

At any age one can be caught up in Boswell and appreciate the great virtues of his portrait of Johnson; but I suspect that one must be a good way past youth to appreciate the great virtues of Johnson himself.[1] That he was a magnificent talker one knows from the outset; but it needs a certain hard-won knowledge of the world to realize that he was also a magnificent man. For the man represents, on one side, almost everything an enlightened and forward-looking citizen of today must deprecate or condemn. He was not simply a staunch, he was a prejudiced and even to a degree a benighted, Tory. He believed in inequality and championed subordination; Whigs—and all the more as they corresponded to something approaching modern liberals—he detested and denounced; unlike almost every other great Englishman of his day, unlike even such feudal-minded Tories as Boswell, he opposed the claims of Wilkes in the Middlesex elections and the grievances of the American colonists; he supported rank, and

---

[1] I know that is true of myself; even what I put in print about Johnson a few years back seems to me, though sound enough in kind, very inadequate in degree.

showed every formal deference to a lord. Moreover, he
was very nearly as great a bigot in religion as he was
a Tory in politics—so much an adherent of the Established Church that in Scotland he refused to go of a
Sunday to the kirk. And to make matters more difficult, there is not just the rigidity of his beliefs but the
violence with which he espoused them. Which calls up
that last infirmity of a noble mind—Johnson's often in-
defensible social behavior. He could be both the worst
of boors and the worst of bullies. "Those," said Wraxall,
"whom Johnson could not . . . vanquish . . . by his
intellect, he silenced by his rudeness." He very often
"talked for victory," and then might say anything that
came into his head, and less say than shout it. He could
get violently angry; he could be shamefully unjust; he
could become outrageously insulting; and between being testy and taurine, he could disrupt—it is strange
that he did not sometimes empty—a drawing room. And
when he left the drawing room for the dinner table, he
might easily double the offense, for then one might be
as disgusted watching him bolt his food as one was ap-
palled hearing him whiplash his neighbors.

Yet if Dr. Johnson was all these things, he was im-
measurably more than the sum of them. He had, I think,
a larger nature, a truer benignity, a profounder humane-
ness than any other English writer of his age. Even his
faults live understandably inside the framework of his
mind, or can be ascribed in part to the infirmities of his
body. Johnson's religious bigotry, for example, was actuated not by passionate belief but by a strong tendency
toward disbelief. He, like Swift, had to be a rigid
churchman because he was not naturally a religious one;
each had a skeptical mind, and sensed that if he ever
conceded anything, he might wind up conceding all.
Johnson happened also to be weighed down by his

moral sense; he was painfully aware of how far he fell short of perfect virtue, and dreaded the thought that at the Judgment Day he might be held to have fallen too far short. Relative goodness offered no consolation: "The better a man is, the more afraid he is of death, having a clearer view of infinite purity." God, for Johnson, was someone not to love but to fear; no man ever got less comfort from his faith, or more perturbation. In the famous colloquy with Dr. Adams there was no talking for effect: Johnson meant literally what he said. "I am afraid," he remarked, "I may be one of those who shall be damned." "What do you mean," inquired Adams, "by being damned?" "Sent to Hell, Sir," Johnson thundered back, "and punished everlastingly." Johnson's morbid horror of death was certainly as much founded on the idea of damnation as on the idea of dissolution. His sort of believer could hardly help being his sort of bigot.

Johnson, again, was a Tory on principles that must be rejected but need not be misunderstood. To begin with, one can fairly point out that there was almost no self-interest in his Toryism. Rather was it rooted in that perfectly empirical view of life which concludes that all men are created *un*equal—not in worldly position alone, but in physique, in personality, in moral stamina, in intellectual capacity. Johnson saw life so; he also saw life much too pessimistically to have any faith in progress; and so saw nothing iniquitous in making the structure of society loosely conform to a "law" of nature. And in Johnson's view, the more arbitrarily it conformed to it, the less cause there was for individual resentment. If it is by pure accident that a man is born a lord, then the man who is not born one is far less stigmatized than if he had had the chance to become one and failed. Johnson really believed that accepting one's place in society

—at least as a convention—tended in the long run to make the individual happier. He saw in "the perpetual struggle for precedence" all the seeds of human dissatisfaction and rancor; while the new democratic conception of equality he thought mere cant. Everybody, he declared, talked of leveling *up*, but nobody of leveling down; and when, to test Mrs. Macaulay's equalitarian professions, he bade her invite her footman sit down and dine with them, he was smugly pleased to note how irritated she became. Moreover, it was one of Johnson's contentions that the ordinary man cares little about political equality; what he wants is personal liberty, the right to live his day-by-day life as he pleases. So far as he went, Johnson was probably right; only it seems never to have occurred to him that the two things might be crucially interdependent; his political obtuseness quite canceled out his psychological insight. The dangers of despotism Johnson airily disposed of by declaring that whenever a ruler becomes too despotic, the people will rise up and cut off his head.

He was, I am afraid—even for his own age—an archconservative. But despite the foolish pamphlets he wrote and the ingenious nonsense he talked (a good deal of it largely for effect), his practices often contraverted his principles, and his ethics were vastly superior to his politics. He could defy a lord as well as defer to one, and denounce injustice even more strenuously than he supported privilege. He would certainly have agreed with that monstrously undemocratic but not irresponsible belief of Burke's, that "though nothing should be done by the people, everything should be done for them." He himself did for them everything he could; whatever must be charged against Johnson's ability to think, very little can be levied against his capacity to feel. For the poor and disinherited and oppressed he

had more than profound compassion; he had real understanding. He had lived very much in the world, he had
been poor and miserable himself; and in respect of poverty, the pompous moralist was never imposed upon,
was always roused to anger, by the glib moralizing of
others:

"Sir," run the famous words, "all the arguments which are
brought to represent poverty as no evil show it to be evidently a great evil. You never find people laboring to convince you that you may live very happily upon a plentiful
fortune."

Indeed, the plight of the poor only made him impatient
with the dislocations of the well-off:

"The sight of people who want food and raiment is so
common in great cities, that a surly fellow like me has no
compassion to spare for wounds given only to vanity and
softness."

And Johnson did much more than abhor such outrages
as the slave trade or imprisonment for debt; he did
much more than relieve such patent distresses as home-
lessness and hunger. He loathed every pseudo-pious and
sanctimonious move to curtail or condemn the pleasures
of the poor. He knew to what crumbs of enjoyment the
poor were reduced; he knew *why* they got unruly, he
knew why they got drunk. He cast no stones, first or
last, at them: instead he spoke up for the few "sweeteners of their existence," he consorted with the "Laurin-
das" and Bet Flints, and took streetwalkers under his
own roof to be nursed back to health, and when he came
upon better days, spent on himself a mere fraction of his
income. We all remember how he filled his house with
dependents, but we may have forgotten the sort of
atmosphere they created: "Williams hates everybody.
Levet hates Desmoulines, and does not love Williams.

Desmoulines hates them both. Poll loves none of them."
Yet the surly fellow bore patiently with them all.

Johnson, moreover, rather did good by stealth than
ever seek to paint himself as better than he was. He detested what seemed to him false or fulsome sentiment.
"When a butcher," he remarked, "tells you that his heart
bleeds for his country, he has in fact no uneasy feeling."
Time and again he insisted that other people's troubles
never really disturb our own enjoyments; that one never
slept the worse, or ate the less, for this friend's sufferings or that friend's loss. It was in matters of this sort
that he rang all the changes on "Clear your mind of
cant"; in condemning fictitious virtue, Johnson even
contrived a kind of fictitious cynicism. In the matter of
"cant," Johnson himself may have indulged in a measure of cant-in-reverse; the word, at any rate, acquired a
pretty loose meaning in Johnson's mouth, and was made
to embrace some things that simply aroused his impatience. Such a famous statement as "No man but a
blockhead ever wrote except for money" is not to be
taken quite literally. It does not signify the philistine's
contempt for the artist, but rather, as Leslie Stephen
says, the professional's contempt for the amateur. And
fundamentally Johnson's war against cant constitutes a
sound protest against flattering self-deceptions, against
man's desire to seem finer-grained or sweeter-natured
than he is.

As for Johnson's personal faults—his bullying, his
boorishness, his abusive manner when opposed—they
may, while staining the brightness of his aura, light up
a little the darkness of his soul. For Johnson was all his
life a scarred and sick and deeply melancholy man. He
could not see or hear well; he had been disfigured in infancy by scrofula; he was wracked by dropsy and
asthma and gout, and tormented by sleeplessness; and

he must always have inwardly suffered from an appearance that earned him such sobriquets as Polyphemus and Caliban. Such a man had only the force of mind, only the power of personality, wherewith to leave his mark on others; and, burdened with pain, was not likely to be too nice in how he did it. Then too, as many people have observed, with his blunted sight and hearing he was not very aware of his behavior, of how fiercely he glared and how furiously he bellowed. But the worst of all the maladies besetting Johnson was that profound melancholy which so often overpowered him and which, save only at intervals, he never threw off. Swift had had something like it, too—though in Swift there was great frustration of living and rancor against life—and in the end it drove Swift mad; but Johnson fought indomitably against it, and against the madness he forever feared. "I will be conquered; I will not capitulate," said Johnson on his deathbed—Johnson who elsewhere asserted that there had never been a week he would choose to live over again. He had, if anyone ever had it, character; far more than he was a moralist, he was a man. The moralist might speak in abstractions from the mind; but time and again the man spoke out, with intense feeling, from the heart. We do not easily forget such things as Johnson's comment on his marriage, "I have known what it was to have a wife, and I have known what it was *to lose a wife"*; or his comment about drunkenness—"He who makes a *beast* of himself, gets rid of the pain of being a *man.*"

And irascible and ill-humored as Johnson could be, he was not ill-natured. It is almost a proof of how little real malevolence was in him that he played up his "hatreds" with humorous ostentation, making fun of Scotchmen, fulminating against Whigs. And in the very noise of such explosions there dwelt that terrific gusto that coun-

tervailed against melancholy and, along with his strength
of character, saved Johnson from despair. For, sad and
sick, Johnson yet loved life in every part of him, body
and belly, heart and mind.

And if the boor and the bully were largely the product of his ills, they were almost the conscious product.
In referring to the contretemps with Chesterfield, he
acutely distinguished his pride from Chesterfield's as
defensive pride; and so might we distinguish much of
his high-handedness as defensive high-handedness. As
Joseph Wood Krutch more or less remarks in his very
discerning biography, Johnson had to be a bully to
avoid being a butt, for the penalty of not enforcing
people's rather terrified respect must have been to court
their merciless derision. A stranger could only be ap-
palled by Johnson's looks; even his most devoted admirers could barely keep a straight face at moments
when this grotesque wall of flesh too grandly pontificated. Once, indeed, Henry Thrale was downright cutting about it: "There, there," he broke in, "now we have
had enough for one lecture, Dr. Johnson; we will not
be upon education any more till after dinner, if you
please." The grotesque appearance and the pompous
manner were a ludicrous combination; yet everything
considered, the manner was better suited to the appearance than any other would have been. It was sound
in Johnson, who must have failed with an informal
approach, to assume a magisterial one. Not that there
was anything studied about it: in Johnson's bullying
there was something defensive, and shaped by vanity;
but his high manner, his symposiarch role, were largely
born with him, concomitants of his enormous self-respect.
He was by nature eminent as he was by nature odd.

But his eminence and his oddness alike made him a
very lonely man, one who hungered to be loved and

longed to be "normal." The craving to be loved, to be
remembered, to be included, breaks out again and again,
never more poignantly than in some of the later letters
to Mrs. Thrale. But the less exposed pathos of his life
lay in how gratified he was, not by what was extraordinary in him, but in what he fancied might seem normal.
He undoubtedly took pleasure in those various displays
of physical strength and health that are preserved of
him—the riding to hounds, the swimming in the sea,
the midnight "frisks," the boyish rolls downhill; but
how much more he took pride. We smile, watching him
bustle about as one of Thrale's executors; but it was not
mere self-importance that made him delight in his
bourgeois role; it was also the sense of being a normal
man of the world. So too his light and playful manner
toward young girls and pretty women masks something
stronger than playfulness. Even though his marriage
with a woman almost twice his age be accepted as a
real love match, Johnson may have partly cherished it
—a little more than he knew—as the primary experience of normal life. For his was never really a normal
life; and deep down, Johnson knew it. And he knew it
for what was odd no less than for what was eminent
about him; beyond feeling the pangs of illness and the
clutch of melancholy and the fear of madness and the
terror of death, Johnson felt—more than most of us—
how painfully each man lives in this world alone. His
was not even a normal nature: "Have you not observed,"
he wrote to Mrs. Thrale, ". . . that my *genius* is always
in extremes; that I am very noisy, or very silent; very
gloomy, or very merry; very sour, or very kind?" With
all he had to face and fight off, his was indeed a very
great achievement in living. The sick man never became
an invalid. The pessimist never became a cynic. The
sufferer, though not free from self-pity, never ceased

to feel compassion for others. The rigid moralist never turned into a puritan; no man, in fact, of such narrow views ever had broader sympathies. And few men with such turbulent natures ever showed greater self-control. As I have said elsewhere, it was a wonderful triumph of character that such a man confined his gluttony to food and repartee.

Of Johnson the talker, there can be little new to say. Other men have displayed greater wisdom in conversation, and even greater wit; but I can think of no one who has been so consistently pointed and pungent, electrical and alive; or who, by his spoken words, has conveyed so much personality and character. For what he goes on being, Johnson chiefly has Boswell to thank; but not for what he was. Johnson's own age, an age very notable for conversation, considered him every bit as great a talker as we do; indeed, his talk was one of the wonders of that age. And what is finest about Johnson's talk is the sheer talk itself, not the substance, not the significance of it. On that score, we can only be delighted that Johnson was often wrongheaded in conversation, and sometimes absurd. We can only be delighted that people regarded Johnson as a sage, for he exerted himself to hold forth like a sage, and could be almost more rewarding when he pontificated than when he actually was wise. In him the power of expression was very nearly an equivalent of the power of thought —though there could also be, on occasion, most decided power of thought. But the pith and picturesqueness, the energy and ingenuity,[1] stand out as something great in itself; and it is no wonder that Johnson's constant

---

[1] In his prose, Johnson frequently turns the concrete into the abstract, but in his talk he does the reverse, clothing most of his ideas in vivid images and metaphors.

concern in discussion was not what arguments he should muster but which side he should take.

There can be little question, I think, that in his pronouncements Johnson was nearly as often wrong as he was right; or, which is as unsatisfactory, that he usually insisted on things being black or white, where more judicious men would allow that they were gray. Once he had unraveled (as he thought) the threads, and unknotted the kinks; once, that is, he had displayed to the full his dialectical skill, the matter was settled, the truth stood revealed. And certainly it must have seemed the truth to all but the most obstinate or perspicacious of his hearers. In talk Johnson had so superlative a gift for being pointed that it needed sharp judgment to grasp whether what he said was also to the point. Quite often it was not; Johnson's arguments could be as irrelevant as they were dazzling.

Yet we do get from his talk far more than just gymnastics or boldness or wit; we get a man with a considered view of the world,[1] a man who was enormously intelligent[2] about many things and remarkably unillusioned about many more; and we get a downrightness that is almost as valuable as it is engaging. What answer could be better than Johnson's when asked if he would write a preface to the work of a dunce: "Yes, Sir; and *say* he was a dunce." What could be more winningly honest or generally true than: "Mrs. Montagu has dropt me. Now, Sir, there are people whom one should like very well to drop, but would not wish to be dropt by." But all this particularizing seems of small account beside the great central fact about Johnson's

---

[1] "Human life is everywhere a state, in which much is to be endured and little to be enjoyed."

[2] Sir Walter Raleigh wrote in one of his letters of "Johnson's amazing intelligence, which, while he lived, made what he thought of you more important than what you thought of him."

talk—its sheer fascination. It is almost literally magnetic, in that it draws us to it, even where we have it by heart, over and over again.

Johnson occupied a very distinguished place in the London of his later days; but even in an age that regarded his writings as highly as his talk, that place was anything but absolute. Many important people of his time, some for sound reasons and some for snobbish ones, some from clashing temperament and some from injured vanity, could not abide him. He, who so strongly defended rank, refused to flatter the highborn and so, all too often, failed to please them. "Great lords and great ladies," he remarked, "don't like to have their mouths stopped": and the fact is worth repeating that "only one man of hereditary title," Sir Charles Bunbury, attended Johnson's funeral. But the lords and ladies, and many people who were neither, had good reason for resenting the *way* their mouths were stopped; and Mrs. Boswell is not to be wondered at for saying she had seen many a bear led by a man, but never before a man led by a bear. We know too, though fortunately Johnson did not, that even some of the titled folk who courted him did so very much on their own terms: Lady Lucan used to suggest sending for Dr. Johnson when there was to be no other company. Late in his life he became so overbearing and ill-mannered that people refused invitations to the Thrales if they knew he was to be there. Beyond all that, we may suppose that certain people always found Johnson's ideas uncongenial and repressive; in literature as in politics and religion his thought traveled backward; and a man who loudly execrated Voltaire, Hume, and Rousseau must have seemed, to his modern-minded contemporaries, a pretty obstructive anachronism.

Yet Johnson did have a very large and distinguished

circle—a fact, indeed, that is constantly flung at us as part proof of how great and conquering he was. Such "proof" has never carried as much weight with me as I daresay it should—not only because Johnson triumphs without it but because a large part of Johnson's circle leaves me cold. Rattle off the big names how you will, they still fail, most of them, to be very enticing. They seem—for all they came together to be edified—a little smug; and simply for so coming together, a little priggish. The Literary Club, with its phalanx of bishops and bishops-to-be, shows a decided ecclesiastical tinge; and, all in all, many of Johnson's friends had a very robust sense of their own moral superiority. One of the great virtues of Johnson's strongly charged presence is that he saved various gatherings from becoming stuffy. (On the other hand, it may have been an awareness of the Great Moralist's presence that induced some of the stuffiness.) Still, it is a question how much we should have liked a good many of Johnson's friends—not only Thrale and Sir John Hawkins, Fanny Burney and Hannah More, or from the earlier days, Richardson and Savage; but even that sinuous climber and polished hypocrite, Sir Joshua, even the illustrious Burke.[1] In some ways, the two most maligned of Johnson's intimates, Boswell and Mrs. Thrale, seem among the most congenial.

Mrs. Thrale was very much a society hostess and something of a lion-hunter; and in bagging Johnson, she and her husband acquired not just a monumental object for display, but someone who brought with him a whole procession of big game. As a hostess, Hetty

[1] Perhaps no century has produced so many distinguished or so many really interesting personalities as the eighteenth; yet among the personages who have survived, very few seem to me genuinely likeable; nor are those we like necessarily those we are able to esteem.

fizzed and foamed and doubtless drew upon all those
artful little insincerities that enhance the enjoyment of
guests. She was a superficial woman, proud of her
family connections (the more so for having married a
brewer) and pleased with her social success. But at
her own level she seems both attractive and amusing;
her prattle must have been far more engaging than the
solemn pronouncements of the *bas bleus;* and her vivacity seems as inborn as its manifestations seem occasionally contrived. In her relations with her husband,
certainly it is she who gains our sympathy. She had
never loved the cold authoritarian to whom she had
been more or less married off; and she must have known
he was constantly unfaithful to her, since she must have
known he was periodically diseased. In her relations
with Johnson, she was amiable and thoughtful until
near the end; and near the end she behaved no more
selfishly, and a good deal more politely, than he did.
Their whole relationship involves as much that is fundamental in human nature as that is fine. Streatham got
from Johnson the prestige of his presence, and its hostess the regard and devotion of a great man; Johnson got
from Streatham all the luxury he delighted in, and that
sense of home he had always craved. On the whole,
the Thrales needed Johnson less than he needed them;
and with the passing years, Mrs. Thrale perhaps found
the lion she had bagged uncomfortably leonine; yet,
even in the full face of his reserving his deepest regard
for her husband, she did all she could to make Johnson
easy and happy. The marriage to Piozzi, so far as it
concerned Hetty herself, was unexceptionable; and, as
it turned out, a genuine success. The marriage, so far
as it concerned Johnson, was one of those unhappy
blows that cannot be condemned, that can only be regretted. For the sick and lonely old man, watching the

door slowly close on what seemed to him his nearest approach to happiness, we can only be deeply sorry; but the man, wrapped up in his aches and infirmities, was decidedly querulous; in his attitude toward Piozzi he was notably unfair; and in his first rebuff of Mrs. Thrale, he was plainly insulting. To take sides in the matter would be to ignore the fact that both people were human beings. In the storybook sense, Hetty might for a year or two have held off marrying Piozzi to minister to Johnson; but that is not how people act, or can even be expected to act, in real life. In any case, her essential consideration for Johnson, and Johnson's essential greatness of heart, alike stand forth in almost the very last words that he ever addressed to her: "Whatever I can contribute to your happiness I am very ready to repay, for that kindness which soothed twenty years of a life radically wretched."

In any rapid view of Boswell, the faults must seem glaring and the man absurd. He could be an offensive toady, and then again could strut like a crow in the gutter. He not only rang the most impressive doorbells, but announced himself as a most desirable caller. And having pushed in among great men, he proceeded to ask them extremely impertinent questions. Most times he was something of a busybody, and sometimes a consummate nuisance. Anything but self-effacing when sober, he grew noisy, silly, and garrulous when drunk. Obsessed with family dignity, he had absolutely no dignity of his own; and pursuing the most ticklish enterprises, proved to be utterly wanting in tact.

Yet this man became, in varying degrees, the friend of Johnson, Reynolds, Goldsmith, Garrick, Burke, Wilkes, Paoli, Hume, Rousseau, Voltaire, of grave bishops and fine ladies, and a diner-out who clearly added to the gaiety and even the solidity of countless gatherings. He was, said Johnson, "a man whom everybody liked," and "the best traveling companion in the world." Since what made him a fool could hardly have made him a favorite, he must have had very saving social virtues. Two such stand out: good nature and high spirits. He could talk well and lead talk on, he could make people feel he was glad to be with them, and perhaps make them feel glad to be with one another. The lively companion was also a pretty skillful catalyst: he was constantly bringing people together that he thought would like each other, or no longer *not* like each other; and this risky and usually unwelcome maneuver for the most part succeeded. Certainly Boswell sought in all this to indulge his curiosity and add to his prestige; but there was present, too, a genuine benevolence. In a world where most meddling hints at mischief, and even the best of us get secret pleasure from seeing our friends at odds, Boswell delighted in watching enemies bury the hatchet. He had too in his relations with people a sympathy and sincerity that went beyond the effusive compliments he paid them. During an age when most people were forced to be on their dignity and to care desperately about appearances—when most people, that is, were under a social strain—Boswell must have offer 1 considerable, though it was only comic, relief. What made him a fool could hardly have made him a favorite; yet it need not have cost him much favor. Most people do not find it hard to like those whom they despise a little.

In solitude as in society, deep down as straight out, the man was a tissue of contrarieties. He was both cocksure and uncertain of himself; painfully self-searching yet comically self-deluded; a Tory in his beliefs and an anarchist in his behavior; unable to curb any of his physical cravings, yet capable of the stupendous discipline needed to complete the *Life;* romantic about love yet rakish about women; an inflexible snob and a born mixer; irrepressibly gay and morbidly gloomy. "Had Boswell been invented by a novelist," Bertrand Bronson has recently written, "we should at once reject the character as an amiable monster": perhaps it is simpler to say that Boswell is a character no novelist would have the audacity to invent. Obviously, Boswell was utterly unstable; and the rush and retreat of his emotions, the surge and collapse of his ego, the veering activities, the shifting goals, the Icarian flights, the broken resolutions, the constant self-recriminations, and always the punctual re-emergence of confidence and hope, made a tangled tragicomedy of Boswell's life. No impulse went unchecked, no emotion long held sway. It was merely fatuous of Boswell to strut about the Stratford Jubilee, or dress up fit to kill when he called on Pitt or Voltaire. It was childish showing-off in him, in the audience at Drury Lane, to imitate the lowing of a cow and become so enraptured with the applause that he attempted "other animals, but with very inferior effect." It was normal rather than not, on hearing of his mother's death, to rush out to a brothel. But there were odder facets. Consider his having two friends try separately to bribe his mistress out of remaining faithful to him; consider his bidding his best friend ask the girl Boswell wanted to marry whether she didn't think the Boswells were a little mad. But if such connivings—and they include things like not writing to Johnson to see whether Johnson would write to him—spring from an almost diseased vanity and a recurring self-doubt, they also bespeak a curiosity nearly as disinterested as it is consuming. There may have been enough of the masochist in Boswell to play with fire out of an obscure wish to be burnt; but there was yet a passionate interest in psychological processes, in human reactions, in whatever provided a clue to behavior or an insight into motive. And with his powerful desire to know went a staggering perseverance to find out. What *is* stable in Boswell is the compulsion to record, to fathom, to compass his instability.

He belongs indeed with those very few beings—Pepys and Rousseau are others—in whom the fierce need to confess the truth was united with the very rare ability. Only these few men have not required some sort of mask, or not wound up striking some sort of attitude. Possibly it was Boswell's permitting himself so much play-acting and fancy dress in public, his lack of inhibitions on the social stage, that helped him not to play-act on paper. We may allow that he possessed that extreme of egoism that preferred stating what was discreditable about himself to suppressing it. Even so, there was something else, something "scientific," some compulsion in the deepest and yet least involved part of his nature that made him ferret out the truth and then hold it boldly up to the light. Anyone both so passionately self-interested and so passionately disinterested in his probing must be accounted, by his very rarity, a kind of genius. Nor need we be surprised if that kind of genius also proves to be a kind of fool, if he has no intellectual values corresponding to his temperamental virtues. Boswell is in a certain sense like Saint-Simon. Neither man had any mind worth talking about, and both men held fast to absurdly outmoded ideas about society. But both were magnificent observers of themselves as well as of others, both could consummately portray, and both were always prepared to face and confess the truth.

In his friendship with Johnson, Boswell found the

most fruitful and fortunate element in his life, but it
was after all only an element. Boswell saw Johnson in-
tensively but infrequently, and even when he rattled
down to London from Scotland, it was to spend much
of his time with a very different sort of people. He
"sallied forth like a roaring Lion after girls" from whom
he all too often caught "the venereal disorder"; he drank
hard and turned up at times in polite society drunk; he
could seldom resist a Tyburn hanging; and on occasion
he hankered as much for the company of a Wilkes as of
a Johnson. It was indeed less his veneration for Johnson
than his love of London and distaste for Scotland that
kept driving him southward; in fact, he moved to London—against his best interests—*after* Johnson died. But
Johnson did bring out the good side of the man. The
two were alike in their politics and their piety, in their
love of talk, in their tremendous gusto, and up to a
point at least—for in Boswell it did not run very deep—
their melancholy. Johnson, too, provided Boswell with
an ideal to strive for, and in some sense served as a
father to a man who found his own father cold and
censorious. It would be quite wrong to suppose that
Boswell played the hypocrite with Johnson: for though
he concealed his wenching that amounted almost to
satyriasis, his desire for the good life was altogether
sincere: if Hell is paved, then Boswell was padded, with
good intentions. The relationship prospered rather more
than less because of Johnson's flare-ups and rebuffs, for
Boswell needed to have a mentor quite as much as
Johnson needed to be one. As for Boswell's dissolute
side, Johnson probably guessed its existence but not its
extent. But who, not knowing, could? To read Boswell's
letters to Temple after reading Boswell's *Life of Johnson*
is to come upon something really schizophrenic. Yet this
was a remarkable schizophrene indeed, one half of him

providing a supreme achievement in art, the other—
in the letters, journals, and private papers—a unique
and astounding revelation in psychology.

II

Though, for the general public, Johnson's pomposity
and polysyllables still stick to him like burs, in the
literary world of our time he has regained much of his
old eminence as a writer. The general reaction against
romanticism has helped; almost every "classical" writer
is more highly regarded today than he was a generation
ago. But Johnson's changed status reflects more than a
change in taste. He is recognized as in many ways a
distinguished and delightful writer; and has been so
recognized chiefly because he has once again been read.
The literary-minded have found what they had every
reason to expect—good sense, keen insight, and tremendous personal force; but they have also found what
may have taken them by surprise—a very full understanding of the ways of men, robust humor and droll
bluntness, prose of uncommon distinction and verse of
actual grandeur.

One must get used to Johnson. Parts of him are downright unreadable; but the parts that are not tend to seem
better with every re-reading. The intellectual framework inside which Johnson operates is not ours; it had
begun, indeed, to be outmoded while it was still current,
and it is just possible to contend that the last literary
age in which Johnson would have been fully at home
was that of Virgil and Horace. Yet inside this framework Johnson operated with great cogency, just as inside the framework of a given style he forged something
like a great one. Doubtless no one today would care to
write like Johnson; but beyond that, no one could.

Johnson lacked what his century generally had: a capacity for prose that was neat yet natural, elegant yet unceremonious, and whose beauty lay not in any overpowering use of language, but in its rhythm and its tone. The best of that prose—Sterne, Goldsmith, Gray—has too much temperament and breeding to tolerate magniloquence. With this style, a sort of domesticated classical one, Johnson's has nothing in common; Johnson's, in everything but sentence structure, is the child of the seventeenth century. Drawing heavily on the Latin element in the language, it can be grave, formal, and sonorous, and shows no affinity to speech (unless it be to Johnson's own). It is a prose that when it lacks the right theme or the right inspiration can become hopelessly heavy:

I have discovered, by a long series of observations, that invention and elocution suffer great impediments from dense and impure vapors, and that the tenuity of a defecated air at a proper distance from the surface of the earth, accelerates the fancy, and sets at liberty those intellectual powers which were before shackled by too strong attraction, and unable to expand themselves under the pressure of a gross atmosphere.

There is enough of this kind of thing in Johnson to explain why his style has become a byword for ponderosity. We may also condemn a side of his prose that, if easier to read, is no easier to relish—that side so overloaded with antithesis that it wears out our patience. And I would concede one thing more: that it is possible, from temperament, to dislike the way Johnson writes, even when it is vigorous or expressive in its kind. Let us take a famous passage, where Johnson almost, but not quite, parodies himself:

A grotto is not often the wish or pleasure of an Englishman, who has more frequent need to solicit than exclude the sun; but Pope's excavation was requisite as an entrance to his garden, and, as some men try to be proud of their defects, he extracted an ornament from an inconvenience, and vanity produced a grotto where necessity enforced a passage.

Nobody can read that sentence without being amused at the author; but where some people will smile and turn aside, others will smile and be drawn irresistibly on. But this particular manner, though many of us would not wish it away, does not always prevail. Johnson can be downright in a way that is almost droll. Refusing to get upset over Dryden's being passed up for a fellowship at Cambridge, Johnson remarks: "Had he thought himself injured, he knew how to complain." Or, noting that a very early work of Congreve's won praise, he concludes: "I would rather praise it than read it." Again and again Johnson's elaborate style becomes thus blunt and abrupt, and the effect is delightful.

But the sesquipedalian style he could also handle with distinction; and the great paragraph which really opens his discussion of Shakespeare ("The Poet, of whose works I have undertaken the revision . . ."), or the last half dozen pages of that Preface, or the conclusion of the Preface to the Dictionary, must take rank as great prose, though of not quite the greatest kind. Here pomposity becomes true pomp; here something Roman is wedded to something English, and sentences that are more fitly termed periods advance their meaning in a swell of sound.

If Johnson is known for anything to the present-day public, he is most likely known for *Rasselas*. Most of us "studied" it at school, and may still recall how Johnson wrote it in the evenings of one week to meet the expenses of his mother's funeral. The tale of the young prince and the old philosopher who escape from a happy, hemmed-in valley to survey the world at large was published the same year and follows much the same plan as *Candide;* but we shall look in vain for the liveliness, the malice, the headlong pace of Voltaire's masterpiece. *Rasselas* has, in fact, none of the interest or entertainment we have the right to expect of a novel. I myself can read any chapter of it with pleasure, but little more than that without fatigue. To be sure, we should not go to it seeking the rewards of a novel; what it has to offer is much sententious wisdom and much grave, even majestic, prose; and more particularly, the substance of Johnson's philosophic thought, of his settled view of life. It is a pessimistic and melancholy view, with the illusoriness—or at least the dissolution—of happiness as its constant burden. If I have used nothing from *Rasselas* here, it is largely because its view of life is formulated as solemnly, and much more succinctly, in the finest of Johnson's poems.

The Vanity of Human Wishes is, moreover, one of the finest poems of its kind that exists, and possibly the only extended thing of Johnson's upon which one can bestow unsullied praise. Its kind is, to be sure, by no means the highest or most magnetic form of poetry; *The Vanity of Human Wishes,* loosely rendering as it does Juvenal's Tenth Satire, is strongly didactic verse. But to it Johnson has given a certain didactic grandeur, and he has deepened it with something torn from his own experience. The famous couplets have the toll of iron bells:

> Yet hope not life from grief or danger free,
> Nor think the doom of man reversed for thee . . .

Johnson's periodical essays obtained for him high praise during his lifetime, when he was only less the author of *The Rambler* than the compiler of the Dictionary. It was chiefly in these papers, and the later *Adventurers* and *Idlers,* that Johnson won his spurs as a writer and his stature as a moralist. Johnson wished, of course, to do more in these essays than instruct and enlighten; following in the wake of the *Spectator,* he certainly at times wished to entertain; but it was not in his make-up, on such terms, to be entertaining. He had neither Addison's temperament nor Addison's touch; there was little about him of the easy, worldly depicter of manners, and even less of the genteelly whimsical humorist. Johnson in a sprightly mood is well-nigh intolerable, and Johnson trying to carve a cherrystone seems rather to be hammering a rock. Only when he comes to consider hope or friendship or fame, does he seem at home with his subject: he loved the grand abstractions, and could often say something gravely witty or oracularly wise about them.

No doubt the essays have a slow, massive, glacier-like force. Yet for a number of reasons—one of them, their glacier-like movement—it is impossible to read them with any real enjoyment. Many of them exhibit Johnson's style at its deadliest; nor is the style generally to be put up with for the sake of the substance. Despite many things that are keenly observed or nobly formulated, too often we fight past the polysyllables only to run head-on into platitudes. Johnson is perhaps liveliest when he writes in the strain of La Rochefoucauld, bringing home to men not how they ought to behave, but how they do:

Self-love is often rather arrogant than blind: it does not hide our faults from ourselves, but persuades us that they escape the notice of others.

Johnson's account of the trip he took with Boswell to the Hebrides—his *Journey to the Western Islands*—was

well summed up by Sir Walter Raleigh as the "most
ceremonious of diaries." It abounds in observations and
reflections that only Johnson would have made; but it
is certainly never chatty, and yet hardly very solid
either. Johnson saw what was to be seen, sometimes
with the care of a man taking notes for a book, sometimes with the complacency of a celebrity being polite,
sometimes with the attentiveness of a traveler storing
up impressions; but he seldom makes *you* see it; and
where the *Journey* does not seem a little perfunctory, it
seems too curious or ponderous. In small stretches it is
enjoyable reading, if only because the nature of the book
is so delightfully ill-suited to the nature of the author;
but one has only to turn to Boswell's account of the
same tour to realize all that Johnson missed, and all
that he mismanaged. The two accounts are indeed so
unlike that my original scheme of setting down Johnson's and Boswell's versions of the same events had to be
discarded; for they produce not a valuable contrast but
almost a disbelief that they are dealing with the same
things.[1]

The Lives of the Poets, written in old age from
neither want of money nor need for fame, are Johnson's
most satisfying and engaging work. The story of how
they came to be written you will find by turning to
Boswell; the proof of how good they can be you will find
by reading the *Pope.* Perhaps the first thing to be said
of them is that they were better suited to Johnson's
genius than anything else, save only *The Vanity of Human Wishes,* that he ever wrote. They were, indeed,
exactly suited to his genius, which was that of a great

---

[1] To be appreciated as a travel book, Boswell's *Hebrides* needs
pretty much to be read as a whole; no drastic abridgement could
preserve the color and continuity of the Tour. The extracts here have,
in the main, been chosen for their value as Johnsoniana.

man of letters rather than, in the narrow sense, of a great biographer, scholar, or critic. In the man of letters was splendidly combined a good deal of all three without providing a supreme example of any one. Johnson had at his command both language and learning, both insight and wit; he had a feeling for literature and an even stronger feeling for the literary world; he loved speculation but equally loved facts; he was interested in poetry, but absorbed by personality; and the *Lives* offered a chance to blend his capacities in a way that best set them off. Moreover, the chance came at just the right period of his life. His perceptions were still sharp but his approach to the world had mellowed, and he wrote, less out of closeted study than out of a lifetime's knowledge. He let himself go; he moved, confidently and a little carelessly, down the long corridor of almost two centuries of poetry. Writing of Rowe's plays, he freely admitted that he had not looked at them for thirty years; and there were other things (like that early novel of Congreve's) that he would not bother to look at at all.

The *Lives* interlard biography with criticism, and remain an example of old-fashioned biography and old-fashioned criticism at its best. Boswell was to revolutionize the one field, and a host of nineteenth-century critics the other, and both fields were to be the richer for the change; but they were also to lose something, and by reading Johnson we can see just what they lost. It was a certain high firmness of touch and fixedness of limits. For Johnson as critic, the earth might still, so to speak, be flat; one never explored far places on the map; but then, one never lost one's way. He knew what he liked, and usually why he liked it; he formulated, he generalized, he summed up with the force of a master. *He* was on firm ground even when his opinions were not; and esthetically, of course, they very often were not. There are regions into which mere good sense cannot penetrate; there are gaps in taste which no amount of ingenuity can conceal; there are times when it is plainly fatal to have too little sensibility. But, as later critics have proved, there are also times when it is fatal to have too much.

That balance of qualities—of toughness and sensibility, of clearsightedness and vision, of being equally at home on earth and in the empyrean—which is at least the theoretical mark of the greatest kind of critic, Johnson never remotely attained to; his powers are limited and too much on one side. Perhaps we may divide imperfect critics into two classes: those who fail to see everything that is there, and those who see things that aren't there at all. The one kind is apt to miss the point, the other to force it. Johnson is a good example of the first kind—a man who makes literature come to him rather than one who goes out to it, a man for whom art is rather a confirmation than an enlargement of experience. Beyond all that—if it is not anterior to all that—he was a good deal of a crustacean in his tastes; he disliked what was new or unorthodox, and was seldom equipped to assess it. Again, too much logic could defeat him: it is "logic," really, rather than prejudice, that arrives at such verdicts as the notorious one on *Lycidas*.

This is to simplify; for on scores of occasions Johnson surprises us by his largeness of grasp, or his sympathy with what seems alien to his nature. But it remains true that Johnson very often went by the rules, were they only rules of his own; and that to a certain rigidity he added a certain literal-mindedness. The moralist in him also harmed the critic, not because the moral qualities of literature can be easily overstressed, but because Johnson insisted that they be overt and didactic. Yet this, like everything else, was born of something in *him*, and not of lip-service to prevailing beliefs. It is, indeed, because Johnson is so independent-minded in his judgments that he is a traditional critic without being in the slightest degree a conventional one. He is one of the boldest critics there are; and hence, despite what seems outmoded in him, still one of the most bracing.

As a biographer, Johnson was old-fashioned in the sense that—from the standpoint of today—biography itself was. It had still to acquire more intimacy of atmosphere, more richness of texture; yet it was in Johnson's plan, as it was in his nature, to banish from biography the pious and adulatory tone that was rendering so much of it worthless. Johnson not only proposed to tell the truth about his poets, but he firmly put telling the truth above everything else. He also enriched, as well as enlivened, his biographies by his love of the vivid anecdote, the eloquent scrap or detail. Still, we must not turn to the *Lives* expecting something beautifully ordered or dramatically heightened; nor should we look for a wholly balanced treatment: Johnson, to a considerable extent, enlarged upon what interested him and excluded what did not.

The *Life of Savage* stands apart from the other *Lives*: beyond having been written some thirty-five years earlier, it is the personal memoir of a friend and the life story of a rascal. It is, indeed, not least enjoyable for setting out to be a kind of vindication and winding up, a kind of exposé. Johnson did his best by his friend: he swallowed not only Savage's claims to be the illegitimate son of a noblewoman, but even his claims to be a poet. Yet all Johnson's affection and magnanimity could not keep him from recognizing—or from reporting—a sizable amount of the truth; and we soon see, all too clearly, what sort of character Savage was. Despite its heavy writing here and there, the *Savage* is perhaps the most entertaining and flavorsome thing that Johnson ever wrote. It remains a classic study of disreputableness.

The Preface to the Shakespeare is Johnson's solidest piece of criticism. It takes an Age-of-Reason view of its subject, which comes at least as close to our own view as the long-enthroned Romantic one; whatever Johnson's limitations, he neither deifies Shakespeare nor re-creates him in his own image. To Johnson, as to us, Shakespeare was a fallible and uneven writer, and a supreme genius rather than a supreme artist. For Johnson, in fact, he was pre-eminently a "poet of Nature," someone who plucked out the universal aspects of human life, "the general passions and principles by which all minds are agitated." ("His story requires Romans or kings, but he thinks only on men.") This is praise, we may note, of Shakespeare the psychologist rather than the poet; and it is praise, once again, of what Johnson could confirm from his own experience. So too, when Johnson makes his famous defense of Shakespeare's violation of the Unities, he is prompted by a logical and not an esthetic view of art. What may possibly be lost in intensity by jumping a thousand miles or a dozen years is not investigated; and it is Johnson's common-sense conclusion that the Unities "have given more trouble to the poet than pleasure to the audience." Yet, so far as it goes, the case Johnson makes out is trenchant.

For the sublime in Shakespeare—as for the sublime generally—Johnson had real feeling; yet it would be foolish to argue that for Shakespeare's poetry as a whole —or for the poetry in relation to the psychology and the drama—Johnson had anything like a full appreciation. He was properly irritated by Shakespeare's way of defacing great scenes with curious ornament, and there is more than a trace of truth in Johnson's dictum that Shakespeare "never has six lines together without a fault." But, by and large, Johnson's responsiveness simply could not keep pace with Shakespeare's imagination, and he seems at times to have pierced through the poetry to the meaning rather than to have found the meaning *in* the poetry. It is this lack in Johnson that leads him to make the most serious, and most astonishing, of his Shakespearean blunders—the setting of Shakespeare's comedy higher than his tragedy. "His tragedy," Johnson summed up, "seems to be skill, his comedy to be instinct." But even were this so, Johnson would be ignoring the fact that Cleopatra and Iago and Lear breathe an air known to no comic character of Shakespeare's but Falstaff. Yet Johnson must have sometimes felt what he did not formulate: consider the most famous of all the Notes on Shakespeare—"He that peruses Shakespeare, looks round alarmed, and starts to find himself alone." That emotion is not born of *As You Like It* or *The Taming of the Shrew.*

Shakespeare also disturbed Johnson because he was not explicitly moral enough; here again we may say that Johnson seems to have pierced through the poetry to the morality rather than to have found the morality *in* the poetry. It is really this objection that underlies such opinions as preferring a happy ending to *Lear:* "I cannot easily be persuaded, that . . . the audience will not always rise better pleased from the final triumph of persecuted virtue." Yet, in spite of himself, Johnson is forced to remark: "A play in which the wicked prosper, and the virtuous miscarry, may doubtless be good, because it is a just representation of the common events of human life." In Johnson the critic, the moralist, and the realist were too often at war not to tarnish the criticism; but the realist was seldom absent, however he might choose to give ground. And though Johnson may not have been the ideal critic of Shakespeare, he wrote about him with a sanity, a fearlessness, a frequent justness of perception, and a deep if partly dissembled love, that constitute a large and lasting service.

In view of Johnson's glaring faults and occasional outrageous blunders, perhaps it must always be his fate to be censured in the very act of being praised. But, after all possible deductions have been made, he is surely a great figure and something like a great force. And to read the best of his writings is to come upon a mind and character scarcely to be imagined from even the best of his talk. The lamps that gave him light were growing dimmer as he wrote, and the wild new glow in the sky was something he stubbornly refused to see; but the light he worked by recovers its brightness in the work he did, and leads us backward, but not astray.

LOUIS KRONENBERGER

JAMES BOSWELL

From THE LIFE
OF SAMUEL JOHNSON, LL.D.

TO WRITE the Life of him who excelled all mankind in writing the lives of others, and who, whether we consider his extraordinary endowments, or his various works, has been equalled by few in any age, is an arduous, and may be reckoned in me a presumptuous task.

Had Dr. Johnson written his own Life, in conformity with the opinion which he has given, that every man's life may be best written by himself; had he employed in the preservation of his own history, that clearness of narration and elegance of language in which he has embalmed so many eminent persons, the world would probably have had the most perfect example of biography that was ever exhibited. But although he at different times, in a desultory manner, committed to writing many particulars of the progress of his mind and fortunes, he never had persevering diligence enough to form them into a regular composition. Of these memorials a few have been preserved; but the greater part was consigned by him to the flames, a few days before his death.

As I had the honour and happiness of enjoying his friendship for upwards of twenty years; as I had the scheme of writing his life constantly in view; as he was well apprised of this circumstance, and from time to time obligingly satisfied my enquiries, by communicating to me the incidents of his early years; as I acquired a facility in recollecting, and was very assiduous in recording, his conversation, of which the extraordinary vigour and vivacity constituted one of the first features of his character; and as I have spared no pains in obtaining materials concerning him, from every quarter where I could discover that they were to be found, and have been favoured with the most liberal communications by his friends; I flatter myself that few biographers have entered upon such a work as this, with more advantages; independent of literary abilities, in which I am not vain enough to compare myself with some great names who have gone before me in this kind of writing.

Instead of melting down my materials into one mass, and constantly speaking in my own person, by which I might have appeared to have more merit in the execution of the work, I have resolved to adopt and enlarge upon the excellent plan of Mr. Mason, in his Memoirs of Gray. Wherever narrative is necessary to explain, connect, and supply, I furnish it to the best of my abilities; but in the chronological series of Johnson's life, which I trace as distinctly as I can, year by year, I produce, wherever it is in my power, his own minutes, letters, or conversation, being convinced that this mode is more lively, and will make my readers better acquainted with him, than even most of those were who actually knew him, but could know him only partially; whereas there is here an accumulation of intelligence from various points, by which his character is more fully understood and illustrated.

Indeed I cannot conceive a more perfect mode of writing any man's life, than not only relating all the most important events of it in their order, but interweaving what he privately wrote, and said, and thought; by which mankind are enabled as it were to see him live, and to "live o'er each scene" with him, as he actually advanced through the several stages of his life. Had his other friends been as diligent and ardent as I was, he might have been almost entirely preserved. As it is, I will venture to say that he will be seen in this work more completely than any man who has ever yet lived.

And he will be seen as he really was; for I profess to write, not his panegyrick, which must be all praise, but his Life; which, great and good as he was, must not be supposed to be entirely perfect. To be as he was, is indeed subject of panegyrick enough to any man in this state of being; but in every picture there should be shade as well as light, and when I delineate him without reserve, I do what he himself recommended, both by his precept and his example.

1709-1727. SAMUEL JOHNSON was born in Lichfield, in Staffordshire, on the 18th of September, N.S. 1709; and his initiation into the Christian church was not delayed; for his baptism is recorded in the register of St. Mary's parish in that city, to have been performed on the day of his birth: His father is there stiled *Gentleman,* a circumstance of which an ignorant panegyrist has praised him for not being proud; when the truth is, that the appellation of Gentleman, though now lost in the indiscriminate assumption of *Esquire,* was commonly taken by those who could not boast of gentility. His father was Michael Johnson, a native of Derbyshire, of obscure extraction, who settled in Lichfield as a bookseller and stationer. His mother was Sarah Ford, descended of an ancient race of substantial yeomanry in Warwickshire. They were well advanced in years when they married, and never had more than two children, both sons, Samuel, their first-born, who lived to be the illustrious character whose various excellence I am to endeavour to record, and Nathanael, who died in his twenty-fifth year.

Mr. Michael Johnson was a man of a large and robust body, and of a strong and active mind; yet, as in the most solid rocks, veins of unsound substance are often discovered, there was in him a mixture of that disease, the nature of which eludes the most minute enquiry, though the effects are well known to be a weariness of life, an unconcern about those things which agitate the greater part of mankind, and a general sensation of gloomy wretchedness. From him then his son inherited, with some other qualities, "a vile melancholy," which in his too strong expression of any disturbance of mind, "made him mad all his life, at least not sober." Michael was, however, forced by the narrowness of his circumstances to be very diligent in business, not only in his shop, but by occasionally resorting to several towns in the neighbourhood, some of which were at a considerable distance from Lichfield. At that time booksellers' shops in the provincial towns of England were very rare, so that there was not one even in Birmingham, in which town old Mr. Johnson used to open a shop every market-day. He was a pretty good Latin scholar, and a citizen so creditable as to be made one of the magistrates of Lichfield; and, being a man of good sense, and skill in his trade, he acquired a reasonable share of wealth, of which however he afterwards lost the greatest part, by engaging unsuccessfully in a manufacture of parchment. He was a zealous high-church man and royalist, and retained his attachment to the unfortunate house of Stuart, though he reconciled himself, by casuistical arguments of expediency and necessity, to take the oaths imposed by the prevailing power.

Johnson's mother was a woman of distinguished understanding. I asked his old school-fellow, Mr. Hector,

surgeon, of Birmingham, if she was not vain of her son.
He said, "she had too much good sense to be vain, but
she knew her son's value." Her piety was not inferiour
to her understanding; and to her must be ascribed those
early impressions of religion upon the mind of her son,
from which the world afterwards derived so much benefit. He told me, that he remembered distinctly having
had the first notice of Heaven, "a place to which good
people went," and hell, "a place to which bad people
went," communicated to him by her, when a little child
in bed with her.

Of the power of his memory, for which he was all his
life eminent to a degree almost incredible, the following
early instance was told me in his presence at Lichfield,
in 1776, by his step-daughter, Mrs. Lucy Porter, as related to her by his mother. When he was a child in petti-
coats, and had learnt to read, Mrs. Johnson one morning
put the common prayer-book into his hands, pointed to
the collect for the day, and said, "Sam, you must get this
by heart." She went up stairs, leaving him to study it:
but by the time she had reached the second floor, she
heard him following her. "What's the matter?" said she.
"I can say it," he replied; and repeated it distinctly,
though he could not have read it more than twice.

Young Johnson had the misfortune to be much afflicted with the scrophula, or king's-evil, which disfigured a countenance naturally well formed, and hurt
his visual nerves so much, that he did not see at all with
one of his eyes, though its appearance was little different
from that of the other. There is amongst his prayers, one
inscribed "*When my* EYE *was restored to its use*," which
ascertains a defect that many of his friends knew he had,
though I never perceived it. I supposed him to be only
near-sighted; and indeed I must observe, that in no
other respect could I discern any defect in his vision; on

the contrary, the force of his attention and perceptive
quickness made him see and distinguish all manner of
objects, whether of nature or of art, with a nicety that is
rarely to be found. When he and I were travelling in the
Highlands of Scotland, and I pointed out to him a mountain which I observed resembled a cone, he corrected
my inaccuracy, by shewing me, that it was indeed
pointed at the top, but that one side of it was larger than
the other. And the ladies with whom he was acquainted
agree, that no man was more nicely and minutely critical
in the elegance of female dress. When I found that he
saw the romantick beauties of Islam, in Derbyshire,
much better than I did, I told him that he resembled an
able performer upon a bad instrument. How false and
contemptible then are all the remarks which have been
made to the prejudice either of his candour or of his
philosophy, founded upon a supposition that he was almost blind. It has been said, that he contracted this
grievous malady from his nurse. His mother, yielding to
the superstitious notion, which, it is wonderful to think,
prevailed so long in this country, as to the virtue of the
regal touch; a notion, which our kings encouraged, and
to which a man of such enquiry and such judgement as
Carte could give credit; carried him to London, where
he was actually touched by Queen Anne. Mrs. Johnson
indeed, as Mr. Hector informed me, acted by the advice
of the celebrated Sir John Floyer, then a physician in
Lichfield. Johnson used to talk of this very frankly; and
Mrs. Piozzi has preserved his very picturesque description of the scene, as it remained upon his fancy. Being
asked if he could remember Queen Anne,—"He had (he
said) a confused, but somehow a sort of solemn recollection of a lady in diamonds, and a long black hood." This
touch, however, was without any effect. I ventured to
say to him, in allusion to the political principles in which

he was educated, and of which he ever retained some odour, that "his mother had not carried him far enough; she should have taken him to ROME."

He was first taught to read English by Dame Oliver, a widow, who kept a school for young children in Lichfield. He told me she could read the black letter, and asked him to borrow for her, from his father, a bible in that character. When he was going to Oxford, she came to take leave of him, brought him, in the simplicity of her kindness, a present of gingerbread, and said he was the best scholar she ever had. He delighted in mentioning this early compliment: adding, with smile, that "this was as high a proof of his merit as he could conceive." His next instructor in English was a master, whom, when he spoke of him to me, he familiarly called Tom Brown, who, said he, "published a spelling-book, and dedicated it to the UNIVERSE; but, I fear, no copy of it can now be had."

He began to learn Latin with Mr. Hawkins, usher, or undermaster of Lichfield school, "a man (said he) very skilful in his little way." With him he continued two years, and then rose to be under the care of Mr. Hunter, the headmaster, who, according to his account, "was very severe, and wrong-headedly severe. He used (said he) to beat us unmercifully; and he did not distinguish between ignorance and negligence; for he would beat a boy equally for not knowing a thing, as for neglecting to know it. He would ask a boy a question, and if he did not answer it, he would beat him, without considering whether he had an opportunity of knowing how to answer it. For instance, he would call up a boy and ask him Latin for a candlestick, which the boy could not expect to be asked. Now, Sir, if a boy could answer every question, there would be no need of a master to teach him."

Indeed Johnson was very sensible how much he owed

to Mr. Hunter. Mr. Langton one day asked him how he
had acquired so accurate a knowledge of Latin, in
which, I believe, he was exceeded by no man of his
time; he said, "My master whipt me very well. Without
that, Sir, I should have done nothing." He told Mr.
Langton, that while Hunter was flogging his boys unmercifully, he used to say, "And this I do to save you
from the gallows." Johnson, upon all occasions, expressed his approbation of enforcing instruction by
means of the rod. "I would rather (said he) have the
rod to be the general terrour to all, to make them learn,
than tell a child, if you do thus, or thus, you will be more
esteemed than your brothers or sisters. The rod produces
an effect which terminates in itself. A child is afraid of
being whipped, and gets his task, and there's an end
on't; whereas, by exciting emulation and comparisons of
superiority, you lay the foundation of lasting mischief;
you make brothers and sisters hate each other."

That superiority over his fellows, which he maintained with so much dignity in his march through life,
was not assumed from vanity and ostentation, but was
the natural and constant effect of those extraordinary
powers of mind, of which he could not but be conscious
by comparison; the intellectual difference, which in
other cases of comparison of characters, is often a matter
of undecided contest, being as clear in his case as the
superiority of stature in some men above others. Johnson did not strut or stand on tip-toe; he only did not
stoop. From his earliest years, his superiority was perceived and acknowledged. He was from the beginning,
Ἄναξ ανδεῶν, a king of men. His favourites used to receive very liberal assistance from him; and such was
the submission and deference with which he was treated,
such the desire to obtain his regard, that three of the
boys, of whom Mr. Hector was sometimes one, used

to come in the morning as his humble attendants, and carry him to school. One in the middle stooped, while he sat upon his back, and one on each side supported him; and thus he was borne triumphant. Such a proof of the early predominance of intellectual vigour is very remarkable, and does honour to human nature.—Talking to me once himself of his being much distinguished at school, he told me, "they never thought to raise me by comparing me to any one; they never said, Johnson is as good a scholar as such a one; but such a one is as good a scholar as Johnson; and this was said but of one, but of Lowe; and I do not think he was as good a scholar."

He discovered a great ambition to excel, which roused him to counteract his indolence. He was uncommonly inquisitive; and his memory was so tenacious, that he never forgot anything that he either heard or read. Mr. Hector remembers having recited to him eighteen verses, which, after a little pause, he repeated *verbatim*, varying only one epithet, by which he improved the line.

He never joined with the other boys in their ordinary diversions: his only amusement was in winter, when he took a pleasure in being drawn upon the ice by a boy barefooted, who pulled him along by a garter fixed around him; no very easy operation, as his size was remarkably large.

After having resided for some time at the house of his uncle, Cornelius Ford, Johnson was, at the age of fifteen, removed to the school of Stourbridge, in Worcestershire, of which Mr. Wentworth was then master. This step was taken by the advice of his cousin, the Rev. Mr. Ford, a man in whom both talents and good dispositions were disgraced by licentiousness, but who was a very able judge of what was right. At this school he did not receive so much benefit as was expected. It has been said, that he acted in the capacity of an assistant to Mr.

Wentworth, in teaching the younger boys. "Mr. Wentworth (he told me) was a very able man, but an idle man, and to me very severe; but I cannot blame him much. I was then a big boy; he saw I did not reverence him; and that he should get no honour by me. I had brought enough with me, to carry me through; and all I should get at his school would be ascribed to my own labour, or to my former master. Yet he taught me a great deal."

He thus discriminated, to Dr. Percy, Bishop of Dromore, his progress at his two grammar-schools. "At one, I learned much in the school, but little from the master; in the other, I learnt much from the master, but little in the school."

1728. That a man in Mr. Michael Johnson's circumstances should think of sending his son to the expensive University of Oxford, at his own charge, seems very improbable. The subject was too delicate to question Johnson upon; but I have been assured by Dr. Taylor, that the scheme never would have taken place, had not a gentleman of Shropshire, one of his school-fellows, spontaneously undertaken to support him at Oxford, in the character of his companion: though, in fact, he never received any assistance whatever from that gentleman.

He, however, went to Oxford, and was entered a Commoner of Pembroke College, on the 31st of October, 1728, being then in his nineteenth year.

His tutor, Mr. Jorden, fellow of Pembroke, was not, it seems, a man of such abilities as we should conceive requisite for the instructor of Samuel Johnson, who gave me the following account of him. "He was a very worthy man, but a heavy man, and I did not profit much by his instructions. Indeed, I did not attend him much. The first day after I came to college, I waited upon him, and then staid away four. On the sixth, Mr. Jorden asked me why I had not attended. I answered, I had been sliding in Christ-Church meadow. And this I said with as much *nonchalance* as I am now talking to you. I had no notion that I was wrong or irreverent to my tutor." BOSWELL. "That, Sir, was great fortitude of mind." JOHNSON. "No, Sir, stark insensibility."

1729. The "morbid melancholy," which was lurking in his constitution, and to which we may ascribe those particularities, and that aversion to regular life, which, at a very early period, marked his character, gathered such strength in his twentieth year, as to afflict him in a dreadful manner. While he was at Lichfield, in the college vacation of the year 1729, he felt himself overwhelmed with an horrible hypochondria, with perpetual irritation, fretfulness, and impatience; and with a dejection, gloom, and despair, which made existence misery. From this dismal malady he never afterwards was perfectly relieved; and all his labours, and all his enjoyments, were but temporary interruptions of its baleful influence.

The particular course of his reading while at Oxford, and during the time of vacation which he passed at home, cannot be traced. Enough has been said of his irregular mode of study. He told me, that from his earliest years he loved to read poetry, but hardly ever read any poem to an end; that he read Shakespeare at a period so early, that the speech of the Ghost in Hamlet terrified him when he was alone; that Horace's Odes were the compositions in which he took most delight, and it was long before he liked his Epistles and Satires. He told me what **he** read *solidly* at Oxford was **Greek; not the**

Grecian historians, but Homer and Euripides, and now and then a little Epigram; that the study of which he was the most fond was Metaphysicks, but he had not read much, even in that way. I always thought that he did himself injustice in his account of what he had read, and that he must have been speaking with reference to the vast portion of study which is possible, and to which a few scholars in the whole history of literature have attained; for when I once asked him whether a person whose name I have now forgotten, studied hard, he answered "No, Sir. I do not believe he studied hard. I never knew a man who studied hard. I conclude, indeed, from the effects, that some men have studied hard, as Bentley and Clarke." Trying him by that criterion upon which he formed his judgement of others, we may be absolutely certain, both from his writings and his conversation, that his reading was very extensive. Dr. Adam Smith, than whom few were better judges on this subject, once observed to me, that "Johnson knew more books than any man alive."

Dr. Adams told me that Johnson, while he was at Pembroke College, "was caressed and loved by all about him, was a gay and frolicksome fellow, and passed there the happiest part of his life." But this is a striking proof of the fallacy of appearances, and how little any of us know of the real internal state even of those whom we see most frequently; for the truth is, that he was then depressed by poverty, and irritated by disease. When I mentioned to him this account as given me by Dr. Adams, he said, "Ah, Sir, I was mad and violent. It was bitterness which they mistook for frolick. I was miserably poor, and I thought to fight my way by my literature and my wit; so I disregarded all power and all authority."

I do not find that he formed any close intimacies with

his fellow-collegians. But Dr. Adams told me, that he contracted a love and regard for Pembroke College, which he retained to the last. Being himself a poet, Johnson was peculiarly happy in mentioning how many of the sons of Pembroke were poets; adding, with a smile of sportive triumph, "Sir, we are a nest of singing birds."

He made enquiry all round the University, and having found that Mr. Bateman, of Christ-Church, was the tutor of highest reputation, Taylor was entered of that College. Mr. Bateman's lectures were so excellent, that Johnson used to come and get them at second-hand from Taylor, till his poverty being so extreme, that his shoes were worn out, and his feet appeared through them, he saw that this humiliating circumstance was perceived by the Christ-Church men, and he came no more. He was too proud to accept of money, and somebody having set a pair of new shoes at his door, he threw them away with indignation.

The *res angusta domi* prevented him from having the advantage of a complete academical education. The friend to whom he had trusted for support had deceived him. His debts in College, though not great, were increasing; and his scanty remittances from Lichfield, which had all along been made with great difficulty, could be supplied no longer, his father having fallen into a state of insolvency. Compelled, therefore, by irresistible necessity, he left the College in autumn, 1731, without a degree, having been a member of it little more than three years.

And now (I had almost said *poor*) Samuel Johnson returned to his native city, destitute, and not knowing how he should gain even a decent livelihood. His father's misfortunes in trade rendered him unable to support his son; and for some time there appeared no means by which he could maintain himself. In the December of this year his father died.

1732. In the forlorn state of his circumstances, he accepted of an offer to be employed as usher in the school of Market-Bosworth, in Leicestershire, to which it appears from one of his little fragments of a diary, that he went on foot, on the 16th of July. This employment was very irksome to him in every respect, and he complained grievously of it in his letters to his friend, Mr. Hector, who was now settled as a surgeon at Birmingham. His general aversion to this painful drudgery was greatly enhanced by a disagreement between him and Sir Wolstan Dixie, the patron of the school, in whose house, I have been told, he officiated as a kind of domestick chaplain, so far, at least, as to say grace at table, but was treated with what he represented as intolerable harshness; and, after suffering for a few months such complicated misery, he relinquished a situation which all his life afterwards he recollected with the strongest aversion, and even a degree of horror.

1736. Johnson had, from his early youth, been sensible to the influence of female charms. His juvenile attachments to the fair sex were, however, very transient: and it is certain, that he formed no criminal connection whatsoever. Mr. Hector, who lived with him in his younger days in the utmost intimacy and social freedom, has assured me, that even at that ardent season his conduct was strictly virtuous in that respect; and that though he loved to exhilarate himself with wine, he never knew him intoxicated but once.

In a man whom religious education has secured from

licentious indulgences, the passion of love, when once it has seized him, is exceedingly strong; being unimpaired by dissipation, and totally concentrated in one object. This was experienced by Johnson, when he became the fervent admirer of Mrs. Porter, after her first husband's death. Miss Porter told me, that when he was first introduced to her mother, his appearance was very forbidding: he was then lean and lank, so that his immense structure of bones was hideously striking to the eye, and the scars of the scrophula were deeply visible. He also wore his hair, which was straight and stiff, and separated behind: and he often had, seemingly, convulsive starts and odd gesticulations, which tended to excite at once surprise and ridicule. Mrs. Porter was so much engaged by his conversation that she overlooked all these external disadvantages, and said to her daughter, "this is the most sensible man that I ever saw in my life."

Though Mrs. Porter was double the age of Johnson, and her person and manner, as described to me by the late Mr. Garrick, were by no means pleasing to others, she must have had a superiority of understanding and talents as she certainly inspired him with a more than ordinary passion; and she having signified her willingness to accept of his hand, he went to Lichfield to ask his mother's consent to the marriage; which he could not but be conscious was a very imprudent scheme, both on account of their disparity of years, and her want of fortune. But Mrs. Johnson knew too well the ardour of her son's temper, and was too tender a parent to oppose his inclinations.

I know not for what reason the marriage ceremony was not performed at Birmingham; but a resolution was taken that it should be at Derby, for which place the bride and bridegroom set out on horseback, I suppose in very good humour. But though Mr. Topham Beau-clerk used archly to mention Johnson's having told him with much gravity, "Sir, it was a love marriage on both sides," I have had from my illustrious friend the follow-ing curious account of their journey to church upon the nuptial morn:—"Sir, she had read the old romances, and had got into her head the fantastical notion that a woman of spirit should use her lover like a dog. So, Sir, at first she told me that I rode too fast, and she could not keep up with me: and, when I rode a little slower, she passed me, and complained that I lagged behind. I was not to be made the slave of caprice; and I resolved to begin as I meant to end. I therefore pushed on briskly, till I was fairly out of her sight. The road lay between two hedges, so I was sure she could not miss it; and I contrived that she should soon come up with me. When she did, I observed her to be in tears."

This, it must be allowed, was a singular beginning of connubial felicity; but there is no doubt that Johnson, though he thus shewed a manly firmness, proved a most affectionate and indulgent husband to the last moment of Mrs. Johnson's life: and in his "Prayers and Medita-tions," we find very remarkable evidence that his regard and fondness for her never ceased, even after her death.

He now set up a private academy, for which purpose he hired a large house, well situated near his native city. In the Gentleman's Magazine for 1736, there is the following advertisement: "At Edial, near Lichfield, in Staffordshire, young gentlemen are boarded and taught the Latin and Greek Languages, by SAMUEL JOHNSON." But the only pupils that were put under his care were the celebrated David Garrick and his brother George, and a Mr. Offely, a young gentleman of good fortune who died early.

Johnson was not more satisfied with his situation as the master of an academy, than with that of the usher of a school; we need not wonder, therefore, that he did not keep his academy above a year and a half. From Mr. Garrick's account he did not appear to have been profoundly reverenced by his pupils. His oddities of manner, and uncouth gesticulations, could not but be the subject of merriment to them; and in particular, the young rogues used to listen at the door of his bed-chamber, and peep through the key-hole, that they might turn into ridicule his tumultuous and awkward fondness for Mrs. Johnson, whom he used to name by the familiar appellation of *Tetty* or *Tetsey*, which, like *Betty* or *Betsey*, is provincially used as a contraction for *Elizabeth*, her christian name, but which to us seems ludicrous, when applied to a woman of her age and appearance. Mr. Garrick described her to me as very fat, with a bosom of more than ordinary protuberance, with swelled cheeks, of a florid red, produced by thick painting, and increased by the liberal use of cordials; flaring and fantastick in her dress, and affected both in her speech and her general behaviour. I have seen Garrick exhibit her, by his exquisite talent of mimickry, so as to excite the heartiest burst of laughter; but he, probably, as is the case in all such representations, considerably aggravated the picture.

Johnson now thought of trying his fortune in London, the great field of genius and exertion, where talents of every kind have the fullest scope, and the highest encouragement. It is a memorable circumstance that his pupil David Garrick went thither at the same time, with intent to complete his education, and follow the profession of the law, from which he was soon diverted by his decided preference for the stage.

1737. How he employed himself upon his first coming to London is not particularly known. I never heard that he found any protection or encouragement by the means of Mr. Colson, to whose academy David Garrick went. Mrs. Lucy Porter told me, that Mr. Walmsley gave him a letter of introduction to Lintot his bookseller, and that Johnson wrote some things for him; but I imagine this to be a mistake, for I have discovered no trace of it, and I am pretty sure he told me, that Mr. Cave was the first publisher by whom his pen was engaged in London.

He had a little money when he came to town, and he knew how he could live in the cheapest manner. His first lodgings were at the house of Mr. Norris, a staymaker, in Exeter-street, adjoining Catharine-street, in the Strand. "I dined (said he) very well for eight-pence, with very good company, at the Pine-Apple in New-street, just by. Several of them had travelled. They expected to meet every day; but did not know one another's names. It used to cost the rest a shilling, for they drank wine; but I had a cut of meat for six-pence, and bread for a penny, and gave the waiter a penny; so that I was quite well served, nay, better than the rest, for they gave the waiter nothing."

His OFELLUS in the *Art of Living in London,* I have heard him relate, was an Irish painter, whom he knew at Birmingham, and who had practiced his own precepts of economy for several years in the British capital. He assured Johnson, who, I suppose, was then meditating to try his fortune in London, but was apprehensive of the expence, "that thirty pounds a year was enough to enable a man to live there without being contemptible. He allowed ten pounds for cloaths and linen. He said a man might live in a garret at eighteen-pence a week;

few people would inquire where he lodged; and if they did, it was easy to say, 'Sir, I am to be found at such a place.' By spending three-pence in a coffee-house, he might be for some hours every day in very good company; he might dine for six-pence, breakfast on bread and milk for a penny, and do without supper. On *clean-shirt* day he went abroad, and paid visits."

Johnson's residence at Lichfield, on his return to it at this time, was only for three months; and as he had as yet seen but a small part of the wonders of the Metropolis, he had little to tell his townsmen. He related to me the following minute anecdote of this period: "In the last age, when my mother lived in London, there were two sets of people, those who gave the wall, and those who took it; the peaceable and the quarrelsome. When I returned to Lichfield, after having been in London, my mother asked me, whether I was one of those who gave the wall, or those who took it. *Now* it is fixed that every man keeps to the right; or, if one is taking the wall, another yields it; and it is never a dispute."

1738. It appears that he was now enlisted by Mr. Cave as a regular coadjutor in his magazine, by which he probably obtained a tolerable livelihood. At what time, or by what means, he had acquired a competent knowledge both of French and Italian, I do not know; but he was so well skilled in them, as to be sufficiently qualified for a translator. That part of his labour which consisted in emendation and improvement of the productions of other contributors, like that employed in levelling ground, can be perceived only by those who had an opportunity of comparing the original with the altered copy. What we certainly know to have been done by him in this way, was the Debates in both houses of Parliament, under the name of "The Senate of Lilliput," sometimes with feigned denominations of the several speakers, sometimes with denominations formed of the letters of their real names, in the manner of what is called anagram, so that they might easily be decyphered. Parliament then kept the press in a kind of mysterious awe, which made it necessary to have recourse to such devices.

But what first displayed his transcendent powers, and "gave the world assurance of the MAN," was his "LONDON, a Poem, in Imitation of the Third Satire of Juvenal;" which came out in May this year, and burst forth with a splendour, the rays of which will forever encircle his name.

It has been generally said, I know not with what truth, that Johnson offered his "London" to several booksellers, none of whom would purchase it. But we have seen that the worthy, modest, and ingenious Mr. Robert Dodsley, had taste enough to perceive its uncommon merit, and thought it creditable to have a share in it. The fact is, that at a future conference, he bargained for the whole property of it, for which he gave Johnson ten guineas; who told me, "I might perhaps have accepted of less; but that Paul Whitehead had a little before got ten guineas for a poem; and I would not take less than Paul Whitehead."

Johnson's "London" was published in May, 1738; and it is remarkable, that it came out on the same morning with Pope's satire, entitled "1738;" so that England had at once its Juvenal and Horace as poetical monitors. POPE, who then filled the poetical throne without a rival, it may reasonably be presumed, must have been particularly struck by the sudden appearance of such a poet; and, to his credit, let it be remembered, that his feelings and conduct on the occasion were candid and

liberal. He requested Mr. Richardson, son of the painter,
to endeavour to find out who this new authour was. Mr.
Richardson, after some inquiry, having informed him
that he had discovered only that his name was Johnson,
and that he was some obscure man, Pope said, "He will
soon be *déterré*."

1744. It does not appear that he wrote anything in
1744 for the Gentleman's Magazine, but the Preface.
But he produced one work this year, fully sufficient to
maintain the high reputation which he had acquired.
This was *The Life of Richard Savage,* a man, of whom
it is difficult to speak impartially, without wondering
that he was for some time the intimate companion of
Johnson; for his character was marked by profligacy,
insolence, and ingratitude: yet, as he undoubtedly had a
warm and vigorous, though unregulated mind, had seen
life in all its varieties, and been much in the company
of the statesmen and wits of his time, he could communicate to Johnson an abundant supply of such materials as his philosophical curiosity most eagerly desired;
and as Savage's misfortunes and misconduct had reduced him to the lowest state of wretchedness as a
writer for bread, his visits to St. John's Gate naturally
brought Johnson and him together.

It is melancholy to reflect, that Johnson and Savage
were sometimes in such extreme indigence, that they
could not pay for a lodging; so that they have wandered
together whole nights in the streets. Yet in these almost
incredible scenes of distress, we may suppose that Savage
mentioned many of the anecdotes with which Johnson
afterwards enriched the life of his unhappy companion,
and those of other Poets.

He told Sir Joshua Reynolds, that one night in particular, when Savage and he walked round St. James's-square for want of a lodging, they were not at all depressed by their situation; but in high spirits and brimful of patriotism, traversed the square for several hours, inveighed against the minister, and "resolved they would *stand by their country.*"

I am afraid, however, that by associating with Savage, who was habituated to the dissipation and licentiousness of the town, Johnson, though his good principles remained steady, did not entirely preserve that conduct, for which, in days of greater simplicity, he was remarked by his friend Mr. Hector; but was imperceptibly led into some indulgences which occasioned much distress to his virtuous mind.

1747. The year 1747 is distinguished as the epoch, when Johnson's arduous and important work, his *Dictionary of the English Language,* was announced to the world, by the publication of its Plan or PROSPECTUS.

How long this immense undertaking had been the object of his contemplation, I do not know. I once asked him by what means he had attained to that astonishing knowledge of our language, by which he was enabled to realise a design of such extent and accumulated difficulty. He told me, that "it was not the effect of particular study; but that it had grown up in his mind insensibly." I have been informed by Mr. James Dodsley, that several years before this period, when Johnson was one day sitting in his brother Robert's shop, he heard his brother suggest to him, that a Dictionary of the English Language would be a work that would be well received by the publick; that Johnson seemed at first to catch at the proposition, but, after a pause, said, in his abrupt decisive manner, "I believe I shall not undertake it."

The booksellers who contracted with Johnson, single
and unaided, for the execution of a work, which in other
countries has not been effected but by the co-operating
exertions of many, were Mr. Robert Dodsley, Mr. Charles
Hitch, Mr. Andrew Millar, the two Messieurs Longman,
and the two Messieurs Knapton. The price stipulated
was fifteen hundred and seventy-five pounds.

The "Plan" was addressed to Philip Dormer, Earl of
Chesterfield, then one of his Majesty's Principal Secre-
taries of State; a nobleman who was very ambitious of
literary distinction, and who, upon being informed of
the design, had expressed himself in terms very favourable to its success. There is, perhaps, in every thing of
any consequence, a secret history which it would be
amusing to know, could we have it authentically communicated. Johnson told me, "Sir, the way in which the
plan of my Dictionary came to be inscribed to Lord
Chesterfield, was this: I had neglected to write it by
the time appointed. Dodsley suggested a desire to have
it addressed to Lord Chesterfield. I laid hold of this as
a pretext for delay, that it might be better done, and let
Dodsley have his desire. I said to my friend, Dr.
Bathurst, 'Now if any good comes of my addressing to
Lord Chesterfield, it will be ascribed to deep policy,'
when, in fact, it was only a casual excuse for laziness."

That he was fully aware of the arduous nature of the
undertaking, he acknowledges; and shews himself perfectly sensible of it in the conclusion of his "Plan;" but
he had a noble consciousness of his own abilities, which
enabled him to go on with undaunted spirit.

Dr. Adams found him one day busy at his Dictionary,
when the following dialogue ensued.—"ADAMS. This is
a great work, Sir. How are you to get all the etymologies? JOHNSON. Why, Sir, here is a shelf with Junius,
and Skinner, and others: and there is a Welch gentleman

who has published a collection of Welch proverbs, who will help me with the Welch. ADAMS. But, Sir, how can you do this in three years? JOHNSON. Sir, I have no doubt that I can do it in three years. ADAMS. But the French Academy, which consists of forty members, took forty years to compile their Dictionary. JOHNSON. Sir, thus it is. This is the proportion. Let me see; forty times forty is sixteen hundred. As three to sixteen hundred, so is the proportion of an Englishman to a Frenchman."

While the Dictionary was going forward, Johnson lived part of the time in Holborn, part in Gough-square, Fleet-street; and he had an upper room fitted up like a counting-house for the purpose, in which he gave to the copyists their several tasks: The words, partly taken from other dictionaries, and partly supplied by himself, having been first written down with spaces left between them, he delivered in writing their etymologies, definitions, and various significations. The authorities were copied from the books themselves, in which he had marked the passages with a black-lead pencil, the traces of which could easily be effaced. I have seen several of them, in which that trouble had not been taken; so that they were just as when used by the copyists. It is remarkable, that he was so attentive in the choice of the passages in which words were authorised, that one may read page after page of his Dictionary with improvement and pleasure; and it should not pass unobserved, that he has quoted no author whose writings had a tendency to hurt sound religion and morality.

1749. In January, he published "THE VANITY OF HUMAN WISHES, being the Tenth Satire of Juvenal imitated." He, I believe, composed it the preceding year. Mrs. Johnson, for the sake of country air, had lodgings at Hampstead, to which he resorted occasionally, and there the greatest part, if not the whole, of this Imitation was written. The fervid rapidity with which it was produced, is scarcely credible. I have heard him say, that he composed seventy lines of it in one day, without putting one of them upon paper till they were finished. I remember when I once regretted to him that he had not given us more of Juvenal's Satires, he said, he probably should give more, for he had them all in his head; by which I understood, that he had the originals and correspondent allusions floating in his mind, which he could, when he pleased, embody and render permanent without much labour. Some of them, however, he observed were too gross for imitation.

The profits of a single poem, however excellent, appear to have been very small in the last reign, compared with what a publication of the same size has since been known to yield. I have mentioned upon Johnson's own authority, that for his LONDON he had only ten guineas; and now, after his fame was established, he got for his "Vanity of Human Wishes" but five guineas more, as is proved by an authentick document in my possession.

Garrick being now vested with theatrical power by being manager of Drury-lane theatre, he kindly and generously made use of it to bring out Johnson's tragedy, which had been long kept back for want of encouragement. But in this benevolent purpose he met with no small difficulty from the temper of Johnson, which could not brook that a drama which he had formed with much study, and had been obliged to keep more than the nine years of Horace, should be revised and altered at the pleasure of an actor. Yet Garrick knew well, that without some alterations it would not be fit for the stage. A violent dispute having ensued between them, Garrick applied to the Reverend Dr. Taylor to interpose. Johnson was at first very obstinate. "Sir, (said he) the fellow wants me to make Mahomet run mad, that he may have an opportunity of tossing his hands and kicking his heels." He was, however, at last, with difficulty, prevailed on to comply with Garrick's wishes, so as to allow of some changes; but still there were not enough.

Dr. Adams was present the first night of the representation of IRENE, and gave me the following account: "Before the curtain drew up, there were catcalls whistling, which alarmed Johnson's friends. The Prologue, which was written by himself in a manly strain, soothed the audience, and the play went off tolerably, till it came to the conclusion, when Mrs. Pritchard, the Heroine of the piece, was to be strangled upon the stage, and was to speak two lines with the bow-string round her neck. The audience cried out 'Murder! Murder!' She several times attempted to speak; but in vain. At last she was obliged to go off the stage alive." This passage was afterwards struck out, and she was carried off to be put to death behind the scenes, as the play now has it. The Epilogue, as Johnson informed me, was written by Sir William Yonge. I know not how his play came to be thus graced by the pen of a person then so eminent in the political world.

Notwithstanding all the support of such performers as Garrick, Barry, Mrs. Cibber, Mrs. Pritchard, and every advantage of dress and decorations, the tragedy of Irene did not please the publick. Mr. Garrick's zeal carried it through for nine nights, so that the authour had his three nights' profits; and from a receipt signed by him, now in the hands of Mr. James Dodsley, it appears that his friend, Mr. Robert Dodsley, gave him one hundred pounds for the copy, with his usual reservation of the right of one edition.

On occasion of this play being brought upon the

stage, Johnson had a fancy that as a dramatick authour his dress should be more gay than what he ordinarily wore; he therefore appeared behind the scenes, and even in one of the side boxes, in a scarlet waistcoat, with rich gold lace, and a gold-laced hat. He humourously observed to Mr. Langton, "that when in that dress he could not treat people with the same ease as when in his usual plain clothes." Dress indeed, we must allow, has more effect even upon strong minds than one should suppose, without having had the experience of it. His necessary attendance while his play was in rehearsal, and during its performance, brought him acquainted with many of the performers of both sexes, which produced a more favourable opinion of their profession than he had harshly expressed in his Life of Savage. With some of them he kept up an acquaintance as long as he and they lived, and was ever ready to shew them acts of kindness. He for a considerable time used to frequent the *Green-Room,* and seemed to take delight in dissipating his gloom, by mixing in the sprightly chit-chat of the motley circle then to be found there. Mr. David Hume related to me from Mr. Garrick, that Johnson at last denied himself this amusement, from considerations of rigid virtue; saying, "I'll come no more behind your scenes, David; for the silk stockings and white bosoms of your actresses excite my amorous propensities." [1]

1750. The first paper of the Rambler was published on Tuesday the 20th of March, 1749-50; and its authour was enabled to continue it, without interruption, every

---

[1] This is one of a few occasions when Boswell softened Johnson's language. His actual words had been: "For the white bubbies and the silk stockings of your Actresses excite my genitals."

Tuesday and Saturday, till Saturday the 17th day of March, 1752, on which day it closed. This is a strong confirmation of the truth of a remark of his, which I have had occasion to quote elsewhere, that "a man may write at any time, if he will set himself doggedly to it;" for, notwithstanding his constitutional indolence, his depression of spirits, and his labour in carrying on his Dictionary, he answered the stated calls of the press twice a week from the stores of his mind, during all that time; having received no assistance, except four billets in No. 10, by Miss Mulso, now Mrs. Chapone; No. 30, by Mrs. Catharine Talbot; No. 97, by Mr. Samuel Richardson, whom he describes in an introductory note as "An authour who has enlarged the knowledge of human nature, and taught the passions to move at the command of virtue;" and Numbers 44 and 100, by Mrs. Elizabeth Carter.

Johnson told me, with an amiable fondness, a little pleasing circumstance relative to this work. Mrs. Johnson, in whose judgement and taste he had great confidence, said to him, after a few numbers of the Rambler had come out, "I thought very well of you before; but I did not imagine you could have written any thing equal to this." Distant praise, from whatever quarter, is not so delightful as that of a wife whom a man loves and esteems. Her approbation may be said to "come home to his *bosom;*" and being so near, its effect is most sensible and permanent.

The Rambler has increased in fame as in age. Soon after its first folio edition was concluded, it was published in six duodecimo volumes; and its authour lived to see ten numerous editions of it in London, beside those of Ireland and Scotland.

Though Johnson's circumstances were at this time far from being easy, his humane and charitable disposition was constantly exerting itself. Mrs. Anna Williams, daughter of a very ingenious Welsh physician, and a woman of more than ordinary talents and literature, having come to London in hopes of being cured of a cataract in both her eyes, which afterwards ended in total blindness, was kindly received as a constant visitor at his house while Mrs. Johnson lived; and, after her death, having come under his roof in order to have an operation upon her eyes performed with more comfort to her than in lodgings, she had an apartment from him during the rest of her life, at all times when he had a house.

1752. That there should be a suspension of his literary labours during a part of the year 1752, will not seem strange, when it is considered that soon after closing his Rambler, he suffered the loss which there can be no doubt, affected him with the deepest distress. For on the 17th of March, O. S., his wife died. Why Sir John Hawkins should unwarrantably take upon him even to *suppose* that Johnson's fondness for her was *dissembled* (meaning simulated or assumed,) and to assert, that if it was not the case, "it was a lesson he had learned by rote," I cannot conceive; unless it proceeded from a want of similar feelings in his own breast. To argue from her being much older than Johnson, or any other circumstances, that he could not really love her, is absurd; for love is not a subject of reasoning, but of feeling, and therefore there are no common principles upon which one can persuade another concerning it. Every man feels for himself, and knows how he is affected by particular qualities in the person he admires, the impressions of which are too minute and delicate to be substantiated in language.

Her wedding-ring, when she became his wife, was, after her death, preserved by him, as long as he lived, with an affectionate care, in a little round wooden box, in the inside of which he pasted a slip of paper, thus inscribed by him in fair characters, as follows:

Eheu!
Eliz. Johnson,
Nupta Jul. 9° 1736,
Mortua, eheu!
Mart. 17° 1752.

I have, indeed, been told by Mrs. Desmoulins, who, before her marriage, lived for some time with Mrs. Johnson at Hampstead, that she indulged herself in country air and nice living, at an unsuitable expence, while her husband was drudging in the smoke of London, and that she by no means treated him with that complacency which is the most engaging quality in a wife. But all this is perfectly compatible with his fondness for her, especially when it is remembered that he had a high opinion of her understanding, and that the impressions which her beauty, real or imaginary, had originally made upon his fancy, being continued by habit, had not been effaced, though she herself was doubtless much altered for the worse. The dreadful shock of separation took place in the night; and he immediately dispatched a letter to his friend, the Reverend Dr. Taylor, which, as Taylor told me, expressed grief in the strongest manner he had ever read; so that it is much to be regretted it has not been preserved. The letter was brought to Dr. Taylor, at his house in the Cloysters, Westminster, about three in the morning; and as it signified an earnest desire to see him, he got up, and went to Johnson as soon as he was dressed, and found him in tears and in extreme agitation. After being a little while together, Johnson requested him to join

with him in prayer. He then prayed extempore, as did
Dr. Taylor; and thus by means of that piety which was
ever his primary object, his troubled mind was, in some
degree, soothed and composed.

The next day he wrote as follows:

To the Reverend Dr. Taylor.

March 18, 1752.

Dear Sir,

Let me have your company and instruction. Do not live
away from me. My distress is great.

Pray desire Mrs. Taylor to inform me what mourning I
should buy for my mother and Miss Porter, and bring a note
in writing with you.

Remember me in your prayers, for vain is the help of man.

I am, dear Sir, &c.

SAM. JOHNSON.

The circle of his friends, indeed, at this time was extensive and various, far beyond what has been generally
imagined. To trace his acquaintance with each particular person, if it could be done, would be a task, of which
the labour would not be repaid by the advantage. But
exceptions are to be made; one of which must be a
friend so eminent as Sir Joshua Reynolds, who was
truly his *dulce decus,* and with whom he maintained
an uninterrupted intimacy to the last hour of his life.
When Johnson lived in Castle-street, Cavendish-square,
he used frequently to visit two ladies who lived opposite
to him, Miss Cotterells, daughters of Admiral Cotterell.
Reynolds used also to visit there, and thus they met.
Mr. Reynolds, as I have observed above, had, from the
first reading of his Life of Savage, conceived a very high
admiration of Johnson's powers of writing. His conversation no less delighted him; and he cultivated his acquaintance with the laudable zeal of one who was ambitious of general improvement. Sir Joshua, indeed, was

lucky enough at their very first meeting to make a remark, which was so much above the commonplace style of conversation, that Johnson at once perceived that Reynolds had the habit of thinking for himself. The ladies were regretting the death of a friend, to whom they owed great obligations; upon which Reynolds observed, "You have however, the comfort of being relieved from a burthen of gratitude." They were shocked a little at this alleviating suggestion, as too selfish; but Johnson defended it in his clear and forcible manner, and was much pleased with the *mind,* the fair view of human nature, which is exhibited, like some of the reflections of Rochefoucauld. The consequence was, that he went home with Reynolds, and supped with him.

Sir Joshua told me a pleasant characteristical anecdote of Johnson about the time of their first acquaintance. When they were one evening together at the Miss Cotterells', the then Duchess of Argyle and another lady of high rank came in. Johnson thinking that the Miss Cotterells were too much engrossed by them, and that he and his friend were neglected, as low company of whom they were somewhat ashamed, grew angry; and resolving to shock their supposed pride, by making their great visitors imagine that his friend and he were low indeed, he addressed himself in a low tone to Mr. Reynolds, saying, "How much do you think you and I could get in a week, if we were to *work as hard* as we could?"—as if they had been common mechanicks.

His acquaintance with Bennet Langton, Esq. of Langton, in Lincolnshire, another much valued friend, commenced soon after the conclusion of his Rambler; which that gentleman, then a youth, had read with so much admiration, that he came to London chiefly with a view of endeavouring to be introduced to its authour. By a fortunate chance he happened to take lodgings in a house where Mr. Levet frequently visited; and having mentioned his wish to his landlady, she introduced him to Mr. Levet, who readily obtained Johnson's permission to bring Mr. Langton to him; as, indeed, Johnson, during the whole course of his life, had no shyness, real or affected, but was easy of access to all who were properly recommended, and even wished to see numbers at his *levee,* as his morning circle of company might, with strict propriety, be called. Mr. Langton was exceedingly surprised when the sage first appeared. He had not received the smallest intimation of his figure, dress, or manner. From perusing his writings, he fancied he should see a decent, well-drest, in short, a remarkably decorous philosopher. Instead of which, down from his bed-chamber, about noon, came, as newly risen, a huge, uncouth figure, with a little dark wig which scarcely covered his head, and his clothes hanging loose about him. But his conversation was so rich, so animated, and so forcible, and his religious and political notions so congenial with those in which Langton had been educated, that he conceived for him that veneration and attachment which he ever preserved. Johnson was not the less ready to love Mr. Langton, for his being of a very ancient family; for I have heard him say, with pleasure, "Langton, Sir, has a grant of free warren from Henry the Second; and Cardinal Stephen Langton, in King John's reign, was of this family."

Mr. Langton afterwards went to pursue his studies at Trinity College, Oxford, where he formed an acquaintance with his fellow-student, Mr. Topham Beauclerk; who, though their opinions and modes of life were so different, that it seemed utterly improbable that they should at all agree, had so ardent a love of literature, so acute an understanding, such elegance of manners, and so well discerned the excellent qualities of Mr.

Langton, a gentleman eminent not only for worth and learning, but for an inexhaustible fund of entertaining conversation, that they became intimate friends.

Johnson, soon after this acquaintance began, passed a considerable time at Oxford. He at first thought it strange that Langton should associate so much with one who had the character of being loose, both in his principles and practice: but, by degrees, he himself was fascinated. Mr. Beauclerk's being of the St. Alban's family, and, having, in some particulars, a resemblance to Charles the Second, contributed, in Johnson's imagination, to throw a lustre upon his other qualities; and in a short time, the moral, pious Johnson, and the gay, dissipated Beauclerk, were companions. "What a coalition! (said Garrick, when he heard of this:) I shall have my old friend to bail out of the Round-house." But I can bear testimony that it was a very agreeable association. Beauclerk was too polite, and valued learning and wit too much, to offend Johnson by sallies of infidelity or licentiousness; and Johnson delighted in the good qualities of Beauclerk, and hoped to correct the evil. Innumerable were the scenes in which Johnson was amused by these young men. Beauclerk could take more liberty with him, than any body with whom I ever saw him; but, on the other hand, Beauclerk was not spared by his respectable companions, when reproof was proper. Beauclerk had such a propensity to satire, that at one time Johnson said to him, "You never open your mouth but with intention to give pain; and you have often given me pain, not from the power of what you said, but from seeing your intention." At another time applying to him, with a slight alteration, a line of Pope, he said,

Thy love of folly, and thy scorn of fools—

Every thing thou dost shews the one, and every thing thou say'st the other." At another time he said to him, "Thy body is all vice, and thy mind all virtue." Beauclerk not seeming to relish the compliment, Johnson said, "Nay, Sir, Alexander the Great, marching in triumph into Babylon, could not have desired to have had more said to him."

Johnson was some time with Beauclerk at his house at Windsor, where he was entertained with experiments in natural philosophy. One Sunday, when the weather was very fine, Beauclerk enticed him, insensibly, to saunter about all the morning. They went into a churchyard, in the time of divine service, and Johnson laid himself down at his ease upon one of the tomb-stones. "Now, Sir, (said Beauclerk) you are like Hogarth's Idle Apprentice." When Johnson got his pension, Beauclerk said to him, in the humourous phrase of Falstaff, "I hope you'll now purge and live cleanly, like a gentleman."

One night, when Beauclerk and Langton had supped at a tavern in London, and sat till about three in the morning, it came into their heads to go and knock up Johnson, and see if they could prevail on him to join them in a ramble. They rapped violently at the door of his chambers in the Temple, till at last he appeared in his shirt, with his little black wig on the top of his head, instead of a night-cap, and a poker in his hand, imagining, probably, that some ruffians were coming to attack him. When he discovered who they were, and was told their errand, he smiled, and with great good humour agreed to their proposal: "What, is it you, you dogs! I'll have a frisk with you." He was soon drest, and they sallied forth together into Covent-Garden, where the greengrocers and fruiterers were beginning to arrange their hampers, just come in from the country.

Johnson made some attempts to help them; but the honest gardeners stared so at his figure and manner, and odd interference, that he soon saw his services were not relished. They then repaired to one of the neighbouring taverns, and made a bowl of that liquor called *Bishop,* which Johnson had always liked; while in joyous contempt of sleep, from which he had been roused, he repeated the festive lines,

> Short, O short then be thy reign,
> And give us to the world again!

They did not stay long, but walked down to the Thames, took a boat, and rowed to Billingsgate. Beauclerk and Johnson were so well pleased with their amusement, that they resolved to persevere in dissipation for the rest of the day: but Langton deserted them, being engaged to breakfast with some young Ladies. Johnson scolded him for "leaving his social friends to go and sit with a set of wretched *un-idea'd* girls." Garrick being told of this ramble, said to him smartly, "I heard of your frolick t'other night. You'll be in the Chronicle." Upon which Johnson afterwards observed, *"He* durst not do such a thing. His *wife* would not *let* him!"

1754. The Dictionary, we may believe, afforded Johnson full occupation this year. As it approached to its conclusion, he probably worked with redoubled vigour, as seamen increase their exertion and alacrity when they have a near prospect of their haven.

Lord Chesterfield, to whom Johnson had paid the high compliment of addressing to his Lordship the Plan of his Dictionary, had behaved to him in such a manner as to excite his contempt and indignation. The world has been for many years amused with a story confidently told, and as confidently repeated with additional circumstances, that a sudden disgust was taken by Johnson upon occasion of his having been one day kept long in waiting in his Lordship's antechamber, for which the reason assigned was, that he had company with him; and that at last, when the door opened, out walked Colley Cibber; and that Johnson was so violently provoked when he found for whom he had been so long excluded, that he went away in a passion, and never would return. I remember having mentioned this story to George Lord Lyttelton, who told me, he was very intimate with Lord Chesterfield; and holding it as a well-known truth, defended Lord Chesterfield by saying, that "Cibber, who had been introduced familiarly by the backstairs, had probably not been there above ten minutes." It may seem strange even to entertain a doubt concerning a story so long and so wildly current, and thus implicitly adopted, if not sanctioned, by the authority which I have mentioned; but Johnson himself assured me, that there was not the least foundation for it. He told me, that there never was any particular incident which produced a quarrel between Lord Chesterfield and him; but that his Lordship's continued neglect was the reason why he resolved to have no connexion with him. When the Dictionary was upon the eve of publication, Lord Chesterfield, who, it is said, had flattered himself with expectations that Johnson would dedicate the work to him, attempted, in a courtly manner, to soothe and insinuate himself with the Sage, conscious, as it should seem, of the cold indifference with which he had treated its learned authour; and further attempted to conciliate him, by writing two papers in "The World," in recommendation of the work; and it must be confessed, that they contain some studied com-

pliments, so finely turned, that if there had been no
previous offence, it is probable that Johnson would have
been highly delighted.

This courtly device failed of its effect. Johnson, who
thought that "all was false and hollow," despised the
honeyed words, and was even indignant that Lord
Chesterfield should, for a moment, imagine, that he
could be the dupe of such an artifice. His expression to
me concerning Lord Chesterfield, upon this occasion,
was, "Sir, after making great professions, he had, for
many years, taken no notice of me; but when my Dictionary was coming out, he fell a scribbling in 'The
World' about it. Upon which, I wrote him a letter expressed in civil terms, but such as might shew him that
I did not mind what he said or wrote, and that I had
done with him."

To the Right Honourable the Earl of Chesterfield.

February 7, 1755.

MY LORD,

I have been lately informed, by the proprietor of the
World, that two papers, in which my Dictionary is recommended to the publick, were written by your Lordship. To
be so distinguished, is an honour, which, being very little
accustomed to favours from the great, I know not well how
to receive, or in what terms to acknowledge.

When, upon some slight encouragement, I first visited
your Lordship, I was overpowered, like the rest of mankind,
by the enchantment of your address, and could not forbear
to wish that I might boast myself *Le vainqueur du vainqueur
de la terre;*—that I might obtain that regard for which I saw
the world contending; but I found my attendance so little
encouraged, that neither pride nor modesty would suffer me
to continue it. When I had once addressed your Lordship in
publick, I had exhausted all the art of pleasing which a retired and uncourtly scholar can possess. I had done all that
I could; and no man is well pleased to have his all neglected,
be it ever so little.

Seven years, my Lord, have now past, since I waited in

your outward rooms, or was repulsed from your door; during which time I have been pushing on my work through difficulties, of which it is useless to complain, and have brought it, at last, to the verge of publication, without one act of assistance, one word of encouragement, or one smile of favour. Such treatment I did not expect, for I never had a Patron before.

The shepherd in Virgil grew at last acquainted with Love, and found him a native of the rocks.

Is not a Patron, my Lord, one who looks with unconcern on a man struggling for life in the water, and, when he has reached ground, encumbers him with help? The notice which you have been pleased to take of my labours, had it been early, had been kind; but it has been delayed till I am indifferent, and cannot enjoy it; till I am solitary, and cannot impart it; till I am known, and do not want it. I hope it is no very cynical asperity, not to confess obligations where no benefit has been received, or to be unwilling that the Publick should consider me as owing that to a Patron, which Providence has enabled me to do for myself.

Having carried on my work thus far with so little obligation to any favourer of learning, I shall not be disappointed though I should conclude it, if less be possible, with less; for I have been long wakened from that dream of hope, in which I once boasted myself with so much exultation,

My Lord,
Your Lordship's most humble
Most obedient servant,
SAM. JOHNSON.

"While this was the talk of the town, (says Dr. Adams, in a letter to me) I happened to visit Dr. Warburton, who finding that I was acquainted with Johnson, desired me earnestly to carry his compliments to him, and to tell him, that he honoured him for his manly behaviour in rejecting these condescensions of Lord Chesterfield, and for resenting the treatment he had received from him with a proper spirit." Johnson was visibly pleased with this compliment, for he had always a high opinion of Warburton. Indeed, the force of mind

which appeared in this letter, was congenial with that
which Warburton himself amply possessed.

There is a curious minute circumstance which struck
me, in comparing the various editions of Johnson's Imitations of Juvenal. In the tenth Satire one of the couplets
upon the vanity of wishes even for literary distinction
stood thus:

> Yet think what ills the scholar's life assail,
> Toil, envy, want, the *garret,* and the jail.

But after experiencing the uneasiness which Lord Chesterfield's fallacious patronage made him feel, he dismissed the word *garret* from the sad group, and in all
the subsequent editions the line stands,

> Toil, envy, want, the *Patron,* and the jail.

That Lord Chesterfield must have been mortified by
the lofty contempt, and polite, yet keen, satire with
which Johnson exhibited him to himself in this letter, it
is impossible to doubt. He, however, with that glossy
duplicity which was his constant study, affected to be
quite unconcerned. Dr. Adams mentioned to Mr. Robert
Dodsley that he was sorry Johnson had written his letter
to Lord Chesterfield. Dodsley, with the true feelings of
trade, said "he was very sorry too; for that he had a
property in the Dictionary, to which his Lordship's
patronage might have been of consequence." He then
told Dr. Adams, that Lord Chesterfield had shewn him
the letter. "I should have imagined (replied Dr. Adams)
that Lord Chesterfield would have concealed it." "Poh!
(said Dodsley) do you think a letter from Johnson
could hurt Lord Chesterfield? Not at all, Sir. It lay upon
his table, where anybody might see it. He read it to
me; said, 'this man has great powers,' pointed out the
severest passages, and observed how well they were

expressed." This air of indifference, which imposed upon
the worthy Dodsley, was certainly nothing but a specimen of that dissimulation which Lord Chesterfield inculcated as one of the most essential lessons for the
conduct of life. His Lordship endeavoured to justify
himself to Dodsley from the charges brought against him
by Johnson; but we may judge of the flimsiness of his
defence, from his having excused his neglect of Johnson, by saying, that "he had heard he had changed his
lodgings, and did not know where he lived;" as if there
could have been the smallest difficulty to inform himself
of that circumstance, by enquiring in the literary circle
with which his Lordship was well acquainted, and was,
indeed, himself, one of its ornaments.

Dr. Adams expostulated with Johnson, and suggested,
that his not being admitted when he called on him, was
probably not to be imputed to Lord Chesterfield; for his
Lordship had declared to Dodsley, that "he would have
turned off the best servant he ever had, if he had known
that he denied him to a man who would have been
always more than welcome;" and in confirmation of this,
he insisted on Lord Chesterfield's general affability and
easiness of access, especially to literary men. "Sir, (said
Johnson) that is not Lord Chesterfield; he is the proudest
man this day existing." "No, (said Dr. Adams) there is
one person, at least, as proud; I think, by your own
account you are the prouder man of the two." "But
mine (replied Johnson instantly) was *defensive* pride."
This, as Dr. Adams well observed, was one of those
happy turns for which he was so remarkably ready.

Johnson having now explicitly avowed his opinion of
Lord Chesterfield, did not refrain from expressing himself concerning that nobleman with pointed freedom:
"This man (said he) I thought had been a Lord among
wits; but, I find, he is only a wit among Lords!" And

when his Letters to his natural son were published, he observed, that "they teach the morals of a whore, and the manners of a dancing-master."

1755. Mr. Andrew Millar, bookseller in the Strand, took the principal charge of conducting the publication of Johnson's Dictionary; and as the patience of the proprietors was repeatedly tried and almost exhausted, by their expecting that the work would be compleated, within the time which Johnson had sanguinely supposed, the learned author was often goaded to dispatch, more especially as he had received all the copy money, by different drafts, a considerable time before he had finished his task. When the messenger who carried the last sheet to Millar returned, Johnson asked him, "Well, what did he say?"—"Sir, (answered the messenger) he said, thank GOD I have done with him." "I am glad (replied Johnson, with a smile,) that he thanks GOD for any thing." It is remarkable, that those with whom Johnson chiefly contracted for his literary labours were Scotchmen, Mr. Millar and Mr. Strahan. Millar, though himself no great judge of literature, had good sense enough to have for his friends very able men, to give him their opinion and advice in the purchase of copyright; the consequence of which was his acquiring a very large fortune, with liberality. Johnson said of him, "I respect Millar, Sir; he has raised the price of literature."

A few of his definitions must be admitted to be erroneous. Thus, *Windward* and *Leeward,* though directly of opposite meaning, are defined identically the same way; as to which inconsiderable specks it is enough to observe, that his Preface announces that he was aware there might be many such in so immense a work; nor was he at all disconcerted when an instance was pointed out to him. A lady once asked him how he came to define *Pastern* the *knee* of a horse: instead of making an elaborate defence, as she expected, he at once answered, "Ignorance, Madam, pure ignorance." His definition of *Network* has been often quoted with sportive malignity,[1] as obscuring a thing in itself very plain. But to these frivolous censures no other answer is necessary than that with which we are furnished by his own Preface. "To explain, requires the use of terms less abstruse than that which is to be explained, and such terms cannot always be found. For as nothing can be proved but by supposing something intuitively known, and evident without proof, so nothing can be defined but by the use of words too plain to admit of definition. Sometimes easier words are changed into harder; as, *burial*, into *sepulture* or *interment; dry*, into *desiccative; dryness*, into *siccity* or *aridity; fit*, into *paroxism;* for, the *easiest* word, whatever it be, can never be translated into one more easy."

His introducing his own opinions, and even prejudices, under general definitions of words, while at the same time the original meaning of the words is not explained, as his *Tory, Whig, Pension, Oats, Excise*,[2] and a few more, cannot be fully defended, and must be placed to the account of capricious and humorous indulgence. Talking to me upon this subject when we were at Ashbourne in 1777, he mentioned a still stronger instance of the predominance of his private feelings in

---

[1] "Anything reticulated or decussated, at equal distances, with interstices between the intersections."

[2] He thus defines *Excise*: "A hateful tax levied upon commodities, and adjudged not by the common judges of property, but wretches hired by those to whom Excise is paid." And *Pension* "is generally understood to mean pay given to a state hireling for treason to his country."

the composition of this work, than any now to be found in it. "You know, Sir, Lord Gower forsook the old Jacobite interest. When I came to the *Renegado*, after telling that it meant 'one who deserts to the enemy, a revolter,' I added, *Sometimes we say a* GOWER. Thus it went to the press: but the printer had more wit than I, and struck it out."

Let it, however, be remembered, that this indulgence does not display itself only in sarcasm towards others, but sometimes in playful allusion to the notions commonly entertained of his own laborious task. Thus: "*Grub-street*, the name of a street in London, much inhabited by writers of small histories, *dictionaries*, and temporary poems; whence, any mean production is called *Grub-street*."—"*Lexicographer*, a writer of dictionaries, *a harmless drudge.*"

1757. He this year resumed his scheme of giving an edition of Shakespeare with notes. He issued proposals of considerable length in which he shewed that he perfectly well knew what variety of research such an undertaking required; but his indolence prevented him from pursuing it with that diligence which alone can collect those scattered facts, that genius, however acute, penetrating, and luminous, cannot discover by its own force. It is remarkable, that at this time his fancied activity was for the moment so vigourous, that he promised his work should be published before Christmas, 1757. Yet nine years elapsed before it saw the light. His throes in bringing it forth had been severe and remittent; and at last we may almost conclude that the Cæsarian operation was performed by the knife of Churchill, whose upbraiding satire, I dare say, made Johnson's friends urge him to dispatch.

> He for subscribers baits his hook,
> And takes your cash; but where's the book?
> No matter where; wise fear, you know,
> Forbids the robbing of a foe;
> But what, to serve our private ends,
> Forbids the cheating of our friends?

On the fifteenth of April he began a new periodical paper, entitled "THE IDLER," which came out every Saturday in a weekly newspaper, called "The Universal Chronicle, or Weekly Gazette," published by Newbery. These essays were continued till April 5, 1760. Many of these excellent essays were written as hastily as an ordinary letter. Mr. Langton remembers Johnson, when on a visit at Oxford, asking him one evening how long it was till the post went out; and on being told about half an hour, he exclaimed, "then we shall do very well." He upon this instantly sat down and finished an Idler, which it was necessary should be in London the next day. Mr. Langton having signified a wish to read it, "Sir, (said he,) you shall not do more than I have done myself." He then folded it up, and sent it off.

1759. In the month of January, his mother died at the great age of ninety, an event which deeply affected him; not that "his mind had acquired no firmness by the contemplation of morality;" but that his reverential affection for her was not abated by years, as indeed he retained all his tender feelings even to the latest period of his life. I have been told, that he regretted much his not having gone to visit his mother for several years previous to her death. But he was constantly engaged in literary labours which confined him to London; and though he had not the comfort of seeing his aged parent, he contributed to her support.

Jan. 20, 1759.
DEAR HONOURED MOTHER,

Neither your condition nor your character make it fit for
me to say much. You have been the best mother, and I believe the best woman in the world. I thank you for your indulgence to me, and beg forgiveness of all that I have done
ill, and all that I have omitted to do well. GOD grant you his
Holy Spirit, and receive you to everlasting happiness, for
Jesus Christ's sake. Amen. Lord Jesus receive your spirit.
Amen.

I am, dear, dear Mother,
Your dutiful Son,
SAM. JOHNSON.

Soon after this event, he wrote his *Rasselas, Prince of
Abyssinia:* concerning the publication of which Sir John
Hawkins guesses vaguely and idly, instead of having
taken the trouble to inform himself with authentick pre-
cision. Not to trouble my readers with a repetition of
the Knight's reveries, I have to mention, that the late
Mr. Strahan the printer told me, that Johnson wrote it,
that with the profits he might defray the expence of his
mother's funeral, and pay some little debts which she
had left. He told Sir Joshua Reynolds, that he composed
it in the evenings of one week, sent it to the press in
portions as it was written, and had never since read it
over. Mr. Strahan, Mr. Johnson, and Mr. Dodsley, purchased it for a hundred pounds, but afterwards paid
him twenty-five pounds more, when it came to a second
edition.

1762. The accession of George the Third to the
throne of these kingdoms, opened a new and brighter
prospect to men of literary merit, who had been honoured with no mark of royal favour in the preceding
reign. His present Majesty's education in this country,

as well as his taste and beneficence, prompted him to be the patron of science and the arts; and early this year Johnson having been represented to him as a very learned and good man, without any certain provision, his Majesty was pleased to grant him a pension of three hundred pounds a year. The Earl of Bute, who was then Prime Minister, had the honour to announce this instance of his Sovereign's bounty, concerning which, many and various stories, all equally erroneous, have been propagated; maliciously representing it as a political bribe to Johnson, to desert his avowed principles, and become the tool of a government which he held to be founded in usurpation. I have taken care to have it in my power to refute them from the most authentick information. Lord Bute told me, that Mr. Wedderburne, now Lord Loughborough, was the person who first mentioned this subject to him. Lord Loughborough told me, that the pension was granted to Johnson solely as the reward of his literary merit, without any stipulation whatever, or even tacit understanding that he should write for administration. His Lordship added, that he was confident the political tracts which Johnson afterwards did write, as they were entirely consonant with his own opinions, would have been written by him, though no pension had been granted to him.

Mr. Thomas Sheridan and Mr. Murphy, who then lived a good deal both with him and Mr. Wedderburne, told me, that they previously talked with Johnson upon this matter, and that it was perfectly understood by all parties that the pension was merely honorary. Sir Joshua Reynolds told me, that Johnson called on him after his Majesty's intention had been notified to him, and said he wished to consult his friends as to the propriety of his accepting this mark of the royal favour, after the definitions which he had given in his Dictionary of *pension* and *pensioners*. He said he should not have Sir Joshua's answer till next day, when he would call again, and desired he might think of it. Sir Joshua answered that he was clear to give his opinion then, that there could be no objection to his receiving from the King a reward for literary merit; and that certainly the definitions in his Dictionary were not applicable to him. Johnson, it should seem, was satisfied, for he did not call again till he had accepted the pension, and had waited on Lord Bute to thank him. He then told Sir Joshua that Lord Bute said to him expressly, "It is not given you for any thing you are to do, but for what you have done." His Lordship, he said, behaved in the handsomest manner. He repeated the words twice, that he might be sure Johnson heard them, and thus set his mind perfectly at ease.

1763. This is to me a memorable year; for in it I had the happiness to obtain the acquaintance of that extraordinary man whose memoirs I am now writing; an acquaintance which I shall ever esteem as one of the most fortunate circumstances in my life. Though then but two-and-twenty, I had for several years read his works with delight and instruction, and had the highest reverence for their authour, which had grown up in my fancy into a kind of mysterious veneration, by figuring to myself a state of solemn elevated abstraction, in which I supposed him to live in the immense metropolis of London. Mr. Gentleman, a native of Ireland, who passed some years in Scotland as a player, and as an instructor in the English language, a man whose talents and worth were depressed by misfortunes, had given me a representation of the figure and manner of DICTIONARY JOHNSON! as he was then generally called; and during my first

visit to London, which was for three months in 1760,
Mr. Derrick the poet, who was Gentleman's friend and
countryman, flattered me with hopes that he would introduce me to Johnson, an honour of which I was very
ambitious. But he never found an opportunity; which
made me doubt that he had promised to do what was
not in his power; till Johnson some years afterwards
told me, "Derrick, Sir, might very well have introduced
you. I had a kindness for Derrick, and am sorry he is
dead."

In the summer of 1761 Mr. Thomas Sheridan was at
Edinburgh, and delivered lectures upon the English
Language and Publick Speaking to large and respectable audiences. I was often in his company, and heard
him frequently expatiate upon Johnson's extraordinary
knowledge, talents, and virtues, repeat his pointed sayings, describe his particularities, and boast of his being
his guest sometimes till two or three in the morning. At
his house I hoped to have many opportunities of seeing
the sage, as Mr. Sheridan obligingly assured me I should
not be disappointed.

When I returned to London in the end of 1762, to my
surprise and regret I found an irreconcileable difference
had taken place between Johnson and Sheridan. A pension of two hundred pounds a year had been given to
Sheridan. Johnson, who, as has been already mentioned,
thought slightingly of Sheridan's art, upon hearing that
he was also pensioned, exclaimed, "What! have they
given *him* a pension? Then it is time for me to give up
mine." Whether this proceeded from a momentary indignation, as if it were an affront to his exalted merit
that a player should be rewarded in the same manner
with him, or was the sudden effect of a fit of peevishness, it was unluckily said, and, indeed, cannot be
justified. Mr. Sheridan's pension was granted to him not

as a player, but as a sufferer in the cause of government, when he was manager of the Theatre Royal in Ireland, when parties ran high in 1753.

Johnson complained that a man who disliked him repeated his sarcasm to Mr. Sheridan, without telling him what followed, which was, that after a pause he added, "However, I am glad that Mr. Sheridan has a pension, for he is a very good man." Sheridan could never forgive this hasty contemptuous expression. It rankled in his mind; and though I informed him of all that Johnson said, and that he would be very glad to meet him amicably, he positively declined repeated offers which I made, and once went off abruptly from a house where he and I were engaged to dine, because he was told that Dr. Johnson was to be there.

Mr. Thomas Davies the actor, who then kept a bookseller's shop in Russel-street, Covent-garden, told me that Johnson was very much his friend, and came frequently to his house, where he more than once invited me to meet him: but by some unlucky accident or other he was prevented from coming to us.

At last, on Monday the 16th of May, when I was sitting in Mr. Davies's back-parlour, after having drunk tea with him and Mrs. Davies, Johnson unexpectedly came into the shop; and Mr. Davies having perceived him through the glass-door in the room in which we were sitting, advancing towards us,—he announced his awful approach to me, somewhat in the manner of an actor in the part of Horatio, when he addresses Hamlet on the appearance of his father's ghost, "Look, my Lord, it comes." I found that I had a very perfect idea of Johnson's figure, from the portrait of him painted by Sir Joshua Reynolds soon after he had published his Dictionary, in the attitude of sitting in his easy chair in deep meditation; which was the first picture his friend did for him, which Sir Joshua very kindly presented to me, and from which an engraving has been made for this work. Mr. Davies mentioned my name, and respectfully introduced me to him. I was much agitated; and recollecting his prejudice against the Scotch, of which I had heard much, I said to Davies, "Don't tell where I come from."—"From Scotland," cried Davies, roguishly. "Mr. Johnson, (said I) I do indeed come from Scotland, but I cannot help it." I am willing to flatter myself that I meant this as light pleasantry to soothe and conciliate him, and not as an humiliating abasement at the expence of my country. But however that might be, this speech was somewhat unlucky; for with that quickness of wit for which he was so remarkable, he seized the expression "come from Scotland," which I used in the sense of being of that country; and, as if I had said that I had come away from it, or left it, retorted, "That, Sir, I find, is what a very great many of your countrymen cannot help." This stroke stunned me a good deal; and when we had sat down, I felt myself not a little embarrassed, and apprehensive of what might come next. He then addressed himself to Davies: "What do you think of Garrick? He has refused me an order for the play for Miss Williams, because he knows the house will be full, and that an order would be worth three shillings." Eager to take any opening to get into conversation with him, I ventured to say, "O, Sir, I cannot think Mr. Garrick would grudge such a trifle to you." "Sir, (said he, with a stern look,) I have known David Garrick longer than you have done: and I know no right you have to talk to me on the subject." Perhaps I deserved this check; for it was rather presumptuous in me, an entire stranger, to express any doubt of the justice of his animadversion upon his old acquaintance and pupil. I now felt myself much mortified, and began to think, that the hope which

I had long indulged of obtaining his acquaintance was blasted. And, in truth, had not my ardour been uncommonly strong, and my resolution uncommonly persevering, so rough a reception might have deterred me for ever from making any further attempts. Fortunately, however, I remained upon the field not wholly discomfited; and was soon rewarded by hearing some of his conversation, of which I preserved the following short minute, without marking the questions and observations by which it was produced.

Speaking of one who with more than ordinary boldness attacked publick measures and the royal family, he said, "I think he is safe from the law, but he is an abusive scoundrel; and instead of applying to my Lord Chief Justice to punish him, I would send half a dozen footmen and have him well ducked."

"The notion of liberty amuses the people of England, and helps to keep off the *tedium vitæ*. When a butcher tells you that *his heart bleeds for his country*, he has, in fact, no uneasy feeling."

"Sheridan will not succeed at Bath with his oratory. Ridicule has gone down before him, and I doubt, Derrick is his enemy."

"Derrick may do very well, as long as he can outrun his character; but the moment his character gets up with him, it is all over."

It is, however, but just to record, that some years afterwards, when I reminded him of this sarcasm, he said, "Well, but Derrick has now got a character that he need not run away from."

I was highly pleased with the extraordinary vigour of his conversation, and regretted that I was drawn away from it by an engagement at another place. I had, for a part of the evening, been left alone with him, and had ventured to make an observation now and then, which he received very civilly; so that I was satisfied that though there was a roughness in his manner, there was no ill-nature in his disposition. Davies followed me to the door, and when I complained to him a little of the hard blows which the great man had given me, he kindly took upon him to console me by saying, "Don't be uneasy. I can see he likes you very well."

A few days afterwards I called on Davies, and asked him if he thought I might take the liberty of waiting on Mr. Johnson at his chambers in the Temple. He said I certainly might, and that Mr. Johnson would take it as a compliment. So on Tuesday the 24th of May, after having been enlivened by the witty sallies of Messieurs Thornton, Wilkes, Churchill, and Lloyd, with whom I had passed the morning, I boldly repaired to Johnson. His chambers were on the first floor of No. 1, Inner-Temple-lane, and I entered them with an impression given me by the Reverend Dr. Blair, of Edinburgh, who had been introduced to him not long before, and described his having "found the Giant in his den"; an expression which, when I came to be pretty well acquainted with Johnson, I repeated to him, and he was diverted at this picturesque account of himself. Dr. Blair had been presented to him by Dr. James Fordyce. At this time the controversy concerning the pieces published by Mr. James Macpherson, as translations of Ossian, was at its height. Johnson had all along denied their authenticity; and, what was still more provoking to their admirers, maintained that they had no merit. The subject having been introduced by Dr. Fordyce, Dr. Blair, relying on the internal evidence of their antiquity, asked Dr. Johnson whether he thought any man of a modern age could have written such poems? Johnson replied, "Yes, Sir, many men, many women, and many children." Johnson at this time, did not know that

Dr. Blair had just published a Dissertation, not only defending their authenticity, but seriously ranking them
with the poems of Homer and Virgil; and when he was
afterwards informed of this circumstance, he expressed
some displeasure at Dr. Fordyce's having suggested the
topick, and said, "I am not sorry that they got thus
much for their pains. Sir, it was like leading one to talk
of a book, when the authour is concealed behind the
door."

He received me very courteously: but, it must be confessed, that his apartment, and furniture, and morning
dress, were sufficiently uncouth. His brown suit of
cloaths looked very rusty: he had on a little old shrivelled unpowdered wig, which was too small for his head;
his shirt-neck and knees of his breeches were loose; his
black worsted stockings ill drawn up; and he had a pair
of unbuckled shoes by way of slippers. But all these
slovenly particularities were forgotten the moment that
he began to talk. Some gentlemen, whom I do not recollect, were sitting with him; and when they went away,
I also rose; but he said to me, "Nay, don't go."—"Sir,
(said I), I am afraid that I intrude upon you. It is benevolent to allow me to sit and hear you." He seemed
pleased with this compliment, which I sincerely paid
him, and answered, "Sir, I am obliged to any man who
visits me."—I have preserved the following short minute
of what passed this day.

"Madness frequently discovers itself merely by unnecessary deviation from the usual modes of the world.
My poor friend Smart showed the disturbance of his
mind, by falling upon his knees, and saying his prayers
in the street, or in any other unusual place. Now although, rationally speaking, it is greater madness not to
pray at all, than to pray as Smart did, I am afraid there

are so many who do not pray, that their understanding is not called in question."

Concerning this unfortunate poet, Christopher Smart, who was confined in a mad-house, he had, at another time, the following conversation with Dr. Burney.— BURNEY. "How does poor Smart do, Sir; is he likely to recover?" JOHNSON. "It seems as if his mind had ceased to struggle with the disease; for he grows fat upon it." BURNEY. "Perhaps, Sir, that may be from want of exercise." JOHNSON. "No, Sir; he has partly as much exercise as he used to have, for he digs in the garden. Indeed, before his confinement, he used for exercise to walk to the alehouse; but he was *carried* back again. I did not think he ought to be shut up. His infirmities were not noxious to society. He insisted on people praying with him; and I'd as lief pray with Kit Smart as any one else. Another charge was, that he did not love clean linen; and I have no passion for it."

Talking of Garrick, he said, "He is the first man in the world for sprightly conversation."

When I rose a second time, he again pressed me to stay, which I did.

He told me, that he generally went abroad at four in the afternoon, and seldom came home till two in the morning. I took the liberty to ask if he did not think it wrong to live thus, and not make more use of his great talents. He owned it was a bad habit.

Before we parted, he was so good as to promise to favour me with his company one evening at my lodgings: and, as I took my leave, shook me cordially by the hand. It was almost needless to add, that I felt no little elation at having now so happily established an acquaintance of which I had been so long ambitious.

My readers will, I trust, excuse me for being thus

minutely circumstantial, when it is considered that the acquaintance of Dr. Johnson was to me a most valuable acquisition, and laid the foundation of whatever instruction and entertainment they may receive from my collections concerning the great subject of the work which they are now perusing.

I did not visit him again till Monday, June 13, at which time I recollect no part of his conversation, except that when I told him I had been to see Johnson ride upon three horses, he said, "Such a man, Sir, should be encouraged; for his performances shew the extent of the human power in one instance, and thus tend to raise our opinion of the faculties of man. He shews what may be attained by persevering application; so that every man may hope, that by giving as much application, although perhaps he may never ride three horses at a time, or dance upon a wire, yet he may be equally expert in whatever profession he has chosen to pursue."

He again shook me by the hand at parting, and asked me why I did not come oftener to him. Trusting that I was now in his good graces, I answered, that he had not given me much encouragement, and reminded him of the check I had received from him at our first interview. "Poh, poh! (said he, with a complacent smile), never mind these things. Come to me as often as you can. I shall be glad to see you."

I had learnt that his place of frequent resort was the Mitre tavern in Fleet-street, where he loved to sit up late, and I begged I might be allowed to pass an evening with him there soon, which he promised I should. A few days afterwards I met him near Temple-bar, about one o'clock in the morning, and asked him if he would then go to the Mitre. "Sir, (said he) it is too late; they won't let us in. But I'll go with you another night with all my heart."

A revolution of some importance in my plan of life had just taken place; for instead of procuring a commission in the foot-guards, which was my own inclination, I had, in compliance with my father's wishes, agreed to study the law, and was soon to set out for Utrecht, to hear the lectures of an excellent Civilian in that University, and then to proceed on my travels. Though very desirous of obtaining Dr. Johnson's advice and instructions on the mode of pursuing my studies, I was at this time so occupied, shall I call it? or so dissipated, by the amusements of London, that our next meeting was not till Saturday, June 25, when happening to dine at Clifton's eating-house, in Butcher-row, I was surprised to perceive Johnson come in and take his seat at another table. He agreed to meet me in the evening at the Mitre. I called on him, and we went thither at nine. We had a good supper, and port wine, of which he then sometimes drank a bottle. I find in my Journal the following minute of our conversation.

"Colley Cibber, Sir, was by no means a blockhead, but by arrogating to himself too much, he was in danger of losing that degree of estimation to which he was entitled. His friends gave out that he *intended* his birthday Odes should be bad: but that was not the case, Sir; for he kept them many months by him, and a few years before he died he shewed me one of them, with great solicitude to render it as perfect as might be, and I made some corrections, to which he was not very willing to submit."

Finding him in a placid humour, and wishing to avail myself of the opportunity which I fortunately had of consulting a sage, to hear whose wisdom, I conceived, in the ardour of youthful imagination, that men filled with a noble enthusiasm for intellectual improvement would gladly have resorted from distant lands;—I opened my mind to him ingenuously, and gave him a little sketch of my life, to which he was pleased to listen with great attention.

I acknowledged, that though educated very strictly in the principles of religion, I had for some time been misled into a certain degree of infidelity; but that I was come now to a better way of thinking, and was fully satisfied of the truth of the Christian revelation, though I was not clear as to every point considered to be orthodox. Being at all times a curious examiner of the human mind, and pleased with an undisguised display of what had passed in it, he called to me with warmth, "Give me your hand; I have taken a liking to you."

When I talked to him of the paternal estate to which I was heir, he said, "Sir, let me tell you, that to be a Scotch landlord, where you have a number of families dependent upon you, and attached to you, is, perhaps as high a situation as humanity can arrive at. A merchant upon the 'Change of London, with a hundred thousand pounds, is nothing; an English Duke, with an immense fortune, is nothing: he has no tenants who consider themselves as under his patriarchal care, and who will follow him to the field upon an emergency."

He proceeded: "Your going abroad, Sir, and breaking off idle habits, may be of great importance to you. I would go where there are courts and learned men. There is a good deal of Spain that has not been perambulated. I would have you go thither. A man of inferiour talents to yours may furnish us with useful observations upon that country."

As Dr. Oliver Goldsmith will frequently appear in this narrative I shall endeavour to make my readers in some degree acquainted with his singular character. He was a native of Ireland, and a contemporary with Mr. Burke, at Trinity College, Dublin, but did not then give much promise of future celebrity. He afterwards studied physick at Edinburgh, and upon the Continent: and I have been informed, was enabled to pursue his travels on foot, partly by demanding at Universities to enter the lists as a disputant, by which, according to the custom of many of them, he was entitled to the premium of a crown, when luckily for him his challenge was not accepted; so that, as I once observed to Dr. Johnson, he *disputed* his passage through Europe. He then came to England, and was employed successively in the capacities of an usher to an academy, a corrector of the press, a reviewer, and a writer for a newspaper. He had sagacity enough to cultivate assiduously the acquaintance of Johnson, and his faculties were gradually enlarged by the contemplation of such a model. To me and many others it appeared that he studiously copied the manner of Johnson, though, indeed, upon a smaller scale.

At this time I think he had published nothing with his name, though it was pretty generally known that *one Dr. Goldsmith* was the authour of "An Enquiry into the present State of polite Learning in Europe," and of "The Citizen of the World," a series of letters supposed to be written from London by a Chinese. No man had the art of displaying with more advantage as a writer, whatever literary acquisitions he made. *"Nihil quod tetigit non ornavit."* His mind resembled a fertile, but thin soil. No deep root could be struck. The oak of the forest did not grow there: but the elegant shrubbery and the fragrant parterre appeared in gay succession. It has been generally circulated and believed that he was a mere fool in conversation; but, in truth, this has been greatly exaggerated. He had, no doubt, a more than common share of that hurry of ideas which we often find in his countrymen, and which sometimes produces a laughable confusion in expressing them. His person was short, his countenance coarse and vulgar, his deportment that of a scholar awkwardly affecting the easy gentleman. Those who were in any way distinguished, excited envy in him to so ridiculous an excess, that the instances of it are hardly credible. When accompanying two beautiful young ladies with their mother on a tour in France, he was seriously angry that more attention was paid to them than to him; and once at the exhibition of the *Fantoccini* in London, when those who sat next him observed with what dexterity a puppet was made to toss a pike, he could not bear that it should have such praise, and exclaimed with some warmth, "Pshaw! I can do it better myself."

He, I am afraid, had no settled system of any sort, so that his conduct must not be strictly scrutinized; but his affections were social and generous, and when he had money he gave it away very liberally. His desire of imaginary consequence predominated over his attention to truth. When he began to rise into notice, he said he had a brother who was Dean of Durham, a fiction so easily detected, that it is wonderful how he should have been so inconsiderate as to hazard it. He boasted to me at this time of the power of his pen in commanding money, which I believe was true in a certain degree, though in the instance he gave he was by no means correct. He told me that he had sold a novel for four hundred pounds. This was his "Vicar of Wakefield." But Johnson informed me, that he had made the bargain for Goldsmith, and the price was sixty pounds. "And, Sir, (said he,) a sufficient price too, when it was sold; for then the fame of Goldsmith had not been elevated, as it afterwards was, by his 'Traveller.'"

Mrs. Piozzi and Sir John Hawkins have strangely misstated the history of Goldsmith's situation and Johnson's friendly interference, when this novel was sold. I shall give it authentically from Johnson's own exact narration:

"I received one morning a message from poor Goldsmith that he was in great distress, and as it was not in his power to come to me, begging that I would come to him as soon as possible. I sent him a guinea, and promised to come to him directly. I accordingly went as soon as I was drest, and found that his landlady had arrested him for his rent, at which he was in a violent passion. I perceived that he had already changed my guinea, and had got a bottle of Madeira and a glass before him. I put the cork into the bottle, desired he would be calm, and began to talk to him of the means by which he might be extricated. He then told me that he had a novel ready for the press, which he produced to me. I looked into it, and saw its merit; told the landlady I should soon return, and having gone to a bookseller sold it for sixty pounds. I brought Goldsmith the money, and he discharged his rent, not without rating his landlady in a high tone for having used him so ill."

My next meeting with Johnson was on Friday the 1st of July, when he and I and Dr. Goldsmith supped at the Mitre. I was before this time pretty well acquainted with Goldsmith, who was one of the brightest ornaments of the Johnsonian school. Goldsmith's respectful attachment to Johnson was then at its height; for his own literary reputation had not yet distinguished him so much as to excite a vain desire of competition with his great Master. He had increased my admiration of the goodness of Johnson's heart, by incidental remarks in the course of conversation, such as, when I mentioned Mr. Levet, whom he entertained under his roof, "He is poor and honest, which is recommendation enough to Johnson;" and when I wondered that he was very kind to a man of whom I had heard a very bad character, "He is now become miserable, and that insures the protection of Johnson."

Dr. John Campbell, the celebrated political and biographical writer, being mentioned, Johnson said, "Campbell is a man of much knowledge, and has a good share of imagination. Campbell is a good man, a pious man. I am afraid he has not been in the inside of a church for many years; but he never passes a church without pulling off his hat. This shews that he has good principles. I used to go pretty often to Campbell's on a Sunday evening till I began to consider that the shoals of Scotchmen who flocked about him might probably say, when any thing of mine was well done, 'Ay, ay, he has learnt this of CAWMELL!' "

He talked very contemptuously of Churchill's poetry, observing, that "it had a temporary currency, only from its audacity of abuse, and being filled with living names, that it would sink into oblivion." I ventured to hint that he was not quite a fair judge, as Churchill had attacked him violently. JOHNSON. "Nay, Sir, I am a very fair judge. He did not attack me violently till he found I did not like his poetry; and his attack on me shall not prevent me from continuing to say what I think of him, from an apprehension that it may be ascribed to resentment. No, Sir, I called the fellow a blockhead at first, and I will call him a blockhead still. However, I will acknowledge that I have a better opinion of him now, than I once had; for he has shown more fertility than I expected. To be sure, he is a tree that cannot produce good fruit; he only bears crabs. But, Sir, a tree that produces a great many crabs is better than a tree which produces only a few."

Let me here apologize for the imperfect manner in which I am obliged to exhibit Johnson's conversation at this period. In the early part of my acquaintance with him, I was so wrapt in admiration of his extraordinary colloquial talents, and so little accustomed to his peculiar mode of expression, that I found it extremely difficult to recollect and record his conversation with its genuine vigour and vivacity. In progress of time, when my mind was, as it were, *strongly impregnated with the Johnsonian æther,* I could with much more facility and exactness, carry in my memory and commit to paper the exuberant variety of his wisdom and wit.

At this time, *Miss* Williams, as she was then called, though she did not reside with him in the Temple under his roof, but had lodgings in Bolt-court, Fleet-street, had so much of his attention, that he every night drank tea with her before he went home, however late it might be, and she always sat up for him. This, it may be fairly conjectured, was not alone a proof of his regard for *her,* but of his own unwillingness to go into solitude, before that unseasonable hour at which he had habituated himself to expect the oblivion of repose. Dr. Goldsmith, being a privileged man, went with him this night, strutting away, and calling to me with an air of superiority, like that of an esoterick over an exoterick disciple of a sage of antiquity, "I go to see Miss Williams." I confess, I then envied him this mighty privilege, of which he seemed so proud; but it was not long before I obtained the same mark of distinction.

On Wednesday, July 6, he was engaged to sup with me at my lodgings in Downing-street, Westminster. But on the preceding night my landlord having behaved very rudely to me and some company who were with me, I had resolved not to remain another night in his house. I was exceedingly uneasy at the awkward appearance I supposed I should make to Johnson and the other gentlemen whom I had invited, not being able to receive them at home, and being obliged to order supper at the Mitre. I went to Johnson in the morning, and talked of it as of a serious distress. He laughed, and said, "Consider, Sir, how insignificant this will appear a twelvemonth hence."—Were this consideration to be applied to most of the little vexatious incidents of life, by which our quiet is too often disturbed, it would prevent many painful sensations. I have tried it frequently with good effect. "There is nothing (continued he) in this mighty misfortune; nay, we shall be better at the Mitre."

I had as my guests this evening at the Mitre tavern, Dr. Johnson, Dr. Goldsmith, Mr. Thomas Davies, Mr. Eccles, an Irish gentleman, for whose agreeable company I was obliged to Mr. Davies, and the Reverend Mr. John Ogilvie, who was desirous of being in company with my illustrious friend, while I in my turn, was proud to have the honour of shewing one of my countrymen upon what easy terms Johnson permitted me to live with him.

Goldsmith, as usual, endeavoured, with too much eagerness, to *shine*, and disputed very warmly with Johnson against the well-known maxim of the British constitution, "the King can do no wrong;" affirming, that, "what was morally false could not be politically true; and as the King might, in the exercise of his regal power, command and cause the doing of what was wrong, it certainly might be said, in sense and in reason, that he could do wrong." JOHNSON. "Sir, you are to consider, that in our constitution, according to its true principles, the King is the head, he is supreme: he is above every thing, and there is no power by which he can be tried. Therefore, it is, Sir, that we hold the King can do no wrong; that whatever may happen to be wrong in government may not be above our reach, by being ascribed to Majesty. Redress is always to be had against oppression, by punishing the immediate agents. The King, though he should command, cannot force a Judge to condemn a man unjustly; therefore it is the Judge whom we prosecute and punish. Political institutions are formed upon the consideration of what will most frequently tend to the good of the whole, although now and then exceptions may occur. Thus it is better in general that a nation should have a supreme legislative power, although it may at times be abused. And then, Sir, there is this consideration, that *if the abuse be enormous, Nature will rise up, and claiming her original rights, overturn a corrupt political system.*" I mark this animated sentence with peculiar pleasure, as a noble instance of that truly dignified spirit of freedom which ever glowed in his heart, though he was charged with slavish tenets by superficial observers; because he was at all times indignant against that false patriotism, that pretended love of freedom, that unruly restlessness which is inconsistent with the stable authority of any good government.

Mr. Ogilvie was unlucky enough to choose for the topick of his conversation the praises of his native country. He began with saying, that there was very rich land around Edinburgh. Goldsmith, who had studied physick there, contradicted this, very untruly, with a sneering laugh. Disconcerted a little by this, Mr. Ogilvie then took a new ground, where, I suppose, he thought himself perfectly safe; for he observed, that Scotland had a great many noble wild prospects. JOHNSON. "I believe, Sir, you have a great many. Norway, too, has noble wild prospects; and Lapland is remarkable for prodigious noble wild prospects. But, Sir, let me tell you, the noblest prospect which a Scotchman ever sees, is the high road that leads him to England!" This unexpected and pointed sally produced a roar of applause. After all, however, those who admire the rude grandeur of Nature, cannot deny it to Caledonia.

On Saturday, July 9, I found Johnson surrounded with a numerous levee, but have not preserved any part of his conversation. On the 14th we had another evening by ourselves at the Mitre.

Feeling myself now quite at ease as his companion, though I had all possible reverence for him, I expressed a regret that I could not be so easy with my father, though he was not much older than Johnson, and certainly however respectable had not more learning and greater abilities to depress me. I asked him the reason of this. JOHNSON. "Why, Sir, I am a man of the world. I live in the world, and I take in some degree, the colour of the world as it moves along. Your father is a Judge in a remote part of the island, and all his notions are taken from the old world. Besides, Sir, there must always be a struggle between a father and son, while one aims at power and the other at independence."

He enlarged very convincingly upon the excellence of rhyme over blank verse in English poetry. I mentioned to him that Dr. Adam Smith, in his lectures upon composition, when I studied under him in the College of Glasgow, had maintained the same opinion strenuously, and I repeated some of his arguments. JOHNSON. "Sir, I was once in company with Smith, and we did not take to each other; but had I known that he loved rhyme as much as you tell me he does, I should have HUGGED him."

To such a degree of unrestrained frankness had he now accustomed me, that in the course of this evening I talked of the numerous reflections which had been thrown out against him on account of his having accepted a pension from his present Majesty. "Why, Sir, (said he, with a hearty laugh,) it is a mighty foolish noise that they make. I have accepted of a pension as a reward which has been thought due to my literary merit; and now that I have this pension, I am the same man in every respect that I have ever been; I retain the same principles. It is true, that I cannot now curse (smiling) the House of Hanover; nor would it be decent for me to drink King James's health in the wine that King George gives me money to pay for. But, Sir, I think that the pleasure of cursing the House of Hanover, and drinking King James's health, are amply overbalanced by three hundred pounds a year."

There was here, most certainly, an affectation of more Jacobitism than he really had. Yet there is no doubt that at earlier periods he was wont often to exercise both his pleasantry and ingenuity in talking Jacobitism. My much respected friend, Dr. Douglas, now Bishop of Salisbury, has favoured me with the following admirable instance from his Lordship's own recollection. One day when dining at old Mr. Langton's, where Miss Roberts, his niece, was one of the company, Johnson, with his usual complacent attention to the fair sex, took her by the hand and said, "My dear, I hope you are a Jacobite." Old Mr. Langton, who, though a high and steady Tory, was attached to the present Royal Family, seemed offended, and asked Johnson, with great warmth, what he could mean by putting such a question to his niece! "Why, Sir, (said Johnson) I meant no offence to your niece, I meant her a great compliment. A Jacobite, Sir, believes in the divine right of Kings. He that believes in the divine right of Kings believes in a Divinity. A Jacobite believes in the divine right of Bishops. He that believes in the divine right of Bishops believes in the divine authority of the Christian religion. Therefore, Sir, a Jacobite is neither an Atheist nor a Deist. That cannot be said of a Whig; for *Whiggism is a negation of all principle.*"

I added that the same person maintained that there was no distinction between virtue and vice. JOHNSON. "Why, Sir, if the fellow does not think as he speaks, he is lying; and I see not what honour he can propose to himself from having the character of a lyar. But if he does really think that there is no distinction between virtue and vice, why, Sir, when he leaves our houses let us count our spoons."

Mr. Levet this day showed me Dr. Johnson's library, which was contained in two garrets over his Chambers, where Lintot, son of the celebrated bookseller of that name, had formerly his warehouse. I found a number of good books, but very dusty and in great confusion. The floor was strewed with manuscript leaves, in Johnson's own hand-writing, which I beheld with a degree of veneration, supposing they perhaps might contain portions of the Rambler, or of Rasselas. I observed an apparatus for chymical experiments, of which Johnson was all his life very fond. The place seemed to be very favourable for retirement and meditation. Johnson told me, that he went up thither without mentioning it to his servant when he wanted to study, secure from interruption; for he would not allow his servant to say he was not at home when he really was. "A servant's strict regard for truth, (said he) must be weakened by such a practice. A philosopher may know that it is merely a form of denial; but few servants are such nice distinguishers. If I accustom a servant to tell a lie for *me,* have I not reason to apprehend that he will tell many lies for *himself?*"

On Wednesday, July 20, Dr. Johnson, Mr. Dempster, and my uncle Dr. Boswell, who happened to be now in London, supped with me at these Chambers. JOHNSON. "Pity is not natural to man. Children are always cruel.

Savages are always cruel. Pity is acquired and improved by the cultivation of reason. We may have uneasy sensations for seeing a creature in distress, without pity; for we have not pity unless we wish to relieve them. When I am on my way to dine with a friend, and finding it late, have bid the coachman make haste, if I happen to attend when he whips his horses, I may feel unpleasantly that the animals are put to pain, but I do not wish him to desist. No, Sir, I wish him to drive on."

Rousseau's treatise on the inequality of mankind was at this time a fashionable topick. It gave rise to an observation by Mr. Dempster, that the advantages of fortune and rank were nothing to a wise man, who ought to value only merit. JOHNSON. "If man were savage, living in the woods by himself, this might be true; but in civilised society we all depend upon each other, and our happiness is very much owing to the good opinion of mankind. Now, Sir, in civilised society, external advantages make us more respected. A man with a good coat upon his back meets with a better reception than he who has a bad one. Sir, you may analyse this, and say what is there in it? But that will avail you nothing, for it is a part of a general system. Pound St. Paul's church into atoms, and consider any single atom; it is, to be sure, good for nothing; but, put all these atoms together, and you have St. Paul's church. So it is with human felicity, which is made up of many ingredients, each of which may be shewn to be very insignificant. In civilised society, personal merit will not serve you so much as money will. Sir, you may make the experiment. Go into the street, and give one man a lecture on morality, and another a shilling, and see which will respect you most. If you wish only to support nature, Sir William Petty fixes your allowance at three pounds a year; but as times are much altered, let us call it six pounds. This sum will fill your belly, shelter you from the weather, and even get you a strong lasting coat, supposing it to be made of good bull's hide. Now, Sir, all beyond this is artificial, and is desired in order to obtain a greater degree of respect from our fellow-creatures. And, Sir, if six hundred pounds a year procure a man more consequence, and, of course, more happiness than six pounds a year, the same proportion will hold as to six thousand, and so on, as far as opulence can be carried. Perhaps he who has a large fortune may not be so happy as he who has a small one; but that must proceed from other causes than from his having the large fortune: for, *cœteris paribus,* he who is rich in a civilised society, must be happier than he who is poor; as riches, if properly used, (and it is a man's own fault if they are not,) must be productive of the highest advantages. Money, to be sure, of itself is of no use; for its only use is to part with it. Rousseau, and all those who deal in paradoxes, are led away by a childish desire of novelty. When I was a boy, I used always to choose the wrong side of a debate, because most ingenious things, that is to say, most new things, could be said upon it. Sir, there is nothing for which you may not muster up more plausible arguments, than those which are urged against wealth and other external advantages. Why, now, there is stealing; why should it be thought a crime? When we consider by what unjust methods property has been often acquired, and that what was unjustly got it must be unjust to keep, where is the harm in one man's taking the property of another from him? Besides, Sir, when we consider the bad use that many people make of their property, and how much better use the thief may make of it, it may be defended as a very allowable practice. Yet, Sir, the experience of mankind has discovered stealing to be so very bad a thing, that they make no scruple to hang a man for it. When I was running about this town a very poor fellow, I was a great arguer for the advantages of poverty; but I was, at the same time, very sorry to be poor. Sir, all the arguments which are brought to represent poverty as no evil, shew it to be evidently a great evil. You never find people labouring to convince you that you may live very happily upon a plentiful fortune.—So you hear people talking how miserable a King must be; and yet they all wish to be in his place."

It was suggested that Kings must be unhappy, because they are deprived of the greatest of all satisfactions, easy and unreserved society. JOHNSON. "That is an ill-founded notion. Being a King does not exclude a man from such society. Great Kings have always been social. The King of Prussia, the only great King at present, is very social. Charles the Second, the last King of England who was a man of parts, was social; and our Henrys and Edwards were all social."

Mr. Dempster having endeavoured to maintain that intrinsick merit *ought* to make the only distinction amongst mankind. JOHNSON. "Why, Sir, mankind have found that this cannot be. How shall we determine the proportion of intrinsick merit? Were that to be the only distinction amongst mankind, we should soon quarrel about the degrees of it. Were all distinctions abolished, the strongest would not long acquiesce, but would endeavour to obtain a superiority by their bodily strength. But, Sir, as subordination is very necessary for society, and contentions for superiority very dangerous, mankind, that is to say, all civilised nations, have settled it upon a plain invariable principle. A man is born to hereditary rank; or his being appointed to certain offices, gives him a certain rank. Subordination tends greatly to human happiness. Were we all upon an equality, we should have no other enjoyment than mere animal pleasure."

I said, I considered distinction of rank to be of so much importance in civilised society, that if I were asked on the same day to dine with the first Duke in England, and with the first man in Britain for genius, I should hesitate which to prefer. JOHNSON. "To be sure, Sir, if you were to dine only once, and it were never to be known where you dined, you would choose rather to dine with the first man for genius; but to gain most respect, you should dine with the first Duke in England. For nine people in ten that you meet with, would have a higher opinion of you for having dined with a Duke; and the great genius himself would receive you better, because you had been with the great Duke."

He took care to guard himself against any possible suspicion that his settled principles of reverence for rank and respect for wealth were at all owing to mean or interested motives; for he asserted his own independence as a literary man. "No man (said he) who ever lived by literature, has lived more independently than I have done." He said he had taken longer time than he needed to have done in composing his Dictionary. He received our compliments upon that great work with complacency, and told us that the Academy *della Crusca* could scarcely believe that it was done by one man.

Next morning I found him alone, and have preserved the following fragments of his conversation. Of a gentleman who was mentioned, he said, "I have not met with any man for a long time who has given me such general displeasure. He is totally unfixed in his principles, and wants to puzzle other people." I said his principles had been poisoned by a noted infidel writer, but that he was, nevertheless, a benevolent good man. JOHNSON. "We can have no dependance upon that instinctive, that constitutional goodness which is not founded upon principle. I grant you that such a man may be a very amiable member of society. I can conceive him placed in such a situation that he is not much tempted to deviate from what is right; and as every man prefers virtue, when there is not some strong incitement to transgress its precepts, I can conceive him doing nothing wrong. But if such a man stood in need of money, I should not like to trust him; and I should certainly not trust him with young ladies, for *there* there is always temptation. Hume, and other sceptical innovators, are vain men, and will gratify themselves at any expence. Truth will not afford sufficient food to their vanity; so they have betaken themselves to errour. Truth, Sir, is a cow which will yield such people no more milk, and so they are gone to milk the bull."

At night, Mr. Johnson and I supped in a private room at the Turk's Head coffee-house, in the Strand. "I encourage this house (said he,) for the mistress of it is a good civil woman, and has not much business."

"Sir, I love the acquaintance of young people; because, in the first place, I don't like to think myself growing old. In the next place, young acquaintances must last longest, if they do last; and then, Sir, young men have more virtue than old men; they have more generous sentiments in every respect. I love the young dogs of this age, they have more wit and humour and knowledge of life than we had; but then the dogs are not so good scholars. Sir, in my early years I read very hard. It is a sad reflection but a true one, that I knew almost as much at eighteen as I do now. My judgement, to be sure, was not so good; but, I had all the facts. I remember very well, when I was at Oxford, an old gentleman said to me, 'Young man, ply your book diligently now, and acquire a stock of knowledge; for when years come upon you, you will find that poring upon books will be but an irksome task.' "

He again insisted on the duty of maintaining sub-ordination of rank. "Sir, I would no more deprive a nobleman of his respect, than of his money. I consider my-self as acting a part in the great system of society, and I do to others as I would have them to do to me. I would behave to a nobleman as I should expect he would be-have to me, were I a nobleman and he Sam. Johnson. Sir, there is one Mrs. Macaulay in this town, a great re-publican. One day when I was at her house, I put on a very grave countenance, and said to her, 'Madam, I am now become a convert to your way of thinking. I am convinced that all mankind are upon an equal footing; and to give you an unquestionable proof, Madam, that I am in earnest, here is a very sensible, civil, well-be-haved fellow-citizen, your footman; I desire that he may be allowed to sit down and dine with us.' I thus, Sir, shewed her the absurdity of the levelling doctrine. She has never liked me since. Sir, your levellers wish to level *down* as far as themselves; but they cannot bear lev-elling *up* to themselves. They would all have some peo-ple under them; why not then have some people above them?"

I spoke of Sir James Macdonald as a young man of most distinguished merit, who united the highest repu-tation at Eton and Oxford, with the patriarchal spirit of a great Highland Chieftain. I mentioned that Sir James had said to me, that he had never seen Mr. Johnson, but he had a great respect for him, though at the same time it was mixed with some degree of terrour. JOHN-SON. "Sir, if he were to be acquainted with me, it might lessen both."

The mention of this gentleman led us to talk of the

Western Islands of Scotland, to visit which he expressed
a wish that then appeared to be a very romantick fancy,
which I little thought would be afterwards realised. He
told me, that his father had put Martin's account of
those islands into his hands when he was very young,
and that he was highly pleased with it; that he was particularly struck with the St. Kilda man's notion that the
high church of Glasgow had been hollowed out of a
rock; a circumstance to which old Mr. Johnson had directed his attention. He said, he would go to the Hebrides with me, when I returned from my travels, unless
some very good companion should offer when I was absent, which he did not think probable; adding, "There
are few people whom I take so much to, as you." And
when I talked of my leaving England, he said with a
very affectionate air, "My dear Boswell, I should be
very unhappy at parting, did I think we were not to
meet again."

He maintained that a boy at school was the happiest
of human beings. I supported a different opinion, from
which I have never yet varied, that a man is happier:
and I enlarged upon the anxiety and sufferings which
are endured at school. JOHNSON. "Ah! Sir, a boy's being
flogged is not so severe as a man's having the hiss of the
world against him. Men have a solicitude about fame;
and the greater share they have of it, the more afraid
they are of losing it." I silently asked myself, "Is it possible that the great SAMUEL JOHNSON really entertains
any such apprehension, and is not confident that his exalted fame is established upon a foundation never to be
shaken?"

On Thursday, July 28, we again supped in private at
the Turk's Head coffee-house. JOHNSON. "Swift has a
higher reputation than he deserves. His excellence is
strong sense; for his humour, though very well, is not

remarkably good. I doubt whether the 'Tale of a Tub' be his; for he never owned it, and it is much above his usual manner."

He laughed heartily when I mentioned to him a saying of his concerning Mr. Thomas Sheridan, which Foote took a wicked pleasure to circulate. "Why, Sir, Sherry is dull, naturally dull; but it must have taken him a great deal of pains to become what we now see him. Such an excess of stupidity, Sir, is not in Nature." —"So (said he,) I allowed him all his own merit."

He now added, "Sheridan cannot bear me. I bring his declamation to a point. I ask him a plain question, 'What do you mean to teach?' Besides, Sir, what influence can Mr. Sheridan have upon the language of this great country, by his narrow exertions? Sir, it is burning a farthing candle at Dover, to shew light at Calais."

I expressed my opinion of my friend Derrick as but a poor writer. JOHNSON. "To be sure, Sir, he is: but you are to consider that his being a literary man has got for him all that he has. It has made him King of Bath. Sir, he has nothing to say for himself but that he is a writer. Had he not been a writer, he must have been sweeping the crossings in the streets, and asking halfpence from everybody that past."

Johnson said once to me, "Sir, I honour Derrick for his presence of mind. One night, when Floyd, another poor authour, was wandering about the streets in the night, he found Derrick fast asleep upon a bulk; upon being suddenly waked, Derrick started up, 'My dear Floyd, I am sorry to see you in this destitute state: will you go home with me to *my lodgings?*'"

I again begged his advice as to my method of study at Utrecht. "Come, (said he) let us make a day of it. Let us go down to Greenwich and dine, and talk of it there." The following Saturday was fixed for this excursion.

As we walked along the Strand tonight, arm in arm, a woman of the town accosted us, in the usual enticing manner. "No, no, my girl, (said Johnson) it won't do." He, however, did not treat her with harshness; and we talked of the wretched life of such women, and agreed, that much more misery than happiness, upon the whole, is produced by illicit commerce between the sexes.

On Saturday, July 30, Dr. Johnson and I took a sculler at the Temple-stairs, and set out for Greenwich. I asked him if he really thought a knowledge of the Greek and Latin languages an essential requisite to a good education. JOHNSON. "Most certainly, Sir; for those who know them have a very great advantage over those who do not. Nay, Sir, it is wonderful what a difference learning makes upon people even in the common intercourse of life, which does not appear to be much connected with it." "And yet, (said I) people go through the world very well, and carry on the business of life to good advantage, without learning." JOHNSON. "Why, Sir, that may be true in cases where learning cannot possibly be of any use; for instance, this boy rows us as well without learning, as if he could sing the song of Orpheus to the Argonauts, who were the first sailors." He then called to the boy, "What would you give, my lad, to know about the Argonauts?" "Sir, (said the boy) I would give what I have." Johnson was much pleased with his answer, and we gave him a double fare. Dr. Johnson then turning to me, "Sir, (said he) a desire of knowledge is the natural feeling of mankind; and every human being, whose mind is not debauched, will be willing to give all that he has, to get knowledge."

We landed at the Old Swan, and walked to Billingsgate, where we took oars and moved smoothly along the silver Thames. It was a very fine day. We were entertained with the immense number and variety of ships that were lying at anchor, and with the beautiful country on each side of the river.

We walked in the evening in Greenwich Park. He asked me, I suppose, by way of trying my disposition, "Is not this very fine?" Having no exquisite relish of the beauties of Nature, and being more delighted with "the busy hum of men," I answered, "Yes, Sir; but not equal to Fleet-street." JOHNSON. "You are right, Sir."

I am aware that many of my readers may censure my want of taste. Let me, however, shelter myself under the authority of a very fashionable Baronet in the brilliant world, who, on his attention being called to the fragrance of a May evening in the country, observed, "This may be very well; but for my part, I prefer the smell of a flambeau at the play-house."

We staid so long at Greenwich, that our sail up the river, in our return to London, was by no means so pleasant as in the morning; for the night air was so cold that it made me shiver. I was the more sensible of it from having sat up all the night before recollecting and writing in my Journal what I thought worthy of preservation; an exertion, which, during the first part of my acquaintance with Johnson, I frequently made. I remember having sat up four nights in one week, without being much incommoded in the day time.

Johnson, whose robust frame was not in the least affected by the cold, scolded me, as if my shivering had been a paltry effeminacy, saying, "Why do you shiver?" Sir William Scott, of the Commons, told me, that when he complained of a head-ach in the post-chaise, as they were travelling together to Scotland, Johnson treated him in the same manner: "At your age, Sir, I had no head-ach."

We concluded the day at the Turk's Head coffee-house very socially. He was pleased to listen to a particular account which I gave him of my family, and of its hereditary estate, as to the extent and population of which he asked questions, and made calculations; recommending, at the same time, a liberal kindness to the tenantry, as people over whom the proprietor was placed by Providence. He took delight in hearing my description of the romantick seat of my ancestors. "I must be there, Sir, (said he) and we will live in the old castle; and if there is not a room in it remaining, we will build one." I was highly flattered, but could scarcely indulge a hope that Auchinleck would indeed be honoured by his presence, and celebrated by a description, as it afterwards was, in his "Journey to the Western Islands."

After we had again talked of my setting out for Holland, he said, "I must see thee out of England; I will accompany you to Harwich." I could not find words to express what I felt upon this unexpected and very great mark of his affectionate regard.

Next day, Sunday, July 31, I told him I had been that morning at a meeting of the people called Quakers, where I had heard a woman preach. JOHNSON. "Sir, a woman's preaching is like a dog's walking on his hind legs. It is not done well; but you are surprised to find it done at all."

On Tuesday, August 2, (the day of my departure from London having been fixed for the 5th,) Dr. Johnson did me the honour to pass a part of the morning with me at my Chambers. He said, that "he always felt an inclination to do nothing." I observed, that it was strange to think that the most indolent man in Britain had written the most laborious work, *The English Dictionary*.

I mentioned an imprudent publication, by a certain friend of his, at an early period of life, and asked him if he thought it would hurt him. JOHNSON. "No, Sir; not much. It may, perhaps, be mentioned at an election."

I had now made good my title to be a privileged man, and was carried by him in the evening to drink tea with Miss Williams, whom, though under the misfortune of having lost her sight, I found to be agreeable in conversation; for she had a variety of literature, and expressed herself well; but her peculiar value was the intimacy in which she had long lived with Johnson, by which she was well acquainted with his habits, and knew how to lead him on to talk.

On Wednesday, August 3, we had our last social evening at the Turk's Head coffee-house, before my setting out for foreign parts. I had the misfortune, before we parted, to irritate him unintentionally. I mentioned to him how common it was in the world to tell absurd stories of him, and to ascribe to him very strange sayings. JOHNSON. "What do they make me say, Sir?" BOSWELL. "Why, Sir, as an instance very strange indeed, (laughing heartily as I spoke,) David Hume told me, you said that you would stand before a battery of cannon to restore the Convocation to its full powers."— Little did I apprehend that he had actually said this: but I was soon convinced of my errour; for, with a determined look, he thundered out, "And would I not, Sir? Shall the Presbyterian *Kirk* of Scotland have its General Assembly, and the Church of England be denied its Convocation?" He was walking up and down the room, while I told him the anecdote; but when he uttered this explosion of high-church zeal, he had come close to my chair, and his eye flashed with indignation. I bowed to the storm, and diverted the force of it, by leading him to expatiate on the influence which religion derived from maintaining the church with great external respectability.

On Friday, August 5, we set out early in the morning

in the Harwich stage-coach. A fat elderly gentlewoman, and a young Dutchman, seemed the most inclined among us to conversation. At the inn where we dined, the gentlewoman said that she had done her best to educate her children; and, particularly, that she had never suffered them to be a moment idle. JOHNSON. "I wish, Madam, you would educate me too; for I have been an idle fellow all my life." "I am sure, Sir, (said she) you have not been idle." JOHNSON. "Nay, Madam, it is very true; and that gentleman there, (pointing to me,) has been idle. He was idle at Edinburgh. His father sent him to Glasgow, where he continued to be idle. He then came to London, where he has been very idle; and now he is going to Utrecht, where he will be as idle as ever." I asked him privately how he could expose me so. JOHNSON. "Poh, poh! (said he) they knew nothing about you, and will think of it no more." In the afternoon the gentlewoman talked violently against the Roman Catholicks, and of the horrours of the Inquisition. To the utter astonishment of all the passengers but myself, who knew that he could talk upon any side of a question, he defended the Inquisition, and maintained, that "false doctrine should be checked on its first appearance; that the civil power should unite with the church in punishing those who dare to attack the established religion, and that such only were punished by the Inquisition." He had in his pocket *Pomponius Mela de Situ Orbis,* in which he read occasionally, and seemed very intent upon ancient geography. Though by no means niggardly, his attention to what was generally right was so minute, that having observed at one of the stages that I ostentatiously gave a shilling to the coachman, when the custom was for each passenger to give only six-pence, he took me aside and scolded me, saying that what I had done would make the coachman dissatisfied with all the rest of the passengers who gave him no more than his due. This was a just reprimand; for in whatever way a man may indulge his generosity or his vanity in spending his money, for the sake of others he ought not to raise the price of any article for which there is a constant demand.

He talked of Mr. Blacklock's poetry, so far as it was descriptive of visible objects; and observed, that "as its authour had the misfortune to be blind, we may be absolutely sure that such passages are combinations of what he has remembered of the works of other writers who could see. That foolish fellow, Spence, has laboured to explain philosophically how Blacklock may have done, by means of his own faculties, what it is impossible he should do. The solution, as I have given it, is plain. Suppose, I know a man to be so lame that he is absolutely incapable to move himself, and I find him in a different room from that in which I left him; shall I puzzle myself with idle conjectures, that, perhaps, his nerves have by some unknown change all at once become effective? No, Sir, it is clear how he got into a different room: he was *carried*."

At supper this night he talked of good eating with uncommon satisfaction. "Some people (said he,) have a foolish way of not minding, or pretending not to mind, what they eat. For my part, I mind my belly very studiously, and very carefully; for I look upon it, that he who does not mind his belly, will hardly mind any thing else." He now appeared to me *Jean Bull philosophe*, and he was for the moment, not only serious, but vehement. Yet I have heard him, upon other occasions, talk with great contempt of people who were anxious to gratify their palates; and the 206th number of his Rambler is a masterly essay against gulosity. His practice, indeed, I must acknowledge, may be considered as casting the balance of his different opinions upon this subject; for I never knew any man who relished good eating more than he did. When at table, he was totally absorbed in the business of the moment; his looks seemed rivetted to his plate; nor would he, unless when in very high company, say one word, or even pay the least attention to what was said by others, till he had satisfied his appetite: which was so fierce, and indulged with such intenseness, that while in the act of eating, the veins of his forehead swelled, and generally a strong perspiration was visible. To those whose sensations were delicate, this could not but be disgusting; and it was doubtless not very suitable to the character of a philosopher, who should be distinguished by self-command. But it must be owned, that Johnson, though he could be rigidly *abstemious,* was not a *temperate* man either in eating or drinking. He could refrain, but he could not use moderately. He told me, that he had fasted two days without inconvenience, and that he had never been hungry but once. They who beheld with wonder how much he eat upon all occasions, when his dinner was to his taste, could not easily conceive what he must have meant by hunger; and not only was he remarkable for the extraordinary quantity which he eat, but he was, or affected to be, a man of very nice discernment in the science of cookery. He used to descant critically on the dishes which had been at table where he had dined or supped, and to recollect very minutely what he had liked. I remember when he was in Scotland, his praising "*Gordon's palates,*" (a dish of palates at the Honourable Alexander Gordon's) with a warmth of expression which might have done honour to more important subjects. "As for Maclaurin's imitation of a *made dish,* it was a wretched attempt." He about the same time was so much displeased with the performances of a nobleman's French cook, that he exclaimed with vehemence, "I'd throw such a rascal into the river;" and he then proceeded to alarm a lady at whose house he was to sup, by the following manifesto of his skill: "I, Madam, who live at a variety of good tables, am a much better judge of cookery, than any person who has a very tolerable cook, but lives much at home; for his palate is gradually adapted to the taste of his cook: whereas, Madam, in trying by a wider range, I can more exquisitely judge." When invited to dine, even with an intimate friend, he was not pleased if something better than a plain dinner was not prepared for him. I have heard him say on such an occasion, "This was a good dinner enough, to be sure: but it was not a dinner to *ask* a man to." On the other hand, he was wont to express, with great glee, his satisfaction when he had been entertained quite to his mind. One day when he had dined with his neighbour and landlord, in Bolt-court, Mr. Allen, the printer, whose old housekeeper had studied his taste in every thing, he pronounced this eulogy: "Sir, we could not have had a better dinner, had there been a *Synod of Cooks.*"

I teased him with fanciful apprehensions of unhappiness. A moth having fluttered round the candle, and burnt itself, he laid hold of this little incident to admonish me; saying, with a sly look, and in a solemn but a quiet tone, "That creature was its own tormentor, and I believe its name was BOSWELL."

Next day we got to Harwich, to dinner; and my passage in the packet-boat to Helvoetsluys being secured, and my baggage put on board, we dined at our inn by ourselves. I happened to say, it would be terrible if he should not find a speedy opportunity of returning to London, and be confined in so dull a place. JOHNSON. "Don't, Sir, accustom yourself to use big words for little matters. It would *not* be *terrible*, though I *were* to be

detained some time here." The practice of using words
of disproportionate magnitude, is, no doubt, too frequent every where; but, I think, most remarkable among
the French, of which, all who have travelled in France
must have been struck with innumerable instances.

We went and looked at the church, and having gone
into it, and walked up to the altar, Johnson, whose piety
was constant and fervent, sent me to my knees, saying,
"Now that you are going to leave your native country,
recommend yourself to the protection of your CREATOR
and REDEEMER."

After we came out of the church, we stood talking for
some time together of Bishop Berkeley's ingenious sophistry to prove the non-existence of matter, and that every
thing in the universe is merely ideal. I observed, that
though we are satisfied his doctrine is not true, it is impossible to refute it. I never shall forget the alacrity with
which Johnson answered, striking his foot with mighty
force against a large stone, till he rebounded from it,—
"I refute it *thus.*"

My revered friend walked down with me to the
beach, where we embraced and parted with tenderness,
and engaged to correspond by letters. I said, "I hope,
Sir, you will not forget me in my absence." JOHNSON.
"Nay, Sir, it is more likely you should forget me, than
that I should forget you." As the vessel put out to sea,
I kept my eyes upon him for a considerable time, while
he remained rolling his majestic frame in his usual manner; and at last I perceived him walk back into the town,
and he disappeared.

1764. Early in 1764 Johnson paid a visit to the Langton family, at their seat of Langton in Lincolnshire,
where he passed some time, much to his satisfaction.

His friend, Bennet Langton, it will not be doubted, did every thing in his power to make the place agreeable to so illustrious a guest; and the elder Mr. Langton and his lady, being fully capable of understanding his value, were not wanting in attention. He, however, told me, that old Mr. Langton, though a man of considerable learning, had so little allowance to make for his occasional "laxity of talk," that because in the course of discussion he sometimes mentioned what might be said in favour of the peculiar tenets of the Romish church, he went to his grave believing him to be of that communion.

Johnson, during his stay at Langton, had the advantage of a good library, and saw several gentlemen of the neighbourhood. I have obtained from Mr. Langton the following particulars of this period.

To a lady who endeavoured to vindicate herself from blame for neglecting social attention to worthy neighbours, by saying, "I would go to them if it would do them any good;" he said, "What good, Madam, do you expect to have in your power to do them? It is shewing them respect, and that is doing them good."

So socially accommodating was he, that once when Mr. Langton and he were driving together in a coach, and Mr. Langton complained of being sick, he insisted that they should go out, and sit on the back of it in the open air, which they did. And being sensible how strange the appearance must be, observed, that a countryman whom they saw in a field would probably be thinking, "If these two madmen should come down, what would become of me?"

Soon after his return to London, which was in February, was founded that CLUB which existed long without a name, but at Mr. Garrick's funeral became distinguished by the title of THE LITERARY CLUB. Sir Joshua

Reynolds had the merit of being the first proposer of it, to which Johnson acceded; and the original members were, Sir Joshua Reynolds, Dr. Johnson, Mr. Edmund Burke, Dr. Nugent, Mr. Beauclerk, Mr. Langton, Dr. Goldsmith, Mr. Chamier, and Sir John Hawkins. They met at the Turk's Head, in Gerrard-street, Soho, one evening in every week, at seven, and generally continued their conversation till a pretty late hour. This club has been gradually increased to its present number, thirty-five. After about ten years, instead of supping weekly, it was resolved to dine together once a fortnight during the meeting of Parliament. Their original tavern having been converted into a private house, they moved first to Prince's in Sackville-street, then to Le Telier's in Dover-street, and now meet at Parsloe's, St. James's-street. Between the time of its formation, and the time at which this work is passing through the press, (June 1792,) the following persons, now dead, were members of it: Mr. Dunning, (afterwards Lord Ashburton,) Mr. Samuel Dyer, Mr. Garrick, Dr. Shipley Bishop of St. Asaph, Mr. Vesey, Mr. Thomas Warton, and Dr. Adam Smith. The present members are, Mr. Burke, Mr. Langton, Lord Charlemont, Sir Robert Chambers, Dr. Percy Bishop of Dromore, Dr. Barnard Bishop of Killaloe, Dr. Marlay Bishop of Clonfert, Mr. Fox, Dr. George Fordyce, Sir William Scott, Sir Joseph Banks, Sir Charles Bunbury, Mr. Windham of Norfolk, Mr. Sheridan, Mr. Gibbon, Sir William Jones, Mr. Colman, Mr. Steevens, Dr. Burney, Dr. Joseph Warton, Mr. Malone, Lord Ossory, Lord Spencer, Lord Lucan, Lord Palmerston, Lord Eliot, Lord Macartney, Mr. Richard Burke, junior, Sir William Hamilton, Dr. Warren, Mr. Courtenay, Dr. Hinchliffe Bishop of Peterborough, the Duke of Leeds, Dr. Douglas Bishop of Salisbury, and the writer of this account.

Sir John Hawkins represents himself as a *"seceder"* from this society, and assigns as the reason of his *"withdrawing"* himself from it, that its late hours were inconsistent with his domestick arrangements. In this he is not accurate; for the fact was, that he one evening attacked Mr. Burke, in so rude a manner, that all the company testified their displeasure; and at their next meeting his reception was such, that he never came again.

He is equally inaccurate with respect to Mr. Garrick, of whom he says, "he trusted that the least intimation of a desire to come among us, would procure him a ready admission; but in this he was mistaken. Johnson consulted me upon it; and when I could find no objection to receiving him, exclaimed,—'He will disturb us by his buffoonery;'—and afterwards so managed matters, that he was never formally proposed, and, by consequence, never admitted."

In justice both to Mr. Garrick and Dr. Johnson, I think it necessary to rectify this mis-statement. The truth is, that not very long after the institution of our club, Sir Joshua Reynolds was speaking of it to Garrick. "I like it much, (said he,) I think I shall be of you." When Sir Joshua mentioned this to Dr. Johnson, he was much displeased with the actor's conceit. *"He'll be of us,"* (said Johnson) how does he know we will *permit* him? the first Duke in England has no right to hold such language." However, when Garrick was regularly proposed some time afterwards, Johnson, though he had taken a momentary offence at his arrogance, warmly and kindly supported him, and he was accordingly elected, was a most agreeable member, and continued to attend our meetings to the time of his death.

Mrs. Piozzi has also given a similar misrepresentation of Johnson's treatment of Garrick in this particular, as if he had used these contemptuous expressions: if Garrick *does* apply, I'll black-ball him.—Surely, one ought to sit in a society like ours,

> Unelbow'd by a gamester, pimp, or player.

I am happy to be enabled by such unquestionable authority as that of Sir Joshua Reynolds, as well as from my own knowledge, to vindicate at once the heart of Johnson and the social merit of Garrick.

About this time he was afflicted with a very severe return of the hypochondriack disorder, which was ever lurking about him. He was so ill, as, notwithstanding his remarkable love of company, to be entirely averse to society, the most fatal symptom of that malady. Dr. Adams told me, that, as an old friend he was admitted to visit him, and that he found him in a deplorable state, sighing, groaning, talking to himself, and restlessly walking from room to room. He then used this emphatical expression of the misery which he felt: "I would consent to have a limb amputated to recover my spirits."

Talking to himself was, indeed, one of his singularities ever since I knew him. I was certain that he was frequently uttering pious ejaculations; for fragments of the Lord's Prayer have been distinctly overheard. His friend Mr. Thomas Davies, of whom Churchill says,

> That Davies hath a very pretty wife——

when Dr. Johnson muttered—"lead us not into temptation," used with waggish and gallant humour to whisper Mrs. Davies, "You, my dear, are the cause of this."

He had another particularity, of which none of his friends even ventured to ask an explanation. It appeared to me some superstitious habit, which he had contracted early, and from which he had never called upon his reason to disentangle him. This was his anxious

care to go out or in at a door or passage, by a certain
number of steps from a certain point, or at least so as
that either his right or his left foot, (I am not certain
which,) should constantly make the first actual movement when he came close to the door or passage. Thus
I conjecture: for I have, upon innumerable occasions,
observed him suddenly stop, and then seem to count his
steps with a deep earnestness; and when he had neglected or gone wrong in this sort of magical movement,
I have seen him go back again, put himself in a proper
posture to begin the ceremony, and, having gone through
it, break from his abstraction, walk briskly on, and join
his companion. A strange instance of something of this
nature, even when on horseback, happened when he
was in the Isle of Sky. Sir Joshua Reynolds has observed
him to go a good way about, rather than cross a particular alley in Leicesterfields; but this Sir Joshua imputed
to his having had some disagreeable recollection associated with it.

That the most minute singularities which belonged to
him, and made very observable parts of his appearance
and manner, may not be omitted, it is requisite to mention, that while talking or even musing as he sat in his
chair, he commonly held his head to one side towards
his right shoulder, and shook it in a tremulous manner,
moving his body backwards and forwards, and rubbing
his left knee in the same direction, with the palm of his
hand. In the intervals of articulating he made various
sounds with his mouth; sometimes as if ruminating, or
what is called chewing the cud, sometimes giving a half
whistle, sometimes making his tongue play backwards
from the roof of his mouth, as if clucking like a hen, and
sometimes protruding it against his upper gums in front,
as if pronouncing quickly under his breath, *too, too, too:*
all this accompanied sometimes with a thoughtful look,

but more frequently with a smile. Generally when he had concluded a period, in the course of a dispute, by which time he was a good deal exhausted by violence and vociferation, he used to blow out his breath like a whale. This I suppose was a relief to his lungs; and seemed in him to be a contemptuous mode of expression, as if he had made the arguments of his opponent fly like chaff before the wind.

1765. This year was distinguished by his being introduced into the family of Mr. Thrale, one of the most eminent brewers in England, and member of Parliament for the borough of Southwark. Foreigners are not a little amazed, when they hear of brewers, distillers, and men in similar departments of trade, held forth as persons of considerable consequence. In this great commercial country it is natural that a situation which produces much wealth should be considered as very respectable; and, no doubt, honest industry is entitled to esteem. But, perhaps, the too rapid advances of men of low extraction tends to lessen the value of that distinction by birth and gentility, which has ever been found beneficial to the grand scheme of subordination. Johnson used to give this account of the rise of Mr. Thrale's father: "He worked at six shillings a week for twenty years in the great brewery, which afterwards was his own. The proprietor of it had an only daughter, who was married to a nobleman. It was not fit that a peer should continue the business. On the old man's death, therefore, the brewery was to be sold. To find a purchaser for so large a property was a difficult matter; and, after some time, it was suggested, that it would be adviseable to treat with Thrale, a sensible, active, honest man, who had been employed in the house, and to transfer the whole to him for thirty thousand pounds, security being taken upon the property. This was accordingly settled. In eleven years Thrale paid the purchase-money. He acquired a large fortune, and lived to be a member of Parliament for Southwark. But what was most remarkable was the liberality with which he used his riches. He gave his son and daughters the best education. The esteem which his good conduct procured him from the nobleman who had married his master's daughter, made him to be treated with much attention; and his son, both at school and at the University of Oxford, associated with young men of the first rank. His allowance from his father, after he left college, was splendid; not less than a thousand a year. This, in a man who had risen as old Thrale did, was a very extraordinary instance of generosity. He used to say, 'If this young dog does not find so much after I am gone as he expects, let him remember that he has had a great deal in my own time.'"

The son, though in affluent circumstances, had good sense enough to carry on his father's trade, which was of such extent, that I remember he once told me, he would not quit it for an annuity of ten thousand a year; "Not (said he,) that I get ten thousand a year by it, but it is an estate to a family." Having left daughters only, the property was sold for the immense sum of one hundred and thirty-five thousand pounds; a magnificent proof of what may be done by fair trade in a long period of time.

Mr. Thrale had married Miss Hester Lynch Salusbury, of good Welch extraction, a lady of lively talents, improved by education. That Johnson's introduction into Mr. Thrale's family, which contributed so much to the happiness of his life, was owing to her desire for his conversation, is a very probable and the general supposition: but it is not the truth. Mr. Murphy, who was intimate with Mr. Thrale, having spoken very highly of Dr. Johnson, he was requested to make them acquainted. This being mentioned to Johnson, he accepted of an invitation to dinner at Thrale's, and was so much pleased with his reception, both by Mr. and Mrs. Thrale, and they so much pleased with him, that his invitations to their house were more and more frequent, till at last he became one of the family, and an apartment was appropriated to him, both in their house at Southwark and in their villa at Streatham.

Johnson had a very sincere esteem for Mr. Thrale, as a man of excellent principles, a good scholar, well skilled in trade, of a sound understanding, and of manners such as presented the character of a plain independent English 'Squire. As this family will frequently be mentioned in the course of the following pages, and as a false notion has prevailed that Mr. Thrale was inferiour, and in some degree insignificant, compared with Mrs. Thrale, it may be proper to give a true state of the case from the authority of Johnson himself in his own words.

"I know no man, (said he,) who is more master of his wife and family than Thrale. If he but holds up a finger, he is obeyed. It is a great mistake to suppose that she is above him in literary attainments. She is more flippant; but he has ten times her learning: he is a regular scholar; but her learning is that of a school-boy in one of the lower forms." My readers may naturally wish for some representation of the figures of this couple. Mr. Thrale was tall, well proportioned, and stately. As for *Madam,* or *my Mistress,* by which epithets Johnson used to mention Mrs. Thrale, she was short, plump, and brisk. She has herself given us a lively view of the idea which Johnson had of her person, on her appearing before him in a dark-coloured gown: "You little creatures should never wear those sort of clothes, however; they are unsuitable in every way. What! have not all insects gay colours!" Mr. Thrale gave his wife a liberal indulgence, both in the choice of their company, and in the mode of entertaining them. He understood and valued Johnson, without remission, from their first acquaintance to the day of his death. Mrs. Thrale was enchanted with Johnson's conversation for its own sake, and had also a very allowable vanity in appearing to be honoured with the attention of so celebrated a man.

Nothing could be more fortunate for Johnson than this connection. He had at Mr. Thrale's all the comforts and even luxuries of life: his melancholy was diverted, and his irregular habits lessened by association with an agreeable and well ordered family. He was treated with the utmost respect, and even affection. The vivacity of Mrs. Thrale's literary talk roused him to cheerfulness and exertion, even when they were alone. But this was not often the case; for he found here a constant succession of what gave him the highest enjoyment, the society of the learned, the witty, and the eminent in every way; who were assembled in numerous companies; called forth his wonderful powers, and gratified him with admiration, to which no man could be insensible.

1766. I returned to London in February, and found Dr. Johnson in a good house in Johnson's court, Fleet-street, in which he had accommodated Miss Williams with an apartment on the ground floor, while Mr. Levett occupied his post in the garret: his faithful Francis was still attending upon him. He received me with much kindness. The fragments of our first conversation, which I have preserved, are these: I told him that Voltaire, in a conversation with me, had distinguished Pope and

Dryden thus:—"Pope drives a handsome chariot, with a couple of neat trim nags; Dryden a coach, and six stately horses." JOHNSON. "Why, Sir, the truth is they both drive coaches and six; but Dryden's horses are either galloping or stumbling: Pope's go at a steady even trot." He said of Goldsmith's "Traveller," which had been published in my absence, "There has not been so fine a poem since Pope's time."

At night I supped with him at the Mitre Tavern, that we might renew our social intimacy at the original place of meeting. But there was now a considerable difference in his way of living. Having had an illness, in which he was advised to leave off wine, he had, from that period, continued to abstain from it, and drank only water, or lemonade.

I told him that a foreign friend of his, whom I had met with abroad, was so wretchedly perverted to infidelity, that he treated the hopes of immortality with brutal levity; and said, "As man dies like a dog, let him lie like a dog," JOHNSON. "If he dies like a dog, *let* him lie like a dog." I added, that this man said to me, "I hate mankind, for I think myself one of the best of them, and I know how bad I am." JOHNSON. "Sir, he must be very singular in his opinion, if he thinks himself one of the best of men; for none of his friends think him so."—He said, "No honest man could be a Deist; for no man could be so after a fair examination of the proofs of Christianity." I named Hume. JOHNSON. "No, Sir; Hume owned to a clergyman in the bishoprick of Durham, that he had never read the New Testament with attention." —I mentioned Hume's notion, that all who are happy are equally happy; a little Miss with a new gown at a dancing-school ball, a General at the head of a victorious army, and an orator, after having made an eloquent speech in a great assembly. JOHNSON. "Sir, that all who are happy, are equally happy, is not true. A peasant and a philosopher may be equally *satisfied,* but not equally *happy.* Happiness consists in the multiplicity of agreeable consciousness. A peasant has not capacity for having equal happiness with a philosopher." I remember this very question very happily illustrated in opposition to Hume, by the Reverend Mr. Robert Brown, at Utrecht. "A small drinking-glass and a large one, (said he,) may be equally full; but the large one holds more than the small."

I talked of the mode adopted by some to rise in the world, by courting great men, and asked him whether he had ever submitted to it. JOHNSON. "Why, Sir, I never was near enough to great men, to court them. You may be prudently attached to great men, and yet independent. You are not to do what you think wrong; and, Sir, you are to calculate, and not pay too dear for what you get. You must not give a shilling's worth of court for sixpence worth of good. But if you can get a shilling's worth of good for sixpence worth of court, you are a fool if you do not pay court."

Our next meeting at the Mitre was on Saturday the 15th of February, when I presented to him my old and most intimate friend, the Reverend Mr. Temple, then of Cambridge. I having mentioned that I had passed some time with Rousseau in his wild retreat, and having quoted some remark made by Mr. Wilkes, with whom I had spent many pleasant hours in Italy, Johnson said, (sarcastically,) "It seems, Sir, you have kept very good company abroad, Rousseau and Wilkes!" Thinking it enough to defend one at a time, I said nothing as to my gay friend, but answered with a smile, "My dear Sir, you don't call Rousseau bad company. Do you really think *him* a bad man?" JOHNSON. "Sir, if you are talking jestingly of this, I don't talk with you. If you mean to be serious, I think him one of the worst of men; a rascal, who ought to be hunted out of society, as he has been. Three or four nations have expelled him: and it is a shame that he is protected in this country." BOSWELL. "I don't deny, Sir, but that his novel may, perhaps, do harm; but I cannot think his intention was bad." JOHNSON. "Sir, that will not do. We cannot prove any man's intention to be bad. You may shoot a man through the head, and say you intended to miss him; but the Judge will order you to be hanged. An alleged want of intention, when evil is committed, will not be allowed in a court of justice. Rousseau, Sir, is a very bad man. I would sooner sign a sentence for his transportation, than that of any felon who has gone from the Old Bailey these many years. Yes, I should like to have him work in the plantations." BOSWELL. "Sir, do you think him as bad a man as Voltaire?" JOHNSON. "Why, Sir, it is difficult to settle the proportion of iniquity between them."

One evening, when a young gentleman teased him with an account of the infidelity of his servant, who, he said, would not believe the scriptures, because he could not read them in the original tongues, and be sure that they were not invented; "Why, foolish fellow, (said Johnson,) has he any better authority for almost everything that he believes?" BOSWELL. "Then the vulgar, Sir, never can know they are right, but must submit themselves to the learned." JOHNSON. "To be sure, Sir. The vulgar are the children of the State, and must be taught like children." BOSWELL. "Then, Sir, a poor Turk must be a Mahometan, just as a poor Englishman must be a Christian?" JOHNSON. "Why, yes, Sir; and what then? This now is such stuff as I used to talk to my mother, when I first began to think myself a clever fellow; and she ought to have whipt me for it."

Another evening Dr. Goldsmith and I called on him,

with the hope of prevailing on him to sup with us at the Mitre. We found him indisposed, and resolved not to go abroad. "Come then, (said Goldsmith,) we will not go to the Mitre tonight, since we cannot have the big man with us." Johnson then called for a bottle of port, of which Goldsmith and I partook, while our friend, now a water-drinker, sat by us. GOLDSMITH. "I think, Mr. Johnson, you don't go near the theatres now. You give yourself no more concern about a new play, than if you had never had any thing to do with the stage." JOHNSON. "Why, Sir, our tastes greatly alter. The lad does not care for the child's rattle, and the old man does not care for the young man's whore." GOLDSMITH. "Nay, Sir; but your Muse was not a whore." JOHNSON. "Sir, I do not think she was. But as we advance in the journey of life we drop some of the things which have pleased us; whether it be that we are fatigued and don't choose to carry so many things any farther, or that we find other things which we like better." BOSWELL. "But, Sir, why don't you give us something in some other way?" GOLDSMITH. "Ay, Sir, we have a claim upon you." JOHNSON. "No, Sir, I am not obliged to do any more. No man is obliged to do as much as he can do. A man is to have part of his life to himself. If a soldier has fought a good many campaigns, he is not to be blamed, if he retires to ease and tranquillity. A physician, who has practised long in a great city, may be excused, if he retires to a small town, and takes less practice. Now, Sir, the good I can do by my conversation bears the same proportion to the good I can do by my writings, that the practice of a physician, retired to a small town, does to his practice in a great city." BOSWELL. "But I wonder, Sir, you have not more pleasure in writing than in not writing." JOHNSON. "Sir, you *may* wonder."

He talked of making verses, and observed. "The great

difficulty is, to know when you have made good ones. When composing, I have generally had them in my mind, perhaps fifty at a time, walking up and down in my room; and then I have written them down, and often, from laziness, have written only half lines. I have written a hundred lines in a day. I remember, I wrote a hundred lines of 'The Vanity of Human Wishes' in a day. Doctor, (turning to Goldsmith,) I am not quite idle; I made one line t'other day; but I made no more." GOLDSMITH. "Let us hear it; we'll put a bad one to it." JOHNSON. "No, Sir; I have forgot it."

1767. In February there happened one of the most remarkable incidents of Johnson's life, which gratified his monarchical enthusiasm, and which he loved to relate with all its circumstances, when requested by his friends. This was his being honoured by a private conversation with his Majesty, in the library at the Queen's house. He had frequently visited those splendid rooms, and noble collection of books, which he used to say was more numerous and curious than he supposed any person could have made in the time which the King had employed. Mr. Barnard, the librarian, took care that he should have every accommodation that should contribute to his ease and convenience, while indulging his literary taste in that place: so that he had here a very agreeable resource at leisure hours.

His Majesty having been informed of his occasional visits, was pleased to signify a desire that he should be told when Dr. Johnson came next to the library. Accordingly, the next time that Johnson did come, as soon as he was fairly engaged with a book, on which, while he sat by the fire, he seemed quite intent, Mr. Barnard stole round to the apartment where the King was, and, in obedience to his Majesty's commands, mentioned that Dr. Johnson was then in the library. His Majesty said he was at leisure, and would go to him: upon which Mr. Barnard took one of the candles that stood on the King's table, and lighted his Majesty through a suite of rooms, till they came to a private door into the library, of which his Majesty had the key. Being entered, Mr. Barnard stepped forward hastily to Dr. Johnson, who was still in a profound study, and whispered him, "Sir, here is the King." Johnson started up, and stood still. His Majesty approached him, and at once was courteously easy.

His Majesty began by observing, that he understood he came sometimes to the library; and then mentioned his having heard that the Doctor had been lately at Oxford, asked him if he was not fond of going thither. To which Johnson answered, that he was indeed fond of going to Oxford sometimes, but was likewise glad to come back again. The King then asked him what they were doing at Oxford. Johnson answered, he could not much commend their diligence, but that in some respects they were mended, for they had put their press under better regulations, and were at that time printing Polybius. He was then asked whether there were better libraries at Oxford or Cambridge. He answered, he believed the Bodleian was larger than any they had at Cambridge; at the same time adding, "I hope, whether we have more books or not than they have at Cambridge, we shall make as good use of them as they do." Being asked whether All-Souls or Christ-Church library was the largest, he answered, "All-Souls library is the largest we have, except the Bodleian." "Ay, (said the King,) that is the publick library."

His Majesty enquired if he was then writing any thing. He answered, he was not, for he had pretty well told the world what he knew, and must now read to acquire more knowledge. The King, as it should seem with a view to urge him to rely on his own stores as an original writer, and to continue his labours, then said, "I do not think you borrow much from any body." Johnson said, he thought he had already done his part as a writer. "I should have thought so too, (said the King,) if you had not written so well."—Johnson observed to me, upon this, that "No man could have paid a handsomer compliment; and it was fit for a King to pay. It was decisive." When asked by another friend, at Sir Joshua Reynolds's, whether he made any reply to this high compliment, he answered, "No, Sir. When the King had said it, it was to be so. It was not for me to bandy civilities with my Sovereign." Perhaps no man who had spent his whole life in courts could have shewn a more nice and dignified sense of true politeness than Johnson did in this instance.

His Majesty having observed to him that he supposed he must have read a great deal; Johnson answered, that he thought more than he read; that he had read a great deal in the early part of his life, but having fallen into ill health, he had not been able to read much, compared with others: for instance, he said he had not read much, compared with Dr. Warburton. Upon which the King said, that he heard Dr. Warburton was a man of such general knowledge, that you could scarce talk with him on any subject on which he was not qualified to speak; and that his learning resembled Garrick's acting, in its universality. His Majesty then talked of the controversy between Warburton and Lowth, which he seemed to have read, and asked Johnson what he thought of it. Johnson answered, "Warburton has most general, most scholastic learning; Lowth is the more correct scholar. I do not know which of them calls names best." The

King was pleased to say he was of the same opinion; adding, "You do not think, then, Dr. Johnson, that there was much argument in the case." Johnson said, he did not think there was. "Why truly, (said the King,) when once it comes to calling names, argument is pretty well at an end."

His Majesty then asked him what he thought of Lord Lyttelton's history, which was then just published. Johnson said, he thought his style pretty good, but that he had blamed Henry the Second rather too much. "Why, (said the King), they seldom do these things by halves." "No, Sir, (answered Johnson), not to Kings." But fearing to be misunderstood, he proceeded to explain himself; and immediately subjoined, "That for those who spoke worse of Kings than they deserved, he could find no excuse; but that he could more easily conceive how some might speak better of them than they deserved, without any ill intention; for, as Kings had much in their power to give, those who were favoured by them would frequently, from gratitude, exaggerate their praises: and as this proceeded from a good motive, it was certainly excusable, as far as errour could be excusable."

The King then asked him what he thought of Dr. Hill. Johnson answered, that he was an ingenious man, but had no veracity; and immediately mentioned, as an instance of it, an assertion of that writer, that he had seen objects magnified to a much greater degree by using three or four microscopes at a time than by using one. "Now, (added Johnson,) every one acquainted with microscopes knows, that the more of them he looks through, the less the object will appear." "Why, (replied the King,) this is not only telling an untruth, but telling it clumsily; for, if that be the case, every one who can look through a microscope will be able to detect him."

"I now, (said Johnson to his friends, when relating

what had passed,) began to consider that I was deprecating this man in the estimation of his Sovereign, and thought it was time for me to say something that might be more favourable." He added, therefore, that Dr. Hill was, notwithstanding, a very curious observer; and if he would have been contented to tell the world no more than he knew, he might have been a very considerable man, and needed not to have recourse to such mean expedients to raise his reputation.

The King then talked of literary journals, mentioned particularly the *Journal des Savans,* and asked Johnson if it was well done. Johnson said, it was formerly very well done, and gave some account of the persons who began it, and carried it on for some years: enlarging at the same time, on the nature and use of such works. The King asked him if it was well done now. Johnson answered, he had no reason to think that it was. The King then asked him if there were any other literary journals published in this kingdom, except the Monthly and Critical Reviews; and on being answered there was no other, his Majesty asked which of them was the best: Johnson answered, that the Monthly Review was done with most care, the Critical upon the best principles; adding that the authours of the Monthly Review were enemies to the Church. This the King said he was sorry to hear.

The conversation next turned on the Philosophical Transactions, when Johnson observed that they had now a better method of arranging their materials than formerly. "Ay, (said the King), they are obliged to Dr. Johnson for that;" for his Majesty had heard and remembered the circumstance, which Johnson himself had forgot.

His Majesty expressed a desire to have the literary biography of this country ably executed, and proposed to Dr. Johnson to undertake it. Johnson signified his readiness to comply with his Majesty's wishes.

During the whole of this interview, Johnson talked to his Majesty with profound respect, but still in his firm manly manner, with a sonorous voice, and never in that subdued tone which is commonly used at the levee and in the drawing room. After the King withdrew, Johnson shewed himself highly pleased with his Majesty's conversation, and gracious behaviour. He said to Mr. Barnard, "Sir, they may talk of the King as they will; but he is the finest gentleman I have ever seen." And he afterwards observed to Mr. Langton, "Sir, his manners are those of as fine a gentleman as we may suppose Lewis the Fourteenth or Charles the Second."

At Sir Joshua Reynolds's, where a circle of Johnson's friends was collected round him to hear his account of this memorable conversation, Dr. Joseph Warton, in his frank and lively manner, was very active in pressing him to mention the particulars. "Come now, Sir, this is an interesting matter; do favour us with it." Johnson, with great good humour, complied.

He told them, "I found his Majesty wished I should talk and I made it my business to talk. I find it does a man good to be talked to by his sovereign. In the first place, a man cannot be in a passion—." Here some question interrupted him, which is to be regretted, as he certainly would have pointed out and illustrated many circumstances of advantage, from being in a situation, where the powers of the mind are at once excited to vigorous exertion, and tempered by reverential awe.

During all the time in which Dr. Johnson was employed in relating to the circle at Sir Joshua Reynolds's the particulars of what passed between the King and him, Dr. Goldsmith remained unmoved upon a sopha at some distance, affecting not to join in the least in the eager curiosity of the company. He assigned as a reason for his gloom and seeming inattention, that he apprehended Johnson had relinquished his purpose of furnishing him with a Prologue to his play, with the hopes of which he had been flattered; but it was strongly suspected that he was fretting with chagrin and envy at the singular honour Dr. Johnson had lately enjoyed. At length, the frankness, and simplicity of his natural character prevailed. He sprung from the sopha, advanced to Johnson, and in a kind of flutter, from imagining himself in the situation which he had just been hearing described, exclaimed, "Well, you acquitted yourself in this conversation better than I should have done; for I should have bowed and stammered through the whole of it."

I received no letter from Johnson this year; nor have I discovered any of the correspondence he had, except the two letters to Mr. Drummond, which have been inserted, for the sake of connection, with that to the same gentleman in 1766. His diary affords no light as to his employment at this time. He passed three months at Lichfield: and I cannot omit an affecting and solemn scene there, as related by himself:

"Sunday, Oct. 18, 1767. Yesterday, Oct. 17, at about ten in the morning, I took my leave forever of my dear old friend, Catharine Chambers, who came to live with my mother about 1724, and has been but little parted from us since. She buried my father, my brother, and my mother. She is now fifty-eight years old.

"I desired all to withdraw, then told her that we were to part forever; that as Christians, we should part with prayer; and that I would, if she was willing, say a short prayer beside her. She expressed great desire to hear me; and held up her poor hands as she lay in bed, with great fervour, while I prayed, kneeling by her, nearly in the following words:

"Almighty and most merciful Father, whose loving kindness is over all thy works, behold, visit, and relieve this thy servant, who is grieved with sickness. Grant that the sense of her weakness may add strength to her faith, and seriousness to her repentance. And grant that by the help of thy Holy Spirit, after the pains and labours of this short life, we may all obtain everlasting happiness, through JESUS CHRIST our Lord, for whose sake hear our prayers. Amen. Our Father, &c.

"I then kissed her. She told me, that to part was the greatest pain that she had ever felt, and that she hoped we should meet again in a better place. I expressed, with swelled eyes, and great emotion of tenderness, the same hopes. We kissed and parted. I humbly hope to meet again, and to part no more."

1768. He said he had lately been a long while at Lichfield, but had grown very weary before he left it. BOSWELL. "I wonder at that, Sir; it is your native place." JOHNSON. "Why so is Scotland *your* native place."

His prejudice against Scotland appeared remarkably strong at this time. When I talked of our advancement in literature, "Sir, (said he,) you have learnt a little from us, and you think yourselves very great men. Hume would never have written History, had not Voltaire written it before him. He is an echo of Voltaire." BOSWELL. "But, Sir, we have Lord Kames." JOHNSON. "You *have* Lord Kames. Keep him; ha, ha, ha! We don't envy you him. Do you ever see Dr. Robertson?" BOSWELL. "Yes, Sir." JOHNSON. "Does the dog talk of me?"

BOSWELL. "Indeed, Sir, he does, and loves you." Thinking that I now had him in a corner, and being solicitous for the literary fame of my country, I pressed him for his opinion on the merit of Dr. Robertson's History of Scotland. But, to my surprize, he escaped.—"Sir, I love Robertson, and I won't talk of his book."

An essay, written by Mr. Deane, a Divine of the Church of England, maintaining the future life of brutes, by an explication of certain parts of the scriptures, was mentioned, and the doctrine insisted on by a gentleman who seemed fond of curious speculation. Johnson, who did not like to hear of any thing concerning a future state which was not authorized by the regular canons of orthodoxy, discouraged this talk; and being offended at its continuation, he watched an opportunity to give the gentleman a blow of reprehension. So, when the poor speculatist, with a serious metaphysical pensive face, addressed him, "But really, Sir, when we see a very sensible dog, we don't know what to think of him," Johnson, rolling with joy at the thought which beamed in his eye, turned quickly round, and replied, "True, Sir: and when we see a very foolish *fellow,* we don't know what to think of *him.*" He then rose up, strided to the fire, and stood for some time laughing and exulting.

He talked of the heinousness of the crime of adultery, by which the peace of families was destroyed. He said, "Confusion of progeny constitutes the essence of the crime; and therefore a woman who breaks her marriage vows is much more criminal than a man who does it. A man, to be sure, is criminal in the sight of GOD; but he does not do his wife a very material injury, if he does not insult her; if, for instance, from mere wantonness of appetite, he steals privately to her chambermaid. Sir, a wife ought not greatly to resent this. I would not receive home a daughter who had run away from her

husband on that account. A wife should study to re-
claim her husband by more attention to please him. Sir,
a man will not, once in a hundred instances, leave his
wife and go to a harlot, if his wife has not been negligent of pleasing."

Soon afterwards, he supped at the Crown and Anchor
tavern, in the Strand, with a company whom I collected to meet him. They were Dr. Percy, now Bishop of
Dromore, Dr. Douglas, now Bishop of Salisbury, Mr.
Langton, Dr. Robertson the Historian, Dr. Hugh Blair,
and Mr. Thomas Davies, who wished much to be introduced to these eminent Scotch literati; but on the
present occasion, he had very little opportunity of hearing them talk, for with an excess of prudence, for which
Johnson afterwards found fault with them, they hardly
opened their lips, and that only to say something which
they were certain would not expose them to the sword
of Goliath; such was their anxiety for their fame when
in the presence of Johnson.

He was vehement against old Dr. Mounsey, of Chel-
sea College, as "a fellow who swore and talked bawdy."
"I have often been in his company, (said Dr. Percy,)
and never heard him swear or talk bawdy." Mr. Davies
who sat next to Dr. Percy, having after this had some
conversation aside with him, made a discovery which,
in his zeal to pay court to Dr. Johnson, he eagerly proclaimed aloud from the foot of the table: "O, Sir, I have
found out a very good reason why Dr. Percy never
heard Mounsey swear or talk bawdy, for he tells me he
never saw him but at the Duke of Northumberland's
table." "And so, Sir, (said Dr. Johnson loudly to Dr.
Percy) you would shield this man from the charge of
swearing and talking bawdy, because he did not do so
at the Duke of Northumberland's table. Sir, you might
as well tell us that you had seen him hold up his hand

at the Old Bailey, and he neither swore nor talked bawdy; or that you had seen him in the cart at Tyburn, and he neither swore nor talked bawdy. And is it thus, Sir, that you presume to controvert what I have related?" Dr. Johnson's animadversion was uttered in such a manner, that Dr. Percy seemed to be displeased, and soon afterwards left the company, of which Johnson did not at that time take any notice.

Swift having been mentioned, Johnson, as usual, treated him with little respect as an authour. Some of us endeavoured to support the Dean of St. Patrick's, by various arguments. One in particular praised his "Conduct of the Allies." JOHNSON. "Sir, his 'Conduct of the Allies' is a performance of very little ability." "Surely, Sir, (said Dr. Douglas,) you must allow it has strong facts." JOHNSON. "Why yes, Sir; but what is that to the merit of the composition? In the Sessions-paper of the Old Bailey there are strong facts. House-breaking is a strong fact; robbery is a strong fact; and murder is a *mighty strong fact*; but is great praise due to the historian of those strong facts? No, Sir, Swift has told what he had to tell distinctly enough, but that is all. He had to count ten, and he has counted it right."—Then recollecting that Mr. Davies, by acting as an *informer*, had been the occasion of his talking somewhat too harshly to his friend Dr. Percy, for which, probably, when the first ebullition was over, he felt some compunction, he took an opportunity to give him a hit: so added, with a preparatory laugh, "Why, Sir, Tom Davies might have written 'the Conduct of the Allies.'" Poor Tom being thus suddenly dragged into ludicrous notice in presence of the Scottish Doctors, to whom he was ambitious of appearing to advantage, was grievously mortified. Nor did his punishment rest here; for upon subsequent occasions, whenever he, "statesman all o'er," assumed a strutting importance, I used to hail him—*"the Authour of the Conduct of the Allies."*

When I called upon Dr. Johnson next morning, I found him highly satisfied with his colloquial prowess the preceding evening. "Well, (said he,) we had good talk." BOSWELL. "Yes, Sir, you tossed and gored several persons."

The late Alexander Earl of Eglintoune, who loved wit more than wine, and men of genius more than syco-phants, had a great admiration of Johnson; but from the remarkable elegance of his own manners, was, perhaps, too delicately sensible of the roughness which some-times appeared in Johnson's behaviour. One evening about this time, when his Lordship did me the honour to sup at my lodgings with Dr. Robertson and several other men of literary distinction, he regretted that John-son had not been educated with more refinement, and lived more in polished society. "No, no, my Lord, (said Signor Baretti,) do with him what you would, he would always have been a bear." "True, (answered the Earl, with a smile,) but he would have been a *dancing* bear."

To obviate all the reflections which have gone round the world to Johnson's prejudice, by applying to him the epithet of a *bear,* let me impress upon my readers a just and happy saying of my friend Goldsmith, who knew him well: "Johnson, to be sure, has a roughness in his manner: but no man alive has a more tender heart. *He has nothing of the bear but his skin."*

1769. On the 30th of September we dined together at the Mitre. I attempted to argue for the superiour happiness of the savage life, upon the usual fanciful topicks. JOHNSON. "Sir, there can be nothing more false. The savages have no bodily advantages beyond those

of civilised men. They have not better health; and as to
care or mental uneasiness, they are not above it, but
below it, like bears. No, Sir; you are not to talk such
paradox: let me have no more on't. It cannot entertain,
far less can it instruct. Lord Monboddo, one of your
Scotch Judges, talked a great deal of such nonsense. I
suffered *him;* but I will not suffer *you.*" BOSWELL. "But,
Sir, does not Rousseau talk such nonsense?" JOHNSON.
"True, Sir, but Rousseau *knows* he is talking nonsense,
and laughs at the world for staring at him." BOSWELL.
"How so, Sir?" JOHNSON. "Why, Sir, a man who talks
nonsense so well, must know that he is talking nonsense.
But I am *afraid,* (chuckling and laughing,) Monboddo
does *not* know that he is talking nonsense." BOSWELL.
"Is it wrong then, Sir, to affect singularity, in order to
make people stare?" JOHNSON. "Yes, if you do it by
propagating errour; and, indeed, it is wrong in any way.
There is in human nature a general inclination to make
people stare; and every wise man has himself to cure
of it, and does cure himself. If you wish to make people
stare by doing better than others, why make them stare
till they stare their eyes out. But consider how easy it
is to make people stare, by being absurd. I may do it
by going into a drawing-room without my shoes. You
remember the gentleman in 'The Spectator,' who had a
commission of lunacy taken out against him for his extreme singularity, such as never wearing a wig, but a
night-cap. Now, Sir, abstractedly, the night-cap was
best: but, relatively, the advantage was overbalanced
by his making the boys run after him."

Talking of a London life, he said, "The happiness of
London is not to be conceived but by those who have
been in it. I will venture to say, there is more learning
and science within the circumference of ten miles from
where we now sit, than in all the rest of the kingdom.'

BOSWELL. "The only disadvantage is the great distance at which people live from one another." JOHNSON. "Yes, Sir; but that is occasioned by the largeness of it, which is the cause of all the other advantages." BOSWELL. "Sometimes I have been in the humour of wishing to retire to a desert." JOHNSON. "Sir, you have desart enough in Scotland."

We drank tea with Mrs. Williams. I had last year the pleasure of seeing Mrs. Thrale at Dr. Johnson's one morning, and had conversation enough with her to admire her talents; and to shew her that I was as Johnsonian as herself. Dr. Johnson had probably been kind enough to speak well of me, for this evening he delivered me a very polite card from Mr. Thrale and her, inviting me to Streatham.

On the 6th of October I complied with this obliging invitation, and found, at an elegant villa, six miles from town, every circumstance that can make society pleasing. Johnson, though quite at home, was yet looked up to with an awe, tempered by affection, and seemed to be equally the care of his host and hostess. I rejoiced at seeing him so happy.

He played off his wit against Scotland with a good humoured pleasantry, which gave me, though no bigot to national prejudices, an opportunity for a little contest with him. I having said that England was obliged to us for gardeners, almost all their good gardeners being Scotchmen;—JOHNSON. "Why, Sir, that is because gardening is much more necessary amongst you than with us, which makes so many of your people learn it. It is *all* gardening with you. Things which grow wild here, must be cultivated with great care in Scotland. Pray now (throwing himself back in his chair, and laughing,) are you ever able to bring the *sloe* to perfection?"

I boasted that we had the honour of being the first to

abolish the unhospitable, troublesome, and ungracious custom of giving vails to servants. JOHNSON. "Sir, you abolished vails, because you were too poor to be able to give them."

Mrs. Thrale then praised Garrick's talents for light gay poetry; and, as a specimen, repeated his song in "Florizel and Perdita," and dwelt with peculiar pleasure on this line:

I'd smile with the simple, and feed with the poor.

JOHNSON. "Nay, my dear Lady, this will never do. Poor David! Smile with the simple;—What folly is that? And who would feed with the poor that can help it? No, no; let me smile with the wise, and feed with the rich."

He would not allow much merit to Whitfield's oratory. "His popularity, Sir, (said he,) is chiefly owing to the peculiarity of his manner. He would be followed by crowds were he to wear a night-cap in the pulpit, or were he to preach from a tree."

On the evening of October 10, I presented Dr. Johnson to General Paoli. I had greatly wished that two men, for whom I had the highest esteem, should meet. They met with a manly ease, mutually conscious of their own abilities, and of the abilities of each other. The General spoke Italian, and Dr. Johnson English, and understood one another very well, with a little aid of interpretation from me, in which I compared myself to an isthmus which joins two great continents. Upon Johnson's approach, the General said, "From what I have read of your works, Sir, and from what Mr. Boswell has told me of you, I have long held you in great veneration." The General talked of languages being formed on the particular notions and manners of a people, without knowing which, we cannot know the language. We may know the direct signification of single words; but by these no

beauty of expression, no sally of genius, no wit is conveyed to the mind. All this must be by allusion to other
ideas. "Sir, (said Johnson,) you talk of language, as if
you had never done any thing else but study it, instead
of governing a nation." The General said, "*Questo e un
troppo gran complimento;*" this is too great a compliment. Johnson answered, "I should have thought so, Sir,
if I had not heard you talk." The General asked him
what he thought of the spirit of infidelity which was so
prevalent. JOHNSON. "Sir, this gloom of infidelity, I hope,
is only a transient cloud passing through the hemisphere, which will soon be dissipated and the sun will
break forth with his usual splendour." "You think then,
(said the General,) that they will change their principles like their clothes." JOHNSON. "Why, Sir, if they
bestow no more thought on principles than on dress, it
must be so." The General said, that "a great part of the
fashionable infidelity was owing to a desire of showing
courage. Men who have no opportunities of shewing it as
to things in this life, take death and futurity as objects
on which to display it." JOHNSON. "That is mighty foolish affectation. Fear is one of the passions of human
nature, of which it is impossible to divest it. You remember that the Emperour Charles V. when he read upon
the tomb-stone of a Spanish nobleman, 'Here lies one
who never knew fear,' wittily said, 'Then he never
snuffed a candle with his fingers.' "

He honoured me with his company at dinner on the
16th of October, at my lodgings in Old Bond-street,
with Sir Joshua Reynolds, Mr. Garrick, Dr. Goldsmith,
Mr. Murphy, Mr. Bickerstaff, and Mr. Thomas Davies.
Garrick played round him with a fond vivacity, taking
hold of the breasts of his coat, and, looking up in his
face with a lively archness, complimented him on the
good health which he seemed then to enjoy; while the

sage, shaking his head, beheld him with a gentle complacency. One of the company not being come at the appointed hour, I proposed, as usual upon such occasions, to order dinner to be served; adding, "Ought six people to be kept waiting for one?" "Why, yes, (answered Johnson, with a delicate humanity,) if the one will suffer more by your sitting down, than the six will do by waiting." Goldsmith, to divert the tedious minutes, strutted about, bragging of his dress, and I believe was seriously vain of it, for his mind was wonderfully prone to such impressions. "Come, come, (said Garrick,) talk no more of that. You are perhaps, the worst—eh, eh!"—Goldsmith was eagerly attempting to interrupt him, when Garrick went on, laughing ironically, "Nay, you will always *look* like a gentleman; but I am talking of being well or *ill drest*." "Well, let me tell you, (said Goldsmith,) when my taylor brought home my bloom-coloured coat, he said, 'Sir, I have a favour to beg of you. When any body asks you who made your clothes, be pleased to mention John Filby, at the Harrow, in Water-lane.' " JOHNSON. "Why, Sir, that was because he knew the strange colour would attract crowds to gaze at it, and thus they might hear of him, and see how well he could make a coat even of so absurd a colour."

After dinner our conversation first turned upon Pope. Johnson said, his characters of men were admirably drawn, those of women not so well. He repeated to us, in his forcible melodious manner, the concluding lines of the Dunciad. While he was talking loudly in praise of those lines one of the company ventured to say, "Too fine for such a poem:—a poem on what?" JOHNSON, (with a disdainful look,) "Why, on *dunces*. It was worth while being a dunce then. Ah, Sir, hadst *thou* lived in those days! It is not worth while being a dunce now, when there are no wits." Johnson said, that the description of the temple, in "The Mourning Bride," was the finest poetical passage he had ever read; he recollected none in Shakespeare equal to it.—"But, (said Garrick, all alarmed for 'the God of his idolatry,') we know not the extent and variety of his powers. We are to suppose there are such passages in his works. Shakespeare must not suffer from the badness of our memories." Johnson, diverted by this enthusiastick jealousy, went on with great ardour. "No, Sir; Congreve has *nature;*" (smiling on the tragick eagerness of Garrick;) but composing himself, he added, "Sir, this is not comparing Congreve on the whole with Shakespeare on the whole; but only maintaining that Congreve has one finer passage than any that can be found in Shakespeare. Sir, a man may have no more than ten guineas in the world, but he may have those ten guineas in one piece; and so may have a finer piece than a man who has ten thousand pounds: but then he has only one ten-guinea piece.—What I mean is, that you can shew me no passage where there is simply a description of material objects, without any intermixture of moral notions, which produces such an effect." Mr. Murphy mentioned Shakespeare's description of the night before the battle of Agincourt; but it was observed it had *men* in it. Mr. Davies suggested the speech of Juliet, in which she figures herself awakening in the tomb of her ancestors. Some one mentioned the description of Dover Cliff. JOHNSON. "No, Sir; it should be all precipice,—all vacuum. The crows impede your fall. The diminished appearance of the boats, and other circumstances, are all very good description; but do not impress the mind at once with the horrible idea of immense height. The impression is divided; you pass on by computation, from one stage of the tremendous space to another.

Mrs. Montague, a lady distinguished for having written an Essay on Shakespeare, being mentioned;—REYN-OLDS. "I think that essay does her honour." JOHNSON. "Yes, Sir, it does *her* honour, but it would do nobody else honour. I have, indeed, not read it all. But when I take up the end of a web, and find it packthread, I do not expect, by looking further, to find embroidery."

On Thursday, October 19, I passed the evening with him at his house.

I complained that he had not mentioned Garrick in his Preface to Shakespeare; and asked him if he did not admire him. JOHNSON. "Yes, as 'a poor player, who frets and struts his hour upon the stage;'—as a shadow." BOSWELL. "But has he not brought Shakespeare into notice?" JOHNSON. "Sir, to allow that, would be to lampoon the age."

I mentioned to him that I had seen the execution of several convicts at Tyburn, two days before, and that none of them seemed to be under any concern. JOHNSON. "Most of them, Sir, have never thought at all." BOSWELL. "But is not the fear of death natural to man?" JOHNSON. "So much so, Sir, that the whole of life is but keeping away the thoughts of it." He then, in a low and earnest tone, talked of his meditating upon the awful hour of his own dissolution, and in what manner he should conduct himself upon that occasion: "I know not (said he,) whether I should wish to have a friend by me, or have it all between GOD and myself."

Talking of our feeling for the distress of others;—JOHNSON. "Why, Sir, there is much noise made about it, but it is greatly exaggerated. No, Sir, we have a certain degree of feeling to prompt us to do good; more than that, Providence does not intend. It would be misery to no purpose." BOSWELL. "But suppose now, Sir, that one of your intimate friends were apprehended for an offence for which he might be hanged." JOHNSON.

"I should do what I could to bail him, and give him any other assistance; but if he were once fairly hanged, I should not suffer." BOSWELL. "Would you eat your dinner that day, Sir?" JOHNSON. "Yes, Sir; and eat it as if he were eating it with me. Why, there's Baretti, who is to be tried for his life tomorrow, friends have risen up for him on every side; yet if he should be hanged, none of them will eat a slice of plum-pudding the less. Sir, that sympathetick feeling goes a very little way in depressing the mind."

I told him that I had dined lately at Foote's, who shewed me a letter which he had received from Tom Davies, telling him that he had not been able to sleep from the concern he felt on account of *"This sad affair of Baretti,"* begging of him to try if he could suggest any thing that might be of service; and, at the same time, recommending to him an industrious young man who kept a pickle-shop. JOHNSON. "Ay, Sir, here you have a specimen of human sympathy; a friend hanged, and a cucumber pickled. We know not whether Baretti or the pickle-man has kept Davies from sleep: nor does he know himself. And as to his not sleeping, Sir; Tom Davies is a very great man; Tom has been upon the stage and knows how to do those things: I have not been upon the stage, and cannot do those things." BOSWELL. "I have often blamed myself, Sir, for not feeling for others, as sensibly as many say they do." JOHNSON. "Sir, don't be duped by them any more. You will find these very feeling people are not very ready to do you good. They *pay* you by *feeling*."

BOSWELL. "Foote has a great deal of humour." JOHNSON. "Yes, Sir." BOSWELL. "He has a singular talent of exhibiting character." JOHNSON. "Sir, it is not a talent; it is a vice; it is what others abstain from. It is not comedy, which exhibits the character of a species, as that of a miser gathered from many misers: it is a farce which exhibits individuals." BOSWELL. "Did not he think of exhibiting you, Sir?" JOHNSON. "Sir, fear restrained him; he knew I would have broken his bones. I would have saved him the trouble of cutting off a leg; I would not have left him a leg to cut off." BOSWELL. "Pray, Sir, is not Foote an infidel?" JOHNSON. "I do not know, Sir, that the fellow is an infidel; but if he be an infidel, he is an infidel as a dog is an infidel; that is to say, he has never thought upon the subject." BOSWELL. "I suppose, Sir, he has thought superficially, and seized the first notions which occurred to his mind." JOHNSON. "Why, then, Sir, still he is like a dog, that snatches the piece next him. Did you never observe that dogs have not the power of comparing? A dog will take a small bit of meat as readily as a large, when both are before him."

He again talked of the passage in Congreve with high commendation, and said, "Shakespeare never has six lines together without a fault. Perhaps you may find seven; but this does not refute my general assertion. If I come to an orchard, and say there's no fruit here, and then comes a poring man, who finds two apples and three pears, and tells me, 'Sir, you are mistaken, I have found both apples and pears,' I should laugh at him: what would that be to the purpose?"

We went home to his house to tea. Mrs. Williams made it with sufficient dexterity, notwithstanding her blindness, though her manner of satisfying herself that the cups were full enough, appeared to me a little aukward; for I fancied she put her finger down a certain way, till she felt the tea touch it.[1] In my first elation at

---

[1] I have since had reason to think that I was mistaken; for I have been informed by a lady, who was long intimate with her, and likely to be a more accurate observer of such matters, that she had acquired such a niceness of touch, as to know, by the feeling on the outside of the cup, how near it was to being full.

being allowed the privilege of attending Dr. Johnson at his late visits to this lady, which was like being *è secretioribus consiliis,* I willingly drank cup after cup, as if it had been the Heliconian spring. But as the charm of novelty went off, I grew more fastidious; and besides, I discovered that she was of a peevish temper.

There was a pretty large circle this evening. Dr. Johnson was in very good humour, lively, and ready to talk upon all subjects. Mr. Fergusson, the self-taught philosopher, told him of a new invented machine which went without horses: a man who sat in it turned a handle, which worked a spring that drove it forward. "Then, Sir, (said Johnson,) what is gained is, the man has his choice whether he will move himself alone, or himself and the machine too." Dominicetti, being mentioned, he would not allow him any merit. "There is nothing in all this boasted system. No, Sir; medicated baths can be no better than warm water: their only effect can be that of tepid moisture." One of the company took the other side, maintaining that medicines of various sorts, and some too of most powerful effect, are introduced into the human frame by the medium of the pores; and, therefore, when warm water is impregnated with salutiferous substances, it may produce great effects as a bath. This appeared to me very satisfactory. Johnson did not answer it; but talking for victory, and determined to be master of the field, he had recourse to the device which Goldsmith imputed to him in the witty words of one of Cibber's comedies: "There is no arguing with Johnson; for when his pistol misses fire, he knocks you down with the butt end of it." He turned to the gentleman, "Well, Sir, go to Dominicetti, and get thyself fumigated; but be sure that the steam be directed to thy *head,* for *that* is the *peccant part.*" This produced a triumphant roar of laughter from the motley assembly of philosophers, printers, and dependents, male and female.

I know not how so whimsical a thought came into my mind, but I asked, "If, Sir, you were shut up in a castle, and a new-born child with you, what would you do?" JOHNSON. "Why, Sir, I should not much like my company." BOSWELL. "But would you take the trouble of rearing it?" He seemed, as may well be supposed, unwilling to pursue the subject: but upon my persevering in my question, replied, "Why yes, Sir, I would; but I must have all conveniences. If I had no garden, I would make a shed on the roof, and take it there for fresh air. I should feed it, and wash it much, and with warm water to please it, not with cold water to give it pain." BOSWELL. "But, Sir, does not heat relax?" JOHNSON. "Sir, you are not to imagine the water is to be very hot. I would not *coddle* the child. No, Sir, the hardy method of treating children does no good. I'll take you five children from London, who shall cuff five Highland children. Sir, a man bred in London will carry a burthen, or run, or wrestle, as well as a man brought up in the hardest manner in the country." BOSWELL. "Good living, I suppose, makes the Londoners strong." JOHNSON. "Why, Sir, I don't know that it does. Our chairmen from Ireland, who are as strong men as any, have been brought up upon potatoes. Quantity makes up for quality." BOSWELL. "Would you teach this child that I have furnished you with, anything?" JOHNSON. "No, I should not be apt to teach it." BOSWELL. "Would not you have a pleasure in teaching it?" JOHNSON. "No, Sir, I should *not* have a pleasure in teaching it." BOSWELL. "Have you not a pleasure in teaching men!—*There* I have you. You have the same pleasure in teaching men, that I should have in teaching children." JOHNSON. "Why, something about that."

When we were alone, I introduced the subject of death, and endeavoured to maintain that the fear of it might be got over. I told him that David Hume said to me, he was no more uneasy to think he should *not be* after his life, than that he *had not been* before he began to exist. JOHNSON. "Sir, if he really thinks so, his perceptions are disturbed; he is mad; if he does not think so, he lies. He may tell you, he holds his finger in the flame of a candle, without feeling pain; would you believe him? When he dies, he at least gives up all he has." BOSWELL. "Foote, Sir, told me, that when he was very ill he was not afraid to die." JOHNSON. "It is not true, Sir. Hold a pistol to Foote's breast, or to Hume's breast, and threaten to kill them, and you'll see how they behave." BOSWELL. "But may we not fortify our minds for the approach of death?"—Here I am sensible I was in the wrong, to bring before his view what he ever looked upon with horrour; for although when in a celestial frame of mind in his "Vanity of Human Wishes," he has supposed death to be "kind Nature's signal for retreat," from this state of being to "a happier seat," his thoughts upon this awful change were in general full of dismal apprehensions. His mind resembled the vast amphitheatre, the Colisæum at Rome. In the centre stood his judgement, which like a mighty gladiator, combated those apprehensions that, like the wild beasts of the *Arena,* were all around in cells, ready to be let out upon him. After a conflict, he drives them back into their dens; but not killing them, they were still assailing him. To my question, whether we might not fortify our minds for the approach of death, he answered, in a passion, "No, Sir, let it alone. It matters not how a man dies, but how he lives. The act of dying is not of importance, it lasts so short a time." He added, (with an earnest look,) "A man knows it must be so, and submits. It will do him no good to whine."

I attempted to continue the conversation. He was so provoked, that he said: "Give us no more of this;" and was thrown into such a state of agitation, that he expressed himself in a way that alarmed and distressed me; shewed an impatience that I should leave him, and when I was going away, called to me sternly, "Don't let us meet tomorrow."

1772. On Saturday, March 27, I introduced to him Sir Alexander Macdonald, with whom he had expressed a wish to be acquainted. He received him very courteously.

Sir Alexander observed, that the Chancellors in England are chosen from views much inferiour to the office, being chosen from temporary political views. JOHNSON. "Why, Sir, in such a government as ours no man is appointed to an office because he is the fittest for it, nor hardly in any other government; because there are so many connections and dependencies to be studied. A despotick prince may choose a man to an office, merely because he is the fittest for it. The King of Prussia may do it." SIR A. "I think, Sir, almost all great lawyers, such at least as have written upon law, have known only law, and nothing else." JOHNSON. "Why no, Sir; Judge Hale was a great lawyer, and wrote upon law; and yet he knew a great many other things, and has written upon other things. Selden, too." SIR A. "Very true, Sir; and Lord Bacon. But was not Lord Coke a mere lawyer?" JOHNSON. "Why, I am afraid he was; but he would have taken it very ill if you had told him so. He would have prosecuted you for scandal." BOSWELL. "Lord Mansfield is not a mere lawyer." JOHNSON. "No, Sir, I never was in Lord Mansfield's company; but Lord Mansfield was distinguished at the University. Lord Mansfield, when he first came to town, 'drank champagne with the wits,' as Prior says. He was the friend of Pope." SIR A. "I have been correcting several Scotch accents in my friend Boswell. I doubt, Sir, if any Scotchman ever attains to a perfect English pronunciation." JOHNSON. "Why, Sir, few of them do, because they do not persevere after acquiring a certain degree of it. But, Sir, there can be no doubt that they may attain to a perfect English pronunciation, if they will. We find how near they come to it; and certainly, a man who conquers nineteen parts of the Scottish accent, may conquer the twentieth. But, Sir, when a man has got the better of nine tenths he grows weary, he relaxes his diligence, he finds he has corrected his accent so far as not to be disagreeable, and he no longer desires his friends to tell him when he is wrong; nor does he choose to be told. Sir, when people watch me narrowly, and I do not watch myself, they will find me out to be of a particular county. In the same manner, Dunning may be found out to be a Devonshire man. So most Scotchmen may be found out. But, Sir, little aberrations are of no disadvantage. I never catched Mallet in a Scotch accent; and yet Mallet, I suppose, was past five-and-twenty before he came to London."

BOSWELL. "It may be of use, Sir, to have a Dictionary to ascertain the pronunciation." JOHNSON. "Why, Sir, my Dictionary shows you the accent of words, if you can but remember them." BOSWELL. "But, Sir, we want marks to ascertain the pronunciation of the vowels. Sheridan, I believe, has finished such a work." JOHNSON. "Why, Sir, consider how much easier it is to learn a language by the ear, than by any marks. Sheridan's Dictionary may do very well; but you cannot always carry it about with you: and, when you want the word, you have not the Dictionary. It is like a man who has a sword that will not draw. It is an admirable sword, to be sure: but while your enemy is cutting your throat, you are unable to use it. Besides, Sir, what entitles Sheridan to fix the pronunciation of English? He has, in the first place, the disadvantage of being an Irishman: and if he says he will fix it after the example of the best company, why they differ among themselves. I remember an instance: when I published the Plan for my Dictionary, Lord Chesterfield told me that the word *great* should be pronounced so as to rhyme to *state;* and Sir William Yonge sent me word that it should be pronounced so as to rhyme to *seat,* and that none but an Irishman would pronounce it *grait.* Now here were two men of the highest rank, the one, the best speaker in the House of Lords, the other, the best speaker in the House of Commons, differing entirely."

On Tuesday, March 31, he and I dined at General Paoli's.

We then walked to the Pantheon. The first view of it did not strike us so much as Ranelagh, of which he said, the *"coup d'œil* was the finest thing he had ever seen." The truth is, Ranelagh is of a more beautiful form; more of it, or rather indeed the whole *rotunda,* appears at once, and it is better lighted. However, as Johnson observed, we saw the Pantheon in time of mourning, when there was a dull uniformity; whereas we had seen Ranelagh, when the view was enlivened with a gay profusion of colours. Mrs. Bosville, of Gunthwait, in Yorkshire, joined us, and entered into conversation with us. Johnson said to me afterwards, "Sir, this is a mighty intelligent lady."

I said there was not half a guinea's worth of pleasure in seeing this place. JOHNSON. "But, Sir, there is half a guinea's worth of inferiority to other people in not having seen it." Boswell. "I doubt, Sir, whether there are many happy people here." Johnson. "Yes, Sir, there are many happy people here. There are many people here who are watching hundreds, and who think hundreds are watching them."

Happening to meet Sir Adam Ferguson, I presented him to Dr. Johnson. Sir Adam expressed some apprehension that the Pantheon would encourage luxury. "Sir, (said Johnson,) I am a great friend to publick amusements; for they keep people from vice. You now (addressing himself to me,) would have been with a wench, had you not been here.—O! I forgot you were married."

Sir Adam suggested, that luxury corrupts a people, and destroys the spirit of liberty. Johnson. "Sir, that is all visionary. I would not give half a guinea to live under one form of government rather than another. It is of no moment to the happiness of an individual. Sir, the danger of the abuse of power is nothing to a private man. What Frenchman is prevented from passing his life as he pleases?" Sir Adam. "But, Sir, in the British constitution it is surely of importance to keep up a spirit in the people, so as to preserve a balance against the crown." Johnson. "Sir, I perceive you are a vile Whig. —Why all this childish jealousy of the power of the crown? The crown has not power enough. When I say that all governments are alike, I consider that in no government power can be abused long. Mankind will not bear it. If a sovereign oppresses his people to a great degree, they will rise and cut off his head. There is a remedy in human nature against tyranny, that will keep us safe under every form of government. Had not the people of France thought themselves honoured in sharing in the brilliant actions of Louis XIV. they would not have endured him; and we may say the same of the King of Prussia's people."

On Sunday, April 5, after attending divine service at St. Paul's church, I found him alone. I mentioned a cause in which I had appeared as counsel at the bar of the General Assembly of the Church of Scotland, where a *Probationer,* (as one licensed to preach, but not yet ordained, is called,) was opposed in his application to be inducted, because it was alleged that he had been guilty of fornication five years before. JOHNSON. "Why, Sir, if he has repented, it is not a sufficient objection. A man who is good enough to go to heaven, is good enough to be a clergyman."

On Monday, April 6, I dined with him at Sir Alexander Macdonald's. Fielding being mentioned, Johnson exclaimed, "he was a blockhead;" and upon my expressing my astonishment at so strange an assertion, he said, "What I mean by his being a blockhead is, that he was a barren rascal." BOSWELL. "Will you not allow, Sir, that he draws very natural pictures of human life?" JOHNSON. "Why, Sir, it is of very low life. Richardson used to say, that had he not known who Fielding was, he should have believed he was an ostler. Sir, there is more knowledge of the heart in one letter of Richardson's, than in all 'Tom Jones.' I, indeed, never read 'Joseph Andrews.' " ERSKINE. "Surely, Sir, Richardson is very tedious." JOHNSON. "Why, Sir, if you were to read Richardson for the story, your impatience would be so much fretted that you would hang yourself. But you must read him for the sentiment, and consider the story as only giving occasion to the sentiment."

On Friday, April 10, I dined with him at General Oglethorpe's, where we found Dr. Goldsmith.

I started the question, whether duelling was consistent

with moral duty. The brave old General fired at this, and said, with a lofty air, "Undoubtedly a man has a right to defend his honour." GOLDSMITH, (turning to me,) "I ask you first, Sir, what would you do if you were affronted?" I answered, I should think it necessary to fight. "Why then, (replied Goldsmith,) that solves the question." JOHNSON. "No, Sir, it does not solve the question. It does not follow, that what a man would do is therefore right." I said, I wished to have it settled, whether duelling was contrary to the laws of Christianity. Johnson immediately entered on the subject, and treated it in a masterly manner; and so far as I have been able to recollect, his thoughts were these: "Sir, as men become in a high degree refined, various causes of offence arise; which are considered to be of such importance, that life must be staked to atone for them, though in reality they are not so. A body that has received a very fine polish may be easily hurt. Before men arrive at this artificial refinement, if one tells his neighbour— he lies, his neighbour tells him—he lies; if one gives his neighbour a blow, his neighbour gives him a blow: but in a state of highly polished society, an affront is held to be a serious injury. It must, therefore, be resented, or rather a duel must be fought upon it; as men have agreed to banish from their society one who puts up with an affront without fighting a duel. Now, Sir, it is never unlawful to fight in self-defence. He, then, who fights a duel, does not fight from passion against his antagonist, but out of self-defence; to avert the stigma of the world, and to prevent himself from being driven out of society. I could wish there was not that superfluity of refinement; but while such notions prevail, no doubt a man may lawfully fight a duel."

The General told us, that when he was a very young man, I think only fifteen, serving under Prince Eugene of Savoy, he was sitting in a company at table with a Prince of Wirtemberg. The Prince took up a glass of wine, and, by a fillip, made some of it fly in Oglethorpe's face. Here was a nice dilemma. To have challenged him instantly, might have fixed a quarrelsome character upon the young soldier: to have taken no notice of it, might have been considered as cowardice. Oglethorpe, therefore, keeping his eye upon the Prince, and smiling all the time, as if he took what his Highness had done in jest, said *"Mon Prince,—"* (I forget the French words he used, the purport however was,) "That's a good joke: but we do it much better in England;" and threw a whole glass of wine in the Prince's face. An old General who sat by, said, *"Il a bien fait, mon Prince, vous l'avez commencé:"* and thus all ended in good humour.

A question was started, how far people who disagree in a capital point can live in friendship together. Johnson said they might. Goldsmith said they could not, as they had not the *idem velle atque idem nolle*—the same likings and the same aversions. JOHNSON. "Why, Sir, you must shun the subject as to which you disagree. For instance, I can live very well with Burke: I love his knowledge, his genius, his diffusion, and affluence of conversation; but I would not talk to him of the Rockingham party." GOLDSMITH. "But, Sir, when people live together who have something as to which they disagree, and which they want to shun, they will be in the situation mentioned in the story of Bluebeard: 'You may look into all the chambers but one.' But we should have the greatest inclination to look into that chamber, to talk of that subject." JOHNSON, (with a loud voice) "Sir, I am not saying that *you* could live in friendship with a man from whom you differ as to some point: I am only saying that I could do it."

I supped with Dr. Johnson, at the Crown and Anchor

tavern, in the Strand, in company with Mr. Langton and his brother-in-law, Lord Binning. I repeated a sentence of Lord Mansfield's speech, of which, by the aid of Mr. Longlands, the solicitor on the other side, who obligingly allowed me to compare his note with my own, I have a full copy: "My Lords, severity is not the way to govern either boys or men." "Nay (said Johnson,) it is the way to *govern them*. I know not whether it be the way to *mend* them."

I talked of the recent expulsion of six students from the University of Oxford, who were methodists, and would not desist from publickly praying and exhorting. JOHNSON. "Sir, that expulsion was extremely just and proper. What have they to do at an University, who are not willing to be taught, but will presume to teach? Where is religion to be learnt, but at an University? Sir, they were examined, and found to be mighty ignorant fellows." BOSWELL. "But, was it not hard, Sir, to expel them, for I am told they were good beings?" JOHNSON. "I believe they might be good beings; but they were not fit to be in the University of Oxford. A cow is a very good animal in the field; but we turn her out of a garden." Lord Elibank used to repeat this as an illustration uncommonly happy.

Desirous of calling Johnson forth to talk, and exercise his wit, though I should myself be the object of it, I resolutely ventured to undertake the defence of convivial indulgence in wine, though he was not tonight in the most genial humour. After urging the common plausible topicks, I at last had recourse to the maxim, *in vino veritas,* a man who is well warmed with wine will speak truth. JOHNSON. "Why, Sir, that may be an argument for drinking, if you suppose men in general to be liars. But, Sir, I would not keep company with a fellow, who lyes as long as he is sober, and whom you must make drunk before you can get a word of truth out of him."

On Sunday, April 19, being Easter-day, General Paoli and I paid him a visit before dinner. I regretted the reflection in his preface to Shakespeare against Garrick, to whom we cannot but apply the following passage: "I collated such copies as I could procure, and wished for more, but have not found the collectors of these rarities very communicative." I told him, that Garrick had complained to me of it, and had vindicated himself by assuring me, that Johnson was made welcome to the full use of his collection, and that he left the key of it with a servant, with orders to have a fire and every convenience for him. I found Johnson's notion was, that Garrick wanted to be courted for them, and that, on the contrary, Garrick should have courted him, and sent him the plays of his own accord. But, indeed, considering the slovenly and careless manner in which books were treated by Johnson, it could not be expected that scarce and valuable editions should have been lent to him.

A gentleman having to some of the usual arguments for drinking added this: "You know, Sir, drinking drives away care, and makes us forget whatever is disagreeable. Would not you allow a man to drink for that reason?" JOHNSON. "Yes, Sir, if he sat next *you*."

He said, "there is no permanent national character: it varies according to circumstances. Alexander the Great swept India: now the Turks sweep Greece."

A learned gentleman, who in the course of conversation wished to inform us of this simple fact, that the Counsel upon the circuit at Shrewsbury were much bitten by fleas, took, I suppose, seven or eight minutes in relating it circumstantially. He in a plenitude of phrase told us, that large bales of woollen cloth were lodged in the town-hall;—that by reason of this, fleas nestled there in prodigious numbers; that the lodgings of the counsel were near the town-hall:—and that those little animals moved from place to place with wonderful agility. Johnson sat in great impatience till the gentleman had finished his tedious narrative, and then burst out (playfully however,) "It is a pity, Sir, that you have not seen a lion; for a flea has taken you such a time, that a lion must have served you a twelvemonth."

He would not allow Scotland to derive any credit from Lord Mansfield; for he was educated in England. "Much (said he,) may be made of a Scotchman, if he be *caught* young."

1773. To my great surprize he asked me to dine with him on Easter-day. I never supposed that he had a dinner at his house; for I had not then heard of any one of his friends having been entertained at his table. He told me, "I have generally a meat pye on Sunday: it is baked at a publick oven, which is very properly allowed, because one man can attend it; and thus the advantage is obtained of not keeping servants from church to dress dinners."

April 11, being Easter-Sunday, after having attended divine Service at St. Paul's, I repaired to Dr. Johnson's. I had gratified my curiosity much in dining with JEAN JAQUES ROUSSEAU, while he lived in the wilds of Neufchatel: I had as great a curiosity to dine with DR. SAMUEL JOHNSON, in the dusky recess of a court in Fleet-street. I supposed we should scarcely have knives and forks, and only some strange, uncouth, ill-drest fish: but I found every thing in very good order. We had no other company but Mrs. Williams and a young woman whom I did not know. As a dinner here was considered

as a singular phenomenon, and as I was frequently inter-
rogated on the subject, my readers may perhaps be
desirous to know our bill of fare. Foote, I remember, in
allusion to Francis, the *negro*, was willing to suppose
that our repast was *black broth*. But the fact was, that
we had a very good soup, a boiled leg of lamb and
spinach, a veal pye, and a rice pudding.

He owned that he thought Hawkesworth was one of
his imitators, but he did not think Goldsmith was. Goldsmith, he said, had great merit. BOSWELL. "But, Sir, he
is much indebted to you for his getting so high in the
publick estimation." JOHNSON. "Why, Sir, he has perhaps got *sooner* to it by his intimacy with me."

On Tuesday, April 13, he and Dr. Goldsmith and I
dined at General Oglethorpe's. Goldsmith expatiated on
the common topick, that the race of our people was de-
generated, and that this was owing to luxury. JOHNSON.
"Sir, in the first place, I doubt the fact. I believe there
are as many tall men in England now, as ever there
were. But, secondly, supposing the stature of our people
to be diminished, that is not owing to luxury; for, Sir,
consider to how very small a proportion of our people
luxury can reach. Our soldiery, surely, are not luxurious, who live on six-pence a day; and the same remark
will apply to almost all the other classes. Luxury, so far
as it reaches the poor, will do good to the race of people; it will strengthen and multiply them. Sir, no nation was ever hurt by luxury; for, as I said before, it can
reach but to a very few. I admit that the great increase
of commerce and manufactures hurts the military spirit
of a people; because it produces a competition for something else than martial honours,—a competition for
riches. It also hurts the bodies of the people; for you
will observe, there is no man who works at any particular trade, but you may know him from his appearance

to do so. One part or the other of his body being more used than the rest, he is in some degree deformed: but, Sir, that is not luxury. A tailor sits cross-legged; but that is not luxury." GOLDSMITH. "Come, you're just going to the same place by another road." JOHNSON. "Nay, Sir, I say that is not *luxury*. Let us take a walk from Charing-cross to Whitechapel, through, I suppose, the greatest series of shops in the world, what is there in any of these shops, (if you except gin-shops,) that can do any human being any harm?" GOLDSMITH. "Well, Sir, I'll accept your challenge. The very next shop to Northumberland-house is a pickle-shop." JOHNSON. "Well, Sir: do we not know that a maid can in one afternoon make pickles sufficient to serve a whole family for a year? nay, that five pickle-shops can serve all the kingdom? Besides, Sir, there is no harm done to any body by the making of pickles, or the eating of pickles."

On Thursday, April 15, I dined with him and Dr. Goldsmith at General Paoli's. I spoke of Allan Ramsay's "Gentle Shepherd," in the Scottish dialect, as the best pastoral that had ever been written; and I offered to teach Dr. Johnson to understand it. "No, Sir, (said he,) I won't learn it. You shall retain your superiority by my not knowing it."

It having been observed that there was little hospitality in London; JOHNSON. "Nay, Sir, any man who has a name, or who has the power of pleasing, will be very generally invited in London. The man, Sterne, I have been told, has had engagements for three months." GOLDSMITH. "And a very dull fellow." JOHNSON. "Why, no, Sir."

On Monday, April 19, he called on me with Mrs. Williams, in Mr. Strahan's coach, and carried me out to dine with Mr. Elphinston, at his Academy at Kensington. Mr. Elphinston talked of a new book that was much

admired, and asked Dr. Johnson if he had read it. JOHN-
SON. "I have looked into it." "What (said Elphinston,)
have you not read it through?" Johnson, offended at being thus pressed, and so obliged to own his cursory
mode of reading, answered tartly, "No, Sir, do *you* read
books *through?*"

On Wednesday, April 21, I dined with him at Mr.
Thrale's.

He said, "Goldsmith should not be forever attempting to shine in conversation: he has not temper for it, he
is so much mortified when he fails. Sir, a game of jokes
is composed partly of skill, partly of chance, a man may
be beat at times by one who has not the tenth part of
his wit. Now Goldsmith's putting himself against another, is like a man laying a hundred to one who cannot spare the hundred. It is not worth a man's while. A
man should not lay a hundred to one, unless he can
easily spare it, though he has a hundred chances for
him: he can get but a guinea, and he may lose a hundred. Goldsmith is in this state. When he contends, if
he gets the better, it is a very little addition to a man of
his literary reputation: if he does not get the better, he
is miserably vexed."

Johnson's own superlative powers of wit set him
above any risk of such uneasiness. Garrick had remarked
to me of him, a few days before, "Rabelais and all other
wits are nothing compared with him. You may be diverted by them; but Johnson gives you a forcible hug,
and shakes laughter out of you, whether you will or no."

Goldsmith, however, was often very fortunate in his
witty contests, even when he entered the lists with Johnson himself. Sir Joshua Reynolds was in company with
them one day, when Goldsmith said, that he thought
he could write a good fable, mentioned the simplicity
which that kind of composition requires, and observed,

that in most fables the animals introduced seldom talk in character. "For instance, (said he,) the fable of the little fishes, who saw birds fly over their heads, and envying them, petitioned Jupiter to be changed into birds. The skill (continued he,) consists in making them talk like little fishes." While he indulged himself in this fanciful reverie, he observed Johnson shaking his sides, and laughing. Upon which he smartly proceeded, "Why, Dr. Johnson, this is not so easy as you seem to think; for if you were to make little fishes talk, they would talk like WHALES."

On Thursday, April 29, I dined with him at General Oglethorpe's, where were Sir Joshua Reynolds, Mr. Langton, Dr. Goldsmith, and Mr. Thrale. The character of Mallet having been introduced, and spoken of slightingly by Goldsmith; JOHNSON. "Why, Sir, Mallet had talents enough to keep his literary reputation alive as long as he himself lived; and that, let me tell you, is a good deal." GOLDSMITH. "But I cannot agree that it was so. His literary reputation was dead long before his natural death. I consider an authour's literary reputation to be alive only while his name will insure a good price for his copy from the booksellers. I will get you (to Johnson,) a hundred guineas for any thing whatever that you shall write, if you put your name to it."

Dr. Goldsmith's new play, "She Stoops to Conquer," being mentioned; JOHNSON. "I know of no comedy for many years that has so much exhilarated an audience, that has answered so much the great end of comedy— making an audience merry."

SIR JOSHUA REYNOLDS. "I do not perceive why the profession of a player should be despised; for the great and ultimate end of all the employments of mankind is to produce amusement. Garrick produces more amusement than any body." BOSWELL. "You say, Dr. Johnson, that Garrick exhibits himself for a shilling. In this respect he is only on a footing with a lawyer who exhibits himself for his fee, and even will maintain any nonsense or absurdity, if the case require it. Garrick refuses a play or a part which he does not like: a lawyer never refuses." JOHNSON. "Why, Sir, what does this prove? only that a lawyer is worse. Boswell is now like Jack in 'The Tale of a Tub,' who, when he is puzzled by an argument, hangs himself. He thinks I shall cut him down, but I'll let him hang," (laughing vociferously.)

On Friday, April 30, I dined with him at Mr. Beauclerk's, where were Lord Charlemont, Sir Joshua Reynolds, and some more members of the LITERARY CLUB, whom he had obligingly invited to meet me, as I was this evening to be ballotted for as candidate for admission into that distinguished society. Johnson had done me the honour to propose me, and Beauclerk was very zealous for me.

Goldsmith being mentioned; JOHNSON. "It is amazing how little Goldsmith knows. He seldom comes where he is not more ignorant than any one else." SIR JOSHUA REYNOLDS. "Yet there is no man whose company is more liked." JOHNSON. "To be sure, Sir. When people find a man of the most distinguished abilities as a writer, their inferiour while he is with them, it must be highly gratifying to them. What Goldsmith comically says of himself is very true,—he always gets the better when he argues alone; meaning, that he is master of a subject in his study, and can write well upon it; but when he comes into company, grows confused, and unable to talk. Take him as a poet, his 'Traveller' is a very fine performance; ay, and so is his 'Deserted Village,' were it not sometimes too much the echo of his 'Traveller.' Whether, indeed, we take him as a poet,—as a comick writer,—or as an historian, he stands in the first class."

BOSWELL. "An historian! My dear Sir, you surely will not rank his compilation of the Roman History with the works of other historians of this age?" JOHNSON. "Why, who are before him?" BOSWELL. "Hume,—Robertson, —Lord Lyttelton." JOHNSON. (His antipathy to the Scotch beginning to rise.) "I have not read Hume; but, doubtless, Goldsmith's History is better than the *verbiage* of Robertson, or the foppery of Dalrymple." BOSWELL. "Will you not admit the superiority of Robertson, in whose history we find such penetration—such painting?" JOHNSON. "Sir, you must consider how that penetration and that painting are employed. It is not history, it is imagination. He who describes what he never saw, draws from fancy. Robertson paints minds as Sir Joshua paints faces in a history-piece: he imagines an heroick countenance. You must look upon Robertson's work as romance and try it by that standard. History it is not. Besides, Sir, it is the great excellence of a writer to put into his book as much as his book will hold. Goldsmith has done this in his History. Now Robertson might have put twice as much into his book. Robertson is like a man who has packed gold in wool; the wool takes up more room than the gold. I would say to Robertson what an old tutor of a college said to one of his pupils: 'Read over your compositions, and wherever you meet with a passage which you think is particularly fine, strike it out.'"

JOHNSON. "I remember once being with Goldsmith in Westminster-abbey. While we surveyed the Poet's Corner, I said to him, *'Forsitan et nostrum nomen miscebitur istis.'* When we got to Temple-bar, he stopped me, pointed to the heads upon it, and slily whispered me, *'Forsitan et nostrum nomen miscebitur* ISTIS.'"

The gentlemen went away to their club, and I was left at Beauclerk's till the fate of my election should be announced to me. I sat in a state of anxiety which even the charming conversation of Lady Di Beauclerk could not entirely dissipate. In a short time I received the agreeable intelligence that I was chosen. I hastened to the place of meeting, and was introduced to such a society as can seldom be found. Mr. Edmund Burke, whom I then saw for the first time, and whose splendid talents had long made me ardently wish for his acquaintance; Dr. Nugent, Mr. Garrick, Dr. Goldsmith, Mr. (afterwards Sir William) Jones, and the company with whom I had dined. Upon my entrance, Johnson placed himself behind a chair, on which he leaned as on a desk or pulpit, and with humorous formality gave me a *Charge,* pointing out the conduct expected from me as a good member of this club.

On Friday, May 7, I breakfasted with him at Mr. Thrale's in the Borough. While we were alone, I endeavoured as well as I could to apologise for a lady who had been divorced from her husband by act of Parliament. I said, that he had used her very ill, had behaved brutally to her, and that she could not continue to live with him without having her delicacy contaminated; that all affection for him was thus destroyed; that the essence of conjugal union being gone, there remained only a cold form, a mere civil obligation; that she was in the prime of life, with qualities to produce happiness; that these ought not to be lost; and, that the gentleman on whose account she was divorced had gained her heart while thus unhappily situated. Seduced, perhaps, by the charms of the lady in question, I thus attempted to palliate what I was sensible could not be justified; for when I had finished my harangue, my venerable friend gave me a proper check: "My dear Sir, never accustom your mind to mingle virtue and vice. The woman's a whore, and there's an end on't."

I dined with him this day at the house of my friends, Messieurs Edward and Charles Dilly, booksellers in the Poultry; there were present, their elder brother Mr. Dilly of Bedfordshire, Dr. Goldsmith, Mr. Langton, Mr. Claxton, Reverend Dr. Mayo, a dissenting minister, the Reverend Mr. Toplady, and my friend the Reverend Mr. Temple.

Talking of birds, I mentioned Mr. Daines Barrington's ingenious Essay against the received notion of their migration. JOHNSON. "I think we have as good evidence for the migration of woodcocks as can be desired. We find they disappear at a certain time of the year, and appear again at a certain time of the year; and some of them, when weary in their flight, have been known to alight on the rigging of ships far out at sea." One of the company observed, that there had been instances of some of them found in summer in Essex. JOHNSON. "Sir, that strengthens our argument. *Exceptio probat regulam.* Some being found shews, that, if all remained, many would be found. A few sick or lame ones may be found." GOLDSMITH. "There is a partial migration of the swallows; the stronger ones migrate, the others do not."

BOSWELL. "I am well assured that the people of Otaheite who have the bread tree, the fruit of which serves them for bread, laughed heartily when they were informed of the tedious process necessary with us to have bread;—plowing, sowing, harrowing, reaping, threshing, grinding, baking." JOHNSON. "Why, Sir, all ignorant savages will laugh when they are told of the advantages of the civilised life. Were you to tell men who live without houses, how we pile brick upon brick, and rafter upon rafter, and that after a house is raised to a certain height, a man tumbles off a scaffold, and breaks his neck; he would laugh heartily at our folly in building; but it does not follow that men are better without houses. No, Sir, (holding up a slice of a good loaf,) this is better than the bread tree."

I introduced the subject of toleration. JOHNSON. "Every society has a right to preserve publick peace and order, and therefore has a good right to prohibit the propagation of opinions which have a dangerous tendency: To say the *magistrate* has this right, is using an inadequate word: it is the *society* for which the magistrate is agent. He may be morally or theologically wrong in restraining the propagation of opinions which he thinks dangerous, but he is politically right." MAYO. "I am of opinion, Sir, that every man is entitled to liberty of conscience in religion; and that the magistrate cannot restrain that right." JOHNSON. "Sir, I agree with you. Every man has a right to liberty of conscience, and with that the magistrate cannot interfere. People confound liberty of thinking with liberty of talking; nay, with liberty of preaching. Every man has a physical right to think as he pleases; for it cannot be discovered how he thinks. He has not a moral right, for he ought to inform himself, and think justly. But, Sir, no member of a society has a right to *teach* any doctrine contrary to what the society holds to be true. The magistrate, I say, may be wrong in what he thinks; but while he thinks himself right, he may and ought to enforce what he thinks." MAYO. "Then, Sir, we are to remain always in errour, and truth never can prevail; and the magistrate was right in persecuting the first Christians." JOHNSON. "Sir, the only method by which religious truth can be established is by martyrdom. The magistrate has a right to enforce what he thinks; and he who is conscious of the truth has a right to suffer. I am afraid there is no other way of ascertaining the truth, but by persecution on the one hand and enduring it on the other." GOLDSMITH. "But how is a man to act, Sir? Though firmly convinced of the truth of his doctrine, may he not think it wrong to expose himself to persecution? Has he a right to do so? Is it not, as it were, committing voluntary suicide?" JOHNSON. "Sir, as to voluntary suicide, as you call it, there are twenty thousand men in an army who will go without scruple to be shot at, and mount a breach for five-pence a day." GOLDSMITH. "But have they a moral right to do this?" JOHNSON. "Nay, Sir, if you will not take the universal opinion of mankind, I have nothing to say. If mankind cannot defend their own way of thinking, I cannot defend it. Sir, if a man is in doubt whether it would be better for him to expose himself to martyrdom or not, he should not do it. He must be convinced that he has a delegation from heaven." GOLDSMITH. "I would consider whether there is the greater chance of good or evil upon the whole. If I see a man who has fallen into a well, I would wish to help him out; but if there is a greater probability that he shall pull me in, than that I shall pull him out, I would not attempt it. So were I to go to Turkey, I might wish to convert the grand Signor to the Christian faith; but when I considered that I should probably be put to death without effectuating my purpose in any degree, I should keep myself quiet." JOHNSON. "Sir, you must consider that we have perfect and imperfect obligations. Perfect obligations, which are generally not to do something, are clear and positive; as, 'thou shalt not kill.' But charity, for instance, is not definable by limits. It is a duty to give to the poor; but no man can say how much another should give to the poor, or when a man has given too little to save his soul. In the same manner it is a duty to instruct the ignorant, and of consequence to convert infidels to Christianity; but no man in the common course of things is obliged to carry this to such a degree as to incur the danger of martyrdom, as no man is obliged to strip himself to the shirt, in order to give charity. I have said, that a man must be persuaded that he has a particular delegation from heaven." GOLD-SMITH. "How is this to be known? Our first reformers, who were burnt for not believing bread and wine to be CHRIST"—JOHNSON. (interrupting him,) "Sir, they were not burnt for not believing bread and wine to be CHRIST, but for insulting those who did believe it. And, Sir, when the first reformers began, they did not intend to be martyred: as many of them ran away as could." BOSWELL. "But, Sir, there was your countryman Elwal, who you told me challenged King George with his black-guards and his red-guards." JOHNSON. "My countryman, Elwal, Sir, should have been put in the stocks: a proper pulpit for him; and he'd have had a numerous audience. A man who preaches in the stocks will always have hearers enough." BOSWELL. "But Elwal thought himself in the right." JOHNSON. "We are not providing for mad people; there are places for them in the neighbour-hood." (meaning Moorfields.) MAYO. "But, Sir, is it not very hard that I should not be allowed to teach my children what I really believe to be the truth?" JOHN-SON. "Why, Sir, you might contrive to teach your chil-dren *extrà scandalum;* but, Sir, the magistrate, if he knows it, has a right to restrain you. Suppose you teach your children to be thieves?" MAYO. "This is making a joke of the subject." JOHNSON. "Nay, Sir, take it thus:—that you teach them the community of goods: for which there are as many plausible arguments as for most er-roneous doctrines. You teach them that all things at first were in common, and that no man had a right to any-thing but as he laid his hands upon it; and that this still is, or ought to be, the rule amongst mankind. Here, Sir, you sap a great principle in society,—property. And don't you think the magistrate would have a right to prevent you? Or, suppose you should teach your children the notion of the Adamites, and they should run naked into the streets, would not the magistrate have a right to flog 'em into their doublets?" MAYO. "I think the magistrate has no right to interfere till there is some overt act." BOSWELL. "So, Sir, though he sees an enemy to the state charging a blunderbuss, he is not to interfere till it is fired off!" MAYO. "He must be sure of its direction against the state." JOHNSON. "The magistrate is to judge of that.—He has no right to restrain your thinking, because the evil centers in yourself. If a man were sitting at this table, and chopping off his fingers, the magistrate, as guardian of the community, has no authority to restrain him, however he might do it from kindness as a parent.—Though, indeed, upon more consideration, I think he may; as it is probable, that he who is chopping off his own fingers, may soon proceed to chop off those of other people. If I think it right to steal Mr. Dilly's plate, I am a bad man; but he can say nothing to me. If I make an open declaration that I think so, he will keep me out of his house. If I put forth my hand, I shall be sent to Newgate. This is the gradation of thinking, preaching, and acting: if a man thinks erroneously, he may keep his thoughts to himself, and nobody will trouble him; if he preaches erroneous doctrine, society may expel him; if he acts in consequence of it, the law takes place, and he is hanged." MAYO. "But, Sir, ought not Christians to have liberty of conscience?" JOHNSON. "I have already told you so, Sir. You are coming back to where you were." BOSWELL. "Dr. Mayo is always taking a return postchaise, and going the stage over again. He has it at half-price." JOHNSON. "Dr. Mayo, like other champions for unlimited toleration, has got a set of words. Sir, it is no matter, politically, whether

the magistrate be right or wrong. Suppose a club were
to be formed, to drink confusion to King George the
Third, and a happy restoration to Charles the Third;
this would be very bad with respect to the State; but
every member of that club must either conform to its
rules, or be turned out of it. Old Baxter, I remember,
maintains, that the magistrate should 'tolerate all things
that are tolerable.' This is no good definition of toleration upon any principle; but it shews that he thought
some things were not tolerable." TOPLADY. "Sir, you
have untwisted this difficult subject with great dexterity."

During this argument, Goldsmith sat in restless agitation, from a wish to get in and *shine.* Finding himself
excluded, he had taken his hat to go away, but remained for some time with it in his hand, like a gamester,
who, at the close of a long night, lingers for a little
while, to see if he can have a favourable opening to
finish with success. Once when he was beginning to
speak, he found himself overpowered by the loud voice
of Johnson, who was at the opposite end of the table,
and did not perceive Goldsmith's attempt. Thus disappointed of his wish to obtain the attention of the company, Goldsmith in a passion threw down his hat, looking angrily at Johnson, and exclaimed in a bitter tone,
"Take it." When Toplady was going to speak, Johnson
uttered some sound, which led Goldsmith to think that
he was beginning again, and taking the words from
Toplady. Upon which, he seized this opportunity of
venting his own envy and spleen, under the pretext of
supporting another person: "Sir, (said he to Johnson,)
the gentleman has heard you patiently for an hour:
pray allow us now to hear him." JOHNSON. (sternly.)
"Sir, I was not interrupting the gentleman. I was only

giving him a signal of my attention. Sir, you are impertinent." Goldsmith made no reply, but continued in the company for some time.

He and Mr. Langton and I went together to THE CLUB, where we found Mr. Burke, Mr. Garrick, and some other members, and amongst them our friend Goldsmith, who sat silently brooding over Johnson's reprimand to him after dinner. Johnson perceived this, and said aside to some of us, "I'll make Goldsmith forgive me;" and then called to him in a loud voice, "Dr. Goldsmith,—something passed today where you and I dined; I ask your pardon." Goldsmith answered placidly, "It must be much from you, Sir, that I take ill." And so at once the difference was over, and they were on as easy terms as ever, and Goldsmith rattled away as usual.

In our way to the club tonight, when I regretted that Goldsmith would, upon every occasion, endeavour to shine, by which he often exposed himself, Mr. Langton observed, that he was not like Addison, who was content with the fame of his writings, and did not aim also at excellency in conversation, for which he found himself unfit; and that he said to a lady who complained of his having talked little in company, "Madam, I have but nine-pence in ready money, but I can draw for a thousand pounds." I observed that Goldsmith had a great deal of Gold in his cabinet, but, not content with that, was always taking out his purse. JOHNSON. "Yes, Sir, and that so often an empty purse!"

Goldsmith's incessant desire of being conspicuous in company, was the occasion of his sometimes appearing to such disadvantage as one should hardly have supposed possible in a man of his genius. When his literary reputation had risen deservedly high, and his society was much courted, he became very jealous of the extraordinary attention which was every where paid to

Johnson. One evening, in a circle of wits, he found fault with me for talking of Johnson as entitled to the honour of unquestionable superiority. "Sir, (said he,) you are for making a monarchy of what should be a republick."

He was still more mortified, when talking in a company with fluent vivacity, and, as he flattered himself, to the admiration of all who were present; a German who sat next him, and perceived Johnson rolling himself, as if about to speak, suddenly stopped him, saying, "Stay, stay,—Toctor Shonson is going to say something." This was, no doubt, very provoking, especially to one so irritable as Goldsmith, who frequently mentioned it with strong expressions of indignation.

It may also be observed, that Goldsmith was sometimes content to be treated with an easy familiarity, but upon occasions, would be consequential and important. An instance of this occurred in a small particular. Johnson had a way of contracting the names of his friends: as Beauclerk, Beau; Boswell, Bozzy; Langton, Lanky; Murphy, Mur, Sheridan, Shorry. I remember one day, when Tom Davies was telling that Dr. Johnson said, "We are all in labour for a name to *Goldy's* play," Goldsmith seemed displeased that such a liberty should be taken with his name, and said, "I have often desired him not to call me *Goldy*." Tom was remarkably attentive to the most minute circumstance about Johnson. I recollect his telling me once, on my arrival in London, "Sir, our great friend has made an improvement on his appellation of old Mr. Sheridan. He calls him now *Sherry derry*."

On Monday, May 9, as I was to set out on my return to Scotland next morning, I was desirous to see as much of Dr. Johnson as I could. But I first called on Goldsmith to take leave of him. The jealousy and envy which, though possessed of many most amiable qualities, he frankly avowed, broke out violently at this interview. Upon another occasion, when Goldsmith confessed himself to be of an envious disposition, I contended with Johnson that we ought not to be angry with him, he was so candid in owning it. "Nay, Sir, (said Johnson,) we must be angry that a man has such a superabundance of an odious quality, that he cannot keep it within his own breast, but it boils over." In my opinion, however, Goldsmith had not more of it than other people have, but only talked of it freely.

He now seemed very angry that Johnson was going to be a traveller; said "he would be a dead weight for me to carry, and that I should never be able to lug him along through the Highlands and Hebrides." Nor would he patiently allow me to enlarge upon Johnson's wonderful abilities; but exclaimed, "Is he like Burke, who winds into a subject like a serpent?" "But, (said I,) Johnson is the Hercules who strangled serpents in his cradle."

I dined with Dr. Johnson at General Paoli's. He was obliged, by indisposition, to leave the company early; he appointed me, however, to meet him in the evening at Mr. (now Sir Robert) Chambers's in the Temple, where he accordingly came, though he continued to be very ill. Chambers, as is common on such occasions, prescribed various remedies to him. JOHNSON. (fretted by pain,) "Pr'ythee don't tease me. Stay till I am well, and then you shall tell me how to cure myself." He grew better, and talked with a noble enthusiasm of keeping up the representation of respectable families. His zeal on this subject was a circumstance in his character exceedingly remarkable, when it is considered that he himself had no pretensions to blood. I heard him once say, "I have great merit in being zealous for subordination and the honours of birth; for I can hardly tell who was my grandfather." He maintained the dignity and propriety of male succession, in opposition to the opinion of one of our friends, who had that day employed Mr. Chambers to draw his will, devising his estate to his three sisters, in preference to a remote heir male. Johnson called them "three *dowdies*," and said, with as high a spirit as the boldest Baron in the most perfect days of the feudal system, "An ancient estate should always go to males. It is mighty foolish to let a stranger have it because he marries your daughter, and takes your name. As for an estate newly acquired by trade, you may give it, if you will, to the dog *Towser*, and let him keep his *own* name."

I have known him at times exceedingly diverted at what seemed to others a very small sport. He now laughed immoderately, without any reason that we could perceive, at our friend's making his will; called him the *testator*, and added, "I dare say he thinks he has done a mighty thing. He won't stay till he gets home to his seat in the country, to produce this wonderful deed: he'll call up the landlord of the first inn on the road; and, after a suitable preface upon mortality and the uncertainty of life, will tell him that he should not delay making his will; and here, Sir, will he say, is my will, which I have just made, with the assistance of one of the ablest lawyers in the kingdom; and he will read it to him, (laughing all the time.) He believes he has made this will; but he did not make it: you, Chambers, made it for him. I trust you have had more conscience than to make him say, 'being of sound understanding;' ha, ha, ha! I hope he has left me a legacy. I'd have his will turned into verse, like a ballad."

Mr. Chambers did not by any means relish this jocularity upon a matter of which *pars magna fuit*, and seemed impatient till he got rid of us. Johnson could not stop his merriment, but continued it all the way till he got without the Temple-gate. He then burst into such a fit of laughter, that he appeared to be almost in a convulsion; and, in order to support himself, laid hold of one of the posts at the side of the foot pavement, and sent forth peals so loud, that in the silence of the night his voice seemed to resound from Temple-bar to Fleet-ditch.

In a letter from Edinburgh, dated the 29th of May, I pressed him to persevere in his resolution to make this year the projected visit to the Hebrides, of which he and I had talked for many years, and which I was confident would afford us much entertainment.

TO JAMES BOSWELL, ESQ.

Johnson's-court, Fleet-street,
July 5, 1773.

DEAR SIR,

When your letter came to me, I was so darkened by an inflammation in my eye that I could not for some time read it. I can now write without trouble, and can read large prints. My eye is gradually growing stronger; and I hope will be able to take some delight in the survey of a Caledonian loch. . . .

I hope your dear lady and her dear baby are both well. I shall see them too when I come; and I have that opinion of your choice, as to suspect that when I have seen Mrs. Boswell, I shall be less willing to go away.

I am, dear Sir,
Your affectionate humble servant,
SAM. JOHNSON.

I again wrote to him, informing him that the Court of Session rose on the twelfth of August, hoping to see him before that time, and expressing, perhaps in too extravagant terms, my admiration of him, and my expectation of pleasure from our intended tour.

To James Boswell, Esq.

August 3, 1773.

Dear Sir,

I shall set out from London on Friday the sixth of this month, and purpose not to loiter much by the way. Which day I shall be at Edinburgh, I cannot exactly tell. I suppose I must drive to an inn, and send a porter to find you.

I am afraid Beattie will not be at his College soon enough for us, and I shall be sorry to miss him; but there is no staying for the concurrence of all conveniences. We will do as well as we can. I am, Sir,

Your most humble servant,
SAM. JOHNSON.

To James Boswell, Esq.

Nov. 27, 1773.

Dear Sir,

I came home last night, without any incommodity, danger, or weariness, and am ready to begin a new journey. I shall go to Oxford on Monday. I know Mrs. Boswell wished me well to go;[1] her wishes have not been disappointed. Mrs. Williams has received Sir A.'s letter.

Make my compliments to all those to whom my compliments may be welcome.

Let the box be sent as soon as it can, and let me know when to expect it.

Enquire, if you can, the order of the Clans: Macdonald is first, Maclean second; further I cannot go. Quicken Dr. Webster.

I am, Sir,
Yours affectionately,
SAM. JOHNSON.

---

[1] In this he shewed a very acute penetration. My wife paid him the most assiduous and respectful attention, while he was our guest; so that I wonder how he discovered her wishing for his departure. The truth is, that his irregular hours and uncouth habits, such as turning the candles with their heads downwards, when they did not burn bright enough, and letting the wax drop upon the carpet, could not but be disagreeable to a lady. Besides, she had not that high admiration of him which was felt by most of those who knew him; and what was very natural to a female mind, she thought he had too

To James Boswell, Esq.

February 7, 1775.

My Dear Boswell,

I am surprised that, knowing as you do the disposition of your countrymen to tell lies in favour of each other, you can be at all affected by any reports that circulate among them. Macpherson[1] never in his life offered me a sight of any original or of any evidence of any kind; but thought only of intimidating me by noise and threats.

The state of the question is this. He, and Dr. Blair, whom I consider as deceived, say, that he copied the poem from old manuscripts. His copies, if he had them, and I believe him to have none, are nothing. Where are the manuscripts? They can be shewn if they exist, but they were never shown. No man has a claim to credit upon his own word, when better evidence, if he had it, may be easily produced. But so far as we can find, the Erse language was never written till very lately for the purposes of religion. A nation that cannot write, or a language that was never written, has no manuscripts. . . .

I am, Sir,

Your most humble servant,

Sam. Johnson.

What words were used by Mr. Macpherson in his letter to the venerable Sage, I have never heard; but they are generally said to have been of a nature very different from the language of literary contest. Dr. Johnson's answer appeared in the newspapers of the day, and has since been frequently republished; but not with perfect accuracy. I give it as dictated to me by himself, written down in his presence, and authenticated by a note in his own handwriting, *"This, I think, is a true copy."*

---

much influence over her husband. She once in a little warmth, made, with more point than justice, this remark upon that subject: "I have seen many a bear led by a man; but I never before saw a man led by a bear."

[1] The "translator" of Ossian.

Mr. James Macpherson.

I received your foolish and impudent letter. Any violence offered me I shall do my best to repel; and what I cannot do for myself, the law shall do for me. I hope I shall never be deterred from detecting what I think a cheat, by the menaces of a ruffian.

What would you have me retract? I thought your book an imposture; I think it an imposture still. For this opinion I have given my reasons to the publick, which I here dare you to refute. Your rage I defy. Your abilities, since your Homer, are not so formidable; and what I hear of your morals inclines me to pay regard not to what you shall say, but to what you shall prove. You may print this if you will.

Sam. Johnson.

Mr. Macpherson little knew the character of Dr. Johnson, if he supposed that he could be easily intimidated; for no man was ever more remarkable for personal courage. He had, indeed, an awful dread of death, or rather, "of something after death;" and what rational man, who seriously thinks of quitting all that he has ever known, and going into a now and unknown state of being, can be without that dread? But his fear was from reflection; his courage natural. His fear, in that one instance, was the result of philosophical and religious consideration. He feared death, but he feared nothing else, not even what might occasion death. Many instances of his resolution may be mentioned. One day, at Mr. Beauclerk's house in the country, when two large dogs were fighting, he went up to them, and beat them till they separated; and at another time, when told of the danger there was that a gun might burst if charged with many balls, he put in six or seven and fired it off against a wall. Mr. Langton told me, that when they were swimming together near Oxford, he cautioned Dr. Johnson against a pool, which was reckoned particularly dangerous; upon which Johnson directly swam into it. He told me himself that one night he was attacked in the street by four men, to whom he would not yield, but kept them all at bay, till the watch came up, and carried both him and them to the round-house. In the play-house at Lichfield, as Mr. Garrick informed me, Johnson having for a moment quitted a chair which was placed for him between the side-scenes, a gentleman took possession of it, and when Johnson on his return civilly demanded his seat, rudely refused to give it up; upon which Johnson laid hold of it, and tossed him and the chair into the pit. Foote, who so successfully revived the old comedy, by exhibiting living characters, had resolved to imitate Johnson on the stage, expecting great profits from his ridicule of so celebrated a man. Johnson being informed of his intention, and being at dinner at Mr. Thomas Davies's the bookseller, from whom I had the story, he asked Mr. Davies "what was the common price of an oak stick;" and being answered six-pence, "Why then, Sir, (said he,) give me leave to send your servant to purchase me a shilling one. I'll have a double quantity; for I am told Foote means to *take me off*, as he calls it, and I am determined the fellow shall not do it with impunity." Davies took care to acquaint Foote of this, which effectually checked the wantonness of the mimick. Mr. Macpherson's menaces made Johnson provide himself with the same implement of defence; and had he been attacked, I have no doubt that, old as he was, he would have made his corporal prowess be felt as much as his intellectual.

My much-valued friend Dr. Barnard, now Bishop of Killaloe, having once expressed to him an apprehension, that if he should visit Ireland he might treat the people of that country more unfavourably than he had done the Scotch, he answered, with strong pointed double-edged wit, "Sir, you have no reason to be afraid of me. The

Irish are not in a conspiracy to cheat the world by false representations of the merits of their countrymen. No, Sir; the Irish are a FAIR PEOPLE;—they never speak well of one another."

On Friday, March 24, I met him at the LITERARY CLUB, where were Mr. Beauclerk, Mr. Langton, Mr. Colman, Dr. Percy, Mr. Vesey, Sir Charles Bunbury, Dr. George Fordyce, Mr. Steevens, and Mr. Charles Fox. Before he came in, we talked of his "Journey to the Western Islands," and of his coming away, "willing to believe the second sight," which seemed to excite some ridicule. I was then so impressed with the truth of many of the stories of which I had been told, that I avowed my conviction, saying, "He is only *willing* to believe: I *do* believe. The evidence is enough for me, though not for his great mind. What will not fill a quart bottle will fill a pint bottle. I am filled with belief." "Are you? (said Colman,) then cork it up."

Johnson was in high spirits this evening at the club, and talked with great animation and success. He attacked Swift, as he used to do upon all occasions. "The 'Tale of a Tub' is so much superiour to his other writings, that one can hardly believe he was the authour of it: there is in it such a vigour of mind, such a swarm of thoughts, so much of nature, and art, and life." I wondered to hear him say of "Gulliver's Travel," "When once you have thought of big men and little men, it is very easy to do all the rest."

From Swift, there was an easy transition to Mr. Thomas Sheridan.—JOHNSON. "Sheridan is a wonderful admirer of the tragedy of Douglas, and presented its authour with a gold medal. Some years ago, at a coffee-house in Oxford, I called to him, 'Mr. Sheridan, Mr. Sheridan, how came you to give a gold medal to Home, for writing that foolish play?' This, you see, was wanton and insolent; but I *meant* to be wanton and insolent. A medal has no value but as a stamp of merit. And was Sheridan to assume to himself the right of giving that stamp? If Sheridan was magnificent enough to bestow a gold medal as an honorary reward of dramatick excellence, he should have requested one of the Universities to choose the person on whom it should be conferred. Sheridan had no right to give a stamp of merit: it was counterfeiting Apollo's coin."

Next day I dined with Johnson at Mr. Thrale's. He attacked Gray, calling him "a dull fellow." BOSWELL. "I understand he was reserved, and might appear dull in company; but surely he was not dull in poetry." JOHNSON. "Sir, he was dull in company, dull in his closet, dull every where. He was dull in a new way, and that made many people think him GREAT."

A young lady who had married a man much her inferiour in rank being mentioned, a question arose how a woman's relations should behave to her in such a situation; and, while I recapitulate the debate, and recollect what has since happened, I cannot but be struck in a manner that delicacy forbids me to express. While I contended that she ought to be treated with an inflexible steadiness of displeasure, Mrs. Thrale was all for mildness and forgiveness, and, according to the vulgar phrase, "making the best of a bad bargain." JOHNSON. "Madam, we must distinguish. Were I a man of rank, I would not let a daughter starve who had made a mean marriage; but having voluntarily degraded herself from the station which she was originally entitled to hold, I would support her only in that which she herself had chosen; and would not put her on a level with my other daughters. You are to consider, Madam, that it is our duty to maintain the subordination of civilized society; and when there is a gross and shameful deviation from rank, it should be punished so as to deter others from the same perversion."

On Friday, March 31, I supped with him and some friends at a tavern. One of the company attempted, with too much forwardness, to rally him on his late appearance at the theatre; but had reason to repent of his temerity. "Why, Sir, did you go to Mrs. Abington's benefit? Did you see?" JOHNSON. "No, Sir." "Did you hear?" JOHNSON. "No, Sir." "Why, then, Sir, did you go?" JOHNSON. "Because, Sir, she is a favourite of the publick; and when the publick cares the thousandth part for you that it does for her, I will go to your benefit too."

Next morning I won a small bet from Lady Diana Beauclerk, by asking him as to one of his particularities, which her Ladyship laid I durst not do. It seems he had been frequently observed at the club to put into his pocket the Seville oranges, after he had squeezed the juice of them into the drink which he made for himself. Beauclerk and Garrick talked of it to me, and seemed to think that he had a strange unwillingness to be discovered. We could not divine what he did with them; and this was the bold question to be put. I saw on his table the spoils of the preceding night, some fresh peels nicely scraped and cut into pieces. "O, Sir, (said I,) I now partly see what you do with the squeezed oranges which you put into your pocket at the Club." JOHNSON. "I have a great love for them." BOSWELL. "And pray, Sir, what do you do with them? You scrape them it seems, very neatly, and what next?" JOHNSON. "Let them dry, Sir." BOSWELL. "And what next?" JOHNSON. "Nay, Sir, you shall know their fate no further." BOSWELL. "Then the world must be left in the dark. It must be said (assuming a mock solemnity,) he scraped them and let them dry, but what he did with them next, he never could be prevailed upon to tell." JOHNSON. "Nay,

Sir, you should say it more emphatically:—he could not be prevailed upon, even by his dearest friends, to tell."

I talked of the cheerfulness of Fleet-street, owing to the constant quick succession of people which we perceive passing through it. JOHNSON. "Why, Sir, Fleet-street has a very animated appearance; but I think the full tide of human existence is at Charing-cross."

On Thursday, April 6, I dined with him at Mr. Thomas Davies's, with Mr. Hicky, the painter, and my old acquaintance, Mr. Moody, the player.

Dr. Johnson, as usual, spoke contemptuously of Colley Cibber. "It is wonderful that a man, who for forty years had lived with the great and the witty, should have acquired so ill the talents of conversation: and he had but half to furnish; for one half of what he said was oaths." He, however, allowed considerable merit to some of his comedies, and said there was no reason to believe that the "Careless Husband" was not written by himself. Davies said, he was the first dramatick writer who introduced genteel ladies upon the stage. Johnson refuted his observation by instancing several such character in comedies before his time. DAVIES. (trying to defend himself for a charge of ignorance,) "I mean genteel moral characters." "I think (said Hicky,) gentility and morality are inseparable." BOSWELL. "By no means, Sir. The genteelest characters are often the most immoral. Does not Lord Chesterfield give precepts for uniting wickedness and the graces? A man, indeed, is not genteel when he gets drunk; but most vices may be committed very genteely: a man may debauch his friend's wife genteely: he may cheat at cards genteely." HICKY. "I do not think *that* is genteel." BOSWELL. "Sir, it may not be like a gentleman, but it may be genteel." JOHNSON. "You are meaning two different things. One means exteriour grace; the other honour. It is certain that a man may be very immoral with exteriour grace. Lovelace, in 'Clarissa,' is a very genteel and a very wicked character. Tom Hervey, who died t'other day, though a vicious man, was one of the genteelest men that ever lived." Tom Davies instanced Charles the Second. JOHNSON, (taking fire at any attack upon that Prince, for whom he had an extraordinary partiality,) "Charles the Second was licentious in his practice; but he always had a reverence for what was good. Charles the Second knew his people, and rewarded merit. The Church was at no time better filled than in his reign. He was the best King we have had from his time till the reign of his present Majesty, except James the Second, who was a very good King, but unhappily believed that it was necessary for the salvation of his subjects that they should be Roman Catholicks. *He* had the merit of endeavouring to do what he thought was for the salvation of the souls of his subjects, till he lost a great Empire. *We,* who thought that we should *not* be saved if we were Roman Catholicks, had the merit of maintaining our religion, at the expence of submitting ourselves to the government of King William, (for it could not be done otherwise,)—to the government of one of the most worthless scoundrels that ever existed. No; Charles the Second was not such a man as——, (naming another King.) He did not destroy his father's will.

"He took money, indeed, from France: but he did not betray those over whom he ruled. He did not let the French fleet pass ours. George the First knew nothing, and desired to know nothing; did nothing, and desired to do nothing; and the only good thing that is told of him is, that he wished to restore the crown to its hereditary successor." He roared with prodigious violence against George the Second. When he ceased, Moody interjected, in an Irish tone, and with a comick look, "Ah! poor George the Second."

I mentioned that Dr. Thomas Campbell had come from Ireland to London, principally to see Dr. Johnson. He seemed angry at this observation. DAVIES. "Why, you know, Sir, there came a man from Spain to see Livy; and Corelli came to England to see Purcell, and, when he heard he was dead, went directly back again to Italy." JOHNSON. "I should not have wished to be dead to disappoint Campbell, had he been so foolish as you represent him; but I should have wished to have been a hundred miles off." This was apparently perverse; and I do believe it was not his real way of thinking: he could not but like a man who came so far to see him. He laughed with some complacency, when I told him Campbell's odd expression to me concerning him: "That having seen such a man, was a thing to talk of a century hence,"—as if he could live so long.

We got into an argument whether the Judges who went to India might with propriety engage in trade. Johnson warmly maintained that they might, "For why (he urged) should not Judges get riches, as well as those who deserve them less?" I said, they should have sufficient salaries, and have nothing to take off their attention from the affairs of the publick. JOHNSON. "No Judge, Sir, can give his whole attention to his office; and it is very proper that he should employ what time he has to himself, to his own advantage, in the most profitable manner." "Then, Sir, (said Davies, who enlivened the dispute by making it somewhat dramatick,) he may become an insurer; and when he is going to the bench, he may be stopped,—'Your Lordship cannot go yet; here is a bunch of invoices: several ships are about to sail.'" JOHNSON. "Sir, you may as well say a Judge should not have a house; for they may come and tell him, 'Your Lordship's house is on fire;' and so, instead of minding the business of his Court, he is to be occupied in getting the engine with the greatest speed. There is no end of this. Every Judge who has land, trades to a certain extent in corn or in cattle; and in the land itself: undoubtedly his steward acts for him, and so do clerks for a great merchant. A Judge may be a farmer; but he is not to geld his own pigs. A Judge may play a little at cards for his amusement; but he is not to play at marbles, or chuck farthing in the Piazza. No, Sir, there is no profession to which a man gives a very great proportion of his time. It is wonderful when a calculation is made, how little the mind is actually employed in the discharge of any profession. No man would be a Judge, upon the condition of being totally a Judge. The best employed lawyer has his mind at work but for a small proportion of his time: a great deal of his occupation is merely mechanical.—I once wrote for a magazine: I made a calculation, that if I should write but a page a day, at the same rate, I should, in ten years, write nine volumes in folio, of an ordinary size and print." Boswell. "Such as Carte's History?" Johnson. "Yes, Sir. When a man writes from his own mind, he writes very rapidly. The greatest part of a writer's time is spent in reading, in order to write; a man will turn over half a library to make one book."

Friday, April 7, I dined with him at a Tavern, with a numerous company. One of the company suggested an internal objection to the antiquity of the poetry said to be Ossian's, that we do not find the wolf in it, which must have been the case had it been of that age.

The mention of the wolf had led Johnson to think of other wild beasts; and while Sir Joshua Reynolds and Mr. Langton were carrying on a dialogue about some-

thing which engaged them earnestly, he, in the midst
of it, broke out, "Pennant tells of Bears.—" [what he
added, I have forgotten.] They went on, which he being
dull of hearing, did not perceive, or, if he did, was not
willing to break off his talk; so he continued to vocifer-
ate his remarks, and *Bear* ("like a word in a catch"
as Beauclerk said,) was repeatedly heard at intervals,
which coming from him who, by those who did not
know him, had been so often assimilated to that fero-
cious animal, while we who were sitting around could
hardly stifle laughter, produced a very ludicrous effect.
Silence having ensued, he proceeded: "We are told,
that the black bear is innocent; but I should not like to
trust myself with him." Mr. Gibbon muttered, in a low
tone of voice, "I should not like to trust myself with
you." This piece of sarcastick pleasantry was a prudent
resolution, if applied to a competition of abilities.

Patriotism having become one of our topicks, Johnson
suddenly uttered, in a strong determined tone, an apophthegm, at which many will start: "Patriotism is the last
refuge of a scoundrel." But let it be considered, that he
did not mean a real and generous love of our country,
but that pretended patriotism which so many, in all
ages and countries, have made a cloak for self interest.

On Friday, April 14, being Good-Friday, I repaired
to him in the morning, according to my usual custom on
that day, and breakfasted with him. I observed that he
fasted so very strictly, that he did not even taste bread,
and took no milk with his tea; I suppose because it is a
kind of animal food.

He was pleased to say, "If you come to settle here,
we will have one day in the week on which we will
meet by ourselves. That is the happiest conversation
where there is no competition, no vanity, but a calm
quiet interchange of sentiments." In his private register

this evening is thus marked, "Boswell sat with me till night; we had some serious talk." It also appears from the same record, that after I left him he was occupied in religious duties, in "giving Francis, his servant, some directions for preparation to communicate; in reviewing his life, and resolving on better conduct." The humility and piety which he discovers on such occasions, is truly edifying. No saint, however, in the course of his religious warfare, was more sensible of the unhappy failure of pious resolves, than Johnson. He said one day, talking to an acquaintance on this subject, "Sir, Hell is paved with good intentions."

On Tuesday, April 11, he and I were engaged to go with Sir Joshua Reynolds to dine with Mr. Cambridge, at his beautiful villa on the banks of the Thames, near Twickenham. Dr. Johnson's tardiness was such, that Sir Joshua, who had an appointment at Richmond, early in the day, was obliged to go by himself on horseback, leaving his coach to Johnson and me. Johnson was in such good spirits, that every thing seemed to please him as we drove along.

Our conversation turned on a variety of subjects. He thought portrait-painting an improper employment for a woman. "Publick practice of any art, (he observed,) and staring in men's faces, is very indelicate in a female." I happened to start a question, whether when a man knows that some of his intimate friends are invited to the house of another friend, with whom they are all equally intimate, he may join them without an invitation. JOHNSON. "No, Sir; he is not to go when he is not invited. They may be invited on purpose to abuse him" (smiling).

As a curious instance how little a man knows, or wishes to know his own character in the world, or, rather as a convincing proof that Johnson's roughness

was only external, and did not proceed from his heart,
I insert the following dialogue. JOHNSON. "It is wonderful, Sir, how rare a quality good humour is in life. We
meet with very few good humoured men." I mentioned
four of our friends, none of whom he would allow to be
good humoured. One was *acid,* another was *muddy,*
and to the others he had objections which have escaped
me. Then, shaking his head and stretching himself at
ease in the coach, and smiling with much complacency,
he turned to me and said, "I look upon *myself* as a good
humoured fellow." The epithet *fellow,* applied to the
great Lexicographer, the stately Moralist, the Masterly
Critick, as if he had been *Sam* Johnson, a mere pleasant
companion, was highly diverting; and this light notion
of himself struck me with wonder. I answered, also
smiling, "No, no, Sir; that will *not* do. You are good
natured, but not good humoured: you are irascible. You
have not patience with folly and absurdity. I believe you
would pardon them, if there were time to deprecate
your vengeance; but punishment follows so quick after
sentence, that they cannot escape."

He defended his remark upon the general insufficiency
of education in Scotland; and confirmed to me the authenticity of his witty saying on the learning of the Scotch,—
"Their learning is like bread in a besieged town: every
man gets a little, but no man gets a full meal." "There is
(said he,) in Scotland a diffusion of learning, a certain
portion of it widely and thinly spread. A merchant has
as much learning as one of their clergy."

No sooner had we made our bow to Mr. Cambridge,
in his library, than Johnson ran eagerly to one side of the
room intent on poring over the backs of the books. Sir
Joshua observed, (aside,) "He runs to the books as I do
to the pictures: but I have the advantage. I can see
much more of the pictures than he can of the books."

Mr. Cambridge, upon this, politely said, "Dr. Johnson, I am going with your pardon, to accuse myself, for I have the same custom which I perceive you have. But it seems odd that one should have such a desire to look at the backs of books." Johnson, ever ready for contest, instantly started from his reverie, wheeled about and answered, "Sir, the reason is very plain. Knowledge is of two kinds. We know a subject ourselves, or we know where we can find information upon it. When we enquire into any subject, the first thing we have to do is to know what books have treated of it. This leads us to look at catalogues, and the backs of books in libraries." Sir Joshua observed to me the extraordinary promptitude with which Johnson flew upon an argument. "Yes, (said I,) he has no formal preparation, no flourishing with his sword; he is through your body in an instant."

"The Beggar's Opera," and the common question, whether it was pernicious in its effects, having been introduced;—JOHNSON. "As to this matter, which has been very much contested, I myself am of opinion, that more influence has been ascribed to 'The Beggar's Opera,' than it in reality ever had; for I do not believe that any man was ever made a rogue by being present at its representation. At the same time I do not deny that it may have some influence, by making the character of a rogue familiar, and in some degree pleasing." Then collecting himself, as it were, to give a heavy stroke: "There is in it such a *labefactation* of all principles as may be injurious to morality."

On Saturday, May 13, I breakfasted with him by invitation, accompanied by Mr. Andrew Crosbie, a Scotch Advocate, whom he had seen at Edinburgh, and the Hon. Colonel (now General) Edward Stopford, brother to Lord Courtown, who was desirous of being introduced to him. His tea and rolls and butter, and whole breakfast apparatus were all in such decorum, and his behaviour was so courteous, that Colonel Stopford was quite surprized, and wondered at his having heard so much said of Johnson's slovenliness and roughness.

It being asked whether it was reasonable for a man to be angry at another whom a woman had preferred to him?—JOHNSON. "I do not see, Sir, that it is reasonable for a man to be angry at another, whom a woman has preferred to him: but angry he is, no doubt; and he is loath to be angry at himself."

Here let me not forget a curious anecdote, as related to me by Mr. Beauclerk, which I shall endeavour to exhibit as well as I can in that gentleman's lively manner; and in justice to him it is proper to add, that Dr. Johnson told me I might rely both on the correctness of his memory, and the fidelity of his narrative. "When Madame de Boufflers was first in England, (said Beauclerk,) she was desirous to see Johnson. I accordingly went with her to his chambers in the Temple, where she was entertained with his conversation for some time. When our visit was over, she and I left him, and were got into Inner Temple-lane when all at once I heard a noise like thunder. This was occasioned by Johnson, who it seems, upon a little recollection, had taken it into his head that he ought to have done the honours of his literary residence to a foreign lady of quality, and eager to show himself a man of gallantry, was hurrying down the stair-case in violent agitation. He overtook us before we reached the Temple-gate, and brushing in between me and Madame de Boufflers, seized her hand, and conducted her to her coach. His dress was a rusty brown morning suit, a pair of old shoes by way of slippers, a little shrivelled wig sticking on the top of his head, and the sleeves of his shirt and the knees of his breeches hanging loose. A considerable crowd of people gathered round, and were not a little struck by this singular appearance."

In the course of this year Dr. Burney informs me that, "he very frequently met Dr. Johnson at Mr. Thrale's, at Streatham, where fire and candles lasted, and much longer than the patience of the servants subsisted."

A few of Johnson's sayings, which that gentleman recollects, shall here be inserted.

"I never take a nap after dinner but when I have had a bad night, and then the nap takes me."

"The writer of an epitaph should not be considered as saying nothing but what is strictly true. Allowance must be made for some degree of exaggerated praise. In lapidary inscriptions a man is not upon oath."

"There is now less flogging in our great schools than formerly, but then less is learned there; so that what the boys get at one end they lose at the other."

"After having talked slightingly of musick, he was observed to listen very attentively while Miss Thrale played on the harpsichord, and with eagerness he called to her, 'Why don't you dash away like Burney?' Dr. Burney upon this said to him, 'I believe, Sir, we shall make a musician of you at last.' Johnson with candid complacency replied, 'Sir, I shall be glad to have a new sense given to me.'"

"He had come down one morning to the breakfast-room, and been a considerable time by himself before any body appeared. When on a subsequent day he was twitted by Mrs. Thrale for being very late, which he generally was, he defended himself by alluding to the extraordinary morning, when he had been too early. 'Madam, I do not like to come down to *vacuity*.'"

"Dr. Burney having remarked that Mr. Garrick was

beginning to look old, he said, 'Why, Sir, you are not to wonder at that; no man's face has had more wear and tear.'"

1776. Having arrived in London late on Friday, the 15th of March, I hastened next morning to wait on Dr. Johnson, at his house; but found he was removed from Johnson's-court, No. 7, to Bolt-court, No. 8, still keeping to his favourite Fleet-street. My reflection at the time upon this change as marked in my Journal, is as follows: "I felt a foolish regret that he had left a court which bore his name; but it was not foolish to be affected with some tenderness of regard for a place in which I had seen him a great deal, from whence I had often issued a better and a happier man than when I went in, and which had often appeared to my imagination while I trod its pavement, in the solemn darkness of the night, to be sacred to wisdom and piety." Being informed that he was at Mr. Thrale's in the Borough, I hastened thither, and found Mrs. Thrale and him at breakfast. I was kindly welcomed. In a moment he was in a full glow of conversation, and I felt myself elevated as if brought into another state of being. Mrs. Thrale and I looked to each other while he talked, and our looks expressed our congenial admiration and affection for him. I shall ever recollect this scene with great pleasure. I exclaimed to her, "I am now intellectually, *Hermippus redivivus,* I am quite restored by him, by transfusion of mind." "There are many (she replied) who admire and respect Mr. Johnson; but you and I *love* him."

He seemed very happy in the near prospect of going to Italy with Mr. and Mrs. Thrale. "But, (said he,) before leaving England I am to take a jaunt to Oxford,

Birmingham, my native city Lichfield, and my old friend, Dr. Taylor's, at Ashbourne, in Derbyshire. I shall go in a few days, and you, Boswell, shall go with me." I was ready to accompany him; being willing even to leave London to have the pleasure of his conversation.

We got into a boat to cross over to Black-friars; and as we moved along the Thames, I talked to him of a little volume, which, altogether unknown to him, was advertised to be published in a few days, under the title of "*Johnsoniana, or Bon-Mots of Dr. Johnson.*" JOHNSON. "Sir, it is a mighty impudent thing." BOSWELL. "Pray, Sir, could you have no redress if you were to prosecute a publisher for bringing out, under your name, what you never said, and ascribing to you dull stupid nonsense, or making you swear profanely, as many ignorant relaters of your *bon-mots* do?" JOHNSON. "No, Sir; there will always be some truth mixed with the falsehood, and how can it be ascertained how much is true and how much is false? Besides, Sir, what damages would a jury give me for having been represented as swearing?" BOSWELL. "I think, Sir, you should at least disavow such a publication, because the world and posterity might with much plausible foundation say, 'Here is a volume which was publickly advertised and came out in Dr. Johnson's own time, and, by his silence, was admitted by him to be genuine.'" JOHNSON. "I shall give myself no trouble about the matter."

We landed at the Temple-stairs, where we parted.

I found him in the evening in Mrs. Williams's room. We talked of religious orders. He said, "It is as unreasonable for a man to go into a Carthusian convent for fear of being immoral, as for a man to cut off his hands for fear he should steal. There is, indeed, great resolution in the immediate act of dismembering himself; but when that is once done, he has no longer any merit: for though it is out of his power to steal, yet he may all his life be a thief in his heart. So when a man has once become a Carthusian, he is obliged to continue so, whether he chooses it or not. Their silence, too, is absurd. We read in the Gospel of the apostles being sent to preach, but not to hold their tongues. All severity that does not tend to increase good, or prevent evil, is idle. I said to the Lady Abbess of a convent, 'Madam, you are here, not for the love of virtue, but the fear of vice.' She said, 'She should remember this as long as she lived.'" I thought it hard to give her this view of her situation, when she could not help it; and, indeed, I wondered at the whole of what he now said; because, both in his "Rambler" and "Idler," he treats religious austerities with much solemnity of respect.

Finding him still persevering in his abstinence from wine, I ventured to speak to him of it.—JOHNSON. "Sir, I have no objection to a man's drinking wine, if he can do it in moderation. I found myself apt to go to excess in it, and therefore, after having been for some time without it on account of illness, I thought it better not to return to it. Every man is to judge for himself, according to the effects which he experiences. One of the fathers tells us, he found fasting made him so peevish that he did not practise it."

Though he often enlarged upon the evil of intoxication, he was by no means harsh and unforgiving to those who indulged in occasional excess in wine. One of his friends, I well remember, came to sup at a tavern with him and some other gentlemen, and too plainly discovered that he had drunk too much at dinner. When one who loved mischief, thinking to produce a severe censure, asked Johnson, a few days afterwards, "Well, Sir, what did your friend say to you, as an apology for being in such a situation?" Johnson answered, "Sir, he said all that a man *should* say: he said he was sorry for it."

On Tuesday, March 19, which was fixed for our proposed jaunt, we met in the morning at the Somerset coffee-house in the Strand, where we were taken up by the Oxford coach. He was accompanied by Mr. Gwyn, the architect; and a gentleman of Merton College, whom he did not know, had the fourth seat. We soon got into conversation; for it was very remarkable of Johnson, that the presence of a stranger had no restraint upon his talk. I observed that Garrick, who was about to quit the stage, would soon have an easier life. JOHNSON. "I doubt that, Sir." BOSWELL. "Why, Sir, he will be Atlas with the burthen off his back." JOHNSON. "But I know not, Sir, if he will be so steady without his load. However, he should never play any more, but be entirely the gentleman, and not partly the player: he should no longer subject himself to be hissed by a mob, or to be insolently treated by performers, whom he used to rule with a high hand, and who would gladly retaliate." BOSWELL. "I think he should play once a year for the benefit of decayed actors, as it has been said he means to do." JOHNSON. "Alas, Sir! he will soon be a decayed actor himself."

Johnson expressed his disapprobation of ornamental architecture, such as magnificent columns supporting a portico, or expensive pilasters supporting merely their own capitals, "because it consumes labour disproportionate to its utility." For the same reason he satyrised statuary. "Painting (said he,) consumes labour not disproportionate to its effect; but a fellow will hack half a year at a block of marble to make something in stone that hardly resembles a man. The value of statuary is owing to its difficulty. You would not value the finest head cut upon a carrot."

Gwyn was a fine lively rattling fellow. Dr. Johnson kept him in subjection, but with a kindly authority. The spirit of the artist, however, rose against what he thought a Gothick attack, and he made a brisk defence. "What, Sir, you will allow no value to beauty in architecture or in statuary? Why should we allow it then in writing? Why do you take the trouble to give us so many fine allusions, and bright images, and elegant phrases? You might convey all your instruction without these ornaments." Johnson smiled with complacency; but said, "Why, Sir, all these ornaments are useful, because they obtain an easier reception for truth; but a building is not at all more convenient for being decorated with superfluous carved work."

Gwyn at last was lucky enough to make one reply to Dr. Johnson, which he allowed to be excellent. Johnson censured him for taking down a church which might have stood many years, and building a new one at a different place, for no other reason but that there might be a direct road to a new bridge; and his expression was, "You are taking a church out of the way, that the people may go in a straight line to the bridge."—"No, Sir, (said Gwyn,) I am putting the church *in* the way, that the people may not *go out of the way*." JOHNSON. (with a hearty loud laugh of approbation,) "Speak no more. Rest your colloquial fame upon this."

Upon our arrival at Oxford, Dr. Johnson and I went directly to University College, but were disappointed on finding that one of the fellows, his friend, Mr. Scott, who accompanied him from Newcastle to Edinburgh, was gone to the country. We put up at the Angel inn, and passed the evening by ourselves in easy and familiar conversation. Talking of constitutional melancholy, he observed, "A man so afflicted, Sir, must divert distressing thoughts, and not combat with them." BOSWELL.

"May not he think them down, Sir?" JOHNSON. "No, Sir. To attempt to *think them down* is madness. He should have a lamp constantly burning in his bed chamber during the night, and if wakefully disturbed, take a book, and read, and compose himself to rest. To have the management of the mind is a great art, and it may be attained in a considerable degree by experience and habitual exercise." BOSWELL. "Should not he provide amusements for himself? Would it not, for instance, be right for him to take a course of chymistry?" JOHNSON. "Let him take a course of chymistry, or a course of ropedancing, or a course of any thing to which he is inclined at the time. Let him contrive to have as many retreats for his mind as he can, as many things to which it can fly from itself. Burton's 'Anatomy of Melancholy' is a valuable work. It is, perhaps, overloaded with quotation. But there is a great spirit and great power in what Burton says, when he writes from his own mind."

We then went to Pembroke College, and waited on his old friend Dr. Adams, the master of it, whom I found to be a most polite, pleasing, communicative man.

Dr. Adams told us, that in some of the Colleges at Oxford, the fellows had excluded the students from social intercourse with them in the common room. JOHNSON. "They are in the right, Sir: there can be no real conversation, no fair exertion of mind amongst them, if the young men are by; for a man who has a character does not choose to stake it in their presence." BOSWELL. "But, Sir, may there not be very good conversation without a contest for superiority?" JOHNSON. "No animated conversation, Sir, for it cannot be but one or other will come off superiour. I do not mean that the victor must have the better of the argument, for he may take the weak side; but his superiority of parts and knowledge will necessarily appear; and he to whom he thus shews

himself superiour is lessened in the eyes of the young
men. You know it was said, '*Mallem cum Scaligero
errare quam cum Clavio recte sapere.*' In the same manner take Bentley's and Jason de Nores' Comments upon
Horace, you will admire Bentley more when wrong,
than Jason when right."

We walked with Dr. Adams into the master's garden,
and into the common room. JOHNSON. (after a reverie
of meditation,) "Ay! Here I used to play at draughts
with Phil. Jones and Fludyer. Jones loved beer, and did
not get very forward in the church. Fludyer turned out
a scoundrel, a Whig, and said he was ashamed of having
been bred at Oxford. He had a living at Putney, and got
under the eye of some retainers to the court at that time,
and so became a violent Whig: but he had been a scoundrel all along to be sure." BOSWELL. "Was he a scoundrel, Sir, in any other way than that of being a political
scoundrel? Did he cheat at draughts?" JOHNSON. "Sir, we
never played for *money*."

He then carried me to visit Dr. Bentham, Canon
of Christ-Church, and Divinity professor, with whose
learned and lively conversation we were much pleased.
He gave us an invitation to dinner, which Dr. Johnson
told me was a high honour. "Sir, it is a great thing to
dine with the Canons of Christ-Church."

I mentioned Sir Richard Steele having published his
"Christian Hero," with the avowed purpose of obliging
himself to lead a religious life; yet that his conduct was
by no means strictly suitable. JOHNSON. "Steele, I believe, practised the lighter vices."

I censured some ludicrous fantastick dialogues between two coach horses and other such stuff, which
Baretti had lately published. He joined with me, and
said, "Nothing odd will do long. 'Tristram Shandy' did
not last." I expressed a desire to be acquainted with a

lady who had been much talked of, and universally celebrated for extraordinary address and insinuation. JOHN-
SON. "Never believe extraordinary characters which you
hear of people. Depend upon it, Sir, they are exaggerated. You do not see one man shoot a great deal higher
than another." I mentioned Mr. Burke. JOHNSON. "Yes;
Burke *is* an extraordinary man. His stream of mind is
perpetual." And once, when Johnson was ill, and unable
to exert himself as much as usual without fatigue, Mr.
Burke having been mentioned, he said, "That fellow calls
forth all my powers. Were I to see Burke now it would kill
me." So much was he accustomed to consider conversation as a contest, and such was his notion of Burke as an
opponent.

Next morning, Thursday, March 21, we set out in a
post-chaise to pursue our ramble. It was a delightful
day, and we rode through Blenheim park. When I
looked at the magnificent bridge built by John Duke of
Marlborough, over a small rivulet, and recollected the
Epigram made upon it—

> The lofty arch his high ambition shows,
> The stream, an emblem of his bounty flows:

and saw that now, by the genius of Brown, a magnificent body of water was collected, I said, "They have
drowned the Epigram." I observed to him, while in the
midst of the noble scene around us, "You and I, Sir,
have, I think, seen together the extremes of what can
be seen in Britain—the wild rough island of Mull, and
Blenheim park."

We dined at an excellent inn at Chapel-house, where
he expatiated on the felicity of England in its taverns
and inns, and triumphed over the French for not having,
in any perfection, the tavern life. "There is no private
house, (said he,) in which people can enjoy themselves

so well, as at a capital tavern. Let there be ever so great
plenty of good things, ever so much grandeur, ever so
much elegance, ever so much desire that every body
should be easy; in the nature of things it cannot be:
there must always be some degree of care and anxiety.
The master of the house is anxious to entertain his
guests; the guests are anxious to be agreeable to him;
and no man, but a very impudent dog indeed, can as
freely command what is in another man's house, as if it
were his own. Whereas, at a tavern, there is a general
freedom from anxiety. You are sure you are welcome:
and the more noise you make, the more trouble you
give, the more good things you call for, the welcomer
you are. No servants will attend you with the alacrity
which waiters do, who are incited by the prospect of an
immediate reward in proportion as they please. No, Sir;
there is nothing which has yet been contrived by man,
by which so much happiness is produced as by a good
tavern or inn." [1] He then repeated, with great emotion,
Shenstone's lines:

> Whoe'er has travell'd life's dull round,
>   Where'er his stages may have been,
> May sigh to think he still has found
>   The warmest welcome at an inn.

---

[1] Sir John Hawkins has preserved very few *Memorabilia* of Johnson. There is, however, to be found in his bulky tome a very excellent one upon this subject. "In contradistinction to those, who, having a wife and children, prefer domestick enjoyments to those which
a tavern affords, I have heard him assert, *that a tavern chair was the
throne of human felicity.*—'As soon (said he) as I enter the door
of a tavern, I experience an oblivion of care, and a freedom from
solicitude: when I am seated, I find the master courteous, and the
servants obsequious to my call; anxious to know and ready to supply
my wants: wine there exhilarates my spirits, and prompts me to free
conversation and an interchange of discourse with those whom I most
love: I dogmatise and am contradicted, and in this conflict of opinion and sentiments I find delight.' "

In the afternoon, as we were driven rapidly along in the post-chaise, he said to me "Life has not many things better than this."

We stopped at Stratford-upon-Avon, and drank tea and coffee; and it pleased me to be with him upon the classick ground of Shakespeare's native place.

On Friday, March 22, having set out early from Henley, where we had lain the preceding night, we arrived at Birmingham about nine o'clock, and, after breakfast, went to call on his old school-fellow Mr. Hector. A very stupid maid, who opened the door, told us, that, "her master was gone out; he was gone to the country; she could not tell when he would return." In short, she gave us a miserable reception; and Johnson observed, "She would have behaved no better to people who wanted him in the way of his profession." He said to her, "My name is Johnson; tell him I called. Will you remember the name?" She answered with rustick simplicity, in the Warwickshire pronunciation, "I don't understand you, Sir."—"Blockhead, (said he,) I'll write." I never heard the word *blockhead* applied to a woman before, though I do not see why it should not, when there is evident occasion for it. He, however, made another attempt to make her understand him, and roared loud in her ear, "*Johnson,*" and then she catched the sound.

We next called on Mr. Lloyd, one of the people called Quakers. He too was not at home, but Mrs. Lloyd was, and received us courteously, and asked us to dinner. Johnson said to me, "After the uncertainty of all human things at Hector's, this invitation came very well." We walked about the town and he was pleased to see it increasing.

Dr. Johnson said to me in the morning, "You will see, Sir, at Mr. Hector's, his sister, Mrs. Careless, a clergyman's widow. She was the first woman with whom I was in love. It dropt out of my head imperceptibly; but she and I shall always have a kindness for each other." He laughed at the notion that a man can never be really in love but once, and considered it as a mere romantick fancy.

On our return from Mr. Bolton's, Mr. Hector took me to his house, where we found Johnson sitting placidly at tea, with his *first love;* who though now advanced in years, was a genteel woman, very agreeable and well bred.

Johnson lamented to Mr. Hector the state of one of their school-fellows, Mr. Charles Congreve, a clergyman, which he thus described: "He obtained, I believe, considerable preferment in Ireland, but now lives in London, quite as a valetudinarian, afraid to go into any house but his own. He takes a short airing in his post-chaise every day. He has an elderly woman, whom he calls cousin, who lives with him, and jogs his elbow, when his glass has stood too long empty, and encourages him in drinking, in which he is very willing to be encouraged; not that he gets drunk, for he is a very pious man, but he is always muddy. He confesses to one bottle of port every day, and he probably drinks more. He is quite unsocial; his conversation is quite monosyllabical; and when, at my last visit, I asked him what o'clock it was? that signal of my departure had so pleasing an effect on him, that he sprung up to look at his watch, like a greyhound bounding at a hare." When Johnson took leave of Mr. Hector, he said, "Don't grow like Congreve; nor let me grow like him, when you are near me."

When he again talked of Mrs. Careless tonight, he seemed to have had his affection revived; for he said, "If I had married her, it might have been as happy for me." BOSWELL. "Pray, Sir, do you not suppose that there are fifty women in the world, with any one of whom a man may be as happy, as with any one woman in particular?" JOHNSON. "Ay, Sir, fifty thousand." BOSWELL. "Then, Sir, you are not of opinion with some who imagine that certain men and certain women are made for each other; and that they cannot be happy if they miss their counterparts." JOHNSON. "To be sure not, Sir. I believe marriages would in general be as happy, and often more so, if they were all made by the Lord Chancellor, upon a due consideration of the characters and circumstances, without the parties having any choice in the matter."

I wished to have staid at Birmingham tonight, to have talked more with Mr. Hector; but my friend was impatient to reach his native city; so we drove on that stage in the dark, and were long pensive and silent. When we came within the focus of the Lichfield lamps, "Now (said he,) we are getting out of a state of death." We put up at the Three Crowns, not one of the great inns, but a good old fashioned one, which was kept by Mr. Wilkins, and was the very next house to that in which Johnson was born and brought up, and which was still his own property. We had a comfortable supper, and got into high spirits. I felt all my Toryism glow in this old capital of Staffordshire. I could have offered incense *genio loci;* and I indulged in libations of that ale, which Boniface, in "The Beaux Stratagem," recommends with such an eloquent jollity.

Next morning he introduced me to Mrs. Lucy Porter, his step-daughter. She was now an old maid, with much simplicity of manner. She had never been in London. Her brother, a Captain in the navy, had left her a fortune of ten thousand pounds; about a third of which she had laid out in building a stately house, and making a handsome garden, in an elevated situation in Lichfield. Johnson, when here by himself, used to live at her house.

She reverenced him, and he had a parental tenderness for her.

I saw here, for the first time, *oat ale;* and oat cakes, not hard as in Scotland, but soft like a Yorkshire cake, were served at breakfast. It was pleasant to me to find, that *"Oats,"* the *"food of horses,"* [1] were so much used as the *food of the people* in Dr. Johnson's own town. He expatiated in praise of Lichfield and its inhabitants, who, he said, were "the most sober, decent people in England, the genteelest in proportion to their wealth, and spoke the purest English." I doubted as to the last article of this eulogy: for they had several provincial sounds; as *there,* pronounced like *fear,* instead of like *fair; once,* pronounced *woonse,* instead of *wunse* or *wonse.* Johnson himself never got entirely free of those provincial accents. Garrick sometimes used to take him off, squeezing a lemon into a punch-bowl, with uncouth gesticulations, looking round the company, and calling out, "Who's for *poonsh?*"

Very little business appeared to be going forward in Lichfield. I found however two strange manufactures for so inland a place, sail-cloth and streamers for ships; and I observed them making some saddle-cloths, and dressing sheepskins: but upon the whole, the busy hand of industry seemed to be quite slackened. "Surely, Sir, (said I,) you are an idle set of people." "Sir, (said Johnson,) we are a city of philosophers, we work with our heads, and make the boobies of Birmingham work for us with their hands."

He told me, "Forty years ago, Sir, I was in love with an actress here, Mrs. Emmet, who acted Flora, in 'Hob in the Well.'" What merit this lady had as an actress, or

---

[1] In the Dictionary, Johnson had defined oats as "a grain which in England is generally given to horses, but in Scotland supports the people."

what was her figure, or her manner, I have not been informed; but, if we may believe Mr. Garrick, his old master's taste in theatrical merit was by no means refined; he was not an *elegans formarum spectator.* Garrick used to tell, that Johnson said of an actor, who played Sir Harry Wildair at Lichfield, "There is a courtly vivacity about the fellow;" when in fact, according to Garrick's account, "he was the most vulgar ruffian that ever went upon *boards.*"

A physician being mentioned who had lost his practice, because his whimsically changing his religion had made people distrustful of him, I maintained that this was unreasonable, as religion is unconnected with medical skill. JOHNSON. "Sir, it is not unreasonable; for when people see a man absurd in what they understand, they may conclude the same of him in what they do not understand. If a physician were to take to eating of horse-flesh, nobody would employ him; though one may eat horse-flesh, and be a very skilful physician. If a man were educated in an absurd religion, his continuing to profess it would not hurt him, though his changing to it would."

On Monday, March 25, we breakfasted at Mrs. Lucy Porter's. Johnson had sent an express to Dr. Taylor's, acquainting him of our being at Lichfield, and Taylor had returned an answer that his post-chaise should come for us this day. While we sat at breakfast, Dr. Johnson received a letter by the post, which seemed to agitate him very much. When he had read it, he exclaimed, "One of the most dreadful things that has happened in my time." The phrase *my time,* like the word *age,* is usually understood to refer to an event of a publick or general nature. I imagined something like an assassination of the King—like a gunpowder plot carried into execution—or like another fire of London. When asked,

"What is it, Sir?" he answered, "Mr. Thrale has lost his only son!" He said, "This is a total extinction to their family, as much as if they were sold into captivity." Upon my mentioning that Mr. Thrale had daughters, who might inherit his wealth;—"Daughters, (said Johnson, warmly,) he'll no more value his daughters than—" I was going to speak.—"Sir, (said he,) don't you know how you yourself think? Sir, he wishes to propagate his name!" In short, I saw male succession strong in his mind, even where there was no name, no family of any long standing. I said, it was lucky he was not present when this misfortune happened. JOHNSON. "It is lucky for *me*. People in distress never think that you feel enough." BOSWELL. "And, Sir, they will have the hope of seeing you, which will be a relief in the mean time; and when you get to them, the pain will be so far abated, that they will be capable of being consoled by you, which, in the first violence of it, I believe, would not be the case." JOHNSON. "No, Sir; violent pain of mind, like violent pain of body, *must* be severely felt." BOSWELL. "I own, Sir, I have not so much feeling for the distress of others, as some people have, or pretend to have; but I know this, that I would do all in my power to relieve them." JOHNSON. "Sir, it is affectation to pretend to feel the distress of others, as much as they do themselves. It is equally so, as if one should pretend to feel as much pain while a friend's leg is cutting off, as he does. No, Sir; you have expressed the rational and just nature of sympathy. I would have gone to the extremity of the earth to have preserved this boy."

He was soon quite calm. The letter was from Mr. Thrale's clerk, and concluded, "I need not say how much they wish to see you in London." He said, "We shall hasten back from Taylor's."

After dinner Dr. Johnson wrote a letter to Mrs.

Thrale, on the death of her son. I said it would be very distressing to Thrale, but she would soon forget it, as she had so many things to think of. JOHNSON. "No, Sir, Thrale will forget it first. *She* has many things that she *may* think of. *He* has many things that he *must* think of." This was a very just remark upon the different effects of those light pursuits which occupy a vacant and easy mind, and those serious engagements which arrest attention, and keep us from brooding over grief.

He observed of Lord Bute, "it was said of Augustus, that it would have been better for Rome that he had never been born, or had never died. So it would have been better for this nation if Lord Bute had never been minister, or had never resigned."

In the evening we went to the Town-hall, which was converted into a temporary theatre, and saw "Theodosius," with "The Stratford Jubilee." I was happy to see Dr. Johnson sitting in a conspicuous part of the pit, and receiving affectionate homage from all his acquaintance. We were quite gay and merry. I afterwards mentioned to him that I condemned myself for being so, when poor Mr. and Mrs. Thrale were in such distress. JOHNSON. "You are wrong, Sir; twenty years hence Mr. and Mrs. Thrale will not suffer much pain from the death of their son. Now, Sir, you are to consider, that distance of place, as well as distance of time, operates upon the human feelings. I would not have you be gay in the presence of the distressed, because it would shock them; but you may be gay at a distance. Pain for the loss of a friend, or of a relation whom we love, is occasioned by the want which we feel. In time the vacuity is filled with something else; or sometimes the vacuity closes up of itself."

Here I shall record some fragments of my friend's conversation during this jaunt.

"Marriage, Sir, is much more necessary to a man than to a woman: for he is much less able to supply himself with domestick comforts. You will recollect my saying to some ladies the other day, that I had often wondered why young women should marry, as they have so much more freedom, and so much more attention paid to them while unmarried, than when married. I indeed did not mention the *strong* reason for their marrying—the *mechanical* reason." BOSWELL. "Why that *is* a strong one. But does not imagination make it much more important than it is in reality? Is it not, to a certain degree, a delusion in us as well as in women?" JOHNSON. "Why yes, Sir; but it is a delusion that is always beginning again." BOSWELL. "I don't know but there is upon the whole more misery than happiness produced by that passion." JOHNSON. "I don't think so, Sir."

"Never speak of a man in his own presence. It is always indelicate, and may be offensive."

"Questioning is not the mode of the conversation among gentlemen. It is assuming a superiority, and it is particularly wrong to question a man concerning himself. There may be parts of his former life which he may not wish to be made known to other persons, or even brought to his own recollection."

"A man should be careful never to tell tales of himself to his own disadvantage. People may be amused and laugh at the time, but they will be remembered and brought out against him upon some subsequent occasion."

On Tuesday, March 26, there came for us an equipage properly suited to a wealthy well-beneficed clergyman: Dr. Taylor's large, roomy post-chaise, drawn by four stout plump horses, and driven by two steady jolly postillions, which conveyed us to Ashbourne.

Dr. Johnson and Dr. Taylor met with great cordiality;

and Johnson soon gave him the same sad account of their school-fellow, Congreve, that he had given to Mr. Hector; adding a remark of such moment to the rational conduct of a man in the decline of life, that deserves to be imprinted upon every mind: "There is nothing against which an old man should be so much upon his guard as putting himself to nurse."

Dr. Taylor commended a physician who was known to him and Dr. Johnson, and said, "I fight many battles for him, as many people in the country dislike him." JOHNSON. "But you should consider, Sir, that by every one of your victories he is a loser; for, every man of whom you get the better, will be very angry, and resolve not to employ him; whereas if people get the better of you in argument about him, they'll think, "We'll send for Dr. ****** nevertheless." This was an observation deep and sure in human nature.

Next day, as Dr. Johnson had acquainted Dr. Taylor of the reason for his returning speedily to London, it was resolved that we should set out after dinner. A few of Dr. Taylor's neighbours were his guests that day.

Dr. Johnson talked with approbation of one who had attained to the state of the philosophical wise man, that is, to have no want of any thing. "Then, Sir, (said I,) the savage is a wise man." "Sir, (said he,) I do not mean simply being without,—but not having a want." I maintained, against this proposition, that it was better to have fine clothes, for instance, than not to feel the want of them. JOHNSON. "No, Sir; fine clothes are good only as they supply the want of other means of procuring respect. Was Charles the Twelfth, think you, less respected for his coarse blue coat and black stock? And you find the King of Prussia dresses plain, because the dignity of his character is sufficient." I here brought myself into a scrape, for I heedlessly said, "Would not *you*, Sir, be the better for velvet embroidery?" JOHNSON. "Sir, you put an end to all argument when you introduce your opponent himself. Have you no better manners? There is *your want*."

On Thursday, March 28, we pursued our journey. He said, "It is commonly a weak man, who marries for love." We then talked of marrying women of fortune; and I mentioned a common remark, that a man may be, upon the whole, richer by marrying a woman with a very small portion, because a woman of fortune will be proportionately expensive; whereas a woman who brings none will be very moderate in expenses. JOHNSON. "Depend upon it, Sir, this is not true. A woman of fortune being used to the handling of money, spends it judiciously: but a woman who gets the command of money for the first time upon her marriage, has such a gust in spending it, that she throws it away with great profusion."

At Leicester we read in the newspaper that Dr. James was dead. I thought that the death of an old school-fellow, and one with whom he had lived a good deal in London, would have affected my fellow-traveller much: but he only said, "Ah! poor Jamy." Afterwards, however, when we were in the chaise, he said, with more tenderness, "Since I set out on this jaunt, I have lost an old friend and a young one;—Dr. James, and poor Harry," (meaning Mr. Thrale's son.)

Having lain at St. Alban's, on Thursday, March 28, we breakfasted the next morning at Barnet. I expressed to him a weakness of mind which I could not help; an uneasy apprehension that my wife and children, who were at a great distance from me, might, perhaps, be ill. "Sir, (said he,) consider how foolish you would think it in *them* to be apprehensive that *you* are ill." This sudden turn relieved me for the moment; but I afterwards perceived it to be an ingenious fallacy. I might, to be sure, be satisfied that they had no reason to be apprehensive about me, because I *knew* that I myself was well: but we might have a mutual anxiety, without the charge of folly; because each was, in some degree, uncertain as to the condition of the other.

I enjoyed the luxury of our approach to London, that metropolis which we both loved so much, for the high and varied intellectual pleasure which it furnishes. I experienced immediate happiness while whirled along with such a companion, and said to him, "Sir, you observed one day at General Oglethorpe's, that a man is never happy for the present, but when he is drunk. Will you not add,—or when driving rapidly in a post-chaise?" JOHNSON. "No, Sir, you are driving rapidly *from* something, or *to* something."

We stopped at Messieurs Dillys, booksellers in the Poultry; from whence he hurried away, in a hackney coach, to Mr. Thrale's in the Borough. I called at his house in the evening, having promised to acquaint Mrs Williams of his safe return; when, to my surprize, I found him sitting with her at tea, and, as I thought, not in a very good humour: for, it seems, when he had got to Mr. Thrale's, he found the coach was at the door waiting to carry Mrs. and Miss Thrale, and Signor Baretti, their Italian master, to Bath. This was not showing the attention which might have been expected to the "Guide, Philosopher, and Friend;" the *Imlac* who had hastened from the country to console a distressed mother, who he understood was very anxious for his return. They had, I found, without ceremony, proceeded on their intended journey. I was glad to understand from him that it was still resolved that his tour to Italy with Mr. and Mrs. Thrale should take place, of which he had entertained some doubt, on account of the loss which

they had suffered; and his doubts afterwards appeared
to be well-founded. He observed, indeed very justly,
that "their loss was an additional reason for their going
abroad; and if it had not been fixed that he should have
been one of the party, he would force them out; but he
would not advise them unless his advice was asked, lest
they might suspect that he recommended what he
wished on his own account."

On Wednesday, April 3, in the morning I found him
very busy putting his books in order, and as they were
generally very old ones, clouds of dust were flying
around him. He had on a pair of large gloves such as
hedgers use. His present appearance put me in mind of
my uncle, Dr. Boswell's description of him, "A robust
genius, born to grapple with whole libraries."

We agreed to dine today at the Mitre tavern. I
brought with me Mr. Murray, Solicitor-General of Scotland, now one of the Judges of the Court of Session,
with the title of Lord Henderland. I mentioned Mr.
Solicitor's relation, Lord Charles Hay, with whom I
knew Dr. Johnson had been acquainted. JOHNSON. "I
wrote something for Lord Charles; and I thought he had
nothing to fear from a court-martial. I suffered a great
loss when he died; he was a mighty pleasing man in
conversation, and a reading man. The character of a
soldier is high. They who stand forth the foremost in
danger, for the community, have the respect of mankind. An officer is much more respected than any other
man who has as little money. In a commercial country,
money will always purchase respect. But you find, an
officer, who has, properly speaking, no money, is every
where well received and treated with attention. The
character of a soldier always stands him in stead." Bos-
WELL. "Yet, Sir, I think that common soldiers are worse
thought of than other men in the same rank in life; such

as labourers." JOHNSON. "Why, Sir, a common soldier is usually a very gross man, and any quality which procures respect may be overwhelmed by grossness. A man of learning may be so vicious or so ridiculous that you cannot respect him. A common soldier too, generally eats more than he can pay for. But when a common soldier is civil in his quarters, his red coat procures him a degree of respect." The peculiar respect paid to the military character in France was mentioned. BOSWELL. "I should think that where military men were so numerous, they would be less valued as not being rare." JOHNSON. "Nay, Sir, wherever a particular character or profession is high in the estimation of a people, those who are of it will be valued above other men. We value an Englishman high in this country, and yet Englishmen are not rare in it."

MURRAY. "It seems to me that we are not angry at a man for controverting an opinion which we believe and value; we rather pity him." JOHNSON. "Why, Sir, to be sure when you wish a man to have that belief which you think is of infinite advantage, you wish well to him; but your primary consideration is your own quiet. If a madman were to come into this room with a stick in his hand, no doubt we should pity the state of his mind; but our primary consideration would be to take care of ourselves. We should knock him down first, and pity him afterwards. No, Sir, every man will dispute with great good humour upon a subject in which he is not interested. I will dispute very calmly upon the probability of another man's son being hanged; but if a man zealously enforces the probability that my own son will be hanged, I shall certainly not be in a very good humour with him." I added this illustration, "If a man endeavours to convince me that my wife, whom I love very much, and in whom I place great confidence, is a disagreeable woman, and is even unfaithful to me, I shall be very angry, for he is putting me in fear of being unhappy." MURRAY. "But, Sir, truth will always bear an examination." JOHNSON. "Yes, Sir, but it is painful to be forced to defend it. Consider, Sir, how should you like, though conscious of your innocence, to be tried before a jury for a capital crime, once a week."

On Friday, April 5, being Good Friday, after having attended the morning service at St. Clement's church, I walked home with Johnson. We talked of the Roman Catholick religion. JOHNSON. "In the barbarous ages, Sir, priests and people were equally deceived; but afterwards there were gross corruptions introduced by the clergy, such as indulgences to priests to have concubines, and the worship of images, not, indeed, inculcated, but knowingly permitted." He strongly censured the licensed stews at Rome. BOSWELL. "So then, Sir, you would allow of no irregular intercourse whatever between the sexes?" JOHNSON. "To be sure I would not, Sir. I would punish it much more than it is done, and so restrain it. In all countries there has been fornication, as in all countries there has been theft; but there may be more or less of the one, as well as of the other, in proportion to the force of law. All men will naturally commit fornication, as all men will naturally steal. And, Sir, it is very absurd to argue, as has been often done, that prostitutes are necessary to prevent the violent effects of appetite from violating the decent order of life; nay, should be permitted in order to preserve the chastity of our wives and daughters. Depend upon it, severe laws, steadily enforced, would be sufficient against those evils, and would promote marriage."

I stated to him this case:—"Suppose a man has a daughter, who he knows has been seduced, but her misfortune is concealed from the world? should he keep her in his house? Would he not, by doing so, be accessary to imposition? And, perhaps, a worthy, unsuspecting man might come and marry this woman, unless the father inform him of the truth." JOHNSON. "Sir, he is accessary to no imposition. His daughter is in his house; and if a man courts her, he takes his chance. If a friend, or, indeed, if any man asks his opinion whether he should marry her, he ought to advise him against it, without telling why, because his real opinion is then required. Or, if he has other daughters who know of her frailty, he ought not to keep her in his house. You are to consider the state of life is this; we are to judge of one another's characters as well as we can; and a man is not bound in honesty or honour, to tell us the faults of his daughter or of himself. A man who has debauched his friend's daughter is not obliged to say to every body—Take care of me; don't let me into your house without suspicion. I once debauched a friend's daughter. I may debauch yours."

Mr. Thrale called upon him, and appeared to bear the loss of his son with a manly composure. There was no affectation about him; and he talked, as usual, upon indifferent subjects. He seemed to me to hesitate as to the intended Italian tour, on which I flattered myself, he and Mrs. Thrale and Dr. Johnson were soon to set out; and, therefore, I pressed it as much as I could. I mentioned that Mr. Beauclerk had said, that Baretti, whom they were to carry with them, would keep them so long in the little towns of his own district, that they would not have time to see Rome. I mentioned this to put them on their guard. JOHNSON. "Sir, we do not thank Mr. Beauclerk for supposing that we are to be directed by Baretti."

I mentioned a new gaming-club, of which Mr. Beauclerk had given me an account, where the members

played to a desperate extent. JOHNSON. "Depend upon
it, Sir, this is mere talk. *Who* is ruined by gaming? You
will not find six instances in an age. There is a strange
rout made about deep play: whereas you have many
more people ruined by adventurous trade, and yet we
do not hear such an outcry against it." THRALE. "There
may be few people absolutely ruined by deep play; but
very many are much hurt in their circumstances by it."
JOHNSON. "Yes, Sir, and so are very many by other kinds
of expence." I had heard him talk once before in the
same manner; and at Oxford he said, "he wished he had
learned to play at cards." The truth, however, is, that he
loved to display his ingenuity in argument; and therefore would sometimes in conversation maintain opinions
which he was sensible were wrong, but in supporting
which, his reasoning and wit would be most conspicuous.
He would begin thus: "Why, Sir, as to the good or evil
of card-playing—" "Now, (said Garrick,) he is thinking
which side he shall take." He appeared to have a pleasure in contradiction, especially when any opinion whatever was delivered with an air of confidence; so that
there was hardly any topick, if not one of the great
truths of Religion and Morality, that he might not have
been incited to argue, either for or against. Lord Elibank
had the highest admiration of his powers. He once observed to me, "Whatever opinion Johnson maintains, I
will not say that he convinces me; but he never fails to
shew me, that he has good reasons for it." I have heard
Johnson pay his Lordship this high compliment:

"I never was in Lord Elibank's company without
learning something."

On Sunday, April 7, Easter-day, after having been at
St. Paul's cathedral, I came to Dr. Johnson, according to
my usual custom. It seemed to me that there was always
something peculiarly mild and placid in his manner

upon this holy festival, the commemoration of the most joyful event in the history of our world, the resurrection of our LORD and SAVIOUR, who, having triumphed over death and the grave, proclaimed immortality to mankind.

I repeated to him an argument of a lady of my acquaintance who maintained, that her husband's having been guilty of numberless infidelities, released her from conjugal obligations, because they were reciprocal. JOHNSON. "This is miserable stuff, Sir. To the contract of marriage, besides the man and wife, there is a third party—Society; and if it be considered as a vow—GOD: and, therefore, it cannot be dissolved by their consent alone. Laws are not made for particular cases, but for men in general. A woman may be unhappy with her husband; but she cannot be freed from him without the approbation of the civil and ecclesiastical power. A man may be unhappy, because he is not so rich as another; but he is not to seize upon another's property with his own hand." BOSWELL. "But, Sir, this lady does not want that the contract should be dissolved; she only argues that she may indulge herself in gallantries with equal freedom as her husband does, provided she takes care not to introduce a spurious issue into his family. You know, Sir, what Macrobius has told of Julia." JOHNSON. "This lady of yours, Sir, I think, is very fit for a brothel."

Mr. Macbean, authour of the "Dictionary of Ancient Geography," came in. He mentioned that he had been forty years absent from Scotland. "Ah, Boswell! (said Johnson, smiling,) what would you give to be forty years from Scotland?" I said, "I should not like to be so long absent from the seat of my ancestors." This gentleman, Mrs. Williams, and Mr. Levett dined with us.

Dr. Johnson made a remark, which both Mr. Macbean and I thought new. It was this: that "the law against usury is for the protection of creditors as well as debtors; for if there were no such check, people would be apt, from the temptation of great interest, to lend to desperate persons, by whom they would lose their money. Accordingly there are instances of ladies being ruined, by having injudiciously sunk their fortunes for high annuities, which, after a few years, ceased to be paid, in consequence of the ruined circumstances of the borrower."

After coffee, we went to afternoon service in St. Clement's church. Observing some beggars in the street as we walked along, I said to him, I suppose there was no civilised country in the world, where the misery of want in the lowest classes of the people was prevented. JOHNSON. "I believe, Sir, there is not; but it is better that some should be unhappy, than that none should be happy, which would be the case in a general state of equality."

On Wednesday, April 10, I dined with him at Mr. Thrale's, where were Mr. Murphy and some other company. Before dinner, Dr. Johnson and I passed some time by ourselves. I was sorry to find it was now resolved that the proposed journey to Italy should not take place this year. He said, "I am disappointed, to be sure; but it is not a great disappointment." I wondered to see him bear, with a philosophical calmness, what would have made most people peevish and fretful. I perceived, however, that he had so warmly cherished the hope of enjoying classical scenes, that he could not easily part with the scheme; for he said, "I shall probably contrive to get to Italy some other way. But I won't mention it to Mr. and Mrs. Thrale, as it might vex them." I suggested, that going to Italy might have done Mr. and Mrs. Thrale good. JOHNSON. "I rather believe not, Sir. While grief is fresh, every attempt to divert only irritates. You must wait till grief be *digested,* and then amusement will dissipate the remains of it."

I said, I disliked the custom which some people had of bringing their children into company, because it in a manner forced us to pay foolish compliments to please their parents. JOHNSON. "You are right, Sir. We may be excused for not caring much about other people's children, for there are many who care very little about their own children. It may be observed, that men, who from being engaged in business, or from their course of life in whatever way, seldom see their children, do not care much about them. I myself should not have had much fondness for a child of my own." MRS. THRALE. "Nay, Sir, how can you talk so?" JOHNSON. "At least, I never wished to have a child."

On Thursday, April 11, I dined with him at General Paoli's, in whose house I now resided, and where I had ever afterwards the honour of being entertained with the kindest attention as his constant guest, while I was in London, till I had a house of my own there. I mentioned my having that morning introduced to Mr. Garrick, Count Neni, a Flemish Nobleman of great rank and fortune, to whom Garrick talked of Abel Drugger as a *small part;* and related, with pleasant vanity, that a Frenchman, who had seen him in one of his low characters, exclaimed, *"Comment! je ne le crois pas. Ce n'est pas Monsieur Garrick, ce Grand Homme!"* Garrick added, with an appearance of grave recollection, "If I were to begin life again, I think I should not play those low characters." Upon which I observed, "Sir, you would be in the wrong; for your great excellence is your variety of playing, your representing so well, characters so very different." JOHNSON. "Garrick, Sir, was not in earnest in what he said; for, to be sure, his peculiar excellence is his variety; and, perhaps, there is not any one character which has not been as well acted by somebody else, as he could do it." Boswell. "Why then, Sir, did he talk so?" Johnson. "Why, Sir, to make you answer as you did." Boswell. "I don't know, Sir; he seemed to dip deep into his mind for the reflection." Johnson. "He had not far to dip, Sir; he had said the same thing, probably, twenty times before."

Of a nobleman raised at a very early period to high office, he said, "His parts, Sir, are pretty well for a Lord; but would not be distinguished in a man who had nothing else but his parts."

A journey to Italy was still in his thoughts. He said, "A man who has not been in Italy, is always conscious of an inferiority, from his not having seen what it is expected a man should see. The grand object of travelling is to see the shores of the Mediterranean. On those shores were the four great Empires of the world; the Assyrian, the Persian, the Grecian, and the Roman.— All our religion, almost all our law, almost all our arts, almost all that sets us above savages, has come to us from the shores of the Mediterranean." The General observed, that "The Mediterranean would be a noble subject for a poem."

A gentleman maintained that the art of printing had hurt real learning, by disseminating idle writings.— Johnson. "Sir, if it had not been for the art of printing, we should now have no learning at all; for books would have perished faster than they could have been transcribed." This observation seems not just, considering for how many ages books were preserved by writing alone.

The same gentleman maintained, that a general diffusion of knowledge among a people was a disadvantage; for it made the vulgar rise above their humble sphere. Johnson. "Sir, while knowledge is a distinction, those who are possessed of it will naturally rise above those who are not. Merely to read and write was a distinction at first; but we see when reading and writing have become general, the common people keep their stations. And so, were higher attainments to become general, the effect would be the same."

"Goldsmith (he said), referred every thing to vanity; his virtues, and his vices too were from that motive. He was not a social man. He never exchanged mind with you."

We spent the evening at Mr. Hoole's. Mr. Mickle, the excellent translator of "The Lusiad," was there. I have preserved little of the conversation of this evening. Dr. Johnson said, "Thomson had a true poetical genius, the power of viewing every thing in a poetical light. His fault is such a cloud of words sometimes, that the sense can hardly peep through. Shiels, who compiled 'Cibber's Lives of the Poets,' was one day sitting with me. I took down Thomson, and read aloud a large portion of him, and then asked,—Is not this fine? Shiels having expressed the highest admiration, Well, Sir, (said I,) I have omitted every other line."

I related a dispute between Goldsmith and Mr. Robert Dodsley, one day when they and I were dining at Tom Davies's, in 1762. Goldsmith asserted, that there was no poetry produced in this age. Dodsley appealed to his own Collection, and maintained, that though you could not find a palace like Dryden's "Ode on St. Cecilia's Day," you had villages composed of very pretty houses; and he mentioned particularly "The Spleen." JOHNSON. "I think Dodsley gave up the question. He and Goldsmith said the same thing; only he said it in a softer manner than Goldsmith did; for he acknowledged that there was no poetry, nothing that towered above the common mark. You may find wit and humour in verse, and yet no poetry. 'Hudibras' has a profusion of these; yet it is not to be reckoned a poem. 'The Spleen,' in Dodsley's collection, on which you say he chiefly rested, is not poetry." BOSWELL. "Does not Gray's poetry, Sir, tower above the common mark?" JOHNSON. "Yes, Sir; but we must attend to the difference between what men in general cannot do if they would, and what every man may do if he would. Sixteen-string Jack towered above the common mark." BOSWELL. "Then, Sir, what is poetry?" JOHNSON. "Why, Sir, it is much easier to say what it is not. We all *know* what light is; but it is not easy to *tell* what it is."

On Friday, April 12, I dined with him at our friend Tom Davies's.

Davies said of a well known dramatick authour, that "he lived upon *potted stories*, and that he made his way as Hannibal did, by vinegar; having begun by attacking people, particularly the players."

He reminded Dr. Johnson of Mr. Murphy's having paid him the highest compliment that ever was paid to a layman, by asking his pardon for repeating some oaths in the course of telling a story.

Johnson and I supped this evening at the Crown and Anchor tavern, in company with Sir Joshua Reynolds, Mr. Langton, Mr. Nairne, now one of the Scotch Judges, with the title of Lord Dunsinan, and my very worthy friend, Sir William Forbes, of Pitsligo.

We discussed the question, whether drinking improved conversation and benevolence. Sir Joshua maintained it did. JOHNSON. "No, Sir: before dinner men meet with great inequality of understanding; and those who are conscious of their inferiority, have the modesty not to talk. When they have drunk wine, every man feels himself happy, and loses that modesty, and grows impudent and vociferous: but he is not improved: he is only not sensible of his defects." Sir Joshua said the Doctor was talking of the effects of excess in wine; but that a moderate glass enlivened the mind, by giving a proper circulation to the blood. "I am, (said he,) in very good spirits, when I get up in the morning. By dinner-time I am exhausted; wine puts me in the same state as when I got up: and I am sure that moderate drinking makes people talk better." JOHNSON. "No, Sir; wine gives not light, gay, ideal hilarity; but tumultuous, noisy, clamorous merriment. I have heard none of those drunken,—nay, drunken is a coarse word,—none of those *vinous* flights." SIR JOSHUA. "Because you have sat by, quite sober, and felt an envy of the happiness of those who were drinking." JOHNSON. "Perhaps, contempt.—And, Sir, it is not necessary to be drunk one's self, to relish the wit of drunkenness. Do we not judge of the drunken wit of the dialogue between Iago and Cassio, the most excellent in its kind, when we are quite sober? Wit is wit, by whatever means it is produced; and, if good, will appear so at all times. I admit that the spirits are raised by drinking, as by the common participation of any pleasure: cock-fighting, or bear-baiting, will raise the spirits of a company, as drinking does, though surely they will not improve conversation. I also admit, that there are some sluggish men who are improved by drinking; as there are fruits which are not good till they are rotten. There are such men, but they are medlars. I indeed allow that there have been a very few men of talents who were improved by drinking; but I maintain that I am right as to the effects of drinking in general: and let it be considered, that there is no position, however false in its universality, which is not true of some particular man." Sir William Forbes said, "Might not a man warmed with wine be like a bottle of beer, which is made brisker by being set before the fire?"—"Nay, (said Johnson, laughing,) I cannot answer that: that is too much for me."

I observed, that wine did some people harm, by inflaming, confusing, and irritating their minds; but that the experience of mankind had declared in favour of moderate drinking. JOHNSON. "Sir, I do not say it is wrong to produce self-complacency by drinking; I only deny that it improves the mind. When I drank wine, I scorned to drink it when in company. I have drunk many a bottle by myself; in the first place, because I had need of it to raise my spirits: in the second place, because I would have nobody to witness its effects upon me."

He told us, he read Fielding's "Amelia" through, without stopping. He said, "if a man begins to read in the middle of a book, and feels an inclination to go on, let him not quit it, to go to the beginning. He may perhaps not feel again the inclination."

On Monday, April 29, he and I made an excursion to Bristol, where I was entertained with seeing him enquire upon the spot, into the authenticity of "*Rowley's* Poetry," as I had seen him enquire upon the spot into the authenticity of "*Ossian's* Poetry."

Johnson said of Chatterton, "This is the most extraordinary young man that has encountered my knowledge. It is wonderful how the whelp has written such things."

We were by no means pleased with our inn at Bristol. "Let us see now, (said I,) how we should describe it." Johnson was ready with his raillery. "Describe it, Sir?— Why, it was so bad, that Boswell wished to be in Scotland!"

"Garrick (he observed) does not play the part of Archer in 'The Beaux Stratagem' well. The gentleman should break out through the footman, which is not the case as he does it."

"That man is never happy for the present is so true, that all his relief from unhappiness is only forgetting himself for a little while. Life is a progress from want to want, not from enjoyment to enjoyment."

"Lord Chesterfield's Letters to his son, I think, might be made a very pretty book. Take out the immorality, and it should be put in the hands of every young gentleman. An elegant manner and easiness of behaviour are acquired gradually and imperceptibly. No man can say, 'I'll be genteel.' There are ten genteel women for one genteel man, because they are more restrained. A man without some degree of restraint is insufferable; but we are less restrained than women. Were a woman sitting in company to put out her legs before her as most men do, we should be tempted to kick them in." No man was a more attentive and nice observer of behaviour in those in whose company he happened to be, than Johnson; or however strange it may seem to many, had a higher estimation of its refinements. Lord Eliot informs me, that one day when Johnson and he were at dinner in a gentleman's house in London, upon Lord Chesterfield's Letters being mentioned, Johnson surprized the company by this sentence: "Every man of any education would rather be called a rascal, than accused of deficiency in *the graces*." Mr. Gibbon, who was present, turned to a lady who knew Johnson well, and lived much with him, and in his quaint manner, tapping his box, addressed her thus: "Don't you think, Madam, (looking towards Johnson,) that among *all* your acquaintance you could find *one* exception?" The lady smiled, and seemed to acquiesce.

When I complained of having dined at a splendid table without hearing one sentence of conversation worthy of being remembered, he said, "Sir, there seldom is any such conversation." BOSWELL. "Why then meet at table?" JOHNSON. "Why to eat and drink together, and to promote kindness; and, Sir, this is better done when there is no solid conversation: for when there is, people differ in opinion, and get into bad humour, or some of the company who are not capable of such conversation, are left out, and feel themselves uneasy. It was for this reason Sir Robert Walpole said, he always talked bawdy at his table, because in that all could join."

Being irritated by hearing a gentleman[1] ask Mr. Levett a variety of questions concerning him, when he was sitting by, he broke out, "Sir, you have but two topicks, yourself and me. I am sick of both." "A man, (said he,) should not talk of himself, nor much of any particular person. He should take care not to be made a proverb; and, therefore, should avoid having any one topick of which people can say, 'We shall hear him upon it.' There was a Dr. Oldfield, who was always talking of the Duke of Marlborough. He came into a coffee house one day, and told that his Grace had spoken in the House of Lords for half an hour. 'Did he indeed speak for half an hour?' (said Belchier, the surgeon,)—'Yes.'—'And what did he say of Dr. Oldfield?'—'Nothing.'—'Why then, Sir, he was very ungrateful; for Dr. Oldfield could not have spoken for a quarter of an hour, without saying something of him.' "

I am now to record a very curious incident in Dr. Johnson's life, which fell under my own observation; of which *pars magna fui,* and which I am persuaded will, with the liberal-minded, be much to his credit.

My desire of being acquainted with celebrated men of every description, had made me, much about the same time, obtain an introduction to Dr. Samuel Johnson and to John Wilkes, Esq. Two men more different could perhaps not be selected out of all mankind. They

---

[1] Boswell.

had even attacked one another with some asperity in their writings; yet I lived in habits of friendship with both. I could fully relish the excellence of each; for I have ever delighted in that intellectual chymistry, which can separate good qualities from evil in the same person.

Sir John Pringle, "mine own friend and my Father's friend," between whom and Dr. Johnson I in vain wished to establish an acquaintance, as I respected and lived in intimacy with both of them, observed to me once, very ingeniously, "It is not in friendship as in mathematicks, where two things, each equal to a third, are equal between themselves. You agree with Johnson as a middle quality, and you agree with me as a middle quality; but Johnson and I should not agree." Sir John was not sufficiently flexible; so I desisted; knowing, indeed, that the repulsion was equally strong on the part of Johnson; who, I know not from what cause, unless his being a Scotchman, had formed a very erroneous opinion of Sir John. But I conceived an irresistible wish, if possible, to bring Dr. Johnson and Mr. Wilkes together. How to manage it, was a nice and difficult matter.

My worthy booksellers and friends, Messieurs Dilly in the Poultry, at whose hospitable and well-covered table I have seen a greater number of literary men, than at any other, except that of Sir Joshua Reynolds, had invited me to meet Mr. Wilkes and some more gentlemen, on Wednesday, May 15. "Pray (said I,) let us have Dr. Johnson."—"What with Mr. Wilkes? not for the world, (said Mr. Edward Dilly;) Dr. Johnson would never forgive me."—"Come, (said I,) if you'll let me negociate for you, I will be answerable that all shall go well." DILLY. "Nay, if you will take it upon you, I am sure I shall be very happy to see them both here."

Notwithstanding the high veneration which I entertained for Dr. Johnson, I was sensible that he was sometimes a little actuated by the spirit of contradiction, and by means of that I hoped I should gain my point. I was persuaded that if I had come upon him with a direct proposal, "Sir, will you dine in company with Jack Wilkes?" he would have flown into a passion, and would probably have answered, "Dine with Jack Wilkes, Sir! I'd as soon dine with Jack Ketch." I therefore, while we were sitting quietly by ourselves at his house in an evening, took occasion to open my plan thus:—"Mr. Dilly, Sir, sends his respectful compliments to you, and would be happy if you would do him the honour to dine with him on Wednesday next along with me, as I must soon go to Scotland." JOHNSON. "Sir, I am obliged to Mr. Dilly. I will wait upon him—" BOSWELL. "Provided, Sir, I suppose, that the company which he is to have, is agreeable to you." JOHNSON. "What do you mean, Sir? What do you take me for? Do you think I am so ignorant of the world, as to imagine that I am to prescribe to a gentleman what company he is to have at his table?" BOSWELL. "I beg your pardon, Sir, for wishing to prevent you from meeting people whom you might not like. Perhaps he may have some of what he calls his patriotick friends with him." JOHNSON. "Well, Sir, and what then? What care *I* for his *patriotick friends?* Poh!" BOSWELL. "I should not be surprized to find Jack Wilkes there." JOHNSON. "And if Jack Wilkes *should* be there, what is that to *me*, Sir? My dear friend, let us have no more of this. I am sorry to be angry with you; but really it is treating me strangely to talk to me as if I could not meet any company whatever, occasionally." BOSWELL. "Pray, forgive me, Sir: I meant well. But you shall meet whoever comes, for me." Thus I secured him, and told Dilly that he would find him very well pleased to be one of his guests on the day appointed.

Upon the much expected Wednesday, I called on him

about half an hour before dinner, as I often did when we were to dine out together, to see that he was ready in time, and to accompany him. I found him buffeting his books, as upon a former occasion, covered with dust, and making no preparation for going abroad. "How is this, Sir? (said I). Don't you recollect that you are to dine at Mr. Dilly's?" JOHNSON. "Sir, I did not think of going to Dilly's: it went out of my head. I have ordered dinner at home with Mrs. Williams." BOSWELL. "But, my dear Sir, you know you were engaged to Mr. Dilly, and I told him so. He will expect you, and will be much disappointed if you don't come." JOHNSON. "You must talk to Mrs. Williams about this."

Here was a sad dilemma. I feared that what I was so confident I had secured, would yet be frustrated. He had accustomed himself to shew Mrs. Williams such a degree of humane attention, as frequently imposed some restraint upon him; and I knew that if she should be obstinate, he would not stir. I hastened down stairs to the blind lady's room, and told her I was in great uneasiness, for Dr. Johnson had engaged to me to dine this day at Mr. Dilly's, but that he had told me he had forgotten his engagement, and had ordered dinner at home. "Yes, Sir, (said she, pretty peevishly,) Dr. Johnson is to dine at home."—"Madam, (said I,) his respect for you is such, that I know he will not leave you, unless you absolutely desire it. But as you have so much of his company, I hope you will be good enough to forego it for a day: as Mr. Dilly is a very worthy man, has frequently had agreeable parties at his house for Dr. Johnson, and will be vexed if the Doctor neglects him today. And then, Madam, be pleased to consider my situation; I carried the message, and I assured Mr. Dilly that Dr. Johnson was to come; and no doubt he has made a dinner, and invited a company, and boasted of the honour he expected to have. I shall be quite disgraced if the Doctor is not there." She gradually softened to my solicitations, which were certainly as earnest as most entreaties to ladies upon any occasion, and was graciously pleased to empower me to tell Dr. Johnson, "That all things considered, she thought he should certainly go." I flew back to him, still in dust, and careless of what should be the event, "indifferent in his choice to go or stay;" but as soon as I had announced to him Mrs. Williams's consent, he roared, "Frank, a clean shirt," and was very soon drest. When I had him fairly seated in a hackney-coach with me, I exulted as much as a fortune-hunter who has got an heiress into a post-chaise with him to set out for Gretna-Green.

When we entered Mr. Dilly's drawing-room, he found himself in the midst of a company he did not know. I kept myself snug and silent, watching how he would conduct himself. I observed him whispering to Mr. Dilly, "Who is that gentleman, Sir?"—"Mr. Arthur Lee."— JOHNSON. "Too, too, too," (under his breath,) which was one of his habitual mutterings. Mr. Arthur Lee could not but be very obnoxious to Johnson, for he was not only a *patriot,* but an *American.* He was afterwards minister from the United States at the court of Madrid. "And who is the gentleman in lace?"—"Mr. Wilkes, Sir." This information confounded him still more; he had some difficulty to restrain himself, and taking up a book, sat down upon a window-seat and read, or at least kept his eye upon it intently for some time, till he composed himself. His feelings, I dare say, were aukward enough. But he no doubt recollected his having rated me for supposing that he could be at all disconcerted by any company, and he, therefore, resolutely set himself to behave quite as an easy man of the world, who could adapt himself at once to the disposition and manners of those whom he might chance to meet.

The cheering sound of "Dinner is upon the table," dissolved his reverie, and we *all* sat down without any symptom of ill humour. There were present, beside Mr. Wilkes, and Mr. Arthur Lee, who was an old companion of mine when he studied physick at Edinburgh, Mr. (now Sir John) Miller, Dr. Lettsom, and Mr. Slater, the druggist. Mr. Wilkes placed himself next to Dr. Johnson, and behaved to him with so much attention and politeness, that he gained upon him insensibly. No man eat more heartily than Johnson, or loved better what was nice and delicate. Mr. Wilkes was very assiduous in helping him to some fine veal. "Pray give me leave, Sir; —It is better here—A little of the brown—Some fat, Sir—A little of the stuffing—Some gravy—Let me have the pleasure of giving you some butter—Allow me to recommend a squeeze of this orange;—or the lemon, perhaps, may have more zest."—"Sir, Sir, I am obliged to you, Sir," cried Johnson, bowing, and turning his head to him with a look for some time of "surly virtue," but, in a short while, of complacency.

Foote being mentioned, Johnson said, "He is not a good mimick." One of the company added, "A merry Andrew, a buffoon." JOHNSON. "But he has wit too, and is not deficient in ideas, or in fertility and variety of imagery, and not empty of reading; he has knowledge enough to fill up his part. One species of wit he has in an eminent degree, that of escape. You drive him into a corner with both hands; but he's gone, Sir, when you think you have got him—like an animal that jumps over your head. Then he has a great range for wit; he never lets truth stand between him and a jest, and he is some- times mighty coarse. Garrick is under many restraints from which Foote is free." WILKES. "Garrick's wit is more like Lord Chesterfield's." JOHNSON. "The first time I was in company with Foote was at Fitzherbert's. Having no good opinion of the fellow, I was resolved not to be pleased; and it is very difficult to please a man against his will. I went on eating my dinner pretty sullenly, affecting not to mind him. But the dog was so very comical, that I was obliged to lay down my knife and fork, throw myself back upon my chair, and fairly laugh it out. No, Sir, he was irresistible. He upon one occasion experienced, in an extraordinary degree, the efficacy of his powers of entertaining. Amongst the many and various modes which he tried of getting money, he became a partner with a small-beer brewer, and he was to have a share of the profits for procuring customers amongst his numerous acquaintance. Fitzherbert was one who took his small-beer; but it was so bad that the servants resolved not to drink it. They were at some loss how to notify their resolution, being afraid of offending their master, who they knew liked Foote much as a companion. At last they fixed upon a little black boy, who was rather a favourite, to be their deputy, and deliver their remonstrance; and having invested him with the whole authority of the kitchen, he was to inform Mr. Fitzherbert, in all their names, upon a certain day, that they would drink Foote's small-beer no longer. On that day Foote happened to dine at Fitzherbert's, and this boy served at table; he was so delighted with Foote's stories, and merriment, and grimace, that when he went down stairs, he told them, "This is the finest man I have ever seen. I will not deliver your message. I will drink his small-beer."

Somebody observed that Garrick could not have done this. WILKES. "Garrick would have made the small-beer still smaller. He is now leaving the stage; but he will play *Scrub* all his life." I knew that Johnson would let nobody attack Garrick but himself, as Garrick said to me, and I had heard him praise his liberality; so to bring out his commendation of his celebrated pupil, I said, loudly, "I have heard Garrick is liberal." JOHNSON. "Yes, Sir, I know that Garrick has given away more money than any man in England that I am acquainted with, and that not from ostentatious views. Garrick was very poor when he began life; so when he came to have money, he probably was very unskilful in giving away, and saved when he should not. But Garrick began to be liberal as soon as he could; and I am of opinion, the reputation of avarice which he has had, has been very lucky for him, and prevented his having many enemies. You despise a man for avarice, but do not hate him. Garrick might have been much better attacked for living with more splendour than is suitable to a player: if they had had the wit to have assaulted him in that quarter, they might have galled him more. But they have kept clamouring about his avarice, which has rescued him from much obloquy and envy."

Talking of the great difficulty of obtaining authentick information for biography, Johnson told us, "When I was a young fellow I wanted to write the 'Life of Dryden,' and in order to get materials, I applied to the only two persons then alive who had seen him; these were old Swinney, and old Cibber. Swinney's information was no more than this, 'That at Will's coffee-house Dryden had a particular chair for himself, which was set by the fire in winter, and was then called his winter-chair; and that it was carried out for him to the balcony in summer, and was then called his summer-chair.' Cibber could tell no more but 'That he remembered him a decent old man, arbiter of critical disputes at Will's.' You are to consider that Cibber was then at a great distance from Dryden, had perhaps one leg only in the room, and durst not draw in the other." BOSWELL. "Yet Cibber was a man of observation?" JOHNSON. "I think not." BOSWELL. "You will allow his 'Apology' to be well done." JOHNSON. "Very well done, to be sure, Sir. That book is a striking proof of the justice of Pope's remark:

> Each might his several province well command,
> Would all but stoop to what they understand."

BOSWELL. "And his plays are good." JOHNSON. "Yes; but that was his trade; *l'esprit du corps;* he had been all his life among players and play-writers. I wondered that he had so little to say in conversation, for he had kept the best company, and learnt all that can be got by the ear. He abused Pindar to me, and then shewed me an ode of his own, with an absurd couplet, making a linnet soar on an eagle's wing. I told him that when the ancients made a simile, they always made it like something real."

Mr. Wilkes remarked, that "among all the bold flights of Shakespeare's imagination, the boldest was making Birnamwood march to Dunsinane; creating a wood where there never was a shrub; a wood in Scotland! ha! ha! ha!" And he also observed, that "the clannish slavery of the Highlands of Scotland was the single exception to Milton's remark of 'The Mountain Nymph, sweet Liberty,' being worshipped in all hilly countries."— "When I was at Inverary (said he,) on a visit to my old friend Archibald, Duke of Argyle, his dependents congratulated me on being such a favourite of his Grace. I said, 'It is then, gentlemen, truly lucky for me; for if I had displeased the Duke, and he had wished it, there is not a Campbell among you but would have been ready to bring John Wilkes's head to him in a charger. It would have been only

> Off with his head! so much for *Aylesbury*.

I was then member for Aylesbury."

Mr. Arthur Lee mentioned some Scotch who had taken possession of a barren part of America, and wondered why they should choose it. JOHNSON. "Why, Sir, all barrenness is comparative. The *Scotch* would not know it to be barren." BOSWELL. "Come, come, he is flattering the English. You have now been in Scotland, Sir, and say if you did not see meat and drink enough there." JOHNSON. "Why yes, Sir; meat and drink enough to give the inhabitants sufficient strength to run away from home." All these quick and lively sallies were said sportively, quite in jest, and with a smile, which showed that he meant only wit. Upon this topick he and Mr. Wilkes could perfectly assimilate; here was a bond of union between them, and I was conscious that as both of them had visited Caledonia, both were fully satisfied of the strange narrow ignorance of those who imagine that it is a land of famine. But they amused themselves with persevering in the old jokes. When I claimed a superiority for Scotland over England in one respect, that no man can be arrested there for a debt merely because another swears it against him; but there must first be the judgement of a court of law ascertaining its justice; and that a seizure of the person, before judgement is obtained, can take place only, if his creditor should swear that he is about to fly from the country, or, as it is technically expressed, is *in meditatione fugœ*: WILKES. "That, I should think, may be safely sworn of all the Scotch nation." JOHNSON. (To Mr. Wilkes) "You must know, Sir, I lately took my friend Boswell, and shewed him genuine civilised life in an English provincial town. I turned him loose at Lichfield, my native city, that he might see for once real civility: for you know he lives among savages in Scotland, and among rakes in London." WILKES. "Except when he is with grave, sober, decent people, like you and me." JOHNSON. (smiling) "And we ashamed of him."

1777. On Sunday evening, Sept. 14, I arrived at Ashbourne, and drove directly up to Dr. Taylor's door. Dr. Johnson and he appeared before I had got out of the post-chaise, and welcomed me cordially.

The subject of grief for the loss of relations and friends being introduced, I observed that it was strange to consider how soon it in general wears away. Dr. Taylor mentioned a gentleman of the neighbourhood as the only instance he had ever known of a person who had endeavoured to *retain* grief. He told Dr. Taylor that after his Lady's death, which affected him deeply, he *resolved* that the grief, which he cherished with a kind of sacred fondness, should be lasting; but that he found he could not keep it long. JOHNSON. "All grief for what cannot in the course of nature be helped, soon wears away; in some sooner, indeed, in some later; but it never continues very long, unless where there is madness, such as will make a man have pride so fixed in his mind, as to imagine himself a king; or any other passion in an unreasonable way: for all unnecessary grief is unwise, and therefore will not be long retained by a sound mind. If indeed, the cause of our grief is occasioned by our own misconduct, if grief is mingled with remorse of conscience, it should be lasting." BOSWELL. "But, Sir, we do not approve of a man who very soon forgets the loss of a wife or a friend." JOHNSON. "Sir, we disapprove of him, not because he soon forgets his grief; for the

sooner it is forgotten the better, but because we suppose, that if he forgets his wife or his friend soon, he
has not had much affection for them."

I was somewhat disappointed in finding that the edition of the English Poets, for which he was to write
Prefaces and Lives, was not an undertaking directed by
him: but that he was to furnish a Preface and Life to
any poet the booksellers pleased. I asked him if he
would do this to any dunce's works, if they should ask
him. JOHNSON. "Yes, Sir, and *say* he was a dunce."

Dr. Taylor's nose happening to bleed, he said, it was
because he had omitted to have himself blooded four
days after a quarter of a year's interval. Dr. Johnson,
who was a great dabbler in physick, disapproved much
of periodical bleeding. "For (said he) you accustom
yourself to an evacuation which Nature cannot perform
of herself, and therefore she cannot help you, should
you from forgetfulness or any other cause omit it; so
you may be suddenly suffocated. You may accustom yourself to other periodical evacuations, because should
you omit them, Nature can supply the omission; but
Nature cannot open a vein to blood you."—"I do not
like to take an emetick, (said Taylor,) for fear of breaking some small vessels."—"Poh! (said Johnson,) if you
have so many things that will break, you had better
break your neck at once, and there's an end on't. You
will break no small vessels:" (blowing with high derision.)

I mentioned to Dr. Johnson, that David Hume's per-
sisting in his infidelity, when he was dying, shocked me
much. JOHNSON. "Why should it shock you, Sir? Hume
owned he had never read the New Testament with attention. Here then was a man who had been at no pains
to enquire into the truth of religion, and had continually
turned his mind the other way. It was not to be expected

that the prospect of death would alter his way of thinking, unless GOD should send an angel to set him right."
I said, I had reason to believe that the thought of an-
nihilation gave Hume no pain. JOHNSON. "It was not so,
Sir. He had a vanity in being thought easy. It is more
probable that he should assume an appearance of ease,
than so very improbable a thing should be, as a man
not afraid of going (as, in spite of his delusive theory,
he cannot be sure but he may go), into an unknown
state, and not being uneasy at leaving all he knew. And
you are to consider, that upon his own principle of an-
nihilation he had no motive to speak the truth." The
horrour of death, which I had always observed in Dr.
Johnson, appearing strong tonight. I ventured to tell
him, that I had been, for moments in my life, not afraid
of death; therefore I could suppose another man in that
state of mind for a considerable space of time. He said,
"he never had a moment in which death was not terrible
to him." He added, that it had been observed, that
scarce any man dies in publick, but with apparent resolution; from that desire of praise which never quits us.
I said, Dr. Dodd seemed to be willing to die, and full
of hopes of happiness. "Sir, (said he,) Dr. Dodd would
have given both his hands and both his legs to have
lived. The better a man is, the more afraid is he of
death, having a clearer view of infinite purity."

Talking of biography, I said, in writing a life, a man's
peculiarities should be mentioned, because they mark
his character. JOHNSON. "Sir, there is no doubt as to
peculiarities: the question is, whether a man's vices
should be mentioned; for instance, whether it should be
mentioned that Addison and Parnell drank too freely;
for people will probably more easily indulge in drinking
from knowing this; so that more ill may be done by the

example, than good by telling the whole truth." Here was an instance of his varying from himself in talk; for when Lord Hailes and he sat one morning calmly conversing in my house at Edinburgh, I well remember that Dr. Johnson maintained, that "If a man is to write *A Panegyrick,* he may keep vices out of sight: but if he professes to write *A Life,* he must represent it really as it was;" and when I objected to the danger of telling that Parnell drank to excess, he said, that "it would produce an instructive caution to avoid drinking, when it was seen, that even the learning and genius of Parnell could be debased by it." And in the Hebrides he maintained, as appears from my "Journal," that a man's intimate friend should mention his faults, if he writes his life.

He observed, that a gentleman of eminence in literature had got into a bad style of Poetry of late. "He puts (said he) a very common thing in a strange dress till he does not know it himself, and thinks other people do not know it." BOSWELL. "That is owing to his being so much versant in old English poetry." JOHNSON. "What is that to the purpose, Sir? If I say a man is drunk, and you tell me it is owing to his taking much drink, the matter is not mended. No, Sir, —— has taken to an odd mode. For example; he'd write thus:

> Hermit hoar, in solemn cell,
> Wearing out life's evening gray.

Gray evening is common enough; but *evening gray* he'd think fine.—Stay;—we'll make out the stanza:

> Hermit hoar, in solemn cell,
> Wearing out life's evening gray:
> Smite thy bosom, sage, and tell,
> What is bliss? and which the way?"

BOSWELL. "But why smite his bosom, Sir?" JOHNSON. "Why to shew he was in earnest," (smiling.)—He at an after period added the following stanza:

> "Thus I spoke; and speaking sigh'd;
> —Scarce repress'd the starting tear;
> When the smiling sage reply'd—
> —Come, my lad, and drink some beer."

I cannot help thinking the first stanza very good solemn poetry, as also the first three lines of the second. Its last line is an excellent burlesque surprize on gloomy sentimental enquirers. And, perhaps, the advice is as good as can be given to a low-spirited dissatisfied being:— "Don't trouble your head with sickly thinking: take a cup, and be merry."

Friday, September 19, after breakfast, Dr. Johnson and I set out in Dr. Taylor's chaise to go to Derby. The day was fine, and we resolved to go by Keddleston, the seat of Lord Scarsdale, that I might see his Lordship's fine house.

Dr. Manningham, physician in London, who was visiting at Lord Scarsdale's, accompanied us through many of the rooms, and soon afterwards my Lord himself, to whom Dr. Johnson was known, appeared, and did the honours of the house. We talked of Mr. Langton. Johnson, with a warm vehemence of affectionate regard, exclaimed, "The earth does not bear a worthier man than Bennet Langton." In his Lordship's dressing-room lay Johnson's small Dictionary: he shewed it to me, with some eagerness, saying, "Look'ye! *Quæ regio in terris nostri non plena laboris.*" He observed, also, Goldsmith's "Animated Nature;" and said, "Here's our friend! The poor Doctor would have been happy to hear of this."

In our way, Johnson strongly expressed his love of driving fast in a post-chaise. "If (said he) I had no duties, and no reference to futurity, I would spend my life in driving briskly in a post-chaise with a pretty woman; but she should be one who could understand me, and would add something to the conversation."

I mentioned that Lord Monboddo told me, he awaked every morning at four, and then for his health got up and walked in his room naked, with the window open, which he called taking *an air bath;* after which he went to bed again, and slept two hours more. Johnson, who was always ready to beat down any thing that seemed to be exhibited with disproportionate importance, thus observed: "I suppose, Sir, there is no more in it than this, he wakes at four, and cannot sleep till he chills himself, and makes the warmth of the bed a grateful sensation."

I talked of the difficulty of rising in the morning. Dr. Johnson told me, "that the learned Mrs. Carter, at that period when she was eager in study, did not awake as early as she wished, and she therefore had a contrivance, that, at a certain hour, her chamber-light should burn a string to which a heavy weight was suspended, which then fell with a strong sudden noise: this roused her from sleep, and then she had no difficulty in getting up."

On Saturday, September 20, after breakfast, when Taylor was gone out to his farm, Dr. Johnson and I had a serious conversation by ourselves.

I suggested a doubt, that if I were to reside in London, the exquisite zest with which I relished it in occasional visits might go off, and I might grow tired of it. JOHNSON. "Why, Sir, you find no man, at all intellectual, who is willing to leave London. No, Sir, when a man is tired of London, he is tired of life; for there is in London all that life can afford."

He said, a country gentleman should bring his lady to visit London as soon as he can, that they may have agreeable topicks for conversation when they are by themselves.

We talked of employment being absolutely necessary to preserve the mind from wearying and growing fretful, especially in those who have a tendency to melancholy; and I mentioned to him a saying which somebody had related of an American savage, who, when an European was expatiating on all the advantages of money, put this question: "Will it purchase *occupation?*" JOHNSON. "Depend upon it, Sir, this saying is too refined for a savage. And, Sir, money *will* purchase occupation; it will purchase all the conveniences of life; it will purchase variety of company; it will purchase all sorts of entertainment."

Johnson and Taylor were so different from each other, that I wondered at their preserving an intimacy. Their having been at school and college together, might, in some degree, account for this; but Sir Joshua Reynolds has furnished me with a stronger reason; for Johnson mentioned to him, that he had been told by Taylor he was to be his heir. I shall not take upon me to animadvert upon this; but certain it is that Johnson paid great attention to Taylor. He now, however, said to me, "Sir, I love him; but I do not love him more; my regard for him does not increase. As it is said in the Apocrypha, 'his talk is of bullocks.' I do not suppose he is very fond of my company. His habits are by no means sufficiently clerical: this he knows that I see; and no man likes to live under the eye of perpetual disapprobation."

I shall present my readers with a series of what I gathered this evening from the Johnsonian garden.

"Did we not hear so much said of Jack Wilkes, we should think more highly of his conversation. Jack has a great variety of talk, Jack is a scholar, and Jack has the manners of a gentleman. But after hearing his name sounded from pole to pole, as the phœnix of convivial felicity, we are disappointed in his company. He has always been *at me:* but I would do Jack a kindness, rather than not. The contest is now over."

"Colley Cibber once consulted me as to one of his birth-day Odes, a long time before it was wanted. I objected very freely to several passages. Cibber lost patience, and would not read his Ode to an end. When we had done with criticism, we walked over to Richardson's, the authour of 'Clarissa,' and I wondered to find Richardson displeased that I 'did not treat Cibber with more *respect.*' Now, Sir, to talk of *respect for a player!*" (smiling disdainfully.) BOSWELL. "There, Sir, you are always heretical: you never will allow merit to a player." JOHNSON. "Merit, Sir, what merit? Do you respect a rope-dancer, or a ballad-singer?" BOSWELL. "No, Sir: but we respect a great player, as a man who can conceive lofty sentiments, and can express them gracefully." JOHNSON. "What, Sir, a fellow who claps a hump on his back, and a hump on his leg, and cries, '*I am Richard the Third*'? Nay, sir, a ballad-singer is a higher man, for he does two things; he repeats and he sings: there is both recitation and musick in his performance: the player only recites." BOSWELL. "My dear Sir! you may turn any thing into ridicule. I allow, that a player of farce is not entitled to respect; he does a little thing: but he who can represent exalted characters, and touch the noblest passions, has very respectable powers; and mankind have agreed in admiring great talents for the stage. We must consider, too, that a great player does what very few are capable to do: his art is a very rare faculty. *Who* can repeat Hamlet's soliloquy, 'To be, or not to be,' as Garrick does it?" JOHNSON. "Any body may. Jemmy, there (a boy about eight years old, who was in the room) will do it as well in a week." BOSWELL. "No, no, Sir: and as a proof of the merit of great acting, and of the value which mankind set upon it, Garrick has got a hundred thousand pounds." JOHNSON. "Is getting a hundred thousand pounds a proof of excellence? That has been done by a scoundrel commissary."

This was most fallacious reasoning. I was *sure*, for once, that I had the best side of the argument. I boldly maintained the just distinction between a tragedian and a mere theatrical droll; between those who rouse our terrour and pity, and those who only make us laugh. "If (said I) Betterton and Foote were to walk into this room, you would respect Betterton much more than Foote." JOHNSON. "If Betterton were to walk into this room with Foote, Foote would soon drive him out of it. Foote, Sir, *quatenùs* Foote, has powers superiour to them all."

On Monday, September 22, when at breakfast, I unguardedly said to Dr. Johnson, "I wish I saw you and Mrs. Macaulay together." He grew very angry; and, after a pause, while a cloud gathered on his brow, he burst out, "No, Sir; you would not see us quarrel, to make you sport. Don't you know that it is very uncivil to *pit* two people against one another?" Then, checking himself, and wishing to be more gentle, he added, "I do not say you should be hanged or drowned for this; but it *is* very uncivil." Dr. Taylor thought him in the wrong, and spoke to him privately of it; but I afterwards acknowledged to Johnson that I was to blame, for I candidly owned, that I meant to express a desire to see a contest between Mrs. Macaulay and him; but then I knew how the contest would end; so that I was to see him triumph. JOHNSON. "Sir, you cannot be sure how a contest will end; and no man has a right to engage two people in a dispute by which their passions may be enflamed, and they may part with bitter resentment against each other. I would sooner keep company with a man from whom I must guard my pockets, than with a man who contrives to bring me into a dispute with somebody that he may hear it. This is the great fault of ——, (naming one of our friends) endeavouring to introduce a subject upon which he knows two people in the company differ." BOSWELL. "But he told me, Sir, he does it for instruction." JOHNSON. "Whatever the motive be, Sir, the man who does so, does very wrong. He has no more right to instruct himself at such risk, than he has to make two people fight a duel, that he may learn how to defend himself."

He found great fault with a gentleman of our acquaintance for keeping a bad table. "Sir, (said he,) when a man is invited to dinner, he is disappointed if he does not get something good. I advised Mrs. Thrale, who has no card-parties at her house, to give sweet-meats, and such good things, in an evening, as are not commonly given, and she would find company enough come to her; for every body loves to have things which please the palate put in their way, without trouble or preparation." Such was his attention to the *minutiæ* of life and manners.

In the evening, a gentleman-farmer, who was on a visit at Dr. Taylor's, attempted to dispute with Johnson in favour of Mungo Campbell, who shot Alexander, Earl of Eglintoune, upon his having fallen, when retreating from his Lordship, who he believed was about to seize his gun, as he had threatened to do. He said, he should have done just as Campbell did. JOHNSON. "Whoever would do as Campbell did, deserves to be hanged; not that I could, as a juryman, have found him legally guilty of murder; but I am glad they found means to convict him." The gentleman-farmer said, "A poor man has as much honour as a rich man; and Campbell had *that* to defend." Johnson exclaimed, "A poor man has no honour." The English yeoman, not dismayed, proceeded: "Lord Eglintoune was a damned fool to run on upon Campbell, after being warned that Campbell would shoot him if he did." Johnson, who could not bear anything like swearing, angrily replied, "He was *not a damned fool*: he only thought too well of Campbell. He did not believe Campbell would be such a *damned* scoundrel, as to do so *damned* a thing." His emphasis on *damned*, accompanied with frowning looks, reproved his opponent's want of decorum in *his* presence.

During this interview at Ashbourne, Johnson seemed to be more uniformly social, cheerful, and alert, than I had almost ever seen him. He was prompt on great occasions and on small. Taylor, who praised every thing of his own to excess, in short, "whose geese were all swans," as the proverb says, expatiated on the excellence of his bull-dog, which he told us, was "perfectly well shaped." Johnson, after examining the animal attentively, thus repressed the vain-glory of our host:—"No, Sir, he is *not* well shaped; for there is not the quick transition from the thickness of the fore-part, to the *tenuity*—the thin part—behind,—which a bull-dog ought to have."

Talking of Rochester's Poems, he said, he had given them to Mr. Steevens to castrate for the edition of the poets, to which he was to write Prefaces. Dr. Taylor (the only time I ever heard him say any thing witty) [1] observed, that "if Rochester had been castrated himself, his exceptionable poems would not have been written." I asked if Burnet had not given a good Life of Rochester. JOHNSON. "We have a good *Death:* there is not much *Life*." I asked whether Prior's poems were to be printed

---

[1] I am told, that Horace, Earl of Oxford, has a collection of Bon-Mots by persons who never said but one.

entire: Johnson said, they were. I mentioned Lord Hailes's censure of Prior, in his Preface to a collection of "Sacred Poems," by various hands, published by him at Edinburgh a great many years ago, where he mentions, "those impure tales which will be the eternal opprobrium of their ingenious authour." JOHNSON. "Sir, Lord Hailes has forgot. There is nothing in Prior that will excite to lewdness. If Lord Hailes thinks there is, he must be more combustible than other people." I instanced the tale of "Paulo Purganti and his Wife." JOHNSON. "Sir, there is nothing there, but that his wife wanted to be kissed, when poor Paulo was out of pocket. No, Sir, Prior is a lady's book. No lady is ashamed to have it standing in her library."

This evening, while some of the tunes of ordinary composition were played with no great skill, my frame was agitated, and I was conscious of a generous attachment to Dr. Johnson, as my preceptor and friend, mixed with an affectionate regret that he was an old man, whom I should probably lose in a short time. I thought I could defend him at the point of my sword. My reverence and affection for him were in full glow. I said to him, "My dear Sir, we must meet every year, if you don't quarrel with me." JOHNSON. "Nay, Sir, you are more likely to quarrel with me, than I with you. My regard for you is greater almost than I have words to express; but I do not chuse to be always repeating it; write it down in the first leaf of your pocket-book, and never doubt of it again."

I talked to him of misery being "the doom of man" in this life, as displayed in his "Vanity of Human Wishes." Yet I observed that things were done upon the supposition of happiness; grand houses were built, fine gardens were made, splendid places of publick amusement were contrived, and crowded with company. JOHNSON.

"Alas, Sir, these are all only struggles for happiness. When I first entered Ranelagh, it gave an expansion and gay sensation to my mind, such as I never experienced any where else. But, as Xerxes wept when he viewed his immense army, and considered that not one of that great multitude would be alive a hundred year afterwards, so it went to my heart to consider that there was not one in all that brilliant circle, that was not afraid to go home and think; but that the thoughts of each individual there, would be distressing when alone."

After supper I accompanied him to his apartment, and at my request he dictated to me an argument in favour of the negro who was then claiming his liberty, in an action in the Court of Session in Scotland. He had always been very zealous against slavery in every form, in which I with all deference thought that he discovered "a zeal without knowledge." Upon one occasion, when in company with some very grave men at Oxford, his toast was, "Here's to the next insurrection of the negroes in the West Indies." His violent prejudice against our West Indian and American settlers appeared whenever there was an opportunity. Towards the conclusion of his "Taxation no Tyranny," he says, "how is it that we hear the loudest *yelps* for liberty among the drivers of negroes?"

I cannot omit a curious circumstance which occurred at Edensor-inn, close by Chatsworth, to survey the magnificence of which I had gone a considerable way out of my road to Scotland. The inn was then kept by a very jolly landlord, whose name, I think, was Malton. He happened to mention that "the celebrated Dr. Johnson had been in his house." I enquired *who* this Dr. Johnson was, that I might hear my host's notion of him. "Sir, (said he,) Johnson, the great writer; *Oddity*, as they call him. He's the greatest writer in England; he writes for the ministry; he has a correspondence abroad, and lets them know what's going on."

My friend, who had a thorough dependance upon the authenticity of my relation without any *embellishment,* as *falsehood* or *fiction* is too gently called, laughed a good deal at this representation of himself.

Talking of ghosts, he said, "It is wonderful that five thousand years have now elapsed since the creation of the world, and still it is undecided whether or not there has ever been an instance of the spirit of any person appearing after death. All argument is against it; but all belief is for it."

He said, "John Wesley's conversation is good, but he is never at leisure. He is always obliged to go at a certain hour. This is very disagreeable to a man who loves to fold his legs and have out his talk, as I do."

1778. On Saturday, April 4, I drank tea with Johnson at Dr. Taylor's, where he had dined. He talked of going to Streatham that night. TAYLOR. "You'll be robbed, if you do: or you must shoot a highwayman. Now I would rather be robbed than do that; I would not shoot a highwayman." JOHNSON. "But I would rather shoot him in the instant when he is attempting to rob me, than afterwards swear against him at the Old Bailey, to take away his life, after he has robbed me. I am surer I am right in the one case, than in the other. I may be mistaken as to the man when I swear: I cannot be mistaken, if I shoot him in the act. Besides, we feel less reluctance to take away a man's life, when we are heated by the injury, than to do it at a distance of time by an oath, after we have cooled." BOSWELL. "So, Sir, you would rather act from the motive of private passion, than that of publick advantage." JOHNSON. "Nay, Sir, when I shoot the high-

wayman, I act from both." Boswell. "Very well, very
well.—There is no catching him." Johnson. "At the
same time, one does not know what to say. For perhaps
one may, a year after, hang himself from uneasiness for
having shot a highwayman. Few minds are fit to be
trusted with so great a thing." Boswell. "Then, Sir, you
would not shoot him?" Johnson. "But I might be vexed
afterwards for that too."

Thrale's carriage not having come for him, as he expected, I accompanied him some part of the way home
to his own house. I told him, that I had talked of him to
Mr. Dunning a few days before, and had said, that in his
company we did not so much interchange conversation,
as listen to him; and that Dunning observed, upon this,
"One is always willing to listen to Dr. Johnson;" to
which I answered, "That is a great deal from you, Sir."
—"Yes, Sir, (said Johnson,) a great deal indeed. Here is
a man willing to listen, to whom the world is listening
all the rest of the year." Boswell. "I think, Sir, it is right
to tell one man of such a handsome thing, which has
been said of him by another. It tends to increase benevolence." Johnson. "Undoubtedly it is right, Sir."

On Tuesday, April 7, I breakfasted with him at his
house. He said, "nobody was content." I mentioned to
him a respectable person in Scotland whom he knew;
and I asserted, that I really believed he was always content. Johnson. "No, Sir, he is not content with the present; he has always some new scheme, some new planta-
tion, something which is future. You know he was not
content as a widower; for he married again." Boswell.
"But he is not restless." Johnson. "Sir, he is only locally
at rest. A chymist is locally at rest; but his mind is hard
at work. This gentleman has done with external exertions. It is too late for him to engage in distant projects."
Boswell. "He seems to amuse himself quite well; to

have his attention fixed, and his tranquillity preserved by very small matters. I have tried this; but it would not do with me." JOHNSON (laughing,) "No, Sir; it must be born with a man to be contented to take up with little things. Women have a great advantage that they may take up with little things, without disgracing themselves: a man cannot, except with fiddling. Had I learnt to fiddle, I should have done nothing else." BOSWELL. "Pray, Sir, did you ever play on any musical instrument?" JOHNSON. "So, Sir. I once bought me a flagelet; but I never made out a tune." BOSWELL. "A flagelet, Sir! —so small an instrument? I should have liked to hear you play on the violoncello. *That* should have been *your* instrument." JOHNSON. "Sir, I might as well have played on the violoncello as another; but I should have done nothing else. No, Sir; a man would never undertake great things, could he be amused with small. I once tried knotting. Dempster's sister undertook to teach me; but I could not learn it." BOSWELL. "So, Sir; it will be related in pompous narrative, 'Once for his amusement he tried knotting; nor did this Hercules disdain the distaff.'" JOHNSON. "Knitting of stockings is a good amusement. As a freeman of Aberdeen I should be a knitter of stockings." He asked me to go down with him and dine at Mr. Thrale's at Streatham, to which I agreed.

He talked to me with serious concern of a certain female friend's "laxity of narration, and inattention to truth."—"I am as much vexed (said he) at the ease with which she hears it mentioned to her, as at the thing itself. I told her, 'Madam, you are contented to hear every day said to you, what the highest of mankind have died for, rather than bear.'—You know, Sir, the highest of mankind have died rather than bear to be told they had uttered a falsehood. Do talk to her of it: I am weary."

Talking of drinking wine, he said, "I did not leave off wine, because I could not bear it; I have drunk three bottles of port without being the worse for it. University College has witnessed this." BOSWELL. "Why, then, Sir, did you leave it off?" JOHNSON. "Why, Sir, because it is so much better for a man to be sure that he is never to be intoxicated, never to lose the power over himself. I shall not begin to drink wine again till I grow old, and want it." BOSWELL. "I think, Sir, you once said to me, that not to drink wine was a great deduction from life." JOHNSON. "It is a diminution of pleasure, to be sure; but I do not say a diminution of happiness. There is more happiness in being rational." BOSWELL. "But if we could have pleasure always, should not we be happy? The greatest part of men would compound for pleasure." JOHNSON. "Supposing we could have pleasure always, an intellectual man would not compound for it. The greatest part of men would compound, because the greatest part of men are gross." BOSWELL. "I allow there may be greater pleasure than from wine. I have had more pleasure from your conversation. I have indeed; I assure you I have." JOHNSON. "When we talk of pleasure, we mean sensual pleasure. When a man says, he had pleasure with a woman, he does not mean conversation, but something of a very different nature. Philosophers tell you, that pleasure is *contrary* to happiness. Gross men prefer animal pleasure. So there are men who have preferred living among savages. Now what a wretch must he be, who is content with such conversation as can be had among savages! You may remember, an officer at Fort Augustus, who had served in America, told us of a woman whom they were obliged to *bind*, in order to get her back from savage life." BOSWELL. "She must have been an animal, a beast." JOHNSON. "Sir, she was a speaking cat."

I mentioned to him that I had become very weary in a company where I heard not a single intellectual sentence, except that "a man who had been settled ten years in Minorca was become a much inferiour man to what he was in London, because a man's mind grows narrow in a narrow place." JOHNSON. "A man's mind grows narrow in a narrow place, whose mind is enlarged only because he has lived in a large place: but what is got by books and thinking is preserved in a narrow place as well as in a large place. A man cannot know modes of life as well in Minorca as in London; but he may study mathematics as well in Minorca." BOSWELL. "I don't know, Sir: if you had remained ten years in the Isle of Col, you would not have been the man that you now are." JOHNSON. "Yes, Sir, if I had been there from fifteen to twenty-five; but not if from twenty-five to thirty-five." BOSWELL. "I own, Sir, the spirits which I have in London make me do every thing with more readiness and vigour. I can talk twice as much in London as any where else."

Soon after our arrival at Thrale's, I heard one of the maids calling eagerly on another, to go to Dr. Johnson. I wondered what this could mean. I afterwards learnt, that it was to give her a Bible, which he had brought from London as a present to her.

Sir John Pringle had expressed a wish that I would ask Dr. Johnson's opinion what were the best English sermons for style. I took an opportunity today of mentioning several to him. Atterbury? JOHNSON. "Yes, Sir, one of the best." BOSWELL. "Tillotson?" JOHNSON. "Why, not now. I should not advise a preacher at this day to imitate Tillotson's style; though I don't know; I should be cautious of objecting to what has been applauded by so many suffrages.—South is one of the best, if you except his peculiarities, and his violence, and sometimes coarseness of language.—*Seed* has a very fine style; but he is not very theological.—*Jortin's* sermons are very elegant.—*Sherlock's* style too is very elegant, though he has not made it his principal study.—And you may add *Smallridge*. All the latter preachers have a good style. Indeed, nobody now talks much of style: every body composes pretty well. There are no such inharmonious periods as there were a hundred years ago. I should recommend Dr. *Clarke's* sermons, were he orthodox. However, it is very well known *where* he is not orthodox, which was upon the doctrine of the Trinity, as to which he is a condemned heretick; so one is aware of it." BOSWELL. "I like Ogden's Sermons on Prayer very much, both for neatness of style and subtilty of reasoning." JOHNSON. "I should like to read all that Ogden has written." BOSWELL. "What I wish to know is, what sermons afford the best specimens of English pulpit eloquence." JOHNSON. "We have no sermons addressed to the passions, that are good for anything; if you mean that kind of eloquence." A CLERGYMAN: (whose name I do not recollect.) "Were not Dodd's sermons addressed to the passions?" JOHNSON. "They were nothing, Sir, be they addressed to what they may."

On Thursday, April 9, I dined with him at Sir Joshua Reynolds's.

When we went to the drawing-room, there was a rich assemblage. Besides the company who had been at dinner, there were Mr. Garrick, Mr. Harris of Salisbury, Dr. Percy, Dr. Burney, the Honourable Mrs. Cholmondeley, Miss Hannah More, &c. &c.

After wandering about in a kind of pleasing distraction for some time, I got into a corner, with Johnson, Garrick, and Harris. GARRICK. (to Harris.) "Pray, Sir, have you read Potter's Æschylus?" HARRIS. "Yes; and think it pretty." GARRICK. (to Johnson.) "And what think you, Sir, of it?" JOHNSON. "I thought what I read of it *verbiage:* but upon Mr. Harris's recommendation, I will read a play. (To Mr. Harris.) Don't prescribe two." Mr. Harris suggested one, I do not remember which. JOHNSON. "We must try its effect as an English poem; that is the way to judge of the merit of a translation. Translations are, in general, for people who cannot read the original." I mentioned the vulgar saying, that Pope's Homer was not a good representation of the original. JOHNSON. "Sir, it is the greatest work of the kind that has ever been produced." GARRICK. "Of all the translations that ever were attempted, I think Elphinstone's Martial the most extraordinary. He consulted me upon it, who am a little of an epigrammatist myself, you know. I told him freely, 'You don't seem to have that turn.' I asked him if he was serious; and finding he was, I advised him against publishing. Why, his translation is more difficult to understand than the original. I thought him a man of some talents; but he seems crazy in this." JOHNSON. "Sir, you have done what I had not courage to do. But he did not ask my advice, and I did not force it upon him, to make him angry with me." GARRICK. "But as a friend, Sir—" JOHNSON. "Why, such a friend as I am with him—no." GARRICK. "But if you see a friend going to tumble over a precipice?" JOHNSON. "That is an extravagant case, Sir. You are sure a friend will thank you for hindering him from tumbling over a precipice: but, in the other case, I should hurt his vanity, and do him no good. He would not take my advice. His brother-in-law, Strahan, sent him a subscription of fifty pounds, and said he would send him fifty more, if he would not publish." GARRICK. "What! eh! is Strahan a good judge of an Epigram? Is not he rather an *obtuse* man, eh?" JOHNSON. "Why, Sir, he may not be a judge of an Epigram: but you see he is a judge of what is *not* an Epigram." BOSWELL. "It is easy for you, Mr. Garrick, to talk to an authour as you talked to Elphinstone; you, who have been so long the manager of a theatre, rejecting the plays of poor authours. You are an old Judge, who have often pronounced sentence of death. You are a practised surgeon, who have often amputated limbs; and though this may have been for the good of your patients, they cannot like you. Those who have undergone a dreadful operation are not very fond of seeing the operator again." GARRICK. "Yes, I know enough of that. There was a reverend gentleman, (Mr. Hawkins,) who wrote a tragedy, the SIEGE of something, which I refused." HARRIS. "So, the siege was raised." JOHNSON. "Ay, he came to me and complained; and told me, that Garrick said his play was wrong in the *concoction*. Now, what is the concoction of a play?" (Here Garrick started, and twisted himself, and seemed sorely vexed; for Johnson told me, he believed the story was true.) GARRICK. "I—I—I—said, *first* concoction." JOHNSON. (smiling.) "Well, he left out *first*. And Rich, he said, refused him *in false English:* he could show it under his hand." GAR-RICK. "He wrote to me in violent wrath, for having refused his play: 'Sir, this is growing a very serious and terrible affair. I am resolved to publish my play. I will appeal to the world; and how will your judgement appear!' I answered, 'Sir, notwithstanding all the seriousness, and all the terrours, I have no objection to your publishing your play; and as you live at a great distance, (Devonshire, I believe,) if you will send it to me, I will convey it to the press.' I never heard more of it, ha! ha! ha!"

On Friday, April 10, I found Johnson at home in the morning. I said to him, "You were yesterday, Sir, in remarkably good humour; but there was nothing to offend you, nothing to produce irritation or violence. There was no bold offender. There was not one capital conviction. It was a maiden assize. You had your white gloves."

He found fault with our friend Langton for having been too silent. "Sir, (said I,) you will recollect that he very properly took up Sir Joshua for being glad that Charles Fox had praised Goldsmith's 'Traveller,' and you joined him." JOHNSON. "Yes, Sir, I knocked Fox on the head, without ceremony. Reynolds is too much under Fox and Burke at present. He is under the *Fox star,* and the *Irish constellation.* He is always under some planet." BOSWELL. "There is no Fox star." JOHNSON. "But there is a dog star." BOSWELL. "They say, indeed, a fox and a dog are the same animal."

We dined together with Mr. Scott (now Sir William Scott, his Majesty's Advocate General,) at his chambers in the Temple, nobody else there. The company being small, Johnson was not in such spirits as he had been the preceding day, and for a considerable time little was said. At last he burst forth: "Subordination is sadly broken down in this age. No man, now, has the same authority which his father had,—except a gaoler. No master has it over his servants: it is diminished in our colleges; nay, in our grammar-schools." BOSWELL. "What is the cause of this, Sir?" JOHNSON. "Why, the coming in of the Scotch," (laughing sarcastically.) BOSWELL. "That is to say, things have been turned topsy-turvy.—But your serious cause." JOHNSON. "Why, Sir, there are many causes, the chief of which is, I think, the great increase of money. No man now depends upon the Lord of the Manour, when he can send to another country, and fetch provisions. The shoe-black at the entry of my court does not depend on me. I can deprive him but of a penny a day, which he hopes somebody else will bring him; and that penny I must carry to another shoe-black, so the trade suffers nothing. I have explained, in my 'Journey to the Hebrides,' how gold and silver destroy feudal subordination. But, besides, there is a general relaxation of reverence. No son now depends upon his father, as in former times. Paternity used to be considered as of itself a great thing, which had a right to many claims. That is, in general, reduced to very small bounds. My hope is, that as anarchy produces tyranny, this extreme relaxation will produce *freni strictio.*"

Talking of fame, for which there is so great a desire, I observed, how little there is of it in reality, compared with the other objects of human attention. "Let every man recollect, and he will be sensible how small a part of his time is employed in talking or thinking of Shakespeare, Voltaire, or any of the most celebrated men that have ever lived, or are now supposed to occupy the attention and admiration of the world. Let this be extracted and compressed; into what a narrow space will it go!" I then slily introduced Mr. Garrick's fame, and his assuming the airs of a great man. JOHNSON. "Sir, it is wonderful how *little* Garrick assumes. No, Sir, Garrick *fortunam reverenter habet.* Consider, Sir; celebrated men, such as you have mentioned, have had their applause at a distance; but Garrick had it dashed in his face, sounded in his ears, and went home every night with the plaudits of a thousand in his *cranium.* Then, Sir, Garrick did not *find,* but *made* his way to the tables, the levees, and almost the bed-chambers of the great. Then, Sir, Garrick had under him a numerous body of people; who, from fear of his power, and hopes of his favour, and admiration of his talents, were constantly submissive to him. And here is a man who has advanced the dignity of his profession. Garrick has made a player a higher character." SCOTT. "And he is a very sprightly writer too." JOHNSON. "Yes, Sir; and all this supported by great wealth of his own acquisition. If all this had happened to me, I should have had a couple of fellows with long poles walking before me, to knock down every body that stood in the way. Consider, if all this had happened to Cibber or Quin, they'd have jumped over the moon.—Yet Garrick speaks to *us*." (smiling.) BOSWELL. "And Garrick is a very good man, a charitable man." JOHNSON. "Sir, a liberal man. He has given away more money than any man in England. There may be a little vanity mixed: but he has shewn, that money is not his first object." BOSWELL. "Yet Foote used to say of him, that he walked out with an intention to do a generous action; but turning the corner of a street, he met with the ghost of a halfpenny, which frightened him." JOHNSON. "Why, Sir, that is very true, too; for I never knew a man of whom it could be said with less certainty to-day, what he will do tomorrow, than Garrick; it depends so much on his humour at the time." SCOTT. "I am glad to hear of his liberality. He has been represented as very saving." JOHNSON. "With his domestick saving we have nothing to do. I remember drinking tea with him long ago, when Peg Woffington made it, and he grumbled at her for making it too strong.[1] He had then begun to feel money in his purse, and did not know when he should have enough of it."

We talked of war. JOHNSON. "Every man thinks meanly of himself for not having been a soldier, or not having been at sea." BOSWELL. "Lord Mansfield does not." JOHNSON. "Sir, if Lord Mansfield were in a company of General Officers and Admirals who have been in service, he would shrink; he'd wish to creep under the table." BOSWELL. "No; he'd think he could *try* them all."

---

[1] When Johnson told this little anecdote to Sir Joshua Reynolds, he mentioned a circumstance which he omitted today:—"Why (said Garrick) it is as red as blood."

JOHNSON. "Yes, if he could catch them: but they'd try him much sooner. No, Sir: were Socrates and Charles the Twelfth of Sweden both present in any company, and Socrates to say, 'Follow me, and hear a lecture in philosophy;' and Charles, laying his hand on his sword, to say, 'Follow me, and dethrone the Czar;' a man would be ashamed to follow Socrates. Sir, the impression is universal: yet it is strange. As to the sailor, when you look down from the quarter-deck to the space below, you see the utmost extremity of human misery: such crowding, such filth, such stench!" BOSWELL. "Yet sailors are happy." JOHNSON. "They are happy as brutes are happy, with a piece of fresh meat—with the grossest sensuality."

He sometimes could not bear being teazed with questions. I was once present when a gentleman asked so many, as, "What did you do, Sir?" "What did you say, Sir?" that he at last grew enraged, and said, "I will not be put to the *question*. Don't you consider, Sir, that these are not the manners of a gentleman? I will not be baited with *what* and *why*; what is this? what is that? why is a cow's tail long? why is a fox's tail bushy?" The gentleman, who was a good deal out of countenance, said, "Why, Sir, you are so good, that I venture to trouble you." JOHNSON. "Sir, my being so *good* is no reason why you should be so *ill*."

On Sunday, April 12, I found him at home before dinner; Dr. Dodd's poem, entitled "Thoughts in Prison," was lying upon his table. This appearing to me an extraordinary effort by a man who was in Newgate for a capital crime, I was desirous to hear Johnson's opinion of it: to my surprize, he told me he had not read a line of it. I took up the book, and read a passage to him. JOHNSON. "Pretty well, if you are previously disposed to like them." I read another passage, with which he was better pleased. He then took the book into his own hands, and having looked at the prayer at the end of it, he said, "What *evidence* is there that this was composed the night before he suffered? *I* do not believe it." He then read aloud where he prays for the King, &c. and observed, "Sir, do you think that a man, the night before he is to be hanged, cares for the succession of a royal family?—Though, he *may* have composed this prayer then. A man who has been canting all his life, may cant to the last.—And yet, a man who has been refused a pardon after so much petitioning, would hardly be praying thus fervently for the King."

He and I, and Mrs. Williams, went to dine with the Reverend Dr. Percy. Talking of Goldsmith, Johnson said, he was very envious. I defended him, by observing that he owned it frankly upon all occasions. JOHNSON. "Sir, you are enforcing the charge. He had so much envy, that he could not conceal it. He was so full of it, that he overflowed. He talked of it to be sure often enough. Now, Sir, what a man avows, he is not ashamed to think; though many a man thinks what he is ashamed to avow. We are all envious naturally; but by checking envy, we get the better of it. So we are all thieves naturally; a child always tries to get at what it wants the nearest way; by good instruction and good habits this is cured, till a man has not even an inclination to seize what is another's; has no struggle with himself about it."

And here I shall record a scene of too much heat between Dr. Johnson and Dr. Percy, which I should have suppressed, were it not that it gave occasion to display the truly tender and benevolent heart of Johnson, who as soon as he found a friend was at all hurt by any thing which he had "said in his wrath," was not only prompt and desirous to be reconciled, but exerted himself to make ample reparation.

Books of Travels having been mentioned, Johnson praised Pennant very highly, as he did at Dunvegan, in the Isle of Skye. Dr. Percy knowing himself to be the heir male of the ancient Percies, and having the warmest and most dutiful attachment to the noble House of Northumberland, could not sit quietly and hear a man praised, who had spoken disrespectfully of Alnwick-Castle and the Duke's pleasure-grounds, especially as he thought meanly of his travels. He therefore opposed Johnson eagerly. JOHNSON. "Pennant, in what he has said of Alnwick, has done what he intended; he has made you very angry." PERCY. "He has said the garden is trim, which is representing it like a citizen's parterre, when the truth is, there is a very large extent of fine turf and gravel walks." JOHNSON. "According to your own account, Sir, Pennant is right. It *is* trim. Here is grass cut close, and gravel rolled smooth. Is not that trim? The extent is nothing against that; a mile may be as trim as a square yard. Your extent puts me in mind of the citizen's enlarged dinner, two pieces of roast-beef, and two puddings. There is no variety, no mind exerted in laying out the ground, no trees." PERCY. "He pretends to give the natural history of Northumberland, and yet takes no notice of the immense number of trees planted there of late." JOHNSON. "That, Sir, has nothing to do with the *natural* history; that is *civil* history. A man who gives the natural history of the oak, is not to tell how many oaks have been planted in this place or that. A man who gives the natural history of the cow, is not to tell how many cows are milked at Islington. The animal is the same, whether milked in the Park or at Islington." PERCY. "Pennant does not describe well; a carrier who goes along the side of Lochlomond would describe it better." JOHNSON. "I think he describes very well." PERCY. "I travelled after him." JOHNSON. "And *I* trav-

elled after him." PERCY. "But, my good friend, you are
short-sighted, and do not see so well as I do." I wondered
at Dr. Percy's venturing thus. Dr. Johnson said nothing
at the time: but inflammable particles were collecting
for a cloud to burst. In a little while Dr. Percy said
something more in disparagement of Pennant. JOHNSON.
(pointedly) "This is the resentment of a narrow mind,
because he did not find every thing in Northumberland."
PERCY. (feeling the stroke) "Sir, you may be as rude as
you please." JOHNSON. "Hold, Sir! don't talk of rudeness;
remember, Sir, you told me, (puffing hard with passion
struggling for a vent) I was short-sighted. We have
done with civility. We are to be as rude as we please."
PERCY. "Upon my honour, Sir, I did not mean to be uncivil." JOHNSON. "I cannot say so, Sir; for I *did* mean to
be uncivil, thinking *you* had been uncivil." Dr. Percy
rose, ran up to him, and taking him by the hand, assured
him affectionately that his meaning had been misunderstood; upon which a reconciliation instantly took place.
JOHNSON. "My dear Sir, I am willing you shall *hang*
Pennant." PERCY. (resuming the former subject) "Pennant complains that the helmet is not hung out to invite
to the hall of hospitality. Now I never heard that it was
a custom to hang out a *helmet*." JOHNSON. "Hang him
up, hang him up." BOSWELL. (humouring the joke)
"Hang out his skull instead of a helmet, and you may
drink ale out of it in your hall of Odin, as he is your
enemy; that will be truly ancient. *There* will be 'Northern Antiquities.'" JOHNSON. "He's a *Whig*, Sir; a *sad
dog*, (smiling at his own violent expressions, merely for
political difference of opinion.) But he's the best traveller I ever read; he observes more things than any one
else does."

We had a calm after the storm, staid the evening and
supped, and were pleasant and gay. But Dr. Percy told

me he was very uneasy at what had passed; for there
was a gentleman there who was well acquainted with
the Northumberland family, to whom he hoped to have
appeared more respectable, by shewing how intimate
he was with Dr. Johnson, and who might now, on the
contrary, go away with an opinion to his disadvantage.
He begged I would mention this to Dr. Johnson, which
I afterwards did. His observation upon it was, "This
comes of *stratagem;* had he told me that he wished to
appear to advantage before that gentleman, he should
have been at the top of the house all the time." He
spoke of Dr. Percy in the handsomest manner.

On Monday, April 13, I dined with Johnson at Mr.
Langton's, where were Dr. Porteus, then Bishop of
Chester, now of London, and Dr. Stinton. He was at
first in a very silent mood. Before dinner he said nothing
but "Pretty baby," to one of the children. Langton said
very well to me afterwards, that he could repeat Johnson's conversation before dinner, as Johnson had said
that he could repeat a complete chapter of "The Natural
History of Iceland," from the Danish of *Horrebow,* the
whole of which was exactly thus:

"CHAP. LXXII. *Concerning Snakes.*
"There are no snakes to be met with throughout the
whole island."

At Mr. Dilly's today were Mrs. Knowles, the ingenious Quaker lady, Miss Seward, the poetess of Lichfield,
the Reverend Dr. Mayo, and the Rev. Mr. Beresford,
Tutor to the Duke of Bedford. Before dinner Dr. Johnson seized upon Mr. Charles Sheridan's "Account of the
late Revolution in Sweden," and seemed to read it ravenously, as if he devoured it, which was to all appearance his method of studying. "He knows how to read

better than any one (said Mrs. Knowles); he gets at the substance of a book directly; he tears out the heart of it." He kept it wrapt up in the tablecloth in his lap during the time of dinner, from an avidity to have one entertainment in readiness, when he should have finished another; resembling (if I may use so coarse a simile) a dog who holds a bone in his paws in reserve, while he eats something else which has been thrown to him.

The subject of cookery having been very naturally introduced at a table where Johnson, who boasted of the niceness of his palate, owned that "he always found a good dinner," he said, "I could write a better book of cookery than has ever yet been written; it should be a book upon philosophical principles. Pharmacy is now made much more simple. Cookery may be made so too. A prescription which is now compounded of five ingredients, had formerly fifty in it. So in cookery, if the nature of the ingredients be well known, much fewer will do. Then, as you cannot make bad meat good, I would tell what is the best butcher's meat, the best beef, the best pieces; how to choose young fowls; the proper seasons of different vegetables; and then how to roast and boil and compound." DILLY. "Mrs. Glasse's 'Cookery,' which is the best, was written by Dr. Hill. Half the *trade* know this." JOHNSON. "Well, Sir. This shews how much better the subject of Cookery may be treated by a philosopher. I doubt if the book be written by Dr. Hill; for, in Mrs. Glasse's 'Cookery,' which I have looked into, salt-petre and sal-prunella are spoken of as different substances, whereas sal-prunella is only salt-petre burnt on charcoal; and Hill could not be ignorant of this. However, as the greatest part of such a book is made by transcription, this mistake may have been carelessly adopted. But you shall see what a Book of Cookery I shall make! I shall agree with Mr. Dilly for the copy-right." Miss Seward. "That would be Hercules with the distaff indeed." Johnson. "No, Madam. Women can spin very well; but they cannot make a good book of Cookery."

Mrs. Knowles affected to complain that men had much more liberty allowed them than women. Johnson. "Why, Madam, women have all the liberty they should wish to have. We have all the labour and the danger, and the women all the advantage. We go to sea, we build houses, we do every thing, in short, to pay our court to the women." Mrs. Knowles. "The Doctor reasons very wittily, but not convincingly. Now, take the instance of building; the mason's wife, if she is ever seen in liquor, is ruined; the mason may get himself drunk as often as he pleases, with little loss of character; nay, may let his wife and children starve." Johnson. "Madam, you must consider, if the mason does get himself drunk, and let his wife and children starve, the parish will oblige him to find security for their maintenance. We have different modes of restraining evil. Stocks for the men, a ducking-stool for women, and a pound for beasts. If we require more perfection from women than from ourselves, it is doing them honour. And women have not the same temptations that we have; they may always live in virtuous company; men must live in the world indiscriminately. If a woman has no inclination to do what is wrong, being secured from it is no restraint to her. I am at liberty to walk into the Thames; but if I were to try it, my friends would restrain me in Bedlam, and I should be obliged to them." Mrs. Knowles. "Still, Doctor, I cannot help thinking it a hardship that more indulgence is allowed to men than to women. It gives a superiority to men, to which I do not see how they are entitled." Johnson. "It is plain, Madam, one or other must have the superiority. As

Shakespeare says, 'If two men ride on a horse, one must ride behind.'" DILLY. "I suppose, Sir, Mrs. Knowles would have them ride in panniers, one on each side." JOHNSON. "Then, Sir, the horse would throw them both." MRS. KNOWLES. "Well, I hope that in another world the sexes will be equal." BOSWELL. "That is being too ambitious, Madam. *We* might as well desire to be equal with the angels. We shall all, I hope, be happy in a future state, but we must not expect to be all happy in the same degree. It is enough, if we be happy according to our several capacities. A worthy carman will get to heaven as well as Sir Isaac Newton. Yet, though equally good, they will not have the same degrees of happiness." JOHNSON. "Probably not."

Upon this subject I had once before sounded him, by mentioning the late Reverend Mr. Brown, of Utrecht's image; that a great and small glass, though equally full, did not hold an equal quantity; which he threw out to refute David Hume's saying, that a little miss, going to dance at a ball, in a fine new dress, was as happy as a great oratour, after having made an eloquent and applauded speech. After some thought, Johnson said, "I come over to the parson."

Dr. Mayo having asked Johnson's opinion of Soame Jenyns's "View of the Internal Evidence of the Christian Religion;"—JOHNSON. "I think it a pretty book; not very theological indeed; and there seems to be an affectation of ease and carelessness, as if it were not suitable to his character to be very serious about the matter." BOSWELL. "He may have intended this to introduce his book the better among genteel people, who might be unwilling to read too grave a treatise. There is a general levity in the age. We have physicians now with bag-wigs; may we not have airy divines, at least somewhat less solemn in their appearance than they used to be?" JOHNSON.

"Jenyns might mean as you say." BOSWELL. "*You* should like his book, Mrs. Knowles, as it maintains, as you *friends* do, that courage is not a Christian virtue." MRS. KNOWLES. "Yes, indeed, I like him there; but I cannot agree with him, that friendship is not a Christian virtue." JOHNSON. "Why, Madam, strictly speaking, he is right. All friendship is preferring the interest of a friend, to the neglect, or, perhaps, against the interests of others; so that an old Greek said, 'He that has *friends* has *no friend.*' Now Christianity recommends universal benevolence,—to consider all men as our brethren; which is contrary to the virtue of friendship, as described by the ancient philosophers. Surely, Madam, your sect must approve of this; for, you call all men *friends.*" MRS. KNOWLES. "We are commanded to do good to all men, 'but especially to them who are of the household of Faith.'" JOHNSON. "Well, Madam. The household of Faith is wide enough." MRS. KNOWLES. "But, Doctor, our Saviour had twelve Apostles, yet there was *one* whom he *loved.* John was called 'the disciple whom JESUS loved.'" JOHNSON. (with eyes sparkling benignantly) "Very well, indeed, Madam. You have said very well." BOSWELL. "A fine application. Pray, Sir, had you ever thought of it?" JOHNSON. "I had not, Sir."

From this pleasing subject, he, I know not how or why, made a sudden transition to one upon which he was a violent aggressor; for he said, "I am willing to love all mankind, *except an American:*" and his inflammable corruption bursting into horrid fire, he "breathed out threatenings and slaughter;" calling them, "Rascals —Robbers—Pirates;" and exclaiming, he'd "burn and destroy them." Miss Seward, looking to him with mild but steady astonishment, said, "Sir, this is an instance that we are always most violent against those whom we have injured."—He was irritated still more by this delicate and keen reproach; and roared out another tremendous volley which one might fancy could be heard across the Atlantick. During this tempest I sat in great uneasiness, lamenting his heat of temper; till, by degrees, I diverted his attention to other topicks.

Talking of Miss ——, a literary lady, he said, "I was obliged to speak to Miss Reynolds, to let her know that I desired she would not flatter me so much." Somebody now observed, "She flatters Garrick." JOHNSON. "She is in the right to flatter Garrick. She is in the right for two reasons; first, because she has the world with her, who have been praising Garrick these thirty years; and secondly, because she is rewarded for it by Garrick. Why should she flatter *me?* I can do nothing for her. Let her carry her praise to a better market. (Then turning to Mrs. Knowles.) You, Madam, have been flattering me all the evening; I wish you would give Boswell a little now. If you knew his merit as well as I do, you would say a great deal; he is the best travelling companion in the world."

April 17, being Good-Friday, I waited on Johnson, as usual. I observed at breakfast that although it was a part of his abstemious discipline on this most solemn fast, to take no milk in his tea, yet when Mrs. Desmoulins inadvertently poured it in, he did not reject it. I talked of the strange indecision of mind, and imbecility in the common occurrences of life, which we may observe in some people. JOHNSON. "Why, Sir, I am in the habit of getting others to do things for me." BOSWELL. "What, Sir! have you that weakness?" JOHNSON. "Yes, Sir. But I always think afterwards I should have done better for myself."

I told him that at a gentleman's house where there was thought to be such extravagance or bad management, that he was living much beyond his income, his lady had objected to the cutting of a pickled mango, and that I had taken an opportunity to ask the price of it, and found it was only two shillings; so here was a very poor saving. JOHNSON. "Sir, that is the blundering œconomy of a narrow understanding. It is stopping one hole in a sieve."

I expressed some inclination to publish an account of my *Travels* upon the continent of Europe, for which I had a variety of materials collected. JOHNSON. "I do not say, Sir, you may not publish your travels; but I give you my opinion, that you would lessen yourself by it. What can you tell of countries so well known as those upon the continent of Europe, which you have visited?" BOSWELL. "But I can give an entertaining narrative, with many incidents, anecdotes, *jeux d'esprit*, and remarks, so as to make very pleasant reading." JOHNSON. "Why, Sir, most modern travellers in Europe who have published their travels, have been laughed at: I would not have you added to the number. The world is now not contented to be merely entertained by a traveller's narrative; they want to learn something. Now some of my friends asked me, why I did not give some account of my travels in France. The reason is plain; intelligent readers had seen more of France than I had. *You* might have liked my travels in France, and THE CLUB might have liked them; but, upon the whole, there would have been more ridicule than good produced by them." BOSWELL. "I cannot agree with you, Sir. People would like to read what you say of any thing. Suppose a face has been painted by fifty painters before; still we love to see it done by Sir Joshua." JOHNSON. "True, Sir, but Sir Joshua cannot paint a face when he has not time to look on it." BOSWELL. "Sir, a sketch of any sort by him is valuable. And, Sir, to talk to you in your own style (raising my voice, and shaking my head,) you *should* have given us your travels in France. I am *sure* I am right, and *there's an end on't.*"

I said to him that it was certainly true, as my friend Dempster had observed in his letter to me upon the subject, that a great part of what was in his "Journey to the Western Islands of Scotland," had been in his mind before he left London. JOHNSON. "Why yes, Sir, the topicks were; and books of travels will be good in proportion to what a man has previously in his mind; his knowing what to observe; his power of contrasting one mode of life with another. As the Spanish proverb says, 'He, who would bring home the wealth of the Indies, must carry the wealth of the Indies with him.' So it is in travelling; a man must carry knowledge with him, if he would bring home knowledge." BOSWELL. "The proverb, I suppose, Sir, means, he must carry a large stock with him to trade with." JOHNSON. "Yes, Sir."

It was a delightful day: as we walked to St. Clement's church, I again remarked that Fleet-street was the most cheerful scene in the world. "Fleet-street (said I,) is in my mind more delightful than Tempé." JOHNSON. "Ay, Sir; but let it be compared with Mull."

There was a very numerous congregation today at St. Clement's church, which Dr. Johnson said he observed with pleasure.

And now I am to give a pretty full account of one of the most curious incidents in Johnson's life, of which he himself has made the following minute on this day: "In my return from church, I was accosted by Edwards, an old fellow-collegian, who had not seen me since 1729. He knew me, and asked if I remembered one Edwards; I did not at first recollect the name, but gradually as we walked along, recovered it, and told him a conversation that had passed at an alehouse between us. My purpose is to continue our acquaintance."

It was in Butcher-row that this meeting happened. Mr. Edwards, who was a decent-looking elderly man in grey clothes, and a wig of many curls, accosted Johnson with familiar confidence, knowing who he was, while Johnson returned his salutation with a courteous formality, as to a stranger. But as soon as Edwards had brought to his recollection their having been at Pembroke-College together nine-and-forty years ago, he seemed much pleased, asked where he lived, and said he should be glad to see him in Bolt-court. EDWARDS. "Ah, Sir! we are old men now." JOHNSON, (who never liked to think of being old:) "Don't let us discourage one another." EDWARDS. "Why, Doctor, you look stout and hearty, I am happy to see you so; for the newspapers told us you were very ill." JOHNSON. "Ay, Sir, they are always telling lies of *us old fellows.*"

Wishing to be present at more of so singular a conversation as that between two fellow-collegians, who had lived forty years in London without ever having chanced to meet, I whispered to Mr. Edwards that Dr. Johnson was going home, and that he had better accompany him now. So Edwards walked along with us, I eagerly assisting to keep up the conversation. Mr. Edwards informed Dr. Johnson that he had practised long as a solicitor in Chancery, but that he now lived in the country upon a little farm, about sixty acres, just by Stevenage in Hertfordshire, and that he came to London (to Barnard's Inn, No. 6,) generally twice a week. Johnson appearing to be in a reverie, Mr. Edwards addressed himself to me, and expatiated on the pleasure of living in the country. BOSWELL. "I have no notion of this, Sir. What you have to entertain you, is, I think, exhausted in half an hour." EDWARDS. "What? don't you love to have hope realized? I see my grass, and my corn, and my trees growing. Now, for instance, I am curious to see if this frost has not nipped my fruit-trees." JOHNSON, (who we did not imagine was attending:) "You find, Sir, you have fears as well as hopes."—So well did he see the whole, when another saw but the half of a subject.

When we got to Dr. Johnson's house, and were seated in his library, the dialogue went on admirably. EDWARDS. "Sir, I remember you would not let us say *prodigious* at College. For even then, Sir, (turning to me,) he was delicate in language, and we all feared him." JOHNSON, (to Edwards:) "From your having practised the law long, Sir, I presume you must be rich." EDWARDS. "No, Sir; I got a good deal of money; but I had a number of poor relations to whom I gave a great part of it." JOHNSON. "Sir, you have been rich in the most valuable sense of the word." EDWARDS. "But I shall not die rich." JOHNSON. "Nay, sure, Sir, it is better to *live* rich, than to *die* rich." EDWARDS. "I wish I had continued at College." JOHNSON. "Why do you wish that, Sir?" EDWARDS. "Because I think I should have had a much easier life than mine has been. I should have been a parson, and had a good living, like Bloxham and several others, and lived comfortably." JOHNSON. "Sir, the life of a parson, of a conscientious clergyman, is not easy. I have always considered a clergyman as the father of a larger family than he is able to maintain. I would rather have Chancery suits upon my hands than the cure of souls. No, Sir, I do not envy a clergyman's life as an easy life, nor do I envy the clergyman who makes it an easy life."—Here taking himself up all of a sudden, he exclaimed, "O! Mr. Edwards! I'll convince you that I recollect you. Do you remember our drinking together at an alehouse near Pembroke gate? At that time, you told me of the

Eton boy, who, when verses on our SAVIOUR's turning water into wine were prescribed as an exercise, brought up a single line, which was highly admired:

Vidit et erubuit lympha pudica DEUM.

and I told you of another fine line in 'Camden's Remains,' an eulogy upon one of our Kings, who was succeeded by his son, a prince of equal merit:

Mira cano, Sol occubuit, nox nulla secuta est.

EDWARDS. "You are a philosopher, Dr. Johnson. I have tried too in my time to be a philosopher; but, I don't know how, cheerfulness was always breaking in." —Mr. Burke, Sir Joshua Reynolds, Mr. Courtenay, Mr. Malone, and, indeed, all the eminent men to whom I have mentioned this, have thought it an exquisite trait of character. The truth is, that philosophy, like religion, is too generally supposed to be hard and severe, at least so grave as to exclude all gaiety.

EDWARDS. "I have been twice married, Doctor. You, I suppose, have never known what it was to have a wife." JOHNSON. "Sir, I have known what it was to have a wife, and (in a solemn tender faultering tone) I have known what it was to *lose a wife*.—It had almost broke my heart."

EDWARDS. "How do you live, Sir? For my part, I must have my regular meals, and a glass of good wine. I find I require it." JOHNSON. "I now drink no wine, Sir. Early in life I drank wine: for many years I drank none. I then for some years drank a great deal." EDWARDS. "Some hogsheads, I warrant you." JOHNSON. "I then had a severe illness, and left it off, and I have never begun it again. I never felt any difference upon myself from eating one thing rather than another, nor from one kind of weather rather than another. There are people, I believe, who feel a difference; but I am not one of them. And as to regular meals, I have fasted from the Sunday's dinner to the Tuesday's dinner, without any inconvenience. I believe it is best to eat just as one is hungry: but a man who is in business, or a man who has a family, must have stated meals. I am a straggler. I may leave this town and go to Grand Cairo, without being missed here or observed there." EDWARDS. "Don't you eat supper, Sir?" JOHNSON. "No, Sir." EDWARDS. "For my part, now, I consider supper as a turn-pike through which one must pass, in order to get to bed."

JOHNSON. "You are a lawyer, Mr. Edwards. Lawyers know life practically. A bookish man should always have them to converse with. They have what he wants." EDWARDS. "I am grown old: I am sixty-five." JOHNSON. "I shall be sixty-eight next birthday. Come, Sir, drink water, and put in for a hundred."

This interview confirmed my opinion of Johnson's most humane and benevolent heart. His cordial and placid behavior to an old fellow-collegian, a man so different from himself; and his telling him that he would go down to his farm and visit him, shewed a kindness of disposition very rare at an advanced age. He observed, "how wonderful it was that they had both been in London forty years, without having ever once met, and both walkers in the street too!" Mr. Edwards, when going away, again recurred to his consciousness of senility, and looking full in Johnson's face, said to him, "You'll find in Dr. Young,

O my coevals! remnants of yourselves."

Johnson did not relish this at all; but shook his head with impatience. Edwards walked off seemingly highly-pleased with the honour of having been thus noticed by Dr. Johnson. When he was gone, I said to Johnson, I thought him but a weak man. JOHNSON. "Why, yes, Sir. Here is a man who has passed through life without experience: yet I would rather have him with me than a more sensible man who will not talk readily. This man is always willing to say what he has to say." Yet Dr. Johnson had himself by no means that willingness which he praised so much, and I think so justly; for who has not felt the painful effect of the dreary void, when there is a total silence in a company, for any length of time; or, which is as bad, or perhaps worse, when the conversation is with difficulty kept up by a perpetual effort?

Johnson once observed to me, "Tom Tyers described me the best: 'Sir, (said he,) you are like a ghost; you never speak till you are spoken to.'"

Mr. Edwards had said to me aside, that Dr. Johnson should have been of a profession. I repeated the remark to Johnson that I might have his own thoughts on the subject. JOHNSON. "Sir, it *would* have been better that I had been of a profession. I ought to have been a lawyer." BOSWELL. "I do not think, Sir, it would have been better, for we should not have had the English Dictionary." JOHNSON. "But you would have had Reports." BOSWELL. "Aye; but there would not have been another, who could have written the Dictionary. There have been very many good Judges. Suppose you had been Lord Chancellor; you would have delivered opinions with more extent of mind, and in a more ornamented manner, than perhaps any Chancellor ever did, or ever will do. But, I believe, causes have been as judiciously decided as you could have done." JOHNSON. "Yes, Sir. Property has been as well settled."

Johnson, however, had a noble ambition floating in his mind, and had, undoubtedly, often speculated on the possibility of his super-eminent powers being rewarded in this great and liberal country by the highest

honours of the State. Sir William Scott informs me, that
upon the death of the late Lord Lichfield, who was
Chancellor of the University of Oxford, he said to Johnson. "What a pity it is, Sir, that you did not follow the
profession of the law. You might have been Lord Chancellor of Great Britain, and attained to the dignity of
the peerage; and now that the title of Lichfield, your
native city, is extinct, you might have had it." Johnson,
upon this, seemed much agitated; and, in an angry tone,
exclaimed, "Why will you vex me by suggesting this,
when it is too late?"

But he did not repine at the prosperity of others. The
late Dr. Thomas Leland told Mr. Courtenay, that when
Mr. Edmund Burke shewed Johnson his fine house and
lands near Beaconsfield, Johnson coolly said, *"Non equi-
dem invideo; miror magis."*

Yet no man had a higher notion of the dignity of
literature than Johnson, or was more determined in
maintaining the respect which he justly considered as due
to it. Of this, besides the general tenor of his conduct
in society, some characteristical instances may be mentioned.

He told Sir Joshua Reynolds, that once when he dined
in a numerous company of booksellers, where the room
being small, the head of the table, at which he sat, was
almost close to the fire, he persevered in suffering a
great deal of inconvenience from the heat, rather than
quit his place, and let one of them sit above him.

Goldsmith, in his diverting simplicity, complained one
day, in a mixed company, of Lord Camden. "I met him
(said he) at Lord Clare's house in the country, and he
took no more notice of me than if I had been an ordinary
man." The company having laughed heartily, Johnson
stood forth in defence of his friend. "Nay, Gentlemen,
(said he,) Dr. Goldsmith is in the right. A nobleman

ought to have made up to such a man as Goldsmith; and I think it is much against Lord Camden that he neglected him."

Nor could he patiently endure to hear, that such respect as he thought due only to higher intellectual qualities, should be bestowed on men of slighter, though perhaps more amusing, talents. I told him, that one morning, when I went to breakfast with Garrick, who was very vain of his intimacy with Lord Camden, he accosted me thus:—"Pray now, did you—did you meet a little lawyer turning the corner, eh?"—"No, Sir, (said I.) Pray what do you mean by the question?"—"Why, (replied Garrick, with an affected indifference, yet as if standing on tip-toe,) Lord Camden has this moment left me. We have had a long walk together." JOHNSON. "Well, Sir, Garrick talked very properly. Lord Camden *was a little lawyer* to be associating so familiarly with a player."

Sir Joshua Reynolds observed, with great truth, that Johnson considered Garrick to be as it were his *property*. He would allow no man either to blame or to praise Garrick in his presence, without contradicting him.

On Saturday, April 14, I drank tea with him. He praised the late Mr. Duncombe, of Canterbury, as a pleasing man. "He used to come to me; I did not seek much after *him*. Indeed I never sought much after any body." BOSWELL. "Lord Orrery, I suppose." JOHNSON. "No, Sir; I never went to him but when he sent for me." BOSWELL. "Richardson?" JOHNSON. "Yes, Sir. But I sought after George Psalmanazar the most. I used to go and sit with him at an alehouse in the city."

I am happy to mention another instance which I discovered of his *seeking after* a man of merit. Soon after the Honourable Daines Barrington had published his excellent "Observations on the Statutes," Johnson waited on that worthy and learned gentleman; and, having told him his name, courteously said, "I have read your book, Sir, with great pleasure, and wish to be better known to you." Thus began an acquaintance, which was continued with mutual regard as long as Johnson lived.

Talking of a recent seditious delinquent, he said, "They should set him in the pillory, that he may be punished in a way that would disgrace him." I observed, that the pillory does not always disgrace. And I mentioned an instance of a gentleman, who I thought was not dishonoured by it. JOHNSON. "Ay, but he was, Sir. He could not mouth and strut as he used to do, after having been there. People are not willing to ask a man to their tables, who has stood in the pillory."

The gentleman who had dined with us at Dr. Percy's came in. Johnson attacked the Americans with intemperate vehemence of abuse. I said something in their favour; and added, that I was always sorry, when he talked on that subject. This, it seems, exasperated him; though he said nothing at the time. The cloud was charged with sulphureous vapour, which was afterwards to burst in thunder.—We talked of a gentleman who was running out his fortune in London; and I said, "We must get him out of it. All his friends must quarrel with him, and that will soon drive him away." JOHNSON. "Nay, Sir, we'll send *you* to him. If your company does not drive a man out of his house, nothing will." This was a horrible shock, for which there was no visible cause. I afterwards asked him why he had said so harsh a thing. JOHNSON. "Because, Sir, you made me angry about the Americans." BOSWELL. "But why did you not take your revenge directly?" JOHNSON (smiling) "Because, Sir, I had nothing ready. A man cannot strike till he has his weapons." This was a candid and pleasant confession.

He shewed me tonight his drawing-room, very genteelly fitted up; and said, "Mrs. Thrale sneered, when I talked of my having asked you and your lady to live at my house. I was obliged to tell her, that you would be in as respectable a situation in my house as in hers. Sir, the insolence of wealth will creep out." Boswell. "She has a little both of the insolence of wealth, and the conceit of parts." Johnson. "The insolence of wealth is a wretched thing; but the conceit of parts has some foundation. To be sure, it should not be. But who is without it?" Boswell. "Yourself, Sir." Johnson. "Why, I play no tricks: I lay no traps." Boswell. "No, Sir. You are six feet high, and you only do not stoop."

We talked of the numbers of people that sometimes have composed the households of great families. I mentioned that there were a hundred in the family of the present Earl of Eglintoune's father. Dr. Johnson seeming to doubt it, I began to enumerate. "Let us see: my Lord and my Lady two." Johnson. "Nay, Sir, if you are to count by twos, you may be long enough." Boswell. "Well, but now I add two sons and seven daughters, and a servant for each, that will make twenty; so we have the fifth part already." Johnson. "Very true. You get at twenty pretty readily; but you will not so easily get further on. We grow to five feet pretty readily; but it is not so easy to grow to seven."

On Saturday, April 25, I dined with him at Sir Joshua Reynolds's, with the learned Dr. Musgrave, Counsellor Leland of Ireland, son to the historian, Mrs. Cholmondeley, and some more ladies. I happened, I know not how, to say that a pamphlet meant a prose piece. Johnson. "No, Sir. A few sheets of poetry unbound are a pamphlet, as much as a few sheets of prose." Musgrave. "A pamphlet may be understood to mean a poetical piece in Westminster-Hall, that is, in formal language; but in common language it is understood to mean prose."

JOHNSON. (and here was one of the many instances of his knowing clearly and telling exactly how a thing is,) "A pamphlet is understood in common language to mean prose, only from this, that there is so much more prose written than poetry; as when we say a *book,* prose is understood for the same reason, though a book may as well be in poetry as in prose. We understand what is most general, and we name what is less frequent."

We talked of a lady's verses on Ireland. MISS REYNOLDS. "Have you seen them, Sir?" JOHNSON. "No, Madam, I have seen a translation from Horace, by one of her daughters. She shewed it me." MISS REYNOLDS. "And how was it, Sir?" JOHNSON. "Why, very well for a young Miss's verses;—that is to say, compared with excellence, nothing; but, very well, for the person who wrote them. I am vexed at being shewn verses in that manner." MISS REYNOLDS. "But if they should be good, why not give them hearty praise?" JOHNSON. "Why, Madam, because I have not then got the better of my bad humour from having been shewn them. You must consider, Madam, before-hand they may be bad as well as good. Nobody has a right to put another under such a difficulty, that he must either hurt the person by telling the truth, or hurt himself by telling what is not true." BOSWELL. "A man often shews his writings to people of eminence, to obtain from them, either from their good-nature, or from their not being able to tell the truth firmly, a commendation, of which he may afterwards avail himself." JOHNSON. "Very true, Sir. Therefore the man, who is asked by an authour what he thinks of his work, is put to the torture, and is not obliged to speak the truth; so that what he says is not considered as his opinion; yet he has said it, and cannot retract it; and this authour, when mankind are hunting him with a cannister at his tail, can say, 'I would not have published, had not Johnson, or Reynolds, or Musgrave, or some other good judge commended the work.' Yet I consider it as a very difficult question in conscience, whether one should advise a man not to publish a work, if profit be his object; for the man may say, 'Had it not been for you, I should have had the money.' Now you cannot be sure; for you have only your own opinion, and the publick may think very differently." SIR JOSHUA REYNOLDS. "You must upon such an occasion have two judgements; one as to the real value of the work, the other as to what may please the general taste at the time." JOHNSON. "But you can be *sure* of neither; and therefore I should scruple much to give a suppressive vote. Both Goldsmith's comedies were once refused; his first by Garrick, his second by Colman, who was prevailed on at last by much solicitation, nay, a kind of force, to bring it on. His 'Vicar of Wakefield' I myself did not think would have had much success. It was written and sold to a bookseller, before his 'Traveller;' but published after; so little expectation had the bookseller from it. Had it been sold after the 'Traveller,' he might have had twice as much money for it, though sixty guineas was no mean price. The bookseller had the advantage of Goldsmith's reputation from 'The Traveller' in the sale, though Goldsmith had it not in selling the copy." SIR JOSHUA REYNOLDS. "The Beggar's Opera affords a proof how strangely people will differ in opinion about a literary performance. Burke thinks it has no merit." JOHNSON. "It was refused by one of the houses; but I should have thought it would succeed, not from any great excellence in the writing, but from the novelty, and the general spirit and gaiety of the piece, which keeps the audience always attentive, and dismisses them in good humour."

We went to the drawing-room, where was a considerable increase of company. It was observed, that avarice was inherent in some dispositions. JOHNSON. "No man was born a miser, because no man was born to possession. Every man is born *cupidus*—desirous of getting; but not *avarus*—desirous of keeping." BOSWELL. "I have heard old Mr. Sheridan maintain, with much ingenuity, that a complete miser is a happy man; a miser who gives himself wholly to the one passion of saving." JOHNSON. "That is flying in the face of all the world, who have called an avaricious man a *miser,* because he is miserable. No, Sir, a man who both spends and saves money is the happiest man, because he has both enjoyments."

The conversation having turned on *Bon-Mots,* he quoted, from one of the *Ana,* an exquisite instance of flattery in a maid of honour in France, who being asked by the Queen what o'clock it was, answered, "What your Majesty pleases."

He observed, "A man cannot with propriety speak of himself, except he relates simple facts; as, 'I was at Richmond:' or what depends on mensuration; as, 'I am six feet high.' He is sure he has been at Richmond; he is sure he is six feet high, but he cannot be sure he is wise, or that he has any other excellence. Then, all censure of a man's self is oblique praise. It is in order to shew how much he can spare. It has all the invidiousness of self-praise, and all the reproach of falsehood." BOSWELL. "Sometimes it may proceed from a man's strong consciousness of his faults being observed. He knows that others would throw him down, and therefore he had better lie down softly of his own accord."

On Tuesday, April 28, he was engaged to dine at General Paoli's, where, as I have already observed, I was still entertained in elegant hospitality, and with all the ease and comfort of a home. I called on him, and accompanied him in a hackney-coach. We stopped first at the bottom of Hedge-lane, into which he went to leave a letter, "with good news for a poor man in distress," as he told me. I did not question him particularly as to this. He himself often resembled Lady Bolingbroke's lively description of Pope: that "he was *un politique aux choux et aux raves.*" He would say, "I dine today in Grosvenor-square;" this might be with a Duke; or, perhaps, "I dine today at the other end of the town:" or, "A gentleman of great eminence called on me yesterday."—He loved thus to keep things floating in conjecture: *Omne ignotum pro magnifico est.* I believe I ventured to dissipate the cloud, to unveil the mystery, more freely and frequently than any of his friends. We stopped again at Wirgman's, the well-known *toy-shop,* in St. James's-Street, at the corner of St. James's-Place, to which he had been directed, but not clearly, for he searched about some time, and could not find it at first; and said, "To direct one only to a corner shop is *toying* with one." I suppose he meant this as a play upon the word *toy;* it was the first time that I knew him to stoop to such sport. After he had been some time in the shop, he sent for me to come out of the coach, and help him to choose a pair of silver buckles, as those he had were too small. Probably this alteration in dress had been suggested by Mrs. Thrale, by associating with whom, his external appearance was much improved. He got better cloaths; and the dark colour, from which he never deviated, was enlivened by metal buttons. His wigs, too, were much better; and during their travels in France, he was furnished with a Paris-made wig, of handsome construction. This choosing of silver buckles was a negociation: "Sir, (said he,) I will not have the ridiculous large ones now in fashion; and I will give no more than a guinea for a pair." Such were the *principles* of the business; and, after some examination, he was fitted. As we drove along, I found him in a talking humour, of which I availed myself. BOSWELL. "I was this morning in Ridley's shop, Sir; and was told, that the collection called '*Johnsoniana*' has sold very much." JOHNSON. "Yet the 'Journey to the Hebrides' has not had a great sale." BOSWELL. "That is strange." JOHNSON. "Yes, Sir; for in that book I have told the world a great deal that they did not know before."

BOSWELL. "I drank chocolate, Sir, this morning with Mr. Eld; and, to my no small surprize, found him to be a *Staffordshire Whig*, a being which I did not believe had existed." JOHNSON. "Sir, there are rascals in all countries." BOSWELL. "Eld said, a Tory was a creature generated between a non-juring parson and one's grandmother." JOHNSON. "And I have always said, the first Whig was the Devil."

At General Paoli's were Sir Joshua Reynolds, Mr. Langton, Marchese Gherardi of Lombardy, and Mr. John Spottiswoode the younger, of Spottiswoode, the solicitor. At this time fears of an invasion were circulated; to obviate which, Mr. Spottiswoode observed, that Mr. Fraser the engineer, who had lately come from Dunkirk, said, that the French had the same fears of us. JOHNSON. "It is thus that mutual cowardice keeps us in peace. Were one-half of mankind brave, and one-half cowards, the brave would be always beating the cowards. Were all brave, they would lead a very uneasy life; all would be continually fighting: but being all cowards, we go on very well."

We talked of drinking wine. JOHNSON. "I require wine, only when I am alone. I have then often wished for it, and often taken it." SPOTTISWOODE. "What, by way of a companion, Sir?" JOHNSON. "To get rid of myself, to send myself away. Wine gives great pleasure;

and every pleasure is of itself a good. It is a good, unless counterbalanced by evil. A man may have a strong reason not to drink wine; and that may be greater than the pleasure. Wine makes a man better pleased with himself. I do not say that it makes him more pleasing to others. Sometimes it does. But the danger is, that while a man grows better pleased with himself, he may be growing less pleasing to others. Wine gives a man nothing. It neither gives him knowledge nor wit; it only animates a man, and enables him to bring out what a dread of the company has repressed. It only puts in motion what has been locked up in frost. But this may be good, or it may be bad." SPOTTISWOODE. "So, Sir, wine is a key which opens a box; but this box may be either full or empty?" JOHNSON. "Nay, Sir, conversation is the key: wine is a pick-lock, which forces open the box, and injures it. A man should cultivate his mind so as to have that confidence and readiness without wine, which wine gives." BOSWELL. "The great difficulty of resisting wine is from benevolence. For instance, a good worthy man asks you to taste his wine, which he has had twenty years in his cellar." JOHNSON. "Sir, all this notion about benevolence arises from a man's imagining himself to be of more importance to others, than he really is. They don't care a farthing whether he drinks wine or not." SIR JOSHUA REYNOLDS. "Yes, they do for the time." JOHNSON. "For the time!—If they care this minute, they forget it the next. And as for the good worthy man; how do you know he is good and worthy? No good and worthy man will insist upon another man's drinking wine. As to the wine twenty years in the cellar, —of ten men, three say this, merely because they must say something; three are telling a lie, when they say they have had the wine twenty years;—three would rather save the wine;—one, perhaps, cares. I allow it is something to please one's company; and people are always pleased with those who partake pleasure with them. But after a man has brought himself to relinquish the great personal pleasure which arises from drinking wine, any other consideration is a trifle. To please others by drinking wine, is something only, if there be nothing against it. I should, however, be sorry to offend worthy men:

> Curst be the verse, how well so e'er it flow,
> That tends to make one worthy man my foe."

BOSWELL. "Curst be the *spring*, the water." JOHNSON. "But let us consider what a sad thing it would be, if we were obliged to drink or do any thing else that may happen to be agreeable to the company where we are." LANGTON. "By the same rule you must join with a gang of cut-purses." JOHNSON. "Yes, Sir: but yet we must do justice to wine; we must allow it the power it possesses. To make a man pleased with himself, let me tell you, is doing a very great thing;

> *Si patriæ volumus, si* NOBIS *vivere cari.*"

I was at this time myself a water-drinker, upon trial, by Johnson's recommendation. JOHNSON. "Boswell is a bolder combatant than Sir Joshua: he argues for wine without the help of wine; but Sir Joshua with it." SIR JOSHUA REYNOLDS. "But to please one's company is a strong motive." JOHNSON. (who, from drinking only water, supposed every body who drank wine to be elevated,) "I won't argue any more with you, Sir. You are too far gone." SIR JOSHUA. "I should have thought so indeed, Sir, had I made such a speech as you have now done." JOHNSON. (drawing himself in, and, I really thought blushing,) "Nay, don't be angry. I did not mean to offend you." SIR JOSHUA. "At first the taste of wine was disagreeable to me; but I brought myself to drink it, that I might be like other people. The pleasure of drinking wine is so connected with pleasing your company, that altogether there is something of social goodness in it." JOHNSON. "Sir, this is only saying the same thing over again." SIR JOSHUA. "No, this is new." JOHNSON. "You put it in new words, but it is an old thought. This is one of the disadvantages of wine, it makes a man mistake words for thoughts." BOSWELL. "I think it is a new thought; at least, it is in a new *attitude*." JOHNSON. "Nay, Sir, it is only in a new coat; or an old coat with a new facing. (Then laughing heartily.) It is the old dog in a new doublet.—An extraordinary instance, however, may occur where a man's patron will do nothing for him, unless he will drink: *there* may be a good reason for drinking."

I mentioned a nobleman, who I believed was really uneasy, if his company would not drink hard. JOHNSON. "That is from having had people about him whom he has been accustomed to command." BOSWELL. "Supposing I should be *tête-à-tête* with him at table." JOHNSON. "Sir, there is no more reason for your drinking with *him,* than his being sober with *you.*" BOSWELL. "Why, that is true; for it would do him less hurt to be sober, than it would do me to get drunk." JOHNSON. "Yes, Sir; and from what I have heard of him, one would not wish to sacrifice himself to such a man. If he must always have somebody to drink with him, he should buy a slave, and then he would be sure to have it. They who submit to drink as another pleases, make themselves his slaves." BOSWELL. "But, Sir, you will surely make allowance for the duty of hospitality. A gentleman who loves drinking, comes to visit me." JOHNSON. "Sir, a man knows whom he visits; he comes to the table of a sober man." BOSWELL. "But, Sir, you and I should not have been so well received in the Highlands and Hebrides, if

I had not drunk with our worthy friends. Had I drunk water only as you did, they would not have been so cordial." JOHNSON. "Sir William Temple mentions, that in his travels through the Netherlands he had two or three gentlemen with him; and when a bumper was necessary, he put it on *them*. Were I to travel again through the islands, I would have Sir Joshua with me to take the bumpers." BOSWELL. "But, Sir, let me put a case. Suppose Sir Joshua should take a jaunt into Scotland; he does me the honour to pay me a visit at my house in the country; I am overjoyed at seeing him; we are quite by ourselves; shall I unsociably and churlishly let him sit drinking by himself? No, no, my dear Sir Joshua, you shall not be treated so, I *will* take a bottle with you."

On Wednesday, April 29, I dined with him at Mr. Allan Ramsay's. Johnson harangued against drinking wine. "A man (said he,) may choose whether he will have abstemiousness and knowledge, or claret and ignorance." Dr. Robertson, (who is very companionable,) was beginning to dissent as to the proscription of claret. JOHNSON: (with a placid smile.) "Nay, Sir, you shall not differ with me; as I have said that the man is most perfect who takes in the most things, I am for knowledge and claret." ROBERTSON: (holding a glass of generous claret in his hand.) "Sir, I can only drink your health." JOHNSON. "Sir, I should be sorry if *you* should be ever in such a state as to be able to do nothing more." ROBERTSON. "Dr. Johnson, allow me to say, that in one respect I have the advantage of you; when you were in Scotland you would not come to hear any of our preachers, whereas, when I am here, I attend your publick worship without scruple, and indeed with great satisfaction." JOHNSON. "Why, Sir, that is not so extraordinary; the King of Siam sent ambassadors to Louis the

Fourteenth; but Louis the Fourteenth sent none to the King of Siam."

Here my friend for once discovered a want of knowledge or forgetfulness; for Louis the Fourteenth did send an embassy to the King of Siam, and the Abbé Choisi, who was employed in it, published an account of it in two volumes.

Next day, Thursday, April 30, I found him at home by himself. JOHNSON. "Well, Sir, Ramsay gave us a splendid dinner. I love Ramsay. You will not find a man in whose conversation there is more instruction, more information, and more elegance, than in Ramsay's." BOSWELL. "What I admire in Ramsay, is his continuing to be so young." JOHNSON. "Why, yes, Sir; it is to be admired. I value myself upon this, that there is nothing of the old man in my conversation. I am now sixty-eight, and I have no more of it than at twenty-eight." BOSWELL. "But, Sir, would not you wish to know old age? He who is never an old man, does not know the whole of human life; for old age is one of the divisions of it." JOHNSON. "Nay, Sir, what talk is this?" BOSWELL. "I mean, Sir, the Sphinx's description of it;—morning, noon, and night. I would know night, as well as morning and noon." JOHNSON. "What, Sir, would you know what it is to feel the evils of old age? Would you have the gout? Would you have decrepitude?"—Seeing him heated, I would not argue any farther; but I was confident that I was in the right. I would, in due time, be a Nestor, an elder of the people; and there *should* be some difference between the conversation of twenty-eight and sixty-eight. A grave picture should not be gay. There is a serene, solemn, placid old age. JOHNSON. "Mrs. Thrale's mother said of me what flattered me much. A clergyman was complaining of want of society in the country where he lived; and said, 'They talk of *runts*;'

(that is, young cows.) 'Sir, (said Mrs. Salusbury,) Mr. Johnson would learn to talk of runts:' meaning that I was a man who would make the most of my situation, whatever it was." He added, "I think myself a very polite man."

On Saturday, May 2, I dined with him at Sir Joshua Reynolds's, where there was a very large company, and a great deal of conversation; but owing to some circumstances which I cannot now recollect, I have no record of any part of it, except that there were several people there by no means of the Johnsonian school; so that less attention was paid to him than usual, which put him out of humour; and upon some imaginary offence from me, he attacked me with such rudeness, that I was vexed and angry, because it gave those persons an opportunity of enlarging upon his supposed ferocity, and ill-treatment of his best friends. I was so much hurt, and had my pride so much roused, that I kept away from him for a week; and perhaps, might have kept away much longer, nay, gone to Scotland without seeing him again, had not we fortunately met and been reconciled. To such unhappy chances are human friendships liable.

On Friday, May 8, I dined with him at Mr. Langton's. I was reserved and silent, which I suppose he perceived, and might recollect the cause. After dinner, when Mr. Langton was called out of the room, and we were by ourselves, he drew his chair near to mine, and said in a tone of conciliating courtesy, "Well, how have you done?" BOSWELL. "Sir, you have made me very uneasy by your behaviour to me when we last were at Sir Joshua Reynolds's. You know, my dear Sir, no man has a greater respect and affection for you, or would sooner go to the end of the world to serve you. Now to treat me so—." He insisted that I had interrupted him, which I assured him was not the case; and proceeded—"But why treat me so before people who neither love you nor me?" JOHNSON. "Well, I am sorry for it. I'll make it up to you twenty different ways, as you please." BOSWELL. "I said today to Sir Joshua, when he observed that you *tossed* me sometimes—I don't care how often, or how high he tosses me, when only friends are present, for then I fall upon soft ground: but I do not like falling on stones, which is the case when enemies are present.—I think this is a pretty good image, Sir." JOHNSON. "Sir, it is one of the happiest I have ever heard."

Mr. Langton having repeated the anecdote of Addison having distinguished between his powers in conversation and in writing, by saying "I have only ninepence in my pocket; but I can draw for a thousand pounds;"—JOHNSON. "He had not that retort ready, Sir: he had prepared it beforehand." LANGTON: (turning to me.) "A fine surmise. Set a thief to catch a thief."

On Tuesday, May 12, I waited on the Earl of Marchmont, to know if his Lordship would favour Dr. Johnson with information concerning Pope, whose Life he was about to write. Johnson had not flattered himself with the hopes of receiving any civility from this nobleman; for he said to me, when I mentioned Lord Marchmont as one who could tell him a great deal about Pope, —"Sir, he will tell *me* nothing." I had the honour of being known to his Lordship, and applied to him of myself, without being commissioned by Johnson. His Lordship behaved in the most polite and obliging manner, promised to tell all he recollected about Pope, and was so very courteous as to say, "Tell Dr. Johnson, I have a great respect for him, and am ready to shew it in any way I can. I am to be in the city tomorrow, and will call at his house as I return." His Lordship however asked, "Will he write the Lives of the Poets impartially? He was the first that brought Whig and Tory into a Dic-

tionary. And what do you think of his definition of Excise? Do you know the history of his aversion to the
word *transpire?*" Then taking down the folio Dictionary,
he shewed it with this censure on its secondary sense:
"To escape from secrecy to notice; a sense lately in-
novated from France, without necessity." The truth was,
Lord Bolingbroke, who left the Jacobites, first used it;
therefore, it was to be condemned. He should have
shewn what word would do for it, if it was unnecessary.
I afterwards put the question to Johnson: "Why, Sir,
(said he,) *get abroad.*" BOSWELL. "That, Sir, is using
two words." JOHNSON. "Sir, there is no end of this. You
may as well insist to have a word for old age." BOSWELL.
"Well, Sir, Senectus." JOHNSON. "Nay, Sir, to insist always that there should be one word to express a thing
in English, because there is one in another language, is
to change the language."

I availed myself of this opportunity to hear from his
Lordship many particulars both of Pope and Lord Bolingbroke, which I have in writing.

I proposed to Lord Marchmont, that he should revise
Johnson's Life of Pope: "So (said his Lordship) you
would put me in a dangerous situation. You know he
knocked down Osborne, the bookseller."

Elated with the success of my spontaneous exertion
to procure material and respectable aid to Johnson for
his very favourite work, "The Lives of the Poets," I
hastened down to Mr. Thrale's at Streatham, where he
now was, that I might insure his being at home next
day; and after dinner, when I thought he would receive
the good news in the best humour, I announced it
eagerly: "I have been at work for you today, Sir. I have
been with Lord Marchmont. He bade me tell you, he
has a great respect for you, and will call on you tomorrow, at one o'clock, and communicate all he knows

about Pope."—Here I paused, in full expectation that he would be pleased with this intelligence, would praise my active merit, and would be alert to embrace such an offer from a nobleman. But whether I had shewn an over-exultation, which provoked his spleen, or whether he was seized with a suspicion that I had obtruded him on Lord Marchmont, and humbled him too much; or whether there was any thing more than an unlucky fit of ill-humour, I know not; but to my surprise, the result was,—JOHNSON. "I shall not be in town tomorrow. I don't care to know about Pope." MRS. THRALE: (surprised as I was, and a little angry.) "I suppose, Sir, Mr. Boswell thought, that as you are to write Pope's Life, you would wish to know about him." JOHNSON. "Wish! why yes. If it rained knowledge, I'd hold out my hand; but I would not give myself the trouble to go in quest of it." There was no arguing with him at the moment. Some time afterwards he said, "Lord Marchmont will call on me, and then I shall call on Lord Marchmont." Mrs. Thrale was uneasy at his unaccountable caprice; and told me, that if I did not take care to bring about a meeting between Lord Marchmont and him, it would never take place, which would be a great pity. I sent a card to his Lordship, to be left at Johnson's house, acquainting him, that Dr. Johnson could not be in town next day, but would do himself the honour of waiting on him at another time.

Talking of divorces, I asked if Othello's doctrine was not plausible:

> He that is robb'd, not wanting what is stolen,
> Let him not know't, and he's not robbed at all.

Dr. Johnson and Mrs. Thrale joined against this. JOHNSON. "Ask any man if he'd wish not to know of such an injury." BOSWELL. "Would you tell your friend to make him unhappy?" JOHNSON. "Perhaps, Sir, I should not; but that would be from prudence on my own account. A man would tell his father." BOSWELL. "Yes; because he would not have spurious children to get any share of the family inheritance." MRS. THRALE. "Or he would tell his brother." BOSWELL. "Certainly, his *elder* brother." JOHNSON. "You would tell your friend of a woman's infamy, to prevent his marrying a whore: there is the same reason to tell him of his wife's infidelity when he is married, to prevent the consequences of imposition. It is a breach of confidence not to tell a friend." BOSWELL. "Would you tell Mr. ——?" (naming a gentleman who assuredly was not in the least danger of such a miserable disgrace, though married to a fine woman.) JOHNSON. "No, Sir; because it would do no good; he is so sluggish, he'd never go to parliament and get a divorce."

He said of one of our friends, "He is ruining himself without pleasure. A man who loses at play, or who runs out his fortune at court, makes his estate less, in hopes of making it bigger: (I am sure of this word, which was often used by him:) but it is a sad thing to pass through the quagmire of parsimony, to the gulph of ruin. To pass over the flowery path of extravagance, is very well."

After Mrs. Thrale was gone to bed, Johnson and I sat up late. We resumed Sir Joshua Reynolds's argument on the preceding Sunday, that a man would be virtuous, though he had no other motive than to preserve his character. JOHNSON. "Sir, it is not true; for as to this world, vice does not hurt a man's character." BOSWELL. "Yes, Sir, debauching a friend's wife will." JOHNSON. "No, Sir. Who thinks the worse of —— for it?" BOSWELL. "Lord —— was not his friend." JOHNSON. "That is only a circumstance, Sir; a slight distinction. He could not get into the house but by Lord ——. A man is chosen Knight of the shire, not the less for having debauched ladies." Boswell. "What, Sir, if he debauched the ladies of gentlemen in the county, will not there be a general resentment against him?" Johnson. "No, Sir. He will lose those particular gentlemen; but the rest will not trouble their heads about it," (warmly). Boswell. "Well, Sir, I cannot think so." Johnson. "Nay, Sir, there is no talking with a man who will dispute what every body knows, (angrily.) Don't you know this?" Boswell. "No, Sir; and I wish to think better of your country than you represent it. I knew in Scotland a gentleman obliged to leave it for debauching a lady; and in one of our counties an Earl's brother lost his election, because he had debauched the lady of another Earl in that county, and destroyed the peace of a noble family."

Still he would not yield. He proceeded: "Will you not allow, Sir, that vice does not hurt a man's character so as to obstruct his prosperity in life, when you know that —— was loaded with wealth and honours; a man who had acquired his fortune by such crimes, that his consciousness of them impelled him to cut his own throat?" Boswell. "You will recollect, Sir, that Dr. Robertson said, he cut his throat because he was weary of still life; little things not being sufficient to move his great mind." Johnson, (very angry.) "Nay, Sir, what stuff is this? You had no more this opinion after Robertson said it, than before. I know nothing more offensive than repeating what one knows to be foolish things, by way of continuing a dispute, to see what a man will answer,—to make him your butt!" (angrier still.) Boswell. "My dear Sir, I had no such intention as you seem to suspect; I had not indeed. Might not this nobleman have felt every thing 'weary, stale, flat, and unprofitable,' as Hamlet says?" Johnson. "Nay, if you are to bring in gabble, I'll talk no more. I will not, upon my honour."—My readers will decide upon this dispute.

1779. I arrived [in London] on Monday, March 15, and next morning at a late hour, found Dr. Johnson sitting over his tea, attended by Mrs. Desmoulins, Mr. Levett, and a clergyman, who had come to submit some poetical pieces to his revision. I found that the subject under immediate consideration was a translation, yet in manuscript, of the *Carmen Seculare* of Horace, which had this year been set to musick, and performed at a publick entertainment in London, for the joint benefit of Monsieur Philidor and Signor Baretti. When Johnson had done reading, the authour asked him bluntly, "If upon the whole it was a good translation?" Johnson, whose regard for truth was uncommonly strict, seemed to be puzzled for a moment, what answer to make; as he certainly could not honestly commend the performance: with exquisite address he evaded the question thus, "Sir, I do not say that it may not be made a very good translation." Here nothing whatever in favour of the performance was affirmed, and yet the writer was not shocked. A printed "Ode to the Warlike Genius of Britain" came next in review; the bard was a lank bony figure, with short black hair; he was writhing himself in agitation, while Johnson read, and shewing his teeth in a grin of earnestness, exclaimed in broken sentences, and in a keen sharp tone, "Is that poetry, Sir?—Is it Pindar?" JOHNSON. "Why, Sir, there is here a great deal of what is called poetry." Then, turning to me, the poet cried, "My muse has not been long upon the town, and (pointing to the Ode) it trembles under the hand of the great critick." Johnson, in a tone of displeasure, asked him, "Why do you praise Anson?" I did not trouble him by asking his reason for this question. He proceeded, "Here is an errour, Sir; you have made Genius feminine."

—"Palpable, Sir; (cried the enthusiast) ⸱ know it. But (in a lower tone) it was to pay a compliment to the Duchess of Devonshire, with which her Grace was pleased. She is walking across Coxheath, in the military uniform, and I suppose her to be the Genius of Britain." JOHNSON. "Sir, you are giving a reason for it; but that will not make it right. You may have a reason why two and two should make five; but they will still make but four."

Although I was several times with him in the course of the following days, such it seems were my occupations, or such my negligence, that I have preserved no memorial of his conversation till Friday, March 26, when I visited him. He said he expected to be attacked on account of his "Lives of the Poets," "However (said he) I would rather be attacked than unnoticed. For the worst thing you can do to an authour is to be silent as to his works. An assault upon a town is a bad thing; but starving it is still worse; an assault may be unsuccessful, you may have more men killed than you kill; but if you starve the town, you are sure of victory."

On Wednesday, April 7, I dined with him at Sir Joshua Reynolds's. I have not marked what company was there. Johnson harangued upon the qualities of different liquors; and spoke with great contempt of claret, as so weak, that "a man would be drowned by it before it make him drunk." He was persuaded to drink one glass of it, that he might judge, not from recollection, which might be dim, but from immediate sensation. He shook his head, and said, "Poor stuff! No, Sir, claret is the liquor for boys; port for men; but he who aspires to be a hero (smiling) must drink brandy. In the first place, the flavour of brandy is most grateful to the palate; and then brandy will do soonest for a man what drinking *can* do for him. There are, indeed, few who are able to drink brandy. That is a power rather to be wished for than attained. And yet, (proceeded he) as in all pleasure hope is a considerable part, I know not but fruition comes too quick by brandy. Florence wine I think the worst; it is wine only to the eye; it is wine neither while you are drinking it, nor after you have drunk it; it neither pleases the taste, nor exhilarates the spirits." I reminded him how heartily he and I used to drink wine together, when we were first acquainted; and how I used to have a head-ache after sitting up with him. He did not like to have this recalled, or, perhaps, thinking that I boasted improperly, resolved to have a witty stroke at me; "Nay, Sir, it was not the *wine* that made your head ache, but the *sense* that I put into it." BOSWELL. "What, Sir! will sense make the head ache?" JOHNSON. "Yes, Sir, (with a smile) when it is not used to it."

Lord Graham, while he praised the beauty of Lochlomond, on the banks of which is his family seat, complained of the climate, and said he could not bear it. JOHNSON. "Nay, my Lord, don't talk so: you may bear it well enough. Your ancestors have borne it more years than I can tell." This was a handsome compliment to the antiquity of the House of Montrose. His Lordship told me afterwards, that he had only affected to complain of the climate; lest, if he had spoken as favourably of his country as he really thought, Dr. Johnson might have attacked it. Johnson was very courteous to Lady Margaret Macdonald. "Madam, (said he,) when I was in the Isle of Sky, I heard of the people running to take the stones off the road, lest Lady Margaret's horse should stumble."

Lord Graham commended Dr. Drummond at Naples as a man of extraordinary talents; and added, that he had a great love of liberty. JOHNSON. "He is *young*, my

Lord; (looking to his Lordship with an arch smile) all *boys* love liberty, till experience convinces them they are not so fit to govern themselves as they imagined. We are all agreed as to our own liberty, we would have as much of it as we can get; but we are not agreed as to the liberty of others: for in proportion as we take, others must lose. I believe we hardly wish that the mob should have liberty to govern us. When that was the case some time ago, no man was at liberty not to have candles in his windows." RAMSAY. "The result is, that order is better than confusion." JOHNSON. "The result is, that order cannot be had but by subordination."

On Friday, April 16, I had been present at the trial of the unfortunate Mr. Hackman, who, in a fit of frantick jealous love, had shot Miss Ray, the favourite of a nobleman. Johnson, in whose company I dined today with some other friends, was much interested by my account of what passed, and particularly with his prayer for the mercy of heaven. He said, in a solemn fervid tone, "I hope he *shall* find mercy."

This day a violent altercation arose between Johnson and Beauclerk, which having made much noise at the time, I think it proper, in order to prevent any future misrepresentation, to give a minute account of it.

In talking of Hackman, Johnson argued, as Judge Blackstone had done, that his being furnished with two pistols was a proof that he meant to shoot two persons. Mr. Beauclerk said, "No; for that every wise man who intended to shoot himself, took two pistols, that he might be sure of doing it at once. Lord ———'s cook shot himself with one pistol, and lived ten days in great agony. Mr. ———, who loved buttered muffins, but durst not eat them because they disagreed with his stomach, resolved to shoot himself; and then he eat three buttered muffins for breakfast, before shooting himself, knowing

that he should not be troubled with indigestion; he had
two charged pistols; one was found lying charged upon
the table by him, after he had shot himself with the
other."—"Well, (said Johnson, with an air of triumph,)
you see here one pistol was sufficient." Beauclerk replied smartly, "Because it happened to kill him." And
either then or a very little afterwards, being piqued at
Johnson's triumphant remark, added, "This is what you
don't know, and I do." There was then a cessation of the
dispute; and some minutes intervened, during which,
dinner and the glass went on cheerfully; when Johnson
suddenly and abruptly exclaimed, "Mr. Beauclerk, how
came you to talk so petulantly to me, as 'This is what
you don't know, but what I know?' One thing *I* know,
which *you* don't seem to know, that you are very uncivil." BEAUCLERK. "Because *you* began by being uncivil, (which you always are.)" The words in paren-
theses were, I believe, not heard by Dr. Johnson. Here
again there was a cessation of arms. Johnson told me,
that the reason why he waited at first some time without
taking any notice of what Mr. Beauclerk said, was because he was thinking whether he should resent it. But
when he considered that there were present a young
Lord and an eminent traveller, two men of the world
with whom he had never dined before, he was apprehensive that they might think they had a right to take
such liberties with him as Beauclerk did, and therefore
resolved he would not let it pass; adding, "that he would
not appear a coward." A little while after this, the conversation turned on the violence of Hackman's temper.
Johnson then said, "It was his business to *command* his
temper, as my friend Mr. Beauclerk, should have done
some time ago." BEAUCLERK. "I should learn of *you*,
Sir." JOHNSON. "Sir, you have given *me* opportunities
enough of learning, when I have been in *your* company.

No man loves to be treated with contempt." BEAUCLERK. (with a polite inclination towards Johnson) "Sir, you have known me twenty years, and however I may have treated others, you may be sure I could never treat you with contempt." JOHNSON. "Sir, you have said more than was necessary." Thus it ended; and Beauclerk's coach not having come for him till very late, Dr. Johnson and another gentleman sat with him a long time after the rest of the company were gone; and he and I dined at Beauclerk's on the Saturday se'night following.

On Saturday, April 24, I dined with him at Mr. Beauclerk's, with Sir Joshua Reynolds, Mr. Jones (afterwards Sir William,) Mr. Langton, Mr. Steevens, Mr. Paradise, and Dr. Higgins. I mentioned that Mr. Wilkes had attacked Garrick to me, as a man who had no friend. JOHNSON. "I believe he is right, Sir. Οι φιγοι, ου φιγος—He had friends, but no friend. Garrick was so diffused, he had no man to whom he wished to unbosom himself. He found people always ready to applaud him, and that always for the same thing: so he saw life with great uniformity." I took upon me, for once, to fight with Goliath's weapons, and play the sophist.—"Garrick did not need a friend, as he got from every body all he wanted. What is a friend? One who supports you and comforts you, while others do not. Friendship, you know, Sir, is the cordial drop, 'to make the nauseous draught of life go down:' but if the draught be not nauseous, if it be all sweet, there is no occasion for that drop." JOHNSON. "Many men would not be content to live so. I hope I should not. They would wish to have an intimate friend, with whom they might compare minds, and cherish private virtues." One of the company mentioned Lord Chesterfield, as a man who had no friend. JOHNSON. "There were more materials to make friendship in Garrick, had he not been so diffused." BOSWELL. "Garrick

was pure gold, but beat out to thin leaf. Lord Chesterfield was tinsel." JOHNSON. "Garrick was a very good
man, the cheerfulest man of his age; a decent liver in a
profession which is supposed to give indulgence to
licentiousness; and a man who gave away, freely, money
acquired by himself. He began the world with a great
hunger for money; the son of a half-pay officer, bred in a
family whose study was to make four-pence do as much
as others made four-pence halfpenny do. But, when he
had got money, he was very liberal." I presumed to
animadvert on his eulogy on Garrick, in his "Lives of the
Poets." "You say, Sir, his death eclipsed the gaiety of
nations." JOHNSON. "I could not have said more nor less.
It is the truth; *eclipsed, not extinguished;* and his death
did eclipse; it was like a storm." BOSWELL. "But why
nations? Did his gaiety extend further than his own nation?" JOHNSON. "Why, Sir, some exaggeration must be
allowed. Besides, nations may be said—if we allow the
Scotch to be a nation, and to have gaiety,—which they
have not, *You* are an exception, though, Come, gentlemen, let us candidly admit that there is one Scotchman
who is cheerful."

Johnson being now better disposed to obtain information concerning Pope than he was last year, sent by me
to my Lord Marchmont, a present of those volumes of
his "Lives of the Poets," which were at this time published, with a request to have permission to wait on him;
and his Lordship, who had called on him twice, obligingly appointed Saturday, the first of May, for receiving us.

On that morning Johnson came to me from Streatham, and after drinking chocolate at General Paoli's,
in South-Audley-street, we proceeded to Lord Marchmont's in Curzon-street. His Lordship met us at the door
of his library, and with great politeness said to Johnson,
"I am not going to make an encomium upon *myself,* by

telling you the high respect I have for *you*, Sir." Johnson was exceedingly courteous; and the interview, which lasted about two hours, during which the Earl communicated his anecdotes of Pope, was as agreeable as I could have wished. When we came out, I said to Johnson, that considering his Lordship's civility, I should have been vexed if he had again failed to come. "Sir, (said he,) I would rather have given twenty pounds than not have come."

During this visit to London I had several interviews with him, which it is unnecessary to distinguish particularly.

He said, "Dodsley first mentioned to me the scheme of an English Dictionary; but I had long thought of it." BOSWELL. "You did not know what you were undertaking." JOHNSON. "Yes, Sir, I knew very well what I was undertaking,—and very well how to do it,—and have done it very well." BOSWELL. "An excellent climax! and it *has* availed you. In your Preface you say, 'What would it avail me in this gloom of solitude?' You have been agreeably mistaken."

I mentioned to him a dispute between a friend of mine and his lady, concerning conjugal infidelity, which my friend had maintained was by no means so bad in the husband, as in the wife. JOHNSON. "Your friend was in the right, Sir. Between a man and his Maker it is a different question: but between a man and his wife, a husband's infidelity is nothing. They are connected by children, by fortune, by serious considerations of community. Wise married women don't trouble themselves about infidelity in their husbands." BOSWELL. "To be sure there is a great difference between the offence of infidelity in a man and that of his wife." JOHNSON. "The difference is boundless. The man imposes no bastards upon his wife."

On Tuesday, October 12, I dined with him at Mr. Ramsay's, with Lord Newhaven, and some other company, none of whom I recollect, but a beautiful Miss Graham, a relation of his Lordship's, who asked Dr. Johnson to hob or nob with her. He was flattered by such pleasing attention, and politely told her, he never drank wine; but if she would drink a glass of water, he was much at her service. She accepted. "Oho, Sir! (said Lord Newhaven) you are caught." JOHNSON. "Nay, I do not see *how* I am *caught;* but if I am caught, I don't want to get free again. If I am caught, I hope to be kept." Then when the two glasses of water were brought, smiling placidly to the young lady, he said, "Madam, let us *reciprocate.*"

Lord Newhaven and Johnson carried on an argument for some time, concerning the Middlesex election. Johnson said, "Parliament may be considered as bound by law, as a man is bound where there is nobody to tie the knot. As it is clear that the House of Commons may expel, and expel again and again, why not allow of the power to incapacitate for that parliament, rather than have a perpetual contest kept up between parliament and the people." Lord Newhaven took the opposite side; but respectfully said, "I speak with great deference to you, Dr. Johnson: I speak to be instructed." This had its full effect on my friend. He bowed his head almost as low as the table, to a complimenting nobleman; and called out, "My Lord, my Lord, I do not desire all this ceremony; let us tell our minds to one another quietly." After the debate was over, he said, "I have got lights on the subject today, which I had not before." This was a great deal from him, especially as he had written a pamphlet upon it.

What I have preserved of his conversation during the remainder of my stay in London at this time, is only what follows: I told him that when I objected to keeping company with a notorious infidel, a celebrated friend of ours said to me, "I do not think that men who live laxly in the world, as you and I do, can with propriety assume such an authority: Dr. Johnson may, who is uniformly exemplary in his conduct. But it is not very consistent to shun an infidel today, and get drunk tomorrow." JOHNSON. "Nay, Sir, this is sad reasoning. Because a man cannot be right in all things, is he to be right in nothing? Because a man sometimes gets drunk, is he therefore to steal? This doctrine would very soon bring a man to the gallows."

He, I know not why, shewed upon all occasions an aversion to go to Ireland, where I proposed to him that we should make a tour. JOHNSON. "It is the last place where I should wish to travel." BOSWELL. "Should you not like to see Dublin, Sir?" JOHNSON. "No, Sir; Dublin is only a worse capital." BOSWELL. "Is not the Giant's-causeway worth seeing?" JOHNSON. "Worth seeing? yes; but not worth going to see."

Yet he had a kindness for the Irish nation, and thus generously expressed himself to a gentleman from that country, on the subject of an UNION which artful Politicians have often had in view—"Do not make an union with us, Sir. We should unite with you, only to rob you. We should have robbed the Scotch, if they had had any thing of which we could have robbed them."

1780. From Mr. Langton I received soon after this time a letter, of which I extract a passage, relative both to Mr. Beauclerk and Dr. Johnson.

"The melancholy information you have received concerning Mr. Beauclerk's death is true. Had his talents been directed in any sufficient degree as they ought, I

have always been strongly of opinion that they were calculated to make an illustrious figure; and that opinion,
as it had been in part formed upon Dr. Johnson's judgement, receives more and more confirmation by hearing,
what since his death, Dr. Johnson has said concerning
them; a few evenings ago, he was at Mr. Vesey's, where
Lord Althorpe, who was one of a numerous company
there, addressed Dr. Johnson on the subject of Mr.
Beauclerk's death, saying, 'Our CLUB has had a great loss
since we met last.' He replied, 'A loss, that perhaps the
whole nation could not repair!' The Doctor then went on
to speak of his endowments, and particularly extolled
the wonderful ease with which he uttered what was
highly excellent. He said, that no man ever was so free
when he was going to say a good thing, from a *look* that
expressed that it was coming; or, when he had said it,
from a look that expressed that it had come. At Mr.
Thrale's, some days before, when we were talking on the
same subject, he said, referring to the same idea of his
wonderful facility, 'That Beauclerk's talents were those
which he had felt himself more disposed to envy, than
those of any whom he had known.'

"On the evening I have spoken of above, at Mr.
Vesey's, you would have been much gratified, as it exhibited an instance of the high importance in which Dr.
Johnson's character is held, I think even beyond any I
ever before was witness to. The company consisted
chiefly of ladies, among whom were the Duchess Dow-
ager of Portland, the Duchess of Beaufort, whom I suppose from her rank, I must name before her mother Mrs.
Boscawen, and her elder sister Mrs. Lewson, who was
likewise there; Lady Lucan, Lady Clermont, and others
of note both for their station and understandings. Among
the gentlemen were Lord Althorpe, whom I have before
named, Lord Macartney, Sir Joshua Reynolds, Lord

Lucan, Mr. Wraxal, whose book you have probably seen, '*The Tour to the Northern Parts of Europe;*' a very agreeable ingenious man; Dr. Warren, Mr. Pepys, the Master in Chancery, whom I believe you know, and Dr. Bernard, the Provost of Eton. As soon as Dr. Johnson was come in, and had taken a chair, the company began to collect round him till they became not less than four, if not five, deep; those behind standing, and listening over the heads of those that were sitting near him."

Being disappointed in my hopes of meeting Johnson this year, so that I could hear none of his admirable sayings, I shall compensate for this want by inserting a collection of them, for which I am indebted to my worthy friend Mr. Langton, whose kind communications have been separately interwoven in many parts of this work.

"John Gilbert Cooper related, that soon after the publication of his Dictionary, Garrick being asked by Johnson what people said of it, told him, that among other animadversions, it was objected that he cited authorities which were beneath the dignity of such a work, and mentioned Richardson. 'Nay, (said Johnson,) I have done worse than that: I have cited *thee*, David.' "

"When in good humour, he would talk of his own writings with a wonderful frankness and candour, and would even criticise them with the closest severity. One day, having read over one of his Ramblers, Mr. Langton asked him, how he liked that paper; he shook his head, and answered, 'too wordy.' At another time, when one was reading his tragedy of 'Irene,' to a company at a house in the country, he left the room: and somebody having asked him the reason of this, he replied, 'Sir, I thought it had been better.' "

"He related, that he had once in a dream a contest of wit with some other person, and that he was very much mortified by imagining that his opponent had the better of him. 'Now, (said he,) one may mark here the effect of sleep in weakening the power of reflection; for had not my judgement failed me, I should have seen, that the wit of this supposed antagonist, by whose superiority I felt myself depressed, was as much furnished by me, as that which I thought I had been uttering in my own character.'"

"Talking of the minuteness with which people will record the sayings of eminent persons, a story was told, that when Pope was on a visit to Spence at Oxford, as they looked from the window they saw a gentleman Commoner, who was just come in from riding, amusing himself with whipping at a post. Pope took occasion to say, 'That young gentleman seems to have little to do.' Mr. Beauclerk observed, 'Then, to be sure, Spence turned round and wrote that down;' and went on to say to Dr. Johnson, 'Pope, Sir, would have said the same of you, if he had seen you distilling.' JOHNSON. 'Sir, if Pope had told me of my distilling, I would have told him of his grotto.'"

"He would allow no settled indulgence of idleness upon principle, and always repelled every attempt to urge excuses for it. A friend one day suggested, that it was not wholesome to study soon after dinner. JOHNSON. 'Ah, Sir, don't give way to such a fancy. At one time of my life I had taken it into my head that it was not wholesome to study between breakfast and dinner.'"

"His affection for Topham Beauclerk was so great, that when Beauclerk was labouring under that severe illness which at last occasioned his death, Johnson said, (with a voice faultering with emotion,) 'Sir, I would walk to the extent of the diameter of the earth to save Beauclerk.'"

"He said, that once, when he had a violent toothache, a Frenchman accosted him thus: *'Ah, Monsieur, vous étudiez trop.'* "

"A gentleman who introduced his brother to Dr. Johnson, was earnest to recommend him to the Doctor's notice, which he did by saying, 'When we have sat together some time, you'll find my brother grow very entertaining.'—'Sir, (said Johnson,) I can wait.' "

"Greek, Sir, (said he) is like lace; every man gets as much of it as he can."

"It is well known that there was formerly a rude custom for those who were sailing upon the Thames, to accost each other as they passed, in the most abusive language they could invent, generally, however, with as much satirical humour as they were capable of producing. Addison gives a specimen of this ribaldry, in number 383 of 'The Spectator,' when Sir Roger de Coverly and he are going to Spring-garden. Johnson was once eminently successful in this species of contest; a fellow having attacked him with some coarse raillery, Johnson answered him thus, 'Sir, your wife, *under pretence of keeping a bawdy-house*, is a receiver of stolen goods.' "

"As Johnson always allowed the extraordinary talents of Mr. Burke, so Mr. Burke was fully sensible of the wonderful powers of Johnson. Mr. Langton recollects having passed an evening with both of them, when Mr. Burke repeatedly entered upon topicks which it was evident he would have illustrated with extensive knowledge and richness of expression; but Johnson always seized upon the conversation, in which, however he acquitted himself in a most masterly manner. As Mr. Burke and Mr. Langton were walking home, Mr. Burke observed that Johnson had been very great that night; Mr. Langton joined in this, but added, he could have wished to hear more from another person; (plainly intimating that he meant Mr. Burke.) 'O, no, (said Mr. Burke) it is enough for me to have rung the bell to him.' "

"Supposing (said he) a wife to be of a studious or argumentative turn, it would be very troublesome: for instance,—if a woman should continually dwell upon the subject of the Arian heresy."

1781. I remember once to have heard Johnson say, "Sir, A thousand years may elapse before there shall appear another man with a power of versification equal to that of Pope."

On Monday, March 19, I arrived in London, and on Tuesday, the 20th, met him in Fleet-street, walking, or rather indeed moving along; for his peculiar march is thus described in a very just and picturesque manner, in a short Life of him published very soon after his death: —"When he walked the streets, what with the constant roll of his head, and the concomitant motion of his body, he appeared to make his way by that motion, independent of his feet." That he was often much stared at while he advanced in this manner, may easily be believed; but it was not safe to make sport of one so robust as he was. Mr. Langton saw him one day, in a fit of absence, by a sudden start, drive the load off a porter's back, and walk forward briskly, without being conscious of what he had done. The porter was very angry, but stood still, and eyed the huge figure with much earnestness, till he was satisfied that his wisest course was to be quiet, and take up his burthen again.

Our accidental meeting in the street after a long separation, was a pleasing surprize to us both. He stepped aside with me into Falcon-court, and made kind enquiries about my family, and as we were in a hurry going different ways, I promised to call on him next day; he said he was engaged to go out in the morning. "Early, Sir?" said I. JOHNSON. "Why, Sir, a London morning does not go with the sun."

He said, "Mrs. Montagu has dropt me. Now, Sir, there are people whom one should like very well to drop, but would not wish to be dropped by."

On Sunday, April 1, I dined with him at Mr. Thrale's.

Mrs. Thrale mentioned a gentleman who had acquired a fortune of four thousand a year in trade, but was absolutely miserable, because he could not talk in company; so miserable, that he was impelled to lament his situation in the street to ******, whom he hates, and who he knows despises him. "I am a most unhappy man (said he). I am invited to conversations. I go to conversations; but, alas! I have no conversation."—JOHNSON. "Man commonly cannot be successful in different ways. This gentleman has spent, in getting four thousand pounds a year, the time in which he might have learnt to talk; and now he cannot talk." Mr. Perkins made a shrewd and droll remark: "If he had got his four thousand a year as a mountebank, he might have learnt to talk at the same time that he was getting his fortune."

Some other gentlemen came in. The conversation concerning the person whose character Dr. Johnson had treated so slightingly, as he did not know his merit, was resumed. Mrs. Thrale said, "You think so of him, Sir, because he is quiet, and does not exert himself with force. You'll be saying the same thing of Mr. ***** there, who sits as quiet—." This was not well bred; and Johnson did not let it pass without correction. "Nay, Madam, what right have you to talk thus? Both Mr. ***** and I have reason to take it ill. *You* may talk so of Mr. *****; but why do you make *me* do it? Have I said anything against Mr. *****? You have *set* him, that I might shoot him: but I have not shot him."

Mr. Thrale appeared very lethargick today. I saw him again on Monday evening, at which time he was not thought to be in immediate danger; but early in the morning of Wednesday the 4th, he expired. Johnson was in the house, and thus mentions the event: "I felt almost the last flutter of his pulse, and looked for the last time upon the face that for fifteen years had never been turned upon me but with respect and benignity." Upon that day there was a *Call* of the LITERARY CLUB; but Johnson apologised for his absence by the following note:

Wednesday.

MR. JOHNSON knows that Sir Joshua Reynolds and the other gentlemen will excuse his incompliance with the Call, when they are told that Mr. Thrale died this morning.

Mr. Thrale's death was a very essential loss to Johnson, who, although he did not foresee all that afterwards happened, was sufficiently convinced that the comforts which Mr. Thrale's family afforded him, would now in a great measure cease. He, however, continued to shew a kind attention to his widow and children as long as it was acceptable: and he took upon him, with a very earnest concern, the office of one of his executors, the importance of which seemed greater than usual to him, from his circumstances having been always such, that he had scarcely any share in the real business of life. His friends of the CLUB were in hopes that Mr. Thrale might have made a liberal provision for him for his life, which, as Mr. Thrale left no son, and a very large fortune, it would have been highly to his honour to have done; and, considering Dr. Johnson's age, could not have been of long duration; but he bequeathed him only two hundred pounds, which was the legacy given to each of his executors. I could not but be somewhat diverted by hearing Johnson talk in a pompous manner of his new office, and particularly of the concerns of the brewery, which it was at last resolved should be sold. Lord Lucan tells a very good story, which, if not precisely exact, is certainly characteristical: that when the sale of Thrale's brewery was going forward, Johnson appeared bustling about, with an ink-horn and pen in his button-hole, like an excise-man; and on being asked what he really considered to be the value of the property which was to be disposed of, answered, "We are not here to sell a parcel of boilers and vats, but the potentiality of growing rich beyond the dreams of avarice."

On Thursday, April 12, I dined with him at a Bishop's, where were Sir Joshua Reynolds, Mr. Berenger, and some more company. He had dined the day before at another Bishop's. I have unfortunately recorded none of his conversation at the Bishop's where we dined together: but I have preserved his ingenious defence of his dining twice abroad in Passion-week; a laxity, in which I am convinced he would not have indulged himself at the time when he wrote his solemn paper in "The Rambler," upon that awful season. It appeared to me, that by being much more in company, and enjoying more luxurious living, he had contracted a keener relish for pleasure, and was consequently less rigourous in his religious rites. This he would not acknowledge; but he reasoned with admirable sophistry, as follows: "Why, Sir, a Bishop's calling company together in this week, is, to use the vulgar phrase, not *the thing*. But you must consider laxity is a bad thing; but preciseness is also a bad thing; and your general character may be more hurt by preciseness than by dining with a Bishop in Passion-week. There might be a handle for reflection. It might

be said, 'He refuses to dine with a Bishop in Passion-week, but was three Sundays absent from church.'"
Boswell. "Very true, Sir. But suppose a man to be uniformly of good conduct, would it not be better that he should refuse to dine with a Bishop in this week, and so not encourage a bad practice by his example?" Johnson. "Why, Sir, you are to consider whether you might not do more harm by lessening the influence of a Bishop's character by your disapprobation in refusing him, than by going to him."

On Friday, April 13, being Good-Friday, I went to St. Clement's church with him as usual. There I saw again his old fellow-collegian, Edwards, to whom I said, "I think, Sir, Dr. Johnson and you meet only at Church." "Sir, (said he,) it is the best place we can meet in, except Heaven, and I hope we shall meet there too." Dr. Johnson told me, that there was very little communication between Edwards and him, after their unexpected renewal of acquaintance. "But (said he, smiling) he met me once, and said, 'I am told you have written a very pretty book called *The Rambler.*' I was unwilling that he should leave the world in total darkness, and sent him a set."

Mr. Berenger visited him today, and was very pleasing. We talked of an evening society for conversation at a house in town, of which we were all members, but of which Johnson said, "It will never do, Sir. There is nothing served about there, neither tea, nor coffee, nor lemonade, nor any thing whatever; and depend upon it, Sir, a man does not love to go to a place from whence he comes out exactly as he went in."

On Friday, April 20, I spent with him one of the happiest days that I remember to have enjoyed in the whole course of my life. Mrs. Garrick, whose grief for the loss of her husband was, I believe, as sincere as wounded affection and admiration could produce, had this day, for the first time since his death, a select party of his friends to dine with her. The company was, Miss Hannah More, who lived with her, and whom she called her Chaplain; Mrs. Boscawen, Mrs. Elizabeth Carter, Sir Joshua Reynolds, Dr. Burney, Dr. Johnson, and myself.

Sir Joshua Reynolds praised "Mudge's Sermons." JOHNSON. "Mudge's Sermons are good, but not practical. He grasps more sense than he can hold; he takes more corn than he can make into meal; he opens a wide prospect, but it is so distant, it is indistinct. I love 'Blair's Sermons.' Though the dog is a Scotchman, and a Presbyterian, and every thing he should not be, I was the first to praise them. Such was my candour." (smiling.) MRS. BOSCAWEN. "Such his great merit, to get the better of your prejudices." JOHNSON. "Why, Madam, let us compound the matter; let us ascribe it to my candour, and his merit."

In the evening we had a large company in the drawing-room; several ladies, the Bishop of Killaloe, Dr. Percy, Mr. Chamberlayne of the Treasury, &c. &c. Somebody said, the life of a mere literary man could not be very entertaining. JOHNSON. "But it certainly may. This is a remark which has been made, and repeated, without justice; why should the life of a literary man be less entertaining than the life of any other man? Are there not as interesting varieties in such a life? As a *literary life* it may be very entertaining." BOSWELL. "But it must be better surely, when it is diversified with a little active variety—such as his having gone to Jamaica:—or—his having gone to the Hebrides." Johnson was not displeased at this.

Talking of a very respectable authour, he told us a curious circumstance in his life, which was, that he had married a printer's devil. REYNOLDS. "A Printer's devil,

Sir! Why, I thought a printer's devil was a creature with a black face and in rags." JOHNSON. "Yes, Sir. But I suppose he had her face washed, and put clean clothes on her. (Then looking very serious, and very earnest.) And she did not disgrace him;—the woman had a bottom of good sense." The word *bottom* thus introduced, was so ludicrous when contrasted with his gravity, that most of us could not forbear tittering and laughing; though I recollect that the Bishop of Killaloe kept his countenance with perfect steadiness, while Miss Hannah More slyly hid her face behind a lady's back who sat on the same settee with her. His pride could not bear that any expression of his should excite ridicule, when he did not intend it; he therefore resolved to assume and exercise despotick power, glanced sternly around, and called out in a strong tone, "Where's the merriment?" Then collecting himself, and looking awful, to make us feel how he could impose restraint, and as it were searching his mind for a still more ludicrous word, he slowly pronounced, "I say the *woman* was *fundamentally* sensible;" as if he had said, hear this now, and laugh if you dare. We all sat composed as at a funeral.

On Tuesday, May 8, I had the pleasure of again dining with him and Mr. Wilkes, at Mr. Dilly's. No *negociation* was now required to bring them together; for Johnson was so well satisfied with the former interview, that he was very glad to meet Wilkes again, who was this day seated between Dr. Beattie and Dr. Johnson; (between *Truth* and *Reason,* as General Paoli said, when I told him of it.) WILKES. "I have been thinking, Dr. Johnson, that there should be a bill brought into parliament that the controverted elections for Scotland should be tried in that country, at their own Abbey of Holy-Rood House, and not here; for the consequence of trying them here is, that we have an inundation of

Scotchmen, who come up and never go back again. Now here is Boswell, who is come upon the election for his own country, which will not last a fortnight." JOHNSON. "Nay, Sir, I see no reason why they should be tried at all; for, you know, one Scotchman is as good as another." WILKES. "Pray, Boswell, how much may be got in a year by an Advocate at the Scotch bar?" BOSWELL. "I believe, two thousand pounds." WILKES. "How can it be possible to spend that money in Scotland?" JOHNSON. "Why, Sir, the money may be spent in England; but there is a harder question. If one man in Scotland gets possession of two thousand pounds, what remains for all the rest of the nation?" WILKES. "You know, in the last war, the immense booty which Thurot carried off by the complete plunder of seven Scotch isles; he re-embarked with *three and six-pence.*" Here again Johnson and Wilkes joined in extravagant sportive raillery upon the supposed poverty of Scotland, which Dr. Beattie and I did not think it worth our while to dispute.

The subject of quotation being introduced, Mr. Wilkes censured it as pedantry. JOHNSON. "No, Sir, it is a good thing; there is a community of mind in it. Classical quotation is the *parole* of literary men all over the world." WILKES. "Upon the continent they all quote the vulgate Bible. Shakespeare is chiefly quoted here; and we quote also Pope, Prior, Butler, Waller, and sometimes Cowley."

We talked of Letter-writing. JOHNSON. "It is now become so much the fashion to publish letters, that, in order to avoid it, I put as little into mine as I can." BOSWELL. "Do what you will, Sir, you cannot avoid it. Should you even write as ill as you can, your letters would be published as curiosities:

Behold a miracle! instead of wit,
See two dull lines with Stanhope's pencil writ.

He gave us an entertaining account of *Bet Flint,* a woman of the town, who, with some eccentrick talents and much effrontery, forced herself upon his acquaintance. "Bet (said he) wrote her own Life in verse, which she brought to me, wishing that I would furnish her with a Preface to it. (Laughing.) I used to say of her, that she was generally slut and drunkard;—occasionally, whore and thief. She had, however, genteel lodgings, a spinnet on which she played, and a boy that walked before her chair. Poor Bet was taken up on a charge of stealing a counterpane, and tried at the Old Bailey. Chief Justice ——, who loved a wench, summed up favourably, and she was acquitted. After which, Bet said, with a gay and satisfied air, 'Now that the counterpane is *my own,* I shall make a petticoat of it.'"

Talking of oratory, Mr. Wilkes described it as accompanied with all the charms of poetical expression. JOHNSON. "No, Sir; oratory is the power of beating down your adversary's arguments, and putting better in their place." WILKES. "But this does not move the passions." JOHNSON. "He must be a weak man, who is to be so moved." WILKES. (naming a celebrated orator). "Amidst all the brilliancy of ——'s imagination, and the exuberance of his wit, there is a strange want of *taste.* It was observed of Apelles's Venus, that her flesh seemed as if she had been nourished by roses: his oratory would sometimes make one suspect that he eats potatoes and drinks whisky."

Mr. Wilkes observed, how tenacious we are of forms in this country; and gave as an instance, the vote of the House of Commons for remitting money to pay the army in America *in Portugal pieces,* when, in reality, the remittance is made not in Portugal money, but in our species. JOHNSON. "Is there not a law, Sir, against exporting the current coin of the realm?" WILKES. "Yes, Sir; but might not the House of Commons, in case of real evident necessity, order our own current coin to be sent into our own colonies?"—Here Johnson, with that quickness of recollection which distinguished him so eminently, gave the *Middlesex Patriot* an admirable retort upon his own ground. "Sure, Sir, *you* don't think a *resolution of the House of Commons* equal to the *law of the land.*" WILKES. (at once perceiving the application) "GOD forbid, Sir."—To hear what had been treated with such violence in "The False Alarm," now turned into pleasant repartee, was extremely agreeable. Johnson went on:—"Locke observes well, that a prohibition to export the current coin is impolitick; for when the balance of trade happens to be against a state, the current coin *must* be exported."

Mr. Beauclerk's great library was this season sold in London by auction. Mr. Wilkes said, he wondered to find in it such a numerous collection of sermons: seeming to think it strange that a gentleman of Mr. Beauclerk's character in the gay world, should have chosen to have many compositions of that kind. JOHNSON. "Why, Sir, you are to consider that sermons make a considerable branch of English literature; so that a library must be very imperfect if it has not a numerous collection of sermons: and in all collections, Sir, the desire of augmenting them grows stronger in proportion to the advance in acquisition; as motion is accelerated by the continuance of the *impetus.* Besides, Sir, (looking at Mr. Wilkes with a placid but significant smile,) a man may collect sermons with intention of making himself better by them. I hope Mr. Beauclerk intended that some time or other that should be the case with him."

Mr. Wilkes said to me, loud enough for Dr. Johnson to hear, "Dr. Johnson should make me a present of his 'Lives of the Poets,' as I am a poor patriot, who cannot afford to buy them." Johnson seemed to take no notice of this hint; but in a little while, he called to Mr. Dilly, "Pray, Sir, be so good as to send a set of my Lives to Mr. Wilkes, with my compliments." This was accordingly done; and Mr. Wilkes paid Dr. Johnson a visit, was courteously received, and sat with him a long time.

The company gradually dropped away. Mr. Dilly himself was called down stairs upon business; I left the room for some time; when I returned, I was struck with observing Dr. Samuel Johnson and John Wilkes, Esq. literally *tête-à-tête;* for they were reclined upon their chairs, with their heads leaning almost close to each other, and talking earnestly, in a kind of confidential whisper, of the personal quarrel between George the Second and the King of Prussia. Such a scene of perfectly easy sociality between two such opponents in the war of political controversy, as that which I now beheld would have been an excellent subject for a picture. It presented to my mind the happy days which are foretold in Scripture, when the lion shall lie down with the kid.

After this day there was another pretty long interval, during which Dr. Johnson and I did not meet. When I mentioned it to him with regret, he was pleased to say, "Then, Sir, let us live double."

About this time it was much the fashion for several ladies to have evening assemblies, where the fair sex might participate in conversation with literary and ingenious men, animated by a desire to please. These societies were denominated *Blue-stocking Clubs,* the origin of which title being little known, it may be worth while to relate it. One of the most eminent members of those societies, when they first commenced, was Mr. Stillingfleet, whose dress was remarkably grave, and in particular it was observed, that he wore blue stockings. Such was the excellence of his conversation, that his absence was felt as so great a loss, that it used to be said, "We can do nothing without the *blue-stockings;*" and thus by degrees the title was established. Miss Hannah More has admirably described a *Blue-stocking Club,* in her *"Bas Bleu,"* a poem in which many of the persons who were most conspicuous there are mentioned.

Johnson was prevailed with to come sometimes into these circles, and did not think himself too grave even for the lively Miss Monckton (now Countess of Corke) who used to have the finest *bit of blue* at the house of her mother, Lady Galway. Her vivacity enchanted the Sage, and they used to talk together with all imaginable ease. A singular instance happened one evening, when she insisted that some of Sterne's writings were very pathetick. Johnson bluntly denied it. "I am sure (said she) they have affected *me."*—"Why (said Johnson, smiling, and rolling himself about,) that is, because, dearest, you're a dunce." When she sometimes afterwards mentioned this to him, he said with equal truth and politeness; "Madam, if I had thought so, I certainly should not have said it."

His disorderly habits, when "making provision for the day that was passing over him," appear from the following anecdote, communicated to me by Mr. John Nichols: —"In the year 1763, a young bookseller, who was an apprentice to Mr. Whiston, waited on him with a subscription to his 'Shakespeare:' and observing that the Doctor made no entry in any book of the subscriber's name, ventured diffidently to ask, whether he would please to have the gentleman's address, that it might be properly inserted in the printed list of subscribers.—'I *shall print no List of Subscribers;'* said Johnson, with great abruptness: but almost immediately recollecting himself, added, very complacently, 'Sir, I have two very cogent reasons for not printing any list of subscribers;— one, that I have lost all the names,—the other, that I have spent all the money.'"

Johnson could not brook appearing to be worsted in argument, even when he had taken the wrong side, to shew the force and dexterity of his talents. When, therefore, he perceived that his opponent gained ground, he had recourse to some sudden mode of robust sophistry. Once when I was pressing upon him with visible advantage, he stopped me thus:—"My dear Boswell, let's have no more of this; you'll make nothing of it. I'd rather have you whistle a Scotch tune."

Care, however, must be taken to distinguish between Johnson when he "talked for victory," and Johnson when he had no desire but to inform and illustrate.—"One of Johnson's principal talents (says an eminent friend of his) was shewn in maintaining the wrong side of an argument, and in a splendid perversion of the truth.— If you could contrive to have his fair opinion on a subject, and without any bias from personal prejudice, or from a wish to be victorious in argument, it was wisdom itself, not only convincing, but overpowering."

He had, however, all his life habituated himself to consider conversation as a trial of intellectual vigour and skill; and to this I think, we may venture to ascribe that unexampled richness and brilliancy which appeared in his own. As a proof at once of his eagerness for colloquial distinction, and his high notion of this eminent friend, he once addressed him thus: "——, we now have been several hours together; and you have said but one thing for which I envied you."

I asked him, if he was not dissatisfied with having so small a share of wealth, and none of those distinctions in the state which are the objects of ambition. He had only a pension of three hundred a year. Why was he not in such circumstances as to keep his coach? Why had he not some considerable office? JOHNSON. "Sir, I have never complained of the world; nor do I think that I have reason to complain. It is rather to be wondered at that I have so much. My pension is more out of the usual course of things than any instance that I have known. Here, Sir, was a man avowedly no friend to Government at the time, who got a pension without asking for it. I never courted the great; they sent for me; but I think they now give me up. They are satisfied: they have seen enough of me." Upon my observing that I could not believe this; for they must certainly be highly pleased by his conversation; conscious of his own superiority, he answered, "No, Sir; great Lords and great Ladies don't love to have their mouths stopped." This was very expressive of the effect which the force of his understanding and brilliancy of his fancy could not but produce; and, to be sure, they must have found themselves strangely diminished in his company. When I warmly declared how happy I was at all times to hear him;—"Yes, Sir, (said he); but if you were Lord Chancellor, it would not be so: you would then consider your own dignity."

The death of Mr. Thrale had made a very material alteration with respect to Johnson's reception in that family. The manly authority of the husband no longer curbed the lively exuberance of the lady; and as her vanity had been fully gratified, by having the Colossus of Literature attached to her for many years, she gradually became less assiduous to please him. Whether her attachment to him was already divided by another object, I am unable to ascertain; but it is plain that Johnson's penetration was alive to her neglect or forced attention; for on the 6th of October this year, we find him making a "parting use of the library" at Streatham, and pronouncing a prayer, which he composed on leaving Mr. Thrale's family.

1783. On Friday, March 21, having arrived in London the night before, I was glad to find him at Mrs. Thrale's house, in Argyll-street, appearances of friendship between them being still kept up. I was shewn into his room, and after the first salutation he said, "I am glad you are come: I am very ill." He looked pale, and was distressed with a difficulty of breathing: but after the common inquiries he assumed his usual strong animated style of conversation. Seeing me now for the first time as a *Laird,* or proprietor of land, he began thus: "Sir, the superiority of a country-gentleman over the people upon his estate is very agreeable: and he who says he does not feel it to be agreeable, lies; for it must be agreeable to have a casual superiority over those who are by nature equal with us."

He sent a message to acquaint Mrs. Thrale that I was arrived. I had not seen her since her husband's death. She soon appeared, and favoured me with an invitation to stay to dinner, which I accepted. There was no other company but herself and three of her daughters, Dr. Johnson and I. She too said, she was very glad I was come, for she was going to Bath, and should have been sorry to leave Dr. Johnson before I came. This seemed to be attentive and kind; and I who had not been informed of any change, imagined all to be as well as formerly. He was little inclined to talk at dinner, and went to sleep after it; but when he joined us in the drawing-room, he seemed revived, and was again himself.

Talking of conversation, he said, "There must, in the first place, be knowledge, there must be materials;—in the second place, there must be a command of words;—in the third place, there must be imagination, to place things in such views as they are not commonly seen in; —and in the fourth place, there must be presence of mind, and a resolution that is not to be overcome by failures; this last is an essential requisite; for want of it many people do not excel in conversation. Now *I* want it; I throw up the game upon losing a trick." I wondered to hear him talk thus of himself, and said, "I don't know, Sir, how this may be; but I am sure you beat other people's cards out of their hands." I doubt whether he heard this remark. While he went on talking triumphantly, I was fixed in admiration, and said to Mrs. Thrale, "O, for short-hand to take this down!"—"You'll carry it all in your head, (said she;) a long head is as good as short-hand."

It has been observed and wondered at, that Mr. Charles Fox never talked with any freedom in the presence of Dr. Johnson; though it is well known, and I myself can witness, that his conversation is various, fluent, and exceedingly agreeable. Johnson's own experience, however, of that gentleman's reserve was a sufficient reason for his going on thus: "Fox never talks in private company; not from any determination not to talk, but because he has not the first motion. A man who is used to the applause of the House of Commons, has no wish for that of a private company. A man accustomed to throw for a thousand pounds, if set down to throw for sixpence, would not be at the pains to count his dice. Burke's talk is the ebullition of his mind; he does not talk from a desire of distinction, but because his mind is full."

After musing for some time, he said, "I wonder how I should have any enemies; for I do harm to nobody." BOSWELL. "In the first place, Sir, you will be pleased to recollect, that you set out with attacking the Scotch; so you got a whole nation for your enemies." JOHNSON. "Why, I own, that by my definition of *oats* I meant to vex them." BOSWELL. "Pray, Sir, can you trace the cause of your antipathy to the Scotch?" JOHNSON. "I cannot, Sir." BOSWELL. "Old Mr. Sheridan says, it was because they sold Charles the First." JOHNSON. "Then, Sir, old Mr. Sheridan has found out a very good reason."

On Sunday, March 23, I breakfasted with Dr. Johnson, who seemed much relieved, having taken opium the night before. He however protested against it, as a remedy that should be given with the utmost reluctance, and only in extreme necessity. I mentioned how commonly it was used in Turkey, and that therefore it could not be so pernicious as he apprehended. He grew warm, and said, "Turks take opium, and Christians take opium; but Russell, in his account of Aleppo, tells us, that it is as disgraceful in Turkey to take too much opium, as it is with us to get drunk. Sir, it is amazing how things are exaggerated. A gentleman was lately telling in a company where I was present, that in France as soon as a man of fashion marries, he takes an opera girl into keeping; and this he mentioned as a general custom. 'Pray, Sir, (said I,) how many opera girls may there be?' He answered, 'About fourscore.' 'Well then, Sir, (said I,) you see there can be no more than fourscore men of fashion who can do this.'"

Mrs. Desmoulins made tea; and she and I talked before him upon a topick which he had once borne patiently from me when we were by ourselves,—his not complaining of the world, because he was not called to some great office, nor had attained to great wealth. He flew into a violent passion, I confess with some justice, and commanded us to have done. "Nobody, (said he) has a right to talk in this manner, to bring before a man his own character, and the events of his life, when he does not choose it should be done. I never have sought the world; the world was not to seek me. It is rather wonderful that so much has been done for me. All the complaints which are made of the world are unjust. I never knew a man of merit neglected: it was generally by his own fault that he failed of success. A man may hide his head in a hole: he may go into the country, and publish a book now and then, which nobody reads, and then complain he is neglected. There is no reason why any person should exert himself for a man who has written a good book: he has not written it for any individual. I may as well make a present to the postman who brings me a letter. When patronage was limited, an authour expected to find a Mæcenas, and complained if he did not find one. Why should he complain? This Mæcenas has others as good as he, or others who have got the start of him." BOSWELL. "But surely, Sir, you will allow that there are men of merit at the bar, who never get practice." JOHNSON. "Sir, you are sure that practice is got from an opinion that the person employed deserves it best; so that if a man of merit at the bar does not get practice, it is from errour, not from injustice. He is not neglected. A horse that is brought to market may not be bought, though he is a very good horse: but that is from ignorance, not from intention."

He observed, "There is a wicked inclination in most people to suppose an old man decayed in his intellects. If a young or middle-aged man, when leaving a company, does not recollect where he laid his hat, it is nothing; but if the same inattention is discovered in an old man, people will shrug up their shoulders, and say, 'His memory is going.'"

Johnson thought the poems published as translations from Ossian, had so little merit, that he said, "Sir, a man might write such stuff for ever, if he would *abandon* his mind to it."

He said, "A man should pass a part of his time with *the laughers,* by which means any thing ridiculous or particular about him might be presented to his view, and corrected." I observed, he must have been a bold laugher who would have ventured to tell Dr. Johnson of any of his particularities.

Dr. Goldsmith once said to Dr. Johnson, that he wished for some additional members to the LITERARY CLUB, to give it an agreeable variety; for (said he) there can now be nothing new among us: we have travelled over one another's minds. Johnson seemed a little angry, and said, "Sir, you have not travelled over *my* mind, I promise you."

Sir Joshua once observed to him, that he had talked above the capacity of some people with whom they had been in company together. "No matter, Sir, (said Johnson); they consider it as a compliment to be talked to, as if they were wiser than they are. So true is this, Sir, that Baxter made it a rule in every sermon that he preached, to say something that was above the capacity of his audience."

Johnson's dexterity in retort, when he seemed to be driven to an extremity by his adversary, was very remarkable. Of his power in this respect, our common friend, Mr. Windham, of Norfolk, has been pleased to furnish me with an eminent instance. However unfavourable to Scotland, he uniformly gave liberal praise to

George Buchanan, as a writer. In a conversation concerning the literary merits of the two countries, in which Buchanan was introduced, a Scotchman, imagining that on this ground he should have an undoubted triumph over him, exclaimed, "Ah, Dr. Johnson, what would you have said of Buchanan, had he been an Englishman?" —"Why, Sir, (said Johnson, after a little pause,) I should *not* have said of Buchanan, had he been an *Englishman,* what I will now say of him as a *Scotchman,* —that he was the only man of genius his country ever produced."

And this brings to my recollection another instance of the same nature. I once reminded him that when Dr. Adam Smith was expatiating on the beauty of Glasgow, he had cut him short by saying, "Pray, Sir, have you ever seen Brentford?" and I took the liberty to add, "My dear Sir, surely that was *shocking.*"—"Why, then, Sir, (he replied,) you have never seen Brentford."

Though his usual phrase for conversation was *talk,* yet he made a distinction; for when he once told me that he dined the day before at a friend's house, with "a very pretty company;" and I asked him if there was good conversation, he answered, "No, Sir; we had *talk* enough, but no *conversation;* there was nothing *discussed.*"

He said to Sir William Scott, "The age is running mad after innovation; and all the business of the world is to be done in a new way; men are to be hanged in a new way; Tyburn itself is not safe from the fury of innovation." It having been argued that this was an improvement.—"No, Sir, (said he, eagerly,) it is *not* an improvement; they object, that the old method drew together a number of spectators. Sir, executions are intended to draw spectators. If they do not draw spectators, they don't answer their purpose. The old method was most satisfactory to all parties; the publick was gratified by a procession; the criminal was supported by it. Why is all this to be swept away?"

The heterogeneous composition of human nature was remarkably exemplified in Johnson. His liberality in giving his money to persons in distress was extraordinary. Yet there lurked about him a propensity to paltry saving. One day I owned to him, that "I was occasionally troubled with a fit of *narrowness*." "Why, Sir, (said he,) so am I. *But I do not tell it.*" He has now and then borrowed a shilling of me; and when I asked him for it again, seemed to be rather out of humour. A droll little circumstance once occurred: As if he meant to reprimand my minute exactness as a creditor, he thus addressed me;—"Boswell, *lend* me sixpence—*not to be repaid.*"

Johnson, for sport perhaps, or from the spirit of contradiction, eagerly maintained that Derrick had merit as a writer. Mr. Morgann argued with him directly, in vain. At length he had recourse to this device. "Pray, Sir, (said he,) whether do you reckon Derrick or Smart the best poet?" Johnson at once felt himself roused; and answered, "Sir, there is no settling the point of precedency between a louse and a flea."

I have no minute of any interview with Johnson till Thursday, May 15th, when I find what follows: Boswell. "I wish much to be in Parliament, Sir." Johnson. "Why, Sir, unless you come resolved to support any administration, you would be the worse for being in Parliament, because you would be obliged to live more expensively."—Boswell. "Perhaps, Sir, I should be the less happy for being in Parliament. I never would sell my vote, and I should be vexed if things went wrong." Johnson. "That's cant, Sir. It would not vex you more in the house than in the gallery: publick affairs vex no man." BOSWELL. "Have not they vexed yourself a little, Sir? Have not you been vexed by all the turbulence of this reign, and by that absurd vote of the House of Commons, 'That the influence of the Crown has increased, is increasing, and ought to be diminished?' " JOHNSON. "Sir, I have never slept an hour less, nor eat an ounce less meat. I would have knocked the factious dogs on the head, to be sure; but I was not *vexed*." BOSWELL. "I declare, Sir, upon my honour, I did imagine I was vexed, and took a pride in it; but it *was,* perhaps, cant; for I own I neither eat less, nor slept less." JOHNSON. "My dear friend, clear your *mind* of cant. You may *talk* as other people do: you may say to a man, 'Sir, I am your most humble servant.' You are *not* his most humble servant. You may say, 'These are bad times; it is a melancholy thing to be reserved at such times.' You don't mind the times. You tell a man, 'I am sorry you had such bad weather the last day of your journey, and were so much wet.' You don't care six-pence whether he is wet or dry. You may *talk* in this manner; it is a mode of talking in Society: but don't *think* foolishly."

My anxious apprehensions at parting with him this year, proved to be but too well founded; for not long afterwards he had a dreadful stroke of the palsy, of which there are very full and accurate accounts in letters written by himself to shew with what composure of mind, and resignation to the Divine Will, his steady piety enabled him to behave.

To MR. EDMUND ALLEN.

June 17, 1783.

DEAR SIR,

It has pleased GOD, this morning, to deprive me of the powers of speech; and as I do not know but that it may be his further good pleasure to deprive me soon of my senses,

I request you will on the receipt of this note, come to me, and act for me, as the exigencies of my case may require.

I am,

Sincerely yours,

SAM. JOHNSON.

Two days after he wrote thus to Mrs. Thrale:

"On Monday, the 16th, I sat for my picture, and walked a considerable way with little inconvenience. In the afternoon and evening I felt myself light and easy, and began to plan schemes of life. Thus I went to bed, and in a short time waked and sat up, as has long been my custom, when I felt a confusion and indistinctness in my head, which lasted, I suppose, about half a minute. I was alarmed, and prayed GOD, that however he might afflict my body, he would spare my understanding. This prayer, that I might try the integrity of my faculties, I made in Latin verse. The lines were not very good, but I knew them not to be very good: I made them easily, and concluded myself to be unimpaired in my faculties.

"Soon after I perceived that I had suffered a paralytick stroke, and that my speech was taken from me. I had no pain, and so little dejection in this dreadful state, that I wondered at my own apathy, and considered that perhaps death itself, when it should come, would excite less horrour than seems now to attend it.

"In order to rouse the vocal organs, I took two drams. Wine has been celebrated for the production of eloquence. I put myself into violent motion, and I think repeated it; but all was in vain. I then went to bed, and strange as it may seem, I think slept. When I saw light, it was time to contrive what I should do. Though GOD stopped my speech, he left me my hand; I enjoyed a mercy which was not granted to my dear friend Lawrence, who now perhaps overlooks me as I am writing, and rejoices that I have what he wanted. My first note was necessarily to my servant, who came in talking, and could not immediately comprehend why he should read what I put into his hands.

"I then wrote a card to Mr. Allen, that I might have a discreet friend at hand, to act as occasion should require. In penning this note, I had some difficulty; my hand, I knew not how nor why, made wrong letters. I then wrote to Dr. Taylor to come to me, and bring Dr. Heberden: and I sent to Dr. Brocklesby, who is my neighbour. My physicians are very friendly, and give me great hopes; but you may imagine my situation. I have so far recovered my vocal powers, as to repeat the Lord's Prayer with no very imperfect articulation. My memory, I hope, yet remains as it was! but such an attack produces solicitude for the safety of every faculty."

Such was the general vigour of his constitution, that he recovered from this alarming and severe attack with wonderful quickness; so that in July he was able to make a visit to Mr. Langton at Rochester, where he passed about a fortnight, and made little excursions as easily as at any time of his life. In August he went as far as the neighbourhood of Salisbury, to Heale, the seat of William Bowles, Esq, a gentleman whom I have heard him praise for exemplary religious order in his family.

His fortitude and patience met with severe trials during this year. The stroke of the palsy has been related circumstantially; but he was also afflicted with the gout, and was besides troubled with a complaint which not only was attended with immediate inconvenience, but threatened him with a chirurgical operation, from which most men would shrink. The complaint was a *sarcocele*, which Johnson bore with uncommon firmness, and was not at all frightened while he looked forward to amputation.

He this autumn received a visit from the celebrated Mrs. Siddons. Mr. Kemble has favoured me with the following minute of what passed at this visit.

"When Mrs. Siddons came into the room, there happened to be no chair ready for her, which he observing, said with a smile, 'Madam, you who so often occasion a want of seats to other people, will the more easily excuse the want of one yourself.'

"Having placed himself by her, he with great good humour entered upon a consideration of the English drama; and, among other enquiries, particularly asked her which of Shakespeare's characters she was most pleased with. Upon her answering that she thought the character of Queen Catharine, in Henry the Eighth, the most natural:—'I think so too, Madam, (said he;) and whenever you perform it, I will once more hobble out to the theatre myself.' Mrs. Siddons promised she would do herself the honour of acting his favourite part for him; but many circumstances happened to prevent the representation of King Henry the Eighth during the Doctor's life.

"In the course of the evening he thus gave his opinion upon the merits of some of the principal performers whom he remembered to have seen upon the stage. 'Mrs. Porter, in the vehemence of rage, and Mrs. Clive, in the sprightliness of humour, I have never seen equalled. What Clive did best, she did better than Garrick; but could not do half so many things well; she was a better romp than any I ever saw in nature.—Pritchard, in common life, was a vulgar ideot; she would talk of her *gownd;* but, when she appeared upon the stage, seemed to be inspired by gentility and understanding.—I once talked with Colley Cibber, and thought him ignorant of the principles of his art.—Garrick, Madam, was no de-claimer; there was not one of his own scene-shifters who could not have spoken *To be, or not to be,* better than he did; yet he was the only actor I ever saw, whom I could call a master both in tragedy and comedy; though I liked him best in comedy. A true conception of character, and natural expression of it, were his dis-tinguished excellencies.' Having expatiated, with his usual force and eloquence, on Mr. Garrick's extraor-dinary eminence as an actor, he concluded with this compliment to his social talents; 'And after all, Madam, I thought him less to be envied on the stage than at the head of a table.' "

Johnson, indeed, had thought more upon the subject of acting than might be generally supposed. Talking of it one day to Mr. Kemble, he said, "Are you, Sir, one of those enthusiasts who believe yourself transformed into the very character you represent?" Upon Mr. Kemble's answering—that he had never felt so strong a persua-sion himself; "To be sure not, Sir, (said Johnson;) the thing is impossible. And if Garrick really believed him-self to be that monster, Richard the Third, he deserved to be hanged every time he performed it."

1784. And now I am arrived at the last year of the life of SAMUEL JOHNSON, a year in which, although passed in severe indisposition, he nevertheless gave many evidences of the continuance of those wondrous powers of mind, which raised him so high in the intel-lectual world. His conversation and his letters of this year were in no respect inferiour to those of former years.

On Wednesday, May 5, I arrived in London, and next morning had the pleasure to find Dr. Johnson

greatly recovered. On Saturday, May 15, I dined with
him at Dr. Brocklesby's, where were Colonel Vallancy,
Mr. Murphy, and that ever-cheerful companion Mr.
Devaynes, apothecary to his Majesty. Of these days,
and others on which I saw him, I have no memorials,
except the general recollection of his being able and
animated in conversation, and appearing to relish society as much as the youngest man. I find only these
three small particulars:—When a person was mentioned,
who said, "I have lived fifty-one years in this world,
without having had ten minutes of uneasiness;" he exclaimed, "The man who says so, lies: he attempts to
impose on human credulity." The Bishop of Exeter in
vain observed, that men were very different. His Lordship's manner was not impressive; and I learnt afterwards, that Johnson did not find out that the person who
talked to him was a Prelate; if he had, I doubt not that
he would have treated him with more respect; for once
talking of George Psalmanazar, whom he reverenced for
his piety, he said, "I should as soon think of contradicting a Bishop."

On the evening of Saturday, May 15, he was in fine
spirits at our Essex-Head Club. He told us, "I dined
yesterday at Mrs. Garrick's with Mrs. Carter, Miss Hannah More, and Miss Fanny Burney. Three such women
are not to be found: I know not where I could find a
fourth, except Mrs. Lennox, who is superiour to them
all." Boswell. "What! had you them all to yourself,
Sir?" Johnson. "I had them all, as much as they were
had; but it might have been better had there been more
company there." Boswell. "Might not Mrs. Montagu
have been a fourth?" Johnson. "Sir, Mrs. Montagu does
not make a trade of her wit; but Mrs. Montagu is a very
extraordinary woman: she has a constant stream of conversation, and it is always impregnated; it has always

meaning." BOSWELL. "Mr. Burke has a constant stream of conversation." JOHNSON. "Yes, Sir; if a man were to go by chance at the same time with Burke under a shed, to shun a shower, he would say—'this is an extraordinary man.' If Burke should go into a stable to see his horse drest, the ostler would say—'we have had an extraordinary man here.'" BOSWELL. "Foote was a man who never failed in conversation. If he had gone into a stable—" JOHNSON. "Sir, if he had gone into the stable, the ostler would have said, here has been a comical fellow: but he would not have respected him." BOSWELL. "And, Sir, the ostler would have answered him, would have given him as good as he brought, as the common saying is." JOHNSON. "Yes, Sir; and Foote would have answered the ostler.——When Burke does not descend to be merry, his conversation is very superiour indeed. There is no proportion between the powers which he shews in serious talk and in jocularity. When he lets himself down to that, he is in the kennel." He called to us with a sudden air of exultation, as the thought started into his mind, "O! gentlemen, I must tell you a very great thing. The Empress of Russia has ordered the 'Rambler' to be translated into the Russian language: so I shall be read on the banks of the Wolga. Horace boasts that his fame would extend as far as the banks of the Rhone; now the Wolga is farther from me than the Rhone was from Horace." BOSWELL. "You must certainly be pleased with this, Sir." JOHNSON. "I am pleased, Sir, to be sure. A man is pleased to find he has succeeded in that which he has endeavoured to do."

On Wednesday, May 19, I sat a part of the evening with him, by ourselves. I observed, that the death of our friends might be a consolation against the fear of our own dissolution, because we might have more friends in the other world than in this. He perhaps felt this a reflection upon his apprehension as to death; and said, with heat, "How can a man know *where* his departed friends are, or whether they will be his friends in the other world? How many friendships have you known formed upon principles of virtue? Most friendships are formed by caprice or by chance, mere confederacies in vice or leagues in folly."

We talked of our worthy friend Mr. Langton. He said, "I know not who will go to Heaven if Langton does not. Sir, I could almost say, *Sit anima mea cum Langtono.*" I mentioned a very eminent friend as a virtuous man. JOHNSON. "Yes, Sir; but —— has not the evangelical virtue of Langton. ——, I am afraid, would not scruple to pick up a wench."

He however charged Mr. Langton with what he thought want of judgement upon an interesting occasion. "When I was ill, (said he) I desired he would tell me sincerely in what he thought my life was faulty. Sir, he brought me a sheet of paper, on which he had written down several texts of Scripture, recommending christian charity. And when I questioned him what occasion I had given for such an animadversion, all that he could say amounted to this,—that I sometimes contradicted people in conversation. Now what harm does it do to any man to be contradicted?" BOSWELL. "I suppose he meant the *manner* of doing it; roughly,—and harshly." JOHNSON. "And who is the worse for that?" BOSWELL. "It hurts people of weaker nerves." JOHNSON. "I know no such weak-nerved people." Mr. Burke, to whom I related this conference, said, "It is well, if when a man comes to die, he has nothing heavier upon his conscience than having been a little rough in conversation."

Johnson, at the time when the paper was presented to him, though at first pleased with the attention of his friend, whom he thanked in an earnest manner, soon exclaimed in a loud and angry tone, "What is your drift, Sir?" Sir Joshua Reynolds pleasantly observed, that it was a scene for a comedy, to see a penitent get into a violent passion and belabour his confessor.

On Thursday, June 3, the Oxford post-coach took us up in the morning at Bolt-court. The other two passengers were Mrs. Beresford and her daughter, two very agreeable ladies from America; they were going to Worcestershire, where they then resided. Frank had been sent by his master the day before to take places for us; and I found from the way-bill that Dr. Johnson had made our names be put down. Mrs. Beresford, who had read it, whispered me, "Is this the great Dr. Johnson?" I told her it was; so she was then prepared to listen. As she soon happened to mention in a voice so low that Johnson did not hear it, that her husband had been a member of the American Congress, I cautioned her to beware of introducing that subject, as she must know how very violent Johnson was against the people of that country. He talked a great deal. Miss Beresford was so much charmed, that she said to me aside, "How he does talk! Every sentence is an essay."

I was surprised at his talking without reserve in the publick post-coach of the state of his affairs; "I have (said he) about the world I think above a thousand pounds, which I intend shall afford Frank an annuity of seventy pounds a-year." Indeed his openness with people at a first interview was remarkable. He said once to Mr. Langton, "I think I am like Squire Richard in 'The Journey to London,' *I'm never strange in a strange place.*" He was truly *social*. He strongly censured what is much too common in England among persons of condition,—maintaining an absolute silence, when unknown to each other; as for instance, when occasionally brought together in a room before the master or mistress of the house has appeared. "Sir, that is being so uncivilised as not to understand the common rights of humanity."

At the inn where we stopped he was exceedingly dissatisfied with some roast mutton which he had for dinner. The ladies, I saw, wondered to see the great philosopher, whose wisdom and wit they had been admiring all the way, get into ill humour from such a cause. He scolded the waiter, saying, "It is as bad as bad can be: it is ill-fed, ill-killed, ill-kept, and ill-drest."

He bore the journey very well, and seemed to feel himself elevated as he approached Oxford, that magnificent and venerable seat of Learning, Orthodoxy, and Toryism. Frank came in the heavy coach, in readiness to attend him; and we were received with the most polite hospitality at the house of his old friend Dr. Adams, Master of Pembroke College, who had given us a kind invitation.

We talked at breakfast, of forms of prayer. JOHNSON. "I know of no good prayers but those in the 'Book of Common Prayer.'" DR. ADAMS, (in a very earnest manner,) "I wish, Sir, you would compose some family prayers." JOHNSON. "I will not compose prayers for you, Sir, because you can do it for yourself. But I have thought of getting together all the books of prayers which I could, selecting those which should appear to me the best, putting out some, inserting others, adding some prayers of my own, and prefixing a discourse on prayer." We all now gathered about him, and two or three of us at a time joined in pressing him to execute this plan. He seemed to be a little displeased at the manner of our importunity, and in great agitation called out, "Do not talk thus of what is so awful. I know not what time GOD will allow me in this world. There are many things which I wish to do." Some of us persisted, and Dr. Adams said, "I never was more serious about anything in my life." JOHNSON. "Let me alone, let me alone; I am overpowered." And then he put his hands before his face, and reclined for some time upon the table.

I mentioned Jeremy Taylor's using, in his forms of prayer, "I am the chief of sinners," and other such self-condemning expressions. "Now, (said I) this cannot be said with truth by every man, and therefore is improper for a general printed form. I myself cannot say that I am the worst of men; I *will* not say so." JOHNSON. "A man may know, that physically, that is, in the real state of things, he is not the worst man; but that morally he may be so. Law observes, 'that every man knows something worse of himself, than he is sure of in others.' You may not have committed such crimes as some men have done; but you do not know against what degree of light they have sinned. Besides, Sir, 'the chief of sinners' is a mode of expression for 'I am a great sinner.' So St. Paul, speaking of our SAVIOUR's having died to save sinners, says, 'of whom I am the chief;' yet he certainly did not think himself so bad as Judas Iscariot." BOSWELL. "But, Sir, Taylor means it literally, for he founds a conceit upon it. When praying for the conversion of sinners, and of himself in particular, he says, 'Lord, thou wilt not leave thy *chief* work undone.' " JOHNSON. "I do not approve of figurative expressions in addressing the Supreme Being; and I never use them. Taylor gives a very good advice: 'Never lie in your prayers; never confess more than you really believe; never promise more than you mean to perform.' " I recollected this precept in his "Golden Grove;" but his *example* for prayer contradicts his *precept*.

Dr. Johnson and I went in Dr. Adams's coach to dine with Mr. Nowell, Principal of St. Mary Hall, at his beautiful villa at Iffley, on the banks of the Isis, about two miles from Oxford. While we were upon the road, I had the resolution to ask Johnson whether he thought that the roughness of his manner had been an advantage or not, and if he would not have done more good if he had been more gentle. I proceeded to answer myself thus: "Perhaps it has been of advantage, as it has given weight to what you said: you could not, perhaps, have talked with such authority without it." JOHNSON. "No, Sir; I have done more good as I am. Obscenity and Impiety have always been repressed in my company." BOSWELL. "True, Sir; and that is more than can be said of every Bishop. Greater liberties have been taken in the presence of a Bishop, though a very good man, from his being milder, and therefore not commanding such awe. Yet, Sir, many people who might have been benefited by your conversation, have been frightened away. A worthy friend of ours has told me, that he has often been afraid to talk to you." JOHNSON. "Sir, he need not have been afraid, if he had any thing rational to say. If he had not, it was better he did not talk."

Mr. Henderson, with whom I had sauntered in the venerable walks of Merton-College, and found him a very learned and pious man, supped with us. Dr. Johnson surprised him not a little, by acknowledging with a look of horrour, that he was much oppressed by the fear of death. The amiable Dr. Adams suggested that GOD was infinitely good. JOHNSON. "That he is infinitely good, as far as the perfection of his nature will allow, I certainly believe; but it is necessary for good upon the whole, that individuals should be punished. As to an *individual*, therefore, he is not infinitely good; and as I cannot be *sure* that I have fulfilled the conditions or which salvation is granted, I am afraid I may be one of those who shall be damned." (looking dismally.) DR. ADAMS. "What do you mean by damned!" JOHNSON.

(passionately and loudly) "Sent to Hell, Sir, and punished everlastingly." DR. ADAMS. "I don't believe that doctrine." JOHNSON. "Hold, Sir, do you believe that some will be punished at all?" DR. ADAMS. "Being excluded from Heaven will be a punishment: yet there may be no great positive suffering." JOHNSON. "Well, Sir; but, if you admit any degree of punishment, there is an end of your argument for infinite goodness simply considered; for, infinite goodness would inflict no punishment whatever. There is no infinite goodness physically considered; morally there is." BOSWELL. "But may not a man attain to such a degree of hope as not to be uneasy from the fear of death?" JOHNSON. "A man may have such a degree of hope as to keep him quiet. You see I am not quiet, from the vehemency with which I talk; but I do not despair." MRS. ADAMS. "You seem, Sir, to forget the merits of our Redeemer." JOHNSON. "Madam, I do not forget the merits of my Redeemer; but my Redeemer has said that he will set some on his right hand and some on his left." —He was in gloomy agitation, and said, "I'll have no more on't."

On Sunday, June 13, our philosopher was calm at breakfast. There was something exceedingly pleasing in our leading a College life, without restraint, and with superiour elegance, in consequence of our living in the Master's House, and having the company of ladies. Mrs. Kennicot related, in his presence, a lively saying of Dr. Johnson's to Miss Hannah More, who had expressed a wonder that the poet who had written "Paradise Lost," should write such poor Sonnets:—"Milton, Madam, was a genius that could cut a Colossus from a rock, but could not carve heads upon cherry-stones."

We talked of the casuistical question, "Whether it was allowable at any time to depart from *Truth?*" JOHNSON. "The general rule is, that Truth should never be violated, because it is of the utmost importance to the comfort of life, that we should have a full security by mutual faith; and occasional inconveniences should be willingly suffered, that we may preserve it. There must, however, be some exceptions. If, for instance, a murderer should ask you which way a man is gone, you may tell him what is not true, because you are under a previous obligation not to betray a man to a murderer." BOSWELL. "Supposing the person who wrote *Junius* were asked whether he was the authour, might he deny it?" JOHNSON. "I don't know what to say to this. If you were *sure* that he wrote *Junius*, would you, if he denied it, think as well of him afterwards? Yet it may be urged, that what a man has no right to ask, you may refuse to communicate; and there is no other effectual mode of preserving a secret and an important secret, the discovery of which may be very hurtful to you, but a flat denial; for if you are silent, or hesitate, or evade, it will be held equivalent to a confession. But stay, Sir, here is another case. Supposing the authour had told me confidentially that he had written *Junius*, and I were asked if he had, I should hold myself at liberty to deny it, as being under a previous promise, express or implied, to conceal it. Now what I ought to do for the authour, may I not do for myself? But I deny the lawfulness of telling a lie to a sick man, for fear of alarming him. You have no business with consequences; you are to tell the truth. Besides, you are not sure, what effect your telling him he is in danger may have. It may bring his distemper to a crisis, and that may cure him. Of all lying, I have the greatest abhorrence of this, because I believe it has been frequently practised on myself."

In the morning of Tuesday, June 15, while we sat at Dr. Adams's, we talked of a printed letter from the reverend Herbert Croft, to a young gentleman who had been his pupil, in which he advised him to read to the end of whatever books he should begin to read. JOHNSON. "This is surely a strange advice; you may as well resolve that whatever men you happen to get acquainted with, you are to keep them for life. A book may be good for nothing; or there may be only one thing in it worth knowing; are we to read it all through? These Voyages, (pointing to the three large volumes of 'Voyages to the South Sea,' which were just come out) *who* will read them through? A man had better work his way before the mast, than read them through; they will be eaten by rats and mice, before they are read through. There can be little entertainment in such books; one set of Savages is like another." BOSWELL. "I do not think the people of Otaheité can be reckoned Savages." JOHNSON. "Don't cant in defence of Savages." BOSWELL. "They have the art of navigation." JOHNSON. "A dog or a cat can swim." BOSWELL. "They carve very ingeniously." JOHNSON. "A cat can scratch, and a child with a nail can scratch." I perceived this was none of the *mollia tempora fandi;* so desisted.

Upon his mentioning that when he came to College he wrote his first exercise twice over, but never did so afterwards; MISS ADAMS. "I suppose, Sir, you could not make them better?" JOHNSON. "Yes, Madam, to be sure I could make them better. Thought is better than no thought." MISS ADAMS. "Do you think, Sir, you could make your Ramblers better?" JOHNSON. "Certainly I could." BOSWELL. "I'll lay a bet, Sir, you cannot." JOHNSON. "But I will, Sir, if I choose. I shall make the best of them you shall pick out, better."—BOSWELL. "But you may add to them. I will not allow of that." JOHNSON. "Nay, Sir, there are three ways of making them better; —putting out,—adding,—or correcting."

After his return to London from this excursion, I saw

him frequently, but have few memorandums; I shall therefore here insert some particulars which I collected at various times.

A dull country magistrate gave Johnson a long, tedious account of his exercising his criminal jurisdiction, the result of which was his having sentenced four convicts to transportation. Johnson, in an agony of impatience to get rid of such a companion, exclaimed, "I heartily wish, Sir, that I were a fifth."

Johnson was present when a tragedy was read, in which there occurred this line:

Who rules o'er freemen should himself be free.

The company having admired it much, "I cannot agree with you (said Johnson:) It might as well be said,

Who drives fat oxen should himself be fat."

Johnson having argued for some time with a pertinacious gentleman; his opponent, who had talked in a very puzzling manner, happened to say, "I don't understand you, Sir;" upon which Johnson observed, "Sir, I have found you an argument; but I am not obliged to find you an understanding."

Sir Joshua Reynolds having said that he took the altitude of a man's taste by his stories and his wit, and of his understanding by the remarks which he repeated; being always sure that he must be a weak man, who quotes common things with an emphasis as if they were oracles;—Johnson agreed with him; and Sir Joshua having also observed that the real character of a man was found out by his amusements,—Johnson added, "Yes, Sir; no man is a hypocrite in his pleasures."

He seemed to take a pleasure in speaking in his own style; for when he had carelessly missed it, he would repeat the thought translated into it. Talking of the Comedy of "The Rehearsal," he said, "It has not wit enough to keep it sweet." This was easy;—he therefore caught himself, and pronounced a more round sentence; "It has not vitality enough to preserve it from putrefaction."

His generous humanity to the miserable was almost beyond example. The following instance is well attested: Coming home late one night, he found a poor woman lying in the street, so much exhausted that she could not walk; he took her upon his back, and carried her to his house, where he discovered that she was one of those wretched females who had fallen into the lowest state of vice, poverty, and disease. Instead of harshly upbraiding her, he had her taken care of with all tenderness for a long time, at a considerable expence, till she was restored to health, and endeavoured to put her into a virtuous way of living.

A gentleman having said that a *congé d'elire* has not, perhaps, the force of a command, but may be considered only as a strong recommendation;—"Sir, (replied Johnson, who overheard him,) it is such a recommendation, as if I should throw you out of a two pair of stairs window, and recommend to you to fall soft."

The anxiety of his friends to preserve so estimable a life, as long as human means might be supposed to have influence, made them plan for him a retreat from the severity of a British winter, to the mild climate of Italy. This scheme was at last brought to a serious resolution at General Paoli's, where I had often talked of it. One essential matter, however, I understood was necessary to be previously settled, which was obtaining such an addition to his income, as would be sufficient to enable him to defray the expence in a manner becoming the first literary character of a great nation, and, independent of all his other merits, the Authour of THE DICTIONARY OF

THE ENGLISH LANGUAGE. The person to whom I above all others thought I should apply to negociate this business, was the Lord Chancellor, because I knew that he highly valued Johnson, and that Johnson highly valued his Lordship; so that it was no degradation of my illustrious friend to solicit for him the favour of such a man. I have mentioned what Johnson said of him to me when he was at the bar; and after his Lordship was advanced to the seals, he said of him, "I would prepare myself for no man in England but Lord Thurlow. When I am to meet with him, I should wish to know a day before." How he would have prepared himself, I cannot conjecture. Would he have selected certain topicks, and considered them in every view, so as to be in readiness to argue them at all points? and what may we suppose those topicks to have been? I once started the curious enquiry to the great man who was the subject of this compliment: he smiled, but did not pursue it.

I first consulted with Sir Joshua Reynolds, who perfectly coincided in opinion with me; and I therefore, though personally very little known to his Lordship, wrote to him, stating the case, and requesting his good offices for Dr. Johnson. I mentioned that I was obliged to set out for Scotland early in the following week, so that if his Lordship should have any commands for me as to this pious negociation, he would be pleased to send them before that time; otherwise Sir Joshua Reynolds would give all attention to it.

This application was made not only without any suggestion on the part of Johnson himself, but was utterly unknown to him, nor had he the smallest suspicion of it. Any insinuations, therefore, which since his death have been thrown out, as if he had stooped to ask what was superfluous, are without any foundation.

On Sunday, June 27, I found him rather better. I

mentioned to him a young man who was going to Jamaica with his wife and children, in expectation of being provided for by two of her brothers settled in that island, one a clergyman, and the other a physician. JOHNSON. "It is a wild scheme, Sir, unless he has a positive and deliberate invitation. There was a poor girl, who used to come about me, who had a cousin in Barbadoes, that, in a letter to her, expressed a wish she should come out to that Island, and expatiated on the comforts and happiness of her situation. The poor girl went out: her cousin was much surprized, and asked her how she could think of coming. 'Because, (said she,) you invited me.'—'Not I,' answered the cousin. The letter was then produced. 'I see it is true, (said she,) that I did invite you: but I did not think you would come.' They lodged her in an outhouse, where she passed her time miserably; and as soon as she had an opportunity she returned to England. Always tell this, when you hear of people going abroad to relations, upon a notion of being well received. In the case which you mention, it is probable the clergyman spends all he gets, and the physician does not know how much he is to get."

We this day dined at Sir Joshua Reynolds's, with General Paoli, Lord Eliot, (formerly Mr. Eliot, of Port Eliot,) Dr. Beattie, and some other company. Talking of Lord Chesterfield;—JOHNSON. "His manner was exquisitely elegant, and he had more knowledge than I expected." BOSWELL. "Did you find, Sir, his conversation to be of a superiour style?" JOHNSON. "Sir, in the conversation which I had with him I had the best right to superiority, for it was upon philology and literature."

A young gentleman present took up the argument against him and maintained that no man ever thinks of the *nose of the mind,* not adverting that though that figurative sense seems strange to us, as very unusual, it is truly not more forced than Hamlet's "In my *mind's eye*, Horatio." He persisted much too long, and appeared to Johnson as putting himself forward as his antagonist with too much presumption: upon which he called to him in a loud tone, "What is it you are contending for if you *be* contending?"—And afterwards imagining that the gentleman retorted upon him with a kind of smart drollery, he said, "Mr. * * * *, it does not become you to talk so to me. Besides, ridicule is not your talent; you have *there* neither intuition nor sagacity."—The gentleman protested that he had intended no improper freedom, but had the greatest respect for Dr. Johnson. After a short pause, during which we were somewhat uneasy. —JOHNSON. "Give me your hand, Sir. You were too tedious, and I was too short." Mr. * * * *. "Sir, I am honoured by your attention in any way." JOHNSON. "Come, Sir, let's have no more of it. We offended one another by our contention; let us not offend the company by our compliments."

By a letter from Sir Joshua Reynolds I was informed, that the Lord Chancellor had called on him, and acquainted him that the application had not been successful; but that his Lordship, after speaking highly in praise of Johnson, as a man who was an honour to his country, desired Sir Joshua to let him know, that on granting a mortgage of his pension, he should draw on his Lordship to the amount of five or six hundred pounds; and that his Lordship explained the meaning of the mortgage to be, that he wished the business to be conducted in such a manner, that Dr. Johnson should appear to be under the least possible obligation. Sir Joshua mentioned, that he had by the same post communicated all this to Dr. Johnson.

To the Lord High Chancellor.

September, 1784.

My Lord,

After a long and not inattentive observation of mankind, the generosity of your Lordship's offer raises in me not less wonder than gratitude. Bounty, so liberally bestowed, I should gladly receive, if my condition made it necessary; for, to such a mind, who would not be proud to own his obligations? But it has pleased God to restore me to so great a measure of health, that if I should now appropriate so much of a fortune destined to do good, I could not escape from myself the charge of advancing a false claim. My journey to the continent, though I once thought it necessary, was never much encouraged by my physicians; and I was very desirous that your Lordship should be told of it by Sir Joshua Reynolds, as an event very uncertain; for if I grew much better, I should not be willing, if much worse, not able, to migrate.—Your Lordship was first solicited without my knowledge; but, when I was told that you were pleased to honour me with your patronage, I did not expect to hear of a refusal; yet, as I have had no long time to brood hope, and have not rioted in imaginary opulence, this cold reception has been scarce a disappointment; and, from your Lordship's kindness, I have received a benefit, which only men like you are able to bestow. I shall not live *mihi carior,* with a higher opinion of my own merit.

I am, my Lord,
Your Lordship's most obliged,
Most grateful, and
Most humble servant,
SAM. JOHNSON.

We now behold Johnson for the last time, in his native city, for which he ever retained a warm affection, and which, by a sudden apostrophe, under the word *Lich,* he introduces with reverence, into his immortal Work, THE ENGLISH DICTIONARY:—"*Salve, magna parens!*" While here, he felt a revival of all the tenderness of filial affection, an instance of which appeared in his ordering the gravestone and inscription over Elizabeth Blaney to be substantially and carefully renewed.

To Mr. Henry White, a young clergyman, with whom he now formed an intimacy, so as to talk to him with great freedom, he mentioned that he could not in general accuse himself of having been an undutiful son. "Once, indeed, (said he,) I was disobedient; I refused to attend my father to Uttoxeter-market. Pride was the source of that refusal, and the remembrance of it was painful. A few years ago I desired to atone for this fault. I went to Uttoxeter in very bad weather, and stood for a considerable time bareheaded in the rain, on the spot where my father's stall used to stand. In contrition I stood, and I hope the penance was expiatory."

Soon after Johnson's return to the metropolis, both the asthma and dropsy became more violent and distressful. It is not my intention to give a very minute detail of the particulars of Johnson's remaining days, of whom it was now evident, that the crisis was fast approaching, when he must *die like men, and fall like one of the Princes.* Yet it will be instructive, as well as gratifying to the curiosity of my readers, to record a few circumstances, on the authenticity of which they may perfectly rely, as I have been at the utmost pains to obtain an accurate account of his last illness, from the best authority.

Dr. Heberden, Dr. Brocklesby, Dr. Warren, and Dr. Butter, physicians, generously attended him, without accepting any fees, as did Mr. Cruickshank, surgeon; and all that could be done from professional skill and ability, was tried, to prolong a life so truly valuable. He himself, indeed, having, on account of his very bad constitution, been perpetually applying himself to medical inquiries, united his own efforts with those of the gentlemen who attended him; and imagining that the dropsical collection of water which oppressed him might be drawn off by making incisions in his body, he, with his usual resolute defiance of pain, cut deep, when he thought that his surgeon had done it too tenderly.

About eight or ten days before his death, when Dr. Brocklesby paid him his morning visit, he seemed very low and desponding, and said, "I have been as a dying man all night." He then emphatically broke out in the words of Shakespeare,

> "Can'st thou not minister to a mind diseas'd;
> Pluck from the memory a rooted sorrow;
> Raze out the written troubles of the brain;
> And, with some sweet oblivious antidote,
> Cleanse the stuff'd bosom of that perilous stuff,
> Which weighs upon the heart?"

To which Dr. Brocklesby readily answer'd, from the same great poet:

> "———————— therein the patient
> Must minister to himself."

Johnson expressed himself much satisfied with the application.

On another day after this, when talking on the subject of prayer, Dr. Brocklesby repeated from Juvenal,

> *Orandum est, ut sit mens sana in corpore sano,*

and so on to the end of the tenth satire; but in running it quickly over, he happened, in the line,

> *Qui spatium vitæ extremum inter munera ponat,*

to pronounce *supremum* for *extremum;* at which Johnson's critical ear instantly took offence, and discoursing vehemently on the unmetrical effect of such a lapse, he shewed himself as full as ever of the spirit of the grammarian.

Having no other relations, it had been for some time Johnson's intention to make a liberal provision for his faithful servant, Mr. Francis Barber, whom he looked upon as particularly under his protection, and whom he had all along treated truly as an humble friend. Having asked Dr. Brocklesby what would be a proper annuity to a favourite servant, and being answered that it must depend on the circumstances of the master; and, that in the case of a nobleman, fifty pounds a-year was considered as an adequate reward for many years' faithful service;—"Then, (said Johnson,) shall I be *nobilissimus*, for I mean to leave Frank seventy pounds a-year, and I desire you to tell him so." It is strange, however, to think, that Johnson was not free from that general weakness of being averse to execute a will, so that he delayed it from time to time; and had it not been for Sir John Hawkins's repeatedly urging it, I think it is probable that his kind resolution would not have been fulfilled. After making one, which, as Sir John Hawkins informs us, extended no further than the promised annuity, Johnson's final disposition of his property was established by a Will and Codicil, of which copies are subjoined.

Two very valuable articles, I am sure we have lost, which were two quarto volumes, containing a full, fair, and most particular account of his own life, from his earliest recollection. I owned to him, that having accidentally seen them, I had read a great deal in them; and apologising for the liberty I had taken, asked him if I could help it. He placidly answered, "Why, Sir, I do not think you could have helped it." I said that I had, for once in my life, felt half an inclination to commit theft. It had come into my mind to carry off those two volumes, and never see him more. Upon my enquiring how this would have affected him, "Sir, (said he,) I believe I should have gone mad."

During his last illness, Johnson experienced the steady and kind attachment of his numerous friends. Mr. Hoole has drawn up a narrative of what passed in the visits which he paid him during that time, from the 10th of November to the 13th of December, the day of his death, inclusive, and has favoured me with a perusal of it, with permission to make extracts, which I have done. Nobody was more attentive to him than Mr. Langton, to whom he tenderly said, *Te teneam moriens deficiente manu.* And I think it highly to the honour of Mr. Windham, that his important occupations as an active statesman did not prevent him from paying assiduous respect to the dying Sage whom he revered. Mr. Langton informs me, that, "one day he found Mr. Burke and four or five more friends sitting with Johnson. Mr. Burke said to him, 'I am afraid, Sir, such a number of us may be oppressive to you.'—'No, Sir, (said Johnson,) it is not so; and I must be in a wretched state, indeed, when your company would not be a delight to me.' Mr. Burke, in a tremulous voice, expressive of being very tenderly affected, replied, 'My dear Sir, you have always been too good to me.' Immediately afterwards he went away. This was the last circumstance in the acquaintance of these two eminent men."

The following particulars of his conversation within a few days of his death, I give on the authority of Mr. John Nichols:

"He said, that the Parliamentary Debates were the only part of his writings which then gave him any compunction: but that at the time he wrote them, he had no conception he was imposing upon the world, though they were frequently written from very slender materials, and often, from none at all,—the mere coinage of his own imagination. He never wrote any part of his works with equal velocity. Three columns of the Magazine, in an hour, was no uncommon effort, which was faster than most persons could have transcribed that quantity.

"Of his friend Cave, he always spoke with great affection. 'Yet, (said he), Cave, (who never looked out of his window, but with a view to the Gentleman's Magazine,) was a penurious paymaster; he would contract for lines by the hundred, and expect the long hundred; but he was a good man, and always delighted to have his friends at his table.'

"He said at another time, three or four days only before his death, speaking of the little fear he had of undergoing a chirurgical operation, 'I would give one of these legs for a year more of life, I mean of comfortable life, not such as that which I now suffer;'—and lamented much his inability to read during his hours of restlessness. 'I used formerly, (he added,) when sleepless in bed, *to read like a Turk.*' "

Amidst the melancholy clouds which hung over the dying Johnson, his characteristical manner shewed itself on different occasions.

When Dr. Warren in the usual style, hoped that he was better; his answer was, "No, Sir; you cannot conceive with what acceleration I advance towards death."

A man whom he had never seen before was employed one night to sit up with him. Being asked next morning how he like his attendant, his answer was, "Not at all, Sir: the fellow's an ideot; he is as aukward as a turn-spit when first put into the wheel, and as sleepy as a dormouse."

Mr. Windham having placed a pillow conveniently to support him, he thanked him for his kindness, and said, "That will do,—all that a pillow can do."

As he opened a note which his servant brought to him, he said, "An odd thought strikes me:—we shall receive no letters in the grave."

He requested three things of Sir Joshua Reynolds:— To forgive him thirty pounds which he had borrowed of him;—to read the Bible;—and never to use his pencil on a Sunday. Sir Joshua readily acquiesced.

Johnson, with that native fortitude, which, amidst all his bodily distress and mental sufferings, never forsook him, asked Dr. Brocklesby, as a man in whom he had confidence, to tell him plainly whether he could recover. "Give me (said he) a direct answer." The Doctor having first asked him if he could bear the whole truth, which way soever it might lead, and being answered that he could, declared that, in his opinion, he could not recover without a miracle. "Then, (said Johnson,) I will take no more physick, not even my opiates: for I have prayed that I may render up my soul to GOD unclouded." In this resolution he persevered, and, at the same time, used only the weakest kinds of sustenance. Being pressed by Mr. Windham to take somewhat more generous nourishment, lest too low a diet should have the very effect which he dreaded, by debilitating his mind, he said, "I will take any thing but inebriating sustenance."

Having, as has been already mentioned, made his will on the 8th and 9th of December, and settled all his worldly affairs, he languished till Monday, the 13th of that month, when he expired, about seven o'clock in the evening, with so little apparent pain that his attendants hardly perceived when his dissolution took place.

A few days before his death, he had asked Sir John Hawkins, as one of his executors, where he should be buried; and on being answered, "Doubtless, in Westminster-Abbey," seemed to feel a satisfaction, very natural to a Poet; and indeed in my opinion very natural to every man of any imagination, who has no family sepulchre in which he can be laid with his fathers. Accordingly, upon Monday, December 20, his remains were deposited in that noble and renowned edifice; and over his grave was placed a large blue flag-stone, with this inscription:

> SAMUEL JOHNSON, LL.D.
> *Obit* XIII *die Decembris,*
> *Anno Domini*
> M.DCC.LXXXIV.
> *Ætatis suæ* LXXV.

His funeral was attended by a respectable number of his friends, particularly such of the members of THE LITERARY CLUB as were then in town; and was also honoured with the presence of several of the Reverend Chapters of Westminster. Mr. Burke, Sir Joseph Banks, Mr. Windham, Mr. Langton, Sir Charles Bunbury, and Mr. Coleman, bore his pall. His school-fellow, Dr. Taylor, performed the mournful office of reading the burial service.

I trust, I shall not be accused of affectation, when I declare, that I find myself unable to express all that I felt upon the loss of such a "Guide, Philosopher, and Friend." I shall, therefore, not say one word of my own, but adopt those of an eminent friend, which he uttered with an abrupt felicity, superiour to all studied compositions:—"He has made a chasm, which not only nothing can fill up, but which nothing has a tendency to fill up. —Johnson is dead.—Let us go to the next best:—there is nobody; no man can be said to put you in mind of Johnson."

From THE JOURNAL OF A TOUR
TO THE HEBRIDES
WITH SAMUEL JOHNSON, LL.D.

D R. JOHNSON had for many years given me
hopes that we should go together and visit the
Hebrides. We reckoned there would be some inconveniences and hardships, and perhaps a little danger; but
these we were persuaded were magnified in the imagination of everybody. When I was at Ferney in 1764, I
mentioned our design to Voltaire. He looked at me as
if I had talked of going to the North Pole, and said,
"You do not insist on my accompanying you?" "No, Sir."
"Then I am very willing you should go." I was not afraid
that our curious expedition would be prevented by
such apprehensions, but I doubted that it would not
be possible to prevail on Dr. Johnson to relinquish for
some time the felicity of a London life, which, to a
man who can enjoy it with full intellectual relish, is
apt to make existence in any narrower sphere seem insipid or irksome. I doubted that he would not be willing
to come down from his elevated state of philosophical
dignity; from a superiority of wisdom among the wise
and of learning among the learned; and from flashing
his wit upon minds bright enough to reflect it.

He had disappointed my expectations so long that I
began to despair; but in spring 1773, he talked of coming to Scotland that year with so much firmness that I
hoped he was at last in earnest. I knew that if he were

once launched from the metropolis, he would go forward very well; and I got our common friends there to assist in setting him afloat. To Mrs. Thrale in particular, whose enchantment over him seldom failed, I was much obliged. It was: "I'll give thee a wind." "Thou art kind." To *attract* him we had invitations from the chiefs Macdonald and MacLeod, and for additional aid I wrote to Lord Elibank, Dr. William Robertson, and Dr. Beattie.

On Saturday the fourteenth of August, 1773, late in the evening, I received a note from him that he was arrived at Boyd's Inn, at the head of the Canongate. I went to him directly. He embraced me cordially, and I exulted in the thought that I now had him actually in Caledonia. Mr. Scott's amiable manners and attachment to our Socrates at once united me to him. He told me that before I came in the Doctor had unluckily had a bad specimen of Scottish cleanliness. He then drank no fermented liquor. He asked to have his lemonade made sweeter, upon which the waiter with his greasy fingers lifted a lump of sugar and put it into it. The Doctor in indignation threw it out of the window. Scott said he was afraid he would have knocked the waiter down. Mr. Johnson told me that such another trick was played him at the house of a lady in Paris. He was to do me the honour to lodge under my roof. I regretted sincerely that I had not also a room for Mr. Scott. Mr. Johnson and I walked arm-in-arm up the High Street to my house in James's Court; it was a dusky night; I could not prevent his being assailed by the evening effluvia of Edinburgh. As we marched slowly along, he grumbled in my ear, "I smell you in the dark!" But he acknowledged that the breadth of the street and the loftiness of the buildings on each side made a noble appearance.

My wife had tea ready for him, which it is well known he delighted to drink at all hours, particularly when sitting up late, and of which his able defence against Mr. Jonas Hanway should have obtained him a magnificent reward from the East India Company. He showed much complacency upon finding that the mistress of the house was so attentive to his singular habit; and as no man could be more polite when he chose to be so, his address to her was most courteous and engaging, and his conversation soon charmed her into a forgetfulness of his external appearance. . . .

Sir William Forbes, Mr. Scott, Mr. Arbuthnot, and another gentleman dined with us. "Come, Dr. Johnson," said I, "it is commonly thought that our veal in Scotland is not good. But here is some which I believe you will like." There was no catching him. JOHNSON. "Why, Sir, what is commonly thought I should take to be true. *Your* veal may be good, but that will only be an exception to the general opinion, not a proof against it."

Dr. Robertson, according to the custom of Edinburgh at that time, dined in the interval between the forenoon and afternoon service, which was then later than now; so we had not the pleasure of his company till dinner was over, when he came and drank wine with us. And then began some animated dialogue, of which here follows a pretty full note.

We talked of Mr. Burke. Dr. Johnson said he had great variety of knowledge, store of imagery, copiousness of language. ROBERTSON. "He has wit too." JOHNSON. "No, sir, he never succeeds there. 'Tis low; 'tis conceit. I used to say Burke never once made a good joke. What I most envy Burke for is his being constantly the same. He is never what we call humdrum; never unwilling to begin to talk, nor in haste to leave off." BOSWELL. "Yet he can listen." JOHNSON. "No, I cannot say he is good at that. So desirous is he to talk that if one is speaking at this end of the table, he'll speak to somebody at the other end. Burke, sir, is such a man that if you met him for the first time in a street where you were stopped by a drove of oxen, and you and he stepped aside to take shelter but for five minutes, he'd talk to you in such a manner that when you parted you would say, 'This is an extraordinary man.' Now, you may be long enough with *me* without finding anything extraordinary." He said he believed Burke was intended for the Law, but either had not money enough to follow it or had not diligence enough. He said he could not understand how a man could apply to one thing and not to another. Robertson said one man had more judgment, another more imagination. JOHNSON. "No, sir; it is only one man has more mind than another. He may direct it differently; he may by accident see the success of one kind of study and take a desire to excel in it. I am persuaded that had Sir Isaac Newton applied to poetry, he would have made a very fine epic poem. I could as easily apply to law as to tragic poetry." BOSWELL. "Yet, sir, you *did* apply to tragic poetry, not to law." JOHNSON. "Because, sir, I had not money to study law. Sir, the man who has vigour may walk to the east just as well as to the west, if he happens to turn his head that way." BOSWELL. "But, sir, 'tis like walking up and down a hill; one man will naturally do the one better than the other. A hare will run up a hill best, from her forelegs being short; a dog, down." JOHNSON. "Nay, sir; that is from mechanical powers. If you make mind mechanical, you may argue in that manner. One mind is a vice, and holds fast; there's a good memory. Another is a file, and he is a disputant, a controversialist. Another is a razor, and he is sarcastical." We talked of Whitefield. He said he was at the same college with him and knew him "before he began to be better than other people" (smiling); that he believed he sincerely meant well, but had a mixture of politics and ostentation, whereas Wesley thought of religion only. Robertson said Whitefield had strong natural eloquence, which, if cultivated, would have done great things. JOHNSON. "Why, sir, I take it he was at the height of what his abilities could do, and was sensible of it. He had the ordinary advantages of education, but he chose to pursue that oratory which is for the mob." BOSWELL. "He had great effect on the passions." JOHNSON. "Why, sir, I don't think so. He could not represent a succession of pathetic images. He vociferated and made an impression. *There,* again, was a mind like a hammer." Dr. Johnson now said a certain eminent political friend of ours was wrong in his maxim of sticking to a certain set of *men* on all occasions. "I can see that a man may do right to stick to a *party,*" said he; "that is to say, he is a *Whig,* or he is a *Tory,* and he thinks one of those parties upon the whole the best, and that to make it prevail, it must be generally supported, though in particulars it may be wrong. He takes its faggot of principles, in which there are fewer rotten sticks than in the other, though some rotten sticks, to be sure; and they cannot well be separated. But to bind one's self to one man, or one set of men (who may be right today and wrong tomorrow), without any general preference of system, I must disapprove."

He told us of Cooke who translated Hesiod and lived twenty years on a translation of Plautus for which he was always taking subscriptions; and that he presented Foote to a club in the following singular manner: "This is the nephew of the gentleman who was lately hung in chains for murdering his brother."

In the evening I introduced to Mr. Johnson two good friends of mine, Mr. William Nairne, advocate, and Mr. Hamilton of Sundrum, my neighbour in the country, both of whom supped with us. I have preserved nothing of what passed, except that Dr. Johnson displayed another of his heterodox opinions: a contempt of tragic acting. He said, "The action of all players in tragedy is bad. It should be a man's study to repress those signs of emotion and passion, as they are called." He was of a directly contrary opinion to that of Fielding in his *Tom Jones*, who makes Partridge say of Garrick, "Why, I could act as well as he himself. I am sure if I had seen a ghost, I should have looked in the very same manner, and done just as he did." For when I asked him, "Would not you, sir, start as Mr. Garrick does if you saw a ghost?" he answered, "I hope not. If I did, I should frighten the ghost."

Wednesday 18 August. On this day we set out from Edinburgh. We should gladly have had Mr. Scott to go with us, but he was obliged to return to England. I have given a sketch of Dr. Johnson; my readers may wish to know a little of his fellow-traveller. Think, then, of a gentleman of ancient blood, the pride of which was his predominant passion. He was then in his thirty-third year, and had been about four years happily married. His inclination was to be a soldier, but his father, a respectable judge, had pressed him into the profession of the Law. He had travelled a good deal and seen many varieties of human life. He had thought more than anybody supposed, and had a pretty good stock of general learning and knowledge. He had all Dr. Johnson's principles, with some degree of relaxation. He had rather too little than too much prudence, and his imagination being lively, he often said things of which the effect was very different from the intention.

Dr. Johnson thought it unnecessary to put himself to the additional expense of bringing with him Francis Barber, his faithful black servant, so we were attended only by my man, Joseph Ritter, a Bohemian, a fine stately fellow above six feet high, who had been over a great part of Europe, and spoke many languages. He was the best servant I ever saw. Let not my readers disdain his introduction. For Dr. Johnson gave him this character: "Sir, he is a civil man, and a wise man."

From an erroneous apprehension of violence, Dr. Johnson had provided a pair of pistols, some gunpowder, and a quantity of bullets; but upon being assured we should run no risk of meeting any robbers, he left his arms and ammunition in an open drawer, of which he gave my wife the charge. He also left in that drawer one volume of a pretty full and curious Diary of his Life, of which I have a few fragments, but the book has been destroyed. I wish female curiosity had been strong enough to have had it all transcribed, which might easily have been done; and I should think the theft, being *pro bono publico,* might have been forgiven. But I may be wrong. My wife told me she never once looked into it. She did not seem quite easy when we left her, but away we went!

Monday 30 August. This day we were to begin our *equitation,* as I said, for *I* would needs make a word too. We might have taken a chaise to Fort Augustus. But we could not find horses after Inverness, so we resolved to begin here to ride. We should have set out at seven. But one of the horses needed shoeing; the smith had got drunk the night before at a wedding and could not rise early; so we did not get off till nine.

A good way up the Loch, I perceived a little hut with an oldish woman at the door of it. I knew it would be a scene for Mr. Johnson. So I spoke of it. "Let's go in," said he. So we dismounted, and we and our guides went in. It was a wretched little hovel, of earth only, I think; and for a window had just a hole which was stopped with a piece of turf which could be taken out to let in light. In the middle of the room (or space which we entered) was a fire of peat, the smoke going out at a hole in the roof. She had a pot upon it with goat's flesh boiling. She had at one end, under the same roof but divided with a kind of partition made of wands, a pen or fold in which we saw a good many kids.

Mr. Johnson asked me where she slept. I asked one of the guides, who asked her in Erse. She spoke with a kind of high tone. He told us she was afraid we wanted to go to bed to her. This coquetry, or whatever it may be called, of so wretched a like being was truly ludicrous. Mr. Johnson and I afterwards made merry upon it. I said it was he who alarmed the poor woman's virtue. "No, sir," said he. "She'll say, 'There came a wicked young fellow, a wild young dog, who I believe would have ravished me had there not been with him a grave old gentleman who repressed him. But when he gets out of the sight of his tutor, I'll warrant you he'll spare no woman he meets, young or old.'" "No," said I. "She'll say, 'There was a terrible ruffian who would have forced me, had it not been for a gentle, mild-looking youth, who, I take it, was an angel.'"

Tuesday 31 August. Between twelve and one we set out and travelled eleven wild miles till we came to a house in Glenmoriston kept by one Macqueen. Our landlord was a sensible fellow. He had learnt his grammar, and Mr. Johnson justly observed that a man is the better for that as long as he lives. There were some books here: a treatise against drunkenness, translated from the French, a volume of the *Spectator*, a volume of Prideaux' *Connexion, Cyrus's Travels*. Macqueen said he had more volumes, and his pride seemed to be much piqued that we were surprised at his having books.

Near to this, we had passed a party of soldiers under a sergeant at work upon the road. We gave them two shillings to drink. They came to this house and made merry in the barn. We went out, Mr. Johnson saying, "Come, let's go and give 'em another shilling apiece." We did so, and he was saluted "MY LORD" by all of 'em. He is really generous, loves influence, and has the way of gaining it. He said he was quite feudal. Here I agree with him. I said I regretted I was not head of a clan. I would make my tenants follow me. I could not be a *patriarchal* chief. But I'd be a *feudal* chief.

The poor soldiers got too much liquor. Some of 'em fought and left blood upon the spot, and cursed whisky next morning. The house here was built of thick turfs and thatched with thinner turfs and heath. It had three rooms in length, and a little room projected. Where we sat, the side-walls were *wainscotted*, as Mr. Johnson said, with wands very well plaited. Our landlord had made all with his own hand. We had a broiled chicken, mutton collops or chops, mutton sausage, and eggs, of which Mr. Johnson eat five and nothing else. I eat four, some chicken and some sausage, and drank some rum and water and sugar. Joseph had lemons for Mr. Johnson, so he had lemonade. Mr. Johnson said he was a fine fellow: a civil man and a wise man.

I talked of the officers whom we had left today: how much service they had seen and how little they got for it, even of fame. Mr. Johnson said, "Sir, a soldier gets as little as any man can get." I observed that Goldsmith had more fame than all the officers last war who were not generals. JOHNSON. "Why, sir, you will get ten thousand to do what they did before you get one who does what Goldsmith has done. You must consider a thing is valued according to its rarity. A pebble that paves the street is in itself more useful than the diamond upon a lady's finger." I wish Goldie had heard this.

He said yesterday when I wondered how John Hay, one of our guides, who had been pressed aboard a man-of-war, did not choose to continue longer than nine months, after which time he got off: "Why, sir, no man will be a sailor who has contrivance to get himself into a jail, for being in a ship is being in a jail with the chance of being drowned."

We had tea in the afternoon, and our landlord's daughter, a modest civil girl very neatly dressed, made it to us. She told us she had been a year at Inverness and learnt reading and writing, sewing, knotting, working lace, and pastry. Mr. Johnson made her a present of a book of arithmetic which he had bought at Inverness.

The room had some deals laid as a kind of ceiling. There were two beds in the room. A woman's gown was hung on a rope to make a curtain of separation between them. Joseph had the sheets which we brought with us laid on them. We had much hesitation whether to undress or lie down with our clothes on. I said at last, "I'll plunge in! I shall have less room for vermin to settle about me when I strip!" Mr. Johnson said he was like one hesitating whether to go into the cold bath. At last he resolved too. I observed he might serve a campaign. Said he, "I could do all that can be done by patience. Whether I should have strength enough, I know not." He was in excellent humour. To see the Rambler as I saw him tonight was really a curiosity. I yesterday told him I was thinking to write an Epistle to him *on his return from Scotland,* in the style of Mrs. Gulliver to Captain Lemuel Gulliver—

Sullen you turn from both and call for *oats.*

He laughed and asked in whose name I'd write it. I said Mrs. Thrale's. He was angry and said, "Sir, if you have

any sense of decency or delicacy, you won't do that."
"Then," said I, "let it be Cole, the landlord of the Mitre
Tavern." "Ay, that may do," said he.

Tonight each offered up his private devotions. After
we had chatted a little from our beds, Mr. Johnson said,
"GOD bless us both for Jesus Christ's sake. Good night."
I pronounced "Amen." Mr. Johnson fell asleep immediately. I could not have that good fortune for a long time.
I fancied myself bit by innumerable vermin under the
clothes, and that a spider was travelling from the *wain-
scot* towards my mouth. At last I fell into insensibility.

Wednesday 1 September. We got away about eight.
We passed through Glen Shiel, with prodigious mountains on each side. We saw where the battle was in the
year 1715. Mr. Johnson owned he was now in a scene
of as wild nature as he could see. But he corrected me
sometimes in my observations. "There," said I, "is a
mountain like a cone." "No, sir," said he. "It would be
called so in a book; and when a man comes to look at
it, he sees 'tis not so. It is indeed pointed at the top. But
one side of it is much longer than the other." Another
mountain I called immense. "No," said he, "but 'tis a
considerable protuberance."

We came to a rich green valley, comparatively speaking, and stopped at Auchnashiel, a kind of rural village,
a number of cottages being built together, as we saw all
along in the Highlands. We passed many many miles today without seeing a house, but only little summer-huts
or *shielings*. Ewan Campbell, servant to Mr. Murchison,
factor to the Laird of MacLeod in Glenelg, run along
with us today. He was a fine obliging little fellow. At
this Auchnashiel, we sat down on a green turf seat at
the end of a house, and they brought us out two wooden
dishes of milk. One of them was frothed like a sillabub.
I saw a woman preparing it with such a stick as is used

for chocolate, and in the same manner. That dish fell to my share; but I put by the froth and took the cream with some wheat-bread which Joseph had brought for us from Fort Augustus. Mr. Johnson imagined my dish was better than his, and desired to taste it. He did so, and was convinced that I had no advantage over him. We had there in a circle all about us, men, women, and children, all Macraes, Lord Seaforth's people. Not one of them could speak English. I said to Mr. Johnson 'twas the same as being with a tribe of Indians. "Yes," said he, "but not so terrifying." I gave all who chose it snuff and tobacco. Governor Trapaud had made us buy a quantity at Fort Augustus and put them up in small parcels. I also gave each person a bit of wheat-bread, which they had never tasted. I then gave a penny apiece to each child. I told Mr. Johnson of this, upon which he called for change for a shilling, and declared that he would distribute among the children. Upon this there was a great stir: not only did some children come running down from neighbouring huts, but I observed one black-headed man, who had been among us all along, coming carrying a very young child. Mr. Johnson then ordered the children to be drawn up in a row, and he distributed his copper and made them and their parents all happy. The poor Macraes, whatever may be their present state, were much thought of in the year 1715, when there was a line in a song,

And aw' the brave McCraas is coming.

There was great diversity in the faces of the circle around us. Some were as black and wild in their appearance as any American savages whatever. One woman was as comely as the figure of Sappho, as we see it painted. We asked the old woman, the mistress of the house where we had the milk (which, by the by, Mr.

Johnson told me, for I did not observe it myself, was built not of turf but of stone), what we should pay. She said, what we pleased. One of our guides asked her in Erse if a shilling was enough. She said, "Yes." But some of the men bid her ask more. This vexed me, because it showed a desire to impose upon strangers, as they knew that even a shilling was high payment. The woman, however, honestly persisted in her first price. So I gave her half-a-crown. Thus we had one good scene of uncommon life to us. The people were very much pleased, gave us many blessings, and said they had not had such a day since the old Laird of MacLeod's time.

Mr. Johnson was much refreshed by this repast. He was pleased when I told him he would make a good chief. He said if he were one, he would dress his servants better than himself, and knock a fellow down if he looked saucy to a Macdonald in rags. But he would not treat men as brutes. He would let them know why all of his clan were to have attention paid to them. He would tell his upper servants why, and make them tell the others.

We rode on well till we came to the high mountain called the Rattachan, by which time both Mr. Johnson and the horses were a good deal fatigued. It is a terrible steep to climb, notwithstanding the road is made slanting along. However, we made it out. On the top of it we met Captain MacLeod of Balmeanach (a Dutch officer come from Skye) riding with his sword slung about him. He asked, "Is this Mr. Boswell?" which was a proof that we were expected. Going down the hill on the other side was no easy task. As Mr. Johnson was a great weight, the two guides agreed that he should ride the horses alternately. Hay's were the two best, and Mr. Johnson would not ride but upon one or other of them, a black or a brown. But as Hay complained much after ascending

the Rattachan, Mr. Johnson was prevailed with to mount
one of Vass's greys. As he rode upon it downhill, it did
not go well, and he grumbled. I walked on a little before, but was excessively entertained with the method
taken to keep him in good humour. Hay led the horse's
head, talking to Mr. Johnson as much as he could; and
just when Mr. Johnson was uttering his displeasure, the
fellow says, "See such pretty goats." Then *whu!* he whis-
tled, and made them jump. Little did he conceive what
Mr. Johnson was. Here was now a common ignorant
horse-hirer imagining that he could divert, as one does
a child, *Mr. Samuel Johnson!* The ludicrousness, absurdity, and extraordinary contrast between what the fellow
fancied and the reality, was as highly comic as anything
that I ever witnessed. I laughed immoderately, and must
laugh as often as I recollect it.

It grew dusky; and we had a very tedious ride for
what was called five miles, but I am sure would measure ten. We spoke none. I was riding forward to the inn
at Glenelg, that I might make some kind of preparation,
or take some proper measures, before Mr. Johnson got
up, who was now advancing in silence, with Hay leading his horse. Mr. Johnson called me back with a tremendous shout, and was really in a passion with me for
leaving him. I told him my intentions. But he was not
satisfied, and said, "Do you know, I should as soon have
thought of picking a pocket as doing so." "I'm diverted
with you," said I. Said he, "I could never be diverted
with incivility." He said doing such a thing made one
lose confidence in him who did it, as one could not tell
what he would do next. I justified myself but lamely to
him. But my intentions were not improper. I wished to
be forward to see if Sir A. Macdonald had sent his boat;
and if not, how we were to sail, and how we were to
lodge, all which I thought I could best settle myself,

without his having any trouble. To apply his great mind to minute particulars is wrong. It is like taking an immense balance, such as you see on a quay for weighing cargoes of ships, to weigh a guinea. I knew I had neat little scales which would do better. That his attention to everything in his way, and his uncommon desire to be always in the right, would make him weigh if he knew of the particulars; and therefore it was right for me to weigh them and let him have them only in effect. I kept by him, since he thought I should.

As we passed the barracks at Bernera, I would fain have put up there; at least I looked at them wishfully, as soldiers have always everything in the best order. But there was only a sergeant and a few men there. We came on to the inn at Glenelg. There was nothing to give the horses, so they were sent to grass with a man to watch them. We found that Sir Alexander had sent his boat to a point which we had passed, at Kintail, or more properly at the King's house—that it had waited several days till their provisions run short, and had returned only this day. So we had nothing to say against that Knight. A lass showed us upstairs into a room raw and dirty; bare walls, a variety of bad smells, a coarse black fir greasy table, forms of the same kind, and from a wretched bed started a fellow from his sleep like Edgar in *King Lear:* "Poor Tom's a-cold."

The landlord was one Munro from Fort Augustus. He pays £8 to MacLeod for the shell of the house, and has not a bit of land in lease. They had no bread, no eggs, no wine, no spirits but whisky, no sugar but brown grown black. They prepared some mutton-chops, but we would not have them. They killed two hens. I made Joseph broil me a bit of one till it was black, and I tasted it. Mr. Johnson would take nothing but a bit of bread, which we had luckily remaining, and some lemonade which he made with a lemon which Joseph had for him, and he got some good sugar; for Mr. Murchison, factor to MacLeod in Glenelg, sent us some, with a bottle of excellent rum, letting us know he was very sorry that his servant had not come and informed him before we passed his house; that we might have been there all night, and that if he were not obliged to set out early next day for Inverness, he would come down and wait upon us.

I took some rum and water and sugar, and grew better; for after my last bad night I hoped much to be well this, and being disappointed, I was uneasy and almost fretful. Mr. Johnson was calm. I said he was so from vanity. "No," said he, " 'tis from philosophy." It was a considerable satisfaction to me to see that the Rambler could practise what he nobly teaches.

I resumed my riding forward, and wanted to defend it. Mr. Johnson was still violent upon that subject, and said, "Sir, had you gone on, I was thinking that I should have returned with you to Edinburgh and then parted, and never spoke to you more."

I sent for fresh hay, with which we made beds to ourselves, each in a room equally miserable. As Wolfe said in his letter from Quebec, we had "choice of difficulties." Mr. Johnson made things better by comparison. At Macqueen's last night he observed that few were so well lodged in a ship. Tonight he said we were better than if we had been upon the hill. He lay down buttoned up in his greatcoat. I had my sheets spread on the hay, and having stripped, I had my clothes and greatcoat and Joseph's greatcoat laid upon me, by way of blankets. Joseph lay in the room by me, upon a bed laid on the floor.

Thursday 2 September. I had slept ill. Mr. Johnson's anger had affected me much. I considered that, without any bad intention, I might suddenly forfeit his friendship. I was impatient to see him this morning. I told him how uneasy he had made me by what he had said. He owned it was said in passion; that he would not have done it; that if he had done it, he would have been ten times worse than me. That it would indeed, as I said, be "limning in water," should such sudden breaks happen (or something to that effect); and said he, "Let's think no more on't." BOSWELL. "Well then, sir, I shall be easy. Remember, I am to have fair warning in case of any quarrel. You are never to spring a mine upon me. It was absurd in me to believe you." JOHNSON. "You deserved about as much as to believe it from night to morning." Mr. MacLeod of Drynoch, to whom we had a letter from Kenneth Macaulay, breakfasted with us.

A quarter before nine we got into a boat for Skye. It rained much when we set off, but cleared up as we advanced. One of the boatmen who spoke English said that a mile at land was two miles at sea. I then said to him that from Glenelg to Armadale in Skye, which was our sail this morning and is called twelve, was only six miles. But this he could not understand. "Well," said Mr. Johnson, "never talk to me of the native good sense of the Highlanders. Here is a fellow who calls one mile two, and yet cannot comprehend that twelve such miles make but six." It was curious to think that now at last Mr. Johnson and I had left the mainland of Scotland and were sailing to the Hebrides, one of which was close in our view; and I had besides a number of youthful ideas, that is to say, ideas which I have had from my youth about the Isle of Skye. We were shown the land of Moidart where Prince Charles first landed. That stirred my mind.

We reached the shore of Armadale before one. Sir Alexander came down and received us. He was in tartan clothes. My lady stood at the top of the bank and made a kind of jumping for joy.

We had an ill-dressed dinner, Sir Alexander not having a cook of any kind from Edinburgh. I alone drank port wine. No claret appeared. We had indeed mountain and Frontignac and Scotch porter. But except what I did myself, there was no hospitable convivial intercourse, no ringing of glasses. Nay, I observed that when Captain Macdonald and Mr. Macqueen came in after we were sat down to dinner, Sir Alexander let them stand round the room and stuck his fork into a liver pudding, instead of getting room made for them. I took care to act as he ought to have done. There was no wheat-loaf, but only a kind of bannock or cake, raw in the heart, as it was so thick. Sir Alexander himself drank punch without souring and with little spirits in it, which he distributed to those men who were accustomed even in their own houses to much better. He gave it with a pewter dividing-spoon which had served the broth. At tea there were few cups and no tea-tongs nor a supernumerary tea-spoon, so we used our fingers.

I was quite hurt with the meanness and unsuitable appearance of everything. I meditated setting out the very next day. At night we had only Rorie and spouse and the naturalist and his son. When Mr. Johnson and I retired for rest, he said it grieved him to see the chief of a great clan in such a state; that he was just as one in a lodging-house in London. However, he resolved that we should weather it out till Monday.

Friday 3 September. The day was very wet. Sir Alexander's piper plays below stairs both at breakfast and dinner, which is the only circumstance of a chief to be found about him. He had two chests of books, of which Mr. Johnson and I ravenously seized some of the contents. It grew fair a little before dinner, and I took a little walk with Captain Macdonald, from whom I found that Sir Alexander was quite unpopular, and that all his deficiencies were well remarked. I made the Captain drink port wine today. Mrs. Macdonald said that I fitted Sir Alexander in several suits better than anybody—a curious expression. I asked her how the old Laird of MacLeod came to be so much in debt. She said, "You may as well read the *Spectator* as begin to tell all that"; and she said it was a pity that this young Laird should lose his *patronomic* estate when he was in no fault; meaning that he was labouring under a load of debt not contracted by himself.

When Sir Alexander was out of the room, I spoke of Sir James. The Highlanders fairly cried. Neither my lady nor Mr. Johnson were then present. I cried too, and we drank a bumper to his memory. It was really melancholy to see the manly, gallant, and generous attachment of clanship going to ruin.

Sir Alexander composed today some Latin verses with which he presented Mr. Johnson. After dinner the Knight and I met in Mr. Johnson's room, where I was looking for pen and ink. I fell upon him with perhaps too great violence upon his behaviour to his people; on the meanness of his appearance here; upon my lady's neither having a maid, nor being dressed better than one. In short, I gave him a volley. He was thrown into a violent passion; said he could not bear it; called in my lady and complained to her, at the same time defending himself with considerable plausibility. Had he been a man of more mind, he and I must have had a quarrel for life. But I knew he would soon come to himself. We had moor-fowl for supper tonight, which comforted me.

We were advised by Rorie, by Donald MacLeod, and everybody to visit Raasay in our way to Dunvegan,

MacLeod's house, to which we looked wishfully forward as expecting more elegance and propriety. The Rev. Mr. Donald Macqueen I heard was the most intelligent man in the island. Sir Alexander should have had him here with us. I had a letter to him from Sir James Foulis. I sent an express to set off early next morning with a letter to him enclosing Sir James's and begging he'd meet us at Raasay on Monday or Tuesday, as also enclosing a card to MacLeod, to inform him that we were to be at Dunvegan.

Mr. Johnson was vexed that he could get no distinct information about anything from any of the people here. He wished that a good comedian saw Rorie and his wife, to take from them a Highland scene.

Saturday 4 September. Sir Alexander was in my room before I got up, with a bowl of buttermilk, of which I drank. Our quarrel was already evanished. I set Mr. Johnson upon him this morning, who said that in seven years he would make this an independent island; that he'd roast oxen whole and hang out a flag as a signal to the Macdonalds to come and get beef and whisky. Poor Sir Alexander was always starting difficulties. "Nay," said Mr. Johnson, "if you're born to object, I have done with you." He would have a magazine of arms. Sir Alexander said they would rust. Said Mr. Johnson, "Let there be men to keep them clean. Your ancestors did not use to let their arms rust."

It was in vain to try to inspirit him. Mr. Johnson said, "Sir, we shall make nothing of him. He has no more ideas of a chief than an attorney who has twenty houses in a street and considers how much he can make of them. All is wrong. He has nothing to say to the people when they come about him." My beauty of a cousin, too, did not escape. Indeed, I was quite disgusted with her nothingness and insipidity. Mr. Johnson said, "This woman would sink a ninety-gun ship. She is so dull—so heavy."

It was fine to see Mr. Johnson light from his horse at Kingsburgh's, who received us most courteously, and after shaking hands supported Mr. Johnson into the house. He was quite the figure of a gallant Highlander —"the graceful mien and manly looks." He had his tartan plaid thrown about him, a large blue bonnet with a knot of black ribbon like a cockade, a brown short coat of a kind of duffle, a tartan vest with gold buttons and gold buttonholes, a bluish filibeg, and tartan hose. He had jet-black hair tied behind and with screwed ringlets on each side, and was a large stately man, with a steady sensible countenance.

There was a comfortable parlour with a good fire, and a dram of admirable Holland's gin went round. By and by supper came, when there appeared his spouse, the celebrated Miss Flora. She was a little woman, of a mild and genteel appearance, mighty soft and well-bred. To see Mr. Samuel Johnson salute Miss Flora Macdonald was a wonderful romantic scene to me. There was a Mrs. Macdonald, wife to James, a brother of Kingsburgh's, and one of his sons. We had as genteel a supper as one would wish to see, in particular an excellent roasted turkey, porter to drink at table, and after supper claret and punch. But what I admired was the perfect ease with which everything went on. My *facility of manners,* as Adam Smith said of me, had fine play.

Miss Flora (for so I shall call her) told me she heard upon the mainland, as she was returning to Skye about a fortnight before this, that Mr. Boswell was coming to Skye, and one Mr. Johnson, a young English buck, with him. He was highly entertained with this event, and speaking of the afternoon which we passed at Anoch, he said, "I, being a *buck,* had Miss in to make tea," or some such expression about Macqueen's daughter. He was rather quiescent tonight and went early to bed. I was in a cordial humour, and promoted a cheerful glass. The punch was superexcellent, and we drank three bowls of it. Honest Mr. Macqueen said of me, "His governor's gone to bed." My heart was sore to recollect that Kingsburgh had fallen sorely back in his affairs, was under a load of debt, and intended to go to America. However, nothing but what was good was present, and I pleased myself in thinking that so fine a fellow would be well everywhere. I slept in the same room with Mr. Johnson. Each had a neat clean bed in an upper chamber.

Monday 13 September. Last night's jovial bout disturbed me somewhat, but not long. The room where we lay was a room indeed. Each bed had tartan curtains, and Mr. Johnson's was the very bed in which the Prince lay. To see Mr. Samuel Johnson lying in Prince Charles's bed, in the Isle of Skye, in the house of Miss Flora Macdonald, struck me with such a group of ideas as it is not easy for words to describe as the mind perceives them. He smiled, and said, "I have had no ambitious thoughts in it." The room was decorated with a great variety of maps and prints. Among others was Hogarth's print of Wilkes grinning with the cap of liberty beside him. That, too, was a curious circumstance in the scene this morning. Such a contrast was Wilkes to the above group! It was like Sir William Chambers's idea of oriental gardening, in which all odd, strange, ugly, and even terrible objects, are to be introduced for the sake of variety, and which is so well ridiculed in an *Epistle* to him. I thought of the two lines in it,

> Here too, O King of vengeance! in thy fane,
> Tremendous Wilkes shall rattle his gold chain.

Upon the table in our room I found a slip of paper in the morning, on which Mr. Johnson had written with his pencil these words: "Quantum cedat virtutibus aurum." What he meant by writing it I could not tell. He had catched cold a day or two ago, and the rain yesterday had made it worse; so he was become very deaf. At breakfast he said he would have given a good deal rather than not have lain in the bed. I said he was the lucky man; and to be sure it had been contrived between Mrs. Macdonald and him. She said, "You know young *bucks* are always favourites of the ladies." He spoke of the Prince being here, and said to Mrs. Macdonald, "*Who* was with him? We were told in England, there was one Miss Flora Macdonald with him." Said she, "They were very right." She then very obligingly told him out of her own mouth, how she had agreed to carry the Prince with her out of Lewis when it was known he was there; the country was full of troops and the coast surrounded with ships. He passed as her maid, an Irish girl, Betty Bourke. They set off in a small boat. The people on shore fired after them to bring them to. But they went forward. They landed in Skye. She got a horse and her maid walked beside her, which it seems is common in this part of the world, but Betty looked somewhat awkward in women's clothes. They came to Monkstadt. She dined at table with Lady Margaret Macdonald, where was an officer who commanded a party watching for the Prince, at whom she often laughed in good humour afterwards as having deceived him; and her maid was—I do not remember where.

Mr. Johnson said all this should be written down. She said Bishop Forbes at Leith had it. Mr. Johnson and I were both visibly of the *old interest* (to use the Oxford expression), kindly affectioned at least, and perhaps too openly so.

At supper, Lady MacLeod mentioned Dr. Cadogan's book on the gout. Mr. Johnson said, " 'Tis a good book in general, but a foolish one as to particulars. 'Tis good in general, as recommending temperance and exercise and cheerfulness. 'Tis only Dr. Cheyne's book told in a new way. And there should come out such a book every thirty years, dressed in the mode of the times. 'Tis foolish, as it says the gout is not hereditary, and one fit of the gout when gone is like a fever when gone." "But," said Lady MacLeod, "he does not practise what he teaches." JOHNSON. "I cannot help that, madam. That does not make his book the worse. People are influenced more by what a man says, if his practice is suitable to it, because they are blockheads. The more intellectual people are, the readier will they attend to what a man tells them. If it is just, they will follow it, be his practice what it will. No man practises so well as he writes. I have, all my life long, been lying till noon. Yet I tell all young men, and tell them with great sincerity, that nobody who does not rise early will ever do any good. Only consider! You read a book; you are convinced by it; you do not know the author. Suppose you afterwards know him, and find that he does not practise what he teaches; are you to give up your former conviction? At this rate you would be kept in a state of *equilibrio* when reading every book, till you knew how the author practised." "But," said Lady MacLeod, "you would think better of Dr. Cadogan if he acted according to his principles." JOHNSON. "Why, madam, to be sure, a man who acts in the face of light is worse than a man who does not know so much. But I think there is something noble in publishing truth, though it condemns one's self." I spoke of Cadogan's recommending good-humour. Mr. Johnson said, "A man grows better-humoured as he grows older, by experience. He learns to think himself of no consequence and little things of little importance; and so he becomes more patient, and better pleased. All good-humour and complaisance is acquired. Naturally a child seizes directly what it sees, and thinks of pleasing itself only. By degrees, it is taught to please others, and to prefer others; and that this will ultimately produce the greatest happiness. If a man is not convinced of that, he never will practise it." Lady MacLeod asked if no man was naturally good. JOHNSON. "No, madam, no more than a wolf." BOSWELL. "Nor no woman, sir?" JOHNSON. "No, sir." Lady MacLeod started, saying low, "This is worse than Swift."

Thursday 16 September. Last night much care was taken of Mr. Johnson. He had hitherto most strangely slept without a night-cap. Miss MacLeod made him a large flannel one, and he was prevailed with to drink a little brandy when he was going to bed—all to do his cold good. He has great virtue in not drinking wine or any fermented liquor, because he could not do it in moderation. He told us so on Tuesday night. Lady MacLeod would hardly believe him, and said, "I'm sure, sir, you would not carry it too far." JOHNSON. "Nay, madam, it carried me." He took the opportunity of a long illness to leave it off. It was prescribed to him then not to drink wine; and having broke off the habit, he has never returned to it. He was in high spirits this morning.

In the argument on Tuesday night about natural goodness, he denied that any child was more so than another, but by difference of instruction; though the greater attention given by one than another, and a variety of imperceptible causes (such as instruction being counteracted by servants) made it be thought that of two children equally well educated, one should be much worse than another. He owned this morning that one might have a greater aptitude to learn than another, and that we inherit dispositions from our parents. Said he, "I inherited a vile melancholy from my father, which has made me mad all my life, at least not sober." Lady MacLeod wondered he should tell this. "Madam," said I, "he knows that with that madness he is superior to other men."

I have often been astonished with what exactness and perspicuity he will explain the whole process of any art. He this morning gave us all the operation of coining, and at night he gave us all the operation of brewing spirits. Mr. Macqueen said when he heard the first he thought he had been bred in the Mint. When he heard the second, that he had been bred a brewer.

It was curious to have him on this remote point of the world. Lady MacLeod was entertained with my simile, that it was like a dog who has got hold of a large piece of meat, and runs away with it to a corner, where he may devour it in peace, without any fear of others taking it from him. "In London, Reynolds, Beauclerk, and all of them are contending who shall have Mr. Johnson. We are feasting upon him undisturbed at Dunvegan."

After the ladies were gone, we talked of the Highlanders' not having sheets; and so on we went to the advantage of wearing linen. Mr. Johnson said, "All animal substances are less cleanly than vegetable. Wool, of which flannel is made, is an animal substance; flannel therefore is not so cleanly as linen. I remember I used to think tar dirty. But when I knew it to be only a preparation of the juice of the pine, I thought so no longer. It is not disagreeable to have the gum that oozes from a plum-tree upon your fingers, because it is vegetable; but if you have any candle-grease, any tallow upon your fingers, you are uneasy till you rub it off." And then he came out with this saying: "I have often thought that if I kept a seraglio, the ladies should all wear linen gowns, or cotton; I mean stuffs made of vegetable substances. I would have no silk; you cannot tell when it is clean. It will be very nasty before it is perceived to be so. Linen detects its own dirtiness."

To hear Mr. Johnson, while sitting solemn in armchair, talk of his keeping a seraglio and saying too, "I have *often* thought," was truly curious. Mr. Macqueen asked him if he would admit me. "Yes," said he, "if he were properly prepared; and he'd make a very good eunuch. He'd be a fine gay animal. He'd do his part well." "I take it," said I, "better than you would do your part." Though he treats his friends with uncommon freedom, he does not like a return. He seemed to me to be a little angry. He got off from my joke by saying, "I have not told you what was to be my part"— and then at once he returned to my office as eunuch and expatiated upon it with such fluency that it really hurt me. . . .

I mentioned a club in London at the Boar's Head in Eastcheap, the very tavern where Falstaff and his joyous companions met; and the members of it all assume Shakespeare's characters. One is Falstaff, another Prince Henry, another Bardolph, and so on. Mr. Johnson said, "Don't be of it. Now that you have a name, you must be careful to avoid many things not bad in themselves, but which will lessen your character. This," said he, "every man who has a name must observe. A man who is not publicly known may live in London as he pleases without any notice being taken of him. But it is wonderful how a person of any consequence is watched. There was a Member of Parliament who wanted to prepare himself to speak on a question that was to come on in the House, and he and I were to talk it over together. He did not wish it should be known that he talked with me; so he would not let me come to his house, but came to me. Some time after he made his speech in the House, Mrs. Cholmondeley, a very airy lady, told me, 'Well, you could make nothing of him,' —naming the gentleman, which was a proof that he was watched. I had once some business to do for Government, and I went to Lord North's. It was dark before I went. Yet a few days after, I was told, 'Well, you have been with Lord North.' That the door of the Prime Minister should be watched is not so wonderful; but that a Member of Parliament should be watched, or my door should be watched, is wonderful."

We set out this morning in Ullinish's boat, having taken leave of him and his family. There was an ease in his house, an appearance as if everything went on daily just as we saw it, that was very agreeable. It made one quite free of the idea that our company was any burden. As we sailed along, Mr. Johnson got into one of his fits of railing at the Scots. He owned that we were a very learned nation for about 100 years, from about 1550 to about 1650. But that we lost our learning during the Civil War and had never recovered it. He said we afforded the only instance of a people among whom the arts of civil life did not advance in proportion with learning; that we had hardly any trade, any money, or any elegance before the Union. That it was strange how with all the advantages that other nations have, we had not any of those arts which are the fruit of industry, till we came in contact with a civilized nation. "We have taught you," said he; "and we'll do the same in time to all barbarous nations—to the Cherokees—and at last to the orangoutangs"—laughing as if Monboddo had been present. I said we had wine before the Union. "No sir," said he: "you had some weak stuff, the refuse of France, which would not make you drunk." BOSWELL. "I assure you, sir, there was a great deal of drunkenness." JOHNSON. "No, sir; there were people who died of dropsies which they contracted in trying to get drunk." . . .

We talked of the assiduity of the Scotch clergy in visiting and privately instructing their people, and how in this they excelled the English clergy. Mr. Johnson would not let this pass. He tried to turn it off by saying, "There are different ways of instructing. Our clergy pray and preach." MacLeod and I pushed the subject, upon which he grew warm, and broke forth, "I do not believe your people are better instructed. If they are, it is the blind leading the blind, for your clergy are not instructed themselves. There is Macaulay—the most ignorant booby and the grossest bastard." (Coll says Mr. Johnson said Macaulay was as obstinate as a mule and as ignorant as a bull, but I do not recollect this.) Mr. Johnson took himself well, and said, "When I talk of the ignorance of your clergy, I speak of them as a body. I do not mean that there are not individuals who are learned" (looking at Mr. Macqueen). "I suppose there are in Muscovy. The clergy of England have produced the most valuable books in support of religion, both in theory and practice. What have your clergy done since you sunk into Presbyterianism? Can you name one book of any value in religion written by them?" We could not. Said he, "I'll help you. Forbes wrote very well, but I believe he wrote before Episcopacy was quite extinguished"; and then pausing a little, he said, "Yes, you have Wishart AGAINST repentance." "But, sir," said I, "we are not contending for the superior learning of our clergy, but for their superior assiduity." He bore us down again with thundering against their ignorance, and said, "I see you have not been well taught, for you have not charity." He had been in a manner forced into this, for when he began, he said, "Since you *will* drive the nail." He again thought of good Mr. Macqueen, and taking him by the hand, said, "Sir, I did not mean any disrespect to you."

Here I must observe that he conquered by leaving the argument, which was just where I put it. The assiduity of the Scottish clergy is certainly greater than that of the English. His taking up the topic of their not having so much learning, was, though most ingenious, yet a fallacy in logic. It was as if there should be a dispute whether a man's hair is well dressed, and Mr. Johnson should say, "Sir, his hair cannot be well dressed, for he has a dirty shirt. No man who has not clean linen has his hair well dressed." [1]

Friday 24 September. This was a good day. Dr. Johnson told us at breakfast that he rode harder at a fox chase than anybody. "The English," said he, "are the only nation who ride hard a-hunting. A Frenchman goes out upon a managed horse, and capers in the field, and no more thinks of leaping a hedge than of mounting a breach. Lord Powerscourt laid a wager, in France, that he would ride a great many miles in a certain short time. The French academicians set to work, and calculated that, from the resistance of the air, it was impossible. His lordship, however, performed it."

I must not forget that in the morning Mr. Johnson told us that the few ancient Irish gentlemen who remain have the highest pride of family. Mr. Sandford, a friend of his, whose mother was Irish, told him that O'Hara, who was true Irish both by father and mother, and he, and Mr. Ponsonby, son to the Earl of Bessborough, the

---

[1] When Johnson read Boswell's script, he commented on this as follows: "I did not say the man's hair could not be well dressed because he had not a clean shirt, but because he was bald."

greatest man of the three, but of an English family, went to see one of those ancient Irish; and that he distinguished them thus: "O'Hara, you are welcome. Mr. Sandford, your mother's son is welcome. Mr. Ponsonby, you may sit down." . . .

Miss Maclean gave us several tunes on a spinet, which, though made so long ago as in 1667, was still very well toned. She sung along with it. Dr. Johnson seemed pleased with the music, though he owns he neither likes it nor has hardly any perception of it. At Mr. Macpherson's, in Sleat, he told us that he knew a drum from a trumpet, and a bagpipe from a guitar, which was about the extent of his knowledge of music. Tonight he said that if he had learnt music he should have been afraid he would have done nothing else than play. It was a method of employing the mind, without the labour of thinking at all, and with some applause from a man's self.

We had the music of the bagpipe every day at Armadale, Dunvegan, and Coll. Dr. Johnson appeared fond of it, and used often to stand for some time with his ear close to the great drone.

The penurious gentleman of our acquaintance,[1] formerly alluded to, afforded us a topic of conversation tonight. Dr. Johnson said I ought to write down a collection of the instances of his narrowness, as they almost exceeded belief. Coll told us that O'Kane, the famous Irish harper, was once at that gentleman's house. He could not find in his heart to give him any money, but gave him a key for a harp, which was finely ornamented with gold and silver and with a precious stone, and was worth eighty or a hundred guineas. He did not know the value of it; and when he came to know it, he would fain have had it back, but O'Kane took care that he

---

[1] Sir Alexander Macdonald.

should not. JOHNSON. "They exaggerate the value; every-body is so desirous that he should be fleeced. I am very willing it should be worth eighty or a hundred guineas, but I do not believe it." BOSWELL. "I do not think O'Kane was obliged to give it back." JOHNSON. "No, sir. If a man with his eyes open, and without any means used to deceive him, gives me a thing, I am not to let him have it again when he grows wiser. I like to see how avarice defeats itself; how, when avoiding to part with money, the miser gives something more valuable." Coll said the gentleman's relations were angry at his giving away the harp-key, for it had been long in the family. JOHNSON. "Sir, he values a new guinea more than an old friend."

Coll also told us that the same person having come up with a sergeant and twenty men working on the high road, he entered into discourse with the sergeant, and then gave him sixpence for the men to drink. The sergeant asked, "Who is this fellow?" Upon being informed, he said, "If I had known who he was, I should have thrown it in his face." JOHNSON. "There is much want of sense in all this. He had no business to speak with the sergeant. He might have been in haste and trotted on. He has not learnt to be a miser; I believe we must take him apprentice." BOSWELL. "He would grudge giving half a guinea to be taught." JOHNSON. "Nay, sir, you must teach him gratis. You must give him an opportunity to practise your precepts."

Let me now go back and glean Johnsoniana. The Saturday before we sailed from Sleat, I sat awhile in the afternoon with Dr. Johnson in his room, in a quiet serious frame. I observed that hardly any man was accurately prepared for dying, but almost every one left something undone, something in confusion; that my father, indeed, told me he knew one man (Carlisle of

Limekilns), after whose death all his papers were found in exact order, and nothing was omitted in his will. JOHNSON. "Sir, I had an uncle who died so, but such attention requires great leisure and great firmness of mind. If one was to think constantly of death, the business of life would stand still. I am no friend to making religion appear too hard. Many good people have done harm by giving severe notions of it. In the same way as to learning: I never frighten young people with difficulties; on the contrary, I tell them that they may very easily get as much as will do very well. I do not indeed tell them that they will be Bentleys."

At Captain Maclean's, I mentioned Pope's friend Spence. JOHNSON. "He was a weak conceited man." BOSWELL. "A good scholar, sir?" JOHNSON. "Why, no, sir." BOSWELL. "He was a pretty scholar." JOHNSON. "You have about reached him."

Last night at the inn, when the factor in Tyree spoke of his having heard that a roof was put on some part of the buildings at Icolmkill, I unluckily said, "It will be fortunate if we find a cathedral with a roof on it." I said this from a foolish anxiety to engage Dr. Johnson's curiosity more. He took me short at once. "What, sir? How can you talk so? If we shall *find* a cathedral roofed! As if we were going to a *terra incognita:* when everything that is at Icolmkill is so well known. You are like some New England men who came to the mouth of the Thames. 'Come,' said they, 'let us go up and see what sort of inhabitants there are here.' They talked, sir, as if they had been to go up the Susquehanna, or any other American river." . . .

I recollect none of his conversation, except that, when talking of dress, he said, "Sir, were I to have anything fine, it should be very fine. Were I to wear a ring, it should not be a bauble but a stone of great value. Were I to wear a laced or embroidered waistcoat, it should be very rich. I had once a very rich laced waistcoat, which I wore the first night of my tragedy."

Tuesday 2 November. We were now in a country not only "of saddles and bridles," but of post-chaises; and having ordered one from Kilmarnock, we got to Auchinleck before dinner.

My father was not quite a year and a half older than Dr. Johnson, but his conscientious discharge of his laborious duty as a judge in Scotland (where the law proceedings are almost all in writing), a severe complaint which ended in his death, and the loss of my mother, a woman of almost unexampled piety and goodness, had before this time in some degree affected his spirits, and rendered him less disposed to exert his faculties; for he had originally a very strong mind and cheerful temper. He assured me he never had felt one moment of what is called low spirits, or uneasiness without a real cause. He had a great many good stories, which he told uncommonly well, and he was remarkable for "humour, *incolumi gravitate*," as Lord Monboddo used to characterize it. His age, his office, and his character had long given him an acknowledged claim to great attention, in whatever company he was; and he could ill brook any diminution of it. He was as sanguine a Whig and Presbyterian as Dr. Johnson was a Tory and Church of England man; and as he had not much leisure to be informed of Dr. Johnson's great merits by reading his works, he had a partial and unfavourable notion of him, founded on his supposed political tenets, which were so discordant to his own that, instead of speaking of him with that respect to which he was entitled, he used to call him "a Jacobite fellow." Knowing all this, I should not have ventured to bring them together, had not my father, out of kindness to me, desired me to invite Dr. Johnson to his house.

I was very anxious that all should be well; and begged of my friend to avoid three topics, as to which they differed very widely: Whiggism, Presbyterianism, and—Sir John Pringle. He said courteously, "I shall certainly not talk on subjects which I am told are disagreeable to a gentleman under whose roof I am; especially, I shall not do so to *your father*."

Our first day went off very smoothly. It rained, and we could not get out; but my father showed Dr. Johnson his library, which, in curious editions of the Greek and Roman classics, is, I suppose, not excelled by any private collection in Great Britain. My father had studied at Leyden and been very intimate with the Gronovii and other learned men there. He was a sound scholar, and, in particular, had collated manuscripts and different editions of Anacreon, and others of the Greek lyric poets, with great care; so that my friend and he had much matter for conversation, without touching on the fatal topics of difference.

Dr. Johnson found here Baxter's Anacreon, which he told me he had long inquired for in vain, and began to suspect there was no such book. Baxter was the keen antagonist of Barnes. His life is in the *Biographia Britannica*. My father has written many notes on this book, and Dr. Johnson and I talked of having it reprinted.

Wednesday 3 November. It rained all day, and gave Dr. Johnson an impression of that incommodiousness of climate in the West, of which he has taken notice in his *Journey;* but, being well accommodated and furnished with variety of books, he was not dissatisfied.

Some gentlemen of the neighbourhood came to visit my father, but there was little conversation. One of them asked Dr. Johnson how he liked the Highlands. The question seemed to irritate him, for he answered, "How, sir, can you ask me what obliges me to speak unfavourably of a country where I have been hospitably entertained? Who *can* like the Highlands? I like the inhabitants very well." The gentleman asked no more questions.

He this day, when we were by ourselves, observed, how common it was for people to talk from books; to retail the sentiments of others, and not their own; in short, to converse without any originality of thinking. He was pleased to say, "You and I do not talk from books."

Friday 5 November. The Reverend Mr. Dun, our parish minister, who had dined with us yesterday with some other company, insisted that Dr. Johnson and I should dine with him today. This gave me an opportunity to show my friend the road to the church, made by my father at a great expense for above three miles on his own estate, through a range of well enclosed farms, with a row of trees on each side of it. He called it the *Via sacra*, and was very fond of it. Dr. Johnson, though he held notions far distant from those of the Presbyterian clergy, yet could associate on good terms with them. One of them discovered a narrowness of information concerning the dignitaries of the Church of England, among whom may be found men of the greatest learning, virtue, and piety, and of a truly apostolic character. He talked before Dr. Johnson of fat bishops and drowsy deans; and, in short, seemed to believe the illiberal and profane scoffings of professed satirists or vulgar railers. Dr. Johnson was so highly offended that he said to him, "Sir, you know no more of our church than a Hottentot." I was sorry that he brought this upon himself.

Saturday 6 November. I cannot be certain whether it was on this day or a former that Dr. Johnson and my father came in collision. If I recollect right, the contest began while my father was showing him his collection of medals; and Oliver Cromwell's coin unfortunately introduced Charles the First, and Toryism. They became exceedingly warm and violent, and I was very much distressed by being present at such an altercation between two men, both of whom I reverenced; yet I durst not interfere. It would certainly be very unbecoming in me to exhibit my honoured father and my respected friend as intellectual gladiators, for the entertainment of the public; and therefore I suppress what would, I dare say, make an interesting scene in this dramatic sketch—this account of the transit of Johnson over the Caledonian Hemisphere.

Yet I think I may, without impropriety, mention one circumstance, as an instance of my father's address. Dr. Johnson challenged him, as he did us all at Talisker, to point out any theological works of merit written by Presbyterian ministers in Scotland. My father, whose studies did not lie much in that way, owned to me afterwards that he was somewhat at a loss how to answer, but that luckily he recollected having read in catalogues the title of *Durham on the Galatians;* upon which he boldly said, "Pray, sir, have you read Mr. Durham's excellent commentary on the Galatians?" "No, sir," said Dr. Johnson. By this lucky thought my father kept him at bay, and for some time enjoyed his triumph; but his antagonist soon made a retort, which I forbear to mention.

In the course of their altercation, Whiggism and Presbyterianism, Toryism and Episcopacy, were terribly buffeted. My worthy hereditary friend, Sir John Pringle, never having been mentioned, happily escaped without a bruise.

My father's opinion of Dr. Johnson may be conjectured from the name he afterwards gave him, which was "Ursa Major."

At Sir Alexander Dick's, from that absence of mind to which every man is at times subject, I told, in a blundering manner, Lady Eglinton's complimentary adoption of Dr. Johnson as her son; for I unfortunately stated that her ladyship adopted him as her son, in consequence of her having been married the year *after* he was born. Dr. Johnson instantly corrected me. "Sir, don't you perceive that you are defaming the Countess? For, supposing me to be her son, and she was not married till the year after my birth, I must have been her *natural* son." A young lady of quality, who was present, very handsomely said, "Might not the son have justified the fault?" My friend was much flattered by this compliment, which he never forgot. When in more than ordinary spirits, and talking of his journey in Scotland, he has called to me, "Boswell, what was it that the young lady of quality said of me at Sir Alexander Dick's?"

From the DIALOGUE
WITH ROUSSEAU

(1764)

EDITOR'S NOTE

As I remarked in the Introduction, I have had to exclude, for reasons of space, all of Boswell's purely autobiographical writings. Had I included enough from the Letters and the Private Papers to reveal Boswell rather than merely parade his peculiarities, there would have been, what with the selections from the *Life* and the *Tour,* almost no space left for representing Johnson. Moreover, the animating principle of this Portable is to combine the best of Johnson's writings with the best of Boswell's about him. But at least one example must be provided of Boswell's non-Johnsonian reporting. The interviews with Rousseau seem to me the finest single example of it—seem to me, indeed, outranked by very little in the *Life.* Here is proof, if proof is demanded, that Boswell was not, Antaeus-like, strong only when in contact with Johnson. And beyond the great vividness of the interviews, they reveal, more than anything in the *Life* does, Boswell's ability to portray himself in the frankest and most foolish light.

The interviews with Rousseau (here very slightly condensed) are taken from the eighteen volumes of Boswell's Private Papers. That these Papers existed was not known until a generation ago; and for a time their owner, Lord Talbot de Malahide (Boswell's great-great-grandson) refused to release them. But in 1927 he sold the entire collection, amounting to more than a million words, to Lt. Col. Ralph H. Isham. Colonel Isham turned them over to the late Geoffrey Scott, and subsequently to Professor Frederick Pottle of Yale, to be edited for private publication. The task involved a great amount of deciphering, annotating and fitting together; and the eighteen volumes were published, in a limited edition, over a period of years.　　　　L. K.

Monday 3 December. One great Object which I have ever had in view since I left Britain, has been to obtain the Acquaintance, and if possible the regard, of Rousseau. I was informed that he lived in a wild Valley, five leagues from Neufchâtel. I set out early this morning, mounted on a little horse with a *Reysesac,* which held some shirts. I was joined by Abraham François, a merchant here. My horse was lazy; he lent me a spur and a whip, and on we jogged very cordially. He taught me a french Song, *"Sous le nom de l'Amitié, Phillis Je vous adore"* to a Minuet tune. I amused myself with him; and this amusement formed an excellent Contrast to the great object which occupied my mind. We had a fine, hard road amidst Mountains covered with snow. We stopped at Bro, the halfway Inn. M. Sando, the Landlord, had a handsom daughter, very lively and very talkative, or rather chatty, to give the Young Lady a lighter word. She told us, *"Monsieur Rousseau vient souvent passer quelques jours ici avec sa Gouvernante, Mademoiselle Vasseur. C'est l'homme le plus aimable. Il a une belle Physionomie. Mais il n'aime pas qu'on vienne le regarder comme un Homme à deux têtes. Mon Dieu! la curiosité des Gens est bien grande. Il y a tant tant du monde qui vient pour le voire; et souvent il ne veut pas le recevoir. Il est malade, et il ne veut pas être incommodé. Voilà un Clus où Je suis allé avec lui et Mademoiselle Vasseur. Nous y avons diné. Il se promène dans ces lieux sauvages toute une journée. Des Messieurs qui sont venus ici m'ont demandé mille questions, 'Et sa Gouvernante, est elle jeune? est elle jolie?'"* All this chat of Mademoiselle helped to frighten me. There was here a Stone-cutter who had wrought for Voltaire. The most stupid of human Beings will remember some Anecdote or other of a Great man whom he has had occasion to see. This Stone cutter told me, "*Monsieur, il y avoit un Cheval à tirer un Char à Fernier, et M. Voltaire disoit toujours, 'Pauvre Cheval! vous êtes maigre, vous êtes comme moi.'*" Any trifle of such a Genius has a value. Abraham François and I drank a glass of good wine, and pursued our journey. We passed one Place exactly like Gillikranky and another where a groupe of broken rocks seemed every moment ready to tumble down upon us. It will most certainly tumble e'er long. M. Rousseau lives in the Village of Môtiers. . . . I advanced with a kind of pleasing trepidation. I wished that I might not see Rousseau till the moment that I had permission to wait upon him. I perceived a white house with green window-boards. He mentions such a one in *Emile.* I imagined it might perhaps be his, and turned away my eyes from it. I rode calmly down the street, and put up at the *Maison de Village.* . . . My Lord Marischal had given me a card with compliments to him, which I was sure would procure me admission. Colonel Chaillet had given me a letter to the *Châtelin,* M. Martinet, the principal Justice of the Place, who could introduce me without difficulty. But my romantic Genius, which will never be extinguished, made me eager to put my own merit to the severest tryal. I had therefore prepared a letter to M. Rousseau, in which I informed him that an ancient Scots Gentleman of twenty four, was come hither with the hopes of seeing him. I assured him that I deserved his regard, that I was ready to stand the test of his penetration. Towards the end of my letter I shewed him that I had a heart and a soul. I have here given no idea of my letter; It can neither be abridged nor transposed, for it is realy a Master-Piece. I shall ever preserve it as a Proof that my Soul can be sublime. I drest and dined and sent my letter *chez* M. Rousseau, ordering the Maid to leave it, and say she'd return for the Answer; so that I might give him time to consider a little, lest perhaps he might be ill and suddenly refuse to see me. I was filled with anxiety. Is not this romantic madness? Was I not sure of admittance by my Reccommendations? Could I not see him as any other Gentleman would do? No: I am above the Vulgar crowd. I would have my merit fairly tried by this Great Judge of human Nature. I must have things in my own way. If my bold attempt succeeds, the recollection of it will be grand as long as I live. But, perhaps, I may appear to him so vain, or so extraordinary, that he may be shocked by such a character and may not admit me. I shall then be in a pretty situation; for I shall be ashamed to present my recommendations. But why all this doubt and uneasiness? It is the effect of my melancholy timidity. What! can the Authour of *Eloïsa* be offended at the enthusiasm of an ingenuous mind? But if he does admit me, I shall have a very difficult character to support; for I have written to him with unusual elevation, and given him an idea of me which I shall hardly come up to.

To prepare myself for the great Interview, I walked out alone. I stroled pensive by the side of the River Ruse in a beautifull Wild Valley surrounded by immense Mountains, some covered with frowning rocks, others with clustering Pines, and others with glittering Snow. The fresh, healthfull air and the romantic Prospect arround me gave me a vigourous and solemn tone. I recalled all my former ideas of J. J. Rousseau, the admiration with which he is regarded over all Europe, his *Héloïse,* his *Emile,* in short, a crowd of great thoughts. This half hour was one of the most remarkable that I ever past.

I returned to my Inn, and the Maid delivered to me

a card with the following Answer from M. Rousseau. *"Je suis malade, souffrant, hors d'état de recevoir des visites. Cependant, Je ne puis me refuser à celle de Monsieur Boswell, pourvu que par égard pour mon état, il veuille bien la faire courte."*

My sensibility dreaded the word *courte*. But I took courage, and went immediatly. I found at the street door Mademoiselle Vasseur waiting for me. She was a little, lively, neat french Girl and did not increase my fear. She conducted me up a darkish stair, then opened a door. I expected, "Now I shall see him"—But it was not so. I entered a room which serves for Vestibule and for Kitchen. My fancy formed many, many a Portrait of the wild Philosopher. At length his door opened and I beheld him, a genteel, black man in the dress of an Armenian. I entered saying, "Many, Many thanks." After the first looks and bows were over, He said, "Will you be seated? Or would you rather take a turn with me in the room?" I chose the last, and happy I was to escape being formally placed upon a chair. I asked him how he was. "Very ill. But I have given up Doctors." "Yes, yes; you have no love for them." As it is impossible for me to relate exactly our conversation, I shall not endeavour at order, but give sentences as I recollect them.

BOSWELL. "The thought of your books, Sir, is a great source of pleasure to you?" ROUSSEAU. "I am fond of them; but when I think of my books so many misfortunes which they have brought upon me are revived in my memory, that really I cannot answer you. My books have saved my life." He spoke of the Parliament of Paris: "If any Society could be covered with disgrace, that would be. I could bring them much into disgrace simply by printing their edict against me on one side, and the Law of Nations and Equity on the side oppo-

site. But I have reasons against doing so at present."
BOSWELL. "We shall have it one day, perhaps?" ROUS-
SEAU. "Perhaps." I was drest in a coat and Waistcoat,
scarlet with Gold lace, Buckskin Breeches, and Boots.
Above all I wore a Great coat of Green Camlet lined
with Fox-skin fur, with the collar and Cuffs of the same
fur. I held under my arm a hat with a sollid gold lace,
at least with the air of being sollid. I had it last winter
at the Hague. I had a free air and spoke well, and when
M. Rousseau said what touched me more than ordinary,
I seised his hand, I thumped him on the shoulder. I was
without restraint. When I found that I realy pleased
him, I said, "Are you aware, Sir, that I am recommended
to you by a man you hold in high regard?" ROUSSEAU.
"Ah! My Lord Marischal?" BOSWELL. "Yes, Sir; My
Lord has furnished me with a Note of introduction to
you." ROUSSEAU. "And you were unwilling to take advantage of it?" BOSWELL. "Nay, Sir; I wished to have a
proof of my merits." ROUSSEAU. "Sir, there would have
been no kind of merit in gaining access to me by a Note
of Lord Marischal's. Whatever he sends will always find
a welcome from me. He is my Protector, my Father; I
would venture to say, my friend." One circumstance
embarrassed me a little: I had forgotten to bring with
me from Neufchâtel My Lord's Billet. But a generous
consciousness of Innocence and honesty gives a freedom
which cannot be counterfeited. I told M. Rousseau, "To
speak truly, I have forgotten to bring his letter with me;
but you accept my word for it?" ROUSSEAU. "Why, certainly. Numbers of people have shown themselves ready
to serve me in their own fashion; My Lord Marischal has
served me in mine. He is the only man on earth to whom
I owe an obligation." *Continuing*, "When I speak of
Kings, I do not include the King of Prussia. He is a King
quite alone and apart. That force of his! Sir, There's the

great matter, to have force—Revenge, even;—You can always find stuff to make something out of. But when force is lacking, when everything is small and split up, there's no hope. The French, for example, are a contemptible nation." BOSWELL. "But the Spaniards, Sir?" ROUSSEAU. "Yes, you will find great souls in Spain." BOSWELL. "And in the Mountains of Scotland. But since our cursed union, Ah . . ." ROUSSEAU. "You undid yourselves." BOSWELL. "Truly, yes. But I must tell you a great satisfaction given me by My Lord. He calls you Jean Jacques out of affection. One day he said to me, 'Jean Jacques is the most grateful man in the world. He wanted to write my brother's life; but I begged him rather to write the Life of Mr. Fletcher of Saultoun, and he promised me he would do so.'" ROUSSEAU. "Yes, Sir; I will write it with the greatest care and pleasure. I shall offend the English, I know. But that is no matter. Will you furnish me with some Anecdotes on the Characters of those who made your Treaty of Union, and details that cannot be found in the Historians?" BOSWELL. "Yes, Sir; but with the warmth of an ancient Scot." ROUSSEAU. "By all means."

He spoke of ecclesiastics; "When one of these Gentlemen provides a new explanation of something incomprehensible, leaving it as incomprehensible as before, everyone cries, 'Here's a great Man.' But, Sir, they will tell you that no single point of Theology may be neglected, that every stone in God's Building, the mystic Jerusalem, must be considered as sacred. But they have added stones to it.—'Here, take off this; take off that! Now you see, the Building is admirably complete, and you have no need to stand there to hold it up.' 'But *we* want to be necessary!' 'Ah! . . .'"

"Sir, you don't see before you the Bear you have

heard tell of. Sir, I have no liking for the world. I live here in a world of fantasies, and I cannot tolerate the world as it is." BOSWELL. "But when you come across fantastical men, are they not to your liking?" ROUSSEAU. "Why, Sir, they have not the same fantasies as myself. Sir, your Country is formed for liberty. I like your habits. You and I feel at liberty to stroll here together without talking. That is more than two Frenchmen can do. Mankind disgusts me. And my Housekeeper tells me that I am in far better humour on the days when I have been alone than on those when I have been in company." BOSWELL. "There has been a great deal written against you, Sir." ROUSSEAU. "They have not understood me. As for Monsieur Vernet at Geneva, he is an Arch-Jesuit, that is all I can say of him."

BOSWELL. "Tell me, Sir, do you not find that I answer to the description I gave you of myself?" ROUSSEAU. "Sir, it is too early for me to judge. But all Appearances are in your favour." BOSWELL. "I fear I have stayed too long. I shall take the honour of returning tomorrow." ROUSSEAU. "O, as to that, I can't tell." BOSWELL. "Sir, I shall stay quietly here in the Village. If you are able to see me, I shall be enchanted; if not, I shall make no complaint." ROUSSEAU. "My Lord Marischal has a perfect understanding of man's feelings, in Solitude no less than in Society. I am overwhelmed with visits from idle people." BOSWELL. "And how do they spend their time?" ROUSSEAU. "In paying Compliments. Also I get a prodigious quantity of letters. And the writer of each of them believes himself the only One." BOSWELL. "You must be greatly surprised, Sir, that a man who has not the honour of your acquaintance, should take the liberty of writing to you?" ROUSSEAU. "No. It gives me no surprise. For I had a similar letter yesterday, the day before yes-

terday and ever so often." BOSWELL. "Sir, Your very
humble Servant— What, you are coming further?"
ROUSSEAU. "I am not coming with you. I am going for
a walk in the passage. Goodbye." . . .

At five I went to M. Rousseau, whom I found more
gay than he had been yesterday. We joked on Mademoiselle Vasseur for keeping him under lock and key.
She, to defend herself, said he had another door to get
out at. Said he, "*Ah Mademoiselle vous dites tout.*" . . .

He gave me the character of the Abbé de St. Pierre,
"a man who did good, simply because he chose to do
good: a man without enthusiasm. One might say that he
was passionately reasonable. He was seen writing his
memoirs, and he used to say, 'I shall be sneered at for
this,' 'I shall get a hissing for that.' It was all one to him.
He carried his principles into the merest trifles. For example, he used to wear his watch suspended from a
button on his coat, because that was more convenient.
As he was precluded from marriage, he kept Mistresses,
and made no secret of it. He had a number of sons. He
would allow them to adopt none but the most strictly
useful professions; for example, he would not allow any
son of his to be a Wig-maker. 'For,' said he, 'so long as
Nature continues to supply us with hair, the profession
of Wig-making must always be full of uncertainty.' He
was completely indifferent to the opinion of men, saying
that they were merely over-grown children. After paying a long visit to a certain Lady, he said to her, 'Madam,
I perceive I am wearisome to you; but that is a matter
of no moment to me. You amuse me.' One of Louis the
XIV's creatures had him turned out of the Academy for
a speech he had made there. Yet he perpetually visited
this man. 'For,' said he, 'he acted in his own interests;

and I bear him no grudge for that. He amuses me. He has no grounds for being offended with me. I have grounds for offence against him; but I am not offended.' In short, he continued to call on this Academician, until the latter put a stop to it because he found it disagreeable to see a man whom he had injured. He had plenty of good sense, but a faulty style: long-winded and diffuse, yet always proving his point. He was a favourite with women; he would go his own way independently, and he won respect. If you become a Member of Parliament, you must resemble the Abbé de St. Pierre. You must stick to your principles." BOSWELL. "But, then, one must be very well instructed." ROUSSEAU. "Ah, sure enough. You must have a well furnished head." BOSWELL. "But, Sir, a Member of Parliament who behaves as a strictly honest man is regarded as a crazy fool." ROUSSEAU. "Well then, you must be a crazy fool of a Member; and believe me, such a man will be respected; —that is, if he holds consistently by his principles. A man who changes round on every occasion, is another affair."

He talked of his *Plan for perpetual Peace, taken from the Abbé de St. Pierre.* I frankly owned that I had not read it. "No?" said he—then took one down from his Book-case and gave it me. I asked him smilingly if he would not put his name upon it. He laughed heartily at me. I talked to him of the German *Album* and how I had been forced to take one; but that except what was written by the Person who gave it me, there was nothing in it. Said he "Then your *Album* is *Album.*" There was a Sally for you. A Precious Pearl; a Pun made by Rousseau. He said, "I have seen the Scottish Highlanders in France. I love the Scots; not because My Lord Marischal is one of them but because he praises them. *You* are

irksome to me. It's my nature. I cannot help it." Bos-
WELL. "Do not stand on ceremony with me." ROUSSEAU.
"Go away."

Wednesday 5 December. When I waited upon Monsieur Rousseau this morning, he said, "My dear Sir, I am
sorry not to be able to talk with you as I would wish."
I took care to wave such excuses, and immediately set
conversation agoing. I told him how I had turned Roman Catholic and had intended to hide myself in a Convent in France. He said, "What madness! I too was
Catholic in my youth. I changed, and then changed
back again. I returned to Geneva and was received as
a Protestant. I went off to the Catholics, and would say
to them, 'I am no longer one of you'; and I got on with
them excellently." I stopped him in the middle of the
room and I said to him, "But tell me, sincerely, are you
a Christian?" I looked at him with a searching eye. His
countenance was no less animated. Each stood steady
and watched the other's looks. He struck his breast, and
replied, "Yes. I pique myself upon being one." BOSWELL.
"Sir, the soul can be sustained by nothing save the Gospel." ROUSSEAU. "I feel that. I am unaffected by all the
objections. I am weak; there may be things beyond my
reach; or perhaps He who made them made a mistake.
I say, God the Father, God the Son and God the Holy
Ghost." BOSWELL. "But tell me, do you suffer from melancholy?" ROUSSEAU. "I was born placid. I have no natural disposition to melancholy. My misfortunes have infected me with it." BOSWELL. "I, for my part, suffer from
it severely. And how can I be happy, I, who have done
so much harm?" ROUSSEAU. "Begin your life anew. God
is good, for He is just. Do good. You will pay off all the
harm you have done. Say to yourself in the morning,
'Come now, I am going to *pay off* so much harm.' Six

well spent years will pay off all the harm you have done." BOSWELL. "What is your view of Cloisters, Penances, and remedies of that sort?" ROUSSEAU. "Mummeries, all of them; invented by men. Do not be guided by men's judgments, or you will find yourself tossed to and fro perpetually. Do not base your life on the judgments of others, first because they are as likely to be mistaken as yourself, and further because you cannot know that they are telling you their true feelings; they may be impelled by motives of interest or convention to talk to you in a way not corresponding to their thoughts." BOSWELL. "Will you, Sir, look after me?" ROUSSEAU. "I cannot. I can be responsible only for myself." BOSWELL. "But I shall come back to you." ROUSSEAU. "I don't promise to see you. I am ill. I need a chamber-pot every minute." BOSWELL. "Yes you will see me." ROUSSEAU. "Be off; and a good journey to you."

Friday 14 December. At eight I got on Horseback and had for my Guide a Smith called Dupuis. I said, "Since when (*depuis quand*) have you had that name?" I past the Mountain Lapidosa which is monstrously steep and in a great measure covered with snow. I was going to Rousseau which consideration levelled the roughest mountains. I arrived at Môtiers before noon. I alighted at Rousseau's door. Up and I went and found Mademoiselle Vasseur who told me, "He is very ill." "But can I see him for a moment?" "I will find out. Step in, Sir." I found him sitting in great pain. ROUSSEAU. "I am overcome with ailments, disappointments, and sorrow. I have my bellyful; everyone thinks it my duty to attend to him." BOSWELL. "That is most natural; and is it not a source of satisfaction to you to find you can be of so much help to others?" He gave a deprecatory shrug. I had left with him when I was last here what I called a *Sketch of my Life,* in which I gave him the important incidents of my History and my melancholy apprehensions, and begged his advice and friendship. It was an interesting Piece. He said, "I have read your Memoir. You have been gulled. You ought never to see a Priest." Boswell. "But can I yet hope to make something of myself?" Rousseau. "Why, yes. Your great difficulty is that you think it so difficult a matter. Come back in the afternoon. But put your watch on the table." Boswell. "For how long?" Rousseau. "A quarter of an hour, and no longer." Boswell. "Twenty minutes." Rousseau. "Be off with you!—Ha! Ha!" Notwithstanding the pain he was in, he was touched with my singular sally, and laughed most realy. He had a gay look immediately. I dined in my old Room with the two Boarders. After dinner I walked out. There had fallen much rain, and the Vallon was all overflowed. Nature looked somewhat different from the time that I was first here. I was sorry that such a scene was subject to any change. At four I went to Monsieur Rousseau. "I have but a moment allowed me; I must use it well. Is it possible to live amongst other men, and to retain singularity?" Rousseau. "Yes, I have done it." Boswell. "But to remain on good terms with them?" Rousseau. "Oh, if you want to be a Wolf, you must howl. I attach very little importance to books." Boswell. "Even to your own Books?" Rousseau. "Oh, they are just Rigmarole." Boswell. "Now you are howling." Rousseau. "When I put my trust in books I was tossed about, as you are (though it is rather by talking that you have been tossed). I had nothing stable here (striking his head) before I began to meditate." Boswell. "But you would not have meditated to such good purpose, if you had not read." Rousseau. "No. I should have meditated to better purpose if I had begun sooner." Boswell. "But I, for example, would never have had the agreeable ideas I possess of the Christian religion, had I not read the *Savoyard's Creed*. To tell the truth, I can find no certain System. Morality appears to me an uncertain thing. For instance, I would like to have thirty women. Could I not satisfy that desire?" ROUSSEAU. "No!" BOSWELL. "Why?" ROUSSEAU. "Ha! Ha! If Mademoiselle were not here, I would give you a most ample reason why." BOSWELL. "But consider, if I am rich, I can take a number of girls; I get them with child; Propagation is thus increased. I give them doweries, and I marry them off to good Peasants who are very happy to have them. Thus they become wives at the same age as would have been the case if they had remained virgins, and I, on my side, have had the benefit of enjoying a great variety of women." ROUSSEAU. "Ah! You will be landed in jealousies, betrayals, and treachery." BOSWELL. "But cannot I follow the oriental usage?" ROUSSEAU. "In the Orient, the women are kept shut up; it means keeping slaves; and, mark you, their women do nothing but harm, whereas ours do much good since they do a great deal of work." BOSWELL. "I should like to follow the example of the old Patriarchs, worthy men whose memory I hold in respect." ROUSSEAU. "But are you not a Citizen? You must not pick and choose one law here and another law there; you must take the laws of your own Society. Fulfill your duties as a Citizen, and if you hold fast, you will win respect." BOSWELL. "I should not tell what I was doing; but I'd do it." . . .

I asked him, "When I get to France and Italy, may I not indulge in the gallantries, usual to those countries, where the husbands do not resent your making love to their wives? Nay, should I not be happier as the citizen of such a nation?" ROUSSEAU. "They are corpses. Do you want to be a Corpse?" He was right. BOSWELL. "But pray tell me, has a virtuous man any true advantages, is he really better off than a man given up to sensuality?" ROUSSEAU. "We cannot doubt that we are spiritual beings; and when the soul escapes from this prison, from this flesh, the virtuous man will find things to his liking. He will enjoy the contemplation of happy souls. nobly employed. He will say, 'I have already lived a life like that.' Whereas those who experience nothing but the vile Passions which have their origin in the body, will be dissatisfied by the spectacle of pleasures which they have no means of enjoying." BOSWELL. "Upon my word, I am at a loss how to act in this world; I cannot determine whether or not I should adopt some profession." ROUSSEAU. "One must have a great Plan." BOSWELL. "What about those Studies, on which so much stress is laid? Such as History, for instance?" ROUSSEAU. "They are just Amusements." BOSWELL. "My Father desires me to be called to the Scottish Bar; I am certainly doing right in satisfying my Father; I have no such certainty if I follow my light inclinations. It follows that I must give my mind to the study of the laws of Scotland." ROUSSEAU. "To be sure; they are your tools. If you mean to be a Carpenter, you must have a plane." BOSWELL. "I do not get on well with my Father. I am not at my ease with him." ROUSSEAU. "To be at ease you need to share some amusement." BOSWELL. "We look after the planting together." ROUSSEAU. "That's too serious a business. You should have some amusement that puts you on an equal footing: shooting, for example. A shot is missed and a joke is made of it, without any infringement of respect; you enjoy a freedom which you take for granted. Once you are involved in a Profession, you must keep on with it even though another, and apparently better, should present itself. If you keep changing, you can achieve nothing." (I should have observed that when I pushed the conversation on women, Mademoiselle went out, and M. Rousseau said, "See now, you are driving Mademoiselle out of the room." She was now returned.) He stopped, and looked at me in a singular manner, "Are you greedy?" BOSWELL. "Yes." ROUSSEAU. "I am sorry to hear it." BOSWELL. "Ha! Ha! I was joking; for in your books, you write in favour of greed. I know what you are about to say, and it is just what I was hoping to hear. I wanted to solicit your soup. I had a great desire to share a meal with you." ROUSSEAU. "Well, if you are not greedy, will you dine here tomorrow? But I give you fair warning, you will find yourself badly off." BOSWELL. "No, I shall not be badly off; I am above all such considerations." ROUSSEAU. "Come then at noon; it will give us time to talk." BOSWELL. "All my thanks." ROUSSEAU. "Good evening." Mademoiselle carried me to the house of a poor woman with a great many children whom M. Rousseau aids with his charity. I contributed my part. I was not pleased to hear Mademoiselle repeat to the Poor Woman just the common consolatory sayings. She should have said something singular.

Saturday 15 December. . . . Gods! Am I now then realy the friend of Rousseau? What a rich assemblage of ideas! I relish my felicity truly in such a scene as this. Shall I not truly relish it at Auchinleck? I was quite gay, my fancy was youthful, and vented its gladness in sportive sallies. I supposed myself in the rude world. I supposed a parcel of young fellows saying, "Come, Boswell, you'll dine with us today?" "No, Gentlemen, excuse me; I'm engaged. I dine today with Rousseau." My tone, my air, my native Pride when I pronounced this! Temple! You would have given half a guinea to see me at that moment. I returned to my Inn where I found the Court of Justice of the Vallon assembled. I entered and was amused to hear a Justice of Peace and honest Farmers and a Country Minister all talking french.

I then went to M. Rousseau. "I hope your health is better today." ROUSSEAU. "Oh don't speak of it." He seemed unusually gay. Before dinner we are all so, if not made to wait too long. A keen appetite gives a vivacity to the whole frame. I said, "You say nothing in regard to a child's duties towards his Parents. You tell us nothing of your Emile's Father." ROUSSEAU. "Oh he hadn't got one. He didn't exist." It is, however, a real pity that M. Rousseau has not treated of the duties between Parents and Children. It is an important and a delicate subject and deserves to be illustrated by a Sage of so clear a Judgment and so elegant a Soul. He praised *the Spectator*. He said, "One comes across Allegories in it. I have no taste for Allegories; though your nation shows a great liking for them." I gave him very fully the character of Mr. Johnson. He said with force, "I would like that man. I would respect him. I would refrain from shattering his principles, were I to find I could do so. I should like to see him; but from far off for fear he might deal me a blow." I told him how averse Mr. Johnson was to write, and how he had his levee. "Ah, (said he,) I understand. He is a man who enjoys holding forth." I told him Mr. Johnson's *Bon Mot* upon the Innovators: That Truth is a Cow which will yield them no more milk, and so they are gone to milk the Bull. He said, "He would detest me. He would say, 'Here is a Corrupter: a Man who comes here to milk the Bull.'" I had diverted myself by pretending to help Mademoiselle Vasseur to make the Soup. We din'd in the Kitchen which was neat and chearfull. There was something singularly agreable in this scene. Here was Rousseau in all his Simplicity, with his Armenian dress which

I have surely mentioned before now. His long coat and
Nightcap made him look easy and well. Our dinner was
as follows: 1 A dish of excellent Soup. 2 A Bouilli of Beef
and Veal. 3 Cabbage, Turnip and Carrot. 4 Cold Pork.
5 Pickled Trout which he jestingly called *Tongue.* 6
Some little dish which I forget. The Dessert consisted of
stoned Pears and of Chestnuts. We had red and white
wines. It was a simple good Repast. We were quite at
our ease. I sometimes forgot myself and became ceremonious. "May I help you to some of this dish?" Rous-
SEAU. "No, Sir. I can help myself to it." Or, "Might I
help myself to some more of that?" ROUSSEAU. "Is your
arm long enough? A man does the honours of his house
from a motive of vanity. He does not want it forgotten
who is the Master. I would like everyone to be his own
Master, and that no one should play the part of Host.
Let each one ask for what he wants; if it is there to give,
let him be given it; otherwise, he must be satisfied without. Here you see true hospitality." BOSWELL. "In England, it is quite another matter. They do not want to be
at ease; they are stiff and silent, in order to win respect."
ROUSSEAU. "In France, you find no such gloom among
folk of distinction. There is even an affectation of the
utmost liberty, as though they would have you understand, 'We stand in no fear of losing our dignity.' That is
a more refined form of self esteem." BOSWELL. "Well,
and do you not share that yourself?" ROUSSEAU. "Yes, 1
allow that I like to be respected; but only in matters of
importance." BOSWELL. "You are so simple. I expected
to find you quite different to this: the great Rousseau.
But you do not see yourself in the same light as others
see you. I counted on finding you enthroned and talking
with a grave authority." ROUSSEAU. "I? Uttering Oracles?
Ha! Ha! Ha!" BOSWELL. "Yes, and I should be much in
awe of you. And, in truth, your simplicity might be open

to criticism; it might be said, 'M. Rousseau does not make himself sufficiently respected.' In Scotland, I can assure you, a very different tone must be taken to escape from the shocking familiarity which is prevalent in that country. Upon my word, I would not put up with it. Should I not be justified in forestalling it by fighting a duel with the first man who should treat me that way, and thus live at peace for the rest of my life?" ROUSSEAU. "No. That is not allowable. It is not right to stake one's life on such follies. Life is given us for objects of importance. Pay no heed to what such men say. They will get tired of talking to a man who does not answer them." BOSWELL. "If you were in Scotland, they would start off by calling you 'Rousseau, Jean Jacques, how goes it?' with the utmost familiarity." ROUSSEAU. "That is perhaps a good thing." BOSWELL. "But they would say, 'Poh! Jean Jacques, why do you allow yourself all these fantasies? You're a pretty man to put forward such claims. Come, Come, settle down in society like other people'; and this they will say to you with a sourness which, for my part, I am quite unable to imitate for you." ROUSSEAU. "Ah, that's bad." There he felt the thistle, when it was applied to himself on the tender part. It was just as if I had said, "Howt Johnie Rousseau man, what for hae ye sae mony figmagairies? Ye're a bony Man indeed to mauk sicana wark; set ye up. Canna ye just live like ither fowk?" It was the best idea could be given in the polite french language of the rude Scots sarcastical vivacity. BOSWELL. "I have leanings towards despotism, let me tell you. On our estates, I am like an ancient Lord, and I insist on respect from the tenants." ROUSSEAU. "But when you see an Old Man with white hair do you, as a young man, have no feelings at all? Have you no respect for age?" BOSWELL. "Yes. I have even, on many occasions, been very affable. I have talked quite freely with the tenants." ROUSSEAU. "Yes, you forgot yourself, and became a man." BOSWELL. "But I was sorry for it afterwards. I used to think, 'I have lowered myself.'" ROUSSEAU. "Ha! Ha! Ha!" BOSWELL. "Yesterday I had in mind to ask a favour of you, to give me credentials as your ambassador to the Corsicans. Will you make me His Excellency? Are you in need of an Ambassador? I offer you my services: Mr. Boswell, Ambassador Extraordinary of M. Rousseau to the Isle of Corsica." ROUSSEAU. "Would you care to be King of Corsica?" BOSWELL. "By my word! Ha! Ha! Not I. It is beyond my powers (with a low bow); all the same, I can say, 'I have refused to be a King.'" ROUSSEAU. "Do you like Cats?" BOSWELL. "No." ROUSSEAU. "I was sure of that. It is my test of character. There you have the despotic instinct of men. They do not like cats because the cat is free, and will never consent to become a slave. He will do nothing to your order, as the other animals do." BOSWELL. "Nor a Chicken, either." ROUSSEAU. "A Chicken would obey your orders if you could make them intelligible to it. But a cat will understand you perfectly, and not obey them." BOSWELL. "But a Cat is ungrateful and treacherous." ROUSSEAU. "No. That's all untrue. A Cat is an animal that can be very attached to you; he will do anything you please out of friendship. I have a Cat here. He has been brought up with my Dog; they play together. The Cat will give the Dog a blow with his tail, and the Dog will offer him his paw." (He described the playing of his dog and cat with exquisite eloquence, as a fine Painter draws a small Piece.) He put some victuals on a trencher, and made his dog dance round it. He sung to him a lively air with a sweet voice and great taste. "You see the Ballet. It is not a gala performance, but a pretty one all the same." I think the Dog's name was Sultan. He stroked him and fed him, and with an arch air said, "He is not much *respected,* but he gets well looked after."

BOSWELL. "Suppose you were to walk in upon a drinking party of young folk, who should treat you with ridicule, would you be above minding it?" ROUSSEAU. "It would put me out of countenance. I am shy by nature. I have often, for example, been overcome by raillery of women. A party such as you describe would be disagreeable to me. I would leave it." I was comforted to find that my sensibility is not despicable weakness.

BOSWELL. "The Anglican Church is the one for me." ROUSSEAU. "Yes. It is no doubt an excellent Religion; but it is not the Gospel, which is all simplicity. It is another kind of religion." BOSWELL. "The Gospel, at the outset, was simple and rigid equally; as when Paul says it is better not to marry, than to marry." ROUSSEAU. "Paul? But that is not the Gospel." BOSWELL. "Then you have no liking for Paul?" ROUSSEAU. "I respect him, but I think he is partly responsible for muddling your head. He would have been an Anglican Clergyman." BOSWELL. "Mr. Johnson is a Jacobite, but he has a Pension of £300 sterling from the King." ROUSSEAU. "He ought not to have accepted a Pension." BOSWELL. "He says that he does not drink the health of King James with the wine given him by King George." ROUSSEAU. "But you should not employ the substance given you by this wine in attacking King George." MLLE. LEVASSEUR. "Shall you, Sir, see M. de Voltaire?" BOSWELL. "Most certainly. *(To Rousseau)* M. de Voltaire has no liking for you. That is natural enough." ROUSSEAU. "Yes. One does not like those whom one has greatly injured. His talk is most enjoyable; it is even better than his books." BOSWELL. "Have you looked at the *Philosophical Dictionary?*" ROUSSEAU. "Yes." BOSWELL. "And what of it?" ROUSSEAU. "I don't like it. I am not intolerant, but he deserves

. . . (I forget his expression here). It is very well to argue against men's opinion; but to show contempt, and to say, 'You are idiots to believe this,' is to be personally offensive. Now go away." BOSWELL. "Not yet. I will leave at three o'clock. I have still five and twenty minutes." ROUSSEAU. "But I can't give you five and twenty minutes." BOSWELL. "I will give you even more than that." ROUSSEAU. "What! Of my own time? All the Kings on earth cannot give me my own time." BOSWELL. "But if I had stayed till tomorrow I should have had five and twenty minutes, and next day another twenty-five. I am not taking these minutes. I am making you a present of them." ROUSSEAU. "Ah! Since you don't steal my money, you are giving it to me." He then repeated part of a french satire ending with, *and whatever they leave you, they count as a gift.* BOSWELL. "Pray speak for me, Mademoiselle. (*To Rousseau*) I have an excellent friend here." ROUSSEAU. "Nay, but this is a league." BOSWELL. "No league at all." MLLE. LEVASSEUR. "Gentlemen, I will tell you the moment the clock strikes." ROUSSEAU. "Come; I need to take the air after eating." We walked out to a gallery pendent upon his wall. BOSWELL. "In old days I was a great mimic. I could imitate everyone I saw. But I do it no longer." ROUSSEAU. "It is a bad quality; for it compels one to seize upon all that is small in a character." BOSWELL. "True; but I assure you there was a nobleness about my art; I carried mimicry to such a point of perfection. I was a kind of Virtuoso. When I espied any singular character I would say, 'It must be added to my collection.'" He laughed with all his nerves: "You are an oddity." BOSWELL. "I am a Physiognomist, believe me. I have studied that art very attentively, I assure you, and I can rely on my conclusions." He seemed to agree to this. ROUSSEAU. "Yet I think the features of the Face vary between one nation and another, as do accent and tone of voice; and these signify different feelings among different peoples." This Observation struck me as new and most ingenious. Bos-WELL. "But, in time, one learns to understand them." ROUSSEAU. "The Roads are bad. You will be late." Bos-WELL. "I take the bad parts on foot; the last league of the way is good. Do you realize that I shall make a good Barrister before a Court of Justice?" ROUSSEAU. "Yes. But I regret you have the talents necessary for defending a bad case." BOSWELL. "Have you any commands for Italy?" ROUSSEAU. "I will send a letter to Geneva for you to carry to Parma." BOSWELL. "Can I send you anything back?" ROUSSEAU. "A few pretty tunes from the Opera." BOSWELL. "By all means. Oh, I have had so much to say, that I have neglected to beg you to play me a tune." ROUSSEAU. "It's too late." MLLE. LEVASSEUR. "Sir, your man is calling for you to start." M. Rousseau embraced me. He was quite the tender St. Preux. He kist me several times, and held me in his arms with elegant cordiality. O! I shall never forget that I have been thus. ROUSSEAU. "Good-bye. You are a fine fellow." BOSWELL. "You have shown me great goodness, but I deserved it." ROUSSEAU. "Yes. You are malicious; but 'tis a pleasant malice, a malice I don't dislike. Write and tell me how you are." BOSWELL. "And you will write to me?" ROUS-SEAU. "I know not how to reach you." BOSWELL. "Yes, you shall write to me in Scotland." ROUSSEAU. "Certainly; and even at Paris." BOSWELL. "Bravo! If I live twenty years, you will write to me for twenty years?" ROUSSEAU. "Yes." BOSWELL. "Good-bye. If you live for seven years, I shall return to Switzerland from Scotland to see you." ROUSSEAU. "Do so. We shall be old acquaintances." BOSWELL. "One word more. Can I feel sure that I am held to you by the slenderest thread? By a hair?" (Seising a hair of my head). ROUSSEAU. "Yes.

Remember always that there are points where our souls are linked." BOSWELL. "It is enough. I, with my melancholy, I, who often look on myself as a despicable being, as a good for nothing creature who should make his escape from life,—I shall be upheld forever by the thought that I am linked to M. Rousseau. Good-bye. Bravo! I will live to the end of my days." ROUSSEAU. "That is undoubtedly a thing one must do. Good-bye."

SAMUEL JOHNSON

RICHARD SAVAGE

IT HAS been observed in all ages that the advantages of nature or of fortune have contributed very little to the promotion of happiness; and that those whom the splendour of their rank, or the extent of their capacity, have placed upon the summit of human life have not often given any just occasion to envy in those who look up to them from a lower station; whether it be that apparent superiority incites great designs, and great designs are naturally liable to fatal miscarriages; or that the general lot of mankind is misery, and the misfortunes of those whose eminence drew upon them an universal attention have been more carefully recorded because they were more generally observed, and have in reality been only more conspicuous than those of others, not more frequent, or more severe.

To these mournful narratives I am about to add the Life of Richard Savage, a man whose writings entitle him to an eminent rank in the classes of learning, and whose misfortunes claim a degree of compassion not always due to the unhappy, as they were often the consequences of the crimes of others rather than his own.

In the year 1697, Anne Countess of Macclesfield, having lived some time upon very uneasy terms with her husband, thought a public confession of adultery the most obvious and expeditious method of obtaining her liberty; and therefore declared that the child with which she was then great was begotten by the Earl Rivers.

This, as may be imagined, made her husband no less desirous of a separation than herself, and he prosecuted his design in the most effectual manner; for he applied not to the ecclesiastical courts for a divorce, but to the parliament for an act by which his marriage might be dissolved, the nuptial contract annulled, and the children of his wife illegitimated. This act, after the usual deliberation, he obtained, though without the approbation of some, who considered marriage as an affair only cognisable by ecclesiastical judges; and, on March 3rd, was separated from his wife, whose fortune, which was very great, was repaid her, and who having, as well as her husband, the liberty of making another choice, was in a short time married to Colonel Brett.

While the Earl of Macclesfield was prosecuting this affair, his wife was, on the 10th of January, 1697-8, delivered of a son; and the Earl Rivers, by appearing to consider him as his own, left none any reason to doubt of the sincerity of her declaration; for he was his godfather and gave him his own name, which was by his direction inserted in the register of St. Andrew's parish in Holborn; but, unfortunately, left him to the care of his mother, whom, as she was now set free from her husband, he probably imagined likely to treat with great tenderness the child that had contributed to so pleasing an event. It is not indeed easy to discover what motives could be found to overbalance that natural affection of a parent, or what interest could be promoted by neglect or cruelty. The dread of shame or of poverty, by which some wretches have been incited to abandon or to murder their children, cannot be supposed to have affected a woman who had proclaimed her crimes and solicited reproach, and on whom the clemency of the legislature had undeservedly bestowed a fortune, which would have been very little diminished by the expenses which the care of her child could have brought upon her. It was therefore not likely that she would be wicked without temptation; that she would look upon her son from his birth with a kind of resentment and abhorrence; and, instead of supporting, assisting, and defending him, delight to see him struggling with misery, or that she would take every opportunity of aggravating his misfortunes and obstructing his resources, and with an implacable and restless cruelty continue her persecution from the first hour of his life to the last.

But, whatever were her motives, no sooner was her son born than she discovered a resolution of disowning him; and in a very short time removed him from her sight by committing him to the care of a poor woman, whom she directed to educate him as her own, and enjoined never to inform him of his true parents.

Such was the beginning of the life of Richard Savage. Born with a legal claim to honour and to affluence, he was in two months illegitimated by the parliament, and disowned by his mother, doomed to poverty and obscurity, and launched upon the ocean of life only that he might be swallowed by its quicksands or dashed upon its rocks.

His mother could not indeed infect others with the same cruelty. As it was impossible to avoid the inquiries which the curiosity or tenderness of her relations made after her child, she was obliged to give some account of the measures she had taken; and her mother, the Lady Mason, whether in approbation of her design or to prevent more criminal contrivances, engaged to transact with the nurse, to pay her for her care, and to superintend the education of the child.

In this charitable office she was assisted by his godmother, Mrs. Lloyd, who while she lived always looked upon him with that tenderness which the barbarity of his mother made peculiarly necessary; but her death, which happened in his tenth year, was another of the misfortunes of his childhood; for though she kindly endeavoured to alleviate his loss by a legacy of 300*l.*, yet, as he had none to prosecute his claim, to shelter him from oppression, or call in law to the assistance of justice, her will was eluded by the executors, and no part of the money was ever paid.

He was, however, not yet wholly abandoned. The Lady Mason still continued her care and directed him to be placed at a small grammar-school near St. Alban's, where he was called by the name of his nurse, without the least intimation that he had a claim to any other.

Here he was initiated in literature, and passed through several of the classes, with what rapidity or with what applause cannot now be known. As he always spoke with respect of his master, it is probable that the mean rank in which he then appeared did not hinder his genius from being distinguished, or his industry from being rewarded; and if in so low a state he obtained distinction and rewards, it is not likely that they were gained but by genius and industry.

It is very reasonable to conjecture that his application was equal to his abilities, because his improvement was more than proportioned to the opportunities which he enjoyed; nor can it be doubted that, if his earliest productions had been preserved like those of happier students, we might in some have found vigorous sallies of that sprightly humour which distinguishes "The Author to be Let," and in others strong touches of that imagination which painted the solemn scenes of "The Wanderer."

While he was thus cultivating his genius, his father, the Earl Rivers, was seized with a distemper which in a short time put an end to his life. He had frequently inquired after his son, and had always been amused with fallacious and evasive answers; but, being now in his own opinion on his death-bed, he thought it his duty to provide for him among his other natural children, and therefore demanded a positive account of him, with an importunity not to be diverted or denied. His mother, who could no longer refuse an answer, determined at least to give such as should cut him off for ever from that happiness which competence affords, and therefore declared that he was dead; which is perhaps the first instance of a lie invented by a mother to deprive her son of a provision which was designed him by another, and which she could not expect herself though he should lose it.

This was therefore an act of wickedness which could not be defeated, because it could not be suspected; the Earl did not imagine there could exist in a human form a mother that would ruin her son without enriching herself, and therefore bestowed upon some other person 6000*l*. which he had in his will bequeathed to Savage.

The same cruelty which incited his mother to intercept this provision which had been intended him prompted her in a short time to another project, a project worthy of such a disposition. She endeavoured to rid herself from the danger of being at any time made known to him, by sending him secretly to the American Plantations.

By whose kindness this scheme was counteracted, or by whose interposition she was induced to lay aside her design, I know not: it is not improbable that the Lady Mason might persuade or compel her to desist; or perhaps she could not easily find accomplices wicked enough to concur in so cruel an action; for it may be conceived that those who had by a long gradation of guilt hardened their hearts against the sense of common wickedness would yet be shocked at the design of a mother to expose her son to slavery and want, to expose him without interest and without provocation; and Savage might on this occasion find protectors and advocates among those who had long traded in crimes, and whom compassion had never touched before.

Being hindered, by whatever means, from banishing him into another country, she formed soon after a scheme for burying him in poverty and obscurity in his own; and, that his station of life, if not the place of his residence, might keep him for ever at a distance from her, she ordered him to be placed with a shoemaker in Holborn, that, after the usual time of trial, he might become his apprentice.

It is generally reported that this project was for some time successful, and that Savage was employed at the awl longer than he was willing to confess; nor was it perhaps any great advantage to him that an unexpected discovery determined him to quit his occupation.

About this time his nurse, who had always treated him as her own son, died; and it was natural for him to take care of those effects which by her death were, as he imagined, become his own: he therefore went to her house, opened her boxes, and examined her papers, among which he found some letters written to her by the Lady Mason, which informed him of his birth, and the reasons for which it was concealed.

He was no longer satisfied with the employment which had been allotted him, but thought he had a right to share the affluence of his mother; and therefore, without scruple, applied to her as her son, and made use of every art to awaken her tenderness and attract her regard. But neither his letters nor the interposition of those friends which his merit or his distress procured him made any impression upon her mind. She still resolved to neglect, though she could no longer disown him.

It was to no purpose that he frequently solicited her to admit him to see her; she avoided him with the most vigilant precaution, and ordered him to be excluded from her house, by whomsoever he might be introduced, and what reason soever he might give for entering it.

Savage was at the same time so touched with the discovery of his real mother that it was his frequent practice to walk in the dark evenings for several hours before her door, in hopes of seeing her as she might come by accident to the window or cross her apartment with a candle in her hand.

But all his assiduity and tenderness were without effect, for he could neither soften her heart nor open her hand, and was reduced to the utmost miseries of want while he was endeavouring to awaken the affection of a mother. He was therefore obliged to seek some other means of support; and, having no profession, became by necessity an author.

At this time the attention of the literary world was engrossed by the Bangorian controversy, which filled the press with pamphlets, and the coffee-houses with disputants. Of this subject, as most popular, he made choice for his first attempt, and, without any other knowledge of the question than he had casually collected from conversation, published [1717] a poem against the Bishop.

What was the success or merit of this performance I know not; it was probably lost among the innumerable pamphlets to which that dispute gave occasion. Mr. Savage was himself in a little time ashamed of it, and endeavoured to suppress it by destroying all the copies that he could collect.

He then attempted a more gainful kind of writing,

and in his eighteenth year offered to the stage a comedy borrowed from a Spanish plot, which was refused by the players, and was therefore given by him to Mr. Bullock, who, having more interest, made some slight alterations, and brought it upon the stage under the title of *Woman's a Riddle,* but allowed the unhappy author no part of the profit.

Not discouraged, however, at his repulse, he wrote, two years afterwards, *Love in a Veil,* another comedy, borrowed likewise from the Spanish, but with little better success than before; for though it was received and acted, yet it appeared so late in the year that the author obtained no other advantage from it than the acquaintance of Sir Richard Steele and Mr. Wilks, by whom he was pitied, caressed, and relieved.

Sir Richard Steele, having declared in his favour with all the ardour of benevolence which constituted his character, promoted his interest with the utmost zeal, related his misfortunes, applauded his merit, took all the opportunities of recommending him, and asserted that "the inhumanity of his mother had given him a right to find every good man his father."

Nor was Mr. Savage admitted to his acquaintance only, but to his confidence, of which he sometimes related an instance too extraordinary to be omitted, as it affords a very just idea of his patron's character.

He was once desired by Sir Richard, with an air of the utmost importance, to come very early to his house the next morning. Mr. Savage came as he had promised, found the chariot at the door, and Sir Richard waiting for him and ready to go out. What was intended, and whither they were to go, Savage could not conjecture, and was not willing to inquire; but immediately seated himself with Sir Richard. The coachman was ordered to drive, and they hurried with the utmost expedition to

Hyde Park Corner, where they stopped at a petty tavern and retired to a private room. Sir Richard then informed him that he intended to publish a pamphlet, and that he had desired him to come thither that he might write for him. He soon sat down to the work. Sir Richard dictated, and Savage wrote, till the dinner that had been ordered was put upon the table. Savage was surprised at the meanness of the entertainment, and after some hesitation ventured to ask for wine, which Sir Richard, not without reluctance, ordered to be brought. They then finished their dinner, and proceeded in their pamphlet, which they concluded in the afternoon.

Mr. Savage then imagined his task over, and expected that Sir Richard would call for the reckoning and return home; but his expectations deceived him, for Sir Richard told him that he was without money, and that the pamphlet must be sold before the dinner could be paid for; and Savage was therefore obliged to go and offer their new production to sale for two guineas, which with some difficulty he obtained. Sir Richard then returned home, having retired that day only to avoid his creditors, and composed the pamphlet only to discharge his reckoning.

Mr. Savage related another fact equally uncommon, which, though it has no relation to his life, ought to be preserved. Sir Richard Steele having one day invited to his house a great number of persons of the first quality, they were surprised at the number of liveries which surrounded the table; and, after dinner, when wine and mirth had set them free from the observation of a rigid ceremony, one of them inquired of Sir Richard how such an expensive train of domestics could be consistent with his fortune. Sir Richard very frankly confessed that they were fellows of whom he would very willingly be rid. And being then asked why he did not discharge them, declared that they were bailiffs, who had introduced themselves with an execution, and whom, since he could not send them away, he had thought it convenient to embellish with liveries, that they might do him credit while they stayed.

His friends were diverted with the expedient, and by paying the debt discharged their attendants, having obliged Sir Richard to promise that they should never again find him graced with a retinue of the same kind.

Under such a tutor, Mr. Savage was not likely to learn prudence or frugality; and perhaps many of the misfortunes which the want of those virtues brought upon him in the following parts of his life might be justly imputed to so unimproving an example.

Nor did the kindness of Sir Richard end in common favours. He proposed to have established him in some settled scheme of life, and to have contracted a kind of alliance with him by marrying him to a natural daughter, on whom he intended to bestow a thousand pounds. But though he was always lavish of future bounties, he conducted his affairs in such a manner that he was very seldom able to keep his promises or execute his own intentions; and, as he was never able to raise the sum which he had offered, the marriage was delayed. In the meantime he was officiously informed that Mr. Savage had ridiculed him; by which he was so much exasperated that he withdrew the allowance which he had paid him, and never afterwards admitted him to his house.

It is not indeed unlikely that Savage might, by his imprudence, expose himself to the malice of a talebearer; for his patron had many follies, which, as his discernment easily discovered, his imagination might sometimes incite him to mention too ludicrously. A little knowledge of the world is sufficient to discover that such weakness is very common, and that there are few who do not sometimes, in the wantonness of thoughtless mirth, or the heat of transient resentment, speak of their friends and benefactors with levity and contempt, though in their cooler moments they want neither sense of their kindness nor reverence for their virtue. The fault therefore of Mr. Savage was rather negligence than ingratitude: but Sir Richard must likewise be acquitted of severity; for who is there that can patiently bear contempt from one whom he has relieved and supported, whose establishment he has laboured, and whose interest he has promoted?

He was now again abandoned to fortune without any other friend than Mr. Wilks; a man who, whatever were his abilities or skill as an actor, deserves at least to be remembered for his virtues, which are not often to be found in the world, and perhaps less often in his profession than in others. To be humane, generous, and candid, is a very high degree of merit in any case; but those qualities deserve still greater praise when they are found in that condition which makes almost every other man, for whatever reason, contemptuous, insolent, petulant, selfish, and brutal.

As Mr. Wilks was one of those to whom calamity seldom complained without relief, he naturally took an unfortunate wit into his protection, and not only assisted him in any casual distresses, but continued an equal and steady kindness to the time of his death.

By his interposition Mr. Savage once obtained from his mother 50*l*., and a promise of 150*l*. more; but it was the fate of this unhappy man that few promises of any advantage to him were performed. His mother was infected, among others, with the general madness of the South Sea traffic; and, having been disappointed in her expectations, refused to pay what perhaps nothing but the prospect of sudden affluence prompted her to promise.

Being thus obliged to depend upon the friendship of Mr. Wilks, he was consequently an assiduous frequenter of the theatres; and in a short time the amusements of the stage took such possession of his mind that he never was absent from a play in several years.

This constant attendance naturally procured him the acquaintance of the players, and, among others, of Mrs. Oldfield, who was so much pleased with his conversation, and touched with his misfortunes, that she allowed him a settled pension of 50*l*. a year, which was during her life regularly paid.

That this act of generosity may receive its due praise, and that the good actions of Mrs. Oldfield may not be sullied by her general character, it is proper to mention that Mr. Savage often declared in the strongest terms, that he never saw her alone, or in any other place than behind the scenes.

At her death [23rd Oct., 1730] he endeavoured to show his gratitude in the most decent manner, by wearing mourning as for a mother; but did not celebrate her in elegies; because he knew that too great profusion of praise would only have revived those faults which his natural equity did not allow him to think less because they were committed by one who favoured him; but of which, though his virtue would not endeavour to palliate them, his gratitude would not suffer him to prolong the memory or diffuse the censure.

In his "Wanderer" he has indeed taken an opportunity of mentioning her; but celebrates her not for her virtue, but her beauty, an excellence which none ever denied her: this is the only encomium with which he has rewarded her liberality, and perhaps he has even in this been too lavish of his praise. He seems to have thought, that never to mention his benefactress would have an appearance of ingratitude, though to have dedicated any particular performance to her memory would have only betrayed an officious partiality, that, without exalting her character, would have depressed his own.

He had sometimes, by the kindness of Mr. Wilks, the advantage of a benefit, on which occasions he often received uncommon marks of regard and compassion; and was once told by the Duke of Dorset that it was just to consider him as an injured nobleman, and that in his opinion the nobility ought to think themselves obliged, without solicitation, to take every opportunity of supporting him by their countenance and patronage. But he had generally the mortification to hear that the whole interest of his mother was employed to frustrate his applications, and that she never left any expedient untried by which he might be cut off from the possibility of supporting life. The same disposition she endeavoured to diffuse among all those over whom nature or fortune gave her any influence, and indeed succeeded too well in her design, but could not always propagate her effrontery with her cruelty, for some of those whom she incited against him were ashamed of their own conduct, and boasted of that relief which they never gave him.

In this censure I do not indiscriminately involve all his relations; for he has mentioned with gratitude the humanity of one lady whose name I am now unable to recollect, and to whom therefore I cannot pay the praises which she deserves for having acted well in opposition to influence, precept, and example.

The punishment which our laws inflict upon those parents who murder their infants is well known, nor has its justice ever been contested; but if they deserve death who destroy a child in its birth, what pains can be severe enough for her who forbears to destroy him only to inflict sharper miseries upon him; who prolongs his life only to make him miserable; and who exposes him, without care and without pity, to the malice of oppression, the caprices of chance, and the temptations of poverty; who rejoices to see him overwhelmed with calamities; and, when his own industry, or the charity of others, has enabled him to rise for a short time above his miseries, plunges him again into his former distress?

The kindness of his friends not affording him any constant supply, and the prospect of improving his fortune by enlarging his acquaintance necessarily leading him to places of expense, he found it necessary to endeavour once more at dramatic poetry, for which he was now better qualified by a more extensive knowledge and longer observation. But having been unsuccessful in comedy, though rather for want of opportunities than genius, he resolved now to try whether he should not be more fortunate in exhibiting a tragedy.

The story which he chose for the subject was that of Sir Thomas Overbury, a story well adapted to the stage, though perhaps not far enough removed from the present age to admit properly the fictions necessary to complete the plan: for the mind, which naturally loves truth, is always most offended with the violation of those truths of which we are most certain; and we of course conceive those facts most certain which approach nearest to our own time.

Out of this story he formed a tragedy, which, if the circumstances in which he wrote it be considered, will afford at once an uncommon proof of strength of genius and evenness of mind, of a serenity not to be ruffled and an imagination not to be suppressed.

During a considerable part of the time in which he was employed upon this performance he was without lodging, and often without meat; nor had he any other conveniences for study than the fields or the streets allowed him; there he used to walk and form his speeches, and afterwards step into a shop, beg for a few moments the use of the pen and ink, and write down what he had composed upon paper which he had picked up by accident.

If the performance of a writer thus distressed is not perfect, its faults ought surely to be imputed to a cause very different from want of genius, and must rather excite pity than provoke censure.

But when under these discouragements the tragedy was finished, there yet remained the labour of introducing it on the stage—an undertaking which, to an ingenuous mind, was in a very high degree vexatious and disgusting; for, having little interest or reputation, he was obliged to submit himself wholly to the players, and admit, with whatever reluctance, the emendations of Mr. Cibber, which he always considered as the disgrace of his performance.

He had indeed in Mr. Hill another critic of a very different class, from whose friendship he received great assistance on many occasions, and whom he never mentioned but with the utmost tenderness and regard. He had been for some time distinguished by him with very particular kindness, and on this occasion it was natural to apply to him as an author of an established character. He therefore sent this tragedy to him, with a short copy of verses, in which he desired his correction. Mr. Hill, whose humanity and politeness are generally known, readily complied with his request; but as he is remarkable for singularity of sentiment, and bold experiments in language, Mr. Savage did not think his play much improved by his innovation, and had even at that time the courage to reject several passages which he could not approve; and, what is still more laudable, Mr. Hill had the generosity not to resent the neglect of his alterations, but wrote the Prologue and Epilogue, in which he touches on the circumstances of the author with great tenderness.

After all these obstructions and compliances he was only able to bring his play upon the stage in the summer, when the chief actors had retired, and the rest were in possession of the house for their own advantage. Among these Mr. Savage was admitted to play the part of Sir Thomas Overbury, by which he gained no great reputation, the theatre being a province for which nature seemed not to have designed him; for neither his voice, look, nor gesture were such as were expected on the stage; and he was so much ashamed of having been reduced to appear as a player, that he always blotted out his name from the list when a copy of his tragedy was to be shown to his friends.

In the publication of his performance he was more successful, for the rays of genius that glimmered in it, that glimmered through all the mists which poverty and Cibber had been able to spread over it, procured him the notice and esteem of many persons eminent for their rank, their virtue, and their wit.

Of this play, acted, printed, and dedicated, the accumulated profits arose to 100*l.*, which he thought at that time a very large sum, having been never master of so much before.

In the Dedication, for which he received ten guineas, there is nothing remarkable. The Preface contains a very liberal encomium on the blooming excellence of Mr. Theophilus Cibber, which Mr. Savage could not in the latter part of his life see his friends about to read without snatching the play out of their hands. The generosity of Mr. Hill did not end on this occasion; for afterwards, when Mr. Savage's necessities returned, he encouraged a subscription to a *Miscellany of Poems* in a very extraordinary manner, by publishing his story in *The Plain Dealer*, with some affecting lines, which he asserts to have been written by Mr. Savage upon the treatment received by him from his mother, but of which he was himself the author, as Mr. Savage afterwards declared. These lines, and the paper in which they were inserted, had a very powerful effect upon all but his mother, whom, by making her cruelty more public, they only hardened in her aversion.

Mr. Hill not only promoted the subscription to the *Miscellany*, but furnished likewise the greatest part of the poems of which it is composed, and particularly "The Happy Man," which he published as a specimen.

The subscriptions of those whom these papers should influence to patronise merit in distress, without any other solicitation, were directed to be left at Button's coffeehouse; and Mr. Savage going thither a few days afterwards, without expectation of any effect from his proposal, found to his surprise seventy guineas, which had been sent him in consequence of the compassion excited by Mr. Hill's pathetic representation.

To this *Miscellany* he wrote a Preface, in which he gives an account of his mother's cruelty in a very uncommon strain of humour, and with a gaiety of imagination which the success of his subscription probably produced.

The Dedication is addressed to the Lady Mary Wortley Montagu, whom he flatters without reserve, and to confess the truth, with very little art. The same observation may be extended to all his dedications: his compliments are constrained and violent, heaped together without the grace of order, or the decency of introduction: he seems to have written his panegyrics for the perusal only of his patrons, and to imagine that he had no other task than to pamper them with praises however gross, and that flattery would make its way to the heart without the assistance of elegance or invention.

Soon afterwards [11th June, 1727] the death of the King furnished a general subject for a poetical contest, in which Mr. Savage engaged, and is allowed to have carried the prize of honour from his competitors: but I know not whether he gained by his performance any other advantage than the increase of his reputation; though it must certainly have been with farther views that he prevailed upon himself to attempt a species of writing of which all the topics had been long before exhausted, and which was made at once difficult by the multitudes that had failed in it, and those that had succeeded.

He was now advancing in reputation, and though frequently involved in very distressful perplexities, appeared however to be gaining upon mankind, when both his fame and his life were endangered by an event, of which it is not yet determined whether it ought to be mentioned as a crime or a calamity.

On the 20th of November, 1727, Mr. Savage came from Richmond, where he then lodged, that he might pursue his studies with less interruption, with an intent to discharge another lodging which he had in Westminster; and accidentally meeting two gentlemen, his acquaintances, whose names were Merchant and Gregory, he went in with them to a neighbouring coffee-house, and sat drinking till it was late, it being in no time of Mr. Savage's life any part of his character to be the first of the company that desired to separate. He would willingly have gone to bed in the same house; but there was not room for the whole company, and therefore they agreed to ramble about the streets, and divert themselves with such amusements as should offer themselves till morning.

In this walk they happened unluckily to discover a light in Robinson's coffee-house, near Charing-Cross, and therefore went in. Merchant with some rudeness demanded a room, and was told that there was a good fire in the next parlour, which the company were about to leave, being then paying their reckoning. Merchant, not satisfied with this answer, rushed into the room, and was followed by his companions. He then petulantly placed himself between the company and the fire, and soon after kicked down the table. This produced a quarrel, swords were drawn on both sides, and one Mr. James Sinclair was killed. Savage having likewise wounded a maid that held him, forced his way with Merchant out of the house, but being intimidated and confused, without resolution either to fly or stay, they were taken in a back court by one of the company and some soldiers, whom he had called to his assistance.

Being secured and guarded that night, they were in the morning carried before three justices, who committed them to the Gatehouse [at Westminster], from whence, upon the death of Mr. Sinclair, which happened the same day, they were removed in the night to Newgate, where they were however treated with some distinction, exempted from the ignominy of chains, and confined, not among the common criminals, but in the Press-yard.

When the day of trial came the court was crowded in a very unusual manner, and the public appeared to interest itself as in a cause of general concern. The witnesses against Mr. Savage and his friends were the woman who kept the house, which was a house of ill fame, and her maid, the men who were in the room with Mr. Sinclair, and a woman of the town, who had been drinking with them, and with whom one of them had been in bed. They swore in general that Merchant gave the provocation, which Savage and Gregory drew their swords to justify; that Savage drew first, and that he stabbed Sinclair when he was not in a posture of defence, or while Gregory commanded his sword; that after he had given the thrust he turned pale, and would have retired, but the maid clung round him, and one of the company endeavoured to detain him, from whom he broke, by cutting the maid on the head, but was afterwards taken in a court.

There was some difference in their depositions: one did not see Savage give the wound, another saw it given when Sinclair held his point towards the ground; and the woman of the town asserted that she did not see Sinclair's sword at all: this difference however was very far from amounting to inconsistency; but it was sufficient to show that the hurry of the dispute was such, that it was not easy to discover the truth with relation to particular circumstances, and that therefore some deductions were to be made from the credibility of the testimonies.

Sinclair had declared several times before his death that he received his wound from Savage; nor did Savage at his trial deny the fact, but endeavoured partly to extenuate it, by urging the suddenness of the whole action, and the impossibility of any ill design or premeditated malice; and partly to justify it by the necessity of self-defence, and the hazard of his own life, if he had lost that opportunity of giving the thrust: he observed that neither reason nor law obliged a man to wait for the blow which was threatened, and which, if he should suffer it, he might never be able to return; that it was always allowable to prevent an assault, and to preserve life by taking away that of the adversary by whom it was endangered.

With regard to the violence with which he endeavoured to escape, he declared that it was not his design to fly from justice, or decline a trial, but to avoid the expenses and severities of a prison; and that he intended to have appeared at the bar without compulsion.

This defence, which took up more than an hour, was heard by the multitude that thronged the court with the most attentive and respectful silence: those who thought he ought not to be acquitted, owned that applause could not be refused him; and those who before pitied his misfortunes, now reverenced his abilities.

The witnesses which appeared against him were proved to be persons of characters which did not entitle them to much credit; a common strumpet, a woman by whom strumpets were entertained, and a man by whom they were supported; and the character of Savage was by several persons of distinction asserted to be that of a modest, inoffensive man, not inclined to broils or to insolence, and who had, to that time, been only known for his misfortunes and his wit.

Had his audience been his judges, he had undoubtedly been acquitted; but Mr. Page, who was then upon the bench, treated him with his usual insolence and severity, and when he had summed up the evidence, endeavoured to exasperate the jury, as Mr. Savage used to relate it, with this eloquent harangue:

"Gentlemen of the jury, you are to consider that Mr. Savage is a very great man, a much greater man than you or I, gentlemen of the jury; that he wears very fine clothes, much finer clothes than you or I, gentlemen of the jury; that he has abundance of money in his pocket, much more money than you or I, gentlemen of the jury;

but, gentlemen of the jury, is it not a very hard case, gentlemen of the jury, that Mr. Savage should therefore kill you or me, gentlemen of the jury?"

Mr. Savage hearing his defence thus misrepresented, and the men who were to decide his fate incited against him by invidious comparisons, resolutely asserted that his cause was not candidly explained, and began to recapitulate what he had before said with regard to his condition, and the necessity of endeavouring to escape the expenses of imprisonment; but the judge having ordered him to be silent, and repeated his orders without effect, commanded that he should be taken from the bar by force.

The jury then heard the opinion of the judge that good characters were of no weight against positive evidence, though they might turn the scale where it was doubtful; and that though, when two men attack each other, the death of either is only manslaughter; but where one is the aggressor, as in the case before them, and, in pursuance of his first attack, kills the other, the law supposes the action, however sudden, to be malicious. They then deliberated upon their verdict, and determined that Mr. Savage and Mr. Gregory were guilty of murder; and Mr. Merchant, who had no sword, only of manslaughter.

Thus ended this memorable trial, which lasted eight hours. Mr. Savage and Mr. Gregory were conducted back to prison, where they were more closely confined, and loaded with irons of fifty pounds weight: four days afterwards they were sent back to the court to receive sentence; on which occasion Mr. Savage made, as far as it could be retained in memory, the following speech:

"It is now, my Lord, too late to offer anything by way of defence or vindication; nor can we expect aught from your Lordships in this court but the sentence which the law requires you, as judges, to pronounce against men of our calamitous condition. But we are also persuaded, that as mere men, and out of this seat of rigorous justice, you are susceptive of the tender passions, and too humane not to commiserate the unhappy situation of those whom the law sometimes, perhaps, exacts from you to pronounce upon. No doubt you distinguish between offences which arise out of premeditation and a disposition habituated to vice or immorality, and transgressions which are the unhappy and unforeseen effects of a casual absence of reason and sudden impulse of passion: we therefore hope you will contribute all you can to an extension of that mercy which the gentlemen of the jury have been pleased to show Mr. Merchant, who (allowing facts as sworn against us by the evidence) has led us into this our calamity. I hope this will not be construed as if we meant to reflect upon that gentleman, or remove anything from us upon him, or that we repine the more at our fate because he has no participation of it: No, my Lord! For my part I declare nothing could more soften my grief than to be without any companion in so great a misfortune."

Mr. Savage had now no hopes of life but from the mercy of the Crown, which was very earnestly solicited by his friends, and which, with whatever difficulty the story may obtain belief, was obstructed only by his mother.

To prejudice the Queen [Caroline, Queen of George II.] against him, she made use of an incident which was omitted in the order of time, that it might be mentioned together with the purpose which it was made to serve. Mr. Savage, when he had discovered his birth, had an incessant desire to speak to his mother, who always avoided him in public, and refused him admission into her house. One evening walking, as it was his custom, in the street that she inhabited, he saw the door of her house by accident open, he entered it, and, finding no person in the passage to hinder him, went up stairs to salute her. She discovered him before he entered her chamber, alarmed the family with the most distressful outcries, and when she had by her screams gathered them about her, ordered them to drive out of the house that villain who had forced himself in upon her and endeavoured to murder her. Savage, who had attempted with the most submissive tenderness to soften her rage, hearing her utter so detestable an accusation, thought it prudent to retire, and, I believe, never attempted afterwards to speak to her.

But, shocked as he was with her falsehood and her cruelty, he imagined that she intended no other use of her lie than to set herself free from his embraces and solicitations, and was very far from suspecting that she would treasure it in her memory as an instrument of future wickedness, or that she would endeavour for this fictitious assault to deprive him of his life.

But when the Queen was solicited for his pardon, and informed of the severe treatment which he had suffered from his judge, she answered, that however unjustifiable might be the manner of his trial, or whatever extenuation the action for which he was condemned might admit, she could not think that man a proper object of the King's mercy who had been capable of entering his mother's house in the night with an intent to murder her.

By whom this atrocious calumny had been transmitted to the Queen; whether she that invented had the front to relate it; whether she found anyone weak enough to credit it, or corrupt enough to concur with her in her hateful design, I know not; but methods had been taken to persuade the Queen so strongly of the truth of it, that she for a long time refused to hear anyone of those who petitioned for his life.

Thus had Savage perished by the evidence of a bawd, a strumpet, and his mother, had not justice and compassion procured him an advocate of rank too great to be rejected unheard, and of virtue too eminent to be heard without being believed. His merit and his calamities happened to reach the ear of the Countess of Hertford, who engaged in his support with all the tenderness that is excited by pity, and all the zeal which is kindled by generosity; and, demanding an audience of the Queen, laid before her the whole series of his mother's cruelty, exposed the improbability of an accusation by which he was charged with an intent to commit a murder that could produce no advantage, and soon convinced her how little his former conduct could deserve to be mentioned as a reason for extraordinary severity.

The interposition of this lady was so successful that he was soon after admitted to bail, and, on the 9th of March, 1728, pleaded the King's pardon.

It is natural to inquire upon what motives his mother could persecute him in a manner so outrageous and implacable; for what reason she could employ all the arts of malice, and all the snares of calumny, to take away the life of her own son, of a son who never injured her, who was never supported by her expense, nor obstructed any prospect of pleasure or advantage; why she should endeavour to destroy him by a lie—a lie which could not gain credit, but must vanish of itself at the first moment of examination, and of which only this can be said to make it probable, that it may be observed from her conduct that the most execrable crimes are sometimes committed without apparent temptation.

This mother is still alive, and may perhaps even yet, though her malice was so often defeated, enjoy the pleasure of reflecting that the life which she often endeavoured to destroy was at last shortened by her maternal offices; that though she could not transport her son to the plantations, bury him in the shop of a mechanic, or hasten the hand of the public executioner, she has yet had the satisfaction of embittering all his hours, and forcing him into exigences that hurried on his death.

It is by no means necessary to aggravate the enormity of this woman's conduct by placing it in opposition to that of the Countess of Hertford; no one can fail to observe how much more amiable it is to relieve than to oppress, and to rescue innocence from destruction than to destroy without an injury.

Mr. Savage, during his imprisonment, his trial, and the time in which he lay under sentence of death, behaved with great firmness and equality of mind, and confirmed by his fortitude the esteem of those who before admired him for his abilities. The peculiar circumstances of his life were made more generally known by a short account, which was then published, and of which several thousands were in a few weeks dispersed over the nation: and the compassion of mankind operated so powerfully in his favour, that he was enabled by frequent presents not only to support himself, but to assist Mr. Gregory in prison; and when he was pardoned and released, he found the number of his friends not lessened.

The nature of the act for which he had been tried was in itself doubtful; of the evidences which appeared against him, the character of the man was not unexceptionable, that of the women notoriously infamous; she whose testimony chiefly influenced the jury to condemn him, afterwards retracted her assertions. He always himself denied that he was drunk, as had been generally reported. Mr. Gregory, who is now (1744) Collector of Antigua, is said to declare him far less criminal than he was imagined, even by some who favoured him; and Page himself afterwards confessed that he had treated him with uncommon rigour. When all these particulars are rated together, perhaps the memory of Savage may not be much sullied by his trial.

Some time after he obtained his liberty, he met in the street the woman that had sworn with so much malignity against him. She informed him that she was in distress, and, with a degree of confidence not easily attainable, desired him to relieve her. He, instead of insulting her misery, and taking pleasure in the calamities of one who had brought his life into danger, reproved her gently for her perjury; and changing the only guinea that he had, divided it equally between her and himself.

This is an action which in some ages would have made a saint, and perhaps in others a hero, and which, without any hyperbolical encomiums, must be allowed to be an instance of uncommon generosity, an act of complicated virtue; by which he at once relieved the poor, corrected the vicious, and forgave an enemy; by which he at once remitted the strongest provocations, and exercised the most ardent charity.

Compassion was indeed the distinguishing quality of Savage; he never appeared inclined to take advantage of weakness, to attack the defenceless, or to press upon the falling: whoever was distressed, was certain at least of his good wishes; and when he could give no assistance to extricate them from misfortunes, he endeavoured to soothe them by sympathy and tenderness.

But when his heart was not softened by the sight of misery, he was sometimes obstinate in his resentment, and did not quickly lose the remembrance of an injury. He always continued to speak with anger of the insolence and partiality of Page, and a short time before his death revenged it by a satire.

It is natural to inquire in what terms Mr. Savage spoke of this fatal action when the danger was over, and he was under no necessity of using any art to set his conduct in the fairest light. He was not willing to dwell upon it; and, if he transiently mentioned it, appeared neither to consider himself as a murderer, nor as a man wholly free from the guilt of blood. How much and how long he regretted it, appeared in a poem which he published many years afterwards. On occasion of a copy of verses, in which the failings of good men were recounted, and in which the author had endeavoured to illustrate his position, that "the best may sometimes deviate from virtue," by an instance of murder committed by Savage in the heat of wine, Savage remarked, that it was no very just representation of a good man, to suppose him liable to drunkenness, and disposed in his riots to cut throats.

He was now indeed at liberty, but was, as before, without any other support than accidental favours and uncertain patronage afforded him; sources by which he was sometimes very liberally supplied, and which at other times were suddenly stopped; so that he spent his life between want and plenty; or, what was yet worse, between beggary and extravagance; for, as whatever he received was the gift of chance, which might as well favour him at one time as another, he was tempted to squander what he had, because he always hoped to be immediately supplied.

Another cause of his profusion was the absurd kindness of his friends, who at once rewarded and enjoyed his abilities by treating him at taverns, and habituating him to pleasures which he could not afford to enjoy, and which he was not able to deny himself, though he purchased the luxury of a single night by the anguish of cold and hunger for a week.

The experience of these inconveniences determined him to endeavour after some settled income, which, having long found submission and entreaties fruitless, he attempted to extort from his mother by rougher methods. He had now, as he acknowledged, lost that tenderness for her which the whole series of her cruelty had not been able wholly to repress, till he found, by the efforts which she made for his destruction, that she was not content with refusing to assist him, and being neutral in his struggles with poverty, but was as ready to snatch every opportunity of adding to his misfortunes; and that she was now to be considered as an enemy implacably malicious, whom nothing but his blood could satisfy. He therefore threatened to harass her with lampoons, and to publish a copious narrative of her conduct, unless she consented to purchase an exemption from infamy by allowing him a pension.

This expedient proved successful. Whether shame still survived, though virtue was extinct, or whether her relations had more delicacy than herself, and imagined that some of the darts which satire might point at her would glance upon them, Lord Tyrconnel, whatever were his motives, upon his promise to lay aside his design of exposing the cruelty of his mother, received him into his family, treated him as his equal, and engaged to allow him a pension of 200*l.* a year.

This was the golden part of Mr. Savage's life, and for some time he had no reason to complain of fortune; his appearance was splendid, his expenses large, and his acquaintance extensive. He was courted by all who endeavoured to be thought men of genius, and caressed by all who valued themselves upon a refined taste. To admire Mr. Savage was a proof of discernment, and to be acquainted with him was a title to poetical reputation. His presence was sufficient to make any place of public entertainment popular, and his approbation and example constituted the fashion. So powerful is genius when it is invested with the glitter of affluence! Men willingly pay to fortune that regard which they owe to merit, and are pleased when they have an opportunity at once of gratifying their vanity and practising their duty.

This interval of prosperity furnished him with opportunities of enlarging his knowledge of human nature, by contemplating life from its highest gradations to its lowest; and, had he afterwards applied to dramatic poetry, he would perhaps not have had many superiors; for as he never suffered any scene to pass before his eyes without notice, he had treasured in his mind all the different combinations of passions, and the innumerable mixtures of vice and virtue, which distinguish one character from another; and, as his conception was strong, his expressions were clear, he easily received impressions from objects, and very forcibly transmitted them to others.

Of his exact observations on human life he has left a proof, which would do honour to the greatest names, in a small pamphlet, called *The Author to be Let*, where he introduces Iscariot Hackney, a prostitute scribbler, giving an account of his birth, his education, his disposition and morals, habits of life, and maxims of conduct. In the Introduction are related many secret histories of the petty writers of that time, but sometimes mixed with ungenerous reflections on their birth, their circumstances, or those of their relations; nor can it be denied that some passages are such as Iscariot Hackney might himself have produced.

He was accused likewise of living in an appearance of friendship with some whom he satirised, and of making use of the confidence which he gained by a seeming kindness, to discover failings and expose them: it must be confessed that Mr. Savage's esteem was no very certain possession, and that he would lampoon at one time those whom he had praised at another.

It may be alleged, that the same man may change his principles; and that he who was once deservedly commended, may be afterwards satirised with equal justice; or that the poet was dazzled with the appearance of virtue, and found the man whom he had celebrated, when he had an opportunity of examining him more narrowly, unworthy of the panegyric which he had too hastily bestowed; and that, as a false satire ought to be recanted for the sake of him whose reputation may be injured, false praise ought likewise to be obviated, lest the distinction between vice and virtue should be lost, lest a bad man should be trusted upon the credit of his encomiast, or lest others should endeavour to obtain the like praises by the same means.

But though these excuses may be often plausible, and sometimes just, they are very seldom satisfactory to mankind; and the writer who is not constant to his subject quickly sinks into contempt, his satire loses its force, and his panegyric its value, and he is only considered at one time as a flatterer, and as a calumniator at another.

To avoid these imputations, it is only necessary to follow the rules of virtue, and to preserve an unvaried regard to truth. For though it is undoubtedly possible that a man, however cautious, may be sometimes deceived by an artful appearance of virtue, or by false evidences of guilt, such errors will not be frequent; and it will be allowed, that the name of an author would never have been made contemptible, had no man ever said what he did not think, or misled others but when he was himself deceived.

The Author to be Let was first published in a single

pamphlet, and afterwards inserted in a collection of pieces relating to the *Dunciad,* which were addressed by Mr. Savage to the Earl of Middlesex, in a Dedication which he was prevailed upon to sign, though he did not write it, and in which there are some positions that the true author would perhaps not have published under his own name, and on which Mr. Savage afterwards reflected with no great satisfaction. The enumeration of the bad effects of the "uncontrolled freedom of the press," and the assertion that the "liberties taken by the writers of journals with their superiors were exorbitant and unjustifiable," very ill became men who have themselves not always shown the exactest regard to the laws of subordination in their writings, and who have often satirised those that at least thought themselves their superiors, as they were eminent for their hereditary rank, and employed in the highest offices of the kingdom. But this is only an instance of that partiality which almost every man indulges with regard to himself: the liberty of the press is a blessing when we are inclined to write against others, and a calamity when we find ourselves overborne by the multitude of our assailants; as the power of the Crown is always thought too great by those who suffer by its influence, and too little by those in whose favour it is exerted; and a standing army is generally accounted necessary by those who command, and dangerous and oppressive by those who support it.

Mr. Savage was likewise very far from believing that the letters annexed to each species of bad poets in the Bathos were, as he was directed to assert, "set down at random"; for when he was charged by one of his friends with putting his name to such an improbability, he had no other answer to make, than that "he did not think of it"; and his friend had too much tenderness to reply, that next to the crime of writing contrary to what he thought, was that of writing without thinking.

After having remarked what is false in this Dedication, it is proper that I observe the impartiality which I recommend, by declaring what Savage asserted; that the account of the circumstances which attended the publication of the *Dunciad*, however strange and improbable, was exactly true.

The publication of this piece at this time raised Mr. Savage a great number of enemies among those that were attacked by Mr. Pope, with whom he was considered as a kind of confederate, and whom he was suspected of supplying with private intelligence and secret incidents: so that the ignominy of an informer was added to the terror of a satirist.

That he was not altogether free from literary hypocrisy, and that he sometimes spoke one thing, and wrote another, cannot be denied; because he himself confessed, that, when he lived with great familiarity with Dennis, he wrote an epigram against him.

Mr. Savage, however, set all the malice of all the pigmy writers at defiance, and thought the friendship of Mr. Pope cheaply purchased by being exposed to their censure and their hatred; nor had he any reason to repent of the preference, for he found Mr. Pope a steady and unalienable friend almost to the end of his life.

About this time, notwithstanding his avowed neutrality with regard to party, he published (1732) a panegyric on Sir Robert Walpole, for which he was rewarded by him with twenty guineas, a sum not very large, if either the excellence of the performance, or the affluence of the patron, be considered; but greater than he afterwards obtained from a person of yet higher rank [Frederick Prince of Wales], and more desirous in appearance of being distinguished as a patron of literature.

As he was very far from approving the conduct of Sir Robert Walpole, and in conversation mentioned him sometimes with acrimony, and generally with contempt; as he was one of those who were always zealous in their assertions of the justice of the late opposition, jealous of the rights of the people, and alarmed by the long-continued triumph of the Court, it was natural to ask him what could induce him to employ his poetry in praise of that man who was, in his opinion, an enemy to liberty, and an oppressor of his country? He alleged, that he was then dependent upon the Lord Tyrconnel, who was an implicit follower of the ministry; and that being enjoined by him, not without menaces, to write in praise of his leader, he had not resolution sufficient to sacrifice the pleasure of affluence to that of integrity.

On this, and on many other occasions, he was ready to lament the misery of living at the tables of other men, which was his fate from the beginning to the end of his life; for I know not whether he ever had, for three months together, a settled habitation, in which he could claim a right of residence.

To this unhappy state it is just to impute much of the inconstancy of his conduct; for though a readiness to comply with the inclination of others was no part of his natural character, yet he was sometimes obliged to relax his obstinacy, and submit his own judgment, and even his virtue, to the government of those by whom he was supported: so that, if his miseries were sometimes the consequences of his faults, he ought not yet to be wholly excluded from compassion, because his faults were very often the effects of his misfortunes.

In this gay period (1729) of his life, while he was surrounded by affluence and pleasure, he published "The Wanderer," a moral poem, of which the design is comprised in these lines:

> I fly all public care, all venal strife,
> To try the still, compar'd with active, life;
> To prove, by these, the sons of men may owe
> The fruits of bliss to bursting clouds of woe;
> That ev'n calamity, by thought refin'd,
> Inspirits and adorns the thinking mind.

And more distinctly in the following passage:

> By woe, the soul to daring action swells;
> By woe, in plaintless patience it excels;
> From patience, prudent clear experience springs,
> And traces knowledge thro' the course of things!
> Thence hope is form'd, thence fortitude, success,
> Renown:—whate'er men covet and caress.

This performance was always considered by himself as his masterpiece; and Mr. Pope, when he asked his opinion of it, told him, that he read it once over, and was not displeased with it; that it gave him more pleasure at the second perusal, and delighted him still more at the third.

Even in this poem he has not been able to forbear one touch upon the cruelty of his mother, which, though remarkably delicate and tender, is a proof how deep an impression it had upon his mind.

From a poem so diligently laboured, and so successfully finished, it might be reasonably expected that he should have gained considerable advantage; nor can it, without some degree of indignation and concern, be told, that he sold the copy for ten guineas, of which he afterwards returned two, that the two last sheets of the work might be reprinted, of which he had in his absence intrusted the correction to a friend, who was too indolent to perform it with accuracy.

A superstitious regard to the correction of his sheets

was one of Mr. Savage's peculiarities: he often altered, revised, recurred to his first reading or punctuation, and again adopted the alteration; he was dubious and irresolute without end, as on a question of the last importance, and at last was seldom satisfied: the intrusion or omission of a comma was sufficient to discompose him, and he would lament an error of a single letter as a heavy calamity. In one of his letters relating to an impression of some verses, he remarks, that he had, with regard to the correction of the proof, "a spell upon him"; and indeed the anxiety with which he dwelt upon the minutest and most trifling niceties deserved no other name than that of fascination.

That he sold so valuable a performance for so small a price, was not to be imputed either to necessity, by which the learned and ingenious are often obliged to submit to very hard conditions; or to avarice, by which the booksellers are frequently incited to oppress that genius by which they are supported; but to that intemperate desire of pleasure, and habitual slavery to his passions, which involved him in many perplexities. He happened at that time to be engaged in the pursuit of some trifling gratification, and, being without money for the present occasion, sold his poem to the first bidder, and perhaps for the first price that was proposed, and would probably have been content with less if less had been offered him.

This poem was addressed to the Lord Tyrconnel, not only in the first lines, but in a formal Dedication filled with the highest strains of panegyric, and the warmest professions of gratitude, but by no means remarkable for delicacy of connexion or elegance of style.

These praises in a short time he found himself inclined to retract, being discarded by the man on whom he had bestowed them, and whom he then immediately discovered not to have deserved them. Of this quarrel, which every day made more bitter, Lord Tyrconnel and Mr. Savage assigned very different reasons, which might perhaps all in reality concur, though they were not all convenient to be alleged by either party. Lord Tyrconnel affirmed that it was the constant practice of Mr. Savage to enter a tavern with any company that proposed it, drink the most expensive wines with great profusion, and when the reckoning was demanded, to be without money: if, as it often happened, his company were willing to defray his part, the affair ended, without any ill consequences; but if they were refractory, and expected that the wine should be paid for by him that drank it, his method of composition was, to take them with him to his own apartment, assume the government of the house, and order the butler in an imperious manner to set the best wine in the cellar before his company, who often drank till they forgot the respect due to the house in which they were entertained, indulged themselves in the utmost extravagance of merriment, practised the most licentious frolics, and committed all the outrages of drunkenness.

Nor was this the only charge which Lord Tyrconnel brought against him. Having given him a collection of valuable books, stamped with his own arms, he had the mortification to see them in a short time exposed to sale upon the stalls, it being usual with Mr. Savage, when he wanted a small sum, to take his books to the pawnbroker.

Whoever was acquainted with Mr. Savage easily credited both these accusations; for having been obliged, from his first entrance into the world, to subsist upon expedients, affluence was not able to exalt him above them; and so much was he delighted with wine and conversation, and so long had he been accustomed to live by chance, that he would at any time go to the tavern without scruple, and trust for the reckoning to the liberality of his company, and frequently of company to whom he was very little known. This conduct indeed very seldom drew upon him those inconveniences that might be feared by any other person; for his conversation was so entertaining, and his address so pleasing, that few thought the pleasure which they received from him dearly purchased by paying for his wine. It was his peculiar happiness that he scarcely ever found a stranger whom he did not leave a friend; but it must likewise be added, that he had not often a friend long without obliging him to become a stranger.

Mr. Savage, on the other hand, declared that Lord Tyrconnel quarrelled with him because he would not subtract from his own luxury and extravagance what he had promised to allow him, and that his resentment was only a plea for the violation of his promise. He asserted that he had done nothing that ought to exclude him from that subsistence which he thought not so much a favour as a debt, since it was offered him upon conditions which he had never broken; and that his only fault was, that he could not be supported with nothing.

He acknowledged that Lord Tyrconnel often exhorted him to regulate his method of life, and not to spend all his nights in taverns, and that he appeared desirous that he would pass those hours with him which he so freely bestowed upon others. This demand Mr. Savage considered as a censure of his conduct, which he could never patiently bear, and which, in the latter and cooler parts of his life, was so offensive to him that he declared it as his resolution "to spurn that friend who should presume to dictate to him"; and it is not likely that in his earlier years he received admonitions with more calmness.

He was likewise inclined to resent such expectations, as tending to infringe his liberty, of which he was very jealous, when it was necessary to the gratification of his passions; and declared that the request was still more unreasonable, as the company to which he was to have been confined was insupportably disagreeable. This assertion affords another instance of that inconsistency of his writings with his conversation which was so often to be observed. He forgot how lavishly he had, in his Dedication to "The Wanderer," extolled the delicacy and penetration, the humanity and generosity, the candour and politeness of the man whom, when he no longer loved him, he declared to be a wretch without understanding, without good nature, and without justice, of whose name he thought himself obliged to leave no trace in any future edition of his writings, and accordingly blotted it out of that copy of "The Wanderer" which was in his hands.

As the reputation of his abilities, the particular circumstances of his birth and life, the splendour of his appearance, and the distinction which was for some time paid him by Lord Tyrconnel, entitled him to familiarity with persons of higher rank than those to whose conversation he had been before admitted, he did not fail to gratify that curiosity, which induced him to take a nearer view of those whom their birth, their employments, or their fortunes necessarily place at a distance from the greatest part of mankind, and to examine whether their merit was magnified or diminished by the medium through which it was contemplated; whether the splendour with which they dazzled their admirers was inherent in themselves, or only reflected on them by the objects that surrounded them; and whether great men were selected for high stations, or high stations made great men.

For this purpose he took all opportunities of conversing familiarly with those who were most conspicuous at that time for their power or their influence; he watched their looser moments, and examined their domestic behaviour with that acuteness which nature had given him, and which the uncommon variety of his life had contributed to increase, and that inquisitiveness which must always be produced in a vigorous mind by an absolute freedom from all pressing or domestic engagements.

His discernment was quick, and therefore he soon found in every person, and in every affair, something that deserved attention; he was supported by others, without any care for himself, and was therefore at leisure to pursue his observations.

More circumstances to constitute a critic on human life could not easily concur; nor indeed could any man, who assumed from accidental advantages more praise than he could justly claim from his real merit, admit any acquaintance more dangerous than that of Savage; of whom likewise it must be confessed, that abilities really exalted above the common level, or virtue refined from passion, or proof against corruption, could not easily find an abler judge, or a warmer advocate.

What was the result of Mr. Savage's inquiry, though he was not much accustomed to conceal his discoveries, it may not be entirely safe to relate, because the persons whose characters he criticised are powerful, and power and resentment are seldom strangers; nor would it perhaps be wholly just, because what he asserted in conversation might, though true in general, be heightened by some momentary ardour of imagination, and, as it can be delivered only from memory, may be imperfectly represented; so that the picture, at first aggravated, and then unskilfully copied, may be justly suspected to retain no great resemblance of the original.

It may, however, be observed that he did not appear to have formed very elevated ideas of those to whom the administration of affairs, or the conduct of parties, has been entrusted—who have been considered as the advocates of the Crown, or the guardians of the people, and who have obtained the most implicit confidence, and the loudest applauses. Of one particular person, who has been at one time so popular as to be generally esteemed, and at another so formidable as to be universally detested, he observed, that his acquisitions had been small, or that his capacity was narrow, and that the whole range of his mind was from obscenity to politics, and from politics to obscenity.

But the opportunity of indulging his speculations on great characters was now at an end. He was banished from the table of Lord Tyrconnel, and turned again adrift upon the world, without prospect of finding quickly any other harbour. As prudence was not one of the virtues by which he was distinguished, he had made no provision against a misfortune like this. And though it is not to be imagined but that the separation must for some time have been preceded by coldness, peevishness, or neglect, though it was undoubtedly the consequence of accumulated provocations on both sides, yet everyone that knew Savage will readily believe that to him it was sudden as a stroke of thunder—that though he might have transiently suspected it, he had never suffered any thought so unpleasing to sink into his mind, but that he had driven it away by amusements, or dreams of future felicity and affluence, and had never taken any measures by which he might prevent a precipitation from plenty to indigence.

This quarrel and separation, and the difficulties to which Mr. Savage was exposed by them, were soon known both to his friends and enemies; nor was it long before he perceived, from the behaviour of both, how much is added to the lustre of genius by the ornaments of wealth.

His condition did not appear to excite much compassion; for he had not always been careful to use the advantages he enjoyed with that moderation which ought to have been with more than usual caution preserved by him, who knew, if he had reflected, that he was only a dependant on the bounty of another, whom he could expect to support him no longer than he endeavoured to preserve his favour by complying with his inclinations, and whom he nevertheless set at defiance, and was continually irritating by negligence or encroachments.

That Mr. Savage was too much elevated by any good fortune is generally known; and some passages of his Introduction to *The Author to be Let* sufficiently show that he did not wholly refrain from such satire as he afterwards thought very unjust when he was exposed to it himself; for, when he was afterwards ridiculed in the character of a distressed poet, he very easily discovered that distress was not a proper subject for merriment, or topic of invective. He was then able to discern that if misery be the effect of virtue, it ought to be reverenced; if of ill fortune, to be pitied; and if of vice, not to be insulted, because it is perhaps itself a punishment adequate to the crime by which it was produced. And the humanity of that man can deserve no panegyric who is capable of reproaching a criminal in the hands of the executioner.

But these reflections, though they readily occurred to him in the first and last parts of his life, were, I am afraid, for a long time forgotten—at least they were, like many other maxims, treasured up in his mind, rather for show than use, and operated very little upon his conduct, however elegantly he might sometimes explain, or however forcibly he might inculcate, them.

His degradation, therefore, from the condition which he had enjoyed with such wanton thoughtlessness was considered by many as an occasion of triumph. Those who had before paid their court to him without success soon returned the contempt which they had suffered; and they who had received favours from him—for of such favours as he could bestow he was very liberal— did not always remember them. So much more certain are the effects of resentment than of gratitude: it is not only to many more pleasing to recollect those faults which place others below them than those virtues by which they are themselves comparatively depressed, but it is likewise more easy to neglect than to recompense; and though there are few who will practise a laborious virtue, there will never be wanting multitudes that will indulge in easy vice.

Savage, however, was very little disturbed at the marks of contempt which his ill fortune brought upon him from those whom he never esteemed, and with whom he never considered himself as levelled by any calamities: and though it was not without some uneasiness that he saw some, whose friendship he valued, change their behaviour, he yet observed their coldness without much emotion, considered them as the slaves of fortune and the worshippers of prosperity, and was more inclined to despise them than to lament himself.

It does not appear that, after this return of his wants, he found mankind equally favourable to him as at his first appearance in the world. His story, though in reality not less melancholy, was less affecting because it was no longer new; it therefore procured him no new friends, and those that had formerly relieved him thought they might now consign him to others. He was now likewise considered by many rather as criminal than as unhappy; for the friends of Lord Tyrconnel, and of his mother, were sufficiently industrious to publish his weaknesses, which were indeed very numerous; and nothing was forgotten that might make him either hateful or ridiculous.

It cannot but be imagined that such representations of his faults must make great numbers less sensible of his distress; many, who had only an opportunity to hear one part, made no scruple to propagate the account which they received; many assisted their circulation from malice or revenge; and perhaps many pretended to credit them that they might with a better grace withdraw their regard, or withhold their assistance.

Savage, however, was not one of those who suffered himself to be injured without resistance, nor was less diligent in exposing the faults of Lord Tyrconnel, over whom he obtained at least this advantage, that he drove him first to the practice of outrage and violence; for he was so much provoked by the wit and virulence of Savage, that he came with a number of attendants, that did no honour to his courage, to beat him at a coffee-house. But it happened that he had left the place a few minutes; and his Lordship had, without danger, the pleasure of boasting how he would have treated him. Mr. Savage went next day to repay his visit at his own house, but was prevailed on by his domestics to retire without insisting upon seeing him.

Lord Tyrconnel was accused by Mr. Savage of some actions which scarcely any provocations will be thought sufficient to justify, such as seizing what he had in his lodgings, and other instances of wanton cruelty, by which he increased the distress of Savage without any advantage to himself.

These mutual accusations were retorted on both sides for many years with the utmost degree of virulence and rage, and time seemed rather to augment than diminish their resentment. That the anger of Mr. Savage should be kept alive is not strange, because he felt every day the consequences of the quarrel; but it might reasonably have been hoped that Lord Tyrconnel might have relented, and at length have forgot those provocations which, however they might have once inflamed him, had not in reality much hurt him.

The spirit of Mr. Savage indeed never suffered him to solicit a reconciliation; he returned reproach for reproach, and insult for insult; his superiority of wit supplied the disadvantages of his fortune, and enabled him to form a party, and prejudice great numbers in his favour.

But though this might be some gratification of his vanity, it afforded very little relief to his necessities; and he was very frequently reduced to uncommon hardships, of which, however, he never made any mean or importunate complaints, being formed rather to bear misery with fortitude than enjoy prosperity with moderation.

He now thought himself again at liberty to expose the cruelty of his mother; and therefore, I believe, about this time published "The Bastard," a poem remarkable for the vivacious sallies of thought in the beginning, where he makes a pompous enumeration of the imagi-

nary advantages of base birth, and the pathetic sentiments at the end, where he recounts the real calamities
which he suffered by the crime of his parents.

The vigour and spirit of the verses, the peculiar circumstances of the author, the novelty of the subject, and
the notoriety of the story to which the allusions are
made, procured this performance a very favourable reception; great numbers were immediately dispersed, and
editions were multiplied with unusual rapidity.

One circumstance attended the publication which
Savage used to relate with great satisfaction. His mother,
to whom the poem was with "due reverence" inscribed,
happened then to be at Bath, where she could not conveniently retire from censure, or conceal herself from
observation; and no sooner did the reputation of the
poem begin to spread, than she heard it repeated in all
places of concourse, nor could she enter the assembly-
rooms, or cross the walks, without being saluted with
some lines from "The Bastard."

This was perhaps the first time that ever she discovered a sense of shame, and on this occasion the
power of wit was very conspicuous: the wretch who
had, without scruple, proclaimed herself an adulteress,
and who had first endeavoured to starve her son, then
to transport him, and afterwards to hang him, was not
able to bear the representation of her own conduct; but
fled from reproach, though she felt no pain from guilt,
and left Bath with the utmost haste, to shelter herself
among the crowds of London.

Thus Savage had the satisfaction of finding, that,
though he could not reform his mother, he could punish
her, and that he did not always suffer alone.

The pleasure which he received from this increase of
his poetical reputation was sufficient for some time to
overbalance the miseries of want, which this perform-

ance did not much alleviate; for it was sold for a very trivial sum to a bookseller [T. Worrall], who, though the success was so uncommon that five impressions were sold, of which many were undoubtedly very numerous, had not generosity sufficient to admit the unhappy writer to any part of the profit.

The sale of this poem was always mentioned by Mr. Savage with the utmost elevation of heart, and referred to by him as an incontestable proof of a general acknowledgment of his abilities. It was indeed the only production of which he could justly boast a general reception.

"The Bastard," however it might provoke or mortify his mother, could not be expected to melt her to compassion, so that he was still under the same want of the necessaries of life; and he therefore exerted all the interest which his wit, or his birth, or his misfortunes could procure, to obtain, upon the death of Eusden, the place of poet-laureat, and prosecuted his application with so much diligence, that the King publicly declared it his intention to bestow it upon him; but such was the fate of Savage, that even the King, when he intended his advantage, was disappointed in his schemes; for the Lord Chamberlain, who has the disposal of the laurel, as one of the appendages of his office, either did not know the King's design, or did not approve it, or thought the nomination of the laureat an encroachment upon his rights, and therefore bestowed the laurel upon Colley Cibber.

Mr. Savage, thus disappointed, took a resolution of applying to the Queen, that, having once given him life, she would enable him to support it, and therefore published a short poem on her birthday, to which he gave the odd title of "Volunteer Laureat." The event of this essay he has himself related in the following letter, which he prefixed to the poem, when he afterwards reprinted it in *The Gentleman's Magazine*, from whence I have copied it entire, as this was one of the few attempts in which Mr. Savage succeeded.

[1738].

Mr. Urban,

In your Magazine for February you published the last *Volunteer Laureat*, written on a very melancholy occasion, viz. the death of the royal patroness of arts and literature in general, and of the author of that poem in particular; I now send you the first that Mr. Savage wrote under that title.— This gentleman, notwithstanding a very considerable interest, being, on the death of Mr. Eusden, disappointed of the Laureat's place, wrote the following verses; which were no sooner published but the late Queen sent to a bookseller for them. The author had not at that time a friend either to get him introduced, or his poem presented at Court; yet such was the unspeakable goodness of that Princess, that, notwithstanding this act of ceremony was wanting, in a few days after publication Mr. Savage received a bank-bill of fifty pounds, and a gracious message from her Majesty, by the Lord North and Guildford, to this effect: "That her Majesty was highly pleased with the verses; that she took particularly kind his lines there relating to the King; that he had permission to write annually on the same subject; and that he should yearly receive the like present till something better (which was her Majesty's intention) could be done for him." After this, he was permitted to present one of his annual poems to her Majesty, had the honour of kissing her hand, and met with the most gracious reception.

Yours, T. B.

Such was the performance, and such its reception; a reception which, though by no means unkind, was yet not in the highest degree generous: to chain down the genius of a writer to an annual panegyric, showed in the Queen too much desire of hearing her own praises, and a greater regard to herself than to him on whom her bounty was conferred. It was a kind of avaricious generosity, by which flattery was rather purchased than genius rewarded.

Mrs. Oldfield had formerly given him the same allowance with much more heroic intention: she had no other view than to enable him to prosecute his studies, and to set himself above the want of assistance, and was contented with doing good without stipulating for encomiums.

Mr. Savage, however, was not at liberty to make exceptions, but was ravished with the favours which he had received, and probably yet more with those which he was promised: he considered himself now as a favourite of the Queen, and did not doubt but a few annual poems would establish him in some profitable employment.

He therefore assumed the title of "Volunteer Laureat," not without some reprehensions from Cibber, who informed him that the title of "Laureat" was a mark of honour conferred by the King, from whom all honour is derived, and which therefore no man has a right to bestow upon himself; and added, that he might, with equal propriety, style himself a Volunteer Lord, or Volunteer Baronet. It cannot be denied that the remark was just; but Savage did not think any title which was conferred upon Mr. Cibber so honourable as that the usurpation of it could be imputed to him as an instance of very exorbitant vanity, and therefore continued to write under the same title, and received every year the same reward.

He did not appear to consider these encomiums as tests of his abilities, or as anything more than annual hints to the Queen of her promise, or acts of ceremony, by the performance of which he was entitled to his pension, and therefore did not labour them with great diligence, or print more than fifty each year, except that for some of the last years he regularly inserted them in *The Gentleman's Magazine,* by which they were dispersed over the kingdom.

Of some of them he had himself so low an opinion, that he intended to omit them in the collection of poems for which he printed proposals, and solicited subscriptions; nor can it seem strange that, being confined to the same subject, he should be at some times indolent, and at others unsuccessful; that he should sometimes delay a disagreeable task till it was too late to perform it well; or that he should sometimes repeat the same sentiment on the same occasion, or at others be misled by an attempt after novelty to forced conceptions and far-fetched images.

He wrote indeed with a double intention, which supplied him with some variety; for his business was to praise the Queen for the favours which he had received, and to complain to her of the delay of those which she had promised: in some of his pieces, therefore, gratitude is predominant, and in some discontent; in some, he represents himself as happy in her patronage; and in others, as disconsolate to find himself neglected.

Her promise, like other promises made to this unfortunate man, was never performed, though he took sufficient care that it should not be forgotten. The publication of his *Volunteer Laureat* procured him no other reward than a regular remittance of 50*l.*

He was not so depressed by his disappointments as to neglect any opportunity that was offered of advancing his interest. When [14th March, 1734] the Princess Anne was married, he wrote a poem upon her departure, only, as he declared, "because it was expected from him," and he was not willing to bar his own prospects by any appearance of neglect.

He never mentioned any advantage gained by this

poem, or any regard that was paid to it; and therefore it is likely that it was considered at court as an act of duty, to which he was obliged by his dependence, and which it was therefore not necessary to reward by any new favour: or perhaps the Queen really intended his advancement, and therefore thought it superfluous to lavish presents upon a man whom she intended to establish for life.

About this time [1735] not only his hopes were in danger of being frustrated, but his pension likewise of being obstructed, by an accidental calumny. The writer of *The Daily Courant*, a paper then published under the direction of the ministry, charged him with a crime, which, though very great in itself, would have been remarkably invidious in him, and might very justly have incensed the Queen against him. He was accused by name of influencing elections against the court, by appearing at the head of a Tory mob; nor did the accuser fail to aggravate his crime, by representing it as the effect of the most atrocious ingratitude, and a kind of rebellion against the Queen, who had first preserved him from an infamous death, and afterwards distinguished him by her favour, and supported him by her charity. The charge, as it was open and confident, was likewise by good fortune very particular. The place of the transaction was mentioned, and the whole series of the rioter's conduct related. This exactness made Mr. Savage's vindication easy; for he never had in his life seen the place which was declared to be the scene of his wickedness, nor ever had been present in any town when its representatives were chosen. This answer he therefore made haste to publish, with all the circumstances necessary to make it credible; and very reasonably demanded that the accusation should be retracted in the same paper, that he might no longer suffer the imputation of sedition and ingratitude. This demand was likewise pressed by him in a private letter to the author of the paper, who, either trusting to the protection of those whose defence he had undertaken, or having entertained some personal malice against Mr. Savage, or fearing lest, by retracting so confident an assertion, he should impair the credit of his paper, refused to give him that satisfaction.

Mr. Savage therefore thought it necessary, to his own vindication, to prosecute him in the King's Bench; but as he did not find any ill effects from the accusation, having sufficiently cleared his innocence, he thought any further procedure would have the appearance of revenge, and therefore willingly dropped it.

He was still in his usual exigences, having no certain support but the pension allowed him by the Queen, which, though it might have kept an exact economist from want, was very far from being sufficient for Mr. Savage, who had never been accustomed to dismiss any of his appetites without the gratification which they solicited, and whom nothing but want of money withheld from partaking of every pleasure that fell within his view.

His conduct with regard to his pension was very particular. No sooner had he changed the bill, than he vanished from the sight of all his acquaintance, and lay for some time out of the reach of all the inquiries that friendship or curiosity could make after him; at length he appeared again penniless as before, but never informed even those whom he seemed to regard most, where he had been; nor was his retreat ever discovered.

This was his constant practice during the whole time that he received the pension from the Queen; he regularly disappeared and returned. He indeed affirmed that he retired to study, and that the money supported him in solitude for many months; but his friends declared that the short time in which it was spent sufficiently confuted his own account of his conduct.

His politeness and his wit still raised him friends, who were desirous of setting him at length free from that indigence by which he had been hitherto oppressed; and therefore solicited Sir Robert Walpole in his favour with so much earnestness, that they obtained a promise of the next place that should become vacant, not exceeding 200*l*. a year. This promise was made with an uncommon declaration, "that it was not the promise of a minister to a petitioner, but of a friend to his friend."

Mr. Savage now concluded himself set at ease for ever, and, as he observes in a poem written on that incident of his life, trusted and was trusted; but soon found that his confidence was ill-grounded, and this friendly promise was not inviolable. He spent a long time in solicitations, and at last despaired and desisted.

He did not indeed deny that he had given the minister some reason to believe that he should not strengthen his own interest by advancing him, for he had taken care to distinguish himself in coffee-houses as an advocate for the ministry of the last years of Queen Anne, and was always ready to justify the conduct and exalt the character of Lord Bolingbroke, whom he mentions with great regard in an Epistle upon Authors, which he wrote about that time; but was too wise to publish, and of which only some fragments have appeared, inserted by him in the *Magazine* after his retirement.

To despair was not, however, the character of Savage; when one patronage failed, he had recourse to another. The Prince was now extremely popular, and had very liberally rewarded the merit of some writers whom Mr. Savage did not think superior to himself, and therefore he resolved to address a poem to him.

For this purpose he made choice of a subject which could regard only persons of the highest rank and greatest affluence, and which was therefore proper for a poem intended to procure the patronage of a prince; and having retired for some time to Richmond, that he might prosecute his design in full tranquillity, without the temptations of pleasure, or the solicitations of creditors, by which his meditations were in equal danger of being disconcerted, he produced [June 1737] a poem "On Public Spirit, with regard to Public Works."

The plan of this poem is very extensive, and comprises a multitude of topics, each of which might furnish matter sufficient for a long performance, and of which some have already employed more eminent writers; but as he was perhaps not fully acquainted with the whole extent of his own design, and was writing to obtain a supply of wants too pressing to admit of long or accurate inquiries, he passes negligently over many public works, which, even in his own opinion, deserved to be more elaborately treated.

In describing villas and gardens, he did not omit to condemn that absurd custom which prevails among the English, of permitting servants to receive money from strangers for the entertainment that they receive, and therefore inserted in his poem these lines:

But what the flowering pride of gardens rare,
However royal, or however fair,
If gates, which to access should still give way,
Ope but, like Peter's paradise, for pay?
If perquisited varlets frequent stand,
And each new walk must a new tax demand?
What foreign eye but with contempt surveys?
What Muse shall from oblivion snatch their praise?

But before the publication of his performance he recollected that the Queen allowed her garden and cave at Richmond to be shown for money, and that she so openly countenanced the practice, that she had bestowed the privilege of showing them as a place of profit on a man whose merit she valued herself upon rewarding, though she gave him only the liberty of disgracing his country.

He therefore thought, with more prudence than was often exerted by him, that the publication of these lines might be officiously represented as an insult upon the Queen, to whom he owed his life and his subsistence; and that the propriety of his observation would be no security against the censures which the unseasonableness of it might draw upon him; he therefore suppressed the passage in the first edition, but after the Queen's death thought the same caution no longer necessary, and restored it to the proper place.

The poem was, therefore, published without any political faults, and inscribed to the Prince; but Mr. Savage, having no friend upon whom he could prevail to present it to him, had no other method of attracting his observation than the publication of frequent advertisements, and therefore received no reward from his patron, however generous on other occasions.

This disappointment he never mentioned without indignation, being by some means or other confident that the Prince was not ignorant of his address to him; and insinuated that, if any advances in popularity could have been made by distinguishing him, he had not written without notice, or without reward.

He was once inclined to have presented his poem in person, and sent to the printer for a copy with that design; but either his opinion changed, or his resolution deserted him, and he continued to resent neglect without attempting to force himself into regard.

Nor was the public much more favourable than his patron, for only seventy-two were sold, though the performance was much commended by some whose judgment in that kind of writing is generally allowed. But Savage easily reconciled himself to mankind without imputing any defect to his work, by observing that his poem was unluckily published two days after the prorogation of the Parliament, and by consequence at a time when all those who could be expected to regard it were in the hurry of preparing for their departure, or engaged in taking leave of others upon their dismission from public affairs.

It must be however allowed, in justification of the public, that this performance is not the most excellent of Mr. Savage's works; and that, though it cannot be denied to contain many striking sentiments, majestic lines, and just observations, it is in general not sufficiently polished in the language, or enlivened in the imagery, or digested in the plan.

Thus his poem contributed nothing to the alleviation of his poverty, which was such as very few could have supported with equal patience; but to which, it must likewise be confessed, that few would have been exposed who received punctually 50*l.* a year: a salary which, though by no means equal to the demands of vanity and luxury, is yet found sufficient to support families above want, and was undoubtedly more than the necessities of life require.

But no sooner had he received his pension than he withdrew to his darling privacy, from which he returned in a short time to his former distress, and for some part of the year generally lived by chance, eating only when he was invited to the tables of his acquaintances, from which the meanness of his dress often excluded him, when the politeness and variety of his conversation would have been thought a sufficient recompense for his entertainment.

He lodged as much by accident as he dined, and passed the night sometimes in mean houses, which are set open at night to any casual wanderers, sometimes in cellars, among the riot and filth of the meanest and most profligate of the rabble; and sometimes, when he had not money to support even the expenses of these receptacles, walked about the streets till he was weary, and lay down in the summer upon a bulk, or in the winter, with his associates in poverty, among the ashes of a glass-house.

In this manner were passed those days and those nights which nature had enabled him to have employed in elevated speculations, useful studies, or pleasing conversations. On a bulk, in a cellar, or in a glass-house, among thieves and beggars, was to be found the author of "The Wanderer," the man of exalted sentiments, extensive views, and curious observations; the man whose remarks on life might have assisted the statesman, whose ideas of virtue might have enlightened the moralist, whose eloquence might have influenced senates, and whose delicacy might have polished courts.

It cannot but be imagined that such necessities might sometimes force him upon disreputable practices; and it is probable that these lines in "The Wanderer" were occasioned by his reflections on his own conduct:

> Though misery leads to happiness, and truth,
> Unequal to the load, this languid youth,
> (O, let none censure, if, untried by grief,
> If, amidst woes, untempted by relief,)
> He stoop'd reluctant to mean acts of shame,
> Which then, ev'n then, he scorn'd, and blush'd to name.

Whoever was acquainted with him was certain to be solicited for small sums, which the frequency of the request made in time considerable, and he was therefore quickly shunned by those who were become familiar enough to be trusted with his necessities; but his rambling manner of life, and constant appearance at houses of public resort, always procured him a new succession of friends, whose kindness had not been exhausted by repeated requests; so that he was seldom absolutely without resources, but had in his utmost exigences this comfort, that he always imagined himself sure of speedy relief.

It was observed, that he always asked favours of this kind without the least submission or apparent consciousness of dependence, and that he did not seem to look upon a compliance with his request as an obligation that deserved any extraordinary acknowledgments; but a refusal was resented by him as an affront, or complained of as an injury; nor did he readily reconcile himself to those who either denied to lend, or gave him afterwards any intimation that they expected to be repaid.

He was sometimes so far compassionated by those who knew both his merit and distresses that they received him into their families, but they soon discovered him to be a very incommodious inmate; for, being always accustomed to an irregular manner of life, he could not confine himself to any stated hours, or pay any regard to the rules of a family, but would prolong his conversation till midnight, without considering that business might require his friend's application in the morning; and, when he had persuaded himself to retire to bed, was not, without equal difficulty, called up to dinner: it was therefore impossible to pay him any distinction without the entire subversion of all economy, a kind of establishment which, wherever he went, he always appeared ambitious to overthrow.

It must therefore be acknowledged, in justification of

mankind, that it was not always by the negligence or
coldness of his friends that Savage was distressed, but
because it was in reality very difficult to preserve him
long in a state of ease. To supply him with money was a
hopeless attempt; for no sooner did he see himself master of a sum sufficient to set him free from care for a day
than he became profuse and luxurious. When once he
had entered a tavern, or engaged in a scheme of pleasure, he never retired till want of money obliged him to
some new expedient. If he was entertained in a family,
nothing was any longer to be regarded there but amusements and jollity; wherever Savage entered he immediately expected that order and business should fly before
him, that all should thenceforward be left to hazard, and
that no dull principle of domestic management should
be opposed to his inclination or intrude upon his gaiety.

His distresses, however afflictive, never dejected him;
in his lowest state he wanted not spirit to assert the natural dignity of wit, and was always ready to repress that
insolence which the superiority of fortune incited, and to
trample on that reputation which rose upon any other
basis than that of merit: he never admitted any gross
familiarities, or submitted to be treated otherwise than
as an equal. Once, when he was without lodging, meat,
or clothes, one of his friends, a man indeed not remarkable for moderation in his prosperity, left a message that
he desired to see him about nine in the morning. Savage
knew that his intention was to assist him; but was very
much disgusted that he should presume to prescribe the
hour of his attendance, and, I believe, refused to visit
him, and rejected his kindness.

The same invincible temper, whether firmness or obstinacy, appeared in his conduct to the Lord Tyrconnel,
from whom he very frequently demanded that the allowance which was once paid him should be restored;

but with whom he never appeared to entertain for a moment the thought of soliciting a reconciliation, and whom he treated at once with all the haughtiness of superiority and all the bitterness of resentment. He wrote to him not in a style of supplication or respect, but of reproach, menace, and contempt; and appeared determined, if he ever regained his allowance, to hold it only by the right of conquest.

As many more can discover that a man is richer than that he is wiser than themselves, superiority of understanding is not so readily acknowledged as that of fortune; nor is that haughtiness which the consciousness of great abilities incites borne with the same submission as the tyranny of affluence; and therefore Savage, by asserting his claim to deference and regard, and by treating those with contempt whom better fortune animated to rebel against him, did not fail to raise a great number of enemies in the different classes of mankind. Those who thought themselves raised above him by the advantages of riches hated him because they found no protection from the petulance of his wit. Those who were esteemed for their writings feared him as a critic and maligned him as a rival; and almost all the smaller wits were his professed enemies.

Among these Mr. Miller so far indulged his resentment as to introduce him in a farce, and direct him to be personated on the stage in a dress like that which he then wore; a mean insult, which only insinuated that Savage had but one coat, and which was therefore despised by him rather than resented; for though he wrote a lampoon against Miller, he never printed it: and as no other person ought to prosecute that revenge from which the person who was injured desisted, I shall not preserve what Mr. Savage suppressed; of which the publication would indeed have been a punishment too severe for so impotent an assault.

The great hardships of poverty were to Savage not the want of lodging or of food, but the neglect and contempt which it drew upon him. He complained that as his affairs grew desperate, he found his reputation for capacity visibly decline; that his opinion in questions of criticism was no longer regarded when his coat was out of fashion; and that those who, in the interval of his prosperity, were always encouraging him to great undertakings by encomiums on his genius and assurances of success, now received any mention of his designs with coldness—thought that the subjects on which he proposed to write were very difficult; and were ready to inform him that the event of a poem was uncertain; that an author ought to employ much time in the consideration of his plan, and not presume to sit down to write in consequence of a few cursory ideas and a superficial knowledge: difficulties were started on all sides, and he was no longer qualified for any performance but "The Volunteer Laureat."

Yet even this kind of contempt never depressed him; for he always preserved a steady confidence in his own capacity, and believed nothing above his reach which he should at any time earnestly endeavour to attain. He formed schemes of the same kind with regard to knowledge and to fortune, and flattered himself with advances to be made in science, as with riches, to be enjoyed in some distant period of his life. For the acquisition of knowledge he was indeed far better qualified than for that of riches; for he was naturally inquisitive and desirous of the conversation of those from whom any information was to be obtained, but by no means solicitous to improve those opportunities that were sometimes offered of raising his fortune; and he was remarkably retentive of his ideas, which, when once he was in possession of them, rarely forsook him; a quality which could never be communicated to his money.

While he was thus wearing out his life in expectation that the Queen would some time recollect her promise, he had recourse to the usual practice of writers, and published proposals for printing his works by subscription, to which he was encouraged by the success of many who had not a better right to the favour of the public; but, whatever was the reason, he did not find the world equally inclined to favour him; and he observed, with some discontent, that though he offered his works at half a guinea, he was able to procure but a small number in comparison with those who subscribed twice as much to Duck.

Nor was it without indignation that he saw his proposals neglected by the Queen, who patronised Mr. Duck's with uncommon ardour, and incited a competition among those who attended the court who should most promote his interest, and who should first offer a subscription. This was a distinction to which Mr. Savage made no scruple of asserting that his birth, his misfortunes, and his genius gave a fairer title than could be pleaded by him on whom it was conferred.

Savage's applications were, however, not universally unsuccessful; for some of the nobility countenanced his design, encouraged his proposals, and subscribed with great liberality. He related of the Duke of Chandos particularly, that upon receiving his proposals he sent him ten guineas.

But the money which his subscriptions afforded him was not less volatile than that which he received from his other schemes; whenever a subscription was paid him he went to a tavern; and, as money so collected is necessarily received in small sums, he never was able to send his poems to the press, but for many years continued his solicitation and squandered whatever he obtained.

This project of printing his works was frequently revived; and, as his proposals grew obsolete, new ones were printed with fresher dates. To form schemes for the publication was one of his favourite amusements; nor was he ever more at ease than when, with any friend who readily fell in with his schemes, he was adjusting the print, forming the advertisements, and regulating the dispersion of his new edition, which he really intended some time to publish, and which, as long as experience had shown him the impossibility of printing the volume together, he at last determined to divide into weekly or monthly numbers, that the profits of the first might supply the expenses of the next.

Thus he spent his time in mean expedients and tormenting suspense, living for the greatest part in fear of prosecutions from his creditors, and consequently skulking in obscure parts of the town, of which he was no stranger to the remotest corners. But, wherever he came, his address secured him friends, whom his necessities soon alienated; so that he had, perhaps, a more numerous acquaintance than any man ever before attained, there being scarcely any person eminent on any account to whom he was not known, or whose character he was not in some degree able to delineate.

To the acquisition of this extensive acquaintance every circumstance of his life contributed. He excelled in the arts of conversation, and therefore willingly practised them. He had seldom any home, or even a lodging in which he could be private; and therefore was driven into public-houses for the common conveniences of life and supports of nature. He was always ready to comply

with every invitation, having no employment to withhold him, and often no money to provide for himself;
and by dining with one company he never failed of obtaining an introduction into another.

Thus dissipated was his life, and thus casual his subsistence; yet did not the distraction of his views hinder
him from reflection, nor the uncertainty of his condition
depress his gaiety. When he had wandered about without any fortunate adventure by which he was led into
a tavern, he sometimes retired into the fields, and was
able to employ his mind in study, to amuse it with pleasing imaginations; and seldom appeared to be melancholy but when some sudden misfortune had just fallen
upon him, and even then in a few moments he would
disentangle himself from his perplexity, adopt the subject of conversation, and apply his mind wholly to the
objects that others presented to it.

This life, unhappy as it may be already imagined, was
yet embittered, in 1738, with new calamities. The death
of the Queen [20th Nov. 1737] deprived him of all the
prospects of preferment with which he so long entertained his imagination; and, as Sir Robert Walpole had
before given him reason to believe that he never intended the performance of his promise, he was now
abandoned again to fortune.

He was, however, at that time supported by a friend;
and as it was not his custom to look out for distant calamities, or to feel any other pain than that which forced
itself upon his senses, he was not much afflicted at his
loss, and perhaps comforted himself that his pension
would be now continued without the annual tribute of a
panegyric.

Another expectation contributed likewise to support
him: he had taken a resolution to write a second tragedy
upon the story of Sir Thomas Overbury, in which he

preserved a few lines of his former play, but made a total alteration of the plan, added new incidents, and introduced new characters; so that it was a new tragedy, not a revival of the former.

Many of his friends blamed him for not making choice of another subject; but, in vindication of himself, he asserted that it was not easy to find a better; and that he thought it his interest to extinguish the memory of the first tragedy, which he could only do by writing one less defective upon the same story; by which he should entirely defeat the artifice of the booksellers, who, after the death of any author of reputation, are always industrious to swell his works by uniting his worst productions with his best.

In the execution of this scheme, however, he proceeded but slowly, and probably only employed himself upon it when he could find no other amusement; but he pleased himself with counting the profits, and perhaps imagined that the theatrical reputation which he was about to acquire would be equivalent to all that he had lost by the death of his patroness.

He did not, in confidence of his approaching riches, neglect the measures proper to secure the continuance of his pension, though some of his favourers thought him culpable for omitting to write on her death; but on her birthday next year [1st March, 1737-8] he gave a proof of the solidity of his judgment and the power of his genius. He knew that the track of elegy had been so long beaten that it was impossible to travel in it without treading in the footsteps of those who had gone before him; and that therefore it was necessary, that he might distinguish himself from the herd of encomiasts, to find out some new walk of funeral panegyric.

This difficult task he performed in such a manner that his poem may be justly ranked among the best pieces that the death of princes has produced. By transferring the mention of her death to her birthday he has formed a happy combination of topics, which any other man would have thought it very difficult to connect in one view, but which he has united in such a manner that the relation between them appears natural; and it may be justly said, that what no other man would have thought on, it now appears scarcely possible for any man to miss.

The beauty of this peculiar combination of images is so masterly that it is sufficient to set this poem above censure; and therefore it is not necessary to mention many other delicate touches which may be found in it, and which would deservedly be admired in any other performance.

To these proofs of his genius may be added, from the same poem, an instance of his prudence, an excellence for which he was not so often distinguished; he does not forget to remind the King, in the most delicate and artful manner, of continuing his pension.

With regard to the success of this address he was for some time in suspense, but was in no great degree solicitous about it, and continued his labour upon his new tragedy with great tranquillity, till the friend who had for a considerable time supported him, removing his family to another place, took occasion to dismiss him. It then became necessary to inquire more diligently what was determined in his affair, having reason to suspect that no great favour was intended him, because he had not received his pension at the usual time.

It is said that he did not take those methods of retrieving his interest which were most likely to succeed; and some of those who were employed in the Exchequer cautioned him against too much violence in his proceedings: but Mr. Savage, who seldom regulated his conduct by the advice of others, gave way to his passion, and demanded of Sir Robert Walpole, at his levee, the reason of the distinction that was made between him and the other pensioners of the Queen, with a degree of roughness which perhaps determined him to withdraw what had been only delayed.

Whatever was the crime of which he was accused or suspected, and whatever influence was employed against him, he received soon after an account that took from him all hopes of regaining his pension; and he had now no prospect of subsistence but from his play, and he knew no way of living for the time required to finish it.

So peculiar were the misfortunes of this man, deprived of an estate and title by a particular law, exposed and abandoned by a mother, defrauded by a mother of a fortune which his father had allotted him, he entered the world without a friend; and though his abilities forced themselves into esteem and reputation, he was never able to obtain any real advantage, and whatever prospects arose were always intercepted as he began to approach them. The King's intentions in his favour were frustrated; his Dedication to the Prince, whose generosity on every other occasion was eminent, procured him no reward; Sir Robert Walpole, who valued himself upon keeping his promise to others, broke it to him without regret; and the bounty of the Queen was, after her death, withdrawn from him, and from him only.

Such were his misfortunes, which yet he bore not only with decency, but with cheerfulness; nor was his gaiety clouded even by his last disappointments, though he was in a short time reduced to the lowest degree of distress, and often wanted both lodging and food. At this time he gave another instance of the insurmountable obstinacy of his spirit: his clothes were worn out, and he received notice that at a coffee-house some clothes and linen were left for him; the person who sent them did not, I believe, inform him to whom he was to be obliged, that he might spare the perplexity of acknowledging the benefit; but though the offer was so far generous, it was made with some neglect of ceremonies, which Mr. Savage so much resented that he refused the present, and declined to enter the house till the clothes that had been designed for him were taken away.

His distress was now publicly known, and his friends, therefore, thought it proper to concert some measures for his relief; and one of them [Pope] wrote a letter to him, in which he expressed his concern "for the miserable withdrawing of his pension," and gave him hopes that in a short time he should find himself supplied with a competence, "without any dependence on those little creatures which we are pleased to call the great."

The scheme proposed for this happy and independent subsistence was, that he should retire into Wales, and receive an allowance of 50l. a year, to be raised by a subscription, on which he was to live privately in a cheap place, without aspiring any more to affluence, or having any further care of reputation.

This offer Mr. Savage gladly accepted, though with intentions very different from those of his friends; for they proposed that he should continue an exile from London for ever, and spend all the remaining part of his life at Swansea; but he designed only to take the opportunity which their scheme offered him of retreating for a short time that he might prepare his play for the stage, and his other works for the press, and then to return to London to exhibit his tragedy, and live upon the profits of his own labour.

With regard to his works, he proposed very great improvements, which would have required much time or great application; and when he had finished them, he designed to do justice to his subscribers by publishing them according to his proposals.

As he was ready to entertain himself with future pleasures, he had planned out a scheme of life for the country, of which he had no knowledge but from pastorals and songs. He imagined that he should be transported to scenes of flowery felicity, like those which one poet has reflected to another; and had projected a perpetual round of innocent pleasures, of which he suspected no interruption from pride, or ignorance, or brutality.

With these expectations he was so enchanted, that when he was once gently reproached by a friend for submitting to live upon a subscription, and advised rather by a resolute exertion of his abilities to support himself, he could not bear to debar himself from the happiness which was to be found in the calm of a cottage, or lose the opportunity of listening without intermission to the melody of the nightingale, which he believed was to be heard from every bramble, and which he did not fail to mention as a very important part of the happiness of a country life.

While this scheme was ripening, his friends directed him to take a lodging in the liberties of the Fleet, that he might be secure from his creditors, and sent him every Monday a guinea, which he commonly spent before the next morning, and trusted, after his usual manner, the remaining part of the week to the bounty of fortune.

He now began very sensibly to feel the miseries of dependence. Those by whom he was to be supported began to prescribe to him with an air of authority, which he knew not how decently to resent, nor patiently to bear; and he soon discovered, from the conduct of most of his subscribers, that he was yet in the hands of "little creatures."

Of the insolence that he was obliged to suffer he gave many instances, of which none appeared to raise his indignation to a greater height than the method which was taken of furnishing him with clothes. Instead of consulting him, and allowing him to send a tailor his orders for what they thought proper to allow him, they proposed to send for a tailor to take his measure, and then to consult how they should equip him.

This treatment was not very delicate, nor was it such as Savage's humanity would have suggested to him on a like occasion; but it had scarcely deserved mention had it not, by affecting him in an uncommon degree, shown the peculiarity of his character. Upon hearing the design that was formed, he came to the lodging of a friend with the most violent agonies of rage; and, being asked what it could be that gave him such disturbance, he replied with the utmost vehemence of indignation, "That they had sent for a tailor to measure him."

How the affair ended was never inquired, for fear of renewing his uneasiness. It is probable that, upon recollection, he submitted with a good grace to what he could not avoid, and that he discovered no resentment where he had no power.

He was, however, not humbled to implicit and universal compliance; for when the gentleman who had first informed him of the design to support him by a subscription attempted to procure a reconciliation with the Lord Tyrconnel, he could by no means be prevailed upon to comply with the measures that were proposed.

A letter was written for him to Sir William Leman, to prevail upon him to interpose his good offices with Lord Tyrconnel, in which he solicited Sir William's assistance "for a man who really needed it as much as any man could well do"; and informed him that he was retiring "for ever to a place where he should no more trouble his relations, friends, or enemies"; he confessed that his passion had betrayed him to some conduct with regard to Lord Tyrconnel for which he could not but heartily ask his pardon; and as he imagined Lord Tyrconnel's passion might be yet so high that he would not "receive a letter from him," begged that Sir William would endeavour to soften him; and expressed his hopes that he would comply with his request, and that "so small a relation would not harden his heart against him."

That any man should presume to dictate a letter to him was not very agreeable to Mr. Savage; and therefore he was, before he had opened it, not much inclined to approve it. But when he read it, he found it contained sentiments entirely opposite to his own, and, as he asserted, to the truth; and, therefore, instead of copying it, wrote his friend a letter full of masculine resentment and warm expostulations. He very justly observed, that the style was too supplicatory, and the representation too abject, and that he ought at least to have made him complain with "the dignity of a gentleman in distress." He declared that he would not write the paragraph in which he was to ask Lord Tyrconnel's pardon, for "he despised his pardon, and therefore could not heartily, and would not hypocritically, ask it." He remarked that his friend made a very unreasonable distinction between himself and him; for, says he, "when you mention men of high rank in your own character," they are "those little creatures whom we are pleased to call the great"; but when you address them "in mine," no servility is sufficiently humble. He then with great propriety explained the ill consequences which might be expected from such a letter, which his relations would print in their own defence, and which would for ever be produced as a full answer to all that he should allege against them; for he always intended to publish a minute account of the treatment which he had received. It is to be remembered, to the honour of the gentleman by whom this letter was drawn up, that he yielded to Mr. Savage's reasons, and agreed that it ought to be suppressed.

After many alterations and delays a subscription was at length raised, which did not amount to 50*l*. a year, though twenty were paid by one gentleman: such was the generosity of mankind, that what had been done by a player without solicitation could not now be effected by application and interest; and Savage had a great number to court and to obey for a pension less than that which Mrs. Oldfield paid him without exacting any servilities.

Mr. Savage, however, was satisfied, and willing to retire, and was convinced that the allowance, though scanty, would be more than sufficient for him, being now determined to commence a rigid economist, and to live according to the exact rules of frugality; for nothing was in his opinion more contemptible than a man who, when he knew his income, exceeded it; and yet he confessed that instances of such folly were too common, and lamented that some men were not to be trusted with their own money.

Full of these salutary resolutions, he left London in July 1739, having taken leave with great tenderness of his friends, and parted from the author of this narrative with tears in his eyes. He was furnished with fifteen guineas, and informed that they would be sufficient, not only for the expense of his journey, but for his support in Wales for some time; and that there remained but little more of the first collection. He promised a strict adherence to his maxims of parsimony, and went away in the stage-coach; nor did his friends expect to hear from him till he informed them of his arrival at Swansea.

But when they least expected, arrived a letter dated the fourteenth day after his departure, in which he sent them word that he was yet upon the road, and without money, and that he therefore could not proceed without a remittance. They then sent him the money that was in their hands, with which he was enabled to reach Bristol, from whence he was to go to Swansea by water.

At Bristol he found an embargo laid upon the shipping, so that he could not immediately obtain a passage; and being therefore obliged to stay there some time, he with his usual felicity ingratiated himself with many of the principal inhabitants, was invited to their houses, distinguished at their public feasts, and treated with a regard that gratified his vanity, and therefore easily engaged his affection.

He began very early after his retirement to complain of the conduct of his friends in London, and irritated many of them so much by his letters that they withdrew, however honourably, their contributions; and it is believed that little more was paid him than the 20*l.* a year which were allowed him by the gentleman who proposed the subscription.

After some stay at Bristol he retired [Sept. 1742] to Swansea, the place originally proposed for his residence, where he lived about a year, very much dissatisfied with the diminution of his salary; but contracted, as in other places, acquaintance with those who were most distinguished in that country, among whom he has celebrated Mr. Powell and Mrs. Jones, by some verses which he inserted in *The Gentleman's Magazine*.

Here he completed his tragedy, of which two acts were wanting when he left London; and was desirous of coming to town to bring it upon the stage. This design was very warmly opposed; and he was advised, by his chief benefactor [Pope], to put it into the hands of Mr. Thomson and Mr. Mallet that it might be fitted for the stage, and to allow his friends to receive the profits, out of which an annual pension should be paid him.

This proposal he rejected with the utmost contempt. He was by no means convinced that the judgment of those to whom he was required to submit was superior to his own. He was now determined, as he expressed it, to be "no longer kept in leading-strings," and had no elevated idea of "his bounty who proposed to pension him out of the profits of his own labours."

He attempted in Wales to promote a subscription for his works, and had once hopes of success; but in a short time afterwards formed a resolution of leaving that part of the country, to which he thought it not reasonable to be confined for the gratification of those who, having promised him a liberal income, had no sooner banished him to a remote corner than they reduced his allowance to a salary scarcely equal to the necessities of life.

His resentment of this treatment, which, in his own opinion at least, he had not deserved, was such that he broke off all correspondence with most of his contributors, and appeared to consider them as persecutors and oppressors; and in the latter part of his life declared that their conduct towards him since his departure from London "had been perfidiousness improving on perfidiousness, and inhumanity on inhumanity."

It is not to be supposed that the necessities of Mr. Savage did not sometimes incite him to satirical exaggerations of the behaviour of those by whom he thought himself reduced to them. But it must be granted that the diminution of his allowance was a great hardship, and that those who withdrew their subscription from a man who, upon the faith of their promise, had gone into a

kind of banishment, and abandoned all those by whom
he had been before relieved in his distresses, will find it
no easy task to vindicate their conduct.

It may be alleged, and perhaps justly, that he was
petulant and contemptuous—that he more frequently
reproached his subscribers for not giving him more, than
thanked them for what he received; but it is to be
remembered that his conduct—and this is the worst
charge that can be drawn up against him—did them no
real injury; and that it therefore ought rather to have
been pitied than resented—at least the resentment it
might provoke ought to have been generous and manly;
epithets which his conduct will hardly deserve that
starves a man whom he has persuaded to put himself
into his power.

It might have been reasonably demanded by Savage
that they should, before they had taken away what they
promised, have replaced him in his former state—that
they should have taken no advantages from the situation to which the appearance of their kindness had reduced him—and that he should have been recalled to
London before he was abandoned. He might justly represent that he ought to have been considered as a lion
in the toils, and demand to be released before the dogs
should be loosed upon him.

He endeavoured, indeed, to release himself, and, with
an intent to return to London, went to Bristol, where a
repetition of the kindness which he had formerly found,
invited him to stay. He was not only caressed and
treated, but had a collection made for him of about 30*l.*,
with which it had been happy if he had immediately departed for London; but his negligence did not suffer him
to consider that such proofs of kindness were not often
to be expected, and that this ardour of benevolence was
in a great degree the effect of novelty, and might, prob-

ably, be every day less; and therefore he took no care to improve the happy time, but was encouraged by one favour to hope for another, till at length generosity was exhausted, and officiousness wearied.

Another part of his misconduct was the practice of prolonging his visits to unseasonable hours, and disconcerting all the families into which he was admitted. This was an error in a place of commerce, which all the charms of his conversation could not compensate: for what trader would purchase such airy satisfaction by the loss of solid gain?—which must be the consequence of midnight merriment, as those hours which were gained at night were generally lost in the morning.

Thus Mr. Savage, after the curiosity of the inhabitants was gratified, found the number of his friends daily decreasing, perhaps without suspecting for what reason their conduct was altered; for he still continued to harass, with his nocturnal intrusions, those that yet countenanced him, and admitted him to their houses.

But he did not spend all the time of his residence at Bristol in visits or at taverns, for he sometimes returned to his studies, and began several considerable designs. When he felt an inclination to write, he always retired from the knowledge of his friends, and lay hid in an obscure part of the suburbs, till he found himself again desirous of company, to which it is likely that intervals of absence made him more welcome.

He was always full of his design of returning to London to bring his tragedy upon the stage; but having neglected to depart with the money that was raised for him, he could not afterwards procure a sum sufficient to defray the expenses of his journey; nor perhaps would a fresh supply have had any other effect than, by putting immediate pleasures into his power, to have driven the thoughts of his journey out of his mind.

While he was thus spending the day in contriving a scheme for the morrow, distress stole upon him by imperceptible degrees. His conduct had already wearied some of those who were at first enamoured of his conversation; but he might, perhaps, still have devolved to others, whom he might have entertained with equal success, had not the decay of his clothes made it no longer consistent with their vanity to admit him to their tables, or to associate with him in public places. He now began to find every man from home at whose house he called, and was therefore no longer able to procure the necessaries of life, but wandered about the town, slighted and neglected, in quest of a dinner, which he did not always obtain.

To complete his misery, he was pursued by the officers for small debts which he had contracted, and was therefore obliged to withdraw from the small number of friends from whom he had still reason to hope for favours. His custom was to lie in bed the greatest part of the day, and to go out in the dark with the utmost privacy, and, after having paid his visit, return again before morning to his lodging, which was in the garret of an obscure inn.

Being thus excluded on one hand, and confined on the other, he suffered the utmost extremities of poverty, and often fasted so long that he was seized with faintness, and had lost his appetite, not being able to bear the smell of meat till the action of his stomach was restored by a cordial.

In this distress he received a remittance of 5*l.* from London, with which he provided himself a decent coat, and determined to go to London, but unhappily spent his money at a favourite tavern. Thus was he again confined to Bristol, where he was every day hunted by bailiffs. In this exigence he once more found a friend, who sheltered him in his house, though at the usual inconveniences with which his company was attended; for he could neither be persuaded to go to bed in the night, nor to rise in the day.

It is observable that in these various scenes of misery he was always disengaged and cheerful: he at some times pursued his studies, and at others continued or enlarged his epistolary correspondence; nor was he ever so far dejected as to endeavour to procure an increase of his allowance by any other methods than accusations and reproaches.

He had now no longer any hopes of assistance from his friends at Bristol, who as merchants, and by consequence sufficiently studious of profit, cannot be supposed to have looked with much compassion upon negligence and extravagance, or to think any excellence equivalent to a fault of such consequence as neglect of economy. It is natural to imagine that many of those who would have relieved his real wants were discouraged from the exertion of their benevolence by observation of the use which was made of their favours, and conviction that relief would only be momentary, and that the same necessity would quickly return.

At last he quitted the house of his friend, and returned to his lodging at the inn, still intending to set out in a few days for London; but on the 10th of January, 1742-3, having been at supper with two of his friends, he was at his return to his lodgings arrested for a debt of about 8*l.*, which he owed at a coffee-house, and conducted to the house of a sheriff's officer. The account which he gives of this misfortune, in a letter to one of the gentlemen with whom he had supped, is too remarkable to be omitted.

"It was not a little unfortunate for me that I spent

yesterday's evening with you, because the hour hindered me from entering on my new lodging; however, I have now got one, but such an one as I believe nobody would choose.

"I was arrested, at the suit of Mrs. Read, just as I was going upstairs to bed at Mr. Bowyer's, but taken in so private a manner, that I believe nobody at the White Lion is apprised of it: though I let the officers know the strength (or rather weakness) of my pocket, yet they treated me with the utmost civility; and even when they conducted me to confinement, it was in such a manner that I verily believe I could have escaped, which I would rather be ruined than have done, notwithstanding the whole amount of my finances was but threepence-halfpenny.

"In the first place I must insist that you will industriously conceal this from Mrs. S——s, because I would not have her good-nature suffer that pain which, I know, she would be apt to feel on this occasion.

"Next, I conjure you, dear Sir, by all the ties of friendship, by no means to have one uneasy thought on my account, but to have the same pleasantry of countenance and unruffled serenity of mind which (God be praised!) I have in this, and have had in a much severer calamity. Furthermore, I charge you, if you value my friendship as truly as I do yours, not to utter, or even harbour, the least resentment against Mrs. Read. I believe she has ruined me, but I freely forgive her; and (though I will never more have any intimacy with her) I would, at a due distance, rather do her an act of good than ill will. Lastly (pardon the expression), I absolutely command you not to offer me any pecuniary assistance, nor to attempt getting me any from any one of your friends. At another time, or on any other occasion, you may, dear friend, be well assured, I would rather write to you in the submissive style of a request, than that of a peremptory command.

"However, that my truly valuable friend may not think I am too proud to ask a favour, let me entreat you to let me have your boy to attend me for this day, not only for the sake of saving me the expense of porters, but for the delivery of some letters to people whose names I would not have known to strangers.

"The civil treatment I have thus far met from those whose prisoner I am makes me thankful to the Almighty, that though he has thought fit to visit me (on my birthnight) with affliction, yet (such is His great goodness!) my affliction is not without alleviating circumstances. I murmur not, but am all resignation to the Divine will. As to the world, I hope that I shall be endued by Heaven with that presence of mind, that serene dignity in misfortune, that constitutes the character of a true nobleman; a dignity far beyond that of coronets; a nobility arising from the just principles of philosophy, refined and exalted by those of Christianity."

He continued five days at the officer's, in hopes that he should be able to procure bail, and avoid the necessity of going to prison. The state in which he passed his time, and the treatment which he received, are very justly expressed by him in a letter which he wrote to a friend: "The whole day," says he, "has been employed in various people's filling my head with their foolish, chimerical systems, which has obliged me coolly (as far as nature will admit) to digest, and accommodate myself to every different person's way of thinking; hurried from one wild system to another, till it has quite made a chaos of my imagination, and nothing done—promised—disappointed—ordered to send every hour from one part of the town to the other."

When his friends, who had hitherto caressed and applauded, found that to give bail and pay the debt was the same, they all refused to preserve him from a prison at the expense of 8*l.*; and therefore, after having been for some time at the officer's house, "at an immense expense," as he observes in his letter, he was at length removed to Newgate.

This expense he was enabled to support by the generosity of Mr. Nash, at Bath, who, upon receiving from him an account of his condition, immediately sent him five guineas, and promised to promote his subscription at Bath with all his interest.

By his removal to Newgate he obtained at least a freedom from suspense, and rest from the disturbing vicissitudes of hope and disappointment; he now found that his friends were only companions who were willing to share his gaiety, but not to partake of his misfortunes; and therefore he no longer expected any assistance from them.

It must, however, be observed of one gentleman that he offered to release him by paying the debt, but that Mr. Savage would not consent, I suppose, because he thought he had before been too burthensome to him.

He was offered by some of his friends that a collection should be made for his enlargement, but he "treated the proposal," and declared "he should again treat it, with disdain. As to writing any mendicant letters, he had too high a spirit, and determined only to write to some ministers of State to try to regain his pension."

He continued to complain of those that had sent him into the country, and objected to them that he had "lost the profits of his play, which had been finished three years"; and in another letter declares his resolution to publish a pamphlet, that the world might know how "he had been used."

This pamphlet was never written; for he in a very short time recovered his usual tranquillity, and cheerfully applied himself to more inoffensive studies. He indeed steadily declared that he was promised a yearly allowance of 50*l*., and never received half the sum; but he seemed to resign himself to that as well as to other misfortunes, and lose the remembrance of it in his amusements and employments.

The cheerfulness with which he bore his confinement appears from the following letter which he wrote, January the 30th [1742-3], to one of his friends in London:

"I now write to you from my confinement in Newgate, where I have been ever since Monday last was se'nnight, and where I enjoy myself with much more tranquillity than I have known for upwards of a twelvemonth past, having a room entirely to myself, and pursuing the amusement of my poetical studies uninterrupted and agreeable to my mind. I thank the Almighty I am now all collected in myself, and though my person is in confinement, my mind can expatiate on ample and useful subjects with all the freedom imaginable. I am now more conversant with the Nine than ever, and if, instead of a Newgate bird, I may be allowed to be a bird of the Muses, I assure you, Sir, I sing very freely in my cage; sometimes indeed in the plaintive notes of the nightingale, but, at others, in the cheerful strains of the lark."

In another letter he observes that he ranges from one subject to another without confining himself to any particular task, and that he was employed one week upon one attempt, and the next upon another.

Surely the fortitude of this man deserves at least to be mentioned with applause; and whatever faults may be imputed to him, the virtue of suffering well cannot be denied him. The two powers which, in the opinion of

Epictetus, constituted a wise man, are those of bearing and forbearing, which it cannot indeed be affirmed to have been equally possessed by Savage; and indeed the want of one obliged him very frequently to practise the other.

He was treated by Mr. Dagge, the keeper of the prison, with great humanity; was supported by him at his own table without any certainty of recompense; had a room to himself to which he could at any time retire from all disturbance; was allowed to stand at the door of the prison, and sometimes taken out into the fields; so that he suffered fewer hardships in prison than he had been accustomed to undergo in the greatest part of his life.

The keeper did not confine his benevolence to a gentle execution of his office, but made some overtures to the creditor for his release, though without effect; and continued, during the whole time of his imprisonment, to treat him with the utmost tenderness and civility.

Virtue is undoubtedly most laudable in that state which makes it most difficult, and therefore the humanity of a gaoler certainly deserves this public attestation; and the man whose heart has not been hardened by such an employment, may be justly proposed as a pattern of benevolence. If an inscription was once engraved "to the honest toll-gatherer," less honours ought not to be paid "to the tender gaoler."

Mr. Savage very frequently received visits, and sometimes presents, from his acquaintances, but they did not amount to a subsistence, for the greater part of which he was indebted to the generosity of this keeper; but these favours, however they might endear to him the particular persons from whom he received them, were very far from impressing upon his mind any advantageous ideas of the people of Bristol, and therefore he thought he could not more properly employ himself in prison than in writing a poem called *London and Bristol delineated.*

When he had brought this poem to its present state, which, without considering the chasm, is not perfect, he wrote to London an account of his design, and informed his friend that he was determined to print it with his name, but enjoined him not to communicate his intention to his Bristol acquaintance. The gentleman, surprised at his resolution, endeavoured to dissuade him from publishing it, at least from prefixing his name; and declared that he could not reconcile the injunction of secrecy with his resolution to own it at its first appearance. To this Mr. Savage returned an answer agreeable to his character in the following terms:

"I received yours this morning, and not without a little surprise at the contents. To answer a question with a question, you ask me concerning London and Bristol, Why will I add *delineated?* Why did Mr. Woolaston add the same word to his *Religion of Nature?* I suppose that it was his will and pleasure to add it in his case; and it is mine to do so in my own. You are pleased to tell me that you understand not why secrecy is enjoined, and yet I intend to set my name to it. My answer is, I have my private reasons, which I am not obliged to explain to anyone. You doubt my friend Mr. S—— would not approve of it. And what is it to me whether he does or not? Do you imagine that Mr. S—— is to dictate to me? If any man who calls himself my friend should assume such an air, I would spurn at his friendship with contempt. You say I seem to think so by not letting him know it. And suppose I do, what then? Perhaps I can give reasons for that disapprobation, very foreign from what you would imagine. You go on in saying, Suppose I should not put my name to it. My answer is, that I will not suppose any such thing, being determined to the contrary: neither, Sir, would I have you suppose that I applied to you for want of another press; nor would I have you imagine that I owe Mr. S—— obligations which I do not."

Such was his imprudence, and such his obstinate adherence to his own resolutions, however absurd! A prisoner! supported by charity! and, whatever insults he might have received during the latter part of his stay at Bristol, once caressed, esteemed, and presented with a liberal collection, he could forget on a sudden his danger and his obligations to gratify the petulance of his wit or the eagerness of his resentment, and publish a satire, by which he might reasonably expect that he should alienate those who then supported him, and provoke those whom he could neither resist nor escape.

This resolution, from the execution of which it is probable that only his death could have hindered him, is sufficient to show how much he disregarded all considerations that opposed his present passions, and how readily he hazarded all future advantages for any immediate gratifications. Whatever was his predominant inclination, neither hope nor fear hindered him from complying with it; nor had opposition any other effect than to heighten his ardour and irritate his vehemence.

This performance was however laid aside while he was employed in soliciting assistance from several great persons; and one interruption succeeding another hindered him from supplying the chasm, and perhaps from retouching the other parts, which he can hardly be imagined to have finished in his own opinion, for it is very unequal, and some of the lines are rather inserted to rhyme to others than to support or improve the sense; but the first and last parts are worked up with great spirit and elegance.

His time was spent in the prison for the most part in study, or in receiving visits; but sometimes he descended to lower amusements, and diverted himself in the kitchen with the conversation of the criminals; for it was not pleasing to him to be much without company; and though he was very capable of a judicious choice, he was often contented with the first that offered; for this he was sometimes reproved by his friends, who found him surrounded with felons; but the reproof was on that, as on other occasions, thrown away; he continued to gratify himself, and to set very little value on the opinion of others.

But here, as in every other scene of his life, he made use of such opportunities as occurred of benefiting those who were more miserable than himself, and was always ready to perform any office of humanity to his fellow-prisoners.

He had now ceased from corresponding with any of his subscribers except one [Pope], who yet continued to remit him the 20*l.* a year which he had promised him, and by whom it was expected that he would have been in a very short time enlarged, because he had directed the keeper to inquire after the state of his debts.

However, he took care to enter his name according to the forms of the court, that the creditor might be obliged to make him some allowance if he was continued a prisoner, and when on that occasion he appeared in the hall, was treated with very unusual respect.

But the resentment of the city was afterwards raised by some accounts that had been spread of the satire; and he was informed that some of the merchants intended to pay the allowance which the law required, and to detain him a prisoner at their own expense. This he treated as an empty menace, and perhaps might have hastened the publication, only to show how much he was superior to their insults, had not all his schemes been suddenly destroyed.

When he had been six months in prison he received from one of his friends [Pope], in whose kindness he had the greatest confidence, and on whose assistance he chiefly depended, a letter that contained a charge of very atrocious ingratitude, drawn up in such terms as sudden resentment dictated. Henley, in one of his advertisements, had mentioned "Pope's treatment of Savage." This was supposed by Pope to be the consequence of a complaint made by Savage to Henley, and was therefore mentioned by him with much resentment. Mr. Savage returned a very solemn protestation of his innocence, but, however, appeared much disturbed at the accusation. Some days afterwards he was seized with a pain in his back and side, which, as it was not violent, was not suspected to be dangerous; but growing daily more languid and dejected, on the 25th of July he confined himself to his room and a fever seized his spirits. The symptoms grew every day more formidable, but his condition did not enable him to procure any assistance. The last time that the keeper saw him was on July the 31st, 1743, when Savage, seeing him at his bedside, said with an uncommon earnestness, "I have something to say to you, Sir," but, after a pause, moved his hand in a melancholy manner, and finding himself unable to recollect what he was going to communicate, said, " 'Tis gone!" The keeper soon after left him, and the next morning he died. He was buried in the churchyard of St. Peter [at Bristol], at the expense of the keeper.

Such were the life and death of Richard Savage, a man equally distinguished by his virtues and vices, and at once remarkable for his weaknesses and abilities.

He was of a middle stature, of a thin habit of body, a long visage, coarse features, and melancholy aspect; of a grave and manly deportment, a solemn dignity of mien, but which, upon a nearer acquaintance, softened into an engaging easiness of manners. His walk was slow, and his voice tremulous and mournful. He was easily excited to smiles, but very seldom provoked to laughter.

His mind was in an uncommon degree vigorous and active. His judgment was accurate, his apprehension quick, and his memory so tenacious that he was frequently observed to know what he had learned from others in a short time, better than those by whom he was informed, and could frequently recollect incidents, with all their combination of circumstances, which few would have regarded at the present time, but which the quickness of his apprehension impressed upon him. He had the art of escaping from his own reflections, and accommodating himself to every new scene.

To this quality is to be imputed the extent of his knowledge, compared with the small time which he spent in visible endeavours to acquire it. He mingled in cursory conversation with the same steadiness of attention as others apply to a lecture; and, amidst the appearance of thoughtless gaiety, lost no new idea that was started, nor any hint that could be improved. He had therefore made in coffee-houses the same proficiency as others in their closets; and it is remarkable that the writings of a man of little education and little reading have an air of learning scarcely to be found in any other performances, but which perhaps as often obscures as embellishes them.

His judgment was eminently exact both with regard to writings and to men. The knowledge of life was indeed his chief attainment; and it is not without some satisfaction that I can produce the suffrage of Savage in favour of human nature, of which he never appeared to entertain such odious ideas as some, who perhaps had neither his judgment nor experience, have published either in ostentation of their sagacity, vindication of their crimes, or gratification of their malice.

His method of life particularly qualified him for conversation, of which he knew how to practise all the graces. He was never vehement or loud, but at once modest and easy, open and respectful; his language was vivacious or elegant, and equally happy upon grave and humorous subjects. He was generally censured for not knowing when to retire; but that was not the defect of his judgment, but of his fortune; when he left his company, he was frequently to spend the remaining part of the night in the street, or at least was abandoned to gloomy reflections, which it is not strange that he delayed as long as he could; and sometimes forgot that he gave others pain to avoid it himself.

It cannot be said that he made use of his abilities for the direction of his own conduct: an irregular and dissipated manner of life had made him the slave of every passion that happened to be excited by the presence of its object, and that slavery to his passions reciprocally produced a life irregular and dissipated. He was not master of his own motions, nor could promise anything for the next day.

With regard to his economy, nothing can be added to the relation of his life. He appeared to think himself born to be supported by others, and dispensed from all necessity of providing for himself; he therefore never prosecuted any scheme of advantage, nor endeavoured even to secure the profits which his writings might have afforded him. His temper was, in consequence of the dominion of his passions, uncertain and capricious; he was easily engaged, and easily disgusted; but he is accused of retaining his hatred more tenaciously than his benevolence.

He was compassionate both by nature and principle, and always ready to perform offices of humanity; but when he was provoked (and very small offences were sufficient to provoke him), he would prosecute his revenge with the utmost acrimony till his passion had subsided.

His friendship was therefore of little value; for though he was zealous in the support or vindication of those whom he loved, yet it was always dangerous to trust him, because he considered himself as discharged by the first quarrel from all ties of honour or gratitude, and would betray those secrets which in the warmth of confidence had been imparted to him. This practice drew upon him an universal accusation of ingratitude: nor can it be denied that he was very ready to set himself free from the load of an obligation; for he could not bear to conceive himself in a state of dependence, his pride being equally powerful with his other passions, and appearing in the form of insolence at one time, and of vanity at another. Vanity, the most innocent species of pride, was most frequently predominant: he could not easily leave off when he had once begun to mention himself or his works; nor ever read his verses without stealing his eyes from the page, to discover in the faces of his audience how they were affected with any favourite passage.

A kinder name than that of vanity ought to be given to the delicacy with which he was always careful to separate his own merit from every other man's, and to reject that praise to which he had no claim. He did not forget, in mentioning his performances, to mark every line that had been suggested or amended; and was so accurate as to relate that he owed *three words* in "The Wanderer" to the advice of his friends.

His veracity was questioned, but with little reason; his accounts, though not indeed always the same, were generally consistent. When he loved any man, he suppressed all his faults; and, when he had been offended by him, concealed all his virtues: but his characters were generally true, so far as he proceeded; though it cannot be denied that his partiality might have sometimes the effect of falsehood.

In cases indifferent, he was zealous for virtue, truth, and justice: he knew very well the necessity of goodness to the present and future happiness of mankind; nor is there perhaps any writer who has less endeavoured to please by flattering the appetites, or perverting the judgment.

As an author, therefore (and he now ceases to influence mankind in any other character), if one piece which he had resolved to suppress be excepted, he has very little to fear from the strictest moral or religious censure. And though he may not be altogether secure against the objections of the critic, it must however be acknowledged that his works are the productions of a genius truly poetical; and, what many writers who have been more lavishly applauded cannot boast, that they have an original air, which has no resemblance of any foregoing writer; that the versification and sentiments have a cast peculiar to themselves, which no man can imitate with success, because what was nature in Savage, would in another be affectation. It must be confessed, that his descriptions are striking, his images animated, his fictions justly imagined, and his allegories artfully pursued; that his diction is elevated, though sometimes forced, and his numbers sonorous and majestic, though frequently sluggish and encumbered. Of his style, the general fault is harshness, and its general excellence is dignity; of his sentiments, the prevailing beauty is simplicity, and uniformity the prevailing defect.

For his life, or for his writings, none, who candidly consider his fortune, will think an apology either necessary or difficult. If he was not always sufficiently instructed in his subject, his knowledge was at least greater than could have been attained by others in the same state. If his works were sometimes unfinished, accuracy cannot reasonably be exacted from a man oppressed with want, which he has no hope of relieving but by a speedy publication. The insolence and resentment of which he is accused were not easily to be avoided by a great mind, irritated by perpetual hardships, and constrained hourly to return the spurns of contempt, and repress the insolence of prosperity; and vanity surely may be readily pardoned in him to whom life afforded no other comforts than barren praises, and the consciousness of deserving them.

Those are no proper judges of his conduct who have slumbered away their time on the down of plenty; nor will any wise man easily presume to say, "Had I been in Savage's condition, I should have lived or written better than Savage."

This relation will not be wholly without its use, if those who languish under any part of his sufferings shall be enabled to fortify their patience by reflecting that they feel only those afflictions from which the abilities of Savage did not exempt him; or those who, in confidence of superior capacities or attainments, disregard the common maxims of life, shall be reminded that nothing will supply the want of prudence; and that negligence and irregularity, long continued, will make knowledge useless, wit ridiculous, and genius contemptible.

ALEXANDER POPE

ALEXANDER POPE was born in London, May
22, 1688, of parents whose rank or station was
never ascertained: we are informed that they were of
"gentle blood"; that his father was of a family of which
the Earl of Downe was the head; and that his mother
was the daughter of William Turner, Esq., of York, who
had likewise three sons, one of whom had the honour
of being killed, and the other of dying, in the service
of Charles the First; the third [the eldest] was made
a general officer in Spain, from whom the sister inherited
what sequestrations and forfeitures had left in the family.

This, and this only, is told by Pope, who is more willing, as I have heard observed, to show what his father
was not, than what he was. It is allowed that he grew
rich by trade, but whether in a shop or on the Exchange
was never discovered till Mr. Tyers told, on the authority of Mrs. Rackett, that he was a linen-draper in the
Strand. Both parents were Papists.

Pope was from his birth of a constitution tender and
delicate, but is said to have shown remarkable gentleness and sweetness of disposition. The weakness of his
body continued through his life; but the mildness of his
mind perhaps ended with his childhood. His voice,
when he was young, was so pleasing, that he was called
in fondness the "little Nightingale."

Being not sent early to school, he was taught to read

by an aunt; and when he was seven or eight years old, became a lover of books. He first learned to write by imitating printed books; a species of penmanship in which he retained great excellence through his whole life, though his ordinary hand was not elegant.

When he was about eight, he was placed in Hampshire under Taverner, a Romish priest, who, by a method very rarely practised, taught him the Greek and Latin rudiments together. He was now first regularly initiated in poetry by the perusal of Ogilby's Homer, and Sandys's Ovid. Ogilby's assistance he never repaid with any praise; but of Sandys he declared in his notes to the Iliad, that English poetry owed much of its beauty to his translations. Sandys very rarely attempted original composition.

From the care of Taverner, under whom his proficiency was considerable, he was removed to a school at Twyford, near Winchester, and again to another school about Hyde Park Corner, from which he used sometimes to stroll to the playhouse, and was so delighted with theatrical exhibitions, that he formed a kind of play from Ogilby's Iliad, with some verses of his own intermixed, which he persuaded his school-fellows to act, with the addition of his master's gardener, who personated Ajax.

At the two last schools he used to represent himself as having lost part of what Taverner had taught him; and on his master at Twyford he had already exercised his poetry in a lampoon. Yet under those masters he translated more than a fourth part of the *Metamorphoses*. If he kept the same proportion in his other exercises, it cannot be thought that his loss was great.

He tells of himself, in his poems, that "he lisp'd in numbers"; and used to say that he could not remember the time when he began to make verses. In the style of fiction it might have been said of him as of Pindar, that when he lay in his cradle, "the bees swarmed about his mouth."

About the time of the Revolution his father, who was undoubtedly disappointed by the sudden blast of Popish prosperity, quitted his trade, and retired to Binfield, in Windsor Forest, with about twenty thousand pounds; for which, being conscientiously determined not to entrust it to the Government, he found no better use than that of locking it up in a chest, and taking from it what his expenses required; and his life was long enough to consume a great part of it before his son came to the inheritance.

To Binfield Pope was called by his father when he was about twelve years old; and there he had for a few months the assistance of one Deane, another priest, of whom he learned only to construe a little of Tully's *Offices*. How Mr. Deane could spend, with a boy who had translated so much of Ovid, some months over a small part of Tully's *Offices*, it is now vain to inquire.

Of a youth so successfully employed, and so conspicuously improved, a minute account must be naturally desired; but curiosity must be contented with confused, imperfect, and sometimes improbable intelligence. Pope, finding little advantage from external help, resolved thenceforward to direct himself, and at twelve formed a plan of study which he completed with little other incitement than the desire of excellence.

His primary and principal purpose was to be a poet, with which his father accidentally concurred by proposing subjects, and obliging him to correct his performances by many revisals; after which the old gentleman, when he was satisfied, would say, "These are good rhymes."

In his perusal of the English poets he soon distinguished the versification of Dryden, which he considered as the model to be studied, and was impressed with such veneration for his instructor, that he persuaded some friends to take him to the coffee-house which Dryden frequented, and pleased himself with having seen him.

Dryden died May 1, 1700, some days before Pope was twelve, so early must he therefore have felt the power of harmony and the zeal of genius. Who does not wish that Dryden could have known the value of the homage that was paid him, and foreseen the greatness of his young admirer?

The earliest of Pope's productions is his "Ode on Solitude," written before he was twelve, in which there is nothing more than other forward boys have attained, and which is not equal to Cowley's performances at the same age.

His time was now wholly spent in reading and writing. As he read the Classics, he amused himself with translating them; and at fourteen made a version of the first book of the *Thebais,* which, with some revision, he afterwards published. He must have been at this time, if he had no help, a considerable proficient in the Latin tongue.

By Dryden's *Fables,* which had then been not long published, and were much in the hands of poetical readers, he was tempted to try his own skill in giving Chaucer a more fashionable appearance, and put *January and May,* and the *Prologue of the Wife of Bath,* into modern English. He translated likewise the *Epistle of Sappho to Phaon* from Ovid, to complete the version which was before imperfect; and wrote some other small pieces which he afterwards printed.

He sometimes imitated the English poets, and professed to have written at fourteen his poem upon "Silence," after Rochester's "Nothing." He had now formed his versification, and the smoothness of his numbers surpassed his original: but this is a small part of his praise; he discovers such acquaintance both with human and public affairs as is not easily conceived to have been attainable by a boy of fourteen in Windsor Forest.

Next year he was desirous of opening to himself new sources of knowledge by making himself acquainted with modern languages, and removed for a time to London, that he might study French and Italian, which, as he desired nothing more than to read them, were by diligent application soon despatched. Of Italian learning he does not appear to have ever made much use in his subsequent studies.

He then returned to Binfield, and delighted himself with his own poetry. He tried all styles and many subjects. He wrote a comedy, a tragedy, an epic poem, with panegyrics on all the princes of Europe; and as he confesses, "thought himself the greatest genius that ever was." Self-confidence is the first requisite to great undertakings. He, indeed, who forms his opinion of himself in solitude, without knowing the powers of other men, is very liable to error; but it was the felicity of Pope to rate himself at his real value.

Most of his puerile productions were, by his maturer judgment, afterwards destroyed: "Alcander," the epic poem, was burned by the persuasion of Atterbury. The tragedy was founded on the legend of St. Genevieve. Of the comedy there is no account.

Concerning his studies it is related that he translated *Tully on Old Age*; and that, besides his books of poetry and criticism, he read Temple's *Essays* and *Locke on Human Understanding*. His reading, though his favourite authors are not known, appears to have been sufficiently extensive and multifarious; for his early pieces show, with sufficient evidence, his knowledge of books.

He that is pleased with himself easily imagines that he shall please others. Sir William Trumbull, who had been ambassador at Constantinople, and Secretary of State when ne retired from business, fixed his residence in the neighbourhood of Binfield. Pope, not yet sixteen, was introduced to the statesman of sixty, and so distinguished himself, that their interviews ended in friendship and correspondence. Pope was, through his whole life, ambitious of splendid acquaintance; and he seems to have wanted neither diligence nor success in attracting the notice of the great; for from his first entrance into the world (and his entrance was very early) he was admitted to familiarity with those whose rank or station made them most conspicuous.

From the age of sixteen the life of Pope, as an author, may be properly computed. He now [1704] wrote his *Pastorals*, which were shown to the poets and critics of that time: as they well deserved, they were read with admiration, and many praises were bestowed upon them and upon the Preface, which is both elegant and learned in a high degree: they were, however, not published till five years afterwards.

Cowley, Milton, and Pope are distinguished among the English poets by the early exertion of their powers; but the works of Cowley alone were published in his childhood, and therefore of him only can it be certain that his puerile performances received no improvement from his maturer studies.

At this time began his acquaintance with Wycherley, a man who seems to have had among his contemporaries his full share of reputation, to have been esteemed without virtue, and caressed without good humour. Pope was proud of his notice; Wycherley wrote verses in his praise, which he was charged by Dennis with writing to himself; and they agreed for a while to flatter one another. It is pleasant to remark how soon Pope learned the cant of an author, and began to treat critics with contempt, though he had yet suffered nothing from them.

But the fondness of Wycherley was too violent to last. His esteem of Pope was such that he submitted some poems to his revision, and when Pope, perhaps proud of such confidence, was sufficiently bold in his criticisms, and liberal in his alterations, the old scribbler was angry to see his pages defaced, and felt more pain from the detection than content from the amendment of his faults. They parted, but Pope always considered him with kindness, and visited him a little time before he died.

Another of his early correspondents was Mr. Cromwell, of whom I have learned nothing particular but that he used to ride a-hunting in a tye-wig. He was fond, and perhaps vain, of amusing himself with poetry and criticism; and sometimes sent his performances to Pope, who did not forbear such remarks as were now and then unwelcome. Pope, in his turn, put the juvenile version of Statius into his hands for correction.

Their correspondence afforded the public its first knowledge of Pope's epistolary powers; for his letters were given by Cromwell to one Mrs. Thomas, and she many years afterwards sold them to Curll, who inserted them [1727] in a volume of his *Miscellanies*.

Walsh, a name yet preserved among the minor poets, was one of his first encouragers. His regard was gained by the *Pastorals*, and from him Pope received the counsel from which he seems to have regulated his studies. Walsh advised him to correctness, which, as he told him, the English poets had hitherto neglected, and which therefore was left to him as a basis of fame; and being delighted with rural poems, recommended to him to write a pastoral comedy, like those which are read so eagerly in Italy; a design which Pope probably did not approve, as he did not follow it.

Pope had now declared himself a poet; and thinking himself entitled to poetical conversation, began at seventeen to frequent Will's, a coffee-house on the north side of Russell-street, in Covent-garden, where the wits of that time used to assemble, and where Dryden had, when he lived, been accustomed to preside.

During this period of his life he was indefatigably diligent, and insatiably curious: wanting health for violent, and money for expensive pleasures, and having excited in himself very strong desires of intellectual eminence, he spent much of his time over his books; but he read only to store his mind with facts and images, seizing all that his authors presented with undistinguishing voracity, and with an appetite for knowledge too eager to be nice. In a mind like his, however, all the faculties were at once involuntarily improving. Judgment is forced upon us by experience. He that reads many books must compare one opinion or one style with another, and when he compares, must necessarily distinguish, reject, and prefer. But the account given by himself of his studies was, that from fourteen to twenty he read only for amusement, from twenty to twenty-seven for improvement and instruction; that in the first part of this time he desired only to know, and in the second he endeavoured to judge.

The *Pastorals,* which had been for some time handed about among poets and critics, were at last printed (1709) in Tonson's [Sixth] *Miscellany,* in a volume which began with the *Pastorals* of Philips, and ended with those of Pope.

The same year [1709] was written the "Essay on Criticism"; a work which displays such extent of comprehension, such nicety of distinction, such acquaint-

ance with mankind, and such knowledge both of ancient
and modern learning, as are not often attained by the
maturest age and longest experience. It was published
about two years afterwards; and being praised by Addison in *The Spectator*, with sufficient liberality, met with
so much favour as enraged Dennis, "who," he says,
"found himself attacked without any manner of provocation on his side, and attacked in his person, instead of
his writings, by one who was wholly a stranger to him,
at a time when all the world knew he was persecuted by
fortune; and not only saw that this was attempted in a
clandestine manner, with the utmost falsehood and calumny, but found that all this was done by a little affected hypocrite, who had nothing in his mouth at the
same time but truth, candour, friendship, good nature,
humanity, and magnanimity."

How the attack was clandestine is not easily perceived, nor how his person is depreciated; but he seems
to have known something of Pope's character, in whom
may be discovered an appetite to talk too frequently of
his own virtues.

The pamphlet is such as rage might be expected to
dictate. He supposes himself to be asked two questions:
whether the "Essay" will succeed, and who or what is
the author.

Its success he admits to be secured by the false opinions then prevalent; the author he concludes to be
"young and raw."

"First; because he discovers a sufficiency beyond his
last ability, and hath rashly undertaken a task infinitely
above his force. Secondly; while this little author struts
and affects the dictatorian air, he plainly shows that at
the same time he is under the rod; and while he pretends to give law to others, is a pedantic slave to authority and opinion. Thirdly; he hath, like schoolboys,

borrowed both from living and dead. Fourthly; he knows not his own mind, and frequently contradicts himself. Fifthly; he is almost perpetually in the wrong."

All these positions he attempts to prove by quotations and remarks; but his desire to do mischief is greater than his power. He has, however, justly criticised some passages in these lines:

> There are whom Heaven has bless'd with store of wit,
> Yet want as much again to manage it;
> For wit and judgment ever are at strife—
> > [First Edition, 4to., 1711, p. 7.]

It is apparent that wit has two meanings, and that what is wanted, though called wit, is truly judgment. So far Dennis is undoubtedly right; but not content with argument, he will have a little mirth, and triumphs over the first couplet in terms too elegant to be forgotten. "By the way, what rare numbers are here! Would not one swear that this youngster had espoused some antiquated muse, who had sued out a divorce on account of impotence from some superannuated sinner; and having been p—xed by her former spouse, has got the gout in her decrepit age, which makes her hobble so damnably." This was the man who would reform a nation sinking into barbarity.

In another place Pope himself allowed that Dennis had detected one of those blunders which are called "bulls." The first edition had this line:

> What is this wit—
> Where wanted, scorned; and envied where acquir'd?

"How," says the critic, "can wit be scorn'd where it is not? Is not this a figure frequently employed in Hibernian land? The person that wants this wit may indeed be scorned, but the scorn shows the honour which the contemner has for wit." Of this remark Pope made the proper use by correcting the passage.

I have preserved, I think, all that is reasonable in Dennis's criticism; it remains that justice be done to his delicacy. "For his acquaintance (says Dennis) he names Mr. Walsh, who had by no means the qualification which this author reckons absolutely necessary to a critic, it being very certain that he was, like this essayer, a very indifferent poet; he loved to be well dressed; and I remember a little young gentleman whom Mr. Walsh used to take into his company, as a double foil to his person and capacity. Inquire between Sunninghill and Oakingham for a young, short, squab gentleman, the very bow of the God of Love, and tell me whether he be a proper author to make personal reflections? He may extol the ancients, but he has reason to thank the gods that he was born a modern; for had he been born of Grecian parents, and his father consequently had by law had the absolute disposal of him, his life had been no longer than that of one of his poems, the life of half a day. Let the person of a gentleman of his parts be never so contemptible, his inward man is ten times more ridiculous; it being impossible that his outward form, though it be that of downright monkey, should differ so much from human shape as his unthinking, immaterial part does from human understanding." Thus began the hostility between Pope and Dennis, which, though it was suspended for a short time, never was appeased. Pope seems, at first, to have attacked him wantonly; but though he always professed to despise him, he discovers, by mentioning him very often, that he felt his force or his venom.

Of this "Essay" Pope declared that he did not expect the sale to be quick, because "not one gentleman in sixty, even of liberal education, could understand it." The gentlemen and the education of that time seem to have been of a lower character than they are of this. He mentioned a thousand copies as a numerous impression.

Dennis was not his only censurer: the zealous Papists thought the monks treated with too much contempt, and Erasmus too studiously praised; but to these objections he had not much regard.

The "Essay" has been translated into French by Hamilton, author of the *Comte de Grammont,* whose version was never printed; by Robotham, secretary to the King for Hanover, and by Resnel; and commented by Dr. Warburton, who has discovered in it such order and connection as was not perceived by Addison, nor, as is said, intended by the author.

Almost every poem consisting of precepts is so far arbitrary and immethodical, that many of the paragraphs may change places with no apparent inconvenience; for of two or more positions, depending upon some remote and general principle, there is seldom any cogent reason why one should precede the other. But for the order in which they stand, whatever it be, a little ingenuity may easily give a reason. "It is possible," says Hooker, "that, by long circumduction from any one truth, all truth may be inferred." Of all homogeneous truths, at least of all truths respecting the same general end, in whatever series they may be produced, a concatenation by intermediate ideas may be formed, such as, when it is once shown, shall appear natural; but if this order be reversed, another mode of connection equally specious may be found or made. Aristotle is praised for naming Fortitude first of the cardinal virtues, as that without which no other virtue can steadily be practised; but he might, with equal propriety, have placed Prudence and Justice before it, since without Prudence Fortitude is mad; without Justice it is mischievous.

As the end of method is perspicuity, that series is sufficiently regular that avoids obscurity; and where there is no obscurity, it will not be difficult to discover method.

In *The Spectator* was published the "Messiah," which he first submitted to the perusal of Steele, and corrected in compliance with his criticisms.

It is reasonable to infer from his Letters that the verses on the "Unfortunate Lady" were written about the time when his "Essay" was published. The lady's name and adventures I have sought with fruitless inquiry.

I can therefore tell no more than I have learned from Mr. Ruffhead, who writes with the confidence of one who could trust his information. She was a woman of eminent rank and large fortune, the ward of an uncle, who, having given her a proper education, expected like other guardians that she should make at least an equal match; and such he proposed to her, but found it rejected in favour of a young gentleman of inferior condition.

Having discovered the correspondence between the two lovers, and finding the young lady determined to abide by her own choice, he supposed that separation might do what can rarely be done by arguments, and sent her into a foreign country, where she was obliged to converse only with those from whom her uncle had nothing to fear.

Her lover took care to repeat his vows, but his letters were intercepted and carried to her guardian, who directed her to be watched with still greater vigilance, till of this restraint she grew so impatient, that she bribed a woman servant to procure her a sword, which she directed to her heart.

From this account, given with evident intention to raise the lady's character, it does not appear that she had any claim to praise, nor much to compassion. She seems to have been impatient, violent, and ungovernable. Her uncle's power could not have lasted long; the hour of liberty and choice would have come in time. But her desires were too hot for delay, and she liked self-murder better than suspense.

Nor is it discovered that the uncle, whoever he was, is with much justice delivered to posterity as "a false Guardian"; he seems to have done only that for which a guardian is appointed; he endeavoured to direct his niece till she should be able to direct herself. Poetry has not often been worse employed than in dignifying the amorous fury of a raving girl.

Not long after he wrote "The Rape of the Lock," the most airy, the most ingenious, and the most delightful of all his compositions, occasioned by a frolic of gallantry rather too familiar, in which Lord Petre cut off a lock of Mrs. Arabella Fermor's hair. This, whether stealth or violence, was so much resented, that the commerce of the two families, before very friendly, was interrupted. Mr. Caryl, a gentleman who, being secretary to King James's Queen, had followed his mistress into France, and who, being the author of *Sir Solomon Single*, a comedy, and some translations, was entitled to the notice of a wit, solicited Pope to endeavour a reconciliation by a ludicrous poem, which might bring both the parties to a better temper. In compliance with Caryl's request, though his name was for a long time marked only by the first and last letters, C—l, a poem of two cantos was written (1711), as is said, in a fortnight, and sent to the offended lady, who liked it well enough to show it:

and, with the usual process of literary transactions, the author, dreading a surreptitious edition, was forced to publish it.

The event is said to have been such as was desired; the pacification and diversion of all to whom it related, except Sir George Brown, who complained with some bitterness that, in the character of Sir Plume, he was made to talk nonsense. Whether all this be true I have some doubt, for at Paris, a few years ago, a niece of Mrs. Fermor, who presided in an English convent, mentioned Pope's work with very little gratitude, rather as an insult than an honour; and she may be supposed to have inherited the opinion of her family.

At its first appearance it was termed by Addison "merum sal." Pope, however, saw that it was capable of improvement; and having luckily contrived to borrow his machinery from the Rosicrucians, imparted the scheme with which his head was teeming to Addison, who told him that his work, as it stood, was "a delicious little thing," and gave him no encouragement to retouch it.

This has been too hastily considered as an instance of Addison's jealousy; for as he could not guess the conduct of the new design, or the possibilities of pleasure comprised in a fiction of which there had been no examples, he might very reasonably and kindly persuade the author to acquiesce in his own prosperity, and forbear an attempt which he considered as an unnecessary hazard.

Addison's counsel was happily rejected. Pope foresaw the future efflorescence of imagery then budding in his mind, and resolved to spare no art or industry of cultivation. The soft luxuriance of his fancy was already shooting, and all the gay varieties of diction were ready at his hand to colour and embellish it.

His attempt was justified by its success. "The Rape of

the Lock" stands forward, in the classes of literature, as the most exquisite example of ludicrous poetry. Berkeley congratulated him upon the display of powers more truly poetical than he had shown before: with elegance of description and justness of precepts he had now exhibited boundless fertility of invention.

He always considered the intermixture of the machinery with the action as his most successful exertion of poetical art. He indeed could never afterwards produce anything of such unexampled excellence. Those performances which strike with wonder, are combinations of skilful genius with happy casualty; and it is not likely that any felicity, like the discovery of a new race of preternatural agents, should happen twice to the same man.

Of this poem the author was, I think, allowed to enjoy the praise for a long time without disturbance. Many years afterwards [1728] Dennis published some remarks upon it, with very little force and with no effect; for the opinion of the public was already settled, and it was no longer at the mercy of criticism.

About this time he published "The Temple of Fame," which, as he tells Steele in their correspondence, he had written two years before; that is, when he was only twenty-two years old, an early time of life for so much learning and so much observation as that work exhibits.

On this poem Dennis afterwards published some remarks, of which the most reasonable is, that some of the lines represent Motion as exhibited by Sculpture.

Of the "Epistle from Eloisa to Abelard" I do not know the date. His first inclination to attempt a composition of that tender kind arose, as Mr. Savage told me, from his perusal of Prior's "Nut-brown Maid." How much he has surpassed Prior's work it is not necessary to mention, when perhaps it may be said with justice that he has excelled every composition of the same kind. The mixture of religious hope and resignation gives an elevation and dignity to disappointed love, which images merely natural cannot bestow. The gloom of a convent strikes the imagination with far greater force than the solitude of a grove.

This piece was, however, not much his favourite in his latter years, though I never heard upon what principle he slighted it.

In the next year (1713) he published "Windsor Forest"; of which part was, as he relates, written at sixteen, about the same time as his *Pastorals;* and the latter part was added afterwards: where the addition begins we are not told. The lines relating to the Peace confess their own date. It is dedicated to Lord Lansdown, who was then high in reputation and influence among the Tories; and it is said that the conclusion of the poem gave great pain to Addison, both as a poet and a politician. Reports like this are often spread with boldness very disproportionate to their evidence. Why should Addison receive any particular disturbance from the last lines of "Windsor Forest"? If contrariety of opinion could poison a politician, he would not live a day; and, as a poet, he must have felt Pope's force of genius much more from many other parts of his works.

The pain that Addison might feel, it is not likely that he would confess; and it is certain that he so well suppressed his discontent that Pope now thought himself his favourite; for, having been consulted in the revisal of *Cato,* he introduced it [14th April, 1713] by a Prologue; and, when Dennis published his *Remarks,* undertook not indeed to vindicate but to revenge his friend, by "Dr. Norris's" *Narrative of the Frenzy of Mr. John Dennis.*

There is reason to believe that Addison gave no en

couragement to this disingenuous hostility; for, says Pope, in a letter to him, "indeed your opinion, that 'tis entirely to be neglected, would have been my own had it been my own case; but I felt more warmth here than I did when I first saw his book against myself (though indeed in two minutes it made me heartily merry)." Addison was not a man on whom such cant of sensibility could make much impression. He left the pamphlet to itself, having disowned it to Dennis, and perhaps did not think Pope to have deserved much by his officiousness.

This year [1713] was printed in *The Guardian* the ironical comparison between the *Pastorals* of Philips and Pope; a composition of artifice, criticism, and literature, to which nothing equal will easily be found. The superiority of Pope is so ingeniously dissembled, and the feeble lines of Philips so skilfully preferred, that Steele, being deceived, was unwilling to print the paper lest Pope should be offended. Addison immediately saw the writer's design; and, as it seems, had malice enough to conceal his discovery and to permit a publication which, by making his friend Philips ridiculous, made him for ever an enemy to Pope.

It appears that about this time Pope had a strong inclination to unite the art of Painting with that of Poetry, and put himself under the tuition of Jervas. He was near-sighted, and therefore not formed by nature for a painter: he tried, however, how far he could advance, and sometimes persuaded his friends to sit. A picture of Betterton, supposed to be drawn by him, was in the possession of Lord Mansfield: if this was taken from life, he must have begun to paint earlier; for Betterton was now dead. Pope's ambition of this new art produced some encomiastic verses to Jervas, which certainly show his power as a poet; but I have been told that they betray his ignorance of painting.

He appears to have regarded Betterton with kindness and esteem; and after his death published, under his name, a version into modern English of Chaucer's Prologues, and one of his Tales, which, as was related by Mr. Harte, were believed to have been the performance of Pope himself by Fenton, who made him a gay offer of 5*l.* if he would show them in the hand of Betterton.

The next year (1713) produced a bolder attempt, by which profit was sought as well as praise. The poems which he had hitherto written, however they might have diffused his name, had made very little addition to his fortune. The allowance which his father made him, though, proportioned to what he had, it might be liberal, could not be large; his religion hindered him from the occupation of any civil employment; and he complained that he wanted even money to buy books.

He therefore resolved [October 1713] to try how far the favour of the public extended, by soliciting a subscription to a version of the Iliad, with large notes.

To print by subscription was, for some time, a practice peculiar to the English. The first considerable work for which this expedient was employed is said to have been Dryden's Virgil; and it had been tried again with great success when *The Tatlers* were collected into volumes.

There was reason to believe that Pope's attempt would be successful. He was in the full bloom of reputation, and was personally known to almost all whom dignity of employment or splendour of reputation had made eminent; he conversed indifferently with both parties, and never disturbed the public with his political opinions; and it might be naturally expected, as each faction then boasted its literary zeal, that the great men, who on other occasions practised all the violence of opposition, would emulate each other in their encouragement of a poet who delighted all, and by whom none had been offended.

With those hopes he offered an English Iliad to subscribers, in six volumes in quarto, for six guineas; a sum, according to the value of money at that time, by no means inconsiderable, and greater than I believe to have been ever asked before. His proposal, however, was very favourably received; and the patrons of literature were busy to recommend his undertaking and promote his interest. Lord Oxford, indeed, lamented that such a genius should be wasted upon a work not original; but proposed no means by which he might live without it. Addison recommended caution and moderation, and advised him not to be content with the praise of half the nation, when he might be universally favoured.

The greatness of the design, the popularity of the author, and the attention of the literary world, naturally raised such expectations of the future sale, that the booksellers made their offers with great eagerness; but the highest bidder was Bernard Lintot, who became proprietor on condition of supplying, at his own expense, all the copies which were to be delivered to subscribers, or presented to friends, and paying 200l. for every volume.

Of the quartos it was, I believe, stipulated that none should be printed but for the author, that the subscription might not be depreciated; but Lintot impressed the same pages upon a small folio, and paper perhaps a little thinner; and sold exactly at half the price, for half a guinea each volume, books so little inferior to the quartos, that by a fraud of trade those folios, being afterwards shortened by cutting away the top and bottom, were sold as copies printed for the subscribers.

Lintot printed 250 on royal paper in folio, for two guineas a volume; of the small folio, having printed 1750 copies of the first volume, he reduced the number in the other volumes to 1000.

It is unpleasant to relate that the bookseller, after all his hopes and all his liberality, was, by a very unjust and illegal action, defrauded of his profit. An edition of the English Iliad was printed in Holland in duodecimo, and imported clandestinely for the gratification of those who were impatient to read what they could not yet afford to buy. This fraud could only be counteracted by an edition equally cheap and more commodious; and Lintot was compelled to contract his folio at once into a duodecimo, and lose the advantage of an intermediate gradation. The notes, which in the Dutch copies were placed at the end of each book, as they had been in the large volumes, were now subjoined to the text in the same page and are therefore more easily consulted. Of this edition 2500 were first printed, and 5000 a few weeks afterwards; but indeed great numbers were necessary to produce considerable profit.

Pope, having now emitted his proposals, and engaged not only his own reputation, but in some degree that of his friends who patronised his subscription, began to be frightened at his own undertaking; and finding himself at first embarrassed with difficulties which retarded and oppressed him, he was for a time timorous and uneasy; had his nights disturbed by dreams of long journeys through unknown ways, and wished, as he said, "that somebody would hang him."

This misery, however, was not of long continuance; he grew by degrees more acquainted with Homer's images and expressions, and practice increased his facility of versification. In a short time he represents himself as despatching regularly fifty verses a day, which would show him by an easy computation the termination of his labour.

His own diffidence was not his only vexation. He that asks a subscription soon finds that he has enemies. All who do not encourage him defame him. He that wants money will rather be thought angry than poor; and he that wishes to save his money conceals his avarice by his malice. Addison had hinted his suspicion that Pope was too much a Tory; and some of the Tories suspected his principles because he had contributed to *The Guardian,* which was carried on by Steele.

To those who censured his politics were added enemies yet more dangerous, who called in question his knowledge of Greek and his qualifications for a translator of Homer. To these he made no public opposition; but in one of his letters escapes from them as well as he can. At an age like his (for he was not more than twenty-five), with an irregular education and a course of life of which much seems to have passed in conversation, it is not very likely that he overflowed with Greek. But when he felt himself deficient, he sought assistance; and what man of learning would refuse to help him? Minute inquiries into the force of words are less necessary in translating Homer than other poets, because his positions are general and his representations natural, with very little dependence on local or temporary customs, on those changeable scenes of artificial life which, by mingling original with accidental notions, and crowding the mind with images which time effaces, produces ambiguity in diction and obscurity in books. To this open display of unadulterated nature it must be ascribed that Homer has fewer passages of doubtful meaning than any other poet either in the learned or in modern languages. I have read of a man, who being, by his ignorance of Greek, compelled to gratify his curiosity with the Latin printed on the opposite page, declared that from the rude simplicity of the lines literally rendered, he formed nobler ideas of the Homeric majesty than from the laboured elegance of polished versions.

Those literal translations were always at hand, and from them he could easily obtain his author's sense with sufficient certainty; and among the readers of Homer the number is very small of those who find much in the Greek more than in the Latin, except the music of the numbers.

If more help was wanting, he had the poetical translation of Eobanus Hessus, an unwearied writer of Latin verses; he had the French Homers of La Valterie and Dacier, and the English of Chapman, Hobbes, and Ogilby. With Chapman, whose work, though now totally neglected, seems to have been popular almost to the end of the last century, he had very frequent consultations, and perhaps never translated any passage till he had read his version, which indeed he has been sometimes suspected of using instead of the original.

Notes were likewise to be provided; for the six volumes would have been very little more than six pamphlets without them. What the mere perusal of the text could suggest, Pope wanted no assistance to collect or methodise; but more was necessary; many pages were to be filled, and learning must supply materials to wit and judgment. Something might be gathered from Dacier; but no man loves to be indebted to his contemporaries, and Dacier was accessible to common readers. Eustathius was therefore necessarily consulted. To read Eustathius, of whose work there was then no Latin version, I suspect Pope, if he had been willing, not to have been able; some other was therefore to be found who had leisure as well as abilities; and he was doubtless most readily employed who would do much work for little money.

The history of the notes has never been traced. Broome, in his Preface to his Poems, declares himself the commentator "in part upon the Iliad"; and it appears from Fenton's letter, preserved in the Museum, that Broome was at first engaged in consulting Eustathius; but that after a time, whatever was the reason, he desisted; another man of Cambridge was then employed, who soon grew weary of the work; and a third, that was recommended by Thirlby, is now discovered to have been Jortin, a man since well known to the learned world, who complained that Pope, having accepted and approved his performance, never testified any curiosity to see him, and who professed to have forgotten the terms on which he worked. The terms which Fenton uses are very mercantile: "I think at first sight that his performance is commendable enough, and have sent word for him to finish the 17th book, and to send it with his demands for his trouble. . . . I have here enclosed the specimen; if the rest come before you return, I will keep them till I receive your orders."

Broome then offered his service a second time, which was probably accepted, as they had afterwards a closer correspondence. Parnell contributed the Life of Homer, which Pope found so harsh that he took great pains in correcting it; and by his own diligence, with such help as kindness or money could procure him, in somewhat more than five years he completed his version of the Iliad, with the notes. He began it in 1712, his twenty-fifth year; and concluded it in 1718, his thirtieth year.

When we find him translating fifty lines a day, it is natural to suppose that he would have brought his work to a more speedy conclusion. The Iliad, containing less than sixteen thousand verses, might have been despatched in less than three hundred and twenty days by fifty verses in a day. The notes, compiled with the assistance of his mercenaries, could not be supposed to require more time than the text. According to this calculation the progress of Pope may seem to have been slow; but the distance is commonly very great between actual performances and speculative possibility. It is natural to suppose that as much as has been done today may be done tomorrow; but on the morrow some difficulty emerges, or some external impediment obstructs. Indolence, interruption, business, and pleasure, all take their turns of retardation; and every long work is lengthened by a thousand causes that can, and ten thousand that cannot, be recounted. Perhaps no extensive and multifarious performance was ever effected within the term originally fixed in the undertaker's mind. He that runs against Time has an antagonist not subject to casualties.

The encouragement given to this translation, though report seems to have overrated it, was such as the world has not often seen. The subscribers were 575. The copies for which subscriptions were given were 654; and only 660 were printed. For those copies Pope had nothing to pay; he therefore received, including the 200*l*. a volume, 5320*l*. 4*s*. without deduction, as the books were supplied by Lintot.

By the success of his subscription Pope was relieved from those pecuniary distresses with which, notwithstanding his popularity, he had hitherto struggled. Lord Oxford had often lamented his disqualification for public employment, but never proposed a pension. While the translation of Homer was in its progress, Mr. Craggs, then Secretary of State, offered to procure him a pension, which, at least during his ministry, might be enjoyed with secrecy. This was not accepted by Pope, who told him, however, that if he should be pressed with want of money he would send to him for occasional supplies. Craggs was not long in power, and was never solicited for money by Pope, who disdained to beg what he did not want.

With the product of this subscription, which he had too much discretion to squander, he secured his future life from want by considerable annuities. The estate of the Duke of Buckingham was found to have been charged with 500*l.* a year, payable to Pope, which doubtless his translation enabled him to purchase.

It cannot be unwelcome to literary curiosity that I deduce thus minutely the history of the English Iliad. It is certainly the noblest version of poetry which the world has ever seen; and its publication must therefore be considered as one of the great events in the annals of learning. . . .

The Iliad was published volume by volume, as the translation proceeded; the four first books appeared in [June] 1715. The expectation of this work was undoubtedly high, and every man who had connected his name with criticism or poetry was desirous of such intelligence as might enable him to talk upon the popular topic. Halifax, who, by having been first a poet and then a patron of poetry, had acquired the right of being a judge, was willing to hear some books while they were yet unpublished. Of this rehearsal Pope afterwards gave the following account:

"The famous Lord Halifax was rather a pretender to taste than really possessed of it.—When I had finished the two or three first books of my translation of the Iliad, that Lord desired to have the pleasure of hearing them read at his house. Addison, Congreve, and Garth were there at the reading. In four or five places Lord Halifax stopt me very civilly, and with a speech each time much of the same kind, 'I beg your pardon, Mr. Pope, but there is something in that passage that does not quite please me. Be so good as to mark the place, and consider it a little at your leisure. I am sure you can give it a better turn.' I returned from Lord Halifax's with Dr. Garth, in his chariot; and, as we were going along, was saying to the Doctor, that my Lord had laid me under a good deal of difficulty by such loose and general observations; that I had been thinking over the passages almost ever since, and could not guess at what it was that offended his Lordship in either of them. Garth laughed heartily at my embarrassment; said I had not been long enough acquainted with Lord Halifax to know his way yet; that I need not puzzle myself about looking those places over and over when I got home. 'All you need do (said he) is to leave them just as they are; call on Lord Halifax two or three months hence, thank him for his kind observations on those passages, and then read them to him as altered. I have known him much longer than you have, and will be answerable for the event.' I followed his advice; waited on Lord Halifax some time after; said, I hoped he would find his objections to those passages removed; read them to him exactly as they were at first: and his Lordship was extremely pleased with them, and cried out, 'Ay, now, Mr. Pope, they are perfectly right; nothing can be better.'"

It is seldom that the great or the wise suspect that they are despised or cheated. Halifax, thinking this a lucky opportunity of securing immortality, made some advances of favour and some overtures of advantage to Pope, which he seems to have received with sullen coldness. All our knowledge of this transaction is derived from a single letter (Dec. 1, 1714), in which Pope says, "I am obliged to you, both for the favours you have done me, and for those you intend me. I distrust neither your will nor your memory when it is to do good; and if I ever become troublesome or solicitous, it must not be out of expectation, but out of gratitude. Your Lordship may either cause me to live agreeably in the town, or contentedly in the country, which is really all the difference I set between an easy fortune and a small one. It is, indeed, a high strain of generosity in you to think of making me easy all my life, only because I have been so happy as to divert you some few hours: but, if I may have leave to add it is because you think me no enemy to my native Country, there will appear a better reason; for I must of consequence be very much (as I sincerely am) yours," etc.

These voluntary offers, and this faint acceptance, ended without effect. The patron was not accustomed to such frigid gratitude, and the poet fed his own pride with the dignity of independence. They probably were suspicious of each other. Pope would not dedicate till he saw at what rate his praise was valued; he would be "troublesome out of gratitude, not expectation." Halifax thought himself entitled to confidence; and would give nothing, unless he knew what he should receive. Their commerce had its beginning in hope of praise on one side, and of money on the other, and ended because Pope was less eager of money than Halifax of praise. It is not likely that Halifax had any personal benevolence to Pope; it is evident that Pope looked on Halifax with scorn and hatred.

The reputation of this great work failed of gaining him a patron; but it deprived him of a friend. Addison and he were now [1715] at the head of poetry and criticism; and both in such a state of elevation, that, like the two rivals in the Roman state, one could no longer bear an equal, nor the other a superior. Of the gradual abatement of kindness between friends the beginning is often scarcely discernible by themselves, and the process is continued by petty provocations, and incivilities sometimes peevishly returned, and sometimes contemptuously neglected, which would escape all attention but that of pride, and drop from any memory but that of resentment. That the quarrel of these two wits should be minutely deduced is not to be expected from a writer to whom, as Homer says, "nothing but rumour has reached, and who has no personal knowledge."

Pope doubtless approached Addison, when the reputation of their wit first brought them together, with the respect due to a man whose abilities were acknowledged, and who having attained that eminence to which he was himself aspiring, had in his hands the distribution of literary fame. He paid court [1713] with sufficient diligence by his Prologue to *Cato*, by his abuse of Dennis [1713], and with praise yet more direct by his poem on the "Dialogues on Medals," of which the immediate publication was then intended. In all this there was no hypocrisy; for he confessed that he found in Addison something more pleasing than in any other man.

It may be supposed that as Pope saw himself favoured by the world, and more frequently compared his own powers with those of others, his confidence increased and his submission lessened; and that Addison felt no delight from the advances of a young wit, who might soon contend with him for the highest place. Every great man, of whatever kind be his greatness, has among his friends those who officiously or insidiously quicken his attention to offences, heighten his disgust, and stimulate his resentment. Of such adherents Addison doubtless had many; and Pope was now too high to be without them.

From the emission and reception of the proposals for the Iliad, the kindness of Addison seems to have abated. Jervas the painter once pleased himself (Aug. 20, 1714) with imagining that he had re-established their friendship; and wrote to Pope that Addison once suspected him of too close a confederacy with Swift, but was now satisfied with his conduct. To this Pope answered, a week after, that his engagements to Swift were such as his services in regard to the subscription demanded, and that the Tories never put him under the necessity of asking leave to be grateful. "But," says he, "as Mr. Addison must be the judge in what regards himself, and has seemed to be no very just one to me, so I must own to you I expect nothing but civility from him." In the same letter he mentions Philips as having been busy to kindle animosity between them; but in a letter to Addison he expresses some consciousness of behaviour inattentively deficient in respect.

Of Swift's industry in promoting the subscription there remains the testimony of Kennet, no friend to either him or Pope:

"Nov. 2, 1713, Dr. Swift came into the coffee-house and had a bow from everybody but me, who, I confess, could not but despise him. When I came to the antechamber to wait, before prayers, Dr. Swift was the principal man of talk and business, and acted as master of requests. Then he instructed a young nobleman that the *best Poet in England* was Mr. Pope (a Papist), who had begun a translation of Homer into English verse, for which *he must have them all subscribe;* for, says he, the author *shall not* begin to print till *I have* a thousand guineas for him."

About this time it is likely that Steele, who was, with

all his political fury, good-natured and officious, procured an interview between these angry rivals, which ended in aggravated malevolence. On this occasion, if the reports be true, Pope made his complaint with frankness and spirit, as a man undeservedly neglected or opposed; and Addison affected a contemptuous unconcern, and, in a calm, even voice, reproached Pope with his vanity, and telling him of the improvements which his early works had received from his own remarks and those of Steele, said that he, being now engaged in public business, had no longer any care for his poetical reputation; nor had any other desire with regard to Pope than that he should not, by too much arrogance, alienate the public.

To this Pope is said to have replied with great keenness and severity, upbraiding Addison with perpetual dependence, and with the abuse of those qualifications which he had obtained at the public cost, and charging him with mean endeavours to obstruct the progress of rising merit. The contest rose so high, that they parted at last without any interchange of civility.

The first volume of Homer was (1715) in time published; and a rival version of the first Iliad, for rivals the time of their appearance inevitably made them, was immediately printed, with the name of Tickell. It was soon perceived that, among the followers of Addison, Tickell had the preference, and the critics and poets divided into factions. "I, like the Tories," says Pope, "have the town in general, that is, the mob, on my side; but 'tis usual with the smaller party to make up in industry what they want in numbers. . . . I appeal to the people as my rightful judges, and while they are not inclined to condemn me, I fear no arbitrary, high-flying proceedings from the small court faction at Button's." This opposition he immediately imputed to Addison, and complained of it in terms sufficiently resentful to Craggs, their common friend.

When Addison's opinion was asked, he declared the versions to be both good, but Tickell's the best that had ever been written; and sometimes said that they were both good, but that Tickell had more of Homer.

Pope was now sufficiently irritated; his reputation and his interest were at hazard. He once intended to print together the four versions of Dryden, Maynwaring, Pope, and Tickell, that they might be readily compared and fairly estimated. This design seems to have been defeated by the refusal of Tonson, who was the proprietor of the other three versions.

Pope intended at another time a rigorous criticism of Tickell's translation, and had marked a copy, which I have seen, in all places that appeared defective. But while he was thus meditating defence or revenge, his adversary sunk before him without a blow; the voice of the public was not long divided, and the preference was universally given to Pope's performance.

He was convinced, by adding one circumstance to another, that the other translation was the work of Addison himself; but if he knew it in Addison's lifetime, it does not appear that he told it. He left his illustrious antagonist to be punished by what has been considered as the most painful of all reflections, the remembrance of a crime perpetrated in vain.

The other circumstances of their quarrel were thus related by Pope:

"Philips seemed to have been encouraged to abuse me in coffee-houses and conversations: Gildon wrote a thing about Wycherley, in which he had abused both me and my relations very grossly. Lord Warwick himself told me one day, that it was in vain for me to endeavour to be well with Mr. Addison; that his jealous temper would never admit of a settled friendship between us: and, to convince me of what he had said, assured me that Addison had encouraged Gildon to publish those scandals, and had given him ten guineas after they were published. The next day, while I was heated with what I had heard, I wrote a letter to Mr. Addison, to let him know that I was not unacquainted with this behaviour of his; that if I was to speak severely of him in return for it, it should be not in such a dirty way; that I should rather tell him, himself, fairly of his faults, and allow his good qualities; and that it should be something in the following manner:—I then subjoined the first sketch of what has been since called my Satire on Addison. He used me very civilly ever after, and never did me any injustice that I know of, from that time to his death, which was about three years after."

The verses on Addison, when they were sent to Atterbury, were considered by him as the most excellent of Pope's performances; and the writer was advised, since he knew where his strength lay, not to suffer it to remain unemployed.

This year (1715) being, by the subscription, enabled to live more by choice, having persuaded his father to sell their estate at Binfield, he purchased, I think only for his life, that house at Twickenham to which his residence afterwards procured so much celebration, and removed thither with his father and mother.

Here he planted the vines and the quincunx which his verses mention; and being under the necessity of making a subterraneous passage to a garden on the other side of the road, he adorned it with fossil bodies, and dignified it with the title of a grotto; a place of silence and retreat, from which he endeavoured to persuade his friends and himself that cares and passions could be excluded.

A grotto is not often the wish or pleasure of an Englishman, who has more frequent need to solicit than exclude the sun; but Pope's excavation was requisite as an entrance to his garden, and, as some men try to be proud of their defects, he extracted an ornament from an inconvenience, and vanity produced a grotto where necessity enforced a passage. It may be frequently remarked of the studious and speculative, that they are proud of trifles, and that their amusements seem frivolous and childish; whether it be that men conscious of great reputation think themselves above the reach of censure, and safe in the admission of negligent indulgences, or that mankind expect from elevated genius an uniformity of greatness, and watch its degradation with malicious wonder; like him who, having followed with his eye an eagle into the clouds, should lament that she ever descended to a perch.

While the volumes of his Homer were annually published, he collected his former works (1717) into one quarto volume, to which he prefixed a Preface, written with great sprightliness and elegance, which was afterwards reprinted, with some passages subjoined that he at first omitted; other marginal additions of the same kind he made in the later editions of his poems. Waller remarks, that poets lose half their praise, because the reader knows not what they have blotted. Pope's voracity of fame taught him the art of obtaining the accumulated honour both of what he had published, and of what he had suppressed.

In this year (1717) his father died suddenly, in his seventy-fifth year, having passed twenty-nine years in privacy. He is not known but by the character which his son has given him. If the money with which he retired was all gotten by himself, he had traded very successfully in times when sudden riches were rarely attainable.

The publication of the Iliad was at last completed in 1720. The splendour and success of this work raised Pope many enemies, that endeavoured to depreciate his abilities. Burnet, who was afterwards a judge of no mean reputation, censured him in a piece called "Homerides" before it was published. Ducket likewise endeavoured to make him ridiculous. Dennis was the perpetual persecutor of all his studies. But, whoever his critics were, their writings are lost; and the names which are preserved, are preserved in "The Dunciad."

In this disastrous year (1720) of national infatuation, when more riches than Peru can boast were expected from the South Sea, when the contagion of avarice tainted every mind, and even poets panted after wealth, Pope was seized with the universal passion, and ventured some of his money. The stock rose in its price; and for a while he thought himself the lord of thousands. But this dream of happiness did not last long; and he seems to have waked soon enough to get clear with the loss of what he once thought himself to have won, and perhaps not wholly of that.

Next year he published some select poems of his friend Dr. Parnell, with a very elegant Dedication to the Earl of Oxford; who, after all his struggles and dangers, then lived in retirement, still under the frown of a victorious faction, who could take no pleasure in hearing his praise.

He gave the same year (1721) an edition of Shakespeare. His name was now of so much authority, that Tonson thought himself entitled, by annexing it, to demand a subscription of six guineas for Shakespeare's Plays in six quarto volumes; nor did his expectation much deceive him; for of 750 which he printed, he dis-

persed a great number at the price proposed. The reputation of that edition indeed sunk afterwards so low, that
140 copies were sold at 16s. each.

On this undertaking, to which Pope was induced by
a reward of 217l. 12s., he seems never to have reflected
afterwards without vexation; for Theobald, a man of
heavy diligence, with very slender powers, first [1726]
in a book called *Shakespeare Restored,* and then [1733]
in a formal edition, detected his deficiencies with all the
insolence of victory; and as he was now high enough to
be feared and hated, Theobald had from others all the
help that could be supplied by the desire of humbling
a haughty character.

From this time Pope became an enemy to editors, col-
lators, commentators, and verbal critics; and hoped to
persuade the world that he miscarried in this undertaking only by having a mind too great for such minute
employment.

Pope in his edition undoubtedly did many things
wrong, and left many things undone; but let him not be
defrauded of his due praise. He was the first that knew,
at least the first that told, by what helps the text might
be improved. If he inspected the early editions negligently, he taught others to be more accurate. In his Preface he expanded with great skill and elegance the character which had been given of Shakespeare by Dryden;
and he drew the public attention upon his works, which,
though often mentioned, had been little read.

Soon after the appearance of the Iliad, resolving not
to let the general kindness cool, he published proposals
for a translation of the Odyssey, in five volumes, for five
guineas. He was willing, however, now to have associates in his labour, being either weary with toiling upon
another's thoughts, or having heard, as Ruffhead relates,
that Fenton and Broome had already begun the work,

and liking better to have them confederates than rivals.

In the patent, instead of saying that he had "translated" the Odyssey, as he had said of the Iliad, he says that he had "undertaken" a translation; and in the proposals, the subscription is said to be not solely for his own use, but for that of "two of his friends who have assisted him in this work."

In 1723, while he was engaged in this new version, he appeared before the Lords at the memorable trial of Bishop Atterbury, with whom he had lived in great familiarity, and frequent correspondence. Atterbury had honestly recommended to him the study of the Popish controversy, in hope of his conversion; to which Pope answered in a manner that cannot much recommend his principles or his judgment. In questions and projects of learning they agreed better. He was called at the trial to give an account of Atterbury's domestic life, and private employment, that it might appear how little time he had left for plots. Pope had but few words to utter, and in those few he made several blunders.

His Letters to Atterbury express the utmost esteem, tenderness, and gratitude: "perhaps," says he, "it is not only in this world that I may have cause to remember the Bishop of Rochester." At their last interview in the Tower, Atterbury presented him with a Bible.

Of the Odyssey Pope translated only twelve books; the rest were the work of Broome and Fenton: the notes were written wholly by Broome, who was not over-liberally rewarded. The public was carefully kept ignorant of the several shares; and an account was subjoined at the conclusion, which is now known not to be true.

The first copy of Pope's books, with those of Fenton, are to be seen in the Museum. The parts of Pope are less interlined than the Iliad; and the latter books of the Iliad less than the former. He grew dexterous by practice, and every sheet enabled him to write the next with more facility. The books of Fenton have very few alterations by the hand of Pope. Those of Broome have not been found; but Pope complained, as it is reported, that he had much trouble in correcting them.

His contract with Lintot was the same as for the Iliad, except that only 100*l.* were to be paid him for each volume. The number of subscribers were 574, and of copies 819; so that his profit, when he paid his assistants, was still very considerable. The work was finished in 1725; and from that time he resolved to make no more translations.

The sale did not answer Lintot's expectation; and he then pretended to discover something of fraud in Pope, and commenced or threatened a suit in Chancery.

On the English Odyssey a criticism was published [1727] by Spence, at that time Prelector of Poetry at Oxford; a man whose learning was not very great, and whose mind was not very powerful. His criticism, however, was commonly just; what he thought, he thought rightly; and his remarks were recommended by his coolness and candour. In him Pope had the first experience of a critic without malevolence, who thought it as much his duty to display beauties as expose faults; who censured with respect, and praised with alacrity.

With this criticism Pope was so little offended that he sought the acquaintance of the writer, who lived with him from that time in great familiarity, attended him in his last hours, and compiled memorials of his conversation. The regard of Pope recommended him to the great and powerful; and he obtained very valuable preferments in the Church.

Not long after [Sept. 1726] Pope was returning home from a visit in a friend's coach, which, in passing a bridge, was overturned into the water; the windows were closed, and being unable to force them open, he was in danger of immediate death, when the postilion snatched him out by breaking the glass, of which the fragments cut two of his fingers in such a manner that he lost their use.

Voltaire, who was then in England, sent him a letter of consolation. He had been entertained by Pope at his table, where he talked with so much grossness that Mrs. Pope was driven from the room. Pope discovered by a trick that he was a spy for the Court, and never considered him as a man worthy of confidence.

He soon afterwards (1727) joined with Swift, who was then in England, to publish three volumes of *Miscellanies,* in which amongst other things he inserted the "Memoirs of a Parish Clerk," in ridicule of Burnet's importance in his own *History,* and a "Debate upon Black and White Horses," written in all the formalities of a legal process by the assistance, as is said, of Mr. Fortescue, afterwards Master of the Rolls. Before these Miscellanies is a Preface signed by Swift and Pope, but apparently written by Pope; in which he makes a ridiculous and romantic complaint of the robberies committed upon authors by the clandestine seizure and sale of their papers. He tells in tragic strains how "the cabinets of the sick and the closets of the dead have been broken open and ransacked"; as if those violences were often committed for papers of uncertain and accidental value, which are rarely provoked by real treasures; as if epigrams and essays were in danger where gold and diamonds are safe. A cat hunted for his musk is, according to Pope's account, but the emblem of a wit winded by booksellers.

His complaint, however, received some attestation;

for the same year the letters written by him to Mr. Cromwell, in his youth, were sold by Mrs. Thomas to Curll, who printed them.

In these *Miscellanies* was first published the "Art of Sinking in Poetry," which, by such a train of consequences as usually passes in literary quarrels, gave in a short time, according to Pope's account, occasion to "The Dunciad."

In the following year (1728) he began to put Atterbury's advice in practice, and showed his satirical powers by publishing "The Dunciad," one of his greatest and most elaborate performances, in which he endeavoured to sink into contempt all the writers by whom he had been attacked, and some others whom he thought unable to defend themselves.

At the head of the Dunces he placed poor Theobald, whom he accused of ingratitude, but whose real crime was supposed to be that of having revised Shakespeare more happily than himself. This satire had the effect which he intended, by blasting the characters which it touched. Ralph, who, unnecessarily interposing in the quarrel, got a place in a subsequent edition, complained that for a time he was in danger of starving, as the booksellers had no longer any confidence in his capacity.

The prevalence of this poem was gradual and slow: the plan, if not wholly new, was little understood by common readers. Many of the allusions required illustration; the names were often expressed only by the initial and final letters, and, if they had been printed at length, were such as few had known or recollected. The subject itself had nothing generally interesting, for whom did it concern to know that one or another scribbler was a dunce? If therefore it had been possible for those who were attacked to conceal their pain and their resentment, "The Dunciad" might have made its way very slowly in the world.

This, however, was not to be expected: every man is of importance to himself, and, therefore, in his own opinion, to others; and, supposing the world already acquainted with all his pleasures and his pains, is perhaps the first to publish injuries or misfortunes which had never been known unless related by himself, and at which those that hear them will only laugh, for no man sympathises with the sorrows of vanity.

The history of "The Dunciad" is very minutely related by Pope himself, in a Dedication which he wrote to Lord Middlesex in the name of Savage:

"I will relate the war of the 'Dunces' (for so it has been commonly called), which began in the year 1727, and ended in 1730.

"When Dr. Swift and Mr. Pope thought it proper, for reasons specified in the Preface to their *Miscellanies,* to publish such little pieces of theirs as had casually got abroad, there was added to them the 'Treatise of the Bathos,' or the 'Art of Sinking in Poetry.' It happened that in one chapter of this piece the several species of bad poets were ranged in classes, to which were prefixed almost all the letters of the alphabet (the greatest part of them at random); but such was the number of poets eminent in that art, that some one or other took every letter to himself: all fell into so violent a fury, that, for half a year or more, the common newspapers (in most of which they had some property, as being hired writers) were filled with the most abusive falsehoods and scurrilities they could possibly devise; a liberty no way to be wondered at in those people, and in those papers, that for many years, during the uncontrolled licence of the press, had aspersed almost all the great characters of the age; and this with impunity, their own persons and names being utterly secret and obscure.

"This gave Mr. Pope the thought that he had now some opportunity of doing good, by detecting and dragging into light these common enemies of mankind; since, to invalidate this universal slander, it sufficed to show what contemptible men were the authors of it. He was not without hopes, that by manifesting the dullness of those who had only malice to recommend them, either the booksellers would not find their account in employing them, or the men themselves, when discovered, want courage to proceed in so unlawful an occupation. This it was that gave birth to 'The Dunciad'; and he thought it an happiness, that, by the late flood of slander on himself, he had acquired such a peculiar right over their names as was necessary to this design.

"On the 12th of March, 1728-9, at St. James's, that poem was presented to the King and Queen (who had before been pleased to read it) by the Right Honourable Sir Robert Walpole; and some days after the whole impression was taken and dispersed by several noblemen and persons of the first distinction.

"It is certainly a true observation, that no people are so impatient of censure as those who are the greatest slanderers, which was wonderfully exemplified on this occasion. On the day the book was first vended, a crowd of authors besieged the shop; entreaties, advices, threats of law and battery, nay cries of treason, were all employed to hinder the coming out of 'The Dunciad'; on the other side the booksellers and hawkers made as great efforts to procure it. What could a few poor authors do against so great a majority as the public? There was no stopping a torrent with a finger; so out it came.

"Many ludicrous circumstances attended it. The 'Dunces' (for by this name they were called) held weekly clubs to consult of hostilities against the author: one wrote a letter to a great minister, assuring him Mr. Pope was the greatest enemy the Government had; and another brought his image in clay to execute him in effigy; with which sad sort of satisfaction the gentlemen were a little comforted.

"Some false editions of the book having an owl in their frontispiece, the true one, to distinguish it, fixed in his stead an ass laden with authors. Then another surreptitious one being printed with the same ass, the new edition in octavo returned for distinction to the owl again. Hence arose a great contest of booksellers against booksellers, and advertisements against advertisements; some recommending the edition of the owl, and others the edition of the ass; by which names they came to be distinguished, to the great honour also of the gentlemen of 'The Dunciad.' "

Pope appears by this narrative to have contemplated his victory over the "Dunces" with great exultation; and such was his delight in the tumult which he had raised, that for a while his natural sensibility was suspended, and he read reproaches and invectives without emotion, considering them only as the necessary effects of that pain which he rejoiced in having given.

It cannot, however, be concealed that, by his own confession, he was the aggressor; for nobody believes that the letters in the "Bathos" were placed at random; and it may be discovered that, when he thinks himself concealed, he indulges the common vanity of common men, and triumphs in those distinctions which he had affected to despise. He is proud that his book was presented to the King and Queen by the Right Honourable Sir Robert Walpole; he is proud that they had read it before; he is proud that the edition was taken off by the nobility and persons of the first distinction.

The edition of which he speaks was, I believe, that which, by telling in the text the names, and in the notes the characters of those whom he had satirised, was made intelligible and diverting. The critics had now declared their approbation of the plan, and the common reader began to like it without fear; those who were strangers to petty literature, and therefore unable to decipher initials and blanks, had now names and persons brought within their view; and delighted in the visible effect of those shafts of malice which they had hitherto contemplated as shot into the air.

Dennis, upon the fresh provocation now given him, renewed the enmity which had for a time been appeased by mutual civilities; and published [1728] remarks, which he had till then suppressed, upon "The Rape of the Lock." Many more grumbled in secret, or vented their resentment in the newspapers by epigrams or invectives.

Ducket, indeed, being mentioned as loving Burnet with "pious passion," pretended that his moral character was injured, and for some time declared his resolution to take vengeance with a cudgel. But Pope appeased him by changing "pious passion" to "cordial friendship," and by a note, in which he vehemently disclaims the malignity of meaning imputed to the first expression.

Aaron Hill, who was represented as diving for the prize, expostulated with Pope, in a manner so much superior to all mean solicitation, that Pope was reduced to sneak and shuffle, sometimes to deny, and sometimes to apologise; he first endeavours to wound, and then is afraid to own that he meant a blow.

"The Dunciad," in the complete edition, is addressed to Dr. Swift: of the notes, part were written by Dr. Arbuthnot, and an apologetical letter was prefixed,

signed by Cleland, but supposed to have been written
by Pope.

After this general war upon Dullness, he seems to
have indulged himself awhile in tranquillity; but his
subsequent productions prove that he was not idle. He
published (1731) a poem on "Taste," in which he very
particularly and severely criticises the house, the furniture, the gardens, and the entertainments of Timon, a
man of great wealth and little taste. By Timon he was
universally supposed, and by the Earl of Burlington, to
whom the poem is addressed, was privately said, to
mean the Duke of Chandos; a man perhaps too much
delighted with pomp and show, but of a temper kind
and beneficent, and who had consequently the voice of
the public in his favour.

A violent outcry was therefore raised against the ingratitude and treachery of Pope, who was said to have
been indebted to the patronage of Chandos for a present
of a thousand pounds, and who gained the opportunity
of insulting him by the kindness of his invitation.

The receipt of a thousand pounds Pope publicly denied; but from the reproach which the attack on a character so amiable brought upon him, he tried all means
of escaping. The name of Cleland was again employed
in an apology, by which no man was satisfied; and he
was at last reduced to shelter his temerity behind dissimulation, and endeavour to make that disbelieved
which he never had confidence openly to deny. He
wrote an exculpatory letter to the Duke, which was answered with great magnanimity, as by a man who accepted his excuse without believing his professions. He
said, that to have ridiculed his taste, or his buildings,
had been an indifferent action in another man; but that
in Pope, after the reciprocal kindness that had been

exchanged between them, it had been less easily excused.

Pope, in one of his letters, complaining of the treatment which his poem had found, "owns that such critics can intimidate him, nay, almost persuade him to write no more, which is a compliment this age deserves." The man who threatens the world is always ridiculous; for the world can easily go on without him, and in a short time will cease to miss him. I have heard of an idiot who used to revenge his vexations by lying all night upon the bridge. "There is nothing," says Juvenal, "that a man will not believe in his own favour." Pope had been flattered till he thought himself one of the moving powers in the system of life. When he talked of laying down his pen, those who sat round him intreated and implored; and self-love did not suffer him to suspect that they went away and laughed.

The following year [4th Dec., 1732] deprived him of Gay, a man whom he had known early, and whom he seemed to love with more tenderness than any other of his literary friends. Pope was now forty-four years old; an age at which the mind begins less easily to admit new confidence, and the will to grow less flexible, and when, therefore, the departure of an old friend is very acutely felt.

In the next year [7th June, 1733] he lost his mother, not by an unexpected death, for she had lasted to the age of ninety-three; but she did not die unlamented. The filial piety of Pope was in the highest degree amiable and exemplary; his parents had the happiness of living till he was at the summit of poetical reputation, till he was at ease in his fortune, and without a rival in his fame, and found no diminution of his respect or tenderness. Whatever was his pride, to them he was obedient; and whatever was his irritability, to them he was gentle.

Life has, among its soothing and quiet comforts, few things better to give than such a son.

One of the passages of Pope's life which seems to deserve some inquiry was a publication of Letters between him and many of his friends, which falling into the hands of Curll, a rapacious bookseller of no good fame, were by him [May 1735] printed and sold. This volume containing some letters from noblemen, Pope incited a prosecution against him in the House of Lords for breach of privilege, and attended himself to stimulate the resentment of his friends. Curll appeared at the bar, and, knowing himself in no great danger, spoke of Pope with very little reverence. "He has," said Curll, "a knack at versifying, but in prose I think myself a match for him." When the orders of the House were examined, none of them appeared to have been infringed; Curll went away triumphant; and Pope was left to seek some other remedy.

Curll's account was, that one evening a man in a clergyman's gown, but with a lawyer's band, brought and offered for sale a number of printed volumes, which he found to be Pope's epistolary correspondence; that he asked no name, and was told none, but gave the price demanded, and thought himself authorised to use his purchase to his own advantage.

That Curll gave a true account of the transaction, it is reasonable to believe, because no falsehood was ever detected; and when some years afterwards I mentioned it to Lintot, the son of Bernard, he declared his opinion to be, that Pope knew better than anybody else how Curll obtained the copies, because another parcel was at the same time sent to himself, for which no price had ever been demanded, and he made known his resolution not to pay a porter, and consequently not to deal with a nameless agent.

Such care had been taken to make them public, that they were sent at once to two booksellers: to Curll, who was likely to seize them as prey; and to Lintot, who might be expected to give Pope information of the seeming injury. Lintot, I believe, did nothing, and Curll did what was expected. That to make them public was the only purpose may be reasonably supposed, because the numbers offered to sale by the private messengers showed that hope of gain could not have been the motive of the impression.

It seems that Pope, being desirous of printing his letters, and not knowing how to do, without imputation of vanity, what has in this country been done very rarely, contrived an appearance of compulsion; that when he could complain that his letters were surreptitiously published, he might decently and defensively publish them himself.

Pope's private correspondence, thus promulgated, filled the nation with praises of his candour, tenderness, and benevolence, the purity of his purposes, and the fidelity of his friendship. There were some letters which a very good or a very wise man would wish suppressed, but, as they had been already exposed, it was impracticable now to retract them.

From the perusal of those Letters, Mr. Allen first conceived the desire of knowing him; and with so much zeal did he cultivate the friendship which he had newly formed, that when Pope told his purpose of vindicating his own property by a genuine edition, he offered to pay the cost.

This, however, Pope did not accept; but in time solicited a subscription for a quarto volume, which appeared (1737), I believe, with sufficient profit. In the Preface he tells that his Letters were reposited in a friend's library, said to be the Earl of Oxford's, and that the copy thence stolen was sent to the press. The story was doubtless received with different degrees of credit. It may be suspected that the Preface to the *Miscellanies* was written to prepare the public for such an incident, and, to strengthen this opinion, James Worsdale, a painter, who was employed in clandestine negotiations, but whose veracity was very doubtful, declared that he was the messenger who carried, by Pope's direction, the books to Curll.

When they were thus published and avowed, as they had relation to recent facts and persons either then living or not yet forgotten, they may be supposed to have found readers; but, as the facts were minute, and the characters, being either private or literary, were little known or little regarded, they awaked no popular kindness or resentment; the book never became much the subject of conversation; some read it as a contemporary history, and some perhaps as a model of epistolary language; but those who read it did not talk of it. Not much therefore was added by it to fame or envy; nor do I remember that it produced either public praise or public censure.

It had, however, in some degree the recommendation of novelty. Our language has few Letters, except those of statesmen. Howel, indeed, about a century ago, published his Letters, which are commended by Morhoff, and which alone of his hundred volumes continue his memory. Loveday's Letters were printed only once; those of Herbert and Suckling are hardly known. Mrs. Phillips's [Orinda's] are equally neglected; and those of Walsh seem written as exercises, and were never sent to any living mistress or friend. Pope's epistolary excellence had an open field; he had no English rival, living or dead.

Pope is seen in this collection as connected with the

other contemporary wits, and certainly suffers no disgrace in the comparison: but it must be remembered that he had the power of favouring himself; he might have originally had publication in his mind, and have written with care, or have afterwards selected those which he had most happily conceived, or most diligently laboured: and I know not whether there does not appear something more studied and artificial in his productions than the rest, except one long letter by Bolingbroke, composed with all the skill and industry of a professed author. It is indeed not easy to distinguish affectation from habit; he that has once studiously formed a style, rarely writes afterwards with complete ease. Pope may be said to write always with his reputation in his head; Swift perhaps like a man who remembered that he was writing to Pope; but Arbuthnot like one who lets thoughts drop from his pen as they rise into his mind.

Before these Letters appeared, he published the first part of what he persuaded himself to think a system of ethics, under the title of an "Essay on Man"; which, if his Letter to Swift (of Sept. 14, 1725) be rightly explained by the commentator, had been eight years under his consideration, and of which he seems to have desired the success with great solicitude. He had now many open and doubtless many secret enemies. The "Dunces" were yet smarting with the war; and the superiority which he publicly arrogated disposed the world to wish his humiliation.

All this he knew, and against all this he provided. His own name, and that of his friend to whom the work is inscribed [Lord Bolingbroke], were in the first editions carefully suppressed; and the poem, being of a new kind, was ascribed to one or another, as favour determined or conjecture wandered: it was given, says Warburton, to every man except him only who could write it. Those who like only when they like the author, and who are under the dominion of a name, condemned it; and those admired it who are willing to scatter praise at random, which while it is unappropriated excites no envy. Those friends of Pope that were trusted with the secret went about lavishing honours on the new-born poet, and hinting that Pope was never so much in danger from any former rival.

To those authors whom he had personally offended, and to those whose opinion the world considered as decisive, and whom he suspected of envy or malevolence, he sent his *Essay* as a present before publication, that they might defeat their own enmity by praises which they could not afterwards decently retract.

With these precautions, in 1732 was published the first part of the "Essay on Man." There had been for some time a report that Pope was busy upon a System of Morality; but this design was not discovered in the new poem, which had a form and a title with which its readers were unacquainted. Its reception was not uniform: some thought it a very imperfect piece, though not without good lines. While the author was unknown, some, as will always happen, favoured him as an adventurer, and some censured him as an intruder; but all thought him above neglect; the sale increased, and editions were multiplied.

The subsequent editions of the first Epistle exhibited two memorable corrections. At first, the poet and his friend

> Expatiate freely o'er this scene of man,
> A mighty maze *of walks without a plan.*

For which he wrote afterwards:

> A mighty maze, *but not without a plan:*

for, if there was no plan, it was in vain to describe or to trace the maze.

The other alteration was of these lines:

> And spite of pride, *and in thy reason's spite,*
> One truth is clear, whatever is, is right:

but having afterwards discovered, or been shown, that the "truth" which subsisted "in spite of reason" could not be very "clear," he substituted:

> And spite of pride, *in erring reason's spite.*

To such oversights will the most vigorous mind be liable when it is employed at once upon argument and poetry.

The second and third Epistles were published; and Pope was, I believe, more and more suspected of writing them: at last, in 1734, he avowed the fourth, and claimed the honour of a moral poet.

In the conclusion it is sufficiently acknowledged that the doctrine of the "Essay on Man" was received from Bolingbroke, who is said to have ridiculed Pope, among those who enjoyed his confidence, as having adopted and advanced principles of which he did not perceive the consequence, and as blindly propagating opinions contrary to his own. That those communications had been consolidated into a scheme regularly drawn, and delivered to Pope, from whom it returned only transformed from prose to verse, has been reported, but hardly can be true. The "Essay" plainly appears the fabric of a poet: what Bolingbroke supplied could be only the first principles; the order, illustration, and embellishments must all be Pope's.

These principles it is not my business to clear from obscurity, dogmatism, or falsehood; but they were not immediately examined; philosophy and poetry have not often the same readers; and the "Essay" abounded in splendid amplifications and sparkling sentences, which were read and admired with no great attention to their ultimate purpose; its flowers caught the eye which did not see what the gay foliage concealed, and for a time flourished in the sunshine of universal approbation. So little was any evil tendency discovered, that, as innocence is unsuspicious, many read it for a manual of piety.

Its reputation soon invited a translator. It was first turned into French prose, and afterwards by Resnel into verse. Both translations fell into the hands of Crousaz, who first, when he had the version in prose, wrote a general censure, and afterwards reprinted Resnel's version, with particular remarks upon every paragraph.

Crousaz was a professor of Switzerland, eminent for his treatise of Logic, and his *Examen de Pyrrhonisme,* and, however little known or regarded here, was no mean antagonist. His mind was one of those in which philosophy and piety are happily united. He was accustomed to argument and disquisition, and perhaps was grown too desirous of detecting faults; but his intentions were always right, his opinions were solid, and his religion pure.

His incessant vigilance for the promotion of piety disposed him to look with distrust upon all metaphysical systems of theology, and all schemes of virtue and happiness purely rational; and therefore it was not long before he was persuaded that the positions of Pope, as they terminated for the most part in natural religion, were intended to draw mankind away from revelation, and to represent the whole course of things as a necessary concatenation of indissoluble fatality: and it is undeniable that, in many passages, a religious eye may easily discover expressions not very favourable to morals or to liberty.

About this time Warburton began to make his appearance in the first ranks of learning. He was a man of vigorous faculties, a mind fervid and vehement, supplied by incessant and unlimited inquiry, with wonderful extent and variety of knowledge, which yet had not oppressed his imagination nor clouded his perspicacity. To every work he brought a memory full fraught, together with a fancy fertile of original combinations, and at once exerted the powers of the scholar, the reasoner, and the wit. But his knowledge was too multifarious to be always exact, and his pursuits too eager to be always cautious. His abilities gave him a haughty confidence, which he disdained to conceal or mollify; and his impatience of opposition disposed him to treat his adversaries with such contemptuous superiority as made his readers commonly his enemies, and excited against the advocate the wishes of some who favoured the cause. He seems to have adopted the Roman emperor's determination, *oderint dum metuant;* he used no allurements of gentle language, but wished to compel rather than persuade.

His style is copious without selection, and forcible without neatness; he took the words that presented themselves; his diction is coarse and impure, and his sentences are unmeasured.

He had in the early part of his life pleased himself with the notice of inferior wits, and corresponded with the enemies of Pope. A letter was produced, when he had perhaps himself forgotten it, in which he tells Concanen, "Dryden, I observe, borrows for want of leisure, and Pope for want of genius; Milton out of pride, and Addison out of modesty." And when [1733] Theobald published Shakespeare, in opposition to Pope, the best notes were supplied by Warburton.

But the time was now come when Warburton was to change his opinion; and Pope was to find a defender in him who had contributed so much to the exaltation of his rival.

The arrogance of Warburton excited against him every artifice of offence, and therefore it may be supposed that his union with Pope was censured as hypocritical inconstancy; but surely to think differently at different times of poetical merit may be easily allowed. Such opinions are often admitted, and dismissed, without nice examination. Who is there that has not found reason for changing his mind about questions of greater importance?

Warburton, whatever was his motive, undertook, without solicitation, to rescue Pope from the talons of Crousaz, by freeing him from the imputation of favouring fatality, or rejecting revelation; and from month to month continued a vindication of the "Essay on Man" in the literary journal of that time called *The Republic of Letters*.

Pope, who probably began to doubt the tendency of his own work, was glad that the positions, of which he perceived himself not to know the full meaning, could by any mode of interpretation be made to mean well. How much he was pleased with his gratuitous defender the following letter evidently shows:

April 11, 1739.

SIR,

I have just received from Mr. R. two more of your letters. It is in the greatest hurry imaginable that I write this; but I cannot help thanking you in particular for your third letter, which is so extremely clear, short, and full, that I think Mr. Crousaz ought never to have another answerer, and deserved not so good an one. I can only say, you do him too much

honour, and me too much right, so odd as the expression
seems; for you have made my system as clear as I ought to
have done, and could not. It is indeed the same system as
mine, but illustrated with a ray of your own, as they say our
natural body is the same still when it is glorified. I am sure
I like it better than I did before, and so will every man else.
I know I meant just what you explain; but I did not explain
my own meaning so well as you. You understand me as well
as I do myself; but you express me better than I could express myself. Pray accept the sincerest acknowledgments.
I cannot but wish these letters were put together in one
book, and intend (with your leave) to procure a translation
of part, at least, or of all of them into French; but I shall
not proceed a step without your consent and opinion, &c.

By this fond and eager acceptance of an exculpatory
comment, Pope testified that, whatever might be the
seeming or real import of the principles which he had
received from Bolingbroke, he had not intentionally attacked religion; and Bolingbroke, if he meant to make
him, without his own consent, an instrument of mischief,
found him now engaged, with his eyes open, on the side
of truth.

It is known that Bolingbroke concealed from Pope his
real opinions. He once discovered them to Mr. Hooke,
who related them again to Pope, and was told by him
that he must have mistaken the meaning of what he
heard; and Bolingbroke, when Pope's uneasiness incited
him to desire an explanation, declared that Hooke had
misunderstood him.

Bolingbroke hated Warburton, who had drawn his
pupil from him; and a little before Pope's death they
had a dispute, from which they parted with mutual
aversion.

From this time Pope lived in the closest intimacy with
his commentator, and amply rewarded his kindness and
his zeal; for he introduced him to Mr. Murray, by whose
interest he became preacher at Lincoln's Inn, and to Mr.

Allen, who gave him his niece and his estate, and by consequence a bishopric. When he died, he left him the property of his works, a legacy which may be reasonably estimated at 4000*l*.

Pope's fondness for the "Essay on Man" appeared by his desire of its propagation. Dobson, who had gained reputation by his version of Prior's "Solomon," was employed by him to translate it into Latin verse, and was for that purpose some time at Twickenham; but he left his work, whatever was the reason, unfinished, and, by Benson's invitation, undertook the longer task of *Paradise Lost*. Pope then desired his friend to find a scholar who should turn his *Essay* into Latin prose, but no such performance has ever appeared.

Pope lived at this time *among the great*, with that reception and respect to which his works entitled him, and which he had not impaired by any private misconduct or factitious partiality. Though Bolingbroke was his friend, Walpole was not his enemy, but treated him with so much consideration as, at his request, to solicit and obtain [1728] from the French Minister an abbey for Mr. Southcott, whom he considered himself as obliged to reward, by this exertion of his interest, for the benefit which he had received from his attendance in a long illness.

It was said that, when the Court was at Richmond, Queen Caroline had declared her intention to visit him. This may have been only a careless effusion, thought on no more: the report of such notice, however, was soon in many mouths; and if I do not forget or misapprehend Savage's account, Pope, pretending to decline what was not yet offered, left his house for a time, not, I suppose, for any other reason than lest he should be thought to stay at home in expectation of an honour which would not be conferred. He was therefore angry at Swift, who represents him as "refusing the visits of a Queen," because he knew that what had never been offered had never been refused.

Beside the general system of morality, supposed to be contained in the "Essay on Man," it was his intention to write distinct poems upon the different duties or conditions of life; one of which is the Epistle to Lord Bathurst (1732) on the "Use of Riches," a piece on which he declared great labour to have been bestowed.

Into this poem some hints are historically thrown, and some known characters are introduced, with others of which it is difficult to say how far they are real or fictitious: but the praise of Kyrle, the Man of Ross, deserves particular examination, who, after a long and pompous enumeration of his public works and private charities, is said to have diffused all those blessings from *five hundred a year*. Wonders are willingly told, and willingly heard. The truth is, that Kyrle was a man of known integrity and active benevolence, by whose solicitation the wealthy were persuaded to pay contributions to his charitable schemes; this influence he obtained by an example of liberality exerted to the utmost extent of his power, and was thus enabled to give more than he had. This account Mr. Victor received from the minister of the place, and I have preserved it, that the praise of a good man, being made more credible, may be more solid. Narrations of romantic and impracticable virtue will be read with wonder, but that which is unattainable is recommended in vain: that good may be endeavoured, it must be shown to be possible.

This is the only piece in which the author has given a hint of his religion by ridiculing the ceremony of burning the Pope, and by mentioning with some indignation the inscription on the Monument.

When this poem was first published, the dialogue, having no letters of direction, was perplexed and obscure. Pope seems to have written with no very distinct idea, for he calls that an "Epistle to Bathurst," in which Bathurst is introduced as speaking.

He afterwards (1733) inscribed to Lord Cobham his "Characters of Men," written with close attention to the operations of the mind and modifications of life. In this poem he has endeavoured to establish and exemplify his favourite theory of the *ruling passion,* by which he means an original direction of desire to some particular object, an innate affection which gives all action a determinate and invariable tendency, and operates upon the whole system of life, either openly, or more secretly by the intervention of some accidental or subordinate propension.

Of any passion, thus innate and irresistible, the existence may reasonably be doubted. Human characters are by no means constant; men change by change of place, of fortune, of acquaintance; he who is at one time a lover of pleasure, is at another a lover of money. Those indeed who attain any excellence commonly spend life in one pursuit; for excellence is not often gained upon easier terms. But to the particular species of excellence men are directed, not by an ascendant planet or predominating humour, but by the first book which they read, some early conversation which they heard, or some accident which excited ardour and emulation.

It must be at least allowed that this *ruling passion,* antecedent to reason and observation, must have an object independent of human contrivance, for there can be no natural desire of artificial good. No man therefore can be born, in the strict acceptation, a lover of money, for he may be born where money does not exist: nor can he be born, in a moral sense, a lover of his country;

for society, politically regulated, is a state contradistinguished from a state of nature, and any attention to that coalition of interests which makes the happiness of a country, is possible only to those whom inquiry and reflection have enabled to comprehend it.

This doctrine is in itself pernicious as well as false: its tendency is to produce the belief of a kind of moral predestination, or overruling principle which cannot be resisted; he that admits it, is prepared to comply with every desire that caprice or opportunity shall excite, and to flatter himself that he submits only to the lawful dominion of Nature, in obeying the resistless authority of his *ruling passion*.

Pope has formed his theory with so little skill, that, in the examples by which he illustrates and confirms it, he has confounded passions, appetites, and habits.

To the "Characters of Men" he added soon after [1735], in an Epistle supposed to have been addressed to Martha Blount, but which the last edition has taken from her, the "Characters of Women." This poem, which was laboured with great diligence, and in the author's opinion with great success, was neglected at its first publication, as the commentator supposes, because the public was informed, by an advertisement, that it contained *no character drawn from the life:* an assertion which Pope probably did not expect or wish to have been believed, and which he soon gave his readers sufficient reason to distrust by telling them in a note that the work was imperfect, because part of his subject was *vice too high* to be yet exposed.

The time, however, soon came in which it was safe to display the Duchess of Marlborough under the name of *Atossa;* and her character was inserted with no great honour to the writer's gratitude.

He published from time to time (between 1733 and

1738) imitations of different poems of Horace, generally with his name, and once, as was suspected, without it. What he was upon moral principles ashamed to own, he ought to have suppressed. Of these pieces it is useless to settle the dates, as they had seldom much relation to the times, and perhaps had been long in his hands.

This mode of imitation, in which the ancients are familiarised, by adapting their sentiments to modern topics, by making Horace say of Shakespeare what he originally said of Ennius, and accommodating his satires on Pantolabus and Nomentanus to the flatterers and prodigals of our own time, was first practised in the reign of Charles the Second by Oldham and Rochester; at least I remember no instances more ancient. It is a kind of middle composition between translation and original design, which pleases when the thoughts are unexpectedly applicable, and the parallels lucky. It seems to have been Pope's favourite amusement, for he has carried it farther than any former poet.

He published likewise a revival, in smoother numbers, of Dr. Donne's *Satires,* which was recommended to him by the Duke of Shrewsbury and the Earl of Oxford. They made no great impression on the public. Pope seems to have known their imbecility, and therefore suppressed them while he was yet contending to rise in reputation, but ventured them when he thought their deficiencies more likely to be imputed to Donne than to himself.

The "Epistle to Dr. Arbuthnot," which seems to be derived in its first design from Boileau's Address *à son Esprit,* was published in January 1734-5, about a month before the death of him to whom it is inscribed. It is to be regretted that either honour or pleasure should have been missed by Arbuthnot,—a man estimable for his learning, amiable for his life, and venerable for his piety.

Arbuthnot was a man of great comprehension, skilful in his profession, versed in the sciences, acquainted with ancient literature, and able to animate his mass of knowledge by a bright and active imagination; a scholar with great brilliance of wit; a wit who, in the crowd of life, retained and discovered a noble ardour of religious zeal.

In this poem Pope seems to reckon with the public. He vindicates himself from censures, and with dignity, rather than arrogance, enforces his own claims to kindness and respect.

Into this poem are interwoven several paragraphs which had been before printed as a fragment, and among them the satirical lines upon Addison, of which the last couplet has been twice corrected. It was at first:

> Who would not smile if such a man there be?
> Who would not laugh if Addison were he?

Then:

> Who would not grieve if such a man there be?
> Who would not laugh if Addison were he?

At last it is:

> Who but must laugh if such a man there be?
> Who would not weep if Atticus were he?

He was at this time at open war with Lord Hervey, who had distinguished himself as a steady adherent to the Ministry, and being offended with a contemptuous answer to one of his pamphlets, had summoned Pulteney to a duel. Whether he or Pope made the first attack perhaps cannot now be easily known; he had written an invective against Pope, whom he calls, "Hard as thy heart, and as thy birth obscure," and hints that his father was a *hatter*. To this Pope wrote a reply in verse and prose; the verses are in this poem, and the prose, though it was never sent, is printed among his Letters, but to a cool reader of the present time exhibits nothing but tedious malignity.

His last Satires, of the general kind, were two Dialogues, named, from the year in which they were published, *Seventeen Hundred and Thirty-eight*. In these poems many are praised and many are reproached. Pope was then entangled in the Opposition; a follower of the Prince of Wales, who dined at his house, and the friend of many who obstructed and censured the conduct of the Ministers. His political partiality was too plainly shown; he forgot the prudence with which he passed, in his earlier years, uninjured and unoffending, through much more violent conflicts of faction.

In the first Dialogue, having an opportunity of praising Allen of Bath, he asked his leave to mention him as a man not illustrious by any merit of his ancestors, and called him in his verses "low-born Allen." Men are seldom satisfied with praise introduced or followed by any mention of defect. Allen seems not to have taken any pleasure in his epithet, which was afterwards softened into "humble Allen."

In the second Dialogue he took some liberty with one of the Foxes, among others; which Fox, in a reply to Lyttelton, took an opportunity of repaying, by reproaching him with the friendship of a lampooner, who scattered his ink without fear or decency, and against whom he hoped the resentment of the Legislature would quickly be discharged.

About this time [1739] Paul Whitehead, a small poet, was summoned before the Lords for a poem called *Manners*, together with Dodsley, his publisher. Whitehead, who hung loose upon society, sculked and escaped; but Dodsley's shop and family made his appearance necessary. He was, however, soon dismissed; and the whole process was probably intended rather to intimidate Pope than to punish Whitehead.

Pope never afterwards attempted to join the patriot with the poet, nor drew his pen upon statesmen. That he desisted from his attempts of reformation is imputed by his commentator to his despair of prevailing over the corruption of the time. He was not likely to have been ever of opinion that the dread of his satire would countervail the love of power or of money; he pleased himself with being important and formidable, and gratified sometimes his pride, and sometimes his resentment; till at last he began to think he should be more safe if he were less busy.

The *Memoirs of Scriblerus,* published about this time, extend only to the first book of a work projected in concert by Pope, Swift, and Arbuthnot, who used to meet in the time of Queen Anne, and denominated themselves the "Scriblerus Club." Their purpose was to censure the abuses of learning by a fictitious Life of an infatuated Scholar. They were dispersed; the design was never completed; and Warburton laments its miscarriage as an event very disastrous to polite letters.

If the whole may be estimated by this specimen, which seems to be the production of Arbuthnot, with a few touches perhaps by Pope, the want of more will not be much lamented; for the follies which the writer ridicules are so little practised, that they are not known: nor can the satire be understood but by the learned; he raises phantoms of absurdity, and then drives them away. He cures diseases that were never felt.

For this reason this joint production of three great writers has never obtained any notice from mankind; it has been little read, or when read has been forgotten, as no man could be wiser, better, or merrier by remembering it.

The design cannot boast of much originality; for besides its general resemblance to Don Quixote, there will be found in it particular imitations of the History of Mr. Ouffle.

Swift carried so much of it into Ireland as supplied him with hints for his travels; and with those the world might have been contented, though the rest had been suppressed.

Pope had sought for images and sentiments in a region not known to have been explored by many other of the English writers; he had consulted the modern writers of Latin poetry, a class of authors whom Boileau endeavoured to bring into contempt, and who are too generally neglected. Pope, however, was not ashamed of their acquaintance, nor ungrateful for the advantages which he might have derived from it. A small selection from the Italians who wrote in Latin had been published at London, about the latter end of the last century, by a man who concealed his name, but whom his Preface shows to have been well qualified for his undertaking. This collection Pope amplified by more than half, and (1740) published it in two volumes, but injuriously omitted his predecessor's Preface. To these books, which had nothing but the mere text, no regard was paid, the authors were still neglected, and the editor was neither praised nor censured.

He did not sink into idleness; he had planned a work, which he considered as subsequent to his "Essay on Man," of which he has given this account to Dr. Swift:

March 25, 1736.

If ever I write more Epistles in verse, one of them shall be addressed to you. I have long concerted it, and begun it; but I would make what bears your name as finished as my last work ought to be, that is to say, more finished than any of the rest. The subject is large, and will divide into four Epistles, which naturally follow the *Essay on Man,* viz.—1. Of the Extent and Limits of Human Reason and Science. 2. A View of the Useful and therefore Attainable, and of the Unuseful and therefore Unattainable Arts. 3. Of the Nature, Ends, Application, and Use of different Capacities. 4. Of the Use of Learning, of the Science, of the World, and of Wit. It will conclude with a Satire against the misapplication of all these, exemplified by Pictures, Characters, and Examples.

This work, in its full extent, being now afflicted with an asthma, and finding the powers of life gradually declining, he had no longer courage to undertake; but, from the materials which he had provided, he added, at Warburton's request, another book to "The Dunciad," of which the design is to ridicule such studies as are either hopeless or useless, as either pursue what is unattainable, or what, if it be attained, is of no use.

When this book was printed (March 1742) the laurel had been for some time upon the head of Cibber; a man whom it cannot be supposed that Pope could regard with much kindness or esteem, though in one of the *Imitations of Horace* he has liberally enough praised "The Careless Husband." In "The Dunciad," among other worthless scribblers, he had mentioned Cibber; who, in his *Apology,* complains of the great poet's unkindness as more injurious, "because," says he, "I never have offended him."

It might have been expected that Pope should have been, in some degree, mollified by this submissive gentleness, but no such consequence appeared. Though he condescended to commend Cibber once, he mentioned him afterwards contemptuously in one of his satires, and again in his "Epistle to Arbuthnot"; and in the fourth book of "The Dunciad" attacked him with acrimony, to which the provocation is not easily discoverable. Perhaps he imagined that, in ridiculing the laureat, he satirised those by whom the laurel had been given, and gratified that ambitious petulance with which he affected to insult the great.

The severity of this satire left Cibber no longer any patience. He had confidence enough in his own powers to believe that he could disturb the quiet of his adversary, and doubtless did not want instigators, who, without any care about the victory, desired to amuse themselves by looking on the contest. He therefore gave the town a pamphlet, in which he declares his resolution from that time never to bear another blow without returning it, and to tire out his adversary by perseverance, if he cannot conquer him by strength.

The incessant and unappeasable malignity of Pope he imputes to a very distant cause. After the *Three Hours after Marriage* had been driven off the stage by the offence which the mummy and crocodile gave the audience, while the exploded scene was yet fresh in memory, it happened that Cibber played Bayes in *The Rehearsal;* and, as it had been usual to enliven the part by the mention of any recent theatrical transactions, he said that he once thought to have introduced his lovers disguised in a mummy and a crocodile. "This," says he, "was received with loud claps, which indicated contempt of the play." Pope, who was behind the scenes, meeting him as he left the stage, attacked him, as he says, with all the virulence of a "wit out of his senses"; to which he replied, "that he would take no other notice of what was said by so particular a man, than to declare, that, as often as he played that part, he would repeat the same provocation."

He shows his opinion to be, that Pope was one of the authors of the play which he so zealously defended; and adds an idle story of Pope's behaviour at a tavern.

The pamphlet was written with little power of thought or language, and, if suffered to remain without notice, would have been very soon forgotten. Pope had now been enough acquainted with human life to know, if his passion had not been too powerful for his understanding, that, from a contention like his with Cibber, the world seeks nothing but diversion, which is given at the expense of the higher character. When Cibber lampooned Pope, curiosity was excited; what Pope would say of Cibber nobody inquired, but in hope that Pope's asperity might betray his pain and lessen his dignity.

He should therefore have suffered the pamphlet to flutter and die, without confessing that it stung him. The dishonour of being shown as Cibber's antagonist could never be compensated by the victory. Cibber had nothing to lose: when Pope had exhausted all his malignity upon him, he would rise in the esteem both of his friends and his enemies. Silence only could have made him despicable; the blow which did not appear to be felt would have been struck in vain.

But Pope's irascibility prevailed, and he resolved to tell the whole English world that he was at war with Cibber; and to show that he thought him no common adversary, he prepared no common vengeance; he published [October 1743] a new edition of "The Dunciad," in which he degraded Theobald from his painful pre-eminence, and enthroned Cibber in his stead. Unhappily the two heroes were of opposite characters, and Pope was unwilling to lose what he had already written; he has therefore depraved his poem by giving to Cibber the old books, the cold pedantry, and sluggish pertinacity of Theobald.

Pope was ignorant enough of his own interest to make another change, and introduced Osborne contending for the prize among the booksellers. Osborne was a man

entirely destitute of shame, without sense of any disgrace but that of poverty. He told me, when he was
doing that which raised Pope's resentment, that he
should be put into "The Dunciad"; but he had the fate
of Cassandra. I gave no credit to his prediction, till in
time I saw it accomplished. The shafts of satire were
directed equally in vain against Cibber and Osborne;
being repelled by the impenetrable impudence of one,
and deadened by the impassive dullness of the other.
Pope confessed his own pain by his anger; but he gave
no pain to those who had provoked him. He was able to
hurt none but himself; by transferring the same ridicule
from one to another he destroyed its efficacy; for by
showing that what he had said of one he was ready to
say of another, he reduced himself to the insignificance
of his own magpie, who from his cage calls cuckold at
a venture.

Cibber, according to his engagement, repaid "The
Dunciad" with another pamphlet, which, Pope said,
"would be as good as a dose of hartshorn to him"; but
his tongue and his heart were at variance. I have heard
Mr. Richardson relate, that he attended his father the
painter on a visit, when one of Cibber's pamphlets came
into the hands of Pope, who said, "These things are my
diversion." They sat by him while he perused it, and
saw his features written with anguish; and young Richardson said to his father, when they returned, that he
hoped to be preserved from such diversion as had been
that day the lot of Pope.

From this time, finding his diseases more oppressive,
and his vital powers gradually declining, he no longer
strained his faculties with any original composition, nor
proposed any other employment for his remaining life
than the revisal and correction of his former works; in

which he received advice and assistance from Warburton, whom he appears to have trusted and honoured in the highest degree.

He laid aside his epic poem, perhaps without much loss to mankind; for his hero was Brutus the Trojan, who, according to a ridiculous fiction, established a colony in Britain. The subject therefore was of the fabulous age; the actors were a race upon whom imagination has been exhausted and attention wearied, and to whom the mind will not easily be recalled when it is invited in blank verse, which Pope had adopted with great imprudence, and I think without due consideration of the nature of our language. The sketch is, at least in part, preserved by Ruffhead; by which it appears that Pope was thoughtless enough to model the names of his heroes with terminations not consistent with the time or country in which he places them.

He lingered through the next year; but perceived himself, as he expresses it, "going down the hill." He had for at least five years been afflicted with an asthma, and other disorders, which his physicians were unable to relieve. Towards the end of his life he consulted Dr. Thomson, a man who had, by large promises and free censures of the common practice of physic, forced himself up into sudden reputation. Thomson declared his distemper to be a dropsy, and evacuated part of the water by tincture of jalap, but confessed that his belly did not subside. Thomson had many enemies, and Pope was persuaded to dismiss him.

While he was yet capable of amusement and conversation, as he was one day sitting in the air with Lord Bolingbroke and Lord Marchmont, he saw his favourite Martha Blount at the bottom of the terrace, and asked Lord Bolingbroke to go and hand her up. Bolingbroke, not liking his errand, crossed his legs and sat still; but

Lord Marchmont, who was younger and less captious, waited on the lady; who, when he came to her, asked, "What, is he not dead yet?" She is said to have neglected him, with shameful unkindness, in the latter time of his decay; yet, of the little which he had to leave, she had a very great part. Their acquaintance began early; the life of each was pictured on the other's mind; their conversation therefore was endearing, for when they met, there was an immediate coalition of congenial notions. Perhaps he considered her unwillingness to approach the chamber of sickness as female weakness or human frailty; perhaps he was conscious to himself of peevishness and impatience, or, though he was offended by her inattention, might yet consider her merit as overbalancing her fault; and if he had suffered his heart to be alienated from her, he could have found nothing that might fill her place; he could have only shrunk within himself; it was too late to transfer his confidence or fondness.

In May 1744 his death was approaching; on the 6th, he was all day delirious, which he mentioned four days afterwards as a sufficient humiliation of the vanity of man; he afterwards complained of seeing things as through a curtain and in false colours, and one day, in the presence of Dodsley, asked what arm it was that came out from the wall. He said that his greatest inconvenience was inability to think.

Bolingbroke sometimes wept over him in this state of helpless decay; and being told by Spence that Pope, at the intermission of his deliriousness, was always saying something kind either of his present or absent friends, and that his humanity seemed to have survived his understanding, answered, "It has so." And added, "I never in my life knew a man that had so tender a heart for his particular friends, or a more general friendship for mankind." At another time he said, "I have known Pope these thirty years, and value myself more in his friendship than"—his grief then suppressed his voice.

Pope expressed undoubting confidence of a future state. Being asked by his friend Mr. Hooke, a Papist, whether he would not die like his father and mother, and whether a priest should not be called, he answered, "I do not think it essential, but it will be very right; and I thank you for putting me in mind of it."

In the morning, after the priest had given him the last sacraments, he said, "There is nothing that is meritorious but virtue and friendship; and indeed friendship itself is only a part of virtue."

He died in the evening of the 30th day of May, 1744, so placidly, that the attendants did not discern the exact time of his expiration. He was buried at Twickenham, near his father and mother, where a monument has been erected to him by his commentator, the Bishop of Gloucester.

He left the care of his papers to his executors; first to Lord Bolingbroke, and if he should not be living, to the Earl of Marchmont; undoubtedly expecting them to be proud of the trust, and eager to extend his fame. But let no man dream of influence beyond his life. After a decent time, Dodsley the bookseller went to solicit preference as the publisher, and was told that the parcel had not been yet inspected; and whatever was the reason, the world has been disappointed of what was "reserved for the next age."

He lost, indeed, the favour of Bolingbroke by a kind of posthumous offence. The political pamphlet called *The Patriot King* had been put into his hands that he might procure the impression of a very few copies, to be distributed, according to the author's direction, among his friends, and Pope assured him that no more had been

printed than were allowed; but, soon after his death,
the printer brought and resigned a complete edition of
fifteen hundred copies, which Pope had ordered him to
print, and to retain in secret. He kept, as was observed,
his engagement to Pope better than Pope had kept it to
his friend; and nothing was known of the transaction till,
upon the death of his employer, he thought himself
obliged to deliver the books to the right owner, who,
with great indignation, made a fire in his yard, and delivered the whole impression to the flames.

Hitherto nothing had been done which was not naturally dictated by resentment of violated faith; resentment more acrimonious, as the violator had been more
loved or more trusted. But here the anger might have
stopped; the injury was private, and there was little
danger from the example.

Bolingbroke, however, was not yet satisfied; his thirst
of vengeance excited him to blast the memory of tho
man over whom he had wept in his last struggles; and
he employed Mallet, another friend of Pope, to tell the
tale to the public, with all its aggravations. Warburton,
whose heart was warm with his legacy, and tender by
the recent separation, thought it proper for him to interpose; and undertook, not indeed to vindicate the action,
for breach of trust has always something criminal, but
to extenuate it by an apology. Having advanced what
cannot be denied, that moral obliquity is made more or
less excusable by the motives that produce it, he in-
quires what evil purpose could have induced Pope to
break his promise. He could not delight his vanity by
usurping the work, which, though not sold in shops, had
been shown to a number more than sufficient to preserve the author's claim; he could not gratify his avarice,
for he could not sell his plunder till Bolingbroke was
dead; and even then, if the copy was left to another, his

fraud would be defeated, and if left to himself, would be useless.

Warburton therefore supposes, with great appearance of reason, that the irregularity of his conduct proceeded wholly from his zeal for Bolingbroke, who might perhaps have destroyed the pamphlet, which Pope thought it his duty to preserve, even without its author's approbation. To this apology an answer was written in *A Letter to the most impudent Man living.*

He brought some reproach upon his own memory by the petulant and contemptuous mention made in his will of Mr. Allen, and an affected repayment of his benefactions. Mrs. Blount, as the known friend and favourite of Pope, had been invited to the house of Allen, where she comported herself with such indecent arrogance, that she parted from Mrs. Allen in a state of irreconcileable dislike, and the door was for ever barred against her. This exclusion she resented with so much bitterness as to refuse any legacy from Pope, unless he left the world with a disavowal of obligation to Allen. Having been long under her dominion, now tottering in the decline of life, and unable to resist the violence of her temper, or perhaps, with the prejudice of a lover, persuaded that she had suffered improper treatment, he complied with her demand, and polluted his will with female resentment. Allen accepted the legacy, which he gave to the hospital at Bath, observing that Pope was always a bad accountant, and that if to 150*l.* he had put a cypher more, he had come nearer to the truth.

The person of Pope is well known not to have been formed by the nicest model. He has, in his account of the "Little Club," compared himself to a spider, and by another is described as protuberant behind and before. He is said to have been beautiful in his infancy; but he was of a constitution originally feeble and weak; and as bodies of a tender frame are easily distorted, his deformity was probably in part the effect of his application. His stature was so low, that, to bring him to a level with common tables, it was necessary to raise his seat. But his face was not displeasing, and his eyes were animated and vivid.

By natural deformity, or accidental distortion, his vital functions were so much disordered, that his life was a "long disease." His most frequent assailant was the headache, which he used to relieve by inhaling the steam of coffee, which he very frequently required.

Most of what can be told concerning his petty peculiarities was communicated by a female domestic of the Earl of Oxford, who knew him perhaps after the middle of life. He was then so weak as to stand in perpetual need of female attendance: extremely sensible of cold, so that he wore a kind of fur doublet under a shirt of a very coarse warm linen with fine sleeves. When he rose, he was invested in bodice made of stiff canvas, being scarce able to hold himself erect till they were laced, and he then put on a flannel waistcoat. One side was contracted. His legs were so slender, that he enlarged their bulk with three pair of stockings, which were drawn on and off by the maid; for he was not able to dress or undress himself, and neither went to bed nor rose without help. His weakness made it very difficult for him to be clean.

His hair had fallen almost all away; and he used to dine sometimes with Lord Oxford, privately, in a velvet cap. His dress of ceremony was black, with a tye-wig and a little sword.

The indulgence and accommodation which his sickness required had taught him all the unpleasing and unsocial qualities of a valetudinary man. He expected that everything should give way to his ease or humour, as a child whose parents will not hear her cry, has an unresisted dominion in the nursery.

C'est que l'enfant toujours est homme,
C'est que l'homme est toujours enfant.

When he wanted to sleep, he "nodded in company"; and once slumbered at his own table while the Prince of Wales was talking of poetry.

The reputation which his friendship gave procured him many invitations; but he was a very troublesome inmate. He brought no servant, and had so many wants that a numerous attendance was scarcely able to supply them. Wherever he was, he left no room for another, because he exacted the attention and employed the activity of the whole family. His errands were so frequent and frivolous that the footmen in time avoided and neglected him; and the Earl of Oxford discharged some of the servants for their resolute refusal of his messages. The maids, when they had neglected their business, alleged that they had been employed by Mr. Pope. One of his constant demands was of coffee in the night, and to the woman that waited on him in his chamber he was very burthensome: but he was careful to recompense her want of sleep; and Lord Oxford's servant declared, that in a house where her business was to answer his call she would not ask for wages.

He had another fault, easily incident to those who, suffering much pain, think themselves entitled to what pleasures they can snatch. He was too indulgent to his appetite; he loved meat highly seasoned and of strong taste; and, at the intervals of the table, amused himself with biscuits and dry conserves. If he sat down to a variety of dishes, he would oppress his stomach with repletion; and though he seemed angry when a dram was offered him, did not forbear to drink it. His friends, who knew the avenues to his heart, pampered him with presents of luxury, which he did not suffer to stand neglected. The death of great men is not always proportioned to the lustre of their lives. Hannibal, says Juvenal, did not perish by a javelin or a sword; the slaughters of Cannæ were revenged by a ring. The death of Pope was imputed by some of his friends to a silver saucepan, in which it was his delight to heat potted lampreys.

That he loved too well to eat is certain; but that his sensuality shortened his life will not be hastily concluded, when it is remembered that a conformation so irregular lasted six and fifty years, notwithstanding such pertinacious diligence of study and meditation.

In all his intercourse with mankind he had great delight in artifice, and endeavoured to attain all his purposes by indirect and unsuspected methods. "He hardly drank tea without a stratagem." If, at the house of his friends, he wanted any accommodation, he was not willing to ask for it in plain terms, but would mention it remotely as something convenient; though, when it was procured, he soon made it appear for whose sake it had been recommended. Thus he teased Lord Orrery till he obtained a screen. He practised his arts on such small occasions, that Lady Bolingbroke used to say, in a French phrase, that "he played the politician about cabbages and turnips." His unjustifiable impression of *The Patriot King*, as it can be imputed to no particular motive, must have proceeded from his general habit of secrecy and cunning; he caught an opportunity of a sly trick, and pleased himself with the thought of outwitting Bolingbroke.

In familiar or convivial conversation it does not appear that he excelled. He may be said to have resembled Dryden as being not one that was distinguished by vivacity in company. It is remarkable that, so near his time, so much should be known of what he has written and so little of what he has said: traditional memory retains no sallies of raillery nor sentences of observation; nothing either pointed or solid, either wise or merry. One apophthegm only stands upon record. When an objection raised against his inscription for Shakespeare was defended by the authority of Patrick, he replied—"*horresco referens*"—that "he would allow the publisher of a Dictionary to know the meaning of a single word, but not of two words put together."

He was fretful and easily displeased, and allowed himself to be capriciously resentful. He would sometimes leave Lord Oxford silently, no one could tell why, and was to be courted back by more letters and messages than the footmen were willing to carry. The table was indeed infested by Lady Mary Wortley, who was the friend of Lady Oxford, and who, knowing his peevishness, could by no intreaties be restrained from contradicting him, till their disputes were sharpened to such asperity that one or the other quitted the house.

He sometimes condescended to be jocular with servants or inferiors; but by no merriment, either of others or his own, was he ever seen excited to laughter.

Of his domestic character frugality was a part eminently remarkable. Having determined not to be dependent, he determined not to be in want, and therefore wisely and magnanimously rejected all temptations to expense unsuitable to his fortune. This general care must be universally approved; but it sometimes appeared in petty artifices of parsimony, such as the practice of writing his compositions on the back of letters, as may be seen in the remaining copy of the Iliad, by which perhaps in five years five shillings were saved; or in a niggardly reception of his friends and scantiness of entertainment, as, when he had two guests in his house, he would set at supper a single pint upon the table; and, having himself taken two small glasses, would retire and say, "Gentlemen, I leave you to your wine." Yet he tells his friends that "he has a heart for all, a house for all, and, whatever they may think, a fortune for all."

He sometimes, however, made a splendid dinner, and is said to have wanted no part of the skill or elegance which such performances require. That this magnificence should be often displayed, that obstinate prudence with which he conducted his affairs would not permit; for his revenue, certain and casual, amounted only to about eight hundred pounds a year, of which however he declares himself able to assign one hundred to charity.

Of this fortune, which, as it arose from public approbation, was very honourably obtained, his imagination seems to have been too full: it would be hard to find a man, so well entitled to notice by his wit, that ever delighted so much in talking of his money. In his letters and in his poems, his garden and his grotto, his quincunx and his vines, or some hints of his opulence, are always to be found. The great topic of his ridicule is poverty; the crimes with which he reproaches his antagonists are their debts, their habitation in the Mint, and their want of a dinner. He seems to be of an opinion not very uncommon in the world, that to want money is to want everything.

Next to the pleasure of contemplating his possessions seems to be that of enumerating the men of high rank with whom he was acquainted, and whose notice he loudly proclaims not to have been obtained by any practices of meanness or servility, a boast which was never denied to be true, and to which very few poets have ever aspired. Pope never set genius to sale; he never flattered those whom he did not love, or praised those whom he did not esteem. Savage however remarked, that he began a little to relax his dignity when he wrote a distich for "his Highness's dog."

His admiration of the great seems to have increased in the advance of life. He passed over peers and statesmen to inscribe his Iliad to Congreve, with a magnanimity of which the praise had been complete, had his friend's virtue been equal to his wit. Why he was chosen for so great an honour it is not now possible to know; there is no trace in literary history of any particular intimacy between them. The name of Congreve appears in the letters among those of his other friends, but without any observable distinction or consequence.

To his latter works, however, he took care to annex names dignified with titles, but was not very happy in his choice; for, except Lord Bathurst, none of his noble friends were such as that a good man would wish to have his intimacy with them known to posterity: he can derive little honour from the notice of Cobham, Burlington, or Bolingbroke.

Of his social qualities, if an estimate be made from his Letters, an opinion too favourable cannot easily be formed; they exhibit a perpetual and unclouded effulgence of general benevolence and particular fondness. There is nothing but liberality, gratitude, constancy, and tenderness. It has been so long said as to be commonly believed, that the true characters of men may be found in their letters, and that he who writes to his friend lays his heart open before him. But the truth is, that such were the simple friendships of the "Golden Age," and are now the friendships only of children. Very few can boast of hearts which they dare lay open to themselves, and of which, by whatever accident exposed, they do not shun a distinct and continued view: and, certainly, what we hide from ourselves we do not show to our friends. There is, indeed, no transaction which offers stronger temptations to fallacy and sophistication than epistolary intercourse. In the eagerness of conversation the first emotions of the mind often burst out before they are considered; in the tumult of business, interest and passion have their genuine effect; but a friendly letter is a calm and deliberate performance, in the cool of leisure, in the stillness of solitude, and surely no man sits down to depreciate by design his own character.

Friendship has no tendency to secure veracity; for by whom can a man so much wish to be thought better than he is, as by him whose kindness he desires to gain or keep? Even in writing to the world there is less constraint; the author is not confronted with his reader, and takes his chance of approbation among the different dispositions of mankind; but a letter is addressed to a single mind, of which the prejudices and partialities are known, and must therefore please, if not by favouring them, by forbearing to oppose them.

To charge those favourable representations which men give of their own minds with the guilt of hypocritical falsehood, would show more severity than knowledge. The writer commonly believes himself. Almost every man's thoughts, while they are general, are right; and most hearts are pure while temptation is away. It is easy to awaken generous sentiments in privacy; to despise death when there is no danger; to glow with benevolence when there is nothing to be given. While such ideas are formed they are felt, and self-love does not suspect the gleam of virtue to be the meteor of fancy.

If the Letters of Pope are considered merely as compositions, they seem to be premeditated and artificial. It is one thing to write, because there is something which the mind wishes to discharge; and another to solicit the imagination, because ceremony or vanity requires something to be written. Pope confesses his early letters to be vitiated with *affectation and ambition:* to know whether he disentangled himself from these perverters of epistolary integrity his book and his life must be set in comparison.

One of his favourite topics is contempt of his own poetry. For this, if it had been real, he would deserve no commendation; and in this he was certainly not sincere, for his high value of himself was sufficiently observed; and of what could he be proud but of his poetry? He writes, he says, when "he has just nothing else to do"; yet Swift complains that he was never at leisure for conversation, because he "had always some poetical scheme in his head." It was punctually required that his writing-box should be set upon his bed before he rose; and Lord Oxford's domestic related, that in the dreadful winter of Forty [1740] she was called from her bed by him four times in one night to supply him with paper lest he should lose a thought.

He pretends insensibility to censure and criticism, though it was observed by all who knew him that every pamphlet disturbed his quiet, and that his extreme irritability laid him open to perpetual vexation; but he wished to despise his critics, and therefore hoped that he did despise them.

As he happened to live in two reigns when the Court paid little attention to poetry, he nursed in his mind a foolish disesteem of Kings, and proclaims that "he never sees Courts." Yet a little regard shown him by the Prince of Wales melted his obduracy; and he had not much to say when he was asked by his Royal Highness, "How he could love a Prince while he disliked Kings?"

He very frequently professes contempt of the world, and represents himself as looking on mankind, sometimes with gay indifference, as on emmets of a hillock, below his serious attention; and sometimes with gloomy indignation, as on monsters more worthy of hatred than of pity. These were dispositions apparently counterfeited. How could he despise those whom he lived by pleasing, and on whose approbation his esteem of himself was superstructed? Why should he hate those to whose favour he owed his honour and his ease? Of things that terminate in human life, the world is the proper judge; to despise its sentence, if it were possible, is not just; and if it were just, is not possible. Pope was far enough from this unreasonable temper; he was sufficiently *a fool to Fame,* and his fault was, that he pretended to neglect it. His levity and his sullenness were only in his Letters; he passed through common life, sometimes vexed, and sometimes pleased, with the natural emotions of common men.

His scorn of the Great is repeated too often to be real; no man thinks much of that which he despises; and as falsehood is always in danger of inconsistency, he makes it his boast at another time that he lives among them.

It is evident that his own importance swells often in his mind. He is afraid of writing, lest the clerks of the Post-office should know his secrets; he has many enemies; he considers himself as surrounded by universal jealousy; "after many deaths, and many dispersions, two or three of us," says he, "may still be brought together, not to plot, but to divert ourselves, and the world too, if it pleases"; and they can live together, and "show what friends wits may be, in spite of all the fools in the world." All this while it was likely that the clerks did not know his hand; he certainly had no more enemies than a public character like his inevitably excites; and with what degree of friendship the wits might live, very few were so much fools as ever to inquire.

Some part of this pretended discontent he learned from Swift, and expresses it, I think, most frequently in his correspondence with him. Swift's resentment was unreasonable, but it was sincere; Pope's was the mere mimicry of his friend, a fictitious part which he began to play before it became him. When he was only twenty-five years old, he related that "a glut of study and retirement had thrown him on the world," and that there was danger lest "a glut of the world should throw him back upon study and retirement." To this Swift answered with great propriety, that Pope had not yet either acted or suffered enough in the world to have become weary of it. And, indeed, it must be some very powerful reason that can drive back to solitude him who has once enjoyed the pleasures of society.

In the Letters both of Swift and Pope there appears such narrowness of mind as makes them insensible of any excellence that has not some affinity with their own, and confines their esteem and approbation to so small a number, that whoever should form his opinion of the age from their representation, would suppose them to have lived amidst ignorance and barbarity, unable to find among their contemporaries either virtue or intelligence, and persecuted by those that could not understand them.

When Pope murmurs at the world, when he professes contempt of fame, when he speaks of riches and poverty, of success and disappointment, with negligent indifference, he certainly does not express his habitual and settled sentiments, but either wilfully disguises his own character, or, what is more likely, invests himself with temporary qualities, and sallies out in the colours of the present moment. His hopes and fears, his joys and sorrows, acted strongly upon his mind; and if he differed from others, it was not by carelessness; he was irritable and resentful; his malignity to Philips, whom he had first made ridiculous, and then hated for being angry, continued too long. Of his vain desire to make Bentley contemptible, I never heard any adequate reason. He was sometimes wanton in his attacks; and, before Chandos, Lady Wortley, and Hill, was mean in his retreat.

The virtues which seem to have had most of his affection were liberality and fidelity of friendship, in which it does not appear that he was other than he describes himself. His fortune did not suffer his charity to be splendid and conspicuous; but he assisted Dodsley with a hundred pounds, that he might open a shop; and of the subscription of forty pounds a year that he raised for Savage, twenty were paid by himself. He was accused of loving money, but his love was eagerness to gain, not solicitude to keep it.

In the duties of friendship he was zealous and constant; his early maturity of mind commonly united him with men older than himself; and therefore, without attaining any considerable length of life, he saw many companions of his youth sink into the grave; but it does not appear that he lost a single friend by coldness or by injury; those who loved him once, continued their kindness. His ungrateful mention of Allen in his will was the effect of his adherence to one whom he had known much longer, and whom he naturally loved with greater fondness. His violation of the trust reposed in him by Bolingbroke could have no motive inconsistent with the warmest affection; he either thought the action so near to indifferent that he forgot it, or so laudable that he expected his friend to approve it.

It was reported, with such confidence as almost to enforce belief, that in the papers intrusted to his executors was found a defamatory Life of Swift, which he had prepared as an instrument of vengeance, to be used if any provocation should be ever given. About this I inquired of the Earl of Marchmont, who assured me that no such piece was among his remains.

The religion in which he lived and died was that of the Church of Rome, to which in his correspondence with Racine he professes himself a sincere adherent. That he was not scrupulously pious in some part of his life, is known by many idle and indecent applications of sentences taken from the Scriptures; a mode of merriment which a good man dreads for its profaneness, and a witty man disdains for its easiness and vulgarity. But to whatever levities he has been betrayed, it does not appear that his principles were ever corrupted, or that he ever lost his belief of Revelation. The positions which he transmitted from Bolingbroke he seems not to have understood, and was pleased with an interpretation that made them orthodox.

A man of such exalted superiority, and so little moderation, would naturally have all his delinquencies observed and aggravated: those who could not deny that he was excellent, would rejoice to find that he was not perfect.

Perhaps it may be imputed to the unwillingness with which the same man is allowed to possess many advantages, that his learning has been depreciated. He certainly was, in his early life, a man of great literary curiosity; and when he wrote his "Essay on Criticism" had, for his age, a very wide acquaintance with books. When he entered into the living world, it seems to have happened to him as to many others, that he was less attentive to dead masters; he studied in the academy of Paracelsus, and made the universe his favourite volume.

He gathered his notions fresh from reality, not from the copies of authors, but the originals of Nature. Yet there is no reason to believe that literature ever lost his esteem; he always professed to love reading; and Dobson, who spent some time at his house translating his "Essay on Man," when I asked him what learning he found him to possess, answered, "More than I expected." His frequent references to history, his allusions to various kinds of knowledge, and his images selected from art and nature, with his observations on the operations of the mind and the modes of life, show an intelligence perpetually on the wing, excursive, vigorous, and diligent, eager to pursue knowledge, and attentive to retain it.

From this curiosity arose the desire of travelling, to which he alludes in his verses to Jervas, and which, though he never found an opportunity to gratify it, did not leave him till his life declined.

Of his intellectual character, the constituent and fundamental principle was good sense, a prompt and intuitive perception of consonance and propriety. He saw immediately, of his own conceptions, what was to be chosen, and what to be rejected; and, in the works of others, what was to be shunned, and what was to be copied.

But good sense alone is a sedate and quiescent quality, which manages its possessions well, but does not increase them; it collects few materials for its own operations, and preserves safety, but never gains supremacy. Pope had likewise genius; a mind active, ambitious, and adventurous, always investigating, always aspiring; in its widest searches still longing to go forward, in its highest flights still wishing to be higher; always imagining something greater than it knows, always endeavouring more than it can do.

To assist these powers, he is said to have had great

strength and exactness of memory. That which he had heard or read was not easily lost; and he had before him not only what his own meditations suggested, but what he had found in other writers, that might be accommodated to his present purpose.

These benefits of nature he improved by incessant and unwearied diligence; he had recourse to every source of intelligence, and lost no opportunity of information; he consulted the living as well as the dead; he read his compositions to his friends, and was never content with mediocrity when excellence could be attained. He considered poetry as the business of his life; and, however he might seem to lament his occupation, he followed it with constancy; to make verses was his first labour, and to mend them was his last.

From his attention to poetry he was never diverted. If conversation offered anything that could be improved, he committed it to paper; if a thought, or perhaps an expression more happy than was common, rose to his mind, he was careful to write it; an independent distich was preserved for an opportunity of insertion; and some little fragments have been found containing lines, or parts of lines, to be wrought upon at some other time.

He was one of those few whose labour is their pleasure: he was never elevated to negligence, nor wearied to impatience; he never passed a fault unamended by indifference, nor quitted it by despair. He laboured his works first to gain reputation and afterwards to keep it.

Of composition there are different methods. Some employ at once memory and invention, and, with little intermediate use of the pen, form and polish large masses by continued meditation, and write their productions only when, in their own opinion, they have completed them. It is related of Virgil, that his custom was to pour out a great number of verses in the morning, and pass

the day in retrenching exuberances and correcting in-
accuracies. The method of Pope, as may be collected
from his translation, was to write his first thoughts in
his first words, and gradually to amplify, decorate, rectify, and refine them.

With such faculties, and such dispositions, he excelled
every other writer in poetical prudence; he wrote in
such a manner as might expose him to few hazards. He
used almost always the same fabric of verse; and, indeed, by those few essays which he made of any other,
he did not enlarge his reputation. Of this uniformity the
certain consequence was readiness and dexterity. By
perpetual practice, language had, in his mind, a system-
atical arrangement; having always the same use for
words, he had words so selected and combined as to be
ready at his call. This increase of facility he confessed
himself to have perceived in the progress of his translation.

But what was yet of more importance, his effusions
were always voluntary, and his subjects chosen by himself. His independence secured him from drudging at a
task, and labouring upon a barren topic: he never exchanged praise for money, nor opened a shop of con-
dolence or congratulation. His poems, therefore, were
scarce ever temporary. He suffered coronations and royal
marriages to pass without a song, and derived no opportunities from recent events, nor any popularity from
the accidental disposition of his readers. He was never
reduced to the necessity of soliciting the sun to shine
upon a birthday, of calling the Graces and Virtues to a
wedding, or of saying what multitudes have said before
him. When he could produce nothing new, he was at
liberty to be silent.

His publications were for the same reason never
hasty. He is said to have sent nothing to the press till it

had lain two years under his inspection: it is at least certain that he ventured nothing without nice examination. He suffered the tumult of imagination to subside, and the novelties of invention to grow familiar. He knew that the mind is always enamoured of its own productions, and did not trust his first fondness. He consulted his friends, and listened with great willingness to criticism; and, what was of more importance, he consulted himself, and let nothing pass against his own judgment.

He professed to have learned his poetry from Dryden, whom, whenever an opportunity was presented, he praised through his whole life with unvaried liberality; and perhaps his character may receive some illustration, if he be compared with his master.

Integrity of understanding and nicety of discernment were not allotted in a less proportion to Dryden than to Pope. The rectitude of Dryden's mind was sufficiently shown by the dismission of his poetical prejudices, and the rejection of unnatural thoughts and rugged numbers. But Dryden never desired to apply all the judgment that he had. He wrote, and professed to write, merely for the people; and when he pleased others, he contented himself. He spent no time in struggles to rouse latent powers; he never attempted to make that better which was already good, nor often to mend what he must have known to be faulty. He wrote, as he tells us, with very little consideration; when occasion or necessity called upon him, he poured out what the present moment happened to supply, and, when once it had passed the press, ejected it from his mind; for when he had no pecuniary interest, he had no further solicitude.

Pope was not content to satisfy; he desired to excel, and therefore always endeavoured to do his best: he did not court the candour, but dared the judgment of his reader, and, expecting no indulgence from others, he showed none to himself. He examined lines and words with minute and punctilious observation, and retouched every part with indefatigable diligence, till he had left nothing to be forgiven.

For this reason he kept his pieces very long in his hands, while he considered and reconsidered them. The only poems which can be supposed to have been written with such regard to the times as might hasten their publication were the two satires of *Thirty-eight;* of which Dodsley told me that they were brought to him by the author, that they might be fairly copied. "Almost every line," he said, "was then written twice over; I gave him a clean transcript, which he sent some time afterwards to me for the press, with almost every line written twice over a second time."

His declaration that his care for his works ceased at their publication was not strictly true. His parental attention never abandoned them; what he found amiss in the first edition, he silently corrected in those that followed. He appears to have revised the Iliad, and freed it from some of its imperfections; and the "Essay on Criticism" received many improvements after its first appearance. It will seldom be found that he altered without adding clearness, elegance, or vigour. Pope had perhaps the judgment of Dryden; but Dryden certainly wanted the diligence of Pope.

In acquired knowledge, the superiority must be allowed to Dryden, whose education was more scholastic, and who before he became an author had been allowed more time for study, with better means of information. His mind has a larger range, and he collects his images and illustrations from a more extensive circumference of science. Dryden knew more of man in his general nature, and Pope in his local manners. The notions of Dryden were formed by comprehensive speculation, and those of Pope by minute attention. There is more dignity in the knowledge of Dryden, and more certainty in that of Pope.

Poetry was not the sole praise of either; for both excelled likewise in prose; but Pope did not borrow his prose from his predecessor. The style of Dryden is capricious and varied; that of Pope is cautious and uniform. Dryden observes the motions of his own mind; Pope constrains his mind to his own rules of composition. Dryden is sometimes vehement and rapid; Pope is always smooth, uniform, and gentle. Dryden's page is a natural field, rising into inequalities, and diversified by the varied exuberance of abundant vegetation; Pope's is a velvet lawn, shaven by the scythe, and levelled by the roller.

Of genius, that power which constitutes a poet; that quality without which judgment is cold, and knowledge is inert; that energy which collects, combines, amplifies, and animates; the superiority must, with some hesitation, be allowed to Dryden. It is not to be inferred that of this poetical vigour Pope had only a little, because Dryden had more; for every other writer since Milton must give place to Pope; and even of Dryden it must be said, that, if he has brighter paragraphs, he has not better poems. Dryden's performances were always hasty, either excited by some external occasion, or extorted by domestic necessity; he composed without consideration, and published without correction. What his mind could supply at call, or gather in one excursion, was all that he sought, and all that he gave. The dilatory caution of Pope enabled him to condense his sentiments, to multiply his images, and to accumulate all that study might produce or chance might supply. If the flights of Dryden therefore are higher, Pope continues longer on the wing. If of Dryden's fire the blaze is brighter, of Pope's the

heat is more regular and constant. Dryden often surpasses expectation, and Pope never falls below it. Dryden is read with frequent astonishment, and Pope with
perpetual delight.

This parallel will, I hope, when it is well considered,
be found just; and if the reader should suspect me, as
I suspect myself, of some partial fondness for the memory of Dryden, let him not too hastily condemn me;
for meditation and inquiry may, perhaps, show him the
reasonableness of my determination.

The Works of Pope are now to be distinctly examined,
not so much with attention to slight faults or petty
beauties, as to the general character and effect of each
performance.

It seems natural for a young poet to initiate himself
by pastorals, which, not professing to imitate real life,
require no experience; and, exhibiting only the simple
operation of unmingled passions, admit no subtle reasoning or deep inquiry. Pope's *Pastorals* are not, however,
composed but with close thought; they have reference
to the time of the day, the seasons of the year, and the
periods of human life. The last, that which turns the
attention upon age and death, was the author's favourite. To tell of disappointment and misery, to thicken the
darkness of futurity, and perplex the labyrinth of uncertainty, has been always a delicious employment of
the poets. His preference was probably just. I wish,
however, that his fondness had not overlooked a line in
which the *Zephyrs* are made *to lament in silence*.

To charge these *Pastorals* with want of invention, is
to require what was never intended. The imitations are
so ambitiously frequent, that the writer evidently means
rather to show his literature than his wit. It is surely
sufficient for an author of sixteen, not only to be able to

copy the poems of antiquity with judicious selection, but to have obtained sufficient power of language and skill in metre to exhibit a series of versification which had in English poetry no precedent, nor has since had an imitation.

The design of "Windsor Forest" is evidently derived from "Cooper's Hill," with some attention to Waller's poem on "The Park"; but Pope cannot be denied to excel his masters in variety and elegance, and the art of interchanging description, narrative, and morality. The objection made by Dennis is the want of plan, of a regular subordination of parts terminating in the principal and original design. There is this want in most descriptive poems, because as the scenes, which they must exhibit successively, are all subsisting at the same time, the order in which they are shown must by necessity be arbitrary, and more is not to be expected from the last part than from the first. The attention, therefore, which cannot be detained by suspense, must be excited by diversity, such as his poem offers to its reader.

But the desire of diversity may be too much indulged; the parts of "Windsor Forest" which deserve least praise, are those which were added to enliven the stillness of the scene, the appearance of Father Thames, and the transformation of Lodona. Addison had in his *Campaign* derided the rivers that "rise from their oozy beds" to tell stories of heroes; and it is therefore strange that Pope should adopt a fiction not only unnatural, but lately censured. The story of Lodona is told with sweetness; but a new metamorphosis is a ready and puerile expedient: nothing is easier than to tell how a flower was once a blooming virgin, or a rock an obdurate tyrant.

The "Temple of Fame" has, as Steele warmly declared. "a thousand beauties." Every part is splendid;

there is great luxuriance of ornaments; the original vision of Chaucer was never denied to be much improved; the allegory is very skilfully continued, the imagery is properly selected, and learnedly displayed: yet, with all this comprehension of excellence, as its scene is laid in remote ages, and its sentiments, if the concluding paragraph be excepted, have little relation to general manners or common life, it never obtained much notice, but is turned silently over, and seldom quoted or mentioned with either praise or blame.

That the *Messiah* excels the *Pollio* is no great praise, if it be considered from what original the improvements are derived.

The "Verses on the Unfortunate Lady" have drawn much attention by the illaudable singularity of treating suicide with respect; and they must be allowed to be written in some parts with vigorous animation, and in others with gentle tenderness; nor has Pope produced any poem in which the sense predominates more over the diction. But the tale is not skilfully told; it is not easy to discover the character of either the Lady or her Guardian. History relates that she was about to disparage herself by a marriage with an inferior; Pope praises her for the dignity of ambition, and yet condemns the uncle to detestation for his pride; the ambitious love of a niece may be opposed by the interest, malice, or envy of an uncle, but never by his pride. On such an occasion a poet may be allowed to be obscure, but inconsistency never can be right.

The "Ode for St. Cecilia's Day" was undertaken at the desire of Steele: in this the author is generally confessed to have miscarried, yet he has miscarried only as compared with Dryden; for he has far outgone other competitors. Dryden's plan is better chosen; history will always take stronger hold of the attention than fable:

the passions excited by Dryden are the pleasures and pains of real life, the scene of Pope is laid in imaginary existence; Pope is read with calm acquiescence, Dryden with turbulent delight; Pope hangs upon the ear, and Dryden finds the passes of the mind.

Both the odes want the essential constituent of metrical compositions, the stated recurrence of settled numbers. It may be alleged, that Pindar is said by Horace to have written *numeris lege solutis:* but as no such lax performances have been transmitted to us, the meaning of that expression cannot be fixed; and perhaps the like return might properly be made to a modern Pindarist, as Mr. Cobb received from Bentley, who, when he found his criticisms upon a Greek Exercise, which Cobb had presented, refuted one after another by Pindar's authority, cried out at last, "Pindar was a bold fellow, but thou art an impudent one."

One of his greatest, though of his earliest works, is the "Essay on Criticism," which, if he had written nothing else, would have placed him among the first critics and the first poets, as it exhibits every mode of excellence that can embellish or dignify didactic composition— selection of matter, novelty of arrangement, justness of precept, splendour of illustration, and propriety of digression. I know not whether it be pleasing to consider that he produced this piece at twenty, and never afterwards excelled it: he that delights himself with observing that such powers may be soon attained, cannot but grieve to think that life was ever after at a stand.

To mention the particular beauties of the "Essay" would be unprofitably tedious; but I cannot forbear to observe, that the comparison of a student's progress in the sciences with the journey of a traveller in the Alps, is perhaps the best that English poetry can show. A simile, to be perfect, must both illustrate and ennoble the subject; must show it to the understanding in a clearer view, and display it to the fancy with greater dignity; but either of these qualities may be sufficient to recommend it. In didactic poetry, of which the great purpose is instruction, a simile may be praised which illustrates, though it does not ennoble; in heroics, that may be admitted which ennobles, though it does not illustrate. That it may be complete, it is required to exhibit, independently of its references, a pleasing image; for a simile is said to be a short episode. To this antiquity was so attentive, that circumstances were sometimes added, which, having no parallels, served only to fill the imagination, and produced what Perrault ludicrously called "comparisons with a long tail." In their similes the greatest writers have sometimes failed: the ship-race, compared with the chariot-race, is neither illustrated nor aggrandised; land and water make all the difference; when Apollo, running after Daphne, is likened to a greyhound chasing a hare, there is nothing gained; the ideas of pursuit and flight are too plain to be made plainer; and a god and the daughter of a god are not represented much to their advantage by a hare and dog. The simile of the Alps has no useless parts, yet affords a striking picture by itself; it makes the foregoing position better understood, and enables it to take faster hold on the attention; it assists the apprehension and elevates the fancy.

Let me likewise dwell a little on the celebrated paragraph in which it is directed that "the sound should seem an echo to the sense"; a precept which Pope is allowed to have observed beyond any other English poet.

This notion of representative metre, and the desire of discovering frequent adaptations of the sound to the sense, have produced, in my opinion, many wild conceits and imaginary beauties. All that can furnish this representation are the sounds of the words considered singly, and the time in which they are pronounced. Every language has some words framed to exhibit the noises which they express, as *thump, rattle, growl, hiss.* These, however, are but few; and the poet cannot make them more, nor can they be of any use but when sound is to be mentioned. The time of pronunciation was in the dactylic measures of the learned languages capable of considerable variety; but that variety could be accommodated only to motion or duration, and different degrees of motion were perhaps expressed by verses rapid or slow, without much attention of the writer, when the image had full possession of his fancy; but our language having little flexibility, our verses can differ very little in their cadence. The fancied resemblances, I fear, arise sometimes merely from the ambiguity of words; there is supposed to be some relation between a *soft* line and *soft* couch, or between *hard* syllables and *hard* fortune.

Motion, however, may be in some sort exemplified; and yet it may be suspected that in such resemblances the mind often governs the ear, and the sounds are estimated by their meaning. One of their most successful attempts has been to describe the labour of Sisyphus:

With many a weary step, and many a groan,
Up the high hill he heaves a huge round stone;
The huge round stone, resulting with a bound,
Thunders impetuous down, and smokes along the ground.

Who does not perceive the stone to move slowly upward, and roll violently back? But set the same numbers to another sense:

While many a merry tale, and many a song,
Cheer'd the rough road, we wish'd the rough road long;

The rough road then, returning in a round,
Mock'd our impatient steps, for all was fairy ground.

We have now surely lost much of the delay, and much
of the rapidity.

To the praises which have been accumulated on "The
Rape of the Lock" by readers of every class, from the
critic to the waiting-maid, it is difficult to make any
addition. Of that which is universally allowed to be the
most attractive of all ludicrous compositions, let it rather
be now inquired from what sources the power of
pleasing is derived.

In this work are exhibited, in a very high degree, the
two most engaging powers of an author. New things are
made familiar, and familiar things are made new. A race
of aerial people, never heard of before, is presented to
us in a manner so clear and easy, that the reader seeks
for no further information, but immediately mingles
with his new acquaintances, adopts their interests, and
attends their pursuits, loves a sylph, and detests a gnome.
That familiar things are made new, every paragraph
will prove. The subject of the poem is an event below
the common incidents of common life; nothing real is
introduced that is not seen so often as to be no longer
regarded; yet the whole detail of a female-day is here
brought before us, invested with so much art of decora-
tion, that, though nothing is disguised, everything is
striking, and we feel all the appetite of curiosity for that
from which we have a thousand times turned fastidi-
ously away.
The purpose of the poet is, as he tells us, to laugh at
"the little unguarded follies of the female sex." It is
therefore without justice that Dennis charges "The Rape
of the Lock" with the want of a moral, and for that rea-

son sets it below the *Lutrin,* which exposes the pride and discord of the clergy. Perhaps neither Pope nor Boileau has made the world much better than he found it; but, if they had both succeeded, it were easy to tell who would have deserved most from public gratitude. The freaks, and humours, and spleen, and vanity of women, as they embroil families in discord, and fill houses with disquiet, do more to obstruct the happiness of life in a year than the ambition of the clergy in many centuries. It has been well observed, that the misery of man proceeds not from any single crush of overwhelming evil, but from small vexations continually repeated.

It is remarked by Dennis likewise that the machinery is superfluous; that, by all the bustle of preternatural operation, the main event is neither hastened nor retarded. To this charge an efficacious answer is not easily made. The Sylphs cannot be said to help or to oppose, and it must be allowed to imply some want of art, that their power has not been sufficiently intermingled with the action. Other parts may likewise be charged with want of connection; the game at *ombre* might be spared; but if the Lady had lost her hair while she was intent upon her cards, it might have been inferred that those who are too fond of play will be in danger of neglecting more important interests. Those perhaps are faults; but what are such faults to so much excellence?

The "Epistle of Eloisa to Abelard" is one of the most happy productions of human wit; the subject is so judiciously chosen, that it would be difficult, in turning over the annals of the world, to find another which so many circumstances concur to recommend. We regularly interest ourselves most in the fortune of those who most deserve our notice. Abelard and Eloisa were conspicuous in their days for eminence of merit. The heart naturally ioves truth. The adventures and misfortunes of this il-

lustrious pair are known from undisputed history. Their
fate does not leave the mind in hopeless dejection, for
they both found quiet and consolation in retirement and
piety. So new and so affecting is their story, that it su-
persedes invention, and imagination ranges at full liberty without straggling into scenes of fable.

The story, thus skilfully adopted, has been diligently
improved. Pope has left nothing behind him which
seems more the effect of studious perseverance and laborious revisal. Here is particularly observable the *curi-
osa felicitas,* a fruitful soil and careful cultivation. Here
is no crudeness of sense, nor asperity of language.

The train of my disquisition has now conducted me to
that poetical wonder, the translation of the Iliad, a performance which no age or nation can pretend to equal.
To the Greeks translation was almost unknown; it was
totally unknown to the inhabitants of Greece. They had
no recourse to the Barbarians for poetical beauties, but
sought for everything in Homer, where indeed there is
but little which they might not find.

The Italians have been very diligent translators, but I
can hear of no version, unless perhaps Anguillara's Ovid
may be excepted, which is read with eagerness. The
Iliad of Salvini every reader may discover to be punctili-
ously exact; but it seems to be the work of a linguist
skilfully pedantic, and his countrymen, the proper judges
of its power to please, reject it with disgust.

Their predecessors the Romans have left some specimens of translation behind them, and that employment
must have had some credit in which Tully and Germani-
cus engaged; but unless we suppose, what is perhaps
true, that the plays of Terence were versions of Me-
nander, nothing translated seems ever to have risen to
high reputation. The French, in the meridian hour of

their learning, were very laudably industrious to enrich their own language with the wisdom of the ancients; but found themselves reduced, by whatever necessity, to turn the Greek and Roman poetry into prose. Whoever could read an author could translate him. From such rivals little can be feared.

The chief help of Pope in this arduous undertaking was drawn from the versions of Dryden. Virgil had borrowed much of his imagery from Homer, and part of the debt was now paid by his translator. Pope searched the pages of Dryden for happy combinations of heroic diction; but it will not be denied that he added much to what he found. He cultivated our language with so much diligence and art that he has left in his Homer a treasure of poetical elegances to posterity. His version may be said to have tuned the English tongue; for since its appearance no writer, however deficient in other powers, has wanted melody. Such a series of lines, so elaborately corrected and so sweetly modulated, took possession of the public ear; the vulgar was enamoured of the poem, and the learned wondered at the translation.

But in the most general applause discordant voices will always be heard. It has been objected by some, who wish to be numbered among the sons of learning, that Pope's version of Homer is not Homerical; that it exhibits no resemblance of the original and characteristic manner of the father of poetry, as it wants his awful simplicity, his artless grandeur, his unaffected majesty. This cannot be totally denied; but it must be remembered that *necessitas quod cogit defendit;* that may be lawfully done which cannot be forborne. Time and place will always enforce regard. In estimating this translation, consideration must be had of the nature of our language, the form of our metre, and above all of the change which two thousand years have made in the modes of life and the habits of thought. Virgil wrote in a language of the same general fabric with that of Homer, in verses of the same measure, and in an age nearer to Homer's time by eighteen hundred years, yet he found, even then, the state of the world so much altered, and the demand for elegance so much increased, that mere nature would be endured no longer; and perhaps, in the multitude of borrowed passages, very few can be shown which he has not embellished.

There is a time when nations emerging from barbarity, and falling into regular subordination, gain leisure to grow wise, and feel the shame of ignorance and the craving pain of unsatisfied curiosity. To this hunger of the mind plain sense is grateful; that which fills the void removes uneasiness, and to be free from pain for a while is pleasure; but repletion generates fastidiousness; a saturated intellect soon becomes luxurious, and knowledge finds no willing reception till it is recommended by artificial diction. Thus it will be found, in the progress of learning, that in all nations the first writers are simple, and that every age improves in elegance. One refinement always makes way for another; and what was expedient to Virgil was necessary to Pope.

I suppose many readers of the English Iliad, when they have been touched with some unexpected beauty of the lighter kind, have tried to enjoy it in the original, where, alas! it was not to be found. Homer doubtless owes to his translator many Ovidian graces not exactly suitable to his character; but to have added can be no great crime, if nothing be taken away. Elegance is surely to be desired, if it be not gained at the expense of dignity. A hero would wish to be loved as well as to be reverenced.

To a thousand cavils one answer is sufficient: the purpose of a writer is to be read, and the criticism which would destroy the power of pleasing must be blown aside. Pope wrote for his own age and his own nation; he knew that it was necessary to colour the images and point the sentiments of his author; he therefore made him graceful, but lost him some of his sublimity.

The copious notes with which the version is accompanied, and by which it is recommended to many readers, though they were undoubtedly written to swell the volumes, ought not to pass without praise: commentaries which attract the reader by the pleasure of perusal have not often appeared; the notes of others are read to clear difficulties, those of Pope to vary entertainment.

It has, however, been objected, with sufficient reason, that there is in the commentary too much of unseasonable levity and affected gaiety; that too many appeals are made to the ladies, and the ease which is so carefully preserved is sometimes the ease of a trifler. Every art has its terms, and every kind of instruction its proper style; the gravity of common critics may be tedious, but is less despicable than childish merriment.

Of the Odyssey nothing remains to be observed: the same general praise may be given to both translations, and a particular examination of either would require a large volume. The notes were written by Broome, who endeavoured, not unsuccessfully, to imitate his master.

Of "The Dunciad" the hint is confessedly taken from Dryden's "Mac Flecknoe"; but the plan is so enlarged and diversified as justly to claim the praise of an original, and affords perhaps the best specimen that has yet appeared of personal satire ludicrously pompous.

That the design was moral, whatever the author might tell either his readers or himself, I am not convinced. The first motive was the desire of revenging the contempt with which Theobald had treated his Shakespeare, and regaining the honour which he had lost, by crushing his opponent. Theobald was not of bulk enough to fill a poem, and therefore it was necessary to find other enemies with other names, at whose expense he might divert the public.

In this design there was petulance and malignity enough; but I cannot think it very criminal. An author places himself uncalled before the tribunal of criticism, and solicits fame at the hazard of disgrace. Dullness or deformity are not culpable in themselves, but may be very justly reproached when they pretend to the honour of wit or the influence of beauty. If bad writers were to pass without reprehension, what should restrain them? *impune diem consumpserit ingens Telephus;* and upon bad writers only will censure have much effect. The satire which brought Theobald and Moore into contempt, dropped impotent from Bentley like the javelin of Priam.

All truth is valuable, and satirical criticism may be considered as useful when it rectifies error and improves judgment; he that refines the public taste is a public benefactor.

The beauties of this poem are well known; its chief fault is the grossness of its images. Pope and Swift had an unnatural delight in ideas physically impure, such as every other tongue utters with unwillingness, and of which every ear shrinks from the mention.

But even this fault, offensive as it is, may be forgiven for the excellence of other passages—such as the formation and dissolution of Moore, the account of the Traveller, the misfortune of the Florist, and the crowded thoughts and stately numbers which dignify the concluding paragraph.

The alterations which have been made in "The Dunciad," not always for the better, require that it should be published, as in the present collection, with all its variations.

The "Essay on Man" was a work of great labour and long consideration, but certainly not the happiest of Pope's performances. The subject is perhaps not very proper for poetry, and the poet was not sufficiently master of his subject; metaphysical morality was to him a new study, he was proud of his acquisitions, and, supposing himself master of great secrets, was in haste to teach what he had not learned. Thus he tells us, in the first epistle, that from the nature of the Supreme Being may be deduced an order of beings such as mankind, because Infinite Excellence can do only what is best. He finds out that these beings must be "somewhere," and that "all the question is whether man be in a wrong place." Surely if, according to the poet's Leibnitian reasoning, we may infer that man ought to be, only because he is, we may allow that his place is the right place because he has it. Supreme Wisdom is not less infallible in disposing than in creating. But what is meant by *somewhere* and *place,* and *wrong place,* it had been vain to ask Pope, who probably had never asked himself.

Having exalted himself into the chair of wisdom, he tells us much that every man knows, and much that he does not know himself: that we see but little, and that the order of the universe is beyond our comprehension —an opinion not very uncommon; and that there is a chain of subordinate beings "from infinite to nothing," of which himself and his readers are equally ignorant. But he gives us one comfort which, without his help, he supposes unattainable, in the position "that though we are fools, yet God is wise."

This essay affords an egregious instance of the predominance of genius, the dazzling splendour of imagery,

and the seductive powers of eloquence. Never was pen-
ury of knowledge and vulgarity of sentiment so happily
disguised. The reader feels his mind full, though he
learns nothing; and when he meets it in its new array,
no longer knows the talk of his mother and his nurse.
When these wonder-working sounds sink into sense, and
the doctrine of the "Essay," disrobed of its ornaments, is
left to the powers of its naked excellence, what shall we
discover? That we are, in comparison with our Creator,
very weak and ignorant—that we do not uphold the
chain of existence—and that we could not make one
another with more skill than we are made. We may
learn yet more—that the arts of human life were copied
from the instinctive operations of other animals—that if
the world be made for man, it may be said that man
was made for geese. To these profound principles of
natural knowledge are added some moral instructions
equally new: that self-interest, well understood, will
produce social concord—that men are mutual gainers
by mutual benefits—that evil is sometimes balanced by
good—that human advantages are unstable and fallacious, of uncertain duration and doubtful effect—that
our true honour is, not to have a great part, but to act it
well—that virtue only is our own—and that happiness is
always in our power.

Surely a man of no very comprehensive search may
venture to say that he has heard all this before; but it
was never till now recommended by such a blaze of embellishments, or such sweetness of melody. The vigorous
contraction of some thoughts, the luxuriant amplification
of others, the incidental illustrations, and sometimes the
dignity, sometimes the softness of the verses, enchain
philosophy, suspend criticism, and oppress judgment by
overpowering pleasure.

This is true of many paragraphs; yet if I had undertaken to exemplify Pope's felicity of composition before a rigid critic, I should not select the "Essay on Man"; for it contains more lines unsuccessfully laboured, more harshness of diction, more thoughts imperfectly expressed, more levity without elegance, and more heaviness without strength, than will easily be found in all his other works.

The "Epistle to Arbuthnot," now arbitrarily called the "Prologue to the Satires," is a performance consisting, as it seems, of many fragments wrought into one design, which by this union of scattered beauties contains more striking paragraphs than could probably have been brought together into an occasional work. As there is no stronger motive to exertion than self-defence, no part has more elegance, spirit, or dignity than the poet's vindication of his own character. The meanest passage is the satire upon Sporus.

Of the two poems which derived their names from the year, and which are called the "Epilogue to the Satires," it was very justly remarked by Savage, that the second was in the whole more strongly conceived, and more equally supported, but that it had no single passages equal to the contention in the first for the dignity of Vice, and the celebration of the triumph of Corruption.

The *Imitations of Horace* seem to have been written as relaxations of his genius. This employment became his favourite by its facility; the plan was ready to his hand, and nothing was required but to accommodate as he could the sentiments of an old author to recent facts or familiar images; but what is easy is seldom excellent; such imitations cannot give pleasure to common readers; the man of learning may be sometimes surprised and delighted by an unexpected parallel; but the comparison requires knowledge of the original, which will likewise often detect strained applications. Between Roman images and English manners there will be an irreconcileable dissimilitude, and the works will be generally uncouth and party-coloured; neither original nor translated, neither ancient nor modern.

Pope had, in proportions very nicely adjusted to each other, all the qualities that constitute genius. He had *Invention,* by which new trains of events are formed, and new scenes of imagery displayed, as in "The Rape of the Lock"; and by which extrinsic and adventitious embellishments and illustrations are connected with a known subject, as in the "Essay on Criticism." He had *Imagination,* which strongly impresses on the writer's mind, and enables him to convey to the reader, the various forms of nature, incidents of life, and energies of passion, as in his "Eloisa," "Windsor Forest," and the "Ethic Epistles." He had *Judgment,* which selects from life or nature what the present purpose requires, and by separating the essence of things from its concomitants, often makes the representation more powerful than the reality: and he had colours of language always before him, ready to decorate his matter with every grace of elegant expression, as when he accommodates his diction to the wonderful multiplicity of Homer's sentiments and descriptions.

Poetical expression includes sound as well as meaning. "Music," says Dryden, "is inarticulate poetry"; among the excellences of Pope, therefore, must be mentioned the melody of his metre. By perusing the works of Dryden, he discovered the most perfect fabric of English verse, and habituated himself to that only which he found the best; in consequence of which restraint, his poetry has been censured as too uniformly musical, and as glutting the ear with unvaried sweetness. I suspect this objection to be the cant of those who judge by principles rather than perception; and who would even themselves have less pleasure in his works, if he had tried to relieve attention by studied discords, or affected to break his lines and vary his pauses.

But though he was thus careful of his versification, he did not oppress his powers with superfluous rigour. He seems to have thought with Boileau, that the practice of writing might be refined till the difficulty should overbalance the advantage. The construction of his language is not always strictly grammatical; with those rhymes which prescription had conjoined he contented himself, without regard to Swift's remonstrances, though there was no striking consonance; nor was he very careful to vary his terminations, or to refuse admission, at a small distance, to the same rhymes.

To Swift's edict for the exclusion of alexandrines and triplets he paid little regard; he admitted them, but, in the opinion of Fenton, too rarely; he uses them more liberally in his translation than his poems.

He has a few double rhymes; and always, I think, unsuccessfully, except once in "The Rape of the Lock."

Expletives he very early ejected from his verses; but he now and then admits an epithet rather commodious than important.

Each of the six first lines of the Iliad might lose two syllables with very little diminution of the meaning; and sometimes, after all his art and labour, one verse seems to be made for the sake of another. In his latter productions the diction is sometimes vitiated by French idioms, with which Bolingbroke had perhaps infected him.

I have been told that the couplet by which he declared his own ear to be most gratified was this:

> Lo, where Mæotis sleeps, and hardly flows
> The freezing Tanais through a waste of snows.

But the reason of this preference I cannot discover.

It is remarked by Watts, that there is scarcely a happy combination of words, or a phrase poetically elegant in the English language, which Pope has not inserted into his version of Homer. How he obtained possession of so many beauties of speech, it were desirable to know. That he gleaned from authors, obscure as well as eminent, what he thought brilliant or useful, and preserved it all in a regular collection, is not unlikely. When, in his last years, Hall's Satires were shown him, he wished that he had seen them sooner.

New sentiments and new images others may produce; but to attempt any further improvement of versification will be dangerous. Art and diligence have now done their best, and what shall be added will be the effort of tedious toil and needless curiosity.

After all this, it is surely superfluous to answer the question that has once been asked, Whether Pope was a poet? otherwise than by asking in return, If Pope be not a poet, where is poetry to be found? To circumscribe poetry by a definition will only show the narrowness of the definer, though a definition which shall exclude Pope will not easily be made. Let us look round upon the present time, and back upon the past; let us inquire to whom the voice of mankind has decreed the wreath of poetry; let their productions be examined, and their claim stated, and the pretensions of Pope will be no more disputed. Had he given the world only his version, the name of poet must have been allowed him: if the writer of the Iliad were to class his successors, he would assign a very high place to his translator, without requiring any other evidence of Genius. . . .

CONCLUSION TO THE
PREFACE TO THE DICTIONARY

IN HOPE of giving longevity to that which its own nature forbids to be immortal, I have devoted this book, the labour of years, to the honour of my country, that we may no longer yield the palm of philology, without a contest, to the nations of the continent. The chief glory of every people arises from its authors: whether I shall add anything by my own writings to the reputation of English literature, must be left to time: much of my life has been lost under the pressures of disease; much has been trifled away; and much has always been spent in provision for the day that was passing over me; but I shall not think my employment useless or ignoble, if, by my assistance, foreign nations, and distant ages, gain access to the propagators of knowledge, and understand the teachers of truth; if my labours afford light to the repositories of science, and add celebrity to Bacon, to Hooker, to Milton, and to Boyle.

When I am animated by this wish, I look with pleasure on my book, however defective, and deliver it to the world with the spirit of a man that has endeavoured well. That it will immediately become popular I have not promised to myself: a few wild blunders, and risible absurdities, from which no work of such multiplicity was ever free, may, for a time, furnish folly with laughter, and harden ignorance into contempt; but useful diligence will at last prevail, and there never can be wanting some who distinguish desert; who will consider that no dictionary of a living tongue ever can be perfect, since, while it is hastening to publication, some words are budding, and some falling away; that a whole life cannot be spent upon syntax and etymology, and that even a whole life would not be sufficient; that he, whose design includes whatever language can express, must often speak of what he does not understand; that a writer will sometimes be hurried by eagerness to the end, and sometimes faint with weariness under a task, which Scaliger compares to the labours of the anvil and the mine; that what is obvious is not always known, and what is known is not always present; that sudden fits of inadvertency will surprise vigilance, slight avocations will seduce attention, and casual eclipses of the mind will darken learning; and that the writer shall often in vain trace his memory, at the moment of need, for that which yesterday he knew with intuitive readiness, and which will come uncalled into his thoughts tomorrow.

In this work, when it shall be found that much is omitted, let it not be forgotten that much likewise is performed; and though no book was ever spared out of tenderness to the author, and the world is little solicitous to know whence proceeded the faults of that which it condemns; yet it may gratify curiosity to inform it, that the English Dictionary was written with little assistance of the learned, and without any patronage of the great; not in the soft obscurities of retirement, or under the shelter of academick bowers, but amidst inconvenience and distraction, in sickness and in sorrow. It may repress the triumph of malignant criticism to observe, that if our language is not here fully displayed, I have only failed in an attempt, which no human powers have hitherto completed. If the lexicons of ancient tongues, now immutably fixed, and comprised in a few volumes, be yet, after the toil of successive ages, inadequate and delusive; if the aggregated knowledge, and co-operating diligence of the Italian academicians, did not secure them from the censure of Beni; if the embodied criticks of France, when fifty years had been spent upon their work, were obliged to change its economy, and give their second edition another form, I may surely be contented without the praise of perfection, which, if I could obtain, in this gloom of solitude, what would it avail me? I have protracted my work till most of those, whom I wished to please, have sunk into the grave, and success and miscarriage are empty sounds: I, therefore, dismiss it with frigid tranquillity, having little to fear or hope from censure or from praise.

From the REVIEW OF

"A FREE ENQUIRY INTO THE NATURE
AND ORIGIN OF EVIL"
BY SOAME JENYNS

THIS is a treatise, consisting of six letters, upon a very difficult and important question, which, I am afraid, this authour's endeavours will not free from the perplexity which has entangled the speculatists of all ages, and which must always continue while *we see* but *in part*. He calls it a *Free Enquiry*, and, indeed, his *freedom* is, I think, greater than his modesty. Though he is far from the contemptible arrogance, or the impious licentiousness of Bolingbroke, yet he decides, too easily, upon questions out of the reach of human determination, with too little consideration of mortal weakness, and with too much vivacity for the necessary caution.

In the first letter, on evil in general, he observes, that, "it is the solution of this important question, whence came *evil?* alone, that can ascertain the moral characteristic of God, without which there is an end of all distinction between good and evil." Yet he begins this inquiry by this declaration: "That there is a supreme being, infinitely powerful, wise, and benevolent, the great creator and preserver of all things, is a truth so clearly demonstrated, that it shall be here taken for granted." What is this, but to say, that we have already reason to grant the existence of those attributes of God, which the present inquiry is designed to prove? The present inquiry is, then, surely made to no purpose. The attributes, to the demonstration of which the solution of this great question is necessary, have been demonstrated, without any solution, or by means of the solution of some former writer . . .

The second letter, on the evils of imperfection, is little more than a paraphrase of Pope's epistles, or yet less than a paraphrase, a mere translation of poetry into prose. This is, surely, to attack difficulty with very disproportionate abilities, to cut the Gordian knot with very blunt instruments. When we are told of the insufficiency of former solutions, why is one of the latest, which no man can have forgotten, given us again? I am told, that this pamphlet is not the effort of hunger; what can it be, then, but the product of vanity? and yet, how can vanity be gratified by plagiarism or transcription? When this speculatist finds himself prompted to another performance, let him consider, whether he is about to disburden his mind, or employ his fingers; and, if I might venture to offer him a subject, I should wish, that he would solve this question: Why he, that has nothing to write, should desire to be a writer?

Yet is not this letter without some sentiments, which, though not new, are of great importance, and may be read, with pleasure, in the thousandth repetition . . .

"No system can possibly be formed, even in imagination, without a subordination of parts. Every animal body must have different members, subservient to each other; every picture must be composed of various colours, and of light and shade; all harmony must be formed of trebles, tenours, and bases; every beautiful and useful edifice must consist of higher and lower, more and less magnificent apartments. This is in the very essence of all created things, and, therefore, cannot be prevented, by any means whatever, unless by not creating them at all."

These instances are used, instead of Pope's oak and weeds, or Jupiter and his satellites; but neither Pope, nor this writer, have much contributed to solve the difficulty. Perfection, or imperfection, of unconscious beings has no meaning, as referred to themselves; the base and the treble are equally perfect; the mean and magnificent apartments feel no pleasure or pain from the comparison. Pope might ask the weed, why it was less than the oak? but the weed would never ask the question for itself. The base and treble differ only to the hearer, meanness and magnificence only to the inhabitant. There is no evil but must inhere in a conscious being, or be referred to it; that is, evil must be felt, before it is evil. Yet, even on this subject, many questions might be offered, which human understanding has not yet answered, and which the present haste of this extract will not suffer me to dilate . . .

We are next entertained with Pope's alleviations of those evils which we are doomed to suffer.

"Poverty, or the want of riches, is generally compensated by having more hopes, and fewer fears, by a greater share of health, and a more exquisite relish of the smallest enjoyments, than those who possess them are usually blessed with. The want of taste and genius, with all the pleasures that arise from them, are commonly recompensed by a more useful kind of common sense, together with a wonderful delight, as well as success, in the busy pursuits of a scrambling world. The sufferings of the sick are greatly relieved by many trifling gratifications, imperceptible to others, and, sometimes, almost repaid by the inconceivable transports occasioned by the return of health and vigour. Folly cannot be very grievous, because imperceptible; and I doubt not but there is some truth in that rant of a mad poet, that there is a pleasure in being mad, which none but madmen know. Ignorance, or the want of knowledge and literature, the appointed lot of all born to poverty and the drudgeries of life, is the only opiate capable of infusing that insensibility, which can enable them to endure the miseries of the one, and the fatigues of the other. It is a cordial, administered by the gracious hand of providence, of which they ought never to be deprived by an ill-judged and improper education . . ."

Much of these positions is, perhaps, true; and the whole paragraph might well pass without censure, were not objections necessary to the establishment of knowledge. Poverty is very gently paraphrased by want of riches. In that sense, almost every man may, in his own opinion, be poor. But there is another poverty, which is want of competence of all that can soften the miseries of life, of all that can diversify attention, or delight imagination. There is yet another poverty, which is want of necessaries, a species of poverty which no care of the public, no charity of particulars, can preserve many from feeling openly, and many secretly.

That hope and fear are inseparably, or very frequently, connected with poverty and riches, my surveys of life have not informed me. The milder degrees of poverty are, sometimes, supported by hope; but the more severe often sink down in motionless despondence. Life must be seen, before it can be known. This authour and Pope, perhaps, never saw the miseries which they imagine thus easy to be borne. The poor, indeed, are insensible of many little vexations, which sometimes imbitter the possessions, and pollute the enjoyments, of the rich. They are not pained by casual incivility, or mortified by the mutilation of a compliment; but this happiness is like that of a malefactor, who ceases to feel the cords that bind him, when the pincers are tearing his flesh.

That want of taste for one enjoyment is supplied by the pleasures of some other, may be fairly allowed; but the compensation of sickness I have never found near to equivalence, and the transports of recovery only prove the intenseness of the pain.

With folly, no man is willing to confess himself very intimately acquainted, and, therefore, its pains and pleasures are kept secret. But what the authour says of its happiness, seems applicable only to fatuity, or gross dulness; for that inferiority of understanding, which makes one man, without any other reason, the slave, or tool, or property of another, which makes him sometimes useless, and sometimes ridiculous, is often felt with very quick sensibility. On the happiness of madmen, as the case is not very frequent, it is not necessary to raise a disquisition, but I cannot forbear to observe, that I never yet knew disorders of mind increase felicity: every madman is either arrogant and irascible, or gloomy and suspicious, or possessed by some passion, or notion, destructive to his quiet. He has always discontent in his look, and malignity in his bosom. And, if he had the power of choice, he would soon repent who should resign his reason to secure his peace.

Concerning the portion of ignorance necessary to make the condition of the lower classes of mankind safe to the publick, and tolerable to themselves, both morals and policy exact a nicer inquiry than will be very soon or very easily made. There is, undoubtedly, a degree of knowledge which will direct a man to refer all to providence, and to acquiesce in the condition with which omniscient goodness has determined to allot him; to consider this world as a phantom, that must soon glide from before his eyes, and the distresses and vexations that encompass him, as dust scattered in his path, as a blast that chills him for a moment, and passes off for ever.

Such wisdom, arising from the comparison of a part with the whole of our existence, those that want it most cannot possibly obtain from philosophy; nor, unless the method of education, and the general tenour of life are changed, will very easily receive it from religion. The bulk of mankind is not likely to be very wise or very good; and I know not, whether there are not many states of life, in which all knowledge, less than the highest wisdom, will produce discontent and danger. I believe it may be sometimes found, that a *little learning* is, to a poor man, a *dangerous thing*. But such is the condition of humanity, that we easily see, or quickly feel the wrong, but cannot always distinguish the right. Whatever knowledge is superfluous, in irremediable poverty, is hurtful, but the difficulty is to determine when poverty is irremediable, and at what point superfluity begins. Gross ignorance every man has found equally dangerous with perverted knowledge. Men, left wholly to their appetites and their instincts, with little sense of moral or religious obligation, and with very faint distinctions of right and wrong, can never be safely employed, or confidently trusted; they can be honest only by obstinacy, and diligent only by compulsion or caprice. Some instruction, therefore, is necessary, and much, perhaps, may be dangerous.

Though it should be granted, that those who are *born to poverty and drudgery,* should not be *deprived,* by an *improper education,* of the *opiate of ignorance;* even this concession will not be of much use to direct our practice, unless it be determined, who are those that are *born to poverty.* To entail irreversible poverty upon generation after generation, only because the ancestor happened to be poor, is, in itself, cruel, if not unjust, and is wholly contrary to the maxims of a commercial nation, which always suppose and promote a rotation of property, and offer every individual a chance of mending his condition by his diligence. Those, who communicate literature to the son of a poor man consider him, as one not born to poverty, but to the necessity of deriving a better fortune from himself. In this attempt, as in others, many fail and many succeed. Those that fail, will feel their misery more acutely; but since poverty is now confessed to be such a calamity, as cannot be borne without the opiate of insensibility, I hope the happiness of those whom education enables to escape from it, may turn the balance against that exacerbation which the others suffer.

I am always afraid of determining on the side of envy or cruelty. The privileges of education may, sometimes, be improperly bestowed, but I shall always fear to withhold them, lest I should be yielding to the suggestions of pride, while I persuade myself that I am following the maxims of policy; and, under the appearance of salutary restraints, should be indulging the lust of dominion, and that malevolence which delights in seeing others depressed . . .

Having thus despatched the consideration of particular evils, he comes, at last, to a general reason, for which *evil* may be said to be *our good*. He is of opinion, that there is some inconceivable benefit in pain, abstractedly considered; that pain, however inflicted, or wherever felt, communicates some good to the general system of being, and, that every animal is, some way or other, the better of the pain of every other animal. This opinion he carries so far, as to suppose, that there passes some principle of union through all animal life, as attraction is communicated to all corporeal nature; and, that the evils suffered on this globe may, by some inconceivable means, contribute to the felicity of the inhabitants of the remotest planet.

How the origin of evil is brought nearer to human conception, by any *inconceivable* means, I am not able to discover. We believed, that the present system of creation was right, though we could not explain the adaptation of one part to the other, or for the whole succession of causes and consequences. Where has this inquirer added to the little knowledge that we had before? He has told us of the benefits of evil, which no man feels, and relations between distant parts of the universe, which he cannot himself conceive. There was enough in the question inconceivable before, and we have little advantage from a new inconceivable solution.

I do not mean to reproach this authour for not knowing what is equally hidden from learning and from ignorance. The shame is, to impose words, for ideas, upon ourselves or others. To imagine, that we are going forward, when we are only turning round. To think, that there is any difference between him that gives no reason, and him that gives a reason, which, by his own confession, cannot be conceived.

But, that he may not be thought to conceive nothing but things inconceivable, he has, at last, thought on a way, by which human sufferings may produce good effects. He imagines, that as we have not only animals for food, but choose some for our diversion, the same privilege may be allowed to some beings above us, *who may deceive, torment, or destroy us, for the ends, only, of their own pleasure or utility.* This he again finds impossible to be conceived, *but that impossibility lessens not the probability of the conjecture, which, by analogy, is so strongly confirmed.*

I cannot resist the temptation of contemplating this

analogy, which, I think, he might have carried further, very much to the advantage of his argument. He might have shown, that these "hunters, whose game is man," have many sports analogous to our own. As we drown whelps and kittens, they amuse themselves, now and then, with sinking a ship, and stand round the fields of Blenheim, or the walls of Prague, as we encircle a cockpit. As we shoot a bird flying, they take a man in the middle of his business or pleasure, and knock him down with an apoplexy. Some of them, perhaps, are virtuosi, and delight in the operations of an asthma, as a human philosopher in the effects of the air-pump. To swell a man with a tympany is as good sport as to blow a frog. Many a merry bout have these frolick beings at the vicissitudes of an ague, and good sport it is to see a man tumble with an epilepsy, and revive and tumble again, and all this he knows not why. As they are wiser and more powerful than we, they have more exquisite diversions; for we have no way of procuring any sport so brisk and so lasting, as the paroxysms of the gout and stone, which, undoubtedly, must make high mirth, especially if the play be a little diversified with the blunders and puzzles of the blind and deaf. We know not how far their sphere of observation may extend. Perhaps, now and then, a merry being may place himself in such a situation, as to enjoy, at once, all the varieties of an epidemical disease, or amuse his leisure with the tossings and contortions of every possible pain, exhibited together.

One sport the merry malice of these beings has found means of enjoying, to which we have nothing equal or similar. They now and then catch a mortal, proud of his parts, and flattered either by the submission of those who court his kindness, or the notice of those who suffer him to court theirs. A head, thus prepared for the reception of false opinions, and the projection of vain designs, they easily fill with idle notions, till, in time, they make their plaything an authour; their first diversion commonly begins with an ode or an epistle, then rises, perhaps, to a political irony, and is, at last, brought to its height, by a treatise of philosophy. Then begins the poor animal to entangle himself in sophisms, and flounder in absurdity, to talk confidently of the scale of being, and to give solutions which himself confesses impossible to be understood. Sometimes, however, it happens, that their pleasure is without much mischief. The authour feels no pain, but while they are wondering at the extravagance of his opinion, and pointing him out to one another, as a new example of human folly, he is enjoying his own applause and that of his companions, and, perhaps, is elevated with the hope of standing at the head of a new sect.

Many of the books which now crowd the world, may be justly suspected to be written for the sake of some invisible order of beings, for surely they are of no use to any of the corporeal inhabitants of the world. Of the productions of the last bounteous year, how many can be said to serve any purpose of use or pleasure! The only end of writing is to enable the readers better to enjoy life, or better to endure it; and how will either of those be put more in our power, by him who tells us, that we are puppets, of which some creature, not much wiser than ourselves, manages the wires! That a set of beings, unseen and unheard, are hovering about us, trying experiments upon our sensibility, putting us in agonies, to see our limbs quiver; torturing us to madness, that they may laugh at our vagaries; sometimes obstructing the bile, that they may see how a man looks, when he is yellow; sometimes breaking a traveller's bones, to try how he will get home; sometimes wasting a man to a skeleton, and sometimes killing him fat, for the greater elegance of his hide . . .

Thus, after having clambered, with great labour, from one step of argumentation to another, instead of rising into the light of knowledge, we are devolved back into dark ignorance; and all our effort ends in belief, that for the evils of life there is some good reason, and in confession, that the reason cannot be found. This is all that has been produced by the revival of Chrysippus's untractableness of matter, and the Arabian scale of existence. A system has been raised, which is so ready to fall to pieces of itself, that no great praise can be derived from its destruction. To object, is always easy, and, it has been well observed by a late writer, that "the hand which cannot build a hovel, may demolish a temple."

PREFACE TO SHAKESPEARE

THAT praises are without reason lavished on the dead, and that the honours due only to excellence are paid to antiquity, is a complaint likely to be always continued by those, who, being able to add nothing to truth, hope for eminence from the heresies of paradox; or those, who, being forced by disappointment upon consolatory expedients, are willing to hope from posterity what the present age refuses, and flatter themselves that the regard which is yet denied by envy, will be at last bestowed by time.

Antiquity, like every other quality that attracts the notice of mankind, has undoubtedly votaries that reverence it, not from reason, but from prejudice. Some seem to admire indiscriminately whatever has been long preserved, without considering that time has sometimes cooperated with chance; all perhaps are more willing to honour past than present excellence; and the mind contemplates genius through the shades of age, as the eye surveys the sun through artificial opacity. The great contention of criticism is to find the faults of the moderns, and the beauties of the ancients. While an authour is yet living we estimate his powers by his worst performance, and when he is dead, we rate them by his best.

To works, however, of which the excellence is not absolute and definite, but gradual and comparative; to works not raised upon principles demonstrative and scientifick, but appealing wholly to observation and experience, no other test can be applied than length of duration and continuance of esteem. What mankind have long possessed they have often examined and compared; and if they persist to value the possession, it is because frequent comparisons have confirmed opinion in its favour. As among the works of nature no man can properly call a river deep, or a mountain high, without the knowledge of many mountains, and many rivers; so in the productions of genius, nothing can be stiled excellent till it has been compared with other works of the same kind. Demonstration immediately displays its power, and has nothing to hope or fear from the flux of years; but works tentative and experimental must be estimated by their proportion to the general and collective ability of man, as it is discovered in a long succession of endeavours. Of the first building that was raised, it might be with certainty determined that it was round or square; but whether it was spacious or lofty must have been referred to time. The Pythagorean scale of numbers was at once discovered to be perfect; but the poems of Homer we yet know not to transcend the common limits of human intelligence, but by remarking, that nation after nation, and century after century, has been able to do little more than transpose his incidents, new-name his characters, and paraphrase his sentiments.

The reverence due to writings that have long subsisted arises therefore not from any credulous confidence in the superior wisdom of past ages, or gloomy persuasion of the degeneracy of mankind, but is the consequence of acknowledged and indubitable positions, that what has been longest known has been most considered, and what is most considered is best understood.

The Poet, of whose works I have undertaken the revision, may now begin to assume the dignity of an ancient, and claim the privilege of established fame and prescriptive veneration. He has long outlived his century, the term commonly fixed as the test of literary merit. Whatever advantages he might once derive from personal allusions, local customs, or temporary opinions, have for many years been lost; and every topick of merriment, or motive of sorrow, which the modes of artificial life afforded him, now only obscure the scenes which they once illuminated. The effects of favour and competition are at an end; the tradition of his friendships and his enmities has perished; his works support no opinion with arguments, nor supply any faction with invectives; they can neither indulge vanity nor gratify malignity; but are read without any other reason than the desire of pleasure, and are therefore praised only as pleasure is obtained; yet, thus unassisted by interest or passion, they have past through variations of taste and changes of manners, and, as they devolved from one generation to another, have received new honours at every transmission.

But because human judgment, though it be gradually gaining upon certainty, never becomes infallible; and approbation, though long continued, may yet be only the approbation of prejudice or fashion; it is proper to inquire, by what peculiarities of excellence Shakespeare has gained and kept the favour of his countrymen.

Nothing can please many, and please long, but just representations of general nature. Particular manners can be known to few, and therefore few only can judge how nearly they are copied. The irregular combinations of fanciful invention may delight a while, by that novelty of which the common satiety of life sends us all in quest; but the pleasures of sudden wonder are soon exhausted, and the mind can only repose on the stability of truth.

Shakespeare is above all writers, at least above all modern writers, the poet of nature; the poet that holds up to his readers a faithful mirrour of manners and of life. His characters are not modified by the customs of particular places, unpractised by the rest of the world; by the peculiarities of studies or professions, which can operate but upon small numbers; or by the accidents of transient fashions or temporary opinions: they are the genuine progeny of common humanity, such as the world will always supply, and observation will always find. His persons act and speak by the influence of those general passions and principles by which all minds are agitated, and the whole system of life is continued in motion. In the writings of other poets a character is too often an individual; in those of Shakespeare it is commonly a species.

It is from this wide extension of design that so much instruction is derived. It is this which fills the plays of Shakespeare with practical axioms and domestick wisdom. It was said of Euripides, that every verse was a precept; and it may be said of Shakespeare, that from his works may be collected a system of civil and oeconomical prudence. Yet his real power is not shewn in the splendour of particular passages, but by the progress of his fable, and the tenour of his dialogue; and he that tries to recommend him by select quotations, will succeed like the pedant in Hierocles, who, when he offered his house to sale, carried a brick in his pocket as a specimen.

It will not easily be imagined how much Shakespeare excells in accommodating his sentiments to real life, but by comparing him with other authours. It was observed of the ancient schools of declamation, that the more diligently they were frequented, the more was the student disqualified for the world, because he found nothing there which he should ever meet in any other place. The same remark may be applied to every stage but that of Shakespeare. The theatre, when it is under any other direction, is peopled by such characters as were never seen, conversing in a language which was never heard, upon topicks which will never arise in the commerce of mankind. But the dialogue of this authour is often so evidently determined by the incident which produces it, and is pursued with so much ease and simplicity, that it seems scarcely to claim the merit of fiction, but to have been gleaned by diligent selection out of common conversation, and common occurrences.

Upon every other stage the universal agent is love, by whose power all good and evil is distributed, and every action quickened or retarded. To bring a lover, a lady, and a rival into the fable; to entangle them in contradictory obligations, perplex them with oppositions of interest, and harrass them with violence of desires inconsistent with each other; to make them meet in rapture and part in agony; to fill their mouths with hyperbolical joy and outrageous sorrow; to distress them as nothing human ever was distressed; to deliver them as nothing human ever was delivered; is the business of a modern dramatist. For this probability is violated, life is misrepresented, and language is depraved. But love is only one of many passions; and as it has no great influence upon the sum of life, it has little operation in the dramas of a poet, who caught his ideas from the living world, and exhibited only what he saw before him. He knew, that any other passion, as it was regular or exorbitant, was a cause of happiness or calamity.

Characters thus ample and general were not easily discriminated and preserved, yet perhaps no poet ever kept his personages more distinct from each other. I will not say with Pope, that every speech may be assigned to the proper speaker, because many speeches there are which have nothing characteristical; but perhaps, though some may be equally adapted to every person, it will be difficult to find, any that can be properly transferred from the present possessor to another claimant. The choice is right, when there is reason for choice.

Other dramatists can only gain attention by hyperbolical or aggravated characters, by fabulous and unexampled excellence or depravity, as the writers of barbarous romances invigorated the reader by a giant and a dwarf; and he that should form his expectations of human affairs from the play, or from the tale, would be equally deceived. Shakespeare has no heroes; his scenes are occupied only by men, who act and speak as the reader thinks that he should himself have spoken or acted on the same occasion: Even where the agency is supernatural the dialogue is level with life. Other writers disguise the most natural passions and most frequent incidents; so that he who contemplates them in the book will not know them in the world: Shakespeare approximates the remote, and familiarizes the wonderful; the event which he represents will not happen, but it it were possible, its effects would probably be such as he has assigned; and it may be said, that he has not only shewn human nature as it acts in real exigencies, but as it would be found in trials, to which it cannot be exposed.

This therefore is the praise of Shakespeare, that his drama is the mirrour of life; that he who has mazed his imagination, in following the phantoms which other writers raise up before him, may here be cured of his delirious extasies, by reading human sentiments in human language, by scenes from which a hermit may estimate the transactions of the world, and a confessor predict the progress of the passions.

His adherence to general nature has exposed him to the censure of criticks, who form their judgments upon narrower principles. Dennis and Rhymer think his *Ro-*

mans not sufficiently *Roman;* and Voltair, censures his kings as not completely royal. Dennis is offended, that Menenius, a senator of Rome, should play the buffoon; and Voltaire perhaps thinks decency violated when the Danish Usurper is represented as a drunkard. But Shakespeare always makes nature predominate over accident; and if he preserves the essential character, is not very careful of distinctions superinduced and adventitious. His story requires Romans or kings, but he thinks only on men. He knew that Rome, like every other city, had men of all dispositions; and wanting a buffoon, he went into the senate-house for that which the senate-house would certainly have afforded him. He was inclined to shew an usurper and a murderer not only odious but despicable, he therefore added drunkenness to his other qualities, knowing that kings love wine like other men, and that wine exerts its natural power upon kings. These are the petty cavils of petty minds; a poet overlooks the casual distinction of country and condition, as a painter, satisfied with the figure, neglects the drapery.

The censure which he has incurred by mixing comick and tragick scenes, as it extends to all his works, deserves more consideration. Let the fact be first stated, and then examined.

Shakespeare's plays are not in the rigorous and critical sense either tragedies or comedies, but compositions of a distinct kind; exhibiting the real state of sublunary nature, which partakes of good and evil, joy and sorrow, mingled with endless variety of proportion and innumerable modes of combination; and expressing the course of the world, in which the loss of one is the gain of another; in which, at the same time, the reveller is hasting to his wine, and the mourner burying his friend; in which the malignity of one is sometimes defeated by the

frolick of another; and many mischiefs and many benefits are done and hindered without design.

Out of this chaos of mingled purposes and casualties
the ancient poets, according to the laws which custom
had prescribed, selected some the crimes of men, and
some their absurdities; some the momentous vicissitudes
of life, and some the lighter occurrences; some the terrours of distress, and some the gayeties of prosperity.
Thus rose the two modes of imitation, known by the
names of *tragedy* and *comedy,* compositions intended to
promote different ends by contrary means, and considered as so little allied, that I do not recollect among
the Greeks or Romans a single writer who attempted
both.

Shakespeare has united the powers of exciting laughter and sorrow not only in one mind, but in one composition. Almost all his plays are divided between serious and ludicrous characters, and, in the successive
evolutions of the design, sometimes produce seriousness
and sorrow, and sometimes levity and laughter.

That this is a practice contrary to the rules of criticism will be readily allowed; but there is always an appeal open from criticism to nature. The end of writing
is to instruct; the end of poetry is to instruct by pleasing.
That the mingled drama may convey all the instruction
of tragedy or comedy cannot be denied, because it includes both in its alternations of exhibition and ap-
proaches nearer than either to the appearance of life, by
shewing how great machinations and slender designs
may promote or obviate one another, and the high and
the low co-operate in the general system by unavoidable
concatenation.

It is objected, that by this change of scenes the passions are interrupted in their progression, and that the

principal event, being not advanced by a due gradation of preparatory incidents, wants at last the power to move, which constitutes the perfection of dramatick poetry. This reasoning is so specious, that it is received as true even by those who in daily experience feel it to be false. The interchanges of mingled scenes seldom fail to produce the intended vicissitudes of passion. Fiction cannot move so much, but that the attention may be easily transferred; and though it must be allowed that pleasing melancholy be sometimes interrupted by unwelcome levity, yet let it be considered likewise, that melancholy is often not pleasing, and that the disturbance of one man may be the relief of another; that different auditors have different habitudes; and that, upon the whole, all pleasure consists in variety.

The players, who in their edition divided our authour's works into comedies, histories, and tragedies, seem not to have distinguished the three kinds by any very exact or definite ideas.

An action which ended happily to the principal persons, however serious or distressful through its intermediate incidents, in their opinion, constituted a comedy. This idea of a comedy continued long amongst us; and plays were written, which, by changing the catastrophe, were tragedies today, and comedies tomorrow.

Tragedy was not in those times a poem of more general dignity or elevation than comedy; it required only a calamitous conclusion, with which the common criticism of that age was satisfied, whatever lighter pleasure it afforded in its progress.

History was a series of actions, with no other than chronological succession, independent on each other, and without any tendency to introduce or regulate the conclusion. It is not always very nicely distinguished from tragedy. There is not much nearer approach to unity of action in the tragedy of *Antony and Cleopatra,* than in the history of *Richard the Second.* But a history might be continued through many plays; as it had no plan, it had no limits.

Through all these denominations of the drama, Shakespeare's mode of composition is the same; an interchange of seriousness and merriment, by which the mind is softened at one time, and exhilarated at another. But whatever be his purpose, whether to gladden or depress, or to conduct the story, without vehemence or emotion, through tracts of easy and familiar dialogue, he never fails to attain his purpose; as he commands us, we laugh or mourn, or sit silent with quiet expectation, in tranquillity without indifference.

When Shakespeare's plan is understood, most of the criticisms of Rhymer and Voltaire vanish away. The play of *Hamlet* is opened, without impropriety, by two sentinels; Iago bellows at Brabantio's window, without injury to the scheme of the play, though in terms which a modern audience would not easily endure; the character of Polonius is seasonable and useful; and the Grave-diggers themselves may be heard with applause.

Shakespeare engaged in dramatick poetry with the world open before him; the rules of the ancients were yet known to few; the publick judgment was unformed; he had no example of such fame as might force him upon imitation, nor criticks of such authority as might restrain his extravagance: He therefore indulged his natural disposition, and his disposition, as Rhymer has remarked, led him to comedy. In tragedy he often writes, with great appearance of toil and study, what is written at last with little felicity; but in his comick scenes, he seems to produce without labour, what no labour can improve. In tragedy he is always struggling after some occasion to be comick; but in comedy he seems to repose, or to luxuriate, as in a mode of thinking congenial to his nature. In his tragick scenes there is always something wanting, but his comedy often surpasses expectation or desire. His comedy pleases by the thoughts and the language, and his tragedy for the greater part by incident and action. His tragedy seems to be skill, his comedy to be instinct.

The force of his comick scenes has suffered little diminution from the changes made by a century and a half, in manners or in words. As his personages act upon principles arising from genuine passion, very little modified by particular forms, their pleasures and vexations are communicable to all times and to all places; they are natural, and therefore durable; the adventitious peculiarities of personal habits, are only superficial dies, bright and pleasing for a little while, yet soon fading to a dim tinct, without any remains of former lustre; but the discriminations of true passion are the colours of nature; they pervade the whole mass, and can only perish with the body that exhibits them. The accidental compositions of heterogeneous modes are dissolved by the chance which combined them; but the uniform simplicity of primitive qualities neither admits increase, nor suffers decay. The sand heaped by one flood is scattered by another, but the rock always continues in its place. The stream of time, which is continually washing the dissoluble fabricks of other poets, passes without injury by the adamant of Shakespeare.

If there be, what I believe there is, in every nation, a stile which never becomes obsolete, a certain mode of phraseology so consonant and congenial to the analogy and principles of its respective language as to remain settled and unaltered; this style is probably to be sought in the common intercourse of life, among those who speak only to be understood, without ambition of elegance. The polite are always catching modish innovations, and the learned depart from established forms of speech, in hope of finding or making better; those who wish for distinction forsake the vulgar, when the vulgar is right; but there is a conversation above grossness and below refinement, where propriety resides, and where this poet seems to have gathered his comick dialogue. He is therefore more agreeable to the ears of the present age than any other authour equally remote, and among his other excellencies deserves to be studied as one of the original masters of our language.

These observations are to be considered not as unexceptionably constant, but as containing general and predominant truth. Shakespeare's familiar dialogue is affirmed to be smooth and clear, yet not wholly without ruggedness or difficulty; as a country may be eminently fruitful, though it has spots unfit for cultivation: His characters are praised as natural, though their sentiments are sometimes forced, and their actions improbable; as the earth upon the whole is spherical, though its surface is varied with protuberances and cavities.

Shakespeare with his excellencies has likewise faults, and faults sufficient to obscure and overwhelm any other merit. I shall shew them in the proportion in which they appear to me, without envious malignity or superstitious veneration. No question can be more innocently discussed than a dead poet's pretensions to renown; and little regard is due to that bigotry which sets candour higher than truth.

His first defect is that to which may be imputed most of the evil in books or in men. He sacrifices virtue to convenience, and is so much more careful to please than to instruct, that he seems to write without any moral purpose. From his writings indeed a system of social duty may be selected, for he that thinks reasonably must think morally; but his precepts and axioms drop casually from him; he makes no just distribution of good or evil, nor is always careful to shew in the virtuous a disapprobation of the wicked; he carries his persons indifferently through right and wrong, and at the close dismisses them without further care, and leaves their examples to operate by chance. This fault the barbarity of his age cannot extenuate; for it is always a writer's duty to make the world better, and justice is a virtue independant on time or place.

The plots are often so loosely formed, that a very slight consideration may improve them, and so carelessly pursued, that he seems not always fully to comprehend his own design. He omits opportunities of instructing or delighting which the train of his story seems to force upon him, and apparently rejects those exhibitions which would be more affecting, for the sake of those which are more easy.

It may be observed, that in many of his plays the latter part is evidently neglected. When he found himself near the end of his work, and, in view of his reward, he shortened the labour to snatch the profit. He therefore remits his efforts where he should most vigorously exert them, and his catastrophe is improbably produced or imperfectly represented.

He had no regard to distinction of time or place, but gives to one age or nation, without scruple, the customs, institutions, and opinions of another, at the expence not only of likelihood, but of possibility. These faults Pope has endeavoured, with more zeal than judgment, to transfer to his imagined interpolators. We need not wonder to find Hector quoting Aristotle, when we see the loves of Theseus and Hippolyta combined with the Gothick mythology of fairies. Shakespeare, indeed, was not the only violator of chronology, for in the same age

Sidney, who wanted not the advantages of learning, has, in his *Arcadia,* confounded the pastoral with the feudal times, the days of innocence, quiet, and security, with those of turbulence, violence, and adventure.

In his comick scenes he is seldom very successful, when he engages his characters in reciprocations of smartness and contests of sarcasm; their jests are commonly gross, and their pleasantry licentious; neither his gentlemen nor his ladies have much delicacy, nor are sufficiently distinguished from his clowns by any appearance of refined manners. Whether he represented the real conversation of his time is not easy to determine; the reign of Elizabeth is commonly supposed to have been a time of stateliness, formality, and reserve; yet perhaps the relaxations of that severity were not very elegant. There must, however, have been always some modes of gayety preferable to others, and a writer ought to chuse the best.

In tragedy his performance seems constantly to be worse, as his labour is more. The effusions of passion which exigence forces out are for the most part striking and energetick; but whenever he solicits his invention, or strains his faculties, the offspring of his throes is tumour, meanness, tediousness, and obscurity.

In narration he affects a disproportionate pomp of diction, and a wearisome train of circumlocution, and tells the incident imperfectly in many words, which might have been more plainly delivered in few. Narration in dramatick poetry is naturally tedious, as it is unanimated and inactive, and obstructs the progress of the action; it should therefore always be rapid, and enlivened by frequent interruption. Shakespeare found it an encumbrance, and instead of lightening it by brevity, endeavoured to recommend it by dignity and splendour.

His declamations or set speeches are commonly cold

and weak, for his power was the power of nature; when he endeavoured, like other tragick writers, to catch opportunities of amplification, and instead of inquiring what the occasion demanded, to show how much his stores of knowledge could supply, he seldom escapes without the pity or resentment of his reader.

It is incident to him to be now and then entangled with an unwieldy sentiment, which he cannot well express, and will not reject; he struggles with it a while, and if it continues stubborn, comprises it in words such as occur, and leaves it to be disentangled and evolved by those who have more leisure to bestow upon it.

Not that always where the language is intricate the thought is subtle, or the image always great where the line is bulky; the equality of words to things is very often neglected, and trivial sentiments and vulgar ideas disappoint the attention, to which they are recommended by sonorous epithets and swelling figures.

But the admirers of this great poet have never less reason to indulge their hopes of supreme excellence, than when he seems fully resolved to sink them in dejection, and mollify them with tender emotions by the fall of greatness, the danger of innocence, or the crosses of love. He is not long soft and pathetick without some idle conceit, or contemptible equivocation. He no sooner begins to move, than he counteracts himself; and terrour and pity, as they are rising in the mind, are checked and blasted by sudden frigidity.

A quibble is to Shakespeare, what luminous vapours are to the traveller; he follows it at all adventures; it is sure to lead him out of his way, and sure to engulf him in the mire. It has some malignant power over his mind, and its fascinations are irresistible. Whatever be the dignity or profundity of his disquisition, whether he be enlarging knowledge or exalting affection, whether he be amusing attention with incidents, or enchaining it in suspense, let but a quibble spring up before him, and he leaves his work unfinished. A quibble is the golden apple for which he will always turn aside from his career, or stoop from his elevation. A quibble, poor and barren as it is, gave him such delight, that he was content to purchase it, by the sacrifice of reason, propriety and truth. A quibble was to him the fatal Cleopatra for which he lost the world, and was content to lose it.

It will be thought strange, that, in enumerating the defects of this writer, I have not yet mentioned his neglect of the unities; his violation of those laws which have been instituted and established by the joint authority of poets and of criticks.

For his other deviations from the art of writing I resign him to critical justice, without making any other demand in his favour, than that which must be indulged to all human excellence: that his virtues be rated with his failings: But, from the censure which this irregularity may bring upon him, I shall, with due reverence to that learning which I must oppose, adventure to try how I can defend him.

His histories, being neither tragedies nor comedies are not subject to any of their laws; nothing more is necessary to all the praise which they expect, than that the changes of action be so prepared as to be understood, that the incidents be various and affecting, and the characters consistent, natural, and distinct. No other unity is intended, and therefore none is to be sought.

In his other works he has well enough preserved the unity of action. He has not, indeed, an intrigue regularly perplexed and regularly unravelled: he does not endeavour to hide his design only to discover it, for this is seldom the order of real events, and Shakespeare is the poet of nature: But his plan has commonly what Aristotle requires, a beginning, a middle, and an end; one event is concatenated with another, and the conclusion follows by easy consequence. There are perhaps some incidents that might be spared, as in other poets there is much talk that only fills up time upon the stage; but the general system makes gradual advances, and the end of the play is the end of expectation.

To the unities of time and place he has shewn no regard; and perhaps a nearer view of the principles on which they stand will diminish their value, and withdraw from them the veneration which, from the time of Corneille, they have very generally received, by discovering that they have given more trouble to the poet, than pleasure to the auditor.

The necessity of observing the unities of time and place arises from the supposed necessity of making the drama credible. The criticks hold it impossible, that an action of months or years can be possibly believed to pass in three hours; or that the spectator can suppose himself to sit in the theatre, while ambassadors go and return between distant kings, while armies are levied and towns besieged, while an exile wanders and returns, or till he whom they saw courting his mistress, shall lament the untimely fall of his son. The mind revolts from evident falsehood, and fiction loses its force when it departs from the resemblance of reality.

From the narrow limitation of time necessarily arises the contraction of place. The spectator, who knows that he saw the first act at Alexandria, cannot suppose that he sees the next at Rome, at a distance to which not the dragons of Medea could, in so short a time, have transported him; he knows with certainty that he has not changed his place, and he knows that place cannot change itself; that what was a house cannot become a plain; that what was Thebes can never be Persepolis.

Such is the triumphant language with which a critick exults over the misery of an irregular poet, and exults commonly without resistance or reply. It is time therefore to tell him by the authority of Shakespeare, that he assumes, as an unquestionable principle, a position, which, while his breath is forming it into words, his understanding pronounces to be false. It is false, that any representation is mistaken for reality; that any dramatick fable in its materiality was ever credible, or, for a single moment, was ever credited.

The objection arising from the impossibility of passing the first hour at Alexandria, and the next at Rome, supposes, that when the play opens, the spectator really imagines himself at Alexandria, and believes that his walk to the theatre has been a voyage to Egypt, and that he lives in the days of Antony and Cleopatra. Surely he that imagines this may imagine more. He that can take the stage at one time for the palace of the Ptolemies, may take it in half an hour for the promontory of Actium. Delusion, if delusion be admitted, has no certain limitation; if the spectator can be once persuaded, that his old acquaintance are Alexander and Cæsar, that a room illuminated with candles is the plain of Pharsalia, or the bank of Granicus, he is in a state of elevation above the reach of reason, or of truth, and from the heights of empyrean poetry, may despise the circumscriptions of terrestrial nature. There is no reason why a mind thus wandering in extasy should count the clock, or why an hour should not be a century in that calenture of the brains that can make the stage a field.

The truth is, that the spectators are always in their senses, and know, from the first act to the last, that the stage is only a stage, and that the players are only players. They came to hear a certain number of lines recited with just gesture and elegant modulation. The lines relate to some action, and an action must be in some place; but the different actions that compleat a story may be in places very remote from each other; and where is the absurdity of allowing that space to represent first Athens, and then Sicily, which was always known to be neither Sicily nor Athens, but a modern theatre?

By supposition, as place is introduced, time may be extended; the time required by the fable elapses for the most part between the acts; for, of so much of the action as is represented, the real and poetical duration is the same. If, in the first act, preparations for war against Mithridates are represented to be made in Rome, the event of the war may, without absurdity, be represented, in the catastrophe, as happening in Pontus; we know that there is neither war, nor preparation for war; we know that we are neither in Rome nor Pontus; that neither Mithridates nor Lucullus are before us. The drama exhibits successive imitations of successive actions; and why may not the second imitation represent an action that happened years after the first, if it be so connected with it, that nothing but time can be supposed to intervene? Time is, of all modes of existence, most obsequious to the imagination; a lapse of years is as easily conceived as a passage of hours. In contemplation we easily contract the time of real actions, and therefore willingly permit it to be contracted when we only see their imitation.

It will be asked, how the drama moves, if it is not credited. It is credited with all the credit due to a drama. It is credited, whenever it moves, as a just picture of a real original; as representing to the auditor what he would himself feel, if he were to do or suffer what is there feigned to be suffered or to be done. The reflection that strikes the heart is not, that the evils before us are real evils, but that they are evils to which we ourselves may be exposed. If there be any fallacy, it is not that we fancy the players, but that we fancy ourselves unhappy for a moment; but we rather lament the possibility than suppose the presence of misery, as a mother weeps over her babe, when she remembers that death may take it from her. The delight of tragedy proceeds from our consciousness of fiction; if we thought murders and treasons real, they would please no more.

Imitations produce pain or pleasure, not because they are mistaken for realities, but because they bring realities to mind. When the imagination is recreated by a painted landscape, the trees are not supposed capable to give us shade, or the fountains coolness; but we consider, how we should be pleased with such fountains playing beside us, and such woods waving over us. We are agitated in reading the history of Henry the Fifth, yet no man takes his book for the field of Agencourt. A dramatick exhibition is a book recited with concomitants that encrease or diminish its effect. Familiar comedy is often more powerful on the theatre, than in the page; imperial tragedy is always less. The humour of Petruchio may be heightened by grimace; but what voice or what gesture can hope to add dignity or force to the soliloquy of Cato.

A play read, affects the mind like a play acted. It is therefore evident, that the action is not supposed to be real; and it follows, that between the acts a longer or shorter time may be allowed to pass, and that no more account of space or duration is to be taken by the auditor of a drama, than by the reader of a narrative, before whom may pass in an hour the life of a hero, or the revolutions of an empire.

Whether Shakespeare knew the unities, and rejected them by design, or deviated from them by happy ignorance, it is, I think, impossible to decide, and useless to enquire. We may reasonably suppose, that, when he rose to notice, he did not want the counsels and admonitions of scholars and criticks, and that he at last deliberately persisted in a practice, which he might have begun by chance. As nothing is essential to the fable, but unity of action, and as the unities of time and place arise evidently from false assumptions, and, by circumscribing the extent of the drama, lessen its variety, I cannot think it much to be lamented, that they were not known by him, or not observed: Nor, if such another poet could arise, should I very vehemently reproach him, that his first act passed at Venice, and his next in Cyprus. Such violations of rules merely positive, become the comprehensive genius of Shakespeare, and such censures are suitable to the minute and slender criticism of Voltaire:

> *Non usque adeo permiscuit imis*
> *Longus summa dies, ut non, si voce Metelli*
> *Serventur leges, malint a Cæsare tolli.*

Yet when I speak thus slightly of dramatick rules, I cannot but recollect how much wit and learning may be produced against me; before such authorities I am afraid to stand, not that I think the present question one of those that are to be decided by mere authority, but because it is to be suspected, that these precepts have not been so easily received but for better reasons than I have yet been able to find. The result of my enquiries, in which it would be ludicrous to boast of impartiality, is, that the unities of time and place are not essential to a just drama, that though they may sometimes conduce to pleasure, they are always to be sacrificed to the nobler beauties of variety and instruction; and that a play, written with nice observation of critical rules, is to be contemplated as an elaborate curiosity, as the product of superfluous and ostentatious art, by which is shewn, rather what is possible, than what is necessary.

He that, without diminution of any other excellence, shall preserve all the unities unbroken, deserves the like applause with the architect, who shall display all the orders of architecture in a citadel, without any deduction from its strength; but the principal beauty of a citadel is to exclude the enemy; and the greatest graces of a play, are to copy nature and instruct life.

Perhaps, what I have here not dogmatically but deliberately written, may recal the principles of the drama to a new examination. I am almost frighted at my own temerity; and when I estimate the fame and the strength of those that maintain the contrary opinion, am ready to sink down in reverential silence; as Æneas withdrew from the defence of Troy, when he saw Neptune shaking the wall, and Juno heading the besiegers.

Those whom my arguments cannot persuade to give their approbation to the judgment of Shakespeare, will easily, if they consider the condition of his life, make some allowance for his ignorance.

Every man's performances, to be rightly estimated, must be compared with the state of the age in which he lived, and with his own particular opportunities; and though to the reader a book be not worse or better for the circumstances of the authour, yet as there is always a silent reference of human works to human abilities, and as the enquiry, how far man may extend his designs, or how high he may rate his native force, is of far greater dignity than in what rank we shall place any particular performance, curiosity is always busy to discover the instruments, as well as to survey the workmanship, to know how much is to be ascribed to original powers, and how much to casual and adventitious help. The palaces of Peru or Mexico were certainly mean and incommodious habitations, if compared to the houses of European monarchs; yet who could forbear to view them with astonishment, who remembered that they were built without the use of iron?

The English nation, in the time of Shakespeare, was yet struggling to emerge from barbarity. The philology of Italy had been transplanted hither in the reign of Henry the Eighth; and the learned languages had been successfully cultivated by Lilly, Linacer, and More; by Pole, Cheke, and Gardiner; and afterwards by Smith, Clerk, Haddon, and Ascham. Greek was now taught to boys in the principal schools; and those who united elegance with learning, read, with great diligence, the Italian and Spanish poets. But literature was yet confined to professed scholars, or to men and women of high rank. The publick was gross and dark; and to be able to read and write, was an accomplishment still valued for its rarity.

Nations, like individuals, have their infancy. A people newly awakened to literary curiosity, being yet unacquainted with the true state of things, knows not how to judge of that which is proposed as its resemblance. Whatever is remote from common appearances is always welcome to vulgar, as to childish credulity; and of a country unenlightened by learning, the whole people is the vulgar. The study of those who then aspired to plebeian learning was laid out upon adventures, giants, dragons, and enchantments. *The Death of Arthur* was the favourite volume.

The mind, which has feasted on the luxurious wonders of fiction, has no taste of the insipidity of truth. A play which imitated only the common occurrences of the world, would, upon the admirers of *Palmerin* and *Guy of Warwick*, have made little impression; he that wrote for such an audience was under the necessity of looking round for strange events and fabulous transactions, and that incredibility, by which maturer knowledge is offended, was the chief recommendation of writings, to unskilful curiosity.

Our authour's plots are generally borrowed from novels, and it is reasonable to suppose, that he chose the most popular, such as were read by many, and related by more; for his audience could not have followed him through the intricacies of the drama, had they not held the thread of the story in their hands.

The stories, which we now find only in remoter authours, were in his time accessible and familiar. The fable of *As you like it,* which is supposed to be copied from Chaucer's Gamelyn, was a little pamphlet of those times; and old Mr. Cibber remembered the tale of *Hamlet* in plain English prose, which the criticks have now to seek in Saxo Grammaticus.

His English histories he took from English chronicles and English ballads; and as the ancient writers were made known to his countrymen by versions, they supplied him with new subjects; he dilated some of Plutarch's lives into plays, when they had been translated by North.

His plots, whether historical or fabulous, are always crouded with incidents, by which the attention of a rude people was more easily caught than by sentiment or argumentation; and such is the power of the marvellous even over those who despise it, that every man finds his mind more strongly seized by the tragedies of Shakespeare than of any other writer; others please us by particular speeches, but he always makes us anxious for the event, and has perhaps excelled all but Homer in securing the first purpose of a writer, by exciting restless and unquenchable curiosity and compelling him that reads his work to read it through.

The shows and bustle with which his plays abound have the same original. As knowledge advances, pleasure passes from the eye to the ear, but returns, as it declines, from the ear to the eye. Those to whom our authour's labours were exhibited had more skill in pomps or processions than in poetical language, and perhaps wanted some visible and discriminated events, as comments on the dialogue. He knew how he should most please; and whether his practice is more agreeable to nature, or whether his example has prejudiced the nation, we still find that on our stage something must be done as well as said, and inactive declamation is very coldly heard, however musical or elegant, passionate or sublime.

Voltaire expresses his wonder, that our authour's extravagances are endured by a nation, which has seen the tragedy of Cato. Let him be answered, that Addison speaks the language of poets, and Shakespeare, of men. We find in Cato innumerable beauties which enamour us of its authour, but we see nothing that acquaints us with human sentiments or human actions; we place it with the fairest and the noblest progeny which judgment propagates by conjunction with learning, but Othello is the vigorous and vivacious offspring of observation impregnated by genius. Cato affords a splendid exhibition of artificial and fictitious manners, and delivers just and noble sentiments, in diction easy, elevated, and harmonious, but its hopes and fears communicate no vibration to the heart; the composition refers us only to the writer; we pronounce the name of Cato, but we think on Addison.

The work of a correct and regular writer is a garden accurately formed and diligently planted, varied with shades, and scented with flowers; the composition of Shakespeare is a forest, in which oaks extend their branches, and pines tower in the air, interspersed some-times with weeds and brambles, and sometimes giving shelter to myrtles and to roses; filling the eye with awful pomp, and gratifying the mind with endless diversity. Other poets display cabinets of precious rarities, mi-nutely finished, wrought into shape, and polished unto brightness. Shakespeare opens a mine which contains gold and diamonds in unexhaustible plenty, though clouded by incrustations, debased by impurities, and mingled with a mass of meaner minerals.

It has been much disputed, whether Shakespeare owed his excellence to his own native force, or whether he had the common helps of scholastick education, the precepts of critical science, and the examples of ancient authours.

There has always prevailed a tradition, that Shake-speare wanted learning, that he had no regular educa-tion, nor much skill in the dead languages. Johnson, his friend, affirms, that *he had small Latin, and no Greek;* who, besides that he had no imaginable temptation to falsehood, wrote at a time when the character and ac-quisitions of Shakespeare were known to multitudes. His evidence ought therefore to decide the controversy, un-less some testimony of equal force could be opposed.

Some have imagined, that they have discovered deep learning in many imitations of old writers; but the ex-amples which I have known urged, were drawn from books translated in his time; or were such easy coin-cidencies of thought, as will happen to all who consider the same subjects; or such remarks on life or axioms of morality as float in conversation, and are transmitted through the world in proverbial sentences.

I have found it remarked, that, in this important sen-tence, "Go before, I'll follow," we read a translation of, "I prae, sequar." I have been told, that when **Caliban,** after a pleasing dream, says, "I cry'd to sleep again," the authour imitates Anacreon, who had, like every other man, the same wish on the same occasion.

There are a few passages which may pass for imitations, but so few, that the exception only confirms the rule; he obtained them from accidental quotations, or by oral communication, and as he used what he had, would have used more if he had obtained it.

The *Comedy of Errors* is confessedly taken from the *Menæchmi* of Plautus; from the only play of Plautus which was then in English. What can be more probable, than that he who copied that, would have copied more; but that those which were not translated were inaccessible?

Whether he knew the modern languages is uncertain. That his plays have some French scenes proves but little; he might easily procure them to be written, and probably, even though he had known the language in the common degree, he could not have written it without assistance. In the story of *Romeo and Juliet* he is observed to have followed the English translation, where it deviates from the Italian; but this on the other part proves nothing against his knowledge of the original. He was to copy, not what he knew himself, but what was known to his audience.

It is most likely that he had learned Latin sufficiently to make him acquainted with construction, but that he never advanced to an easy perusal of the Roman authours. Concerning his skill in modern languages, I can find no sufficient ground of determination; but as no imitations of French or Italian authours have been discovered, though the Italian poetry was then high in esteem, I am inclined to believe, that he read little more than English, and chose for his fables only such tales as he found translated.

That much knowledge is scattered over his works is very justly observed by Pope, but it is often such knowledge as books did not supply. He that will understand Shakespeare, must not be content to study him in the closet, he must look for his meaning sometimes among the sports of the field, and sometimes among the manufactures of the shop.

There is however proof enough that he was a very diligent reader, nor was our language then so indigent of books, but that he might very liberally indulge his curiosity without excursion into foreign literature. Many of the Roman authours were translated, and some of the Greek; the reformation had filled the kingdom with theological learning; most of the topicks of human disquisition had found English writers; and poetry had been cultivated, not only with diligence, but success. This was a stock of knowledge sufficient for a mind so capable of appropriating and improving it.

But the greater part of his excellence was the product of his own genius. He found the English stage in a state of the utmost rudeness; no essays either in tragedy or comedy had appeared, from which it could be discovered to what degree of delight either one or other might be carried. Neither character nor dialogue were yet understood. Shakespeare may be truly said to have introduced them both amongst us, and in some of his happier scenes to have carried them both to the utmost height.

By what gradations of improvement he proceeded, is not easily known; for the chronology of his works is yet unsettled. Rowe is of opinion, that "perhaps we are not to look for his beginning, like those of other writers, in his least perfect works; art had so little, and nature so large a share in what he did, that for ought I know," says he, "the performances of his youth, as they were the most vigorous, were the best." But the power of nature is only the power of using to any certain purpose the materials which diligence procures, or opportunity supplies. Nature gives no man knowledge, and when images are collected by study and experience, can only assist in combining or applying them. Shakespeare, however favoured by nature, could impart only what he had learned; and as he must increase his ideas, like other mortals, by gradual acquisition, he, like them, grew wiser as he grew older, could display life better, as he knew it more, and instruct with more efficacy, as he was himself more amply instructed.

There is a vigilance of observation and accuracy of distinction which books and precepts cannot confer; from this almost all original and native excellence proceeds. Shakespeare must have looked upon mankind with perspicacity, in the highest degree curious and attentive. Other writers borrow their characters from preceding writers, and diversify them only by the accidental appendages of present manners; the dress is a little varied, but the body is the same. Our authour had both matter and form to provide; for except the characters of Chaucer, to whom I think he is not much indebted, there were no writers in English, and perhaps not many in other modern languages, which shewed life in its native colours.

The contest about the original benevolence or malignity of man had not yet commenced. Speculation had not yet attempted to analyse the mind, to trace the passions to their sources, to unfold the seminal principles of vice and virtue, or sound the depths of the heart for the motives of action. All those enquiries, which from that time that human nature became the fashionable study, have been made sometimes with nice discernment, but often with idle subtilty, were yet unattempted. The tales, with which the infancy of learning was satisfied, exhibited only the superficial appearances of action, related the events but omitted the causes, and were formed for such as delighted in wonders rather than in truth. Mankind was not then to be studied in the closet; he that would know the world, was under the necessity of gleaning his own remarks, by mingling as he could in its business and amusements.

Boyle congratulated himself upon his high birth, because it favoured his curiosity, by facilitating his access. Shakespeare had no such advantage; he came to London a needy adventurer, and lived for a time by very mean employments. Many works of genius and learning have been performed in states of life, that appear very little favourable to thought or to enquiry; so many, that he who considers them is inclined to think that he sees enterprise and perseverance predominating over all external agency, and bidding help and hindrance vanish before them. The genius of Shakespeare was not to be depressed by the weight of poverty, nor limited by the narrow conversation to which men in want are inevitably condemned; the incumbrances of his fortune were shaken from his mind, *as dewdrops from a lion's mane*.

Though he had so many difficulties to encounter, and so little assistance to surmount them, he has been able to obtain an exact knowledge of many modes of life, and many casts of native dispositions; to vary them with great multiplicity; to mark them by nice distinctions; and to shew them in full view by proper combinations. In this part of his performances he had none to imitate, but has himself been imitated by all succeeding writers; and it may be doubted, whether from all his successors more maxims of theoretical knowledge, or more rules of practical prudence, can be collected, than he alone has given to his country.

Nor was his attention confined to the actions of men; he was an exact surveyor of the inanimate world; his descriptions have always some peculiarities, gathered by contemplating things as they really exist. It may be observed, that the oldest poets of many nations preserve their reputation, and that the following generations of wit, after a short celebrity, sink into oblivion. The first, whoever they be, must take their sentiments and descriptions immediately from knowledge; the resemblance is therefore just, their descriptions are verified by every eye, and their sentiments acknowledged by every breast. Those whom their fame invites to the same studies, copy partly them, and partly nature, till the books of one age gain such authority, as to stand in the place of nature to another, and imitation, always deviating a little, becomes at last capricious and casual. Shakespeare, whether life or nature be his subject, shews plainly, that he has seen with his own eyes; he gives the image which he receives, not weakened or distorted by the intervention of any other mind; the ignorant feel his representations to be just, and the learned see that they are compleat.

Perhaps it would not be easy to find any authour, except Homer, who invented so much as Shakespeare, who so much advanced the studies which he cultivated, or effused so much novelty upon his age or country. The form, the characters, the language, and the shows of the English drama are his. "He seems," says Dennis, "to have been the very original of our English tragical harmony, that is, the harmony of blank verse, diversified often by dissyllable and trissyllable terminations. For the diversity distinguishes it from heroick harmony, and by bringing it nearer to common use makes it more proper to gain attention, and more fit for action and dialogue.

Such verse we make when we are writing prose; we make such verse in common conversation."

I know not whether this praise is rigorously just. The dissyllable termination, which the critick rightly appropriates to the drama, is to be found, though, I think, not in *Gorboduc* which is confessedly before our authour; yet in *Hieronnymo,* of which the date is not certain, but which there is reason to believe at least as old as his earliest plays. This however is certain, that he is the first who taught either tragedy or comedy to please, there being no theatrical piece of any older writer, of which the name is known, except to antiquaries and collectors of books, which are sought because they are scarce, and would not have been scarce, had they been much esteemed.

To him we must ascribe the praise, unless Spenser may divide it with him, of having first discovered to how much smoothness and harmony the English language could be softened. He has speeches, perhaps sometimes scenes, which have all the delicacy of Rowe, without his effeminacy. He endeavours indeed commonly to strike by the force and vigour of his dialogue, but he never executes his purpose better, than when he tries to sooth by softness.

Yet it must be at last confessed, that as we owe every thing to him, he owes something to us; that, if much of his praise is paid by perception and judgement, much is likewise given by custom and veneration. We fix our eyes upon his graces, and turn them from his deformities, and endure in him what we should in another loath or despise. If we endured without praising, respect for the father of our drama might excuse us; but I have seen, in the book of some modern critick, a collection of anomalies, which shew that he has corrupted language by every mode of depravation, but which his admirer has accumulated as a monument of honour.

He has scenes of undoubted and perpetual excellence, but perhaps not one play, which, if it were now exhibited as the work of a contemporary writer, would be heard to the conclusion. I am indeed far from thinking, that his works were wrought to his own ideas of perfection; when they were such as would satisfy the audience, they satisfied the writer. It is seldom that authours, though more studious of fame than Shakespeare, rise much above the standard of their own age; to add a little of what is best will always be sufficient for present praise, and those who find themselves exalted into fame, are willing to credit their encomiasts, and to spare the labour of contending with themselves.

It does not appear, that Shakespeare thought his works worthy of posterity, that he levied any ideal tribute upon future times, or had any further prospect, than of present popularity and present profit. When his plays had been acted, his hope was at an end; he solicited no addition of honour from the reader. He therefore made no scruple to repeat the same jests in many dialogues, or to entangle different plots by the same knot of perplexity, which may be at least forgiven him, by those who recollect, that of Congreve's four comedies, two are concluded by a marriage in a mask, by a deception, which perhaps never happened, and which, whether likely or not, he did not invent.

So careless was this great poet of future fame, that, though he retired to ease and plenty, while he was yet little *declined into the vale of years*, before he could be disgusted with fatigue, or disabled by infirmity, he made no collection of his works, nor desired to rescue those that had been already published from the depravations that obscured them, or secure to the rest a better destiny, by giving them to the world in their genuine state.

Of the plays which bear the name of Shakespeare in the late editions, the greater part were not published till about seven years after his death, and the few which appeared in his life are apparently thrust into the world without the care of the authour, and therefore probably without his knowledge.

Of all the publishers, clandestine or professed, their negligence and unskilfulness has by the late revisers been sufficiently shown. The faults of all are indeed numerous and gross, and have not only corrupted many passages perhaps beyond recovery, but have brought others into suspicion, which are only obscured by obsolete phraseology, or by the writer's unskilfulness and affectation. To alter is more easy than to explain, and temerity is a more common quality than diligence. Those who saw that they must employ conjecture to a certain degree, were willing to indulge it a little further. Had the authour published his own works, we should have sat quietly down to disentangle his intricacies, and clear his obscurities; but now we tear what we cannot lose, and eject what we happen not to understand.

The faults are more than could have happened without the concurrence of many causes. The stile of Shakespeare was in itself ungrammatical, perplexed, and obscure; his works were transcribed for the players by those who may be supposed to have seldom understood them; they were transmitted by copiers equally unskilful, who still multiplied errours; they were perhaps sometimes mutilated by the actors, for the sake of shortening the speeches; and were at last printed without correction of the press.

In this state they remained, not as Dr. Warburton

supposes, because they were unregarded, but because the editor's art was not yet applied to modern languages, and our ancestors were accustomed to so much negligence of English printers, that they could very patiently endure it. At last an edition was undertaken by Rowe; not because a poet was to be published by a poet, for Rowe seems to have thought very little on correction or explanation, but that our authour's works might appear like those of his fraternity, with the appendages of a life and recommendatory preface. Rowe has been clamorously blamed for not performing what he did not undertake, and it is time that justice be done him, by confessing, that though he seems to have had no thought of corruption beyond the printer's errours, yet he has made many emendations, if they were not made before, which his successors have received without acknowledgement, and which, if they had produced them, would have filled pages and pages with censures of the stupidity by which the faults were committed, with displays of the absurdities which they involved, with ostentatious expositions of the new reading, and self congratulations on the happiness of discovering it.

Of Rowe, as of all the editors, I have preserved the preface, and have likewise retained the authour's life, though not written with much elegance or spirit; it relates however what is now to be known, and therefore deserves to pass through all succeeding publications.

The nation had been for many years content enough with Mr. Rowe's performance, when Mr. Pope made them acquainted with the true state of Shakespeare's text, shewed that it was extremely corrupt, and gave reason to hope that there were means of reforming it. He collated the old copies, which none had thought to examine before, and restored many lines to their integrity; but, by a very compendious criticism, he rejected whatever he disliked, and thought more of amputation than of cure.

I know not why he is commended by Dr. Warburton for distinguishing the genuine from the spurious plays. In this choice he exerted no judgement of his own; the plays which he received, were given by Hemings and Condel, the first editors; and those which he rejected, though, according to the licentiousness of the press in those times, they were printed during Shakespeare's life, with his name, had been omitted by his friends, and were never added to his works before the edition of 1664, from which they were copied by the later printers.

This was a work which Pope seems to have thought unworthy of his abilities, being not able to suppress his contempt of *the dull duty of an editor.* He understood but half his undertaking. The duty of a collator is indeed dull, yet, like other tedious tasks, is very necessary; but an emendatory critick would ill discharge his duty, without qualities very different from dullness. In perusing a corrupted piece, he must have before him all possibilities of meaning, with all possibilities of expression. Such must be his comprehension of thought, and such his copiousness of language. Out of many readings possible, he must be able to select that which best suits with the state of opinions, and modes of language prevailing in every age, and with his authour's particular cast of thought, and turn of expression. Such must be his knowledge, and such his taste. Conjectural criticism demands more than humanity possesses, and he that exercises it with most praise has very frequent need of indulgence. Let us now be told no more of the dull duty of an editor.

Confidence is the common consequence of success. They whose excellence of any kind has been loudly celebrated, are ready to conclude, that their powers are universal. Pope's edition fell below his own expectations, and he was so much offended, when he was found to have left any thing for others to do, that he past the latter part of his life in a state of hostility with verbal criticism.

I have retained all his notes, that no fragment of so great a writer may be lost; his preface, valuable alike for elegance of composition and justness of remark, and containing a general criticism on his authour, so extensive that little can be added, and so exact, that little can be disputed, every editor has an interest to suppress, but that every reader would demand its insertion.

Pope was succeeded by Theobald, a man of narrow comprehension and small acquisitions, with no native and intrinsick splendour of genius, with little of the artificial light of learning, but zealous for minute accuracy, and not negligent in pursuing it. He collated the ancient copies, and rectified many errors. A man so anxiously scrupulous might have been expected to do more, but what little he did was commonly right.

In his report of copies and editions he is not to be trusted, without examination. He speaks sometimes indefinitely of copies, when he has only one. In his enumeration of editions, he mentions the two first folios as of high, and the third folio as of middle authority; but the truth is, that the first is equivalent to all others, and that the rest only deviate from it by the printer's negligence. Whoever has any of the folios has all, excepting those diversities which mere reiteration of editions will produce. I collated them all at the beginning, but afterwards used only the first.

Of his notes I have generally retained those which he retained himself in his second edition, except when they were confuted by subsequent annotators, or were too minute to merit preservation. I have sometimes adopted his restoration of a comma, without inserting the panegyrick in which he celebrated himself for his atchievement. The exuberant excrescence of his diction I have often lopped, his triumphant exultations over Pope and Rowe I have sometimes suppressed, and his contemptible ostentation I have frequently concealed; but I have in some places shewn him, as he would have shewn himself, for the reader's diversion, that the inflated emptiness of some notes may justify or excuse the contraction of the rest.

Theobald, thus weak and ignorant, thus mean and faithless, thus petulant and ostentatious, by the good luck of having Pope for his enemy, has escaped, and escaped alone, with reputation, from this undertaking. So willingly does the world support those who solicite favour, against those who command reverence; and so easily is he praised, whom no man can envy.

Our authour fell then into the hands of Sir Thomas Hanmer, the Oxford editor, a man, in my opinion, eminently qualified by nature for such studies. He had, what is the first requisite to emendatory criticism, that intuition by which the poet's intention is immediately discovered, and that dexterity of intellect which despatches its work by the easiest means. He had undoubtedly read much; his acquaintance with customs, opinions, and traditions, seems to have been large; and he is often learned without shew. He seldom passes what he does not understand, without an attempt to find or to make a meaning, and sometimes hastily makes what a little more attention would have found. He is solicitous to reduce to grammar, what he could not be sure that his authour intended to be grammatical. Shakespeare regarded more the series of ideas, than of words; and his language, not being designed for the reader's desk, was all that he desired it to be, if it conveyed his meaning to the audience.

Hanmer's care of the metre has been too violently censured. He found the measures reformed in so many passages, by the silent labours of some editors, with the silent acquiescence of the rest, that he thought himself allowed to extend a little further the license, which had already been carried so far without reprehension; and of his corrections in general, it must be confessed, that they are often just, and made commonly with the least possible violation of the text.

But, by inserting his emendations, whether invented or borrowed, into the page, without any notice of varying copies, he has appropriated the labour of his predecessors, and made his own edition of little authority. His confidence indeed, both in himself and others, was too great; he supposes all to be right that was done by Pope and Theobald; he seems not to suspect a critick of fallibility, and it was but reasonable that he should claim what he so liberally granted.

As he never writes without careful enquiry and diligent consideration, I have received all his notes, and believe that every reader will wish for more.

Of the last editor it is more difficult to speak. Respect is due to high place, tenderness to living reputation, and veneration to genius and learning; but he cannot be justly offended at that liberty of which he has himself so frequently given an example, nor very solicitous what is thought of notes, which he ought never to have considered as part of his serious employments, and which, I suppose, since the ardour of composition is remitted, he no longer numbers among his happy effusions.

The original and predominant errour of his commentary, is acquiescence in his first thoughts; that precipitation which is produced by consciousness of quick discernment; and that confidence which presumes to do, by surveying the surface, what labour only can perform.

by penetrating the bottom. His notes exhibit sometimes perverse interpretations, and sometimes improbable conjectures; he at one time gives the authour more profundity of meaning, than the sentence admits, and at another discovers absurdities, where the sense is plain to every other reader. But his emendations are likewise often happy and just; and his interpretation of obscure passages learned and sagacious.

Of his notes, I have commonly rejected those, against which the general voice of the publick has exclaimed, or which their own incongruity immediately condemns, and which, I suppose, the authour himself would desire to be forgotten. Of the rest, to part I have given the highest approbation, by inserting the offered reading in the text; part I have left to the judgment of the reader, as doubtful, though specious; and part I have censured without reserve, but I am sure without bitterness of malice, and, I hope, without wantonness of insult.

It is no pleasure to me, in revising my volumes, to observe how much paper is wasted in confutation. Whoever considers the revolutions of learning, and the various questions of greater or less importance, upon which wit and reason have exercised their powers, must lament the unsuccessfulness of enquiry, and the slow advances of truth, when he reflects, that great part of the labour of every writer is only the destruction of those that went before him. The first care of the builder of a new system, is to demolish the fabricks which are standing. The chief desire of him that comments an authour, is to shew how much other commentators have corrupted and obscured him. The opinions prevalent in one age, as truths above the reach of controversy, are confuted and rejected in another, and rise again to reception in remoter times. Thus the human mind is kept in motion without progress. Thus sometimes truth and errour, and sometimes contrarieties of errour, take each other's place by reciprocal invasion. The tide of seeming knowledge which is poured over one generation, retires and leaves another naked and barren; the sudden meteors of intelligence which for a while appear to shoot their beams into the regions of obscurity, on a sudden withdraw their lustre, and leave mortals again to grope their way.

These elevations and depressions of renown, and the contradictions to which all improvers of knowledge must for ever be exposed, since they are not escaped by the highest and brightest of mankind, may surely be endured with patience by cricks and annotators, who can rank themselves but as the satellites of their authours. How canst thou beg for life, says Achilles to his captive, when thou knowest that thou art now to suffer only what must another day be suffered by Achilles?

Dr. Warburton had a name sufficient to confer celebrity on those who could exalt themselves into antagonists, and his notes have raised a clamour too loud to be distinct. His chief assailants are the authours of *the Canons of criticism* and of the *Review of Shakespeare's text;* of whom one ridicules his errours with airy petulance, suitable enough to the levity of the controversy; the other attacks them with gloomy malignity, as if he were dragging to justice an assassin or incendiary. The one stings like a fly, sucks a little blood, takes a gay flutter, and returns for more; the other bites like a viper, and would be glad to leave inflammations and gangrene behind him. When I think on one, with his confederates, I remember the danger of Coriolanus, who was afraid that "girls with spits, and boys with stones, should slay him in puny battle"; when the other crosses my imagination, I remember the prodigy in *Macbeth,*

An eagle tow'ring in his pride of place,
Was by a mousing owl hawk'd at and kill'd.

Let me however do them justice. One is a wit, and one a scholar. They have both shown acuteness sufficient in the discovery of faults, and have both advanced some probable interpretations of obscure passages; but when they aspire to conjecture and emendation, it appears how falsely we all estimate our own abilities, and the little which they have been able to perform might have taught them more candour to the endeavours of others.

Before Dr. Warburton's edition, *Critical observations on Shakespeare* had been published by Mr. Upton, a man skilled in languages, and acquainted with books, but who seems to have had no great vigour of genius or nicety of taste. Many of his explanations are curious and useful, but he likewise, though he professed to oppose the licentious confidence of editors, and adhere to the old copies, is unable to restrain the rage of emendation, though his ardour is ill seconded by his skill. Every cold empirick, when his heart is expanded by a successful experiment, swells into a theorist, and the laborious collator at some unlucky moment frolicks in conjecture.

Critical, historical, and explanatory notes have been likewise published upon Shakespeare by Dr. Grey, whose diligent perusal of the old English writers has enabled him to make some useful observations. What he undertook he has well enough performed, but as he neither attempts judicial nor emendatory criticism, he employs rather his memory than his sagacity. It were to be wished that all would endeavour to imitate his modesty who have not been able to surpass his knowledge.

I can say with great sincerity of all my predecessors,

what I hope will hereafter be said of me, that not one has left Shakespeare without improvement, nor is there one to whom I have not been indebted for assistance and information. Whatever I have taken from them it was my intention to refer to its original authour, and it is certain, that what I have not given to another, I believed when I wrote it to be my own. In some perhaps I have been anticipated; but if I am ever found to encroach upon the remarks of any other commentator, I am willing that the honour, be it more or less, should be transferred to the first claimant, for his right, and his alone, stands above dispute; the second can prove his pretensions only to himself, nor can himself always distinguish invention, with sufficient certainty, from recollection.

They have all been treated by me with candour, which they have not been careful of observing to one another. It is not easy to discover from what cause the acrimony of a scholiast can naturally proceed. The subjects to be discussed by him are of very small importance; they involve neither property nor liberty; nor favour the interest of sect or party. The various readings of copies, and different interpretations of a passage, seem to be questions that might exercise the wit, without engaging the passions. But, whether it be, that "small things make mean men proud," and vanity catches small occasions; or that all contrariety of opinion, even in those that can defend it no longer, makes proud men angry; there is often found in commentaries a spontaneous strain of invective and contempt, more eager and venomous than is vented by the most furious controvertist in politicks against those whom he is hired to defame.

Perhaps the lightness of the matter may conduce to the vehemence of the agency; when the truth to be in-

vestigated is so near to inexistence, as to escape attention, its bulk is to be enlarged by rage and exclamation:
That to which all would be indifferent in its original
state, may attract notice when the fate of a name is ap-
pended to it. A commentator has indeed great temptations to supply by turbulence what he wants of dignity,
to beat his little gold to a spacious surface, to work that
to foam which no art or diligence can exalt to spirit.

The notes which I have borrowed or written are either
illustrative, by which difficulties are explained; or judicial, by which faults and beauties are remarked; or
emendatory, by which depravations are corrected.

The explanations transcribed from others, if I do not
subjoin any other interpretation, I suppose commonly to
be right, at least I intend by acquiescence to confess,
that I have nothing better to propose.

After the labours of all the editors, I found many
passages which appeared to me likely to obstruct the
greater number of readers, and thought it my duty to
facilitate their passage. It is impossible for an expositor
not to write too little for some, and too much for others.
He can only judge what is necessary by his own experience; and how long soever he may deliberate, will at last
explain many lines which the learned will think impossible to be mistaken, and omit many for which the ignorant will want his help. These are censures merely relative, and must be quietly endured. I have endeavoured
to be neither superfluously copious, nor scrupulously reserved, and hope that I have made my authour's meaning accessible to many who before were frighted from
perusing him, and contributed something to the publick,
by diffusing innocent and rational pleasure.

The compleat explanation of an authour not sys-
tematick and consequential, but desultory and vagrant,
abounding in casual allusions and light hints, is not to be

expected from any single scholiast. All personal reflections, when names are suppressed, must be in a few years irrecoverably obliterated; and customs, too minute to attract the notice of law, such as modes of dress, formalities of conversation, rules of visits, disposition of furniture, and practices of ceremony, which naturally find places in familiar dialogue, are so fugitive and unsubstantial, that they are not easily retained or recovered. What can be known, will be collected by chance, from the recesses of obscure and obsolete papers, perused commonly with some other view. Of this knowledge every man has some, and none has much; but when an authour has engaged the publick attention, those who can add any thing to his illustration, communicate their discoveries, and time produces what had eluded diligence.

To time I have been obliged to resign many passages, which, though I did not understand them, will perhaps hereafter be explained, having, I hope, illustrated some, which others have neglected or mistaken, sometimes by short remarks, or marginal directions, such as every editor has added at his will, and often by comments more laborious than the matter will seem to deserve; but that which is most difficult is not always most important, and to an editor nothing is a trifle by which his authour is obscured.

The poetical beauties or defects I have not been very diligent to observe. Some plays have more, and some fewer judicial observations, not in proportion to their difference of merit, but because I gave this part of my design to chance and to caprice. The reader, I believe, is seldom pleased to find his opinion anticipated; it is natural to delight more in what we find or make, than in what we receive. Judgement, like other faculties, is improved by practice, and its advancement is hindered by submission to dictatorial decisions, as the memory grows torpid by the use of a table book. Some initiation is however necessary; of all skill, part is infused by precept, and part is obtained by habit; I have therefore shewn so much as may enable the candidate of criticism to discover the rest.

To the end of most plays, I have added short strictures, containing a general censure of faults, or praise of excellence; in which I know not how much I have concurred with the current opinion; but I have not, by any affectation of singularity, deviated from it. Nothing is minutely and particularly examined, and therefore it is to be supposed, that in the plays which are condemned there is much to be praised, and in those which are praised much to be condemned.

The part of criticism in which the whole succession of editors has laboured with the greatest diligence, which has occasioned the most arrogant ostentation, and excited the keenest acrimony, is the emendation of corrupted passages, to which the publick attention having been first drawn by the violence of contention between Pope and Theobald, has been continued by the persecution, which, with a kind of conspiracy, has been since raised against all the publishers of Shakespeare.

That many passages have passed in a state of depravation through all the editions is indubitably certain; of these the restoration is only to be attempted by collation of copies or sagacity of conjecture. The collator's province is safe and easy, the conjecturer's perilous and difficult. Yet as the greater part of the plays are extant only in one copy, the peril must not be avoided, nor the difficulty refused.

Of the readings which this emulation of amendment has hitherto produced, some from the labours of every publisher I have advanced into the text; those are to be considered as in my opinion sufficiently supported; some I have rejected without mention, as evidently erroneous; some I have left in the notes without censure or approbation, as resting in equipoise between objection and defence; and some, which seemed specious but not right, I have inserted with a subsequent animadversion.

Having classed the observations of others, I was at last to try what I could substitute for their mistakes, and how I could supply their omissions. I collated such copies as I could procure, and wished for more, but have not found the collectors of these rarities very communicative. Of the editions which chance or kindness put into my hands I have given an enumeration, that I may not be blamed for neglecting what I had not the power to do.

By examining the old copies, I soon found that the later publishers, with all their boasts of diligence, suffered many passages to stand unauthorised, and contented themselves with Rowe's regulation of the text, even where they knew it to be arbitrary, and with a little consideration might have found it to be wrong. Some of these alterations are only the ejection of a word for one that appeared to him more elegant or more intelligible. These corruptions I have often silently rectified; for the history of our language, and the true force of our words, can only be preserved, by keeping the text of authours free from adulteration. Others, and those very frequent, smoothed the cadence, or regulated the measure; on these I have not exercised the same rigour; if only a word was transposed, or a particle inserted or omitted, I have sometimes suffered the line to stand; for the inconstancy of the copies is such, as that some liberties may be easily permitted. But this practice I have not suffered to proceed far, having restored the primitive diction wherever it could for any reason be preferred.

The emendations, which comparison of copies supplied, I have inserted in the text; sometimes where the improvement was slight, without notice, and sometimes with an account of the reasons of the change.

Conjecture, though it be sometimes unavoidable, I have not wantonly nor licentiously indulged. It has been my settled principle, that the reading of the ancient books is probably true, and therefore is not to be disturbed for the sake of elegance, perspicuity, or mere improvement of the sense. For though much credit is not due to the fidelity, nor any to the judgement of the first publishers, yet they who had the copy before their eyes were more likely to read it right, than we who read it only by imagination. But it is evident that they have often made strange mistakes by ignorance or negligence, and that therefore something may be properly attempted by criticism, keeping the middle way between presumption and timidity.

Such criticism I have attempted to practise, and where any passage appeared inextricably perplexed, have endeavoured to discover how it may be recalled to sense, with least violence. But my first labour is, always to turn the old text on every side, and try if there be any interstice, through which light can find its way; nor would Huetius himself condemn me, as refusing the trouble of research, for the ambition of alteration. In this modest industry I have not been unsuccessful. I have rescued many lines from the violations of temerity, and secured many scenes from the inroads of correction. I have adopted the Roman sentiment, that it is more honourable to save a citizen, than to kill an enemy, and have been more careful to protect than to attack.

I have preserved the common distribution of the plays into acts, though I believe it to be in almost all the plays void of authority. Some of those which are divided in the later editions have no division in the first folio, and some that are divided in the folio have no division in the preceding copies. The settled mode of the theatre requires four intervals in the play, but few, if any, of our authour's compositions can be properly distributed in that manner. An act is so much of the drama as passes without intervention of time or change of place. A pause makes a new act. In every real, and therefore in every imitative action, the intervals may be more or fewer, the restriction of five acts being accidental and arbitrary. This Shakespeare knew, and this he practised; his plays were written, and at first printed in one unbroken continuity, and ought now to be exhibited with short pauses, interposed as often as the scene is changed, or any considerable time is required to pass. This method would at once quell a thousand absurdities.

In restoring the authour's works to their integrity, I have considered the punctuation as wholly in my power; for what could be their care of colons and commas, who corrupted words and sentences. Whatever could be done by adjusting points is therefore silently performed, in some plays with much diligence, in others with less; it is hard to keep a busy eye steadily fixed upon evanescent atoms, or a discursive mind upon evanescent truth.

The same liberty has been taken with a few particles, or other words of slight effect. I have sometimes inserted or omitted them without notice. I have done that sometimes, which the other editors have done always, and which indeed the state of the text may sufficiently justify.

The greater part of readers, instead of blaming us for passing trifles, will wonder that on mere trifles so much labour is expended, with such importance of debate, and such solemnity of diction. To these I answer with confidence, that they are judging of an art which they do not understand; yet cannot much reproach them with their ignorance, nor promise that they would become in general, by learning criticism, more useful, happier, or wiser.

As I practised conjecture more, I learned to trust it less; and after I had printed a few plays, resolved to insert none of my own readings in the text. Upon this caution I now congratulate myself, for every day encreases my doubt of my emendations.

Since I have confined my imagination to the margin, it must not be considered as very reprehensible, if I have suffered it to play some freaks in its own dominion. There is no danger in conjecture, if it be proposed as conjecture; and while the text remains uninjured, those changes may be safely offered, which are not considered even by him that offers them as necessary or safe.

If my readings are of little value, they have not been ostentatiously displayed or importunately obtruded. I could have written longer notes, for the art of writing notes is not of difficult attainment. The work is performed, first by railing at the stupidity, negligence, ignorance, and asinine tastelessness of the former editors, and shewing, from all that goes before and all that follows, the inelegance and absurdity of the old reading; then by proposing something, which to superficial readers would seem specious, but which the editor rejects with indignation; then by producing the true reading, with a long paraphrase, and concluding with loud acclamations on the discovery, and a sober wish for the advancement and prosperity of genuine criticism.

All this may be done, and perhaps done sometimes without impropriety. But I have always suspected that the reading is right, which requires many words to prove it wrong; and the emendation wrong, that cannot without so much labour appear to be right. The justness of a happy restoration strikes at once, and the moral precept may be well applied to criticism, *quod dubitas ne feceris.*

To dread the shore which he sees spread with wrecks, is natural to the sailor. I had before my eye, so many critical adventures ended in miscarriage, that caution was forced upon me. I encountered in every page Wit struggling with its own sophistry, and Learning confused by the multiplicity of its views. I was forced to censure those whom I admired, and could not but reflect, while I was dispossessing their emendations, how soon the same fate might happen to my own, and how many of the readings which I have corrected may be by some other editor defended and established.

> Criticks, I saw, that other's names efface,
> And fix their own, with labour, in the place;
> Their own, like others, soon their place resign'd,
> Or disappear'd, and left the first behind.
>
> POPE.

That a conjectural critick should often be mistaken, cannot be wonderful, either to others or himself, if it be considered, that in his art there is no system, no principal and axiomatical truth that regulates subordinate positions. His chance of errour is renewed at every attempt; an oblique view of the passage, a slight misapprehension of a phrase, a casual inattention to the parts connected, is sufficient to make him not only fail, but fail ridiculously; and when he succeeds best, he produces perhaps but one reading of many probable, and he that suggests another will always be able to dispute his claims.

It is an unhappy state, in which danger is hid under pleasure. The allurements of emendation are scarcely resistible. Conjecture has all the joy and all the pride of invention, and he that has once started a happy change, is too much delighted to consider what objections may rise against it.

Yet conjectural criticism has been of great use in the learned world; nor is it my intention to depreciate a study, that has exercised so many mighty minds, from the revival of learning to our own age, from the Bishop of Aleria to English Bentley. The criticks on ancient authours have, in the exercise of their sagacity, many assistances, which the editor of Shakespeare is condemned to want. They are employed upon grammatical and settled languages, whose construction contributes so much to perspicuity, that Homer has fewer passages unintelligible than Chaucer. The words have not only a known regimen, but invariable quantities, which direct and confine the choice. There are commonly more manuscripts than one; and they do not often conspire in the same mistakes. Yet Scaliger could confess to Salmasius how little satisfaction his emendations gave him. *"Illudunt nobis conjecturæ nostræ, quarum nos pudet, posteaquam in meliores codices incidimus."* And Lipsius could complain, that criticks were making faults, by trying to remove them, *"Ut olim vitiis, ita nunc remediis laboratur."* And indeed, where mere conjecture is to be used, the emendations of Scaliger and Lipsius, notwithstanding their wonderful sagacity and erudition, are often vague and disputable, like mine or Theobald's.

Perhaps I may not be more censured for doing wrong, than for doing little; for raising in the publick expectations, which at last I have not answered. The expectation of ignorance is indefinite, and that of knowledge is often tyrannical. It is hard to satisfy those who know not what to demand, or those who demand by design what they think impossible to be done. I have indeed disappointed no opinion more than my own; yet I have endeavoured to perform my task with no slight solicitude. Not a single passage in the whole work has appeared to me corrupt, which I have not attempted to restore; or obscure, which I have not endeavoured to illustrate. In many I have failed like others; and from many, after all my efforts, I have retreated, and confessed the repulse. I have not passed over, with affected superiority, what is equally difficult to the reader and to myself, but where I could not instruct him, have owned my ignorance. I might easily have accumulated a mass of seeming learning upon easy scenes; but it ought not to be imputed to negligence, that, where nothing was necessary, nothing has been done, or that, where others have said enough, I have said no more.

Notes are often necessary, but they are necessary evils. Let him, that is yet unacquainted with the powers of Shakespeare, and who desires to feel the highest pleasure that the drama can give, read every play from the first scene to the last, with utter negligence of all his commentators. When his fancy is once on the wing, let it not stoop at correction or explanation. When his attention is strongly engaged, let it disdain alike to turn aside to the name of Theobald and of Pope. Let him read on through brightness and obscurity, through integrity and corruption; let him preserve his comprehension of the dialogue and his interest in the fable. And when the pleasures of novelty have ceased, let him attempt exactness, and read the commentators.

Particular passages are cleared by notes, but the general effect of the work is weakened. The mind is refrigerated by interruption; the thoughts are diverted from the principal subject; the reader is weary, he suspects not why; and at last throws away the book, which he has too diligently studied.

Parts are not to be examined till the whole has been surveyed; there is a kind of intellectual remoteness necessary for the comprehension of any great work in its full design and its true proportions; a close approach shews the smaller niceties, but the beauty of the whole is discerned no longer.

It is not very grateful to consider how little the succession of editors has added to this authour's power of pleasing. He was read, admired, studied, and imitated, while he was yet deformed with all the improprieties which ignorance and neglect could accumulate upon him; while the reading was yet not rectified, nor his allusions understood; yet then did Dryden pronounce "that Shakespeare was the man, who, of all modern and perhaps ancient poets, had the largest and most comprehensive soul. All the images of nature were still present to him, and he drew them not laboriously, but luckily: When he describes any thing, you more than see it, you feel it too. Those who accuse him to have wanted learning, give him the greater commendation: he was naturally learned: he needed not the spectacles of books to read nature; he looked inwards, and found her there. I cannot say he is every where alike; were he so, I should do him injury to compare him with the greatest of mankind. He is many times flat and insipid; his comick wit degenerating into clenches, his serious swelling into bombast. But he is always great, when some great occasion is presented to him: No man can say, he ever had a fit subject for his wit, and did not then raise himself as high above the rest of poets,

Quantum lenta solent inter viburna cupressi."

It is to be lamented, that such a writer should want a commentary; that his language should become obsolete, or his sentiments obscure. But it is vain to carry wishes beyond the condition of human things; that which must happen to all, has happened to Shakespeare, by accident and time; and more than has been suffered by any other writer since the use of types, has been suffered by him through his own negligence of fame, or perhaps by that superiority of mind, which despised its own performances, when it compared them with its powers, and judged those works unworthy to be preserved, which the criticks of following ages were to contend for the fame of restoring and explaining.

Among these candidates of inferiour fame, I am now to stand the judgment of the publick; and wish that I could confidently produce my commentary as equal to the encouragement which I have had the honour of receiving. Every work of this kind is by its nature deficient, and I should feel little solicitude about the sentence, were it to be pronounced only by the skilful and the learned.

From the NOTES
TO SHAKESPEARE'S PLAYS

A MIDSUMMER-NIGHT'S DREAM

ACT I. SCENE iv. (I. ii. 50-3.)

FLUTE. *Nay, faith, let me not play a woman; I have a beard coming.*
QUINCE. *That's all one; you shall play it in a masque.*

This passage shews how the want of women on the old Stage was supplied. If they had not a young man who could perform the part with a face that might pass for feminine, the character was acted in a mask, which was at that time a part of a Lady's dress so much in use that it did not give any unusual appearance to the Scene; and he that could modulate his voice in a female tone might play the woman very successfully. It is observed in Downes's Memoirs of the Playhouse, that one of these counterfeit heroines moved the passions more strongly than the women that have since been brought upon the stage. Some of the catastrophes of the old comedies, which make Lovers marry the wrong women, are, by recollection of the common use of masks, brought nearer to probability.

MEASURE FOR MEASURE

ACT II. SCENE ix. (II. iii. 11-12.)

> *Who falling in the* flaws *of her own youth,*
> *Hath* blister'd *her report.*

Who does not see that the integrity of the metaphor requires we should read FLAMES *of her own youth.*—WAR-
BURTON.

Who does not see that upon such principles there is
no end of correction.

THE WINTER'S TALE

ACT IV. SCENE iv. (IV. iii. 21-2.)

> *How would he look, to see his work, so noble,*
> *Vilely bound up!*

It is impossible for any man to rid his mind of his
profession. The authourship of Shakespeare has supplied
him with a metaphor, which rather than he would lose
it, he has put with no great propriety into the mouth
of a country maid. Thinking of his own works his mind
passed naturally to the Binder. I am glad that he has no
hint at an Editor.

KING JOHN

ACT IV. SCENE iv. (IV. ii. 197-8.)

> *Slippers, which his nimble haste*
> *Had falsely thrust upon contrary feet.*

I know not how the commentators understand this
important passage, which, in Dr. Warburton's edition,
is marked as eminently beautiful, and, in the whole, not
without justice. But Shakespeare seems to have confounded a man's shoes with his gloves. He that is frighted
or hurried may put his hand into the wrong glove, but
either shoe will equally admit either foot. The authour
seems to be disturbed by the disorder which he describes.

1 HENRY IV

Act III. Scene i. (III. i. 97-8.)

HOTSPUR. *Methinks, my moiety, north from Burton here,*
In quantity equals not one of yours.

Hotspur is here just such a divider as the *Irishman* who
made *three halves;* Therefore, for the honour of *Shakespeare,*
I will suppose, with the *Oxford Editor,* that he wrote *por-*
tion.—WARBURTON.

I will not suppose it.

2 HENRY IV

But Falstaff unimitated, unimitable Falstaff, how shall
I describe thee? Thou compound of sense and vice; of
sense which may be admired but not esteemed, of vice
which may be despised, but hardly detested. Falstaff is
a character loaded with faults, and with those faults
which naturally produce contempt. He is a thief, and a
glutton, a coward, and a boaster, always ready to cheat
the weak, and prey upon the poor; to terrify the timorous and insult the defenceless. At once obsequious and
malignant, he satirises in their absence those whom he
lives by flattering. He is familiar with the prince only as
an agent of vice, but of this familiarity he is so proud
as not only to be supercilious and haughty with common
men, but to think his interest of importance to the duke
of Lancaster. Yet the man thus corrupt, thus despicable,
makes himself necessary to the prince that despises him,
by the most pleasing of all qualities, perpetual gaiety, by
an unfailing power of exciting laughter, which is the
more freely indulged, as his wit is not of the splendid or
ambitious kind, but consists in easy escapes and sallies

of levity, which make sport but raise no envy. It must be observed that he is stained with no enormous or sanguinary crimes, so that his licentiousness is not so offensive but that it may be borne for his mirth.

The moral to be drawn from this representation is, that no man is more dangerous than he that with a will to corrupt, hath the power to please; and that neither wit nor honesty ought to think themselves safe with such a companion when they see Henry seduced by Falstaff.

HENRY V

ACT IV. SCENE viii. (IV. iii. 24.)

KING HENRY. *By* Jove, *I am not covetous of gold.*

The king prays like a christian, and swears like a heathen.

3 HENRY VI

ACT IV. SCENE vii. (IV. vi. 70.)

This pretty lad will prove our country's bliss.

He was afterwards Henry VII. A man who put an end to the civil war of the two houses, but not otherwise remarkable for virtue. Shakespeare knew his trade. Henry VII was Grandfather to Queen Elizabeth, and the King from whom James inherited.

HENRY VIII

To play histories, or to exhibit a succession of events by action and dialogue, was a common entertainment among our rude ancestors upon great festivities. The parish clerks once performed at Clerkenwell a play which lasted three days, containing, *The History of the World.*

MACBETH

Act II. Scene ii. (ii. i. 49-50.)

> *Now o'er one half the world*
> *Nature seems dead.*

That is, *over our hemisphere all action and motion seem to have ceased.* This image, which is perhaps the most striking that poetry can produce, has been adopted by Dryden in his *Conquest of Mexico.*

> *All things are hush'd as Nature's self lay dead,*
> *The mountains seem to nod their drowsy head;*
> *The little birds in dreams their songs repeat,*
> *And sleeping flow'rs beneath the night dews sweat.*
> *Even lust and envy sleep!*

These lines, though so well known, I have transcribed, that the contrast between them and this passage of Shakespeare may be more accurately observed.

Night is described by two great poets, but one describes a night of quiet, the other of perturbation. In the night of Dryden, all the disturbers of the world are laid asleep; in that of Shakespeare, nothing but sorcery, lust, and murder, is awake. He that reads Dryden, finds himself lull'd with serenity, and disposed to solitude and contemplation. He that peruses Shakespeare, looks round alarmed, and starts to find himself alone. One is the night of a lover, the other, of a murderer.

LETTERS ON
MRS. THRALE'S MARRIAGE
TO PIOZZI

MRS. PIOZZI TO DR. JOHNSON

Bath, June 30 [1784]

MY DEAR SIR,

The enclosed is a circular letter which I have sent to all the guardians, but our friendship demands somewhat more; it requires that I should beg your pardon for concealing from you a connexion which you must have heard of by many, but I suppose never believed. Indeed, my dear Sir, it was concealed only to save us both needless pain; I could not have borne to reject that counsel it would have killed me to take, and I only tell it you now because all is irrevocably settled, and out of your power to prevent. I will say, however, that the dread of your disapprobation has given me some anxious moments, and though, perhaps, I am become by many privations the most independent woman in the world, I feel as if acting without a parent's consent till you write kindly to

Your faithful servant.

CIRCULAR

SIR,

As one of the executors of Mr. Thrale's will and guardian to his daughters, I think it my duty to acquaint you that the three eldest left Bath last Friday for their own house at Brighthelmstone in company with an amiable friend, Miss Nicholson, who has sometimes resided with us here, and in whose society they may, I think, find some advantages and certainly no disgrace. I waited on them to Salisbury, Wilton, &c., and offered to attend them to the seaside myself, but they preferred this lady's company to mine, having heard that Mr. Piozzi is coming back from Italy, and judging perhaps by our past friendship and continued correspondence that his return would be succeeded by our marriage.

I have the honour to be, Sir, your obedient servant.

DR. JOHNSON TO MRS. PIOZZI

MADAM,

If I interpret your letter right, you are ignominiously married; if it is yet undone, let us once more talk together. If you have abandoned your children and your religion, God forgive your wickedness: if you have forfeited your fame and your country, may your folly do no further mischief. If the last act is yet to do, I who have loved you, esteemed you, reverenced you, and served you, I who long thought you the first of humankind, entreat that, before your fate is irrevocable, I may once more see you. I was, I once was,

Madam, most truly yours,

SAM. JOHNSON.

I will come down, if you permit it.

MRS. PIOZZI TO DR. JOHNSON

SIR,

I have this morning received from you so rough a letter in reply to one which was both tenderly and respectfully written, that I am forced to desire the conclusion of a correspondence which I can bear to continue no longer. The birth of my second husband is not meaner than that of my first; his sentiments are not meaner; his profession is not meaner, and his superiority in what he professes acknowledged by all mankind. It is want of fortune then that is ignominious; the character of the man I have chosen has no other claim to such an epithet. The religion to which he has always been a zealous adherent will, I hope, teach him to forgive insults he has not deserved; mine will, I hope, enable me to bear them at once with dignity and patience. To hear that I have forfeited my fame is indeed the greatest insult I ever yet received. My fame is as unsullied as snow, or I should think it unworthy of him who is henceforth to protect it.

I write by the coach the more speedily and effectually to prevent your coming hither. Perhaps by my fame (and I hope it is so) you mean only that celebrity which is a consideration of a much lower kind. I care for that only as it may give pleasure to my husband and his friends.

Farewell, dear Sir, and accept my best wishes. You have always commanded my esteem, and long enjoyed the fruits of a friendship never infringed by one harsh expression on my part during twenty years of familiar talk. Never did I oppose your will, or control your wish; nor can your unmerited severity itself lessen my regard; but till you have changed your opinion of Mr. Piozzi let us converse no more. God bless you.

DR. JOHNSON TO MRS. PIOZZI

DEAR MADAM,

What you have done, however I may lament it. I have no pretence to resent, as it has not been injurious to me: I therefore breathe out one sigh more of tenderness, perhaps useless, but at least sincere.

I wish that God may grant you every blessing, that you may be happy in this world for its short continuance, and eternally happy in a better state; and whatever I can contribute to your happiness I am very ready to repay, for that kindness which soothed twenty years of a life radically wretched.

Do not think slightly of the advice which I now presume to offer. Prevail upon Mr. Piozzi to settle in England: you may live here with more dignity than in Italy, and with more security: your rank will be higher, and your fortune more under your own eye. I desire not to detail all my reasons, but every argument of prudence and interest is for England, and only some phantoms of imagination seduce you to Italy.

I am afraid, however, that my counsel is vain, yet I have eased my heart by giving it

When Queen Mary took the resolution of sheltering herself in England, the Archbishop of St. Andrew's, attempting to dissuade her, attended on her journey; and when they came to the irremeable stream that separated the two kingdoms, walked by her side into the water, in the middle of which he seized her bridle, and with earnestness proportioned to her danger and his own affection pressed her to return. The Queen went forward— If the parallel reaches thus far, may it go no further. The tears stand in my eyes.

I am going into Derbyshire, and hope to be followed by your good wishes, for I am, with great affection,

Your, etc.,

SAM. JOHNSON.

POEMS

*Spoken by Mr. Garrick at the Opening of the Theatre Royal,
Drury Lane, 1747*

When Learning's triumph o'er her barb'rous foes
First rear'd the stage, immortal Shakespeare rose;
Each change of many-colour'd life he drew,
Exhausted worlds, and then imagin'd new:
Existence saw him spurn her bounded reign,
And panting Time toil'd after him in vain.
His pow'rful strokes presiding Truth impress'd,
And unresisted Passion storm'd the breast.

   Then Jonson came, instructed from the school,
To please in method, and invent by rule;
His studious patience and laborious art,
By regular approach essay'd the heart:
Cold Approbation gave the ling'ring bays;
For those who durst not censure, scarce could praise.
A mortal born, he met the gen'ral doom,
But left, like Egypt's kings, a lasting tomb.

   The wits of Charles found easier ways to fame,
Nor wish'd for Jonson's art, or Shakespeare's flame.
Themselves they studied; as they felt, they writ:
Intrigue was plot, obscenity was wit.
Vice always found a sympathetic friend;
They pleas'd their age, and did not aim to mend.
Yet bards like these aspir'd to lasting praise,
And proudly hop'd to pimp in future days.
Their cause was gen'ral, their supports were strong,

Their slaves were willing, and their reign was long:
Till Shame regain'd the post that Sense betray'd,
And Virtue call'd Oblivion to her aid.

Then, crush'd by rules, and weaken'd as refin'd,
For years the pow'r of tragedy declin'd;
From bard to bard the frigid caution crept,
Till Declamation roar'd whilst Passion slept;
Yet still did Virtue deign the stage to tread,
Philosophy remain'd though Nature fled.
But forc'd, at length, her ancient reign to quit,
She saw great Faustus lay the ghost of Wit;
Exulting Folly hail'd the joyful day,
And Pantomime and Song confirm'd her sway.

But who the coming changes can presage,
And mark the future periods of the stage?
Perhaps if skill could distant times explore,
New Behns, new Durfeys, yet remain in store;
Perhaps where Lear has rav'd, and Hamlet dy'd,
On flying cars new sorcerers may ride;
Perhaps (for who can guess th' effects of chance)
Here Hunt may box, or Mahomet may dance.

Hard is his lot that here by fortune plac'd,
Must watch the wild vicissitudes of taste;
With ev'ry meteor of caprice must play,
And chase the new-blown bubbles of the day.
Ah! let not censure term our fate our choice,
The stage but echoes back the public voice;
The drama's laws, the drama's patrons give,
For we that live to please, must please to live.

Then prompt no more the follies you decry,
As tyrants doom their tools of guilt to die;
'Tis yours, this night, to bid the reign commence
Of rescued Nature and reviving Sense;
To chase the charms of Sound, the pomp of Show,
For useful Mirth and salutary Woe;

Bid scenic Virtue form the rising age,
And Truth diffuse her radiance from the stage.

THE VANITY OF HUMAN WISHES

In Imitation of the Tenth Satire of Juvenal

Let observation with extensive view,
Survey mankind, from China to Peru;
Remark each anxious toil, each eager strife,
And watch the busy scenes of crowded life;
Then say how hope and fear, desire and hate,
O'erspread with snares the clouded maze of fate,
Where wav'ring man, betray'd by vent'rous pride,
To tread the dreary paths without a guide;
As treach'rous phantoms in the mist delude,
Shuns fancied ills, or chases airy good.
How rarely reason guides the stubborn choice,
Rules the bold hand, or prompts the suppliant voice,
How nations sink, by darling schemes oppress'd,
When Vengeance listens to the fool's request.
Fate wings with ev'ry wish th' afflictive dart,
Each gift of nature, and each grace of art,
With fatal heat impetuous courage glows,
With fatal sweetness elocution flows,
Impeachment stops the speaker's pow'rful breath,
And restless fire precipitates on death.

But scarce observ'd the knowing and the bold,
Fall in the gen'ral massacre of gold;
Wide-wasting pest! that rages unconfin'd,
And crowds with crimes the records of mankind,
For gold his sword the hireling ruffian draws,
For gold the hireling judge distorts the laws;
Wealth heap'd on wealth, nor truth nor safety buys,
The dangers gather as the treasures rise.

Let Hist'ry tell where rival kings command,

And dubious title shakes the madded land,
When statutes glean the refuse of the sword,
How much more safe the vassal than the lord,
Low skulks the hind beneath the rage of pow'r,
And leaves the wealthy traitor in the Tow'r,
Untouch'd his cottage, and his slumbers sound,
Though confiscation's vultures hover round.

   The needy traveller, serene and gay,
Walks the wild heath, and sings his toil away.
Does envy seize thee? crush th' upbraiding joy,
Increase his riches and his peace destroy,
New fears in dire vicissitude invade,
The rustling brake alarms, and quiv'ring shade,
Nor light nor darkness bring his pain relief,
One shows the plunder, and one hides the thief.

   Yet still one gen'ral cry the skies assails,
And gain and grandeur load the tainted gales;
Few know the toiling statesman's fear or care,
Th' insidious rival and the gaping heir.

   Once more, Democritus, arise on earth,
With cheerful wisdom and instructive mirth,
See motley life in modern trappings dress'd,
And feed with varied fools th' eternal jest:
Thou who couldst laugh where want enchain'd caprice.
Toil crush'd conceit, and man was of a piece;
Where wealth unlov'd without a mourner dy'd;
And scarce a sycophant was fed by pride;
Where ne'er was known the form of mock debate,
Or seen a new-made mayor's unwieldy state;
Where change of fav'rites made no change of laws,
And senates heard before they judg'd a cause;
How wouldst thou shake at Britain's modish tribe,
Dart the quick taunt, and edge the piercing gibe?
Attentive truth and nature to descry,
And pierce each scene with philosophic eye.

To thee were solemn toys or empty show,
The robes of pleasure and the veils of woe:
All aid the farce, and all thy mirth maintain,
Whose joys are causeless, or whose griefs are vain.

Such was the scorn that fill'd the sage's mind,
Renew'd at ev'ry glance on humankind;
How just that scorn ere yet thy voice declare,
Search ev'ry state, and canvass ev'ry pray'r.

Unnumber'd suppliants crowd Preferment's gate,
Athirst for wealth, and burning to be great;
Delusive Fortune hears th' incessant call,
They mount, they shine, evaporate, and fall.
On ev'ry stage the foes of peace attend,
Hate dogs their flight, and insult mocks their end.
Love ends with hope, the sinking statesman's door
Pours in the morning worshipper no more;
For growing names the weekly scribbler lies,
To growing wealth the dedicator flies,
From ev'ry room descends the painted face,
That hung the bright palladium of the place,
And smok'd in kitchens, or in auctions sold,
To better features yields the frame of gold;
For now no more we trace in ev'ry line
Heroic worth, benevolence divine:
The form distorted justifies the fall,
And detestation rids th' indignant wall.

But will not Britain hear the last appeal,
Sign her foe's doom, or guard her fav'rite's zeal?
Through Freedom's sons no more remonstrance rings,
Degrading nobles and controlling kings;
Our supple tribes repress their patriot throats,
And ask no questions but the price of votes;
With weekly libels and septennial ale,
Their wish is full to riot and to rail.

In full-blown dignity, see Wolsey stand,

Law in his voice, and fortune in his hand:
To him the church, the realm, their pow'rs consign,
Through him the rays of regal bounty shine,
Turn'd by his nod the stream of honour flows,
His smile alone security bestows:
Still to new heights his restless wishes tow'r,
Claim leads to claim, and pow'r advances pov'r;
Till conquest unresisted ceas'd to please,
And rights submitted, left him none to seize.
At length his sov'reign frowns—the train of state
Mark the keen glance, and watch the sign to hate.
Where'er he turns he meets a stranger's eye,
His suppliants scorn him, and his followers fly;
At once is lost the pride of awful state,
The golden canopy, the glitt'ring plate,
The regal palace, the luxurious board,
The liv'ried army, and the menial lord.
With age, with cares, with maladies oppress'd,
He seeks the refuge of monastic rest.
Grief aids disease, remember'd folly stings,
And his last sighs reproach the faith of kings.

Speak thou, whose thoughts at humble peace repine,
Shall Wolsey's wealth, with Wolsey's end be thine?
Or liv'st thou now, with safer pride content,
The wisest justice on the banks of Trent?
For why did Wolsey near the steeps of fate,
On weak foundations raise th' enormous weight?
Why but to sink beneath misfortune's blow,
With louder ruin to the gulfs below?

What gave great Villiers to th' assassin's knife,
And fix'd disease on Harley's closing life?
What murder'd Wentworth, and what exil'd Hyde,
By kings protected and to kings ally'd?
What but their wish indulg'd in courts to shine,
And pow'r too great to keep or to resign?

When first the college rolls receive his name,
The young enthusiast quits his ease for fame;
Through all his veins the fever of renown
Spreads from the strong contagion of the gown;
O'er Bodley's dome his future labours spread,
And Bacon's mansion trembles o'er his head.
Are these thy views? proceed, illustrious youth,
And Virtue guard thee to the throne of Truth!
Yet should thy soul indulge the gen'rous heat,
Till captive Science yields her last retreat;
Should Reason guide thee with her brightest ray,
And pour on misty Doubt resistless day;
Should no false kindness lure to loose delight,
Nor praise relax, nor difficulty fright;
Should tempting Novelty thy cell refrain,
And Sloth effuse her opiate fumes in vain;
Should Beauty blunt on fops her fatal dart,
Nor claim the triumph of a letter'd heart;
Should no disease thy torpid veins invade,
Nor Melancholy's phantoms haunt thy shade;
Yet hope not life from grief or danger free,
Nor think the doom of man revers'd for thee:
Deign on the passing world to turn thine eyes,
And pause awhile from letters, to be wise;
There mark what ills the scholar's life assail,
Toil, envy, want, the patron, and the gaol.
See nations slowly wise, and meanly just,
To buried merit raise the tardy bust.
If dreams yet flatter, once again attend,
Hear Lydiat's life, and Galileo's end.

Nor deem, when Learning her last prize bestows,
The glitt'ring eminence exempt from foes;
See when the vulgar 'scape, despis'd or aw'd,
Rebellion's vengeful talons seize on Laud.
From meaner minds, though smaller fines content

The plunder'd palace, or sequester'd rent;
Mark'd out by dangerous parts he meets the shock,
And fatal Learning leads him to the block:
Around his tomb let Art and Genius weep,
But hear his death, ye blockheads, hear and sleep.

The festal blazes, the triumphal show,
The ravish'd standard, and the captive foe,
The senate's thanks, the gazette's pompous tale,
With force resistless o'er the brave prevail.
Such bribes the rapid Greek o'er Asia whirl'd,
For such the steady Romans shook the world;
For such in distant lands the Britons shine,
And stain with blood the Danube or the Rhine;
This pow'r has praise, that virtue scarce can warm,
Till fame supplies the universal charm.
Yet Reason frowns on War's unequal game,
Where wasted nations raise a single name,
And mortgag'd states their grandsires' wreaths regret
From age to age in everlasting debt;
Wreaths which at last the dear-bought right convey
To rust on medals, or on stones decay.

On what foundation stands the warrior's pride?
How just his hopes, let Swedish Charles decide;
A frame of adamant, a soul of fire,
No dangers fright him, and no labours tire;
O'er love, o'er fear, extends his wide domain,
Unconquer'd lord of pleasure and of pain;
No joys to him pacific sceptres yield,
War sounds the trump, he rushes to the field;
Behold surrounding kings their pow'rs combine,
And one capitulate, and one resign,
Peace courts his hand, but spreads her charms in vain;
"Think nothing gain'd," he cries, "till nought remain,
On Moscow's walls till Gothic standards fly,
And all be mine beneath the polar sky."

The march begins in military state,
And nations on his eye suspended wait;
Stern Famine guards the solitary coast,
And Winter barricades the realms of Frost;
He comes, not want and cold his course delay;—
Hide, blushing Glory, hide Pultowa's day:
The vanquish'd hero leaves his broken bands,
And shows his miseries in distant lands;
Condemn'd a needy supplicant to wait,
While ladies interpose, and slaves debate.
But did not Chance at length her error mend?
Did no subverted empire mark his end?
Did rival monarchs give the fatal wound?
Or hostile millions press him to the ground?
His fall was destin'd to a barren strand,
A petty fortress, and a dubious hand;
He left the name, at which the world grew pale,
To point a moral, or adorn a tale.

All times their scenes of pompous woes afford,
From Persia's tyrant to Bavaria's lord.
In gay hostility, and barb'rous pride,
With half mankind embattled at his side,
Great Xerxes comes to seize the certain prey,
And starves exhausted regions in his way;
Attendant Flatt'ry counts his myriads o'er,
Till counted myriads soothe his pride no more;
Fresh praise is tried till madness fires his mind,
The waves he lashes, and enchains the wind;
New pow'rs are claim'd, new pow'rs are still bestow'd,
Till rude resistance lops the spreading god;
The daring Greeks deride the martial show,
And heap their valleys with the gaudy foe;
Th' insulted sea with humbler thought he gains,
A single skiff to speed his flight remains;
Th' incumber'd oar scarce leaves the dreaded coast

Through purple billows and a floating host.
　The bold Bavarian, in a luckless hour,
Tries the dread summits of Cæsarean pow'r,
With unexpected legions bursts away,
And sees defenseless realms receive his sway;
Short sway! fair Austria spreads her mournful charms,
The queen, the beauty, sets the world in arms;
From hill to hill the beacon's rousing blaze
Spreads wide the hope of plunder and of praise;
The fierce Croatian, and the wild Hussar,
With all the sons of ravage crowd the war;
The baffled prince, in honour's flatt'ring bloom
Of hasty greatness finds the fatal doom,
His foes' derision, and his subjects' blame,
And steals to death from anguish and from shame.
　Enlarge my life with multitude of days,
In health, in sickness, thus the suppliant prays;
Hides from himself his state, and shuns to know,
That life protracted is protracted woe.
Time hovers o'er, impatient to destroy,
And shuts up all the passages of joy:
In vain their gifts the bounteous seasons pour,
The fruit autumnal, and the vernal flow'r,
With listless eyes the dotard views the store,
He views, and wonders that they please no more;
Now pall the tasteless meats, and joyless wines,
And Luxury with sighs her slave resigns.
Approach, ye minstrels, try the soothing strain,
Diffuse the tuneful lenitives of pain:
No sounds alas would touch th' impervious ear,
Though dancing mountains witness'd Orpheus near;
Nor lute nor lyre his feeble pow'rs attend,
Nor sweeter music of a virtuous friend,
But everlasting dictates crowd his tongue,
Perversely grave, or positively wrong.

The still returning tale, and ling'ring jest,
Perplex the fawning niece and pamper'd guest,
While growing hopes scarce awe the gath'ring sneer,
And scarce a legacy can bribe to hear;
The watchful guests still hint the last offense,
The daughter's petulance, the son's expense,
Improve his heady rage with treach'rous skill,
And mould his passions till they make his will.

Unnumber'd maladies his joints invade,
Lay siege to life and press the dire blockade;
But unextinguish'd Av'rice still remains,
And dreaded losses aggravate his pains;
He turns, with anxious heart and crippled hands,
His bonds of debt, and mortgages of lands;
Or views his coffers with suspicious eyes,
Unlocks his gold, and counts it till he dies.

But grant, the virtues of a temp'rate prime
Bless with an age exempt from scorn or crime;
An age that melts with unperceiv'd decay,
And glides in modest innocence away;
Whose peaceful day Benevolence endears,
Whose night congratulating Conscience cheers;
The gen'ral fav'rite as the gen'ral friend:
Such age there is, and who shall wish its end?

Yet ev'n on this her load Misfortune flings,
To press the weary minutes' flagging wings:
New sorrow rises as the day returns,
A sister sickens, or a daughter mourns.
Now kindred Merit fills the sable bier,
Now lacerated Friendship claims a tear.
Year chases year, decay pursues decay,
Still drops some joy from with'ring life away;
New forms arise, and diff'rent views engage,
Superfluous lags the vet'ran on the stage,
Till pitying Nature signs the last release,

And bids afflicted worth retire to peace.
But few there are whom hours like these await,
Who set unclouded in the gulfs of fate.
From Lydia's monarch should the search descend,
By Solon caution'd to regard his end,
In life's last scene what prodigies surprise,
Fears of the brave, and follies of the wise?
From Marlb'rough's eyes the streams of dotage flow,
And Swift expires a driv'ler and a show.

The teeming mother anxious for her race,
Begs for each birth the fortune of a face:
Yet Vane could tell what ills from beauty spring;
And Sedley curs'd the form that pleas'd a king.
Ye nymphs of rosy lips and radiant eyes,
Whom Pleasure keeps too busy to be wise,
Whom joys with soft varieties invite
By day the frolic, and the dance by night;
Who frown with vanity, who smile with art,
And ask the latest fashion of the heart,
What care, what rules your heedless charms shall save,
Each nymph your rival, and each youth your slave?
Against your fame with fondness hate combines,
The rival batters, and the lover mines.
With distant voice neglected Virtue calls,
Less heard, and less the faint remonstrance falls;
Tir'd with contempt, she quits the slipp'ry reign,
And Pride and Prudence take her seat in vain.
In crowd at once, where none the pass defend,
The harmless freedom, and the private friend.
The guardians yield, by force superior ply'd:
To Int'rest, Prudence; and to Flatt'ry, Pride.
Now Beauty falls betray'd, despis'd, distress'd,
And hissing Infamy proclaims the rest.

Where then shall Hope and Fear their objects find?
Must dull suspense corrupt the stagnant mind?

Must helpless man, in ignorance sedate,
Roll darkling down the torrent of his fate?
Must no dislike alarm, no wishes rise,
No cries invoke the mercies of the skies?
Enquirer, cease, petitions yet remain,
Which Heav'n may hear, nor deem religion vain.
Still raise for good the supplicating voice,
But leave to Heav'n the measure and the choice.
Safe in his pow'r, whose eyes discern afar
The secret ambush of a specious pray'r.
Implore his aid, in his decisions rest,
Secure, whate'er he gives, he gives the best.
Yet when the sense of sacred presence fires,
And strong devotion to the skies aspires,
Pour forth thy fervours for a healthful mind,
Obedient passions, and a will resign'd;
For love, which scarce collective man can fill;
For patience sov'reign o'er transmuted ill;
For faith, that panting for a happier seat,
Counts death kind Nature's signal of retreat:
These goods for man the laws of Heav'n ordain,
These goods he grants, who grants the pow'r to gain;
With these celestial Wisdom calms the mind,
And makes the happiness she does not find.

A SHORT SONG OF CONGRATULATION

Long-expected one and twenty,
Ling'ring year, at last is flown;
Pomp and pleasure, pride and plenty,
Great Sir John, are all your own.

Loosen'd from the minor's tether,
Free to mortgage or to sell,

Wild as wind, and light as feather,
Bid the slaves of thrift farewell.

Call the Betty's, Kate's, and Jenny's,
Ev'ry name that laughs at care,
Lavish of your Grandsire's guineas,
Show the spirit of an heir.

All that prey on vice and folly
Joy to see their quarry fly,
Here the gamester light and jolly,
There the lender grave and sly.

Wealth, Sir John, was made to wander,
Let it wander as it will:
See the jockey, see the pander,
Bid them come, and take their fill.

When the bonny blade carouses,
Pocket full, and spirits high,
What are acres? What are houses?
Only dirt, or wet or dry.

If the guardian or the mother
Tell the woes of wilful waste,
Scorn their counsel and their pother,
You can hang or drown at last.

ON THE DEATH OF MR. ROBERT LEVET
A PRACTISER IN PHYSIC

Condemn'd to Hope's delusive mine,
    As on we toil from day to day,
By sudden blasts, or slow decline,
    Our social comforts drop away.

Well tried through many a varying year,
    See Levet to the grave descend;
Officious, innocent, sincere,
    Of ev'ry friendless name the friend.

Yet still he fills Affection's eye,
    Obscurely wise, and coarsely kind;
Nor, letter'd Arrogance, deny
    Thy praise to merit unrefin'd.

When fainting Nature call'd for aid,
    And hov'ring Death prepar'd the blow,
His vig'rous remedy display'd
    The power of art without the show.

In Misery's darkest cavern known,
    His useful care was ever nigh,
Where hopeless Anguish pour'd his groan,
    And lonely Want retir'd to die.

No summons mock'd by chill delay,
    No petty gain disdain'd by pride,
The modest wants of ev'ry day
    The toil of ev'ry day supplied.

His virtues walk'd their narrow round,
    Nor made a pause, nor left a void;
And sure th' Eternal Master found
    The single talent well employ'd.

The busy day, the peaceful night,
    Unfelt, uncounted, glided by;
His frame was firm, his powers were bright,
    Though now his eightieth year was nigh.

Then with no throbbing fiery pain,
  No cold gradations of decay,
Death broke at once the vital chain,
  And freed his soul the nearest way.

APPENDIX

From MRS. PIOZZI'S ANECDOTES
OF SAMUEL JOHNSON

ONE day when my son was going to school, and dear Dr. Johnson followed as far as the garden gate, praying for his salvation, in a voice which those who listened attentively could hear plain enough, he said to me suddenly, "Make your boy tell you his dreams: the first corruption that entered into my heart was communicated in a dream." What was it, Sir? said I. "*Do* not ask me," replied he with much violence, and walked away in apparent agitation. I never durst make any further enquiries.

Mr. Johnson was himself exceedingly disposed to the general indulgence of children, and was even scrupulously and ceremoniously attentive not to offend them: he had strongly persuaded himself of the difficulty people always find to erase early impressions either of kindness or resentment, and said, "He should never have so loved his mother when a man, had she not given him coffee she could ill afford, to gratify his appetite when a boy." If you had had children Sir, said I, would you have taught them any thing? "I hope," replied he, "that I should have willingly lived on bread and water to obtain instruction for them; but I would not have set their future friendship to hazard for the sake of thrusting into their heads knowledge of things for which they might not perhaps have either taste or necessity. You teach your daughters the diameters of the planets, and wonder when you have done that they do not delight in your company. No science can be communicated by mortal creatures without attention from the scholar; no attention can be obtained from children without the infliction of pain, and pain is never remembered without resentment." That something should be learned, was however so certainly his opinion, that I have heard him say, how education had been often compared to agriculture, yet that it resembled it chiefly in this: "that if nothing is sown, no crop," says he, "can be obtained." His contempt of the lady who fancied her son could be eminent without study, because Shakespeare was found wanting in scholastic learning, was expressed in terms so gross and so well known, I will not repeat them here.

Mr. Johnson caught me . . . reprimanding the daughter of my housekeeper for having sat down unpermitted in her mother's presence. "Why, she gets her living, does she not," said he, "without her mother's help? Let the wench alone," continued he. And when we were again out of the women's sight who were concerned in the dispute: "Poor people's children, dear Lady (said he), never respect them: I did not respect my own mother, though I loved her: and one day, when in anger she called me a puppy, I asked her if she knew what they called a puppy's mother."

Dr. Johnson delighted in his own partiality for Oxford; and one day, at my house, entertained five members of the other university with various instances of the superiority of Oxford, enumerating the gigantic names of many men whom it had produced, with apparent triumph. At last I said to him, Why there happens to be no less than five Cambridge men in the room now. "I did not," said he, "think of that till you told me;

but the wolf don't count the sheep." When the company were retired, we happened to be talking of Dr. Barnard, the Provost of Eton, who died about that time; and after a long and just eulogium on his wit, his learning, and his goodness of heart: "He was the only man too," says Mr. Johnson quite seriously, "that did justice to my good breeding; and you may observe that I am well-bred to a degree of needless scrupulosity. No man," continued he, not observing the amazement of his hearers, "no man is so cautious not to interrupt another; no man thinks it so necessary to appear attentive when others are speaking; no man so steadily refuses preference to himself, or so willingly bestows it on another, as I do; no body holds so strongly as I do the necessity of ceremony, and the ill effects which follow the breach of it: yet people think me rude; but Barnard did me justice."

Says Garrick to him one day, Why did not you make me a tory, when we lived so much together, you love to make people tories? "Why," says Johnson, pulling a heap of halfpence from his pocket, "did not the king make these guineas?"

Dr. Johnson was liberal enough in granting literary assistance to others, I think; and innumerable are the prefaces, sermons, lectures, and dedications which he used to make for people who begged of him. Mr. Murphy related in his and my hearing one day, and he did not deny it, that when Murphy joked him the week before for having been so diligent of late between Dodd's sermon and Kelly's prologue, that Dr. Johnson replied, "Why, Sir, when they come to me with a dead stay-maker and a dying parson, what can a man do?" He *said*, however, that "he hated to give away literary performances, or even to sell them too cheaply: the next generation shall not accuse me," added he, "of beating down the price of literature: one hates, besides, ever to give that which one has been accustomed to sell; would not you, Sir," turning to Mr. Thrale, "rather give away money than porter?"

When I one day lamented the loss of a first cousin killed in America—"Prithee, my dear," said he, "have done with canting: how would the world be worse for it, I may ask, if all your relations were at once spitted like larks, and roasted for Presto's supper?" Presto was the dog that lay under the table while we talked.

When a well-known author published his poems in the year 1777: Such a one's verses are come out, said I: "Yes," replied Johnson, "and this frost has struck them in again. Here are some lines I have written to ridicule them: but remember that I love the fellow dearly, now—for all I laugh at him.

> Wheresoe'er I turn my view,
> All is strange, yet nothing new:
> Endless labour all along,
> Endless labour to be wrong;
> Phrase that Time has flung away;
> Uncouth words in disarray,
> Trick'd in antique ruff and bonnet,
> Ode, and elegy, and sonnet."

I could give another comical instance of caricatura imitation. Recollecting some day, when praising these verses of Lopez de Vega,

> Se a quien los leones vence
> Vence una muger hermosa
> O el de flaco averguençe
> O ella di ser mas furiosa.

more than he thought they deserved, Mr. Johnson instantly observed "that they were founded on a trivial

conceit; and that conceit ill-explained, and ill-expressed
beside.—The lady, we all know, does not conquer in the
same manner as the lion does: 'Tis a mere play of
words," added he, "and you might as well say, that

> If the man who turnips cries,
> Cry not when his father dies,
> 'Tis a proof that he had rather
> Have a turnip than his father."

In the year 1777, or thereabouts, when all the talk
was of an invasion, he said most pathetically one afternoon, "Alas! alas! how this unmeaning stuff spoils all my
comfort in my friends' conversation! Will the people
never have done with it; and shall I never hear a sentence again without the *French* in it? Here is no invasion coming, and you *know* there is none. Let the
vexatious and frivolous talk alone, or suffer it at least to
teach you *one* truth: and learn by this perpetual echo
of even unapprehended distress, how historians magnify
events expected, or calamities endured; when you know
they are at this very moment collecting all the big words
they can find, in which to describe a consternation never
felt, for a misfortune which never happened. Among all
your lamentations, who eats the less? Who sleeps the
worse, for one general's ill success, or another's capitula-
tion? *Oh, pray* let us hear no more of it!"—No man
however was more zealously attached to his party; he
not only loved a tory himself, but he loved a man the
better if he heard he hated a whig. "Dear Bathurst,"
said he to me one day, "was a man to my very heart's
content: he hated a fool, and he hated a rogue, and he
hated a *whig*; he was a very good *hater*."

Severity towards the poor was, in Dr. Johnson's opinion (as is visible in his Life of *Addison* particularly),

an undoubted and constant attendant or consequence upon whiggism; and he was not contented with giving them relief, he wished to add also indulgence. He loved the poor as I never yet saw any one else do, with an earnest desire to make them happy.—What signifies, says some one, giving halfpence to common beggars? they only lay it out in gin or tobacco. "And why should they be denied such sweeteners of their existence?" says Johnson. "It is surely very savage to refuse them every possible avenue to pleasure, reckoned too coarse for our own acceptance. Life is a pill which none of us can bear to swallow without gilding; yet for the poor we delight in stripping it still barer, and are not ashamed to shew even visible displeasure, if ever the bitter taste is taken from their mouths." In consequence of these principles he nursed whole nests of people in his house, where the lame, the blind, the sick, and the sorrowful found a sure retreat from all the evils whence his little income could secure them: and commonly spending the middle of the week at our house, he kept his numerous family in Fleet-street upon a settled allowance; but returned to them every Saturday, to give them three good dinners, and his company, before he came back to us on the Monday night—treating them with the same, or perhaps more ceremonious civility, than he would have done by as many people of fashion.

When at Versailles the people shewed us the theatre. As we stood on the stage looking at some machinery for playhouse purposes: Now we are here, what shall we act, Mr. Johnson,—The Englishman at Paris? "No, no," replied he, "we will try to act Harry the Fifth." His dislike of the French was well known to both nations, I believe; but he applauded the number of their books and the graces of their style. "They have few sentiments," said he, "but they express them neatly; they have little meat too, but they dress it well." Johnson's own notions about eating however was nothing less than delicate; a leg of pork boiled till it dropped from the bone, a veal-pye with plums and sugar, or the outside cut of a salt buttock of beef, were his favourite dainties: with regard to drink, his liking was for the strongest, as it was not the flavour, but the effect he sought for, and professed to desire; and when I first knew him, he used to pour capillaire into his Port wine. For the last twelve years however, he left off all fermented liquors. To make himself some amends indeed, he took his chocolate liberally, pouring in large quantities of cream, or even melted butter; and was so fond of fruit, that though he usually eat seven or eight large peaches of a morning before breakfast began, and treated them with proportionate attention after dinner again, yet I have heard him protest that he never had quite as much as he wished of wall-fruit, except once in his life, and that was when we were all together at Ombersley, the seat of my Lord Sandys. I was saying to a friend one day, that I did not like goose; one smells it so while it is roasting, said I: "But you, Madam," replies the Doctor, "have been at all times a fortunate woman, having always had your hunger so forestalled by indulgence, that you never experienced the delight of smelling your dinner beforehand." Which pleasure, answered I pertly, is to be enjoyed in perfection by such as have the happiness to pass through Porridge-Island of a morning. "Come, come," says he gravely, "let's have no sneering at what is so serious to so many: hundreds of your fellow-creatures, dear Lady, turn another way, that they may not be tempted by the luxuries of

Porridge-Island to wish for gratifications they are not able to obtain: you are certainly not better than all of *them;* give God thanks that you are happier."

Solitude (added he one day) is dangerous to reason, without being favourable to virtue.

"No person," said he one day, "goes under-dressed till he thinks himself of consequence enough to forbear carrying the badge of his rank upon his back." And in answer to the arguments urged by Puritans, Quakers, &c. against showy decorations of the human figure, I once heard him exclaim, "Oh, let us not be found when our Master calls us, ripping the lace off our waistcoats, but the spirit of contention from our souls and tongues! Let us all conform in outward customs, which are of no consequence, to the manners of those whom we live among, and despise such paltry distinctions. Alas, Sir," continued he, "a man who cannot get to heaven in a green coat, will not find his way thither the sooner in a grey one." On an occasion of less consequence, when he turned his back on Lord Bolingbroke in the rooms at Brighthelmstone, he made this excuse: "I am not obliged, Sir," said he to Mr. Thrale, who stood fretting, "to find reasons for respecting the rank of him who will not condescend to declare it by his dress or some other visible mark: what are stars and other signs of superiority made for?"

The truth is, nobody suffered more from pungent sorrow at a friend's death than Johnson, though he would suffer no one else to complain of their losses in the same way; "for," says he, "we must either outlive our friends you know, or our friends must outlive us; and I see no man that would hesitate about the choice."

I asked him upon this, if he ever disputed with his wife? (I had heard that he loved her passionately.) "Perpetually," said he, "my wife had a particular reverence for cleanliness, and desired the praise of neatness in her dress and furniture, as many ladies do, till they become troublesome to their best friends, slaves to their own besoms, and only sigh for the hour of sweeping their husbands out of the house as dirt and useless lumber: a clean floor is *so* comfortable, she would say sometimes, by way of twitting; till at last I told her, that I thought we had had talk enough about the *floor,* we would now have a touch at the *ceiling.*"

Johnson loved his dinner exceedingly, and has often said in my hearing, perhaps for my edification, "that wherever the dinner is ill got there is poverty, or there is avarice, or there is stupidity; in short, the family is somehow grossly wrong: for," continued he, "a man seldom thinks with more earnestness of any thing than he does of his dinner; and if he cannot get that well dressed, he should be suspected of inaccuracy in other things." One day when he was speaking upon the sub-- ject, I asked him, if he ever huffed his wife about his dinner? "So often," replied he, "that at last she called to me, and said, 'Nay, hold Mr. Johnson, and do not make a farce of thanking God for a dinner which in a few minutes you will protest not eatable.'"

Mr. Johnson's hatred of the Scotch is so well known, and so many of his *bons mots* expressive of that hatred have been already repeated in so many books and pamphlets, that 'tis perhaps scarcely worth while to write down the conversation between him and a friend of that nation who always resides in London, and who at his return from the Hebrides asked him, with a firm tone of voice, What he thought of his country? "That it is a very vile country to be sure, Sir," returned for answer Dr. Johnson. "Well, Sir!" replies the other somewhat mortified, "God made it." "Certainly he did," answers Mr. Johnson again; "but we must always remember that he made it for Scotchmen, and comparisons are odious, Mr. S——; but God made hell."

He certainly rode on Mr. Thrale's old hunter with a good firmness, and though he would follow the hounds fifty miles an end sometimes, would never own himself either tired or amused. "I have now learned," said he, "by hunting, to perceive, that it is no diversion at all, nor ever takes a man out of himself for a moment: the dogs have less sagacity than I could have prevailed on myself to suppose; and the gentlemen often call to me not to ride over them. It is very strange, and very melancholy, that the paucity of human pleasures should persuade us ever to call hunting one of them."—He was however proud to be amongst the sportsmen; and I think no praise ever went so close to his heart, as when Mr. Hamilton called out one day upon Brighthelmstone Downs, Why Johnson rides as well, for aught I see, as the most illiterate fellow in England.

One day when he was in a humour to record some of them, he told us the following tale: "A person," said he, "had for these last five weeks often called at my door, but would not leave his name, or other message; but that he wished to speak with me. At last we met, and he told me that he was oppressed by scruples of conscience: I blamed him gently for not applying, as the rules of our church direct, to his parish priest or other discreet clergyman; when, after some compliments on his part, he told me, that he was clerk to a very eminent trader, at whose warehouses much business consisted in packing goods in order to go abroad: that he was often tempted to take paper and packthread enough for his own use, and that he had indeed done so so often, that he could recollect no time when he ever had bought any for himself.—'But probably,' said I, 'your master was wholly indifferent with regard to such trivial emoluments; you had better ask for it at once, and so take your trifles with consent.'—'Oh, Sir!,' replies the visitor, 'my master bid me have as much as I pleased, and was half angry when I talked to him about it.'—'Then pray Sir,' said I, 'teize me no more about such airy nothings' —and was going on to be very angry, when I recollected that the fellow might be mad perhaps; so I asked him, 'When he left the counting-house of an evening?' —'At seven o'clock, Sir.'—'And when do you go to-bed, Sir?'—'At twelve o'clock.'—'Then,' replied I, 'I have at least learned thus much by my new acquaintance;— that five hours of the four-and-twenty unemployed are enough for a man to go mad in; so I would advise you Sir, to study algebra, if you are not an adept already in it: your head would get less *muddy*, and you will leave off tormenting your neighbours about paper and packthread, while we all live together in a world that is bursting with sin and sorrow.' It is perhaps needless to add, that this visitor came no more."

Another strange thing he told me once which there was no danger of forgetting: how a young gentleman called on him one morning, and told him that his father having, just before his death, dropped suddenly into the enjoyment of an ample fortune, he, the son, was willing to qualify himself for genteel society by adding some literature to his other endowments, and wished to be put in an easy way of obtaining it. Johnson recommended the university: "for you read Latin, Sir, with *facility*." "I read it a little to be sure, Sir." "But do you read it *with facility*, I say?" "Upon my word, Sir, I do not very well know, but I rather believe not." Mr. Johnson now began to recommend other branches of science, when he found languages at such an immeasurable distance, and advising him to study natural history, there arose some talk about animals, and their divisions into oviparous and viviparous; "And the cat here, Sir," said the youth who wished for instruction, "pray in which class is she?" Our doctor's patience and desire of doing good began now to give way to the natural roughness of his temper. "You would do well," said he, "to look for some person to be always about you, Sir, who is capable of explaining such matters, and not come to us (there were some literary friends present as I recollect) to know whether the cat lays eggs or not: get a discreet man to keep you company, there are so many who would be glad of your table and fifty pounds a year."

When Sir Joshua Reynolds had painted his portrait looking into the slit of his pen, and holding it almost close to his eye, as was his general custom, he felt displeased, and told me "he would not be known by posterity for his *defects* only, let Sir Joshua do his worst." I said in reply, that Reynolds had no such difficulties about himself, and that he might observe the picture which hung up in the room where we were talking, represented Sir Joshua holding his ear in his hand to catch the sound. "He may paint himself as deaf if he chuses," replied Johnson; "but I will not be *blinking Sam*."

From FANNY BURNEY'S DIARY

28th March [1777]

MY DEAR DADDY,

My dear father seemed well pleased at my returning to my time; and that is no small consolation and pleasure to me. So now, to our Thursday morning party.

Mrs. and Miss Thrale, Miss Owen, and Mr. Seward came long before *Lexiphanes*. Mrs. Thrale is a very pretty woman still; she is extremely lively and chatty; has no supercilious or pedantic airs, and is really gay and agreeable. Her daughter is about twelve years old, (stiff and proud), I believe, (or else shy and reserved: I don't yet know which). Miss Owen, who is a relation, is good-humoured and *sensible enough;* she is a sort of butt, and, as such, a general favourite; for those sort of characters are prodigiously useful in drawing out the wit and pleasantry of others. Mr. Seward is a very polite, agreeable young man.

My sister Burney was invited to meet and play to them. The conversation was supported with a good deal of vivacity (N.B. my father being at home) for about half an hour, and then Hetty and *Susette* for the first time *in public*, played a duet; and in the midst of this performance Dr. Johnson was announced. He is, indeed, very ill-favoured; is tall and stout; but stoops terribly; he is almost bent double. His mouth is almost [continually opening and shutting], as if he was chewing. He has a strange method of frequently twirling his fingers, and twisting his hands. His body is in continual agitation, *see-sawing* up and down; his feet are never a moment quiet; and, in short, his whole person is in *perpetual motion*. His dress, too, considering the times, and that he had meant to put on his *best becomes,* being engaged to dine in a large company, was as much out of the common road as his figure; he had a large wig, snuff-colour coat, and gold buttons, but no ruffles to his [shirt], doughty fists, and black worsted stockings. He is shockingly near-sighted, and did not, till she held out her hand to him, even know Mrs. Thrale. He *poked his nose* over the keys of the harpsichord, till the duet was finished, and then my father introduced Hetty to him as an old acquaintance, and he cordially kissed her! When she was a little girl, he had made her a present of *The Idler.*

His attention, however, was not to be diverted five minutes from the books, as we were in the library; he pored over them, shelf by shelf, almost touching the backs of them with his eye-lashes, as he read their titles. At last, having fixed upon one, he began, without further ceremony, to read to himself, all the time standing at a distance from the company. We were all very much provoked, as we perfectly languished to hear him talk; but it seems he is the most silent creature, when not particularly drawn out, in the world.

My sister then played another duet with my father; but Dr. Johnson was so deep in the *Encyclopédie* that, as he is very deaf, I question if he even knew what was going forward. When this was over, Mrs. Thrale, in a laughing manner, said, "Pray, Dr. Burney, can you tell me what that song was and whose, which Savoi sung last night at Bach's Concert, and which you did not hear?" My father confessed himself by no means so good a diviner, not having had time to consult the stars, though in the house of Sir Isaac Newton. However, wishing to draw Dr. Johnson into some conversation, he told him the question. The Doctor, seeing his drift, good-naturedly put away his book, and said very drolly, "And pray, Sir, *who is Bach?* is he a piper?" Many exclamations of surprise, you will believe, followed this question. "Why you have read his name often in the papers," said Mrs. Thrale; and then she gave him some account of his Concert, and the number of fine performances she had heard at it.

"Pray," said he, gravely, "Madam, what is the expense?"

"O!" answered she, "much trouble and solicitation, to get a Subscriber's Ticket;—or else, half a Guinea."

"Trouble and solicitation," said he, "I will have nothing to do with; but I would be willing to give eighteen pence."

Ha! ha!

Chocolate being then brought, we adjourned to the drawing-room. And here, Dr. Johnson being taken from the books, entered freely and most cleverly into conversation; though it is remarkable he never speaks at all, but when spoken to; nor does he ever *start,* though he so admirably *supports,* any subject.

The whole party was engaged to dine at Mrs. Montagu's. Dr. Johnson said he had received the most flattering note he had ever read, or that any body else had ever read, by way of invitation. "Well! so have I too," cried Mrs. Thrale; "so if a note from Mrs. Montagu is to be boasted of, I beg mine may not be forgot."

"*Your* note," cried Dr. Johnson, "can bear no comparison with *mine;* I am *at the head of the Philosophers,* she says."

"And I," cried Mrs. Thrale, "*have all the Muses in my train!*"

"A fair battle," said my father. "Come, compliment for compliment, and see who will hold out longest."

"Oh! I am afraid for Mrs. Thrale," cried Mr. Seward; "for I know Mrs. Montagu exerts all her forces, when she attacks Dr. Johnson."

"Oh, yes!" said Mrs. Thrale, "she has often, I know, flattered *him,* till he has been ready to faint."

"Well, ladies," said my father, "you must get him between you today, and see which can lay on the paint thickest, Mrs. Thrale or Mrs. Montagu."

"I had rather," cried the Doctor, drily, "go to Bach's Concert!"

The next name that was started, was that of Sir John Hawkins: and Mrs. Thrale said, "Why now, Dr. Johnson, he is another of those whom you suffer nobody to abuse but yourself; Garrick is one, too; for if any other person speaks against him, you browbeat him in a minute!"

"Why, madam," answered he, "they don't know when to abuse him, and when to praise him; I will allow no man to speak ill of David that he does not deserve; and as to Sir John, why really I believe him to be an honest man at the bottom: but to be sure he is penurious, and he is mean, and it must be owned he has a degree of brutality, and a tendency to savageness, that cannot easily be defended."

We all laughed, as he meant we should, at this curious manner of speaking in his favour, and he then related an anecdote that he said he knew to be true in regard to his meanness. He said that Sir John and he once belonged to the same club, but that as he eat no supper after the first night of his admission, he desired to be excused paying his share.

"And was he excused?"

"Oh yes; for no man is angry at another for being inferior to himself; we all scorned him, and admitted his plea. For my part I was such a fool as to pay my share for wine, though I never tasted any. But Sir John was a most *unclubable* man!"

Before dinner, to my great joy, Dr. Johnson returned home from Warley Common. I followed Mrs. Thrale into the library to see him, and he is so near-sighted that he took me for Miss Streatfield: but he did not welcome me less kindly when he found his mistake, which Mrs. Thrale made known by saying, "No, 'tis Miss Streatfield's rival, Miss Burney."

At tea-time the subject turned upon the domestic economy of Dr. Johnson's own household. Mrs. Thrale has often acquainted me that his house is quite filled and overrun with all sorts of strange creatures, whom he admits for mere charity, and because nobody else will admit them—for his charity is unbounded—or, rather, bounded only by his circumstances.

The account he gave of the adventures and absurdities of the set was highly diverting, but too diffused for writing, though one or two speeches I must give. I think I shall occasionally theatricalise my dialogues.

Mrs. Thrale.—Pray, sir, how does Mrs. Williams like all this tribe?

Dr. Johnson.—Madam, she does not like them at all; but their fondness for her is not greater. She and De Mullin quarrel incessantly; but as they can both be occasionally of service to each other, and as neither of them have any other place to go to, their animosity does not force them to separate.

Mrs. T.—And pray, sir, what is Mr. Macbean?

Dr. J.—Madam, he is a Scotchman; he is a man of great learning, and for his learning I respect him, and I wish to serve him. He knows many languages, and knows them well; but he knows nothing of life. I advised him to write a geographical dictionary; but I have lost all hopes of his ever doing anything properly, since I found he gave as much labour to Capua as to Rome.

Mr. T.—And pray who is clerk of your kitchen, sir?

Dr. J.—Why, sir, I am afraid there is none; a general anarchy prevails in my kitchen, as I am told by Mr. Levat, who says it is not now what it used to be!

Mrs. T.—Mr. Levat, I suppose, sir, has the office of keeping the hospital in health? for he is an apothecary.

Dr. J.—Levat, madam, is a brutal fellow, but I have a good regard for him; for his brutality is in his manners, not his mind.

Mr. T.—But how do you get your dinners drest?

Dr. J.—Why, De Mullin has the chief management of the kitchen; but our roasting is not magnificent, for we have no jack.

Mr. T.—No jack? Why, how do they manage without?

Dr. J.—Small joints, I believe, they manage with a string, and larger are done at the tavern. I have some thoughts (with a profound gravity) of buying a jack, because I think a jack is some credit to a house.

Mr. T.—Well, but you'll have a spit, too?

Dr. J.—No, sir, no; that would be superfluous; for we shall never use it; and if a jack is seen, a spit will be presumed!

Mrs. T.—But pray, sir, who is the Poll you talk of? She that you used to abet in her quarrels with Mrs. Williams, and call out, "At her again, Poll! Never flinch, Poll"?

Dr. J.—Why, I took to Poll very well at first, but she won't do upon a nearer examination.

Mrs. T.—How came she among you, sir?

Dr. J.—Why, I don't rightly remember, but we could spare her very well from us. Poll is a stupid slut; I had some hopes of her at first; but, when I talked to her tightly and closely, I could make nothing of her; she was wiggle-waggle, and I could never persuade her to be categorical.

Mrs. T.—Tomorrow, sir, Mrs. Montagu dines here, and then you will have talk enough.

Dr. Johnson began to see-saw, with a countenance strongly expressive of inward fun, and after enjoying it some time in silence, he suddenly and with great animation turned to me and cried,

"Down with her, Burney!—down with her!—spare her not! attack her, fight her, and down with her at once! You are a rising wit, and she is at the top; and when I was beginning the world, and was nothing and nobody, the joy of my life was to fire at all the established wits; and then everybody loved to halloo me on. But there is no game now; everybody would be glad to see me conquered; but then, when I was new, to vanquish the great ones was all the delight of my poor little dear soul! So at her, Burney,—at her, and down with her!"

Norbury Park, Sunday, Nov. 28 [1784]—Last Thursday, Nov. 25, my father set me down at Bolt Court, while he went on upon business. I was anxious to again see poor Dr. Johnson, who has had terrible health since his return from Lichfield. He let me in, though very ill. He was alone, which I much rejoiced at; for I had a longer and more satisfactory conversation with him than I have had for many months. He was in rather better spirits, too, than I have lately seen him; but he told me he was going to try what sleeping out of town might do for him.

"I remember," said he, "that my wife, when she was

near her end, poor woman, was also advised to sleep out of town; and when she was carried to the lodgings that had been prepared for her, she complained that the staircase was in very bad condition—for the plaster was beaten off the walls in many places. 'Oh,' said the man of the house, 'that's nothing but by the knocks against it of the coffins of the poor souls that have died in the lodgings!' "

He laughed, though not without apparent secret anguish, in telling me this. I felt extremely shocked, but, willing to confine my words at least to the literal story, I only exclaimed against the unfeeling absurdity of such a confession.

"Such a confession," cried he, "to a person then coming to try his lodging for her health, contains, indeed, more absurdity than we can well lay our account for."

I had seen Miss T[hrale] the day before.

"So," said he, "did I."

I then said, "Do you ever, sir, hear from her mother?"

"No," cried he, "nor write to her. I drive her quite from my mind. If I meet with one of her letters, I burn it instantly. I have burnt all I can find. I never speak of her, and I desire never to hear of her more. I drive her, as I said, wholly from my mind."

Yet, wholly to change this discourse, I gave him a history of the Bristol milk-woman and told him the tales I had heard of her writing so wonderfully, though she had read nothing but Young and Milton; "though those," I continued, "could never possibly, I should think, be the first authors with anybody. Would children understand them? and grown people who have not read are children in literature."

"Doubtless," said he; "but there is nothing so little comprehended among mankind as what is genius. They give to it all, when it can be but a part. Genius is nothing more than knowing the use of tools; but there must be tools for it to use: a man who has spent all his life in this room will give a very poor account of what is contained in the next."

"Certainly, sir; yet there is such a thing as invention? Shakespeare could never have seen a Caliban."

"No; but he had seen a man, and knew, therefore, how to vary him to a monster. A man who would draw a monstrous cow, must first know what a cow commonly is; or how can he tell that to give her an ass's head or an elephant's tusk will make her monstrous? Suppose you show me a man who is a very expert carpenter; another will say he was born to be a carpenter—but what if he had never seen any wood? Let two men, one with genius, the other with none, look at an overturned waggon:—he who has no genius, will think of the waggon only as he sees it, overturned, and walk on; he who has genius, will paint it to himself before it was overturned,—standing still, and moving on, and heavy loaded, and empty; but both must see the waggon, to think of it at all."

How just and true all this, my dear Susy! He then animated, and talked on, upon this milk-woman, upon a once as famous shoemaker, and upon our immortal Shakespeare, with as much fire, spirit, wit, and truth of criticism and judgment, as ever yet I have heard him. How delightfully bright are his faculties, though the poor and infirm machine that contains them seems alarmingly giving way.

Yet, all brilliant as he was, I saw him growing worse, and offered to go, which, for the first time I ever remember, he did not oppose; but, most kindly pressing both my hands,

"Be not," he said, in a voice of even tenderness, "be not long in coming again for my letting you go now."

I assured him I would be the sooner, and was running off, but he called me back, in a solemn voice, and, in a manner the most energetic, said,

"Remember me in your prayers!"